ORDNANCE SURVEY

STREET A[illegible]

Hertfordshire

Contents

IV *Key to maps*

VI *Administrative boundaries*

1 *Street maps*

178 *Index explanation and abbreviations*

179 *Index of towns, villages and rural localities*

180 *Index of street names*

PHILIP'S

First edition published 1986
Fourth edition published 1994 by

Ordnance Survey	and	Philip's
Romsey Road		an imprint of Reed Consumer Books Limited
Maybush		Michelin House, 81 Fulham Road, London, SW3 6RB
Southampton SO16 4GU		and Auckland, Melbourne, Singapore and Toronto

ISBN 0-540-05995-1 (Philip's, hardback)
ISBN 0-540-05996-X (Philip's, softback)
ISBN 0-319-00472-4 (Ordnance Survey, hardback)
ISBN 0-319-00473-2 (Ordnance Survey, softback)

To the best of the Publishers' knowledge, the information in this atlas was correct at the time of going to press. No responsibility can be accepted for any errors or their consequences.

The representation in this atlas of a road, track or path is no evidence of the existence of a right of way.

Printed and bound in Great Britain by
Butler & Tanner Ltd, Frome and London

Key to map symbols

(British Rail symbol)	**British Rail station**
(London transport symbol)	**London transport station**
(Private railway symbol)	**Private railway station**
(Bus symbol)	**Bus or coach station**
(H)	**Heliport**
♦	**Police station** (may not be open 24 hours)
✚	**Hospital with casualty facilities** (may not be open 24 hours)
□	**Post office**
+	**Place of worship**
(Building symbol)	**Important building**
P	**Parking**
120	**Adjoining page indicator**
(Double lines)	**Motorway or dual carriageway**
A27(T)	**Main or through road** (with Department of Transport number)
(Gate symbol)	**Gate or obstruction to traffic** (restrictions may not apply at all times or to all vehicles)
- - - - -	**Footpath**
— — —	**Bridleway**
– – –	**Path**
(Double thin lines)	**Track**

The representation in this atlas of a road, track or path is no evidence of the existence of a right of way

Amb Sta	**Ambulance station**	LC	**Level crossing**
Coll	**College**	Liby	**Library**
FB	**Footbridge**	Mus	**Museum**
F Sta	**Fire station**	Sch	**School**
Hospl	**Hospital**	TH	**Town hall**

0 | ¼ | ½ | ¾ | 1 mile

0 | 250m | 500m | 250m | 1 Kilometre

The scale of the maps is 3½ inches to 1 mile (1:18103)

The small numbers around the edges of the maps identify the 1 kilometre National Grid lines

Key to map pages

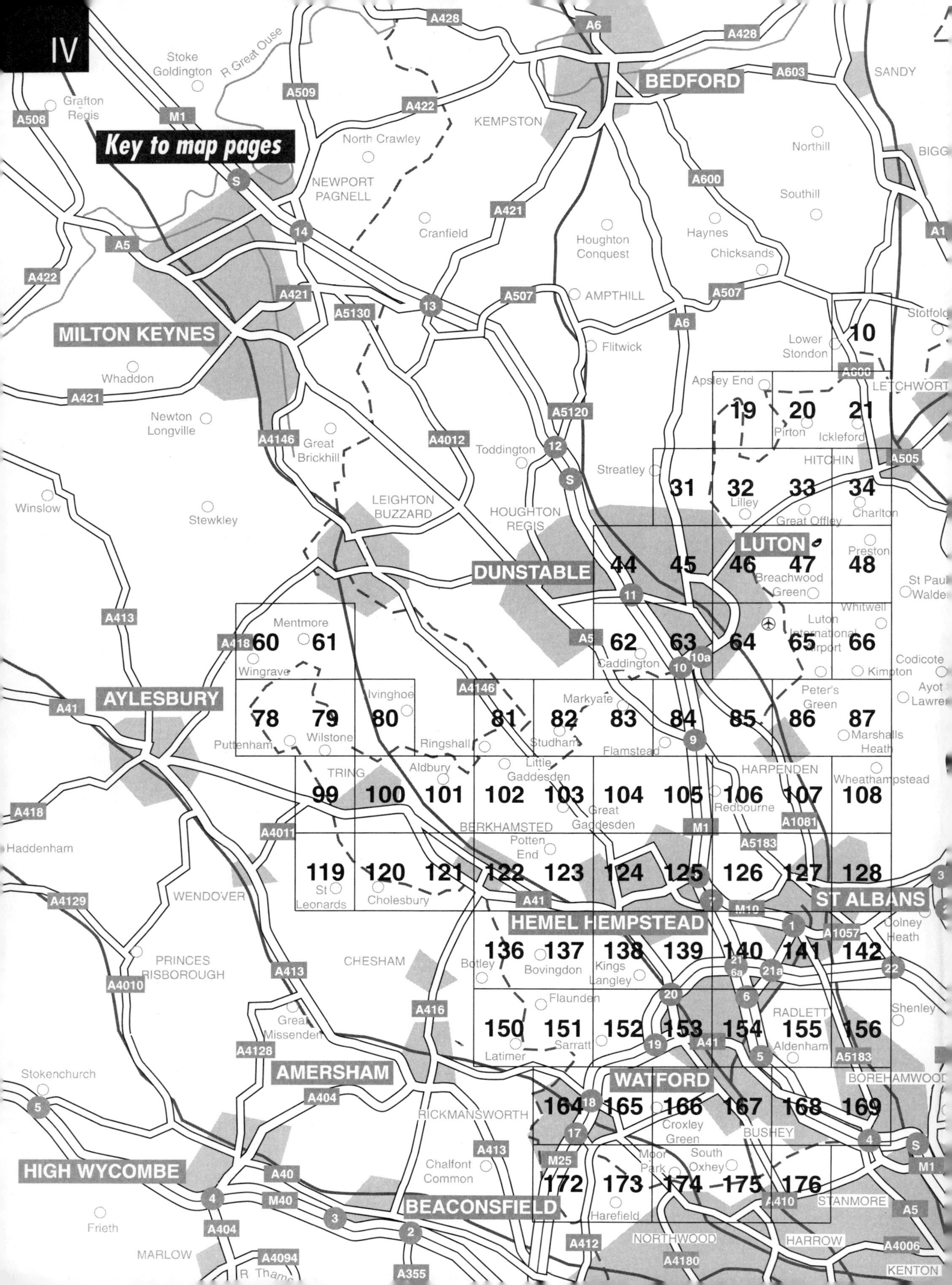

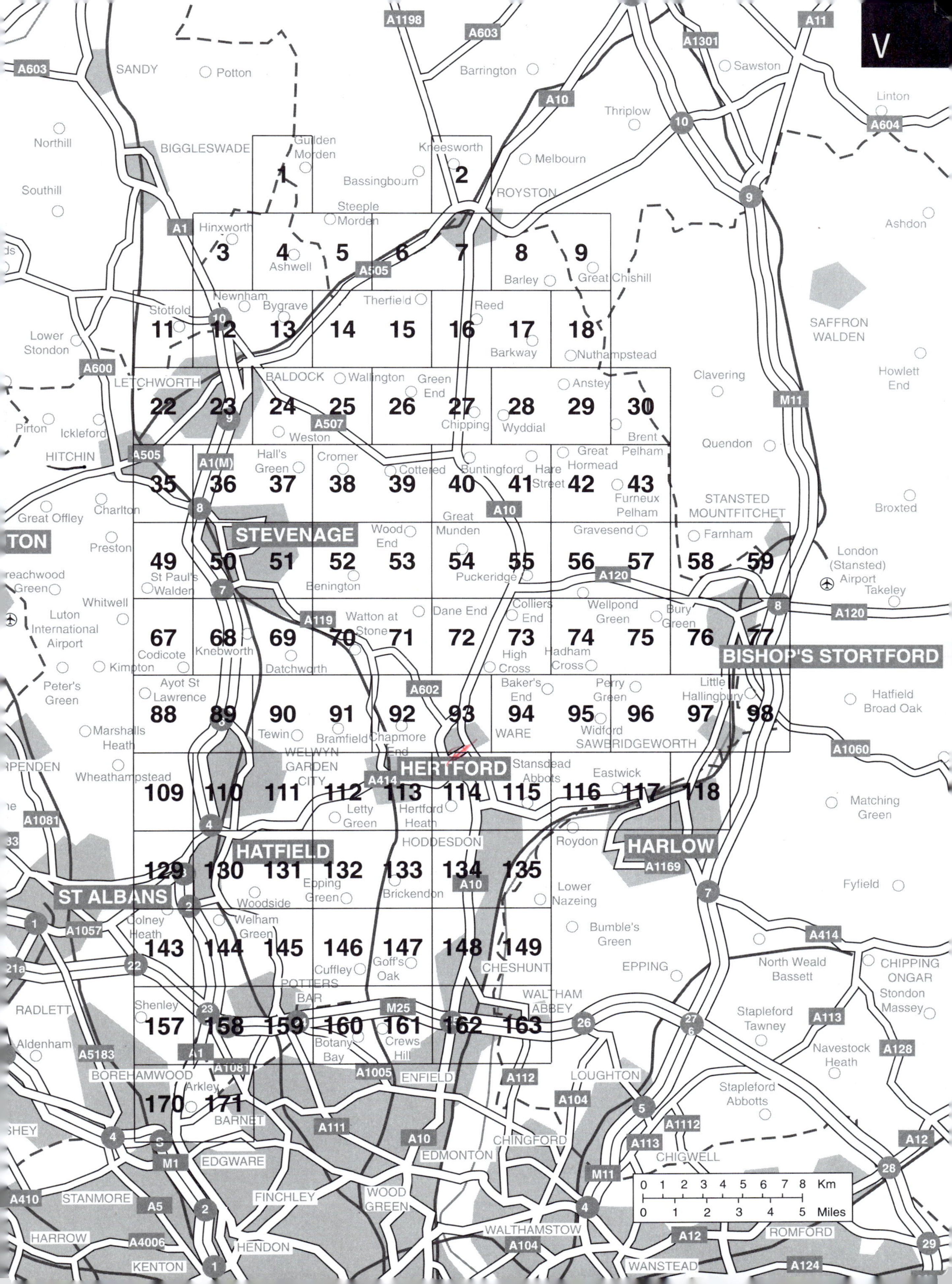
A1198
A603
A11
A1301
A603
SANDY
Potton
Barrington
Sawston
A10
Linton
Thriplow
10
A604
Northill
Gulden
Morden
Kneesworth
BIGGLESWADE
1
2
Melbourn
Bassingbourn
Southill
ROYSTON
9
Steeple
Morden
Ashdon
A1
Hinxworth
3
4
5
6
7
8
9
Ashwell
A505
Barley
Great Chishill
Newnham
Therfield
Reed
Stotfold
Bygrave
10
11
12
13
14
15
16
17
18
SAFFRON
WALDEN
Lower
Stondon
Barkway
Nuthampstead
A600
BALDOCK
Wallington
Green
End
Anstey
Clavering
Howlett
End
LETCHWORTH
22
23
24
25
26
27
28
29
30
M11
Pirton
Ickleford
Weston
A507
Chipping
Wyddial
Brent
Pelham
Quendon
HITCHIN
A505
A1(M)
Hall's
Green
Cromer
Cottered
Buntingford
Hare
Street
Great
Hormead
35
36
37
38
39
40
41
42
43
Furneux
Pelham
STANSTED
MOUNTFITCHET
Broxted
Great Offley
Charlton
8
A10
Great
Munden
TON
Preston
STEVENAGE
Wood
End
Gravesend
Farnham
London
(Stansted)
Airport
49
50
51
52
53
54
55
56
57
58
59
reachwood
Green
St Paul's
Walden
Benington
Puckeridge
A120
Takeley
Whitwell
7
Watton at
Stone
Dane End
Colliers
End
Wellpond
Green
Bury
Green
8
A120
Luton
International
Airport
A119
67
68
69
70
71
72
73
74
75
76
77
Codicote
Knebworth
High
Cross
Hadham
Cross
BISHOP'S STORTFORD
Peter's
Green
Kimpton
Datchworth
Ayot St
Lawrence
A602
Baker's
End
Perry
Green
Little
Hallingbury
Hatfield
Broad Oak
88
89
90
91
92
93
94
95
96
97
98
Marshalls
Heath
Tewin
Bramfield
Chapmore
End
WARE
Widford
SAWBRIDGEWORTH
A1060
RPENDEN
WELWYN
GARDEN
CITY
HERTFORD
Stansdead
Abbots
Eastwick
Wheathampstead
A414
Matching
Green
109
110
111
112
113
114
115
116
117
118
Letty
Green
Hertford
Heath
A1081
4
HODDESDON
Roydon
HATFIELD
HARLOW
A1169
129
130
131
132
133
134
135
Epping
Green
Brickendon
A10
Lower
Nazeing
Fyfield
ST ALBANS
Woodside
7
1
A1057
2
Colney
Heath
Welham
Green
Bumble's
Green
A414
143
144
145
146
147
148
149
21a
22
Cuffley
Goff's
Oak
CHESHUNT
EPPING
North Weald
Bassett
CHIPPING
ONGAR
POTTERS
BAR
WALTHAM
ABBEY
Stondon
Massey
RADLETT
Shenley
23
M25
Stapleford
Tawney
A113
157
158
159
160
161
162
163
26
27
6
Aldenham
Botany
Bay
Crews
Hill
Navestock
Heath
A128
A5183
A1
A1081
BOREHAMWOOD
A1005
ENFIELD
A112
LOUGHTON
Arkley
Stapleford
Abbotts
170
171
BARNET
A104
5
A1112
A111
SHEY
4
3
A10
CHINGFORD
A113
A12
M1
EDGWARE
EDMONTON
CHIGWELL
28
M11
0 1 2 3 4 5 6 7 8 Km
0 1 2 3 4 5 Miles
A410
STANMORE
A5
FINCHLEY
WOOD
GREEN
2
4
HARROW
A4006
WALTHAMSTOW
A12
ROMFORD
A104
HENDON
KENTON
1
WANSTEAD
A124
29

ADMINISTRATIVE BOUNDARIES

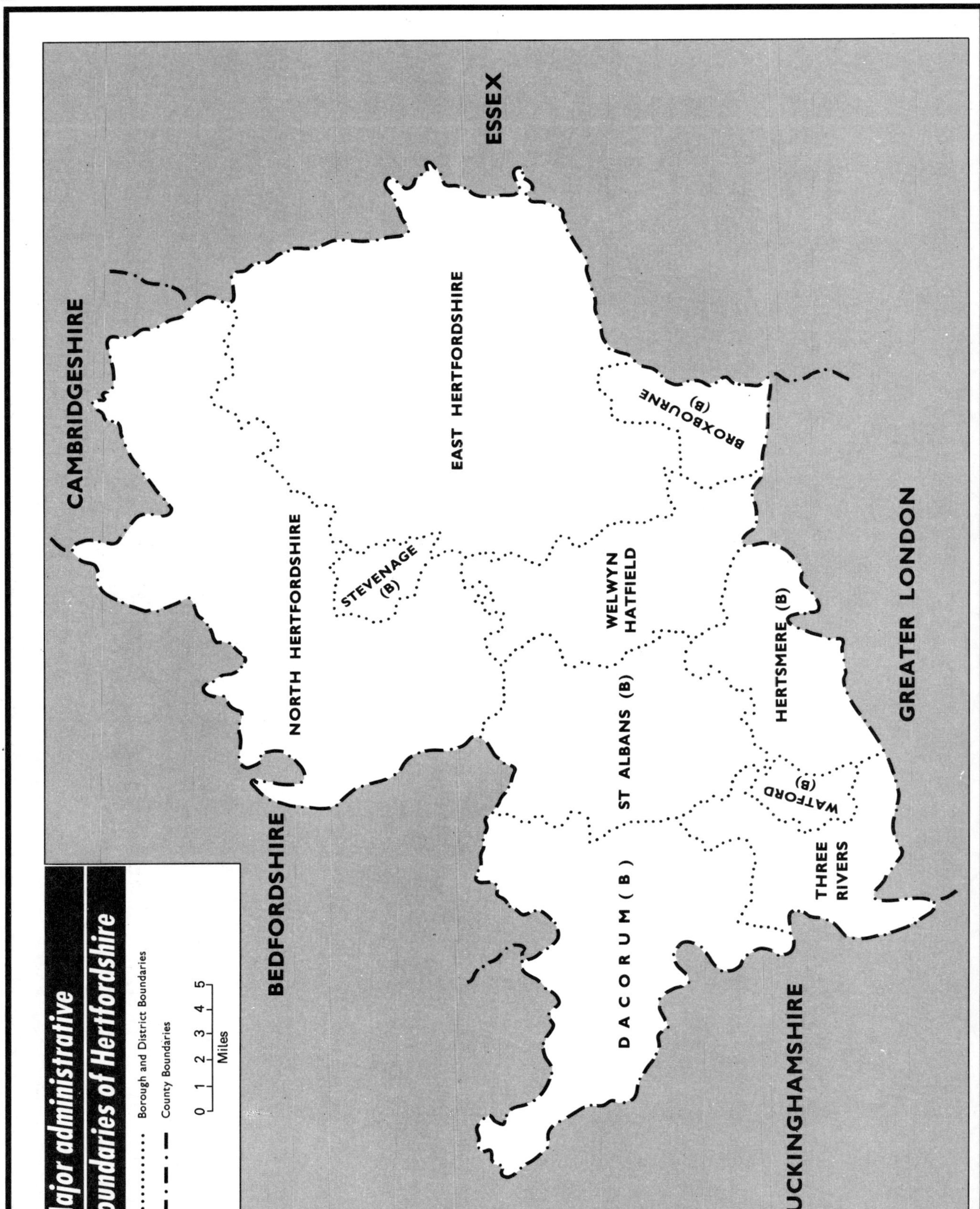

not continued, see key diagram

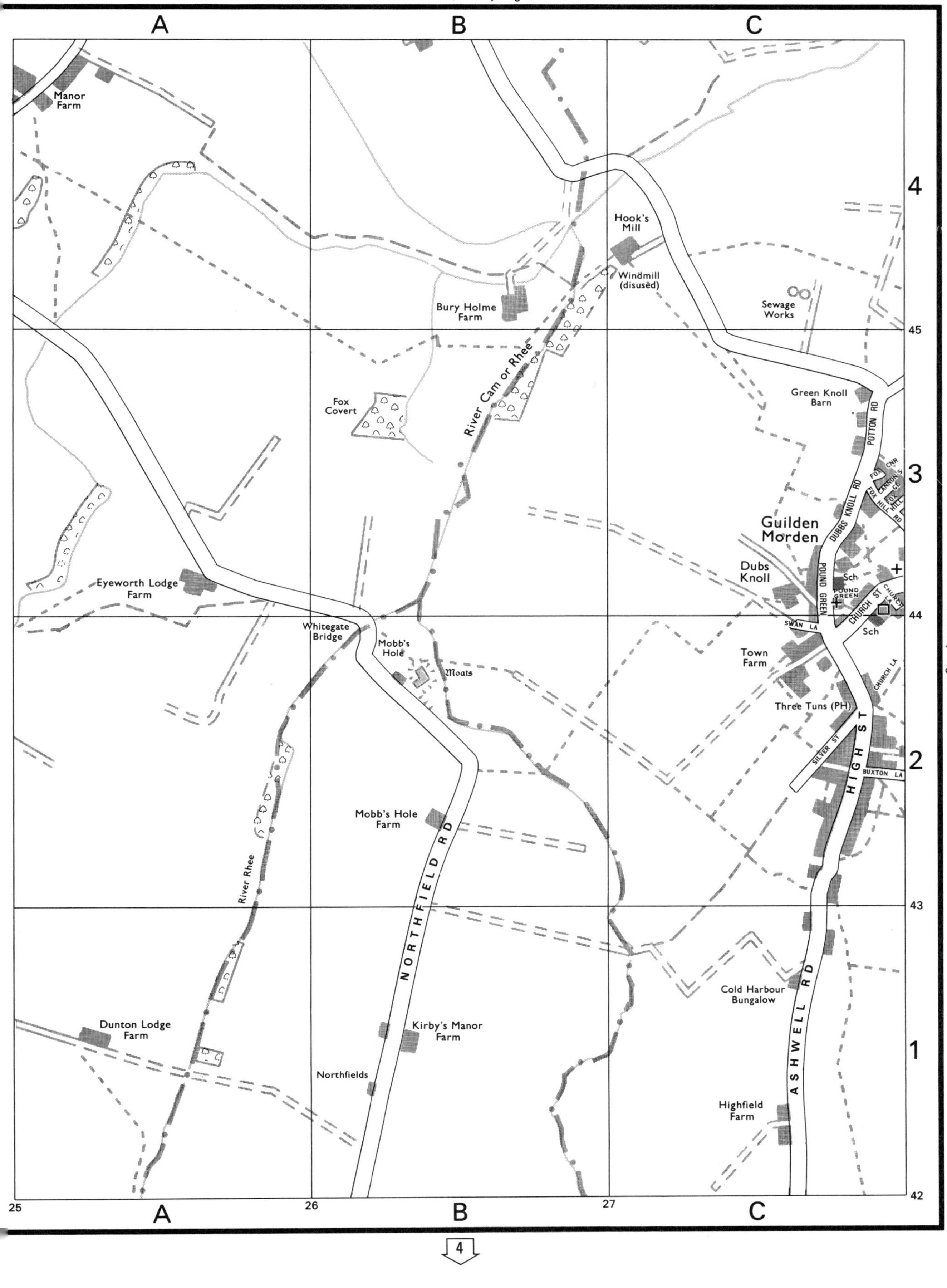

not continued, see key diagram

4

not continued, see key diagram

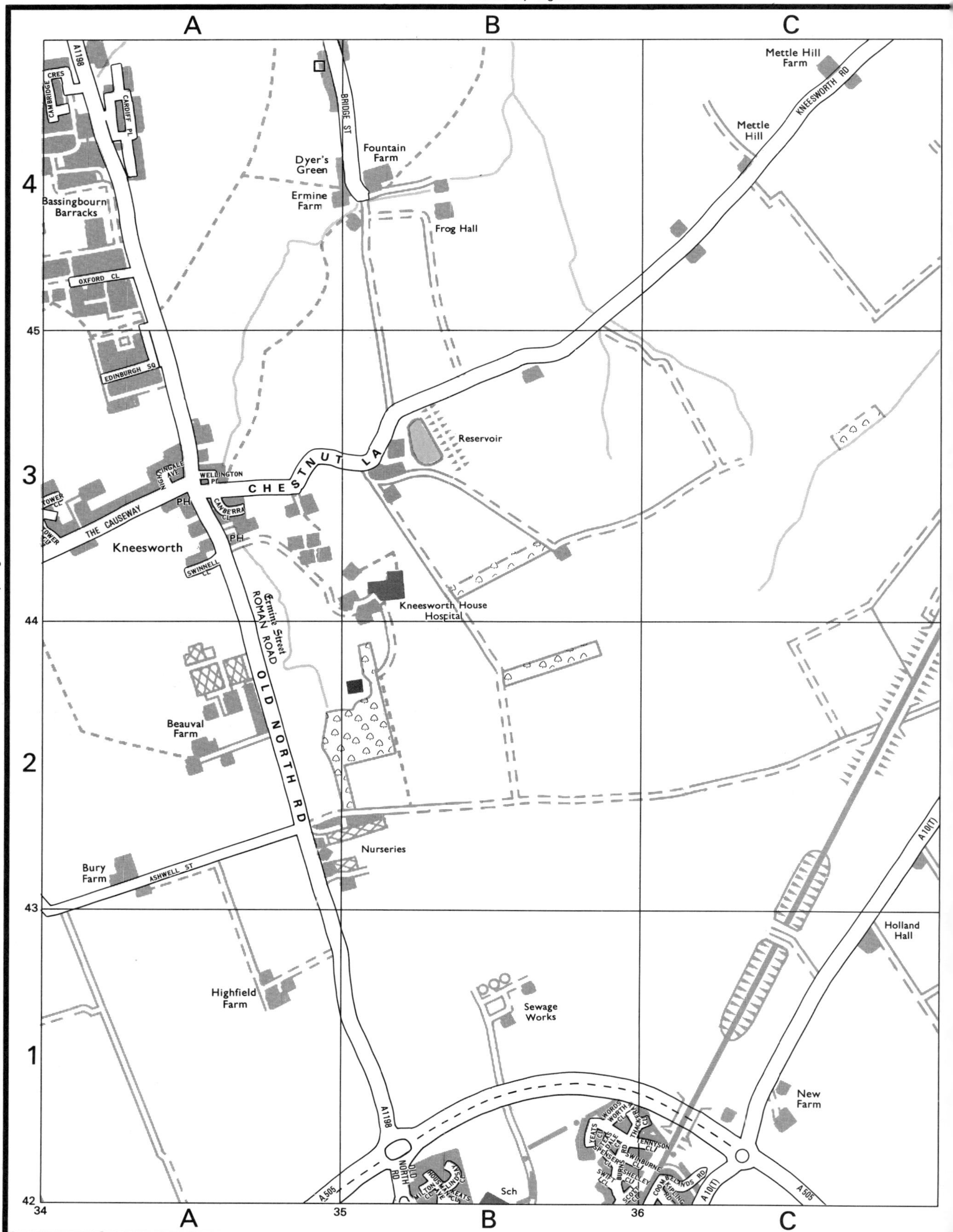

not continued, see key diagram

7

not continued, see key diagram

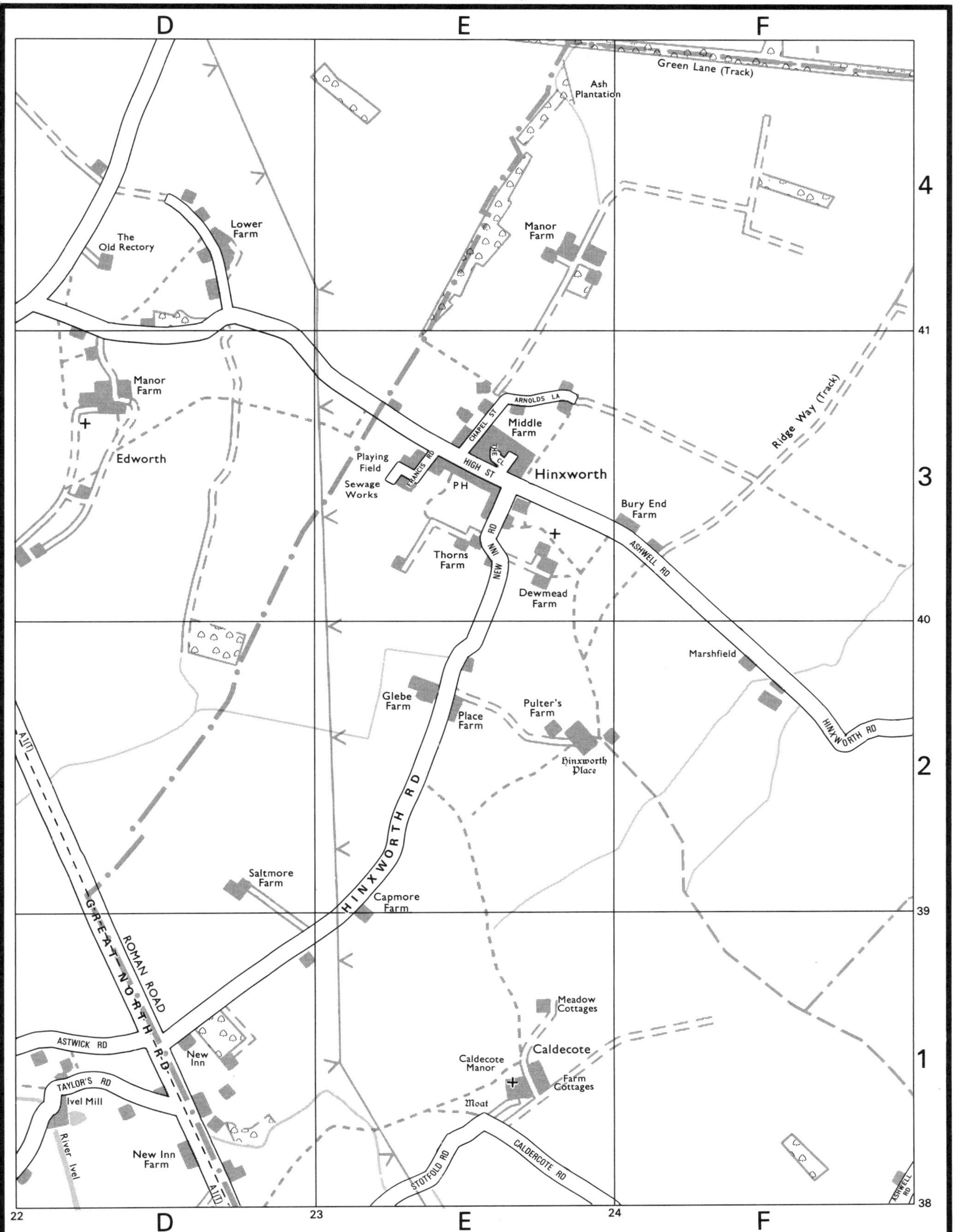

4

12

1

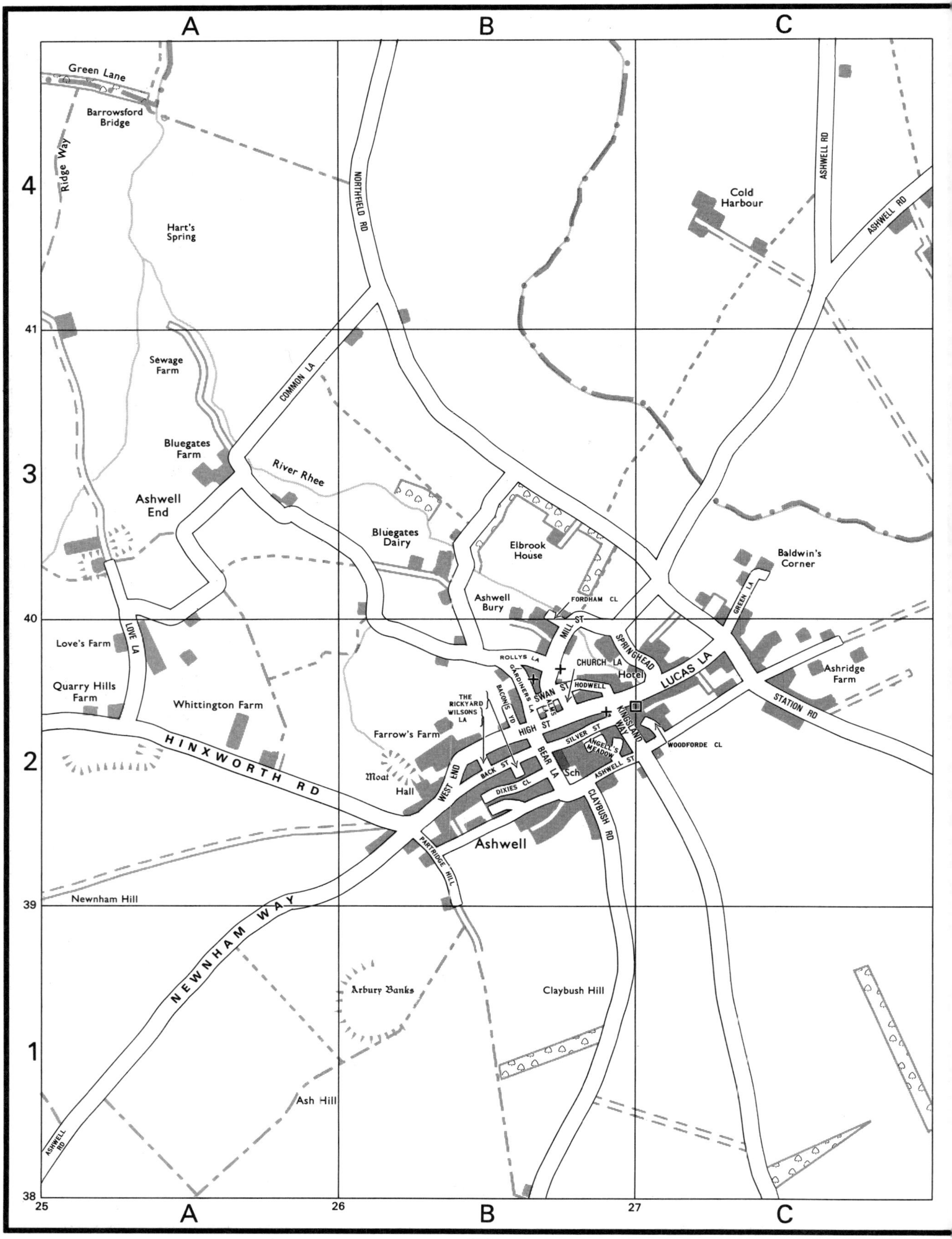
A
B
C
4
3
2
1
41
40
39
38
25
26
27
Green Lane
Barrowsford Bridge
Ridge Way
Hart's Spring
NORTHFIELD RD
ASHWELL RD
Cold Harbour
ASHWELL RD
Sewage Farm
COMMON LA
Bluegates Farm
River Rhee
Ashwell End
Bluegates Dairy
Elbrook House
Baldwin's Corner
GREEN LA
Ashwell Bury
FORDHAM CL
MILL ST
LOVE LA
Love's Farm
ROLLYS LA
CHURCH LA
SPRINGHEAD
Hotel
LUCAS LA
Ashridge Farm
GARDINERS LA
SWAN ST
HODWELL
Quarry Hills Farm
Whittington Farm
THE RICKYARD
WILSONS LA
BACON'S YD
ALMS LA
KINGSLAND WAY
STATION RD
HIGH ST
SILVER ST
Farrow's Farm
ANGELL'S MEADOW
WOODFORDE CL
HINXWORTH RD
Moat
Hall
WEST END
BACK ST
BEAR LA
Sch
ASHWELL ST
DIXIES CL
CLAYBUSH RD
PARTRIDGE HILL
Ashwell
Newnham Hill
NEWNHAM WAY
Arbury Banks
Claybush Hill
Ash Hill
ASHWELL RD

3

13

not continued, see key diagram

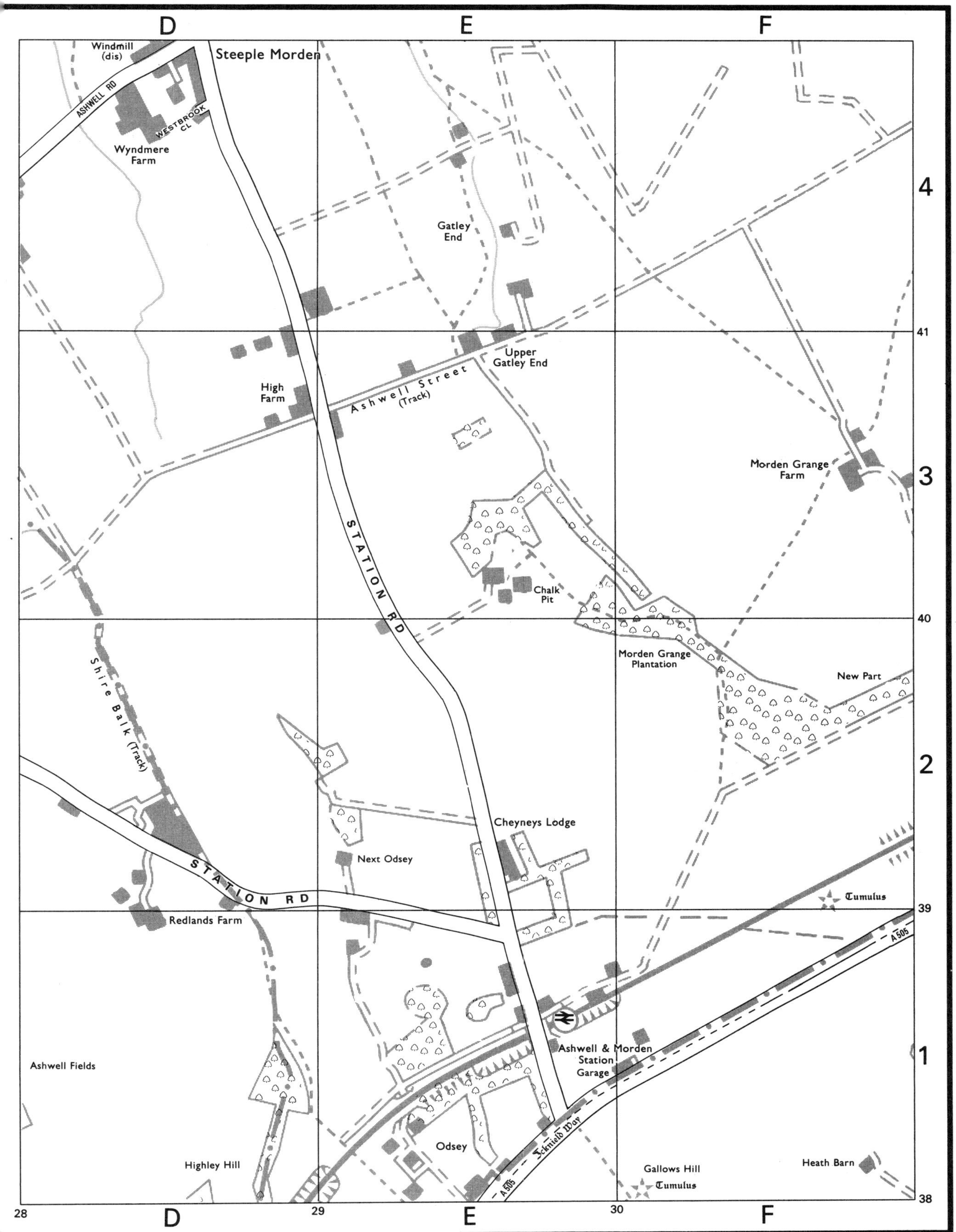

6

14

not continued, see key diagram

5

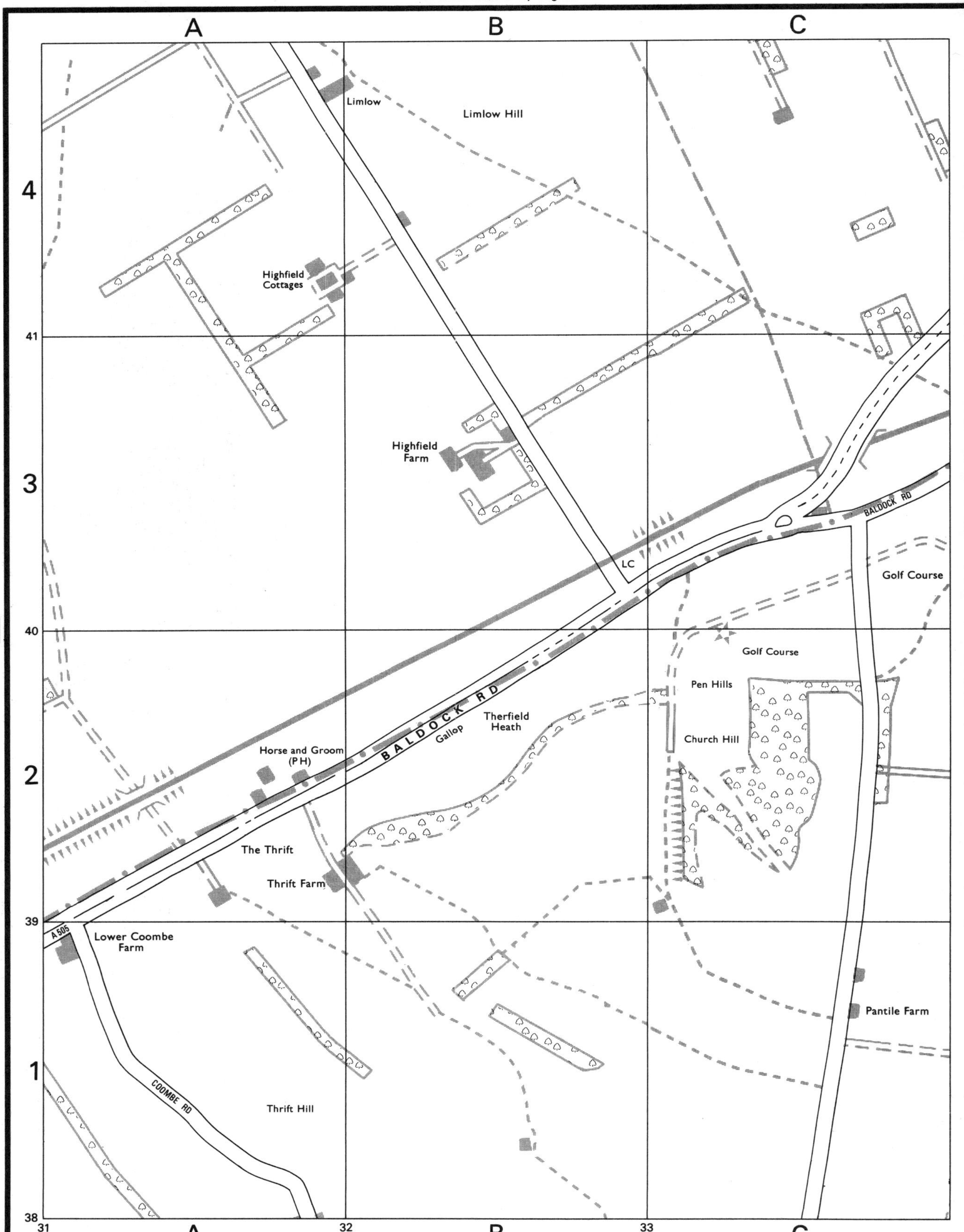

15

2

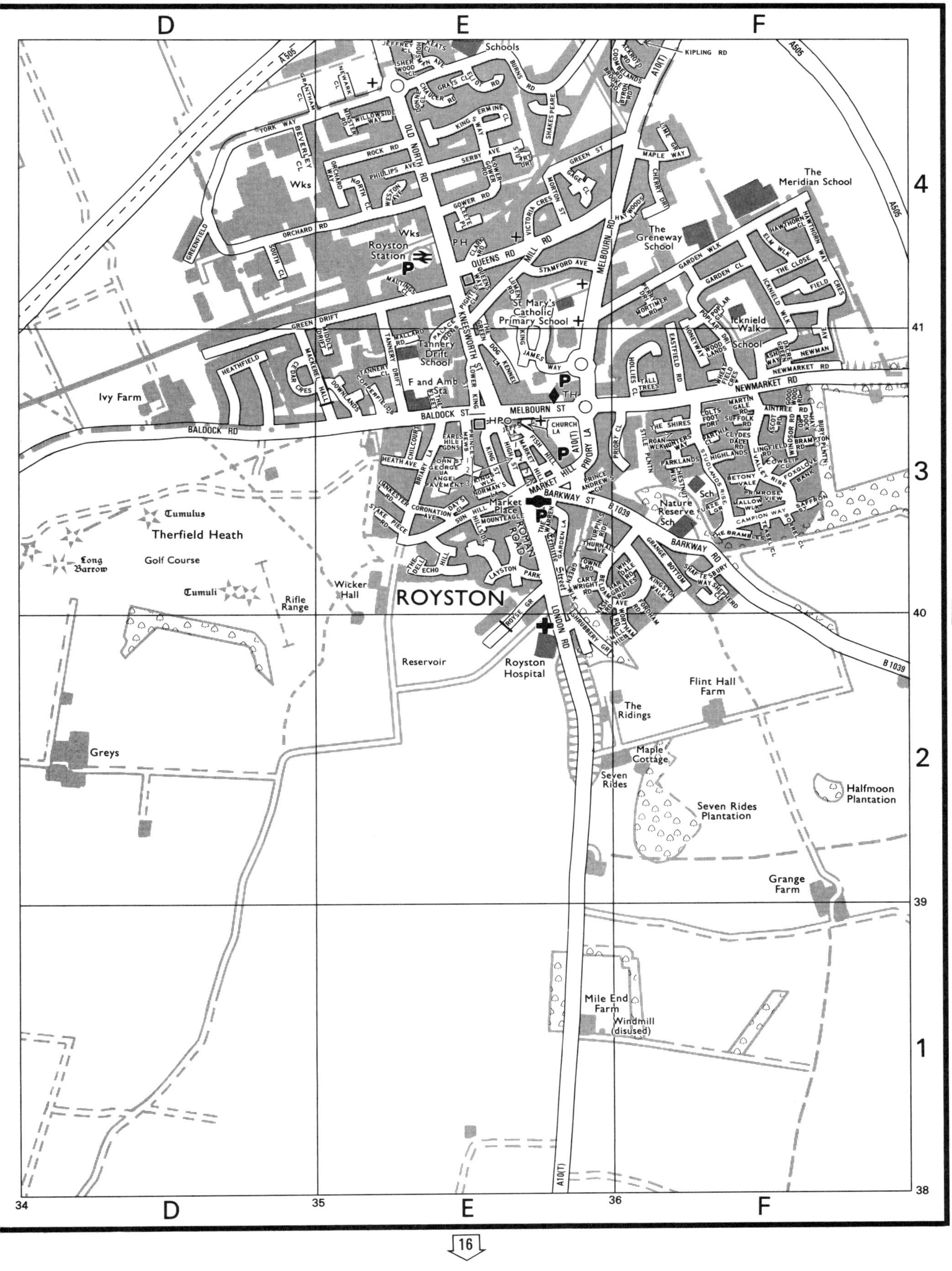
D
E
F
4
3
2
1
41
40
39
38
34
35
36
ROYSTON
Schools
Kipling Rd
A505
A10(T)
B1039
Wks
Royston Station
The Meridian School
The Greneway School
St Mary's Catholic Primary School
Tannery Drift School
Icknield Walk School
F and Amb Sta
Ivy Farm
Baldock Rd
Baldock St
Melbourn St
Newmarket Rd
Barkway St
Barkway Rd
London Rd
Kneesworth St
Old North Rd
Mill Rd
Melbourn Rd
Queens Rd
Orchard Rd
York Way
Rock Rd
Green Drift
Tannery Drift
Priory La
Market Hill
Market Place
Roman Road
Nature Reserve
Sch
Cumulus
Therfield Heath
Golf Course
Long Barrow
Cumuli
Rifle Range
Wicker Hall
Reservoir
Royston Hospital
Flint Hall Farm
The Ridings
Maple Cottage
Seven Rides
Seven Rides Plantation
Halfmoon Plantation
Greys
Grange Farm
Mile End Farm
Windmill (disused)

8

16

not continued, see key diagram

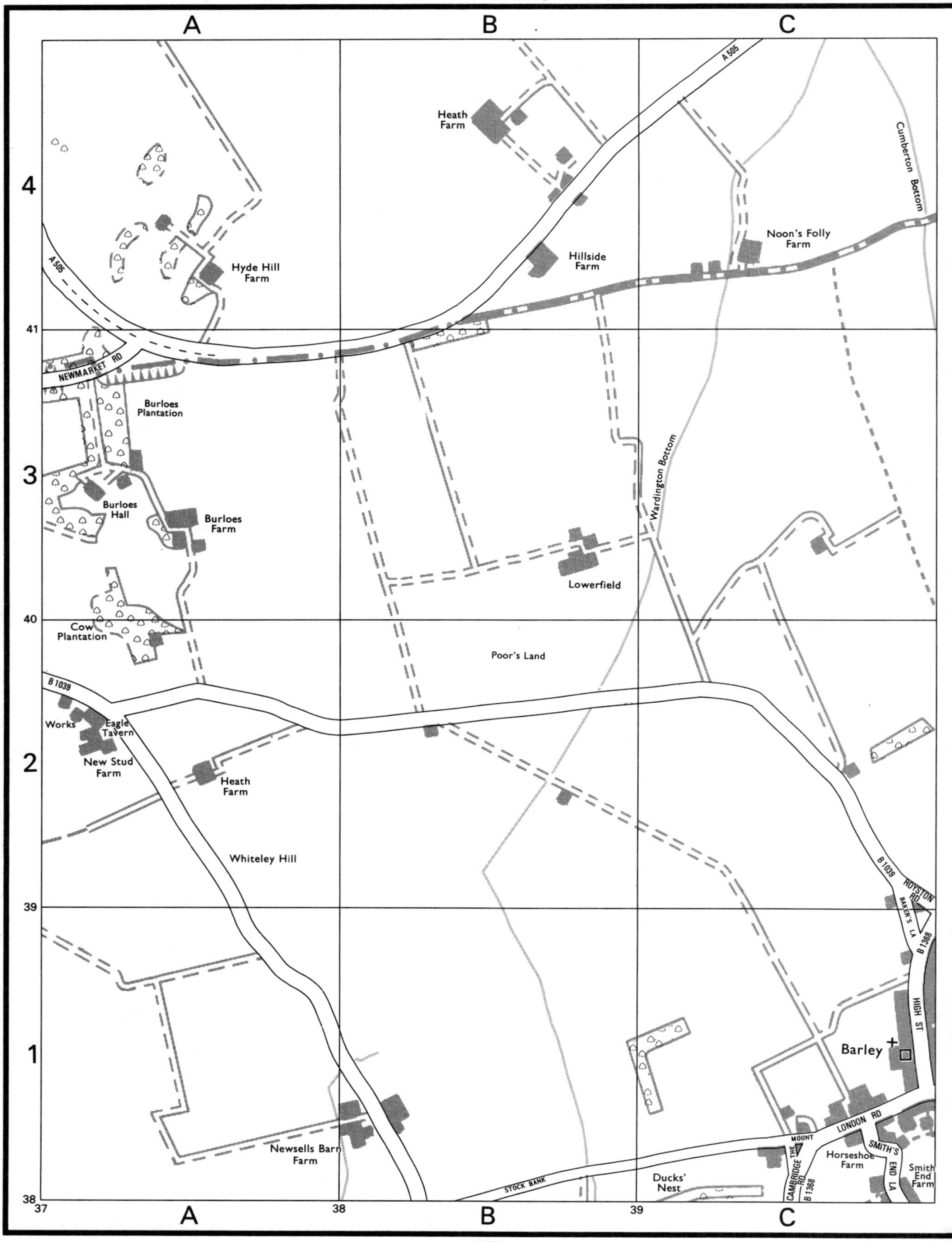

7

17

not continued, see key diagram

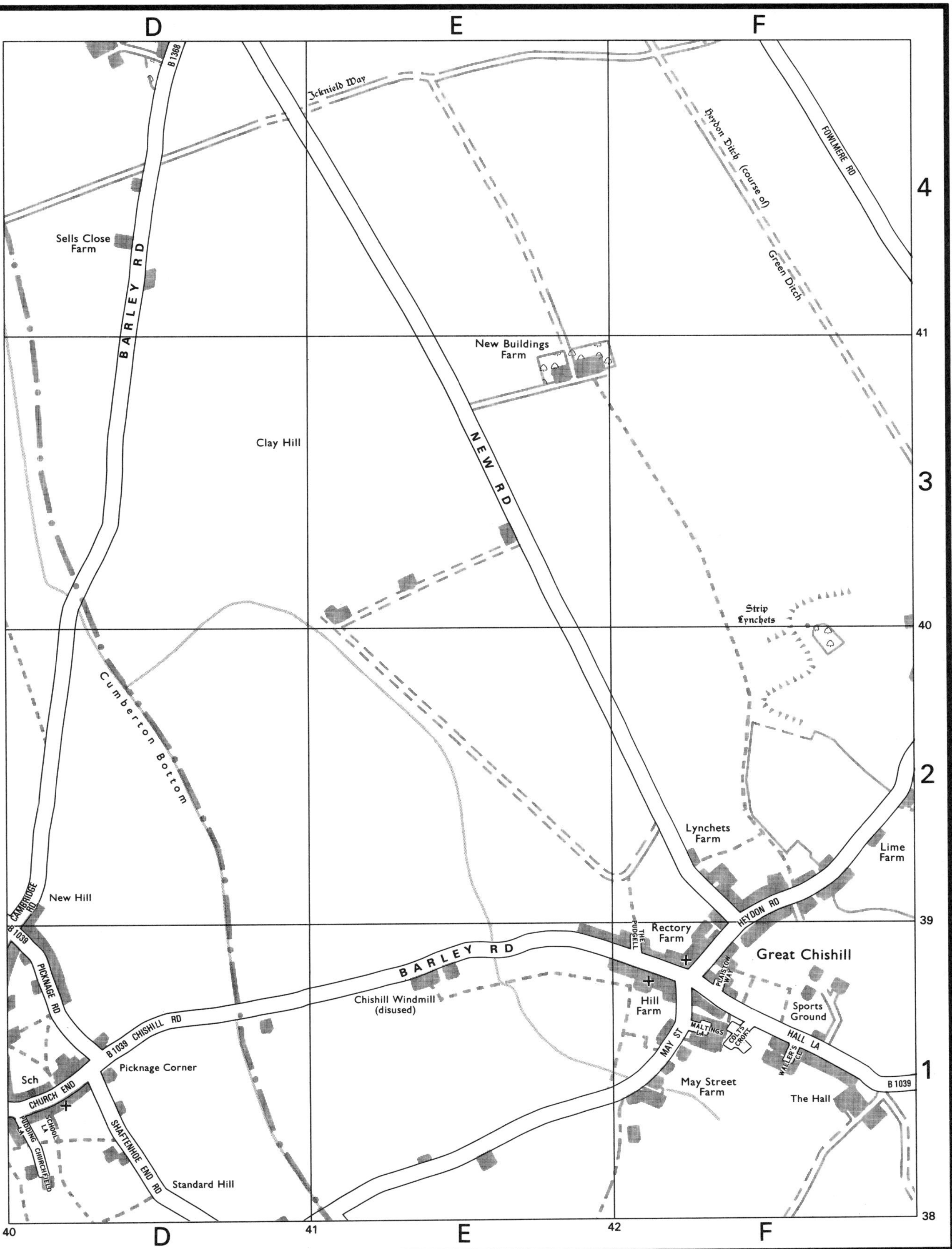

not continued, see key diagram

18

not continued, see key diagram

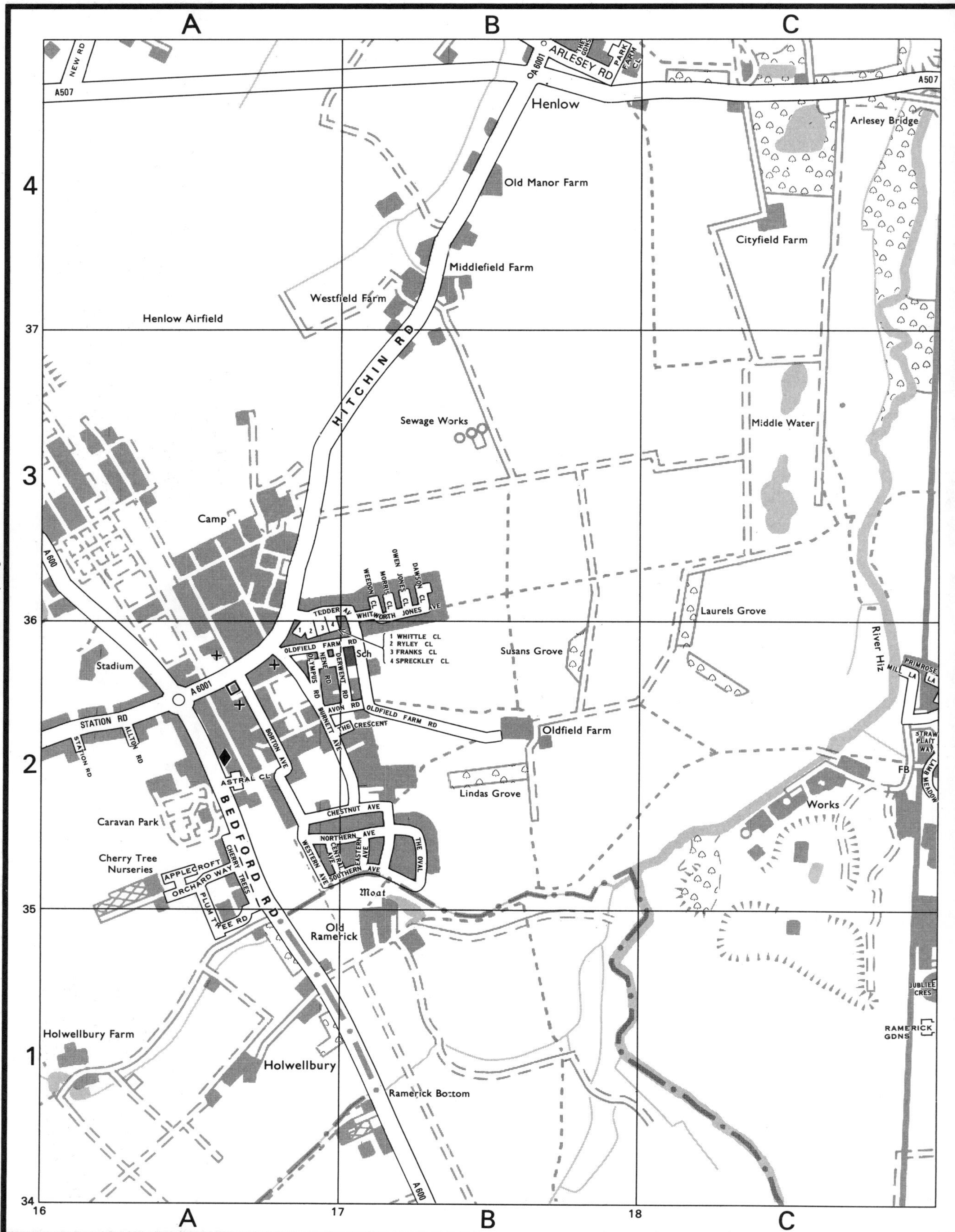

not continued, see key diagram

not continued, see key diagram

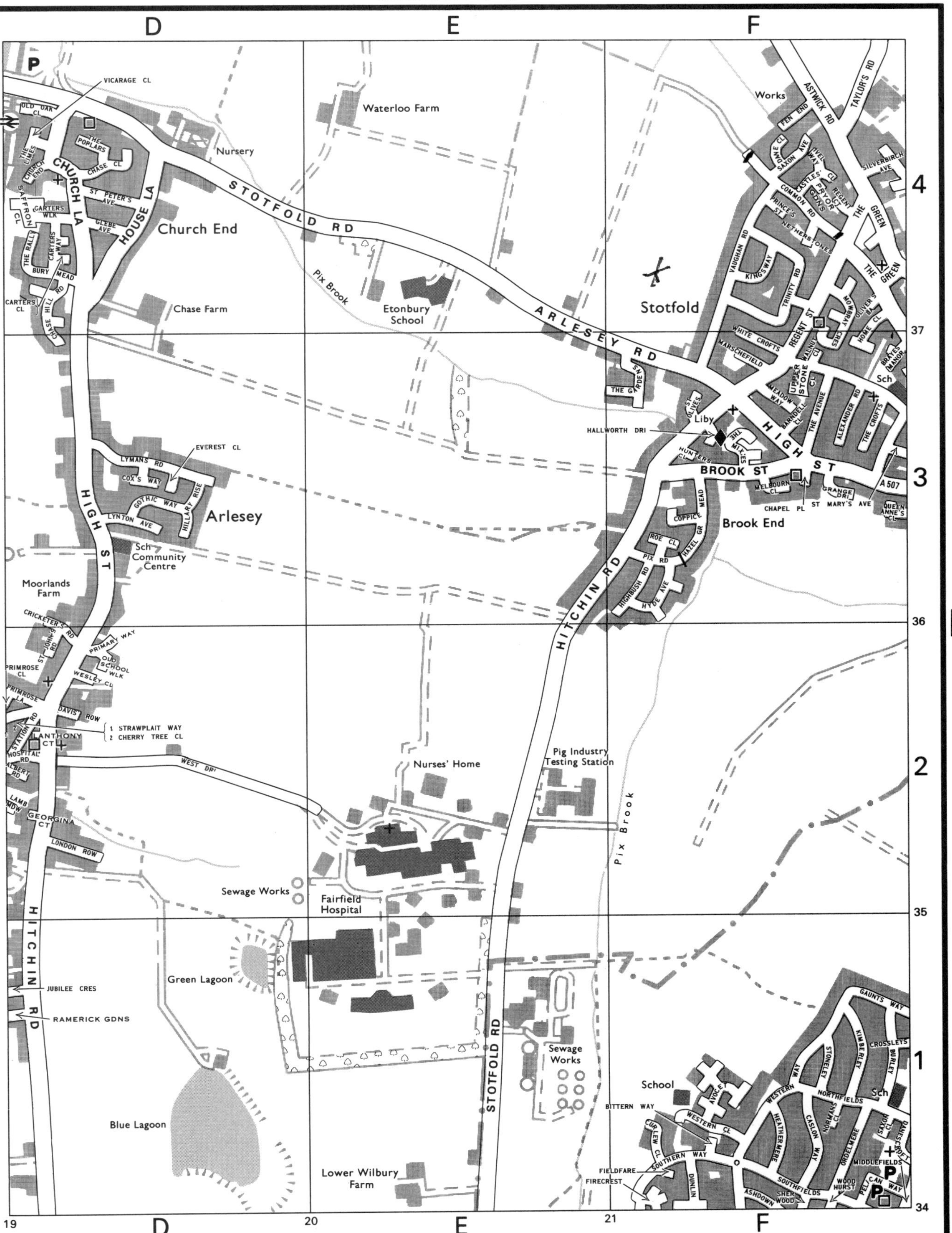

12

22

3

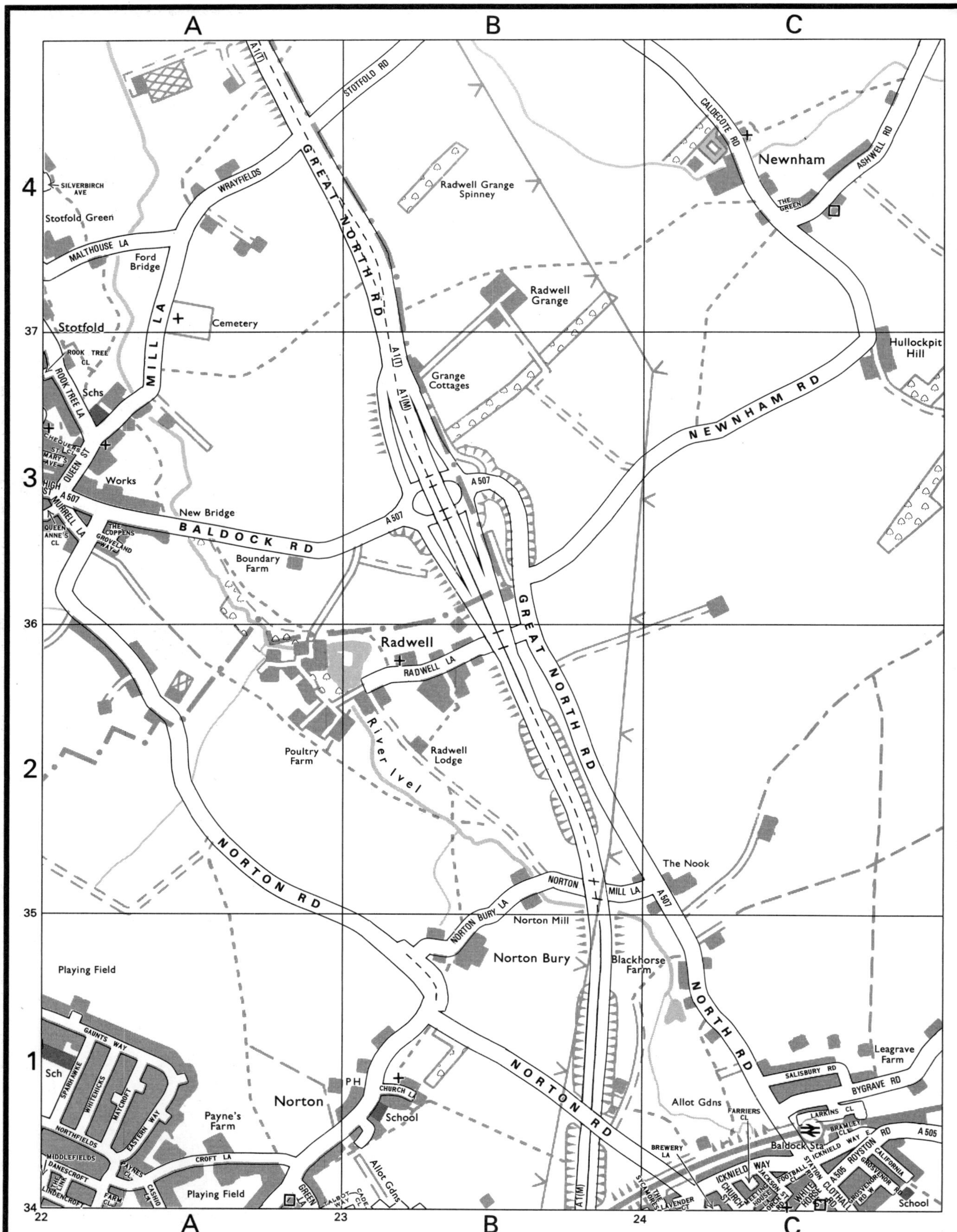
A
B
C
4
3
2
1
37
36
35
34
22
23
24
SILVERBIRCH AVE
Stotfold Green
MALTHOUSE LA
Ford Bridge
WRAYFIELDS
STOTFOLD RD
A1(T)
GREAT NORTH RD
Radwell Grange Spinney
CALDECOTE RD
Newnham
ASHWELL RD
THE GREEN
Radwell Grange
Stotfold
Cemetery
MILL LA
ROOK TREE CL
ROOK TREE LA
Schs
Grange Cottages
A1(M)
Hullockpit Hill
NEWNHAM RD
CHEQUERS CL
ST MARY'S AVE
QUEEN ST
HIGH ST
Works
A 507
MURRELL LA
QUEEN ANNE'S CL
THE COPPENS
GROVELAND WAY
New Bridge
BALDOCK RD
Boundary Farm
Radwell
RADWELL LA
Poultry Farm
River Ivel
Radwell Lodge
NORTON RD
The Nook
NORTON MILL LA
NORTON BURY LA
Norton Mill
Norton Bury
Blackhorse Farm
NORTH RD
Playing Field
GAUNTS WAY
SPARHAWKE
WHITEHICKS
MAYCROFT
EASTERN WAY
Sch
PH
CHURCH LA
Norton
School
Payne's Farm
NORTHFIELDS
MIDDLEFIELDS
DANESCROFT
THE LINK
LINDENCROFT
PAYNES CL
CROFT LA
CASHIO LA
FARM CL
Playing Field
GREEN LA
TALBOT WAY
CADE CL
Allot Gdns
Allot Gdns
FARRIERS CL
BREWERY LA
THE SYCAMORES
LAVENDER CT
ICKNIELD WAY
CHURCH ST
JACKSON ST
MEETING HOUSE
FOOTBALL CL
STATION RD
SALISBURY RD
BYGRAVE RD
Leagrave Farm
LARKINS CL
BRAMLEY CL
ICKNIELD WAY E
Baldock Sta
ROYSTON RD
A 505
CALIFORNIA
GROSVENOR RD
GROSVENOR RD W
WHITE HORSE
CLOTHALL
School

11

23

4

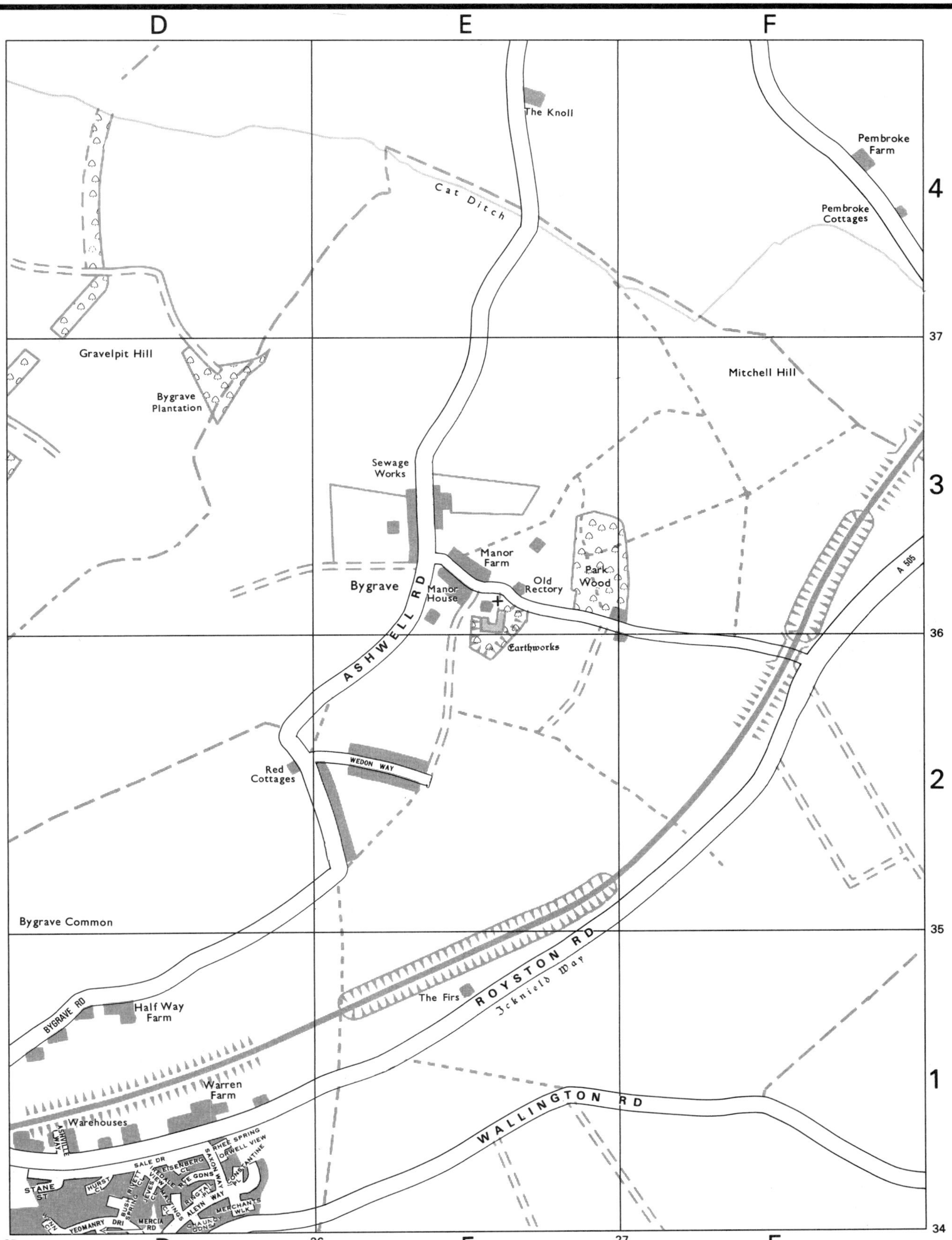
D
E
F
The Knoll
Pembroke Farm
Pembroke Cottages
Cat Ditch
4
37
Gravelpit Hill
Bygrave Plantation
Mitchell Hill
Sewage Works
3
Manor Farm
Old Rectory
Park Wood
Bygrave
Manor House
Earthworks
A 505
ASHWELL RD
36
WEDON WAY
Red Cottages
2
Bygrave Common
35
ROYSTON RD
Icknield Way
The Firs
BYGRAVE RD
Half Way Farm
Warren Farm
Warehouses
1
WALLINGTON RD
ASHVILLE WAY
SALE DR
EISENBERG CL
SAXON WAY
RHEE SPRING
ORWELL VIEW
CONSTANTINE PL
STANE ST
HURST CL
RIVETT CL
BUSH SPRING
YEOMANRY DRI
MERCIA RD
RINGTALE PL
ALEYN WAY
MERCHANTS WLK
CHAUNCY GDNS
34
25
26
27

14

24

5

13

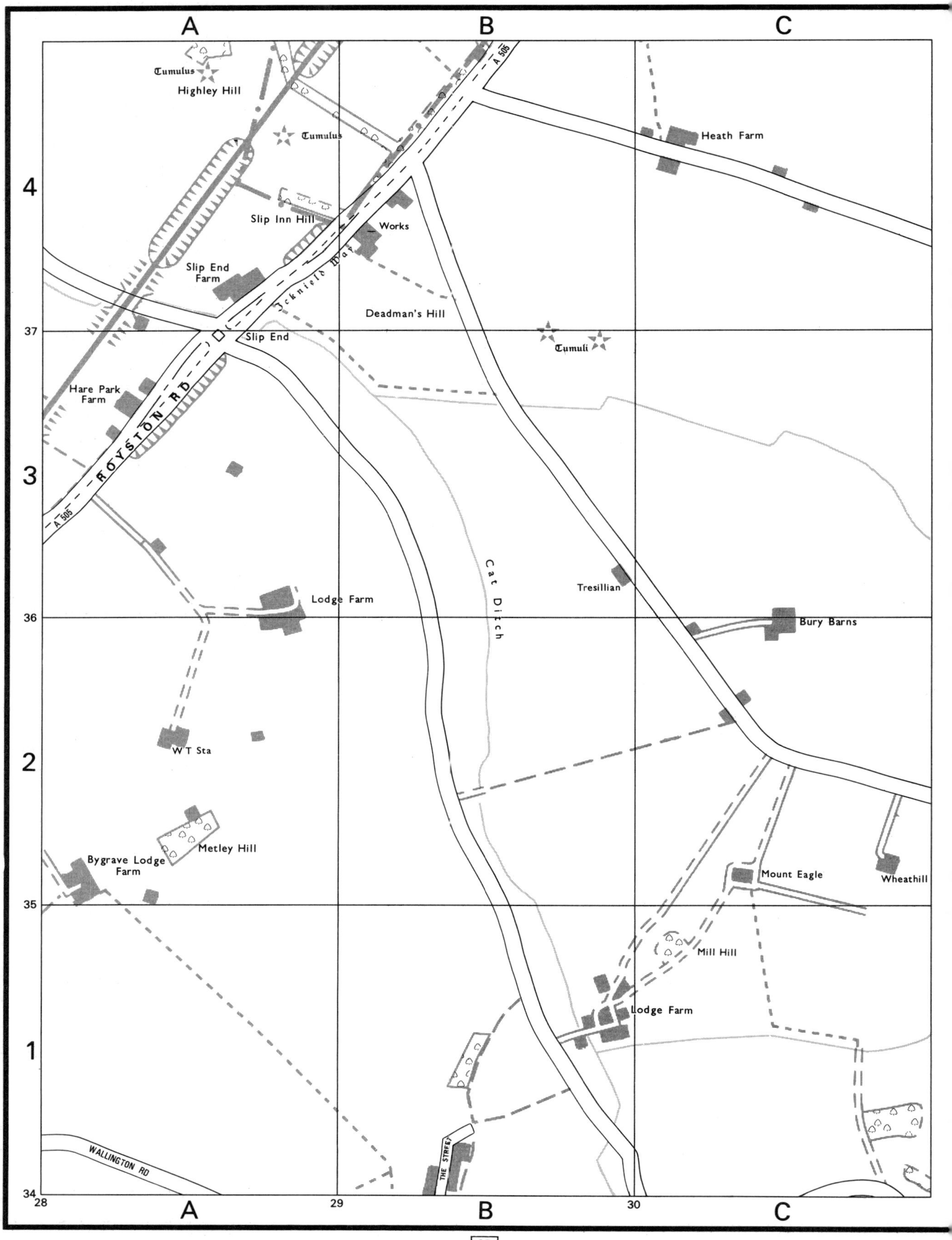
A
B
C
4
3
2
1
37
36
35
34
28
29
30
Tumulus
Highley Hill
Tumulus
Slip Inn Hill
Works
Slip End Farm
Icknield Way
Deadman's Hill
Slip End
A 505
Heath Farm
Tumuli
Hare Park Farm
ROYSTON RD
Lodge Farm
Cat Ditch
Tresillian
Bury Barns
W T Sta
Metley Hill
Bygrave Lodge Farm
Mount Eagle
Wheathill
Mill Hill
Lodge Farm
WALLINGTON RD
THE STREET

25

6

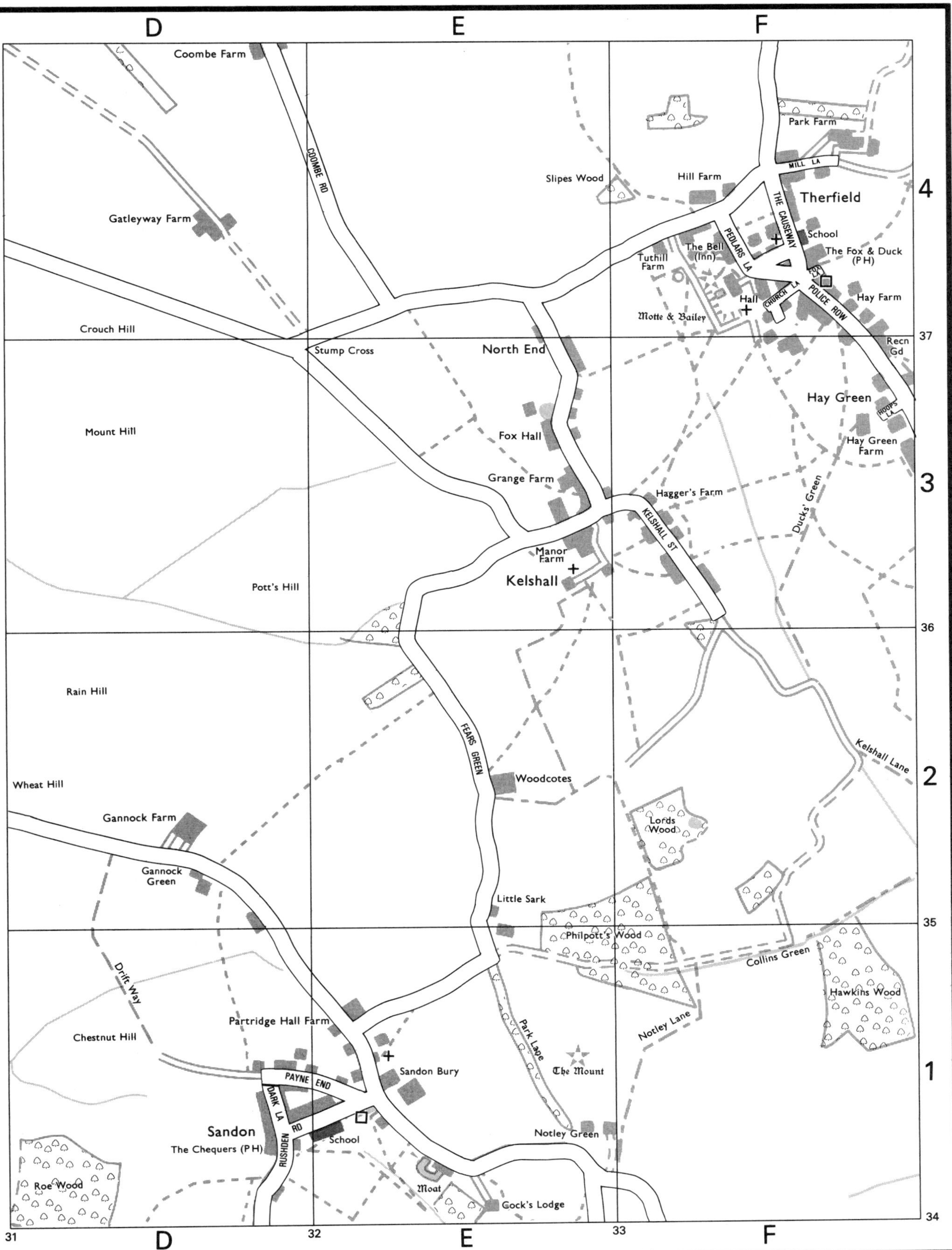
D
E
F
Coombe Farm
COOMBE RD
Gatleyway Farm
Crouch Hill
Stump Cross
North End
Mount Hill
Fox Hall
Grange Farm
Pott's Hill
Manor Farm
Kelshall
KELSHALL ST
Hagger's Farm
Slipes Wood
Hill Farm
Park Farm
MILL LA
Therfield
THE CAUSEWAY
School
The Bell (Inn)
Tuthill Farm
PEDLARS LA
The Fox & Duck (PH)
Hall
CHURCH LA
POLICE ROW
Hay Farm
Motte & Bailey
Recn Gd
Hay Green
HOOPS LA
Hay Green Farm
Ducks' Green
Rain Hill
FEARS GREEN
Woodcotes
Kelshall Lane
Wheat Hill
Gannock Farm
Lords Wood
Gannock Green
Little Sark
Philpott's Wood
Collins Green
Hawkins Wood
Drift Way
Chestnut Hill
Partridge Hall Farm
Park Lane
Notley Lane
Sandon Bury
The Mount
PAYNE END
DARK LA
RD
RUSHDEN
Sandon
The Chequers (PH)
School
Notley Green
Roe Wood
Moat
Gock's Lodge
4
37
3
36
2
35
1
34
31
32
33
D
E
F

16

26

7

15

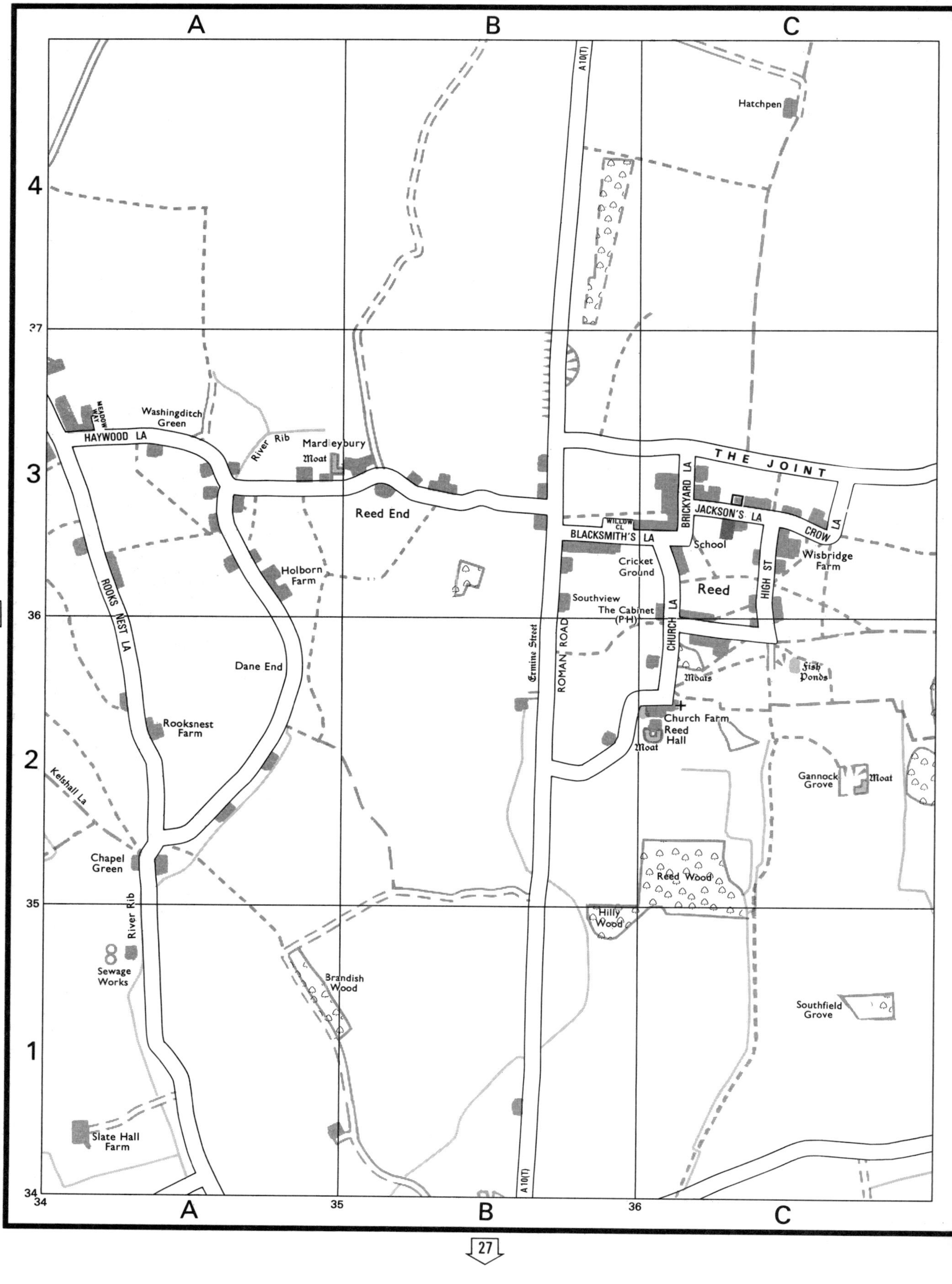
A
B
C
A
B
C
4
3
2
1
37
36
35
34
34
35
36
A 10(T)
Hatchpen
Washingditch Green
MEADOW WAY
HAYWOOD LA
River Rib
Mardleybury
Moat
Reed End
THE JOINT
BRICKYARD LA
JACKSON'S LA
CROW LA
WILLOW CL
BLACKSMITH'S LA
School
Wisbridge Farm
Holborn Farm
Cricket Ground
Reed
HIGH ST
ROOKS NEST LA
Southview
The Cabinet (PH)
CHURCH LA
ROMAN ROAD
Ermine Street
Dane End
Moats
Fish Ponds
Rooksnest Farm
Church Farm
Reed Hall
Moat
Kelshall La
Gannock Grove
Moat
Chapel Green
Reed Wood
Hilly Wood
River Rib
Sewage Works
Brandish Wood
Southfield Grove
Slate Hall Farm

27

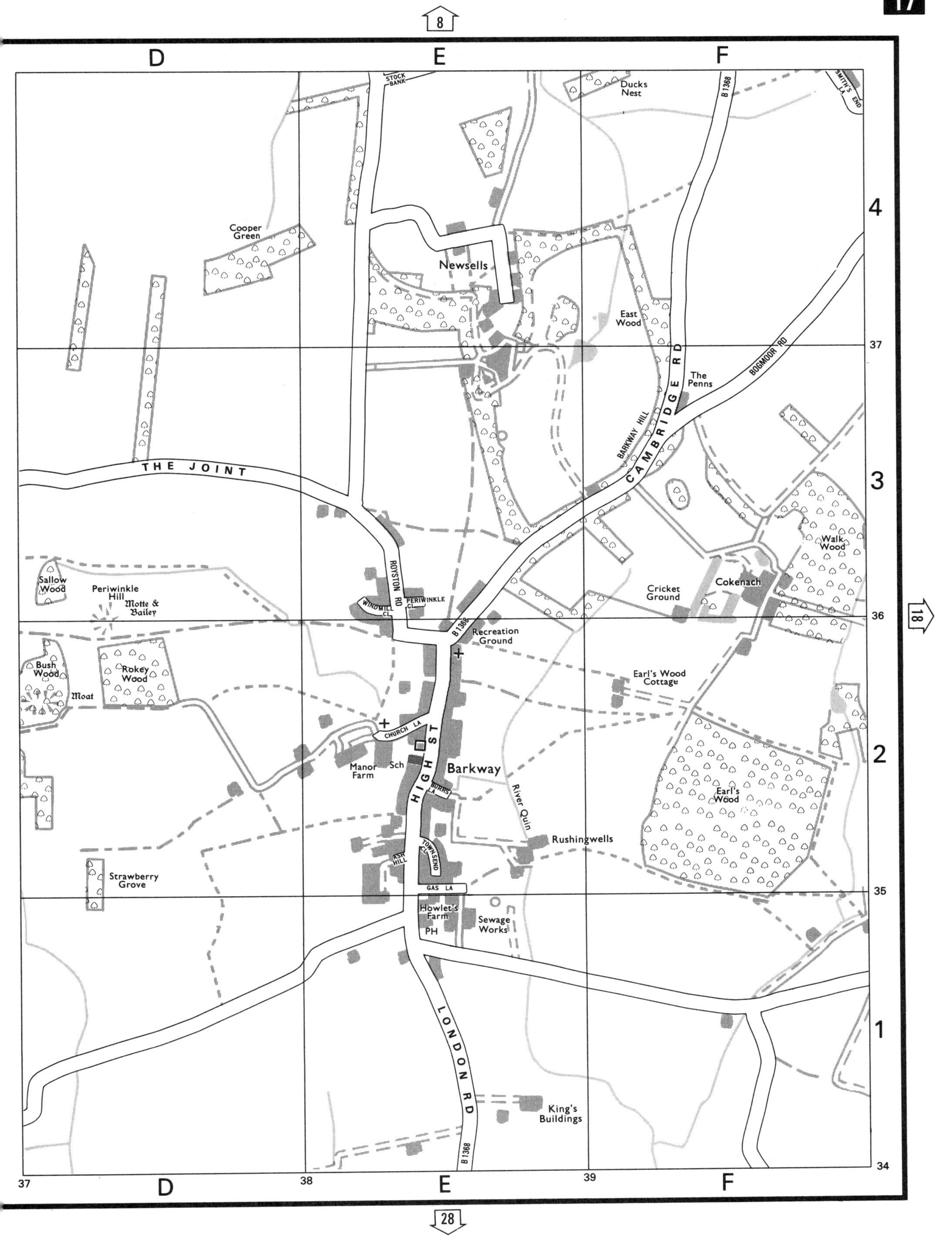
8
D
E
F
STOCK BANK
Ducks Nest
B1368
SMITH'S END LA
Cooper Green
Newsells
East Wood
The Penns
BOGMOOR RD
CAMBRIDGE RD
BARKWAY HILL
THE JOINT
Walk Wood
Sallow Wood
Periwinkle Hill
Motte & Bailey
ROYSTON RD
WINDMILL CL
PERIWINKLE CL
Cricket Ground
Cokenach
Recreation Ground
Bush Wood
Rokey Wood
Moat
Earl's Wood Cottage
CHURCH LA
Manor Farm
Sch
HIGH ST
Barkway
BURRS LA
River Quin
Earl's Wood
Rushingwells
ASH HILL
TOWNSEND CL
Strawberry Grove
GAS LA
Howlet's Farm
PH
Sewage Works
LONDON RD
King's Buildings
B1368
4
37
3
36
2
35
1
34
37
38
39
18
28

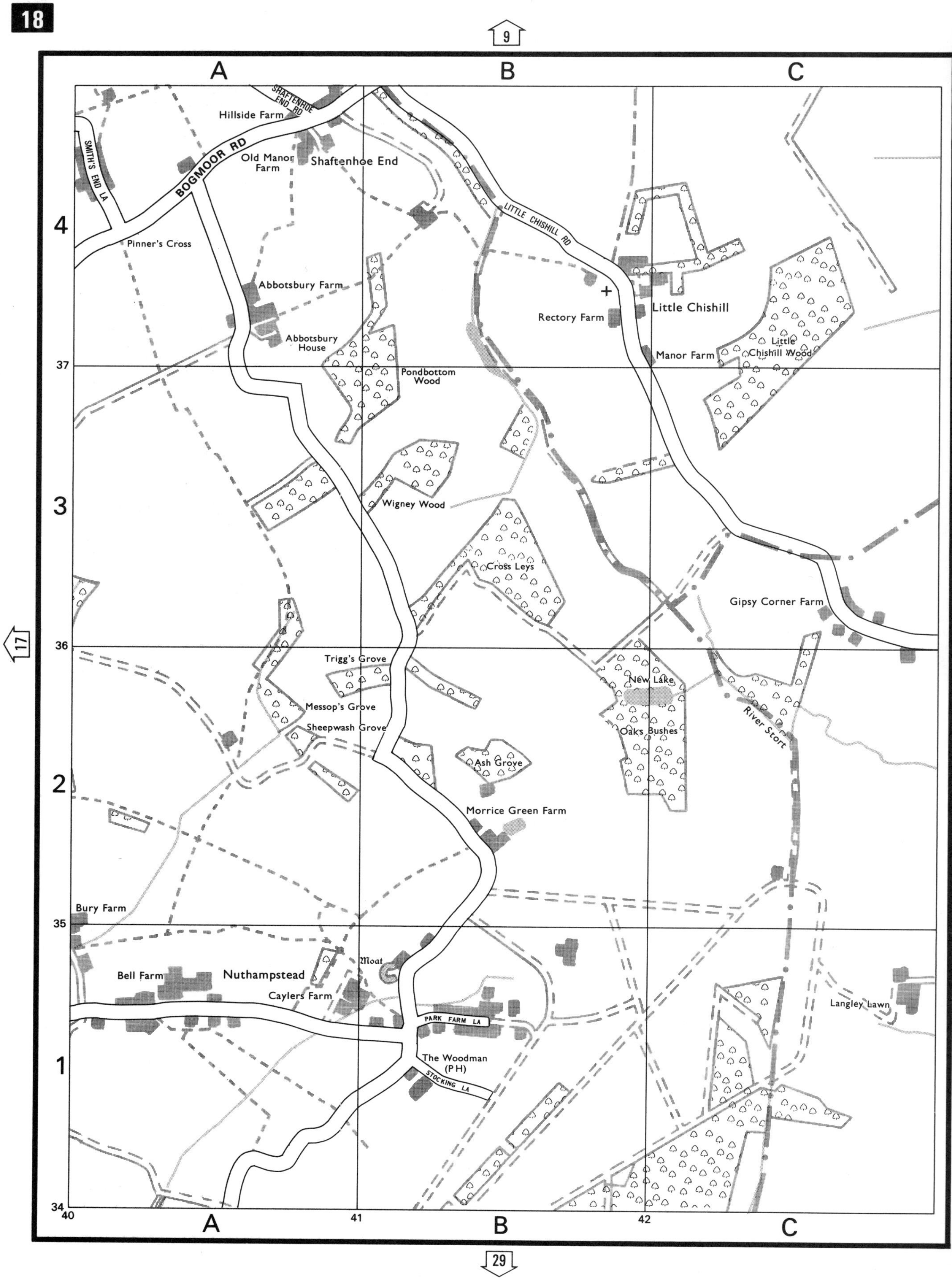
9
17
29
A
B
C
4
3
2
1
37
36
35
34
40
41
42
Hillside Farm
SHAFTENHOE END RD
SMITH'S END LA
BOGMOOR RD
Old Manor Farm
Shaftenhoe End
LITTLE CHISHILL RD
Pinner's Cross
Abbotsbury Farm
Abbotsbury House
Rectory Farm
Little Chishill
Manor Farm
Little Chishill Wood
Pondbottom Wood
Wigney Wood
Cross Leys
Gipsy Corner Farm
Trigg's Grove
Messop's Grove
Sheepwash Grove
New Lake
Oaks Bushes
River Stort
Ash Grove
Morrice Green Farm
Bury Farm
Moat
Bell Farm
Nuthampstead
Caylers Farm
PARK FARM LA
The Woodman (PH)
STOCKING LA
Langley Lawn

not continued, see key diagram

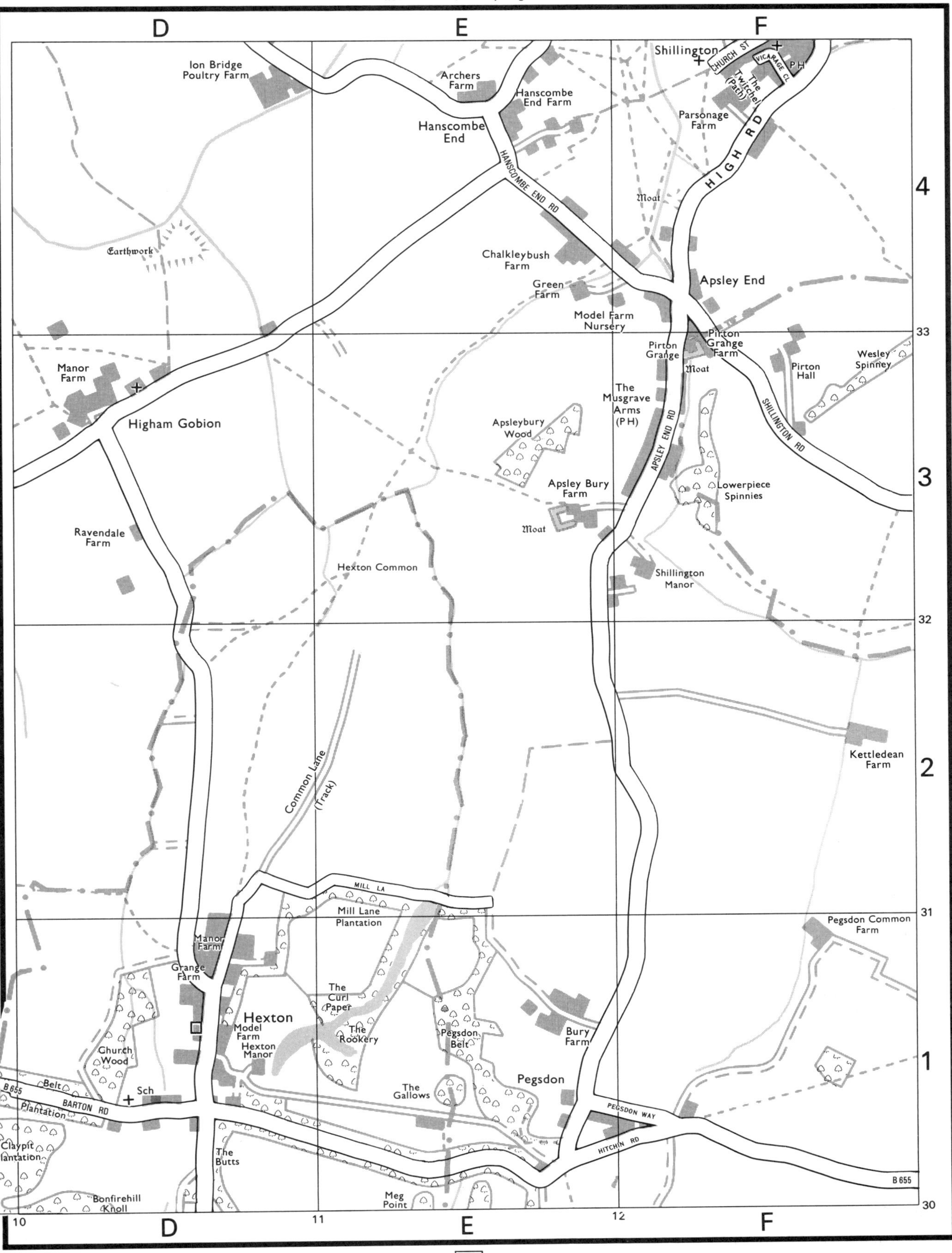

32

not continued, see key diagram

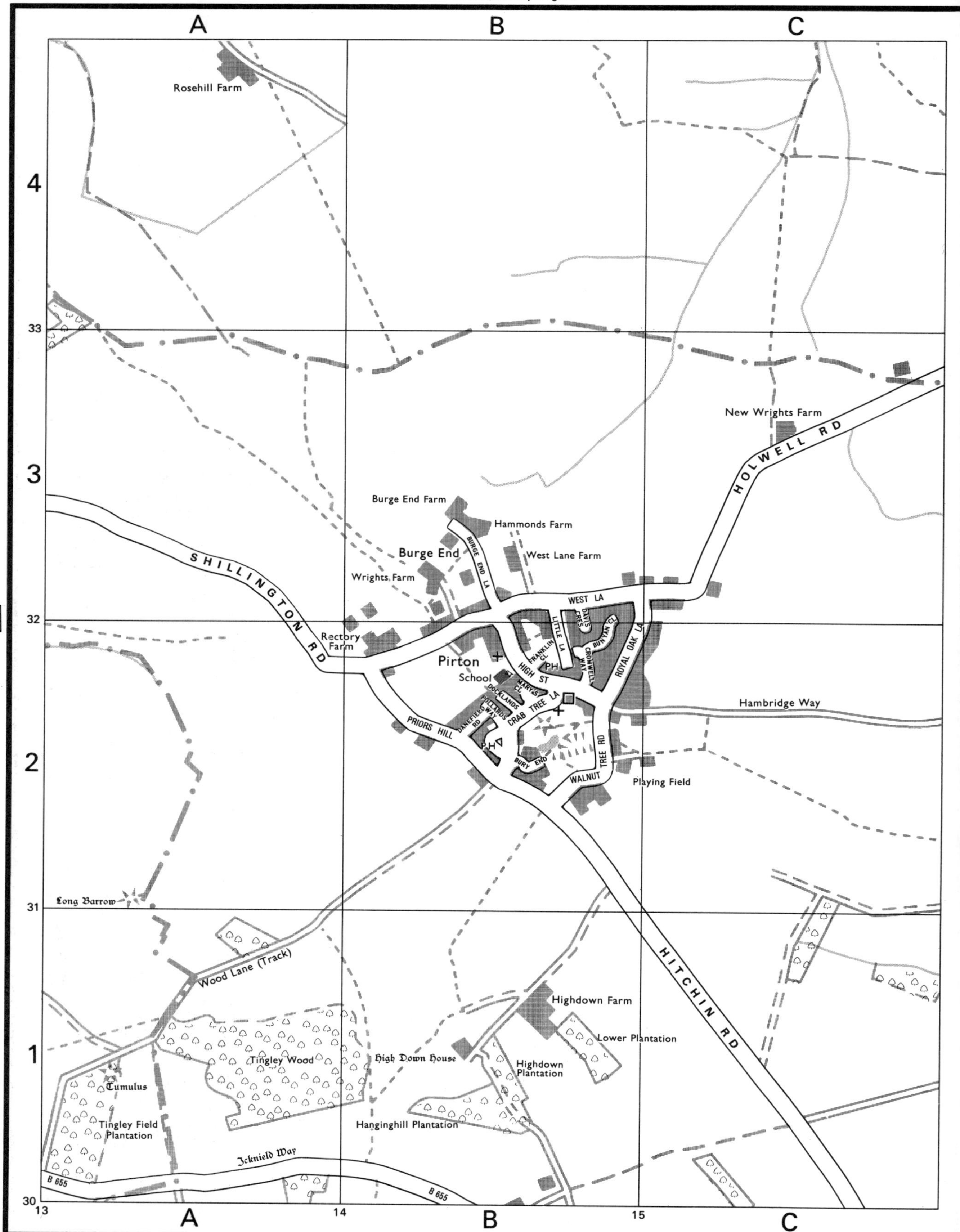

19

33

10

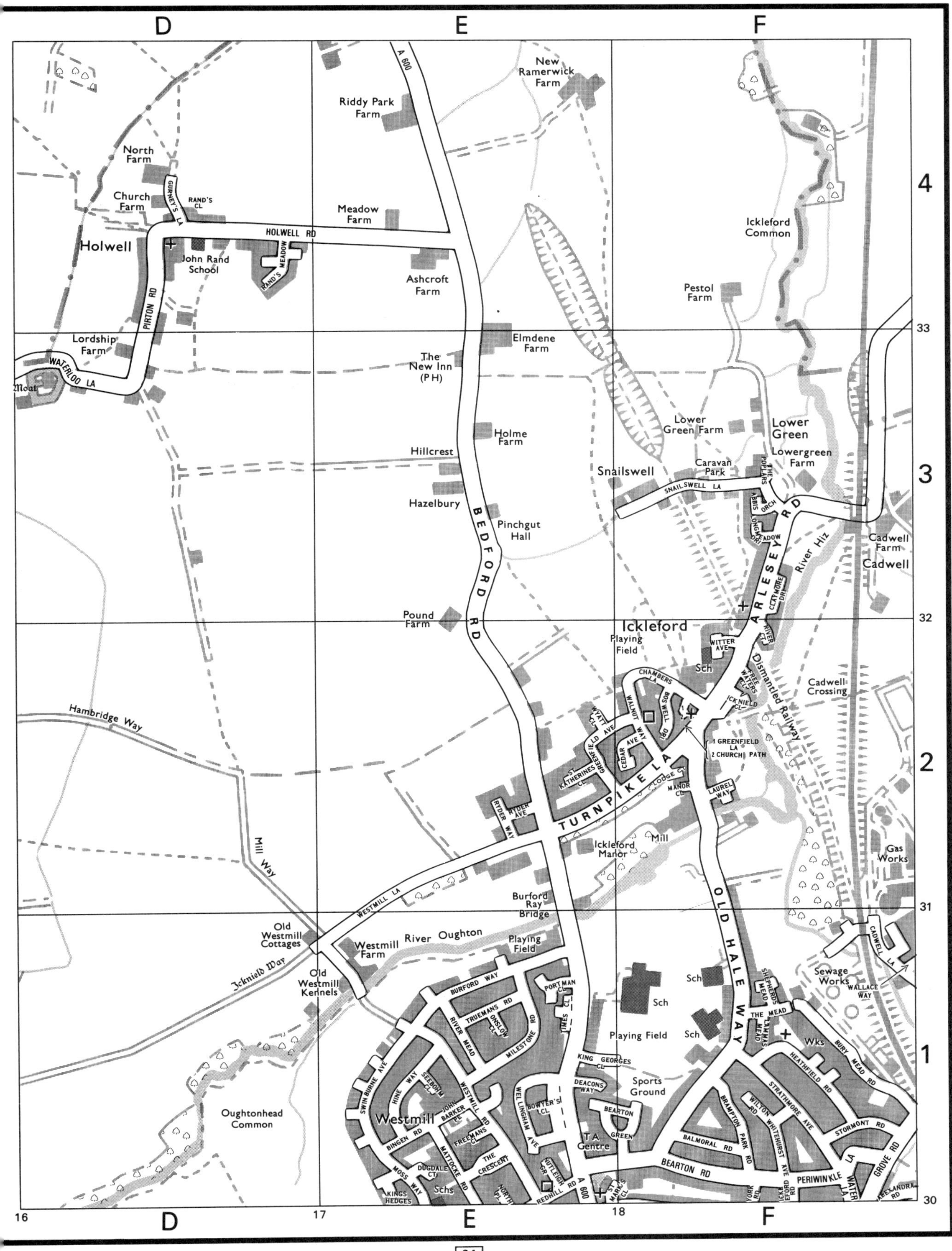

D
E
F
4
3
2
1
33
32
31
30
16
17
18
New Ramerwick Farm
Riddy Park Farm
North Farm
Church Farm
GURNEY'S LA
RAND'S CL
HOLWELL RD
Meadow Farm
Holwell
John Rand School
RAND'S MEADOW
Ashcroft Farm
PIRTON RD
Ickleford Common
Pestol Farm
Lordship Farm
WATERLOO LA
Moat
Elmdene Farm
The New Inn (PH)
Holme Farm
Lower Green Farm
Lower Green
Lowergreen Farm
Hillcrest
Snailswell
Caravan Park
SNAILSWELL LA
THE POPLARS
ABBIS ORCH
Hazelbury
Pinchgut Hall
BEDFORD RD
A 600
ARLESEY RD
Cadwell Farm
Cadwell
River Hiz
Pound Farm
Ickleford
Playing Field
WITTER AVE
Sch
CHAMBERS LA
Dismantled Railway
Cadwell Crossing
ICKNIELD CL
Hambridge Way
WALNUT WAY
BOSWELL DR
WYATT CL
GREENFIELD AVE
CEDAR AVE
1 GREENFIELD LA
2 CHURCH PATH
ST KATHERINES CL
TURNPIKE LA
LODGE CT
MANOR CL
LAUREL WAY
RYDER WAY
RYDER AVE
Ickleford Manor
Mill
Gas Works
Mill Way
WESTMILL LA
Burford Ray Bridge
OLD HALE WAY
Old Westmill Cottages
River Oughton
Westmill Farm
Playing Field
CADWELL LA
Sewage Works
WALLACE WAY
Icknield Way
Old Westmill Kennels
BURFORD WAY
PORTMAN CL
Sch
SHEPHERDS MEAD
TRUEMANS RD
ONSLOW CL
RIVER MEAD
MILESTONE RD
TIMES CL
THE MEAD
LAMMAS MEAD
Playing Field
Wks
BURY MEAD RD
HEATHFIELD RD
KING GEORGES CL
SWINBURNE AVE
HINE WAY
SEEBOHM CL
WESTMILL RD
Sports Ground
STRATHMORE AVE
WILTON RD
JOHN BARKER PL
DEACONS WAY
BOWYER'S CL
WELLINGHAM AVE
BEARTON GREEN
BRAMPTON PARK RD
STORMONT RD
Oughtonhead Common
Westmill
FREEMANS CL
TA Centre
WHITEHURST AVE
BINGEN RD
BALMORAL RD
THE CRESCENT
NUTLEIGH GR
BEARTON RD
MOSS WAY
DUGDALE CT
MATTOCKE RD
PERIWINKLE LA
GROVE RD
KINGS HEDGES
Schs
NORTH PL
REDHILL RD
ST MARKS CL
YORK RD
ICKLEFORD RD
WATER LA
ALEXANDRA RD

22

34

11

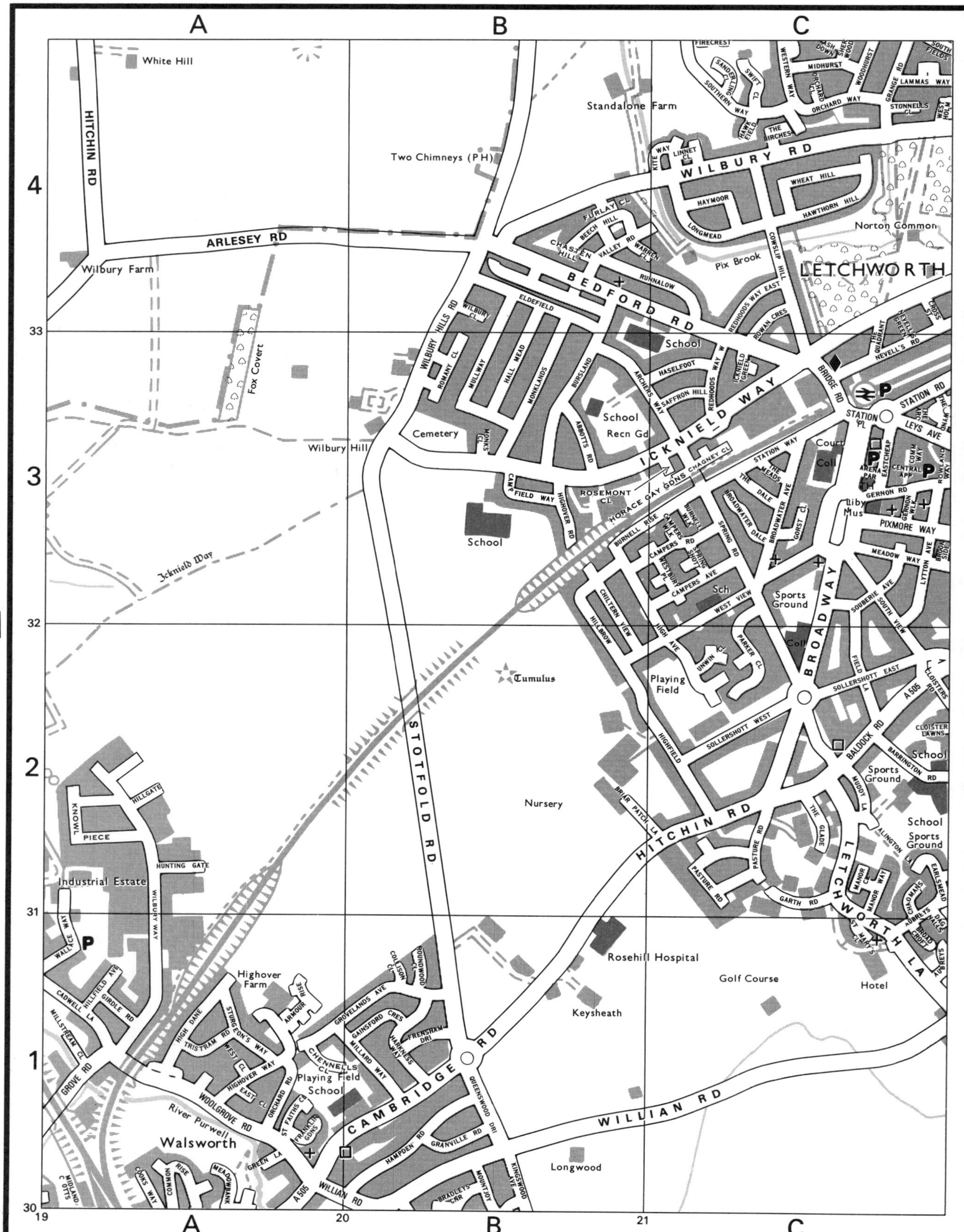
A
B
C
4
3
2
1
33
32
31
30
19
20
21
White Hill
HITCHIN RD
Standalone Farm
Two Chimneys (PH)
ARLESEY RD
Wilbury Farm
Fox Covert
Wilbury Hill
Icknield Way
Cemetery
School
Tumulus
STOTFOLD RD
Nursery
Industrial Estate
HILLGATE
KNOWL PIECE
HUNTING GATE
WILBURY WAY
WALLACE WAY
HILLFIELD AVE
GIRDLE RD
CADWELL LA
MILLSTREAM CL
GROVE RD
HIGH DANE
TRISTRAM RD
STURGEON'S WAY
WEST CL
HIGHOVER WAY
EAST CL
ORCHARD RD
WOOLGROVE RD
River Purwell
Walsworth
GREEN LA
COMMON RISE
MEADOWBANK
MIDLAND COTTS
ST FAITHS CL
FRANKLIN GDNS
Highover Farm
ARMOUR RISE
CHENNELLS CL
Playing Field
School
GROVELANDS AVE
GAINSFORD CRES
MILLARD WAY
HARKNESS WAY
FRENSHAM DRI
COLLISON CL
ROUNDWOOD CL
CAMBRIDGE RD
QUEENSWOOD DRI
HAMPDEN RD
GRANVILLE RD
WILLIAN RD
A505
BRADLEYS CNR
MOUNT JOY
KINGSWOOD AVE
Longwood
Keysheath
Rosehill Hospital
Golf Course
Hotel
HITCHIN RD
BRIAR PATCH LA
PASTURE RD
GARTH RD
THE GLADE
LETCHWORTH LA
ST MARY'S CL
MANOR CL
MANOR WAY
CHAGMANS
AUBREYS
BROAD CROFT
EARLSMEAD
School
Sports Ground
ALINGTON LA
MUDDY LA
BARRINGTON RD
BALDOCK RD
CLOISTER LAWNS
CLOISTERS RD
A505
SOLLERSHOTT EAST
SOLLERSHOTT WEST
FIELD LA
HIGHFIELD
Playing Field
UNWIN CL
PARKER CL
HIGH AVE
CHILTERN VIEW
HILLBROW
WEST VIEW
Sch
Coll
BROADWAY
Sports Ground
SOUBERIE AVE
SOUTH VIEW
LYTTON AVE
MEADOW WAY
PIXMORE WAY
BROOK SIDE
Liby
Mus
GERNON RD
GERNON WLK
CAMPERS AVE
CAMPERS RD
CAMPERS WLK
BURNELL RISE
BURNELL WLK
WESTBURY CL
SPRING SHOTT
SPRING RD
BROADWATER DALE
BROADWATER AVE
GORST CL
THE DALE
THE MEADS
STATION WAY
Court
Coll
EASTCHEAP
ARENA PAR
COMM WAY
CENTRAL APP
LEYS AVE
STATION PL
STATION RD
THE ARC
THE WYND
ROWLAND
HORACE GAY GDNS
CHAGNEY CL
ROSEMONT CL
CAMP FIELD WAY
HIGHOVER RD
ICKNIELD WAY
School
Recn Gd
ABBOTTS RD
BURSLAND
MONKLANDS
HALL MEAD
MULLWAY
ROMANY CL
WILBURY HILLS RD
WILBURY CL
MONKS CL
ELDEFIELD
BEDFORD RD
School
HASELFOOT
SAFFRON HILL
ARCHERS WAY
REDHOODS WAY W
ICKNIELD GREEN
REDHOODS WAY EAST
ROWAN CRES
BRIDGE RD
THE QUADRANT
NEVELLS GREEN
NEVELL'S RD
CROSS ST
CHASTEN HILL
VALLEY RD
BEECH HILL
FURLAY CL
WARREN CL
RUNNALOW
Pix Brook
LETCHWORTH
Norton Common
COWSLIP HILL
LONGMEAD
HAYMOOR
WHEAT HILL
HAWTHORN HILL
WILBURY RD
KITE WAY
LINNET CL
THE BIRCHES
HAWK FIELD
SOUTHERN WAY
SANDERLING CL
SWIFT CL
FIRECREST
WESTERN WAY
MIDHURST
ORCHARD CL
ORCHARD WAY
WOODHURST
GRANGE RD
LAMMAS WAY
STONNELLS CL
SOUTH FIELDS
WEST HOLM

21

35

12

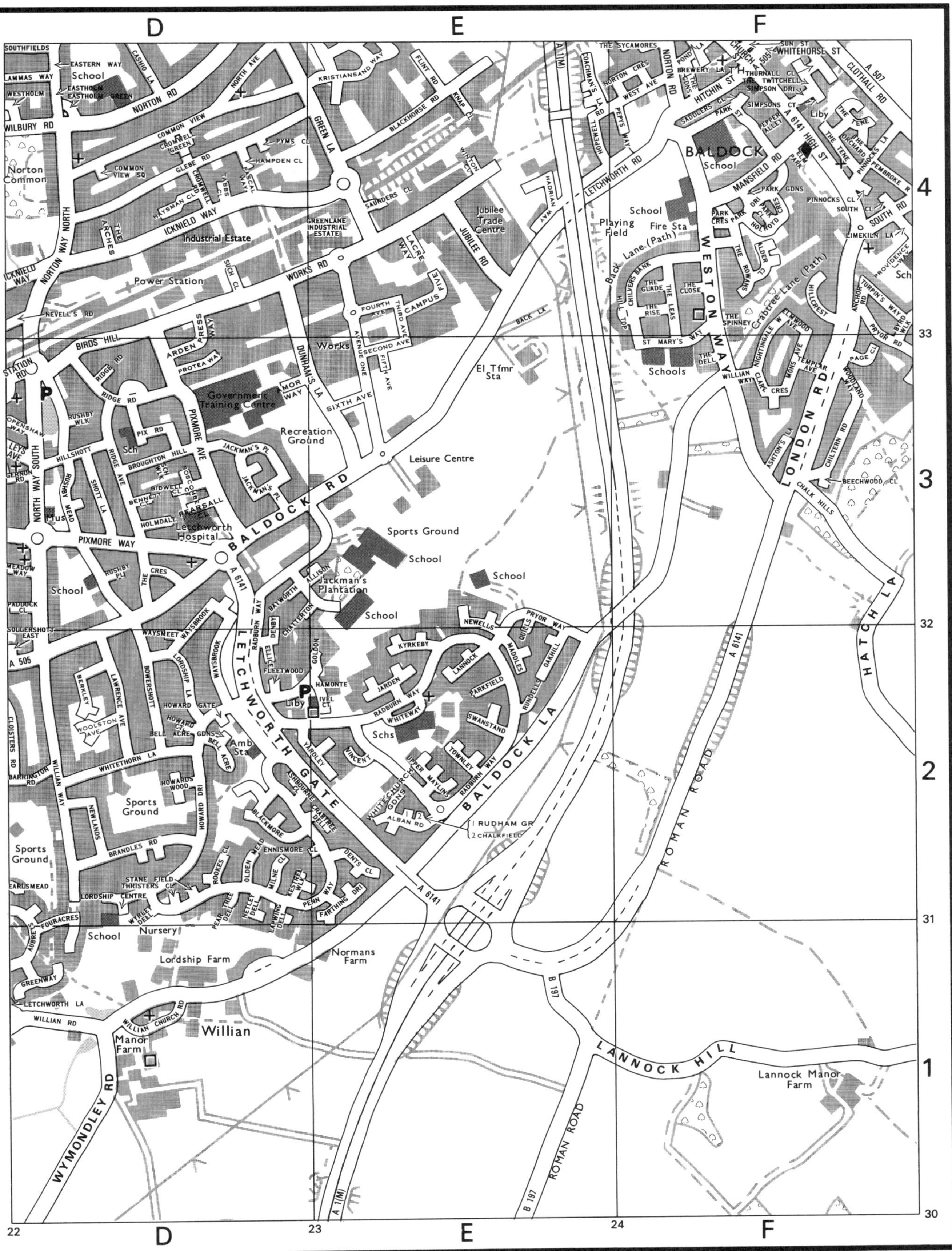
D
E
F
4
3
2
1
33
32
31
30
22
23
24
SOUTHFIELDS
EASTERN WAY
LAMMAS WAY
School
WESTHOLM
EASTHOLM
EASTHOLM GREEN
CASHIO LA
NORTON RD
NORTH AVE
WILBURY RD
Norton Common
COMMON VIEW
CROMWELL GREEN
PYMS CL
GLEBE RD
HAMPDEN CL
COMMON VIEW SQ
CROMWELL
TABBS
ASCAL WAY
HAYSMAN CL
ICKNIELD WAY
THE ARCHES
NORTON WAY NORTH
Industrial Estate
GREENLANE INDUSTRIAL ESTATE
ICKNIELD WAY
Power Station
SUCH CL
WORKS RD
NEVELL'S RD
KRISTIANSAND WAY
FLINT RD
GREEN LA
BLACKHORSE RD
KNAP CL
WINTON CL
SAUNDERS CL
LACRE WAY
Jubilee Trade Centre
JUBILEE RD
FOURTH AVE
THIRD AVE
CAMPUS
FIVE
SECOND AVE
AVENUE ONE
FIFTH AVE
SIXTH AVE
Works
BIRDS HILL
STATION RD
ARDEN PRESS WAY
PROTEA WAY
RIDGE RD
Government Training Centre
AMOR WAY
DUNHAM'S LA
Recreation Ground
Leisure Centre
El Tfmr Sta
BACK LA
HADRIAN WAY
LETCHWORTH RD
A 1(M)
THE SYCAMORES
COACHMAN'S LA
NORTON CRES
WEST AVE
PEPYS WAY
HOPEWELL RD
NORTON RD
POND LA
BREWERY LA
THE GDNS
HITCHIN ST
CHURCH ST
A 505
SUN ST
WHITEHORSE ST
THURNALL CL
THE TWITCHELL
SIMPSON DRI
A 507
CLOTHALL RD
SADDLERS CL
PARK ST
SIMPSONS CT
PEPPER ALLEY
A 6141 HIGH ST
Liby
THE TENE
THE ORCHARD
BALDOCK
School
MANSFIELD RD
ELM PARK
PINNOCKS LA
PEMBROKE RD
PARK GDNS
PINNOCKS CL
SOUTH RD
School
Playing Field
Fire Sta
PARK CRES
PARK DRI
HOLYROOD CL
LIMEKILN LA
Back Lane (Path)
WESTON WAY
THE ROWAN
ALDER CL
PROVIDENCE WAY
Sch
CHILVERS BANK
THE GLADE
THE LEAS
THE CLOSE
HILL TOP
THE RISE
THE SPINNEY
Crabtree Lane (Path)
HILLCREST
ANCHOR RD
TURPIN'S WAY
BYFORD WAY
PRYOR RD
ST MARY'S WAY
THE DELL
Schools
NIGHTINGALE WAY
ELMWOOD AVE
WILLIAN WAY
CLARE CRES
MONS AVE
TEMPLAR AVE
LONDON RD
WOODLAND WAY
PAGE CL
ASHTON'S LA
CHILTERN RD
BEECHWOOD CL
CHALK HILLS
HATCH LA
RUSHBY WLK
OPENSHAW WAY
PIX RD
Sch
LEYS AVE
HILLSHOTT
BROUGHTON HILL
PIXMORE AVE
JACKMAN'S PL
BALDOCK RD
RIDGE AVE
BIDWELL CL
BOSCOMBE CT
PEARSALL CL
BENNETT CT
HOLMDALE
SHOTT LA
RUSHBY MEAD
NORTH WAY SOUTH
Mus
PIXMORE WAY
Letchworth Hospital
Sports Ground
School
Jackman's Plantation
School
School
RUSHBY PL
THE CRES
A 6141
MEADOW WAY
School
PADDOCK CL
SOLLERSHOTT EAST
WAYSMEET
WAYSBROOK
A 505
ALLISON
BAYWORTH
RADBURN WAY
DENBY
CHATTERTON
GOLDON
ELLICE
FLEETWOOD
HAMONTE
Liby
IVEL CT
NEWELLS
PRYOR WAY
QUILLS
KYRKEBY
MADDLES
OAKHILL
LANNOCK
JARDEN
PARKFIELD
RUNDELLS
RADBURN WAY
WHITEWAY
SWANSTAND
Schs
BERKLEY
LAWRENCE AVE
BOWERSHOTT
LORDSHIP LA
HOWARD GATE
HOWARD CT
BELL ACRE GDNS
BELL ACRE
Amb Sta
LETCHWORTH GATE
WOOLSTON AVE
CLOISTERS RD
YARDLEY
VINCENT
TOWNLEY
UPPER MAYLINS
RADBURN WAY
BALDOCK LA
WHITETHORN LA
BARRINGTON RD
WILLIAN WAY
HOWARDS WOOD
HOWARD DRI
Sports Ground
NEWLANDS
ASHBOURNE CL
CRABTREE DELL
WHITECHURCH GDNS
ALBAN RD
1 RUDHAM GR
2 CHALKFIELD
BLACKMORE
Sports Ground
BRANDLES RD
ENNISMORE CL
DENTS CL
ROOKES CL
OLDEN MEAD
MILNE CL
KESTREL WLK
PENN WAY
FARTHING DRI
EARLSMEAD
STANE FIELD
THRISTERS CL
LORDSHIP CENTRE
WYNLEY DELL
PEAR TREE DELL
NETLEY DELL
LAPWING DELL
A 6141
A 6141
ROMAN ROAD
FOURACRES
AUBREYS
School
Nursery
Lordship Farm
Normans Farm
GREENWAY
LETCHWORTH LA
WILLIAN RD
WILLIAN CHURCH RD
Willian
Manor Farm
B 197
LANNOCK HILL
Lannock Manor Farm
WYMONDLEY RD
ROMAN ROAD
B 197
A 1(M)

24

36

13

23

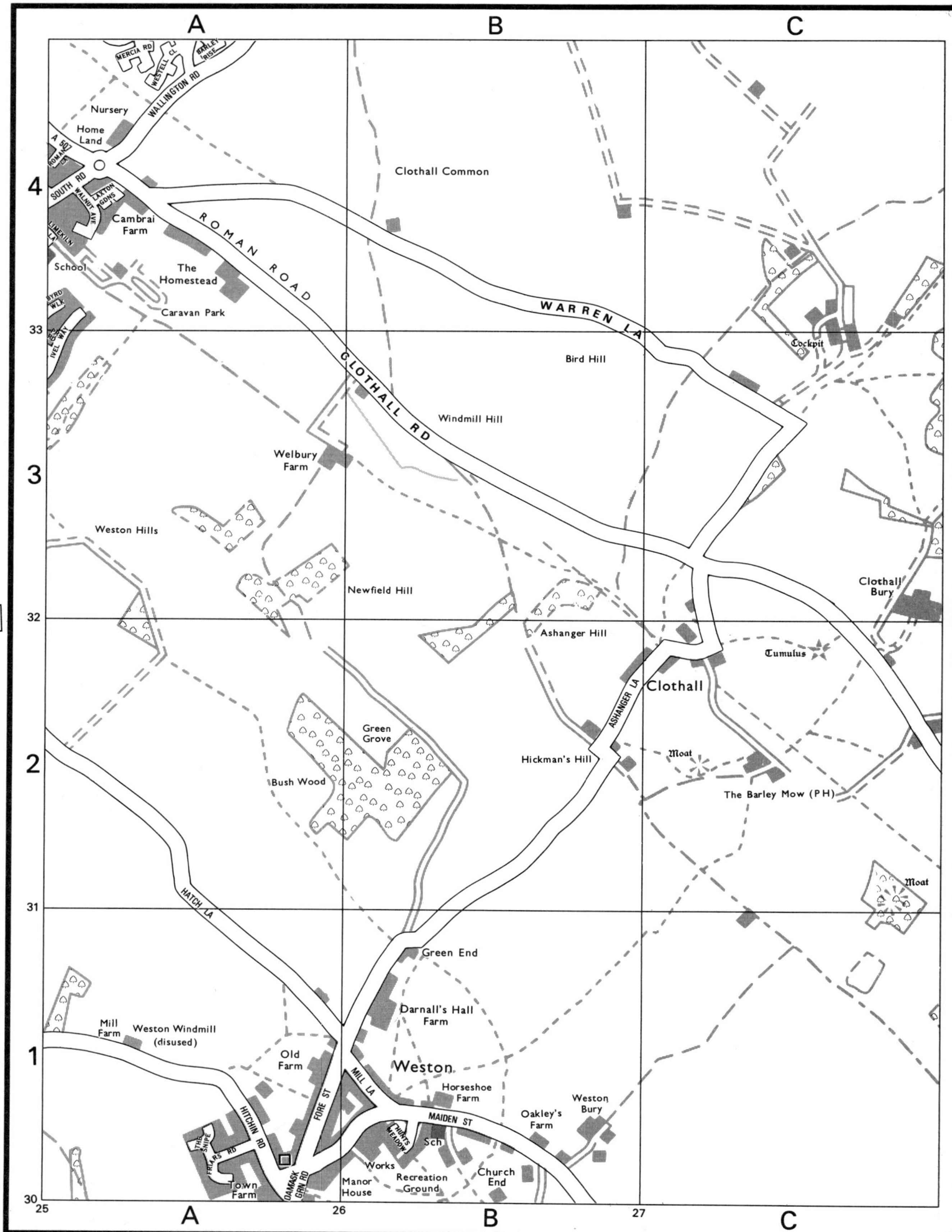
A
B
C
4
3
2
1
33
32
31
30
25
26
27
MERCIA RD
WESTELL CL
BARLEY RISE
WALLINGTON RD
Nursery
Home Land
A 507
ROMAN LA
SOUTH RD
WALNUT AVE
LAXTON GDNS
LIMEKILN LA
Cambrai Farm
School
The Homestead
BYRD WLK
IVEL WAY
Caravan Park
ROMAN ROAD
Clothall Common
WARREN LA
Bird Hill
Cockpit
CLOTHALL RD
Windmill Hill
Welbury Farm
Weston Hills
Newfield Hill
Clothall Bury
Ashanger Hill
Tumulus
ASHANGER LA
Clothall
Green Grove
Bush Wood
Hickman's Hill
Moat
The Barley Mow (PH)
HATCH LA
Green End
Darnall's Hall Farm
Mill Farm
Weston Windmill (disused)
Old Farm
Weston
MILL LA
Horseshoe Farm
Weston Bury
Oakley's Farm
HITCHIN RD
FORE ST
MAIDEN ST
THE SNIPE
FRIARS RD
HUNTS MEADOW
Sch
Works
Recreation Ground
Church End
Town Farm
DAMASK GRN RD
Manor House

37

14

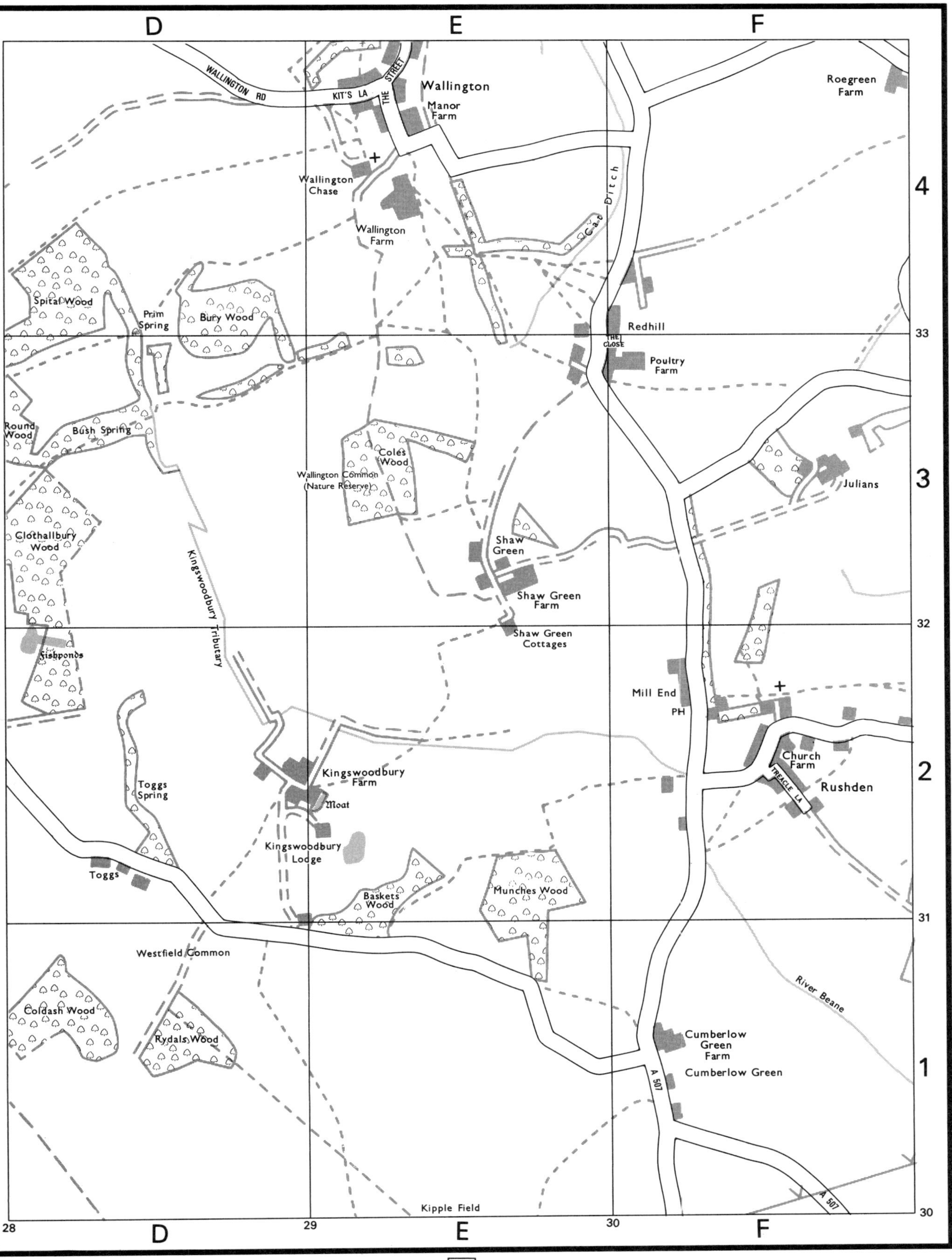
D
E
F
WALLINGTON RD
KIT'S LA
THE STREET
Wallington
Manor Farm
Roegreen Farm
Wallington Chase
Wallington Farm
Cat Ditch
4
Spital Wood
Prim Spring
Bury Wood
Redhill
THE CLOSE
Poultry Farm
33
Round Wood
Bush Spring
Coles Wood
Wallington Common (Nature Reserve)
Julians
3
Clothallbury Wood
Shaw Green
Shaw Green Farm
Kingswoodbury Tributary
Shaw Green Cottages
32
Fishponds
Mill End
PH
Church Farm
TREACLE LA
Rushden
2
Toggs Spring
Kingswoodbury Farm
Moat
Kingswoodbury Lodge
Toggs
Baskets Wood
Munches Wood
31
Westfield Common
River Beane
Coldash Wood
Rydals Wood
Cumberlow Green Farm
Cumberlow Green
1
A 507
A 507
Kipple Field
30
28
29
30
D
E
F

26

38

15

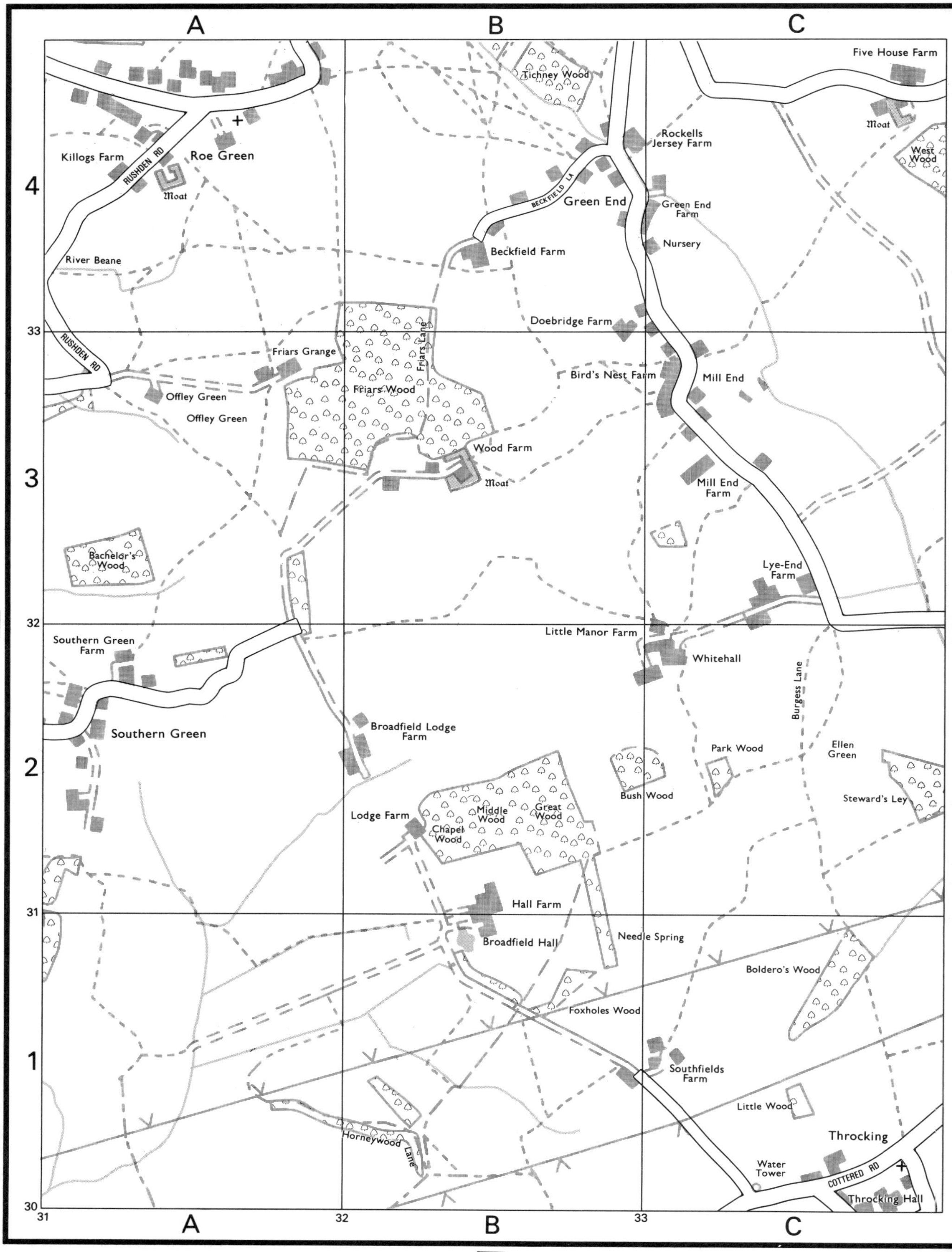

A
B
C
Five House Farm
Tichney Wood
Moat
Rockells
Jersey Farm
West Wood
Killogs Farm
Roe Green
RUSHDEN RD
Moat
4
BECKFIELD LA
Green End
Green End Farm
River Beane
Beckfield Farm
Nursery
Doebridge Farm
33
RUSHDEN RD
Friars Grange
Friars Lane
Bird's Nest Farm
Mill End
Friars Wood
Offley Green
Offley Green
Wood Farm
3
Moat
Mill End Farm
Bachelor's Wood
Lye-End Farm
32
Little Manor Farm
Southern Green Farm
Whitehall
Burgess Lane
Southern Green
Broadfield Lodge Farm
Park Wood
Ellen Green
2
Bush Wood
Steward's Ley
Lodge Farm
Middle Wood
Great Wood
Chapel Wood
Hall Farm
31
Broadfield Hall
Needle Spring
Boldero's Wood
Foxholes Wood
1
Southfields Farm
Little Wood
Horneywood Lane
Throcking
Water Tower
COTTERED RD
Throcking Hall
30
31
32
33
A
B
C

25

39

16

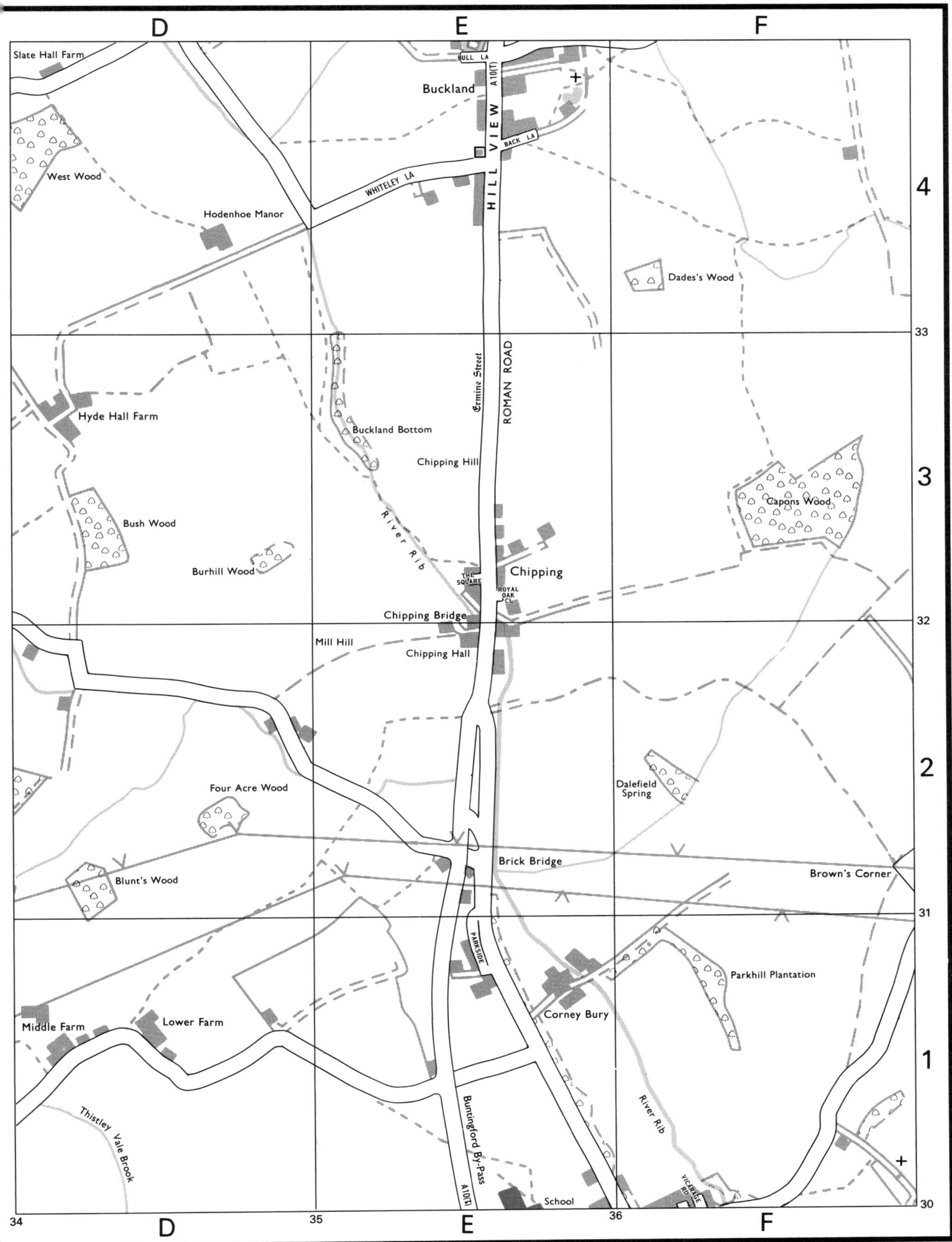
D
E
F
Slate Hall Farm
Buckland
BULL LA
A10(T)
HILL VIEW
BACK LA
WHITELEY LA
West Wood
Hodenhoe Manor
Dades's Wood
4
33
Ermine Street
ROMAN ROAD
Hyde Hall Farm
Buckland Bottom
Chipping Hill
3
Capons Wood
Bush Wood
River Rib
Burhill Wood
THE SQUARE
Chipping
ROYAL OAK CL
Chipping Bridge
32
Mill Hill
Chipping Hall
2
Four Acre Wood
Dalefield Spring
Brick Bridge
Blunt's Wood
Brown's Corner
31
PARKSIDE
Parkhill Plantation
Lower Farm
Middle Farm
Corney Bury
1
Thistley Vale Brook
Buntingford By-Pass
A10(T)
River Rib
VICARAGE RD
School
30
34
35
36
D
E
F

28

40

17

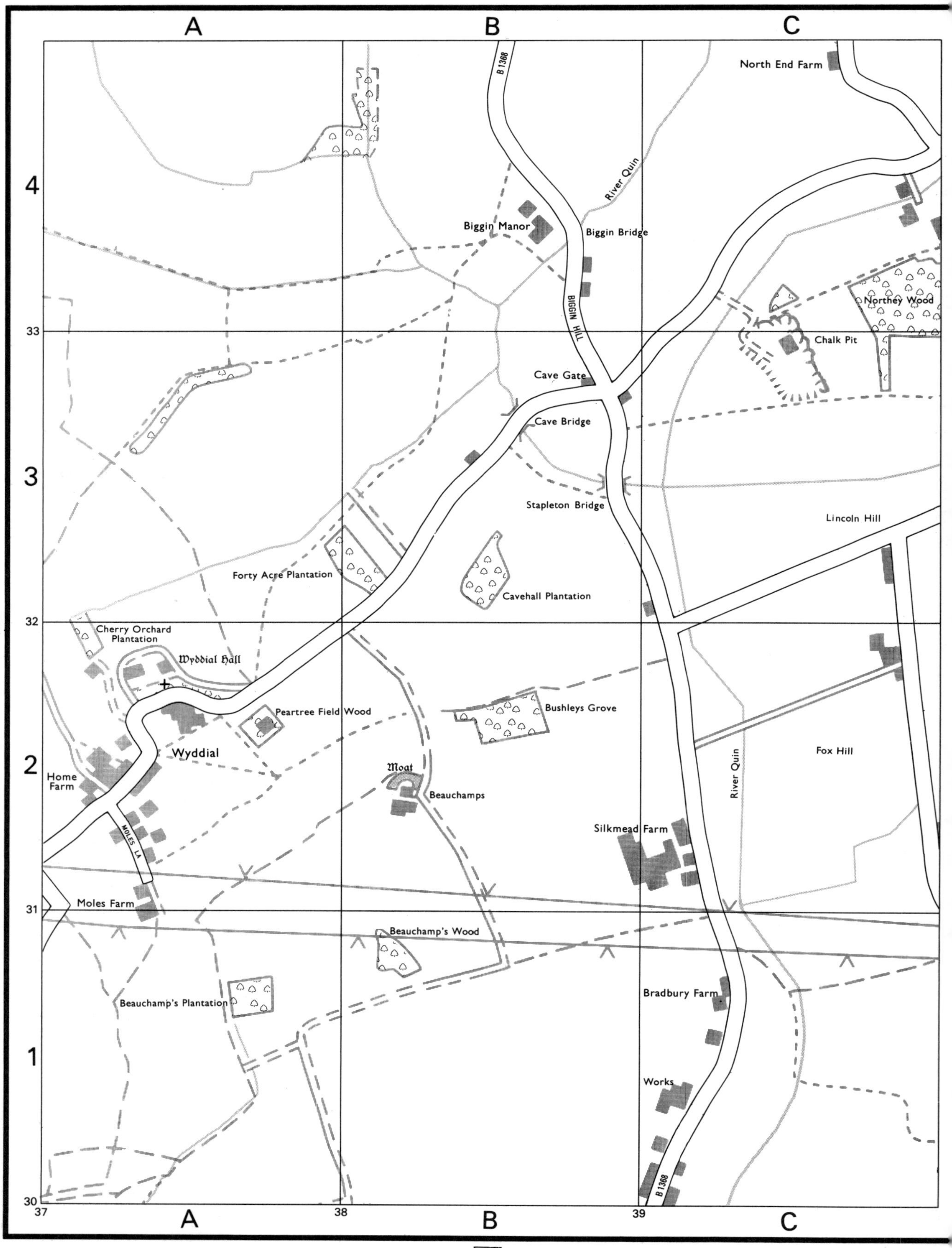
A
B
C
4
3
2
1
33
32
31
30
37
38
39
B 1368
North End Farm
River Quin
Biggin Manor
Biggin Bridge
BIGGIN HILL
Northey Wood
Chalk Pit
Cave Gate
Cave Bridge
Stapleton Bridge
Lincoln Hill
Forty Acre Plantation
Cavehall Plantation
Cherry Orchard Plantation
Wyddial Hall
Peartree Field Wood
Bushleys Grove
Wyddial
Home Farm
Moat
Beauchamps
Fox Hill
River Quin
Silkmead Farm
MOLES LA
Moles Farm
Beauchamp's Wood
Beauchamp's Plantation
Bradbury Farm
Works
B 1368

27

41

18

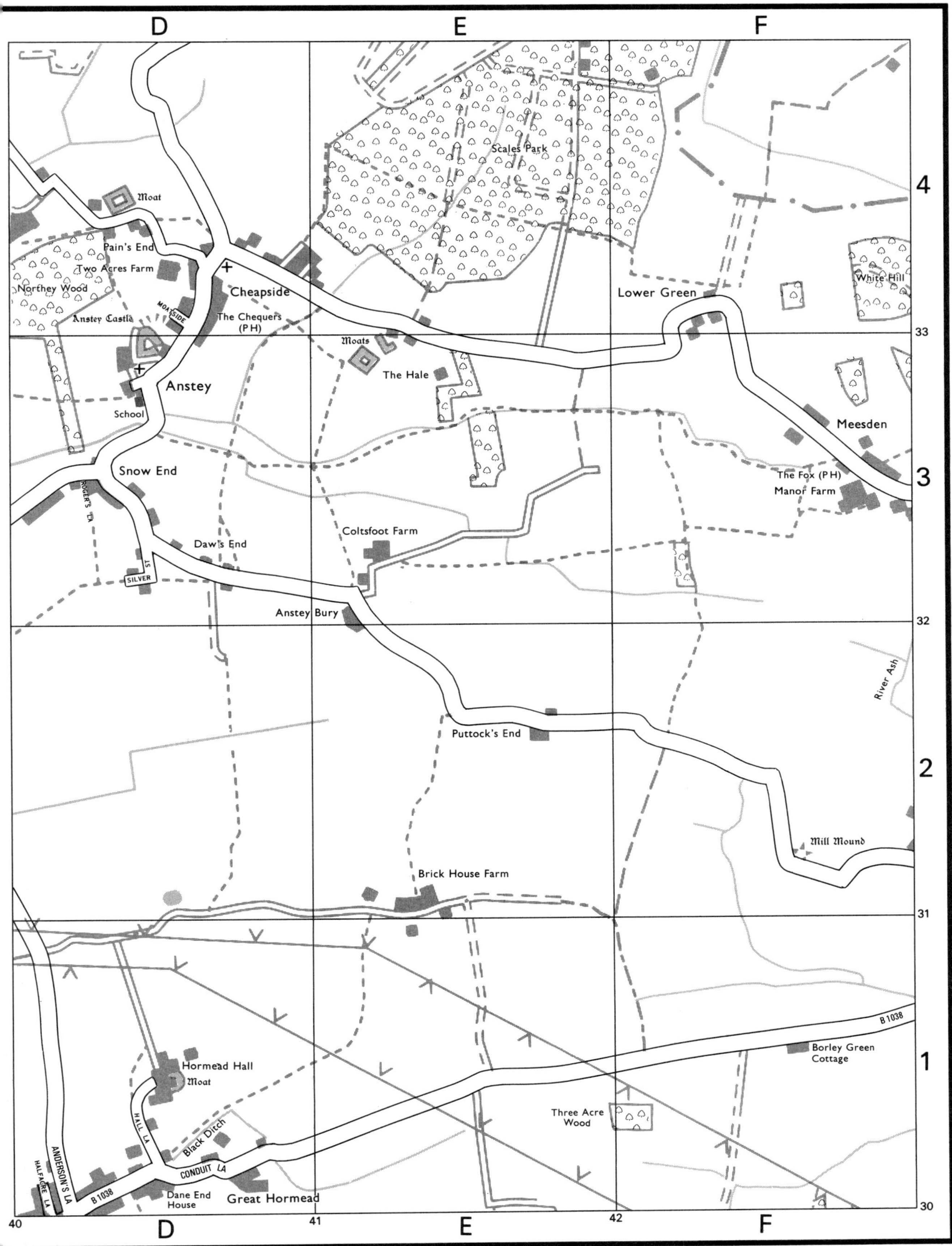

D
E
F
Scales Park
Moat
Pain's End
Two Acres Farm
Northey Wood
Anstey Castle
MOATSIDE
Cheapside
The Chequers (PH)
Lower Green
White Hill
Moats
The Hale
Anstey
School
Snow End
ROGER'S LA
Meesden
The Fox (PH)
Manor Farm
Coltsfoot Farm
Daw's End
SILVER ST
Anstey Bury
River Ash
Puttock's End
Mill Mound
Brick House Farm
Hormead Hall
Moat
HALL LA
Black Ditch
CONDUIT LA
B 1038
B 1038
Borley Green Cottage
Three Acre Wood
ANDERSON'S LA
HALFACRE LA
Dane End House
Great Hormead
4
3
2
1
33
32
31
30
40
41
42

30

42

not continued, see key diagram

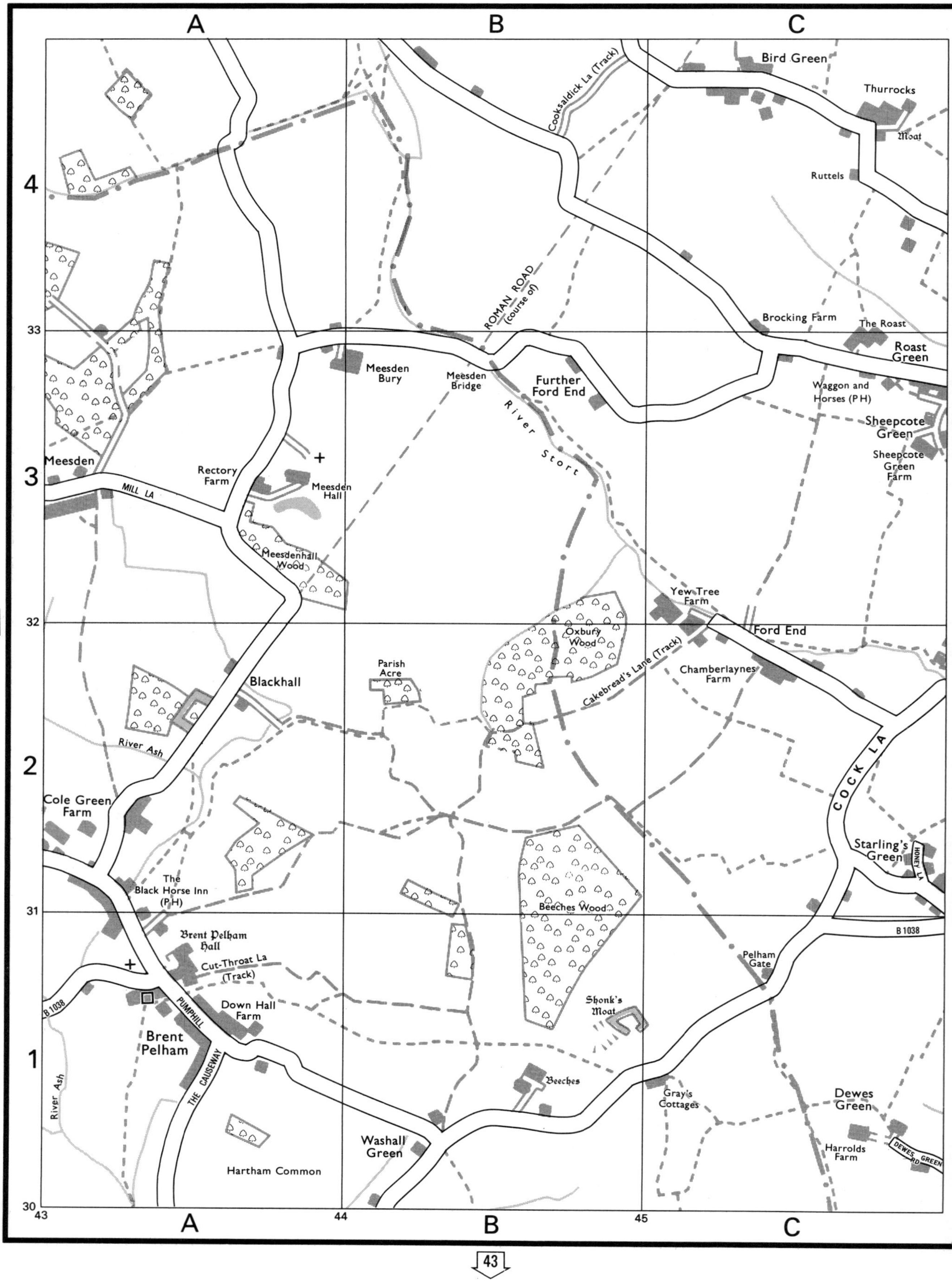

29

43

not continued, see key diagram

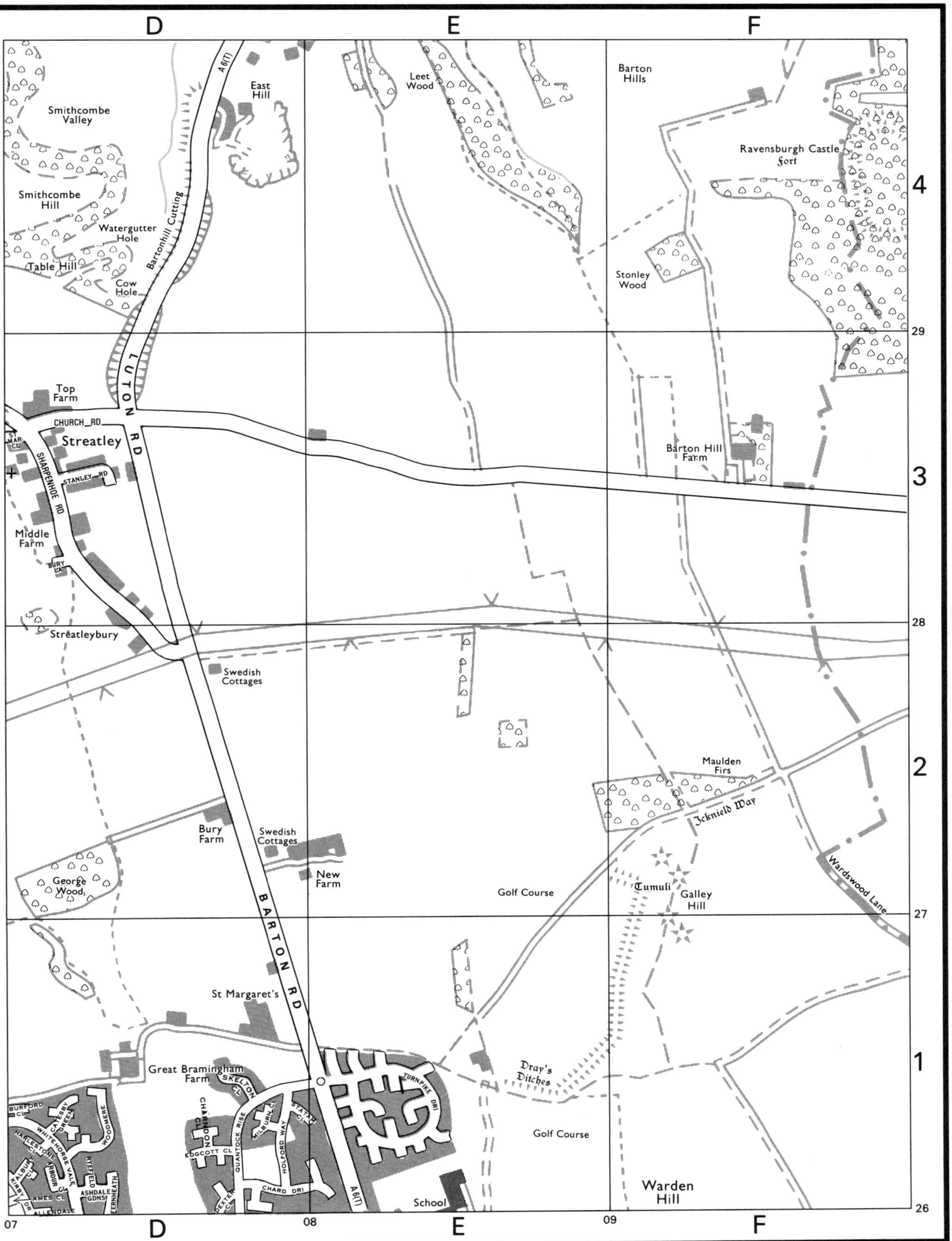

32

45

19

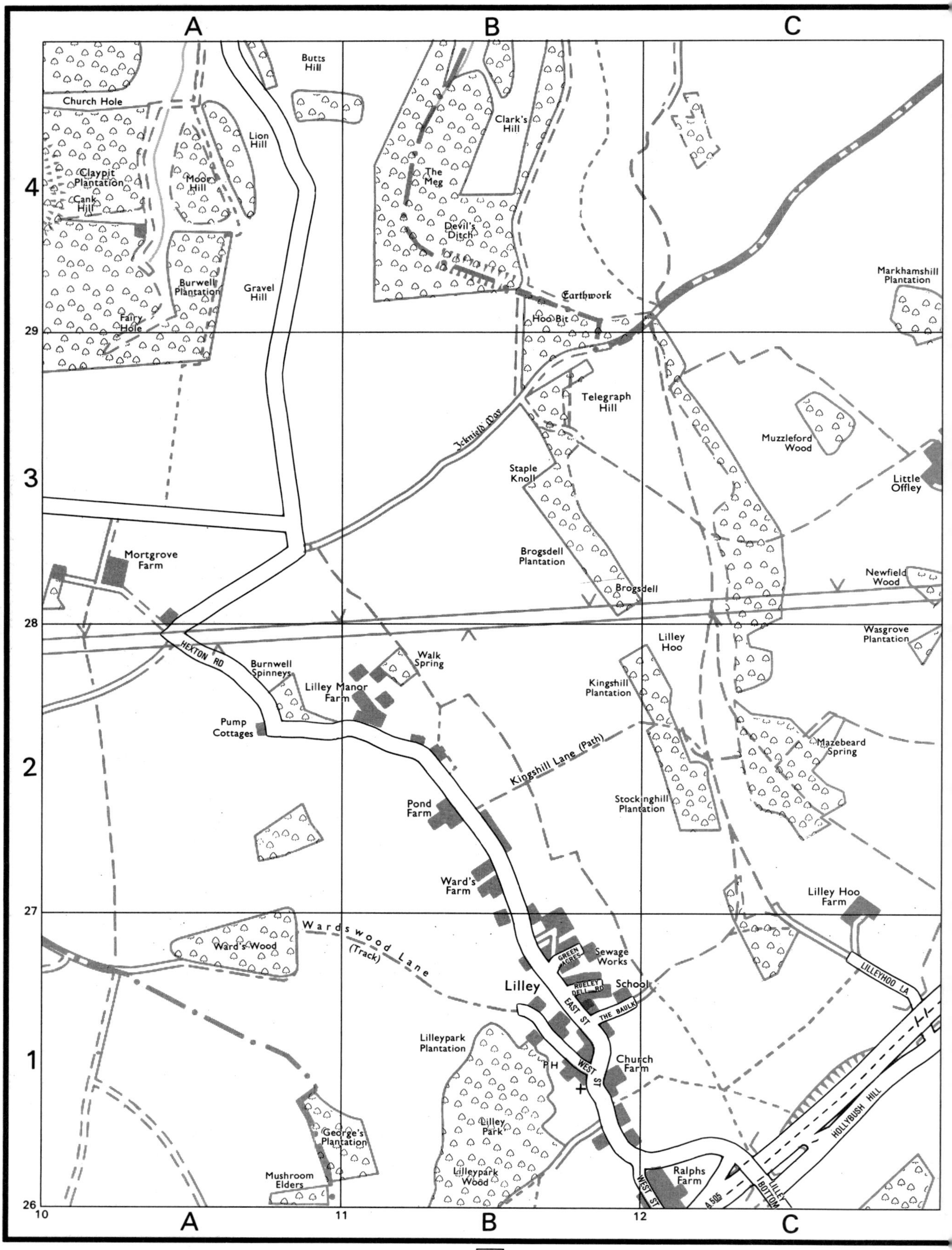
A
B
C
4
3
2
1
29
28
27
26
10
11
12
Church Hole
Butts Hill
Lion Hill
Claypit Plantation
Moor Hill
Cank Hill
Burwell Plantation
Gravel Hill
Fairy Hole
Clark's Hill
The Meg
Devil's Ditch
Earthwork
Hoo Bit
Markhamshill Plantation
Telegraph Hill
Icknield Way
Muzzleford Wood
Staple Knoll
Little Offley
Mortgrove Farm
Brogsdell Plantation
Newfield Wood
Brogsdell
Wasgrove Plantation
Lilley Hoo
HEXTON RD
Burnwell Spinneys
Walk Spring
Lilley Manor Farm
Kingshill Plantation
Pump Cottages
Mazebeard Spring
Kingshill Lane (Path)
Pond Farm
Stockinghill Plantation
Ward's Farm
Lilley Hoo Farm
Wardswood Lane
(Track)
Ward's Wood
GREEN ACRES
Sewage Works
Lilley
HUELEY DELL RD
School
LILLEYHOO LA
EAST ST
THE BAULK
Lilleypark Plantation
PH
WEST ST
Church Farm
HOLLYBUSH HILL
Lilley Park
George's Plantation
Lilleypark Wood
Mushroom Elders
Ralphs Farm
A 505
LILLEY BOTTOM

31

46

20

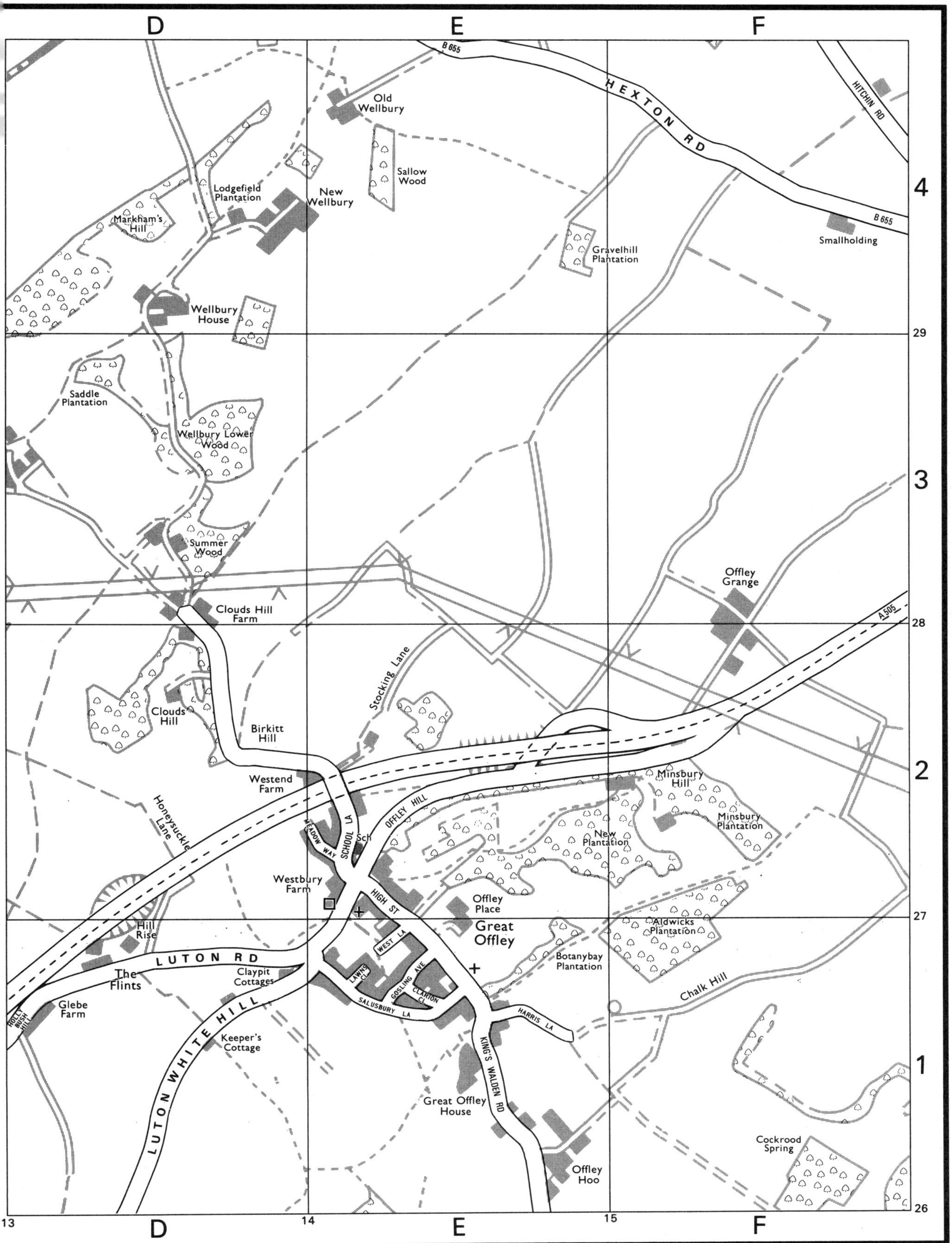
D
E
F
B 655
HEXTON RD
HITCHIN RD
Old Wellbury
Sallow Wood
Lodgefield Plantation
New Wellbury
Markham's Hill
Gravelhill Plantation
Smallholding
Wellbury House
Saddle Plantation
Wellbury Lower Wood
Summer Wood
Clouds Hill Farm
Offley Grange
A 505
Stocking Lane
Clouds Hill
Birkitt Hill
Westend Farm
Minsbury Hill
Minsbury Plantation
Honeysuckle Lane
MEADOW WAY
SCHOOL LA
Sch
OFFLEY HILL
New Plantation
Westbury Farm
HIGH ST
Offley Place
Great Offley
Aldwicks Plantation
Hill Rise
WEST LA
LUTON RD
The Flints
Claypit Cottages
LAWNS CL
GOSLING AVE
CLARION CL
Botanybay Plantation
Chalk Hill
SALUSBURY LA
HARRIS LA
Glebe Farm
HOLLY BUSH HILL
LUTON WHITE HILL
Keeper's Cottage
KING'S WALDEN RD
Great Offley House
Cockrood Spring
Offley Hoo
4
3
2
1
29
28
27
26
13
14
15
D
E
F

34

47

21

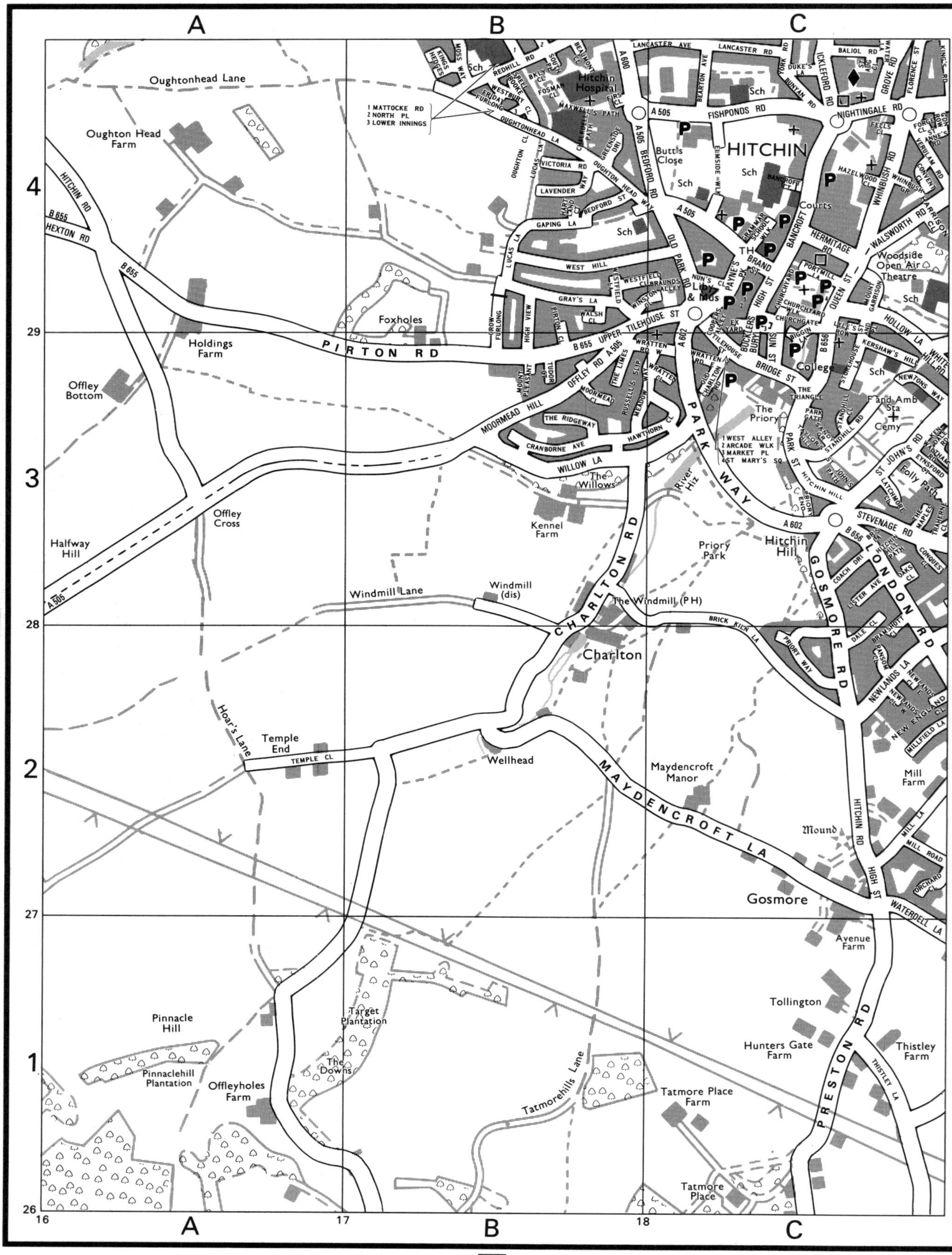
A
B
C
4
3
2
1
29
28
27
26
16
17
18
Oughtonhead Lane
Oughton Head Farm
1 MATTOCKE RD
2 NORTH PL
3 LOWER INNINGS
HITCHIN RD
B 655
HEXTON RD
Holdings Farm
Offley Bottom
Foxholes
PIRTON RD
MOORMEAD HILL
Offley Cross
Halfway Hill
A 505
Kennel Farm
The Willows
Windmill Lane
Windmill (dis)
The Windmill (PH)
CHARLTON RD
Charlton
BRICK KILN LA
Hoar's Lane
Temple End
TEMPLE CL
Wellhead
MAYDENCROFT LA
Maydencroft Manor
Priory Park
Hitchin Hill
River Hiz
PARK WAY
A 602
The Priory
1 WEST ALLEY
2 ARCADE WLK
3 MARKET PL
4 ST MARY'S SQ
HITCHIN
Hitchin Hospital
Butt's Close
Sch
Courts
Liby & Mus
College
Fire and Amb Sta
Cemy
Woodside Open Air Theatre
Folly Path
LANCASTER AVE
LANCASTER RD
FISHPONDS RD
NIGHTINGALE RD
BEDFORD RD
OLD PARK RD
UPPER TILEHOUSE ST
BANCROFT
HERMITAGE RD
WALSWORTH RD
QUEEN ST
HIGH ST
BRIDGE ST
STEVENAGE RD
LONDON RD
GOSMORE RD
HITCHIN RD
Mill Farm
Mound
Gosmore
WATERDELL LA
Avenue Farm
Tollington
Hunters Gate Farm
Thistley Farm
THISTLEY LA
PRESTON RD
Tatmore Place Farm
Tatmore Place
Tatmorehills Lane
Target Plantation
The Downs
Pinnacle Hill
Pinnaclehill Plantation
Offleyholes Farm

33

48

22

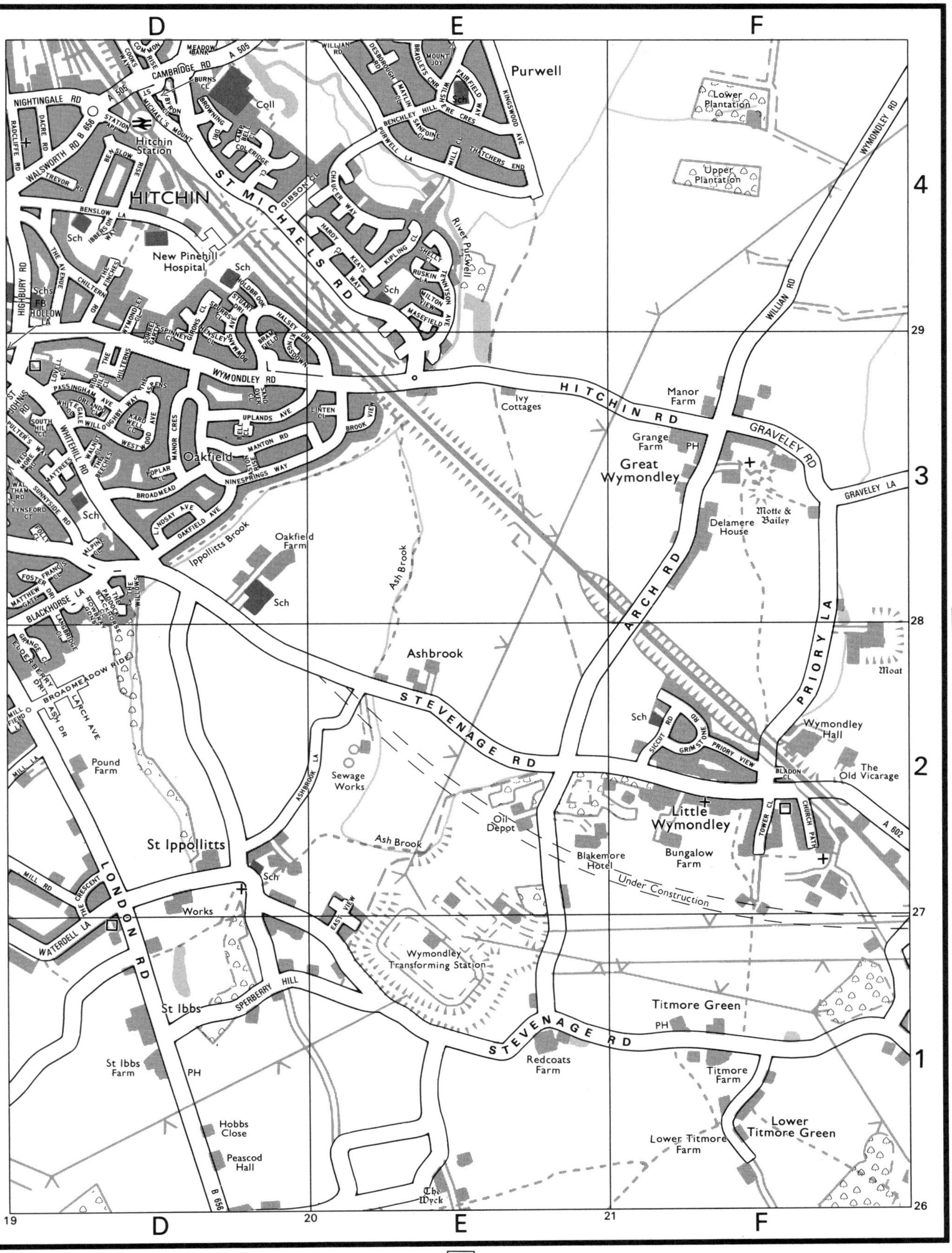

D
E
F
4
3
2
1
29
28
27
26
19
20
21
Purwell
Lower Plantation
Upper Plantation
WYMONDLEY RD
HITCHIN
Hitchin Station
Coll
New Pinehill Hospital
Sch
Schs
FB
HOLLOW LA
CAMBRIDGE RD
A 505
NIGHTINGALE RD
WALSWORTH RD B 656
ST MICHAELS RD
River Purwell
WILLIAN RD
Manor Farm
Ivy Cottages
HITCHIN RD
GRAVELEY RD
GRAVELEY LA
Grange Farm
PH
Great Wymondley
Motte & Bailey
Delamere House
Oakfield
WYMONDLEY RD
UPLANDS AVE
MANTON RD
NINESPRINGS WAY
BROADMEAD
LINDSAY AVE
OAKFIELD AVE
Ippollitts Brook
Oakfield Farm
Ash Brook
ARCH RD
PRIORY LA
Moat
Ashbrook
STEVENAGE RD
Sewage Works
ASHBROOK LA
Sch
GRIMSTONE RD
SICCUT RD
PRIORY VIEW
Wymondley Hall
The Old Vicarage
BLADON CL
Little Wymondley
TOWER CL
CHURCH PATH
A 602
Oil Depot
Blakemore Hotel
Bungalow Farm
Under Construction
Pound Farm
BLACKHORSE LA
BROADMEADOW RIDE
LARCH AVE
ASH DR
St Ippollitts
LONDON RD
MILL RD
THE CRESCENT
WATERDELL LA
Works
EAST VIEW
Wymondley Transforming Station
SPERBERRY HILL
St Ibbs
St Ibbs Farm
PH
Hobbs Close
Peascod Hall
B 656
Titmore Green
PH
STEVENAGE RD
Redcoats Farm
Titmore Farm
Lower Titmore Green
Lower Titmore Farm
The Wyck

36

49

23

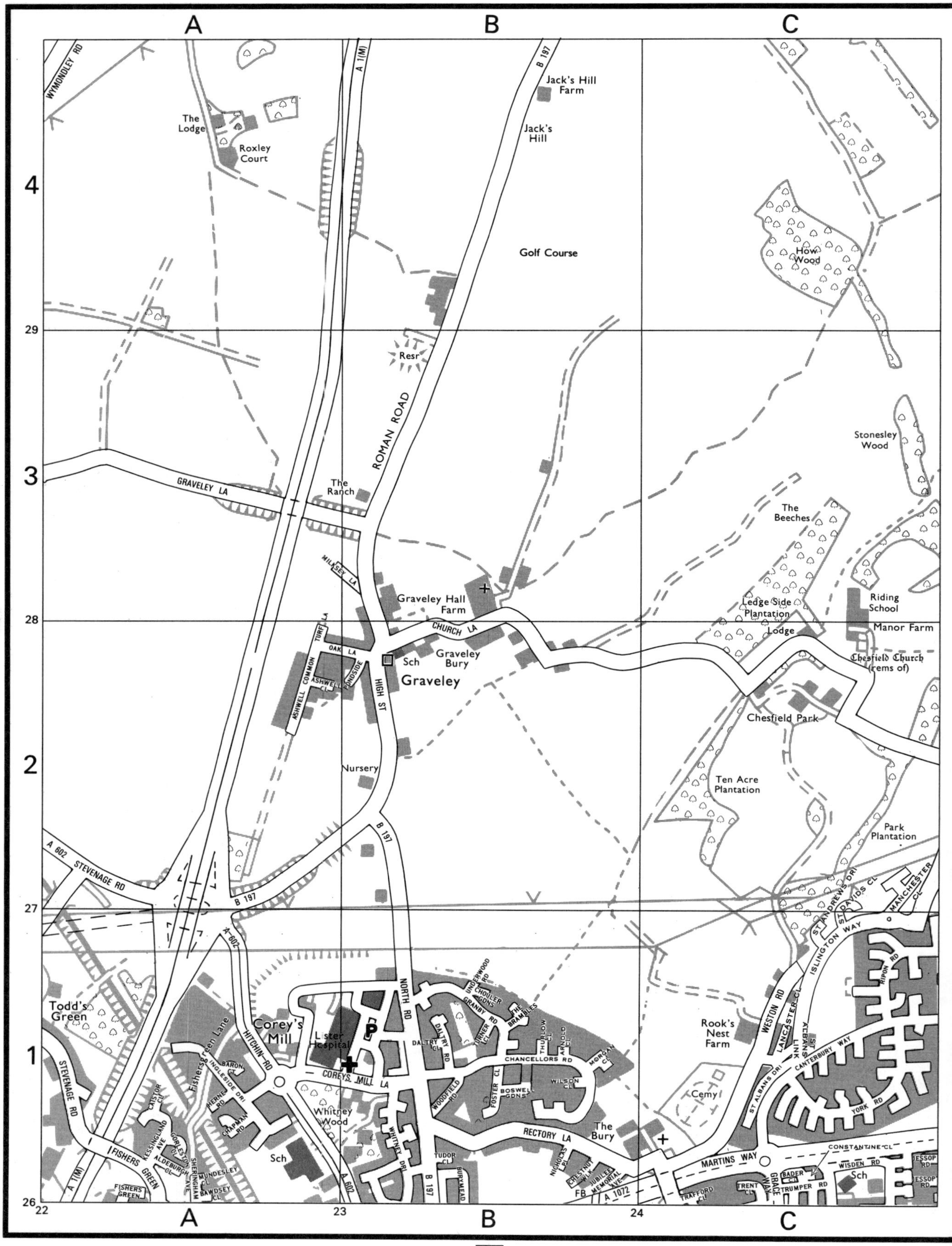
A
B
C
4
3
2
1
29
28
27
26
22
23
24
WYMONDLEY RD
The Lodge
Roxley Court
A 1(M)
B 197
Jack's Hill Farm
Jack's Hill
Golf Course
How Wood
Resr
ROMAN ROAD
Stonesley Wood
GRAVELEY LA
The Ranch
The Beeches
MILKSEY LA
Graveley Hall Farm
Riding School
Ledge Side Plantation
Lodge
Manor Farm
CHURCH LA
TURF LA
OAK LA
Sch
Graveley Bury
Chesfield Church (rems of)
ASHWELL COMMON
ASHWELL CL
PONDSIDE
HIGH ST
Graveley
Chesfield Park
Nursery
Ten Acre Plantation
Park Plantation
A 602
STEVENAGE RD
B 197
ST ANDREWS DRI
ST DAVIDS CL
MANCHESTER CL
ISLINGTON WAY
RIPON RD
Todd's Green
UNDERWOOD RD
CHOULER GDNS
GRANBY RD
THE BRAMBLES
NORTH RD
Corey's Mill
Lister Hospital
P
Fishersgreen Lane
HITCHIN RD
DALTRY RD
DALTRY CL
TURNER CL
THURLOW CL
ARNOLD CL
MORGAN CL
CHANCELLORS RD
Rook's Nest Farm
WESTON RD
LANCASTER CL
ST ALBANS LINK
CANTERBURY WAY
BARON CL
INGLESIDE DRI
COREYS MILL LA
WOODFIELD RD
FOSTER CL
BOSWELL GDNS
WILSON CL
Cemy
ST ALBANS DRI
YORK RD
STEVENAGE RD
CATSTON CL
KESSINGLAND AVE
HERNE RD
CHAPMAN RD
Whitney Wood
WHITNEY DRI
The Bury
RECTORY LA
GORLESTON CL
ALDEBURGH CL
SHERINGHAM AVE
MUNDESLEY CL
BAWDSEY CL
Sch
TUDOR CL
BURYMEAD
NICHOLAS PL
CHESTNUT WLK
JUBILEE AVE
MEMORIAL
FB
A 1072
MARTINS WAY
GRACE WAY
CONSTANTINE CL
JESSOP RD
WISDEN RD
BADER CL
TRUMPER RD
TRENT CL
TRAFFORD CL
Sch
FISHERS GREEN
A 1(M)
A 602

35

50

24

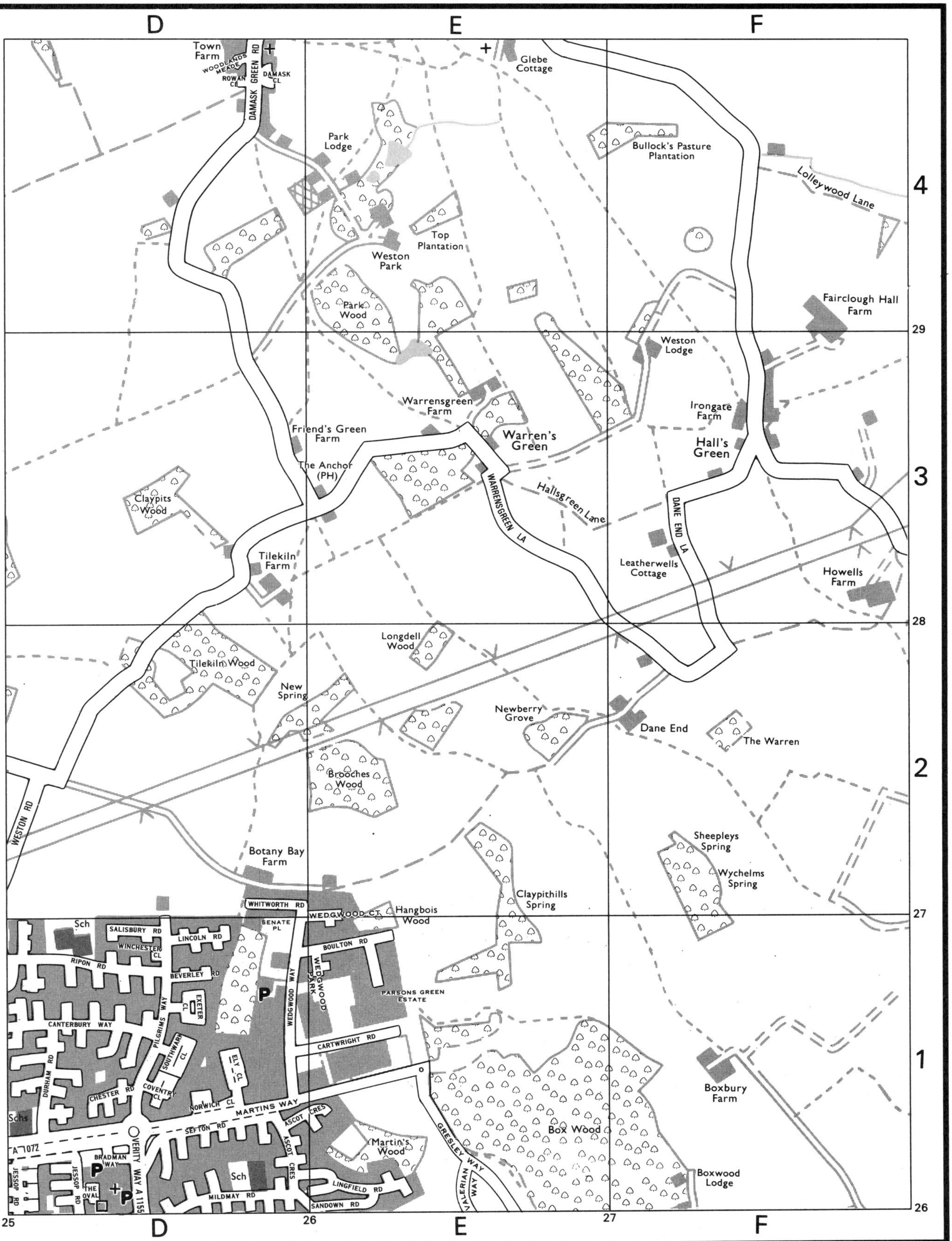
D
E
F
Town Farm
WOODLANDS MEADE
ROWAN CL
DAMASK GREEN RD
DAMASK CL
Glebe Cottage
Park Lodge
Bullock's Pasture Plantation
Lolleywood Lane
Top Plantation
Weston Park
Park Wood
Fairclough Hall Farm
Weston Lodge
Warrensgreen Farm
Warren's Green
Irongate Farm
Hall's Green
Friend's Green Farm
The Anchor (PH)
Claypits Wood
WARRENSGREEN LA
Hallsgreen Lane
DANE END LA
Leatherwells Cottage
Tilekiln Farm
Howells Farm
Longdell Wood
Tilekiln Wood
New Spring
Newberry Grove
Dane End
The Warren
Brooches Wood
WESTON RD
Sheepleys Spring
Wychelms Spring
Botany Bay Farm
Claypithills Spring
WHITWORTH RD
WEDGWOOD CT
Hangbois Wood
Sch
SALISBURY RD
LINCOLN RD
SENATE PL
BOULTON RD
WINCHESTER CL
RIPON RD
BEVERLEY RD
WEDGWOOD PARK
PARSONS GREEN ESTATE
EXETER CL
PILGRIMS WAY
WEDGWOOD WAY
CANTERBURY WAY
CARTWRIGHT RD
SOUTHWARK CL
ELY CL
DURHAM RD
CHESTER RD
COVENTRY CL
NORWICH CL
MARTINS WAY
ASCOT CRES
Boxbury Farm
Schs
SEFTON RD
GRESLEY WAY
Box Wood
A 1072
BRADMAN WAY
VERITY WAY A 1155
Martin's Wood
JESSOP RD
THE OVAL
Sch
VALERIAN WAY
LINGFIELD RD
Boxwood Lodge
MILDMAY RD
SANDOWN RD
4
3
2
1
29
28
27
26
25
26
27

38

51

25

37

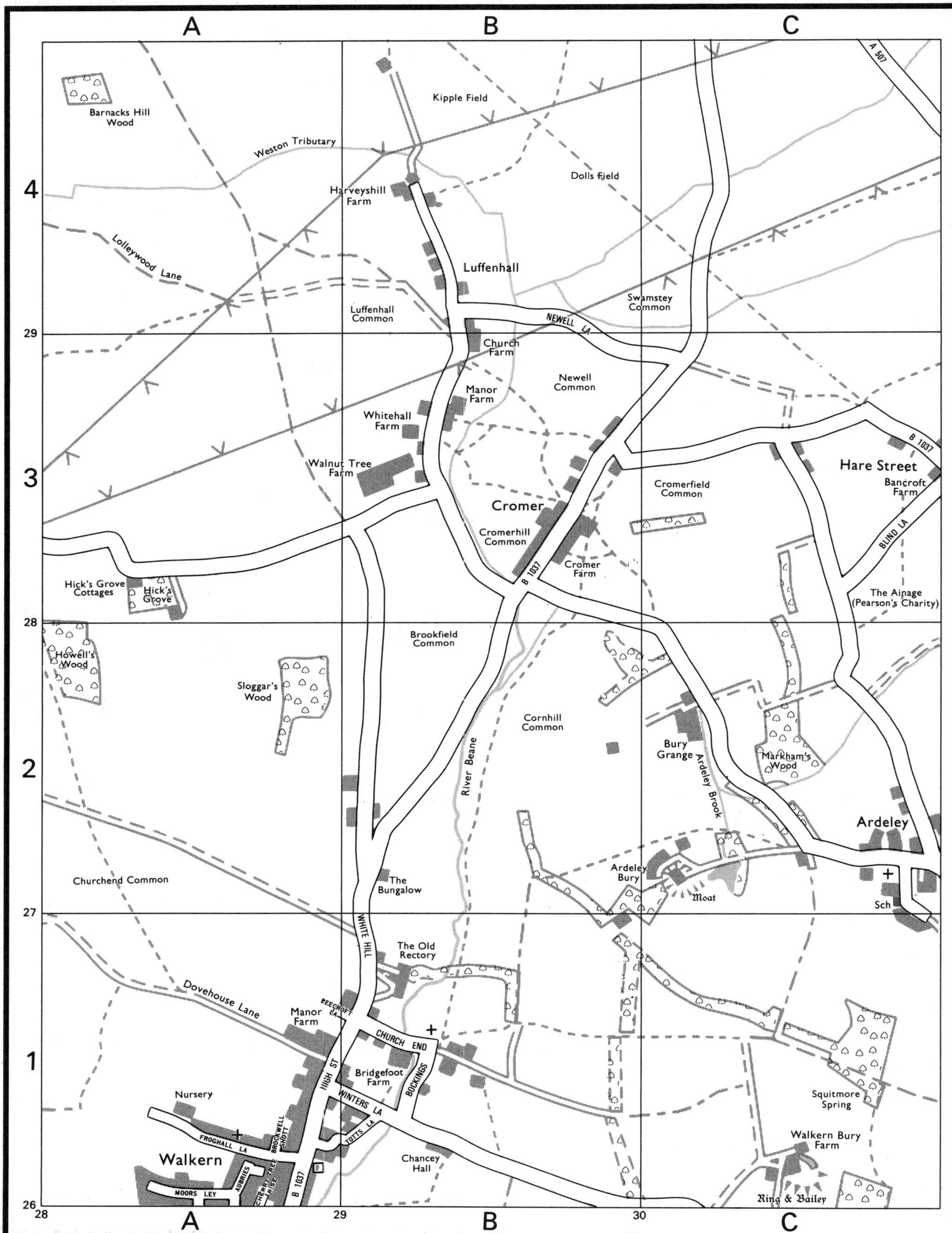
A
B
C
4
3
2
1
29
28
27
26
28
29
30
Barnacks Hill Wood
Kipple Field
A 507
Weston Tributary
Dolls Field
Harveyshill Farm
Lolleywood Lane
Luffenhall
Swamstey Common
Luffenhall Common
NEWELL LA
Church Farm
Newell Common
Manor Farm
Whitehall Farm
Walnut Tree Farm
B 1037
Hare Street
Bancroft Farm
Cromerfield Common
Cromer
Cromerhill Common
BLIND LA
B 1037
Cromer Farm
Hick's Grove Cottages
Hick's Grove
The Ainage (Pearson's Charity)
Brookfield Common
Howell's Wood
Sloggar's Wood
Cornhill Common
Bury Grange
Ardeley Brook
Markham's Wood
River Beane
Ardeley
Churchend Common
The Bungalow
Ardeley Bury
Moat
Sch
WHITE HILL
The Old Rectory
Dovehouse Lane
BEECROFT LA
Manor Farm
CHURCH END
BOCKINGS
Bridgefoot Farm
HIGH ST
WINTERS LA
Nursery
Squitmore Spring
BROOKWELL SHOTT
FROGHALL LA
TOTTS LA
Walkern Bury Farm
Walkern
Chancey Hall
AUBRIES
CHERRY TREE RISE
B 1037
MOORS LEY
Ring & Bailey

52

26

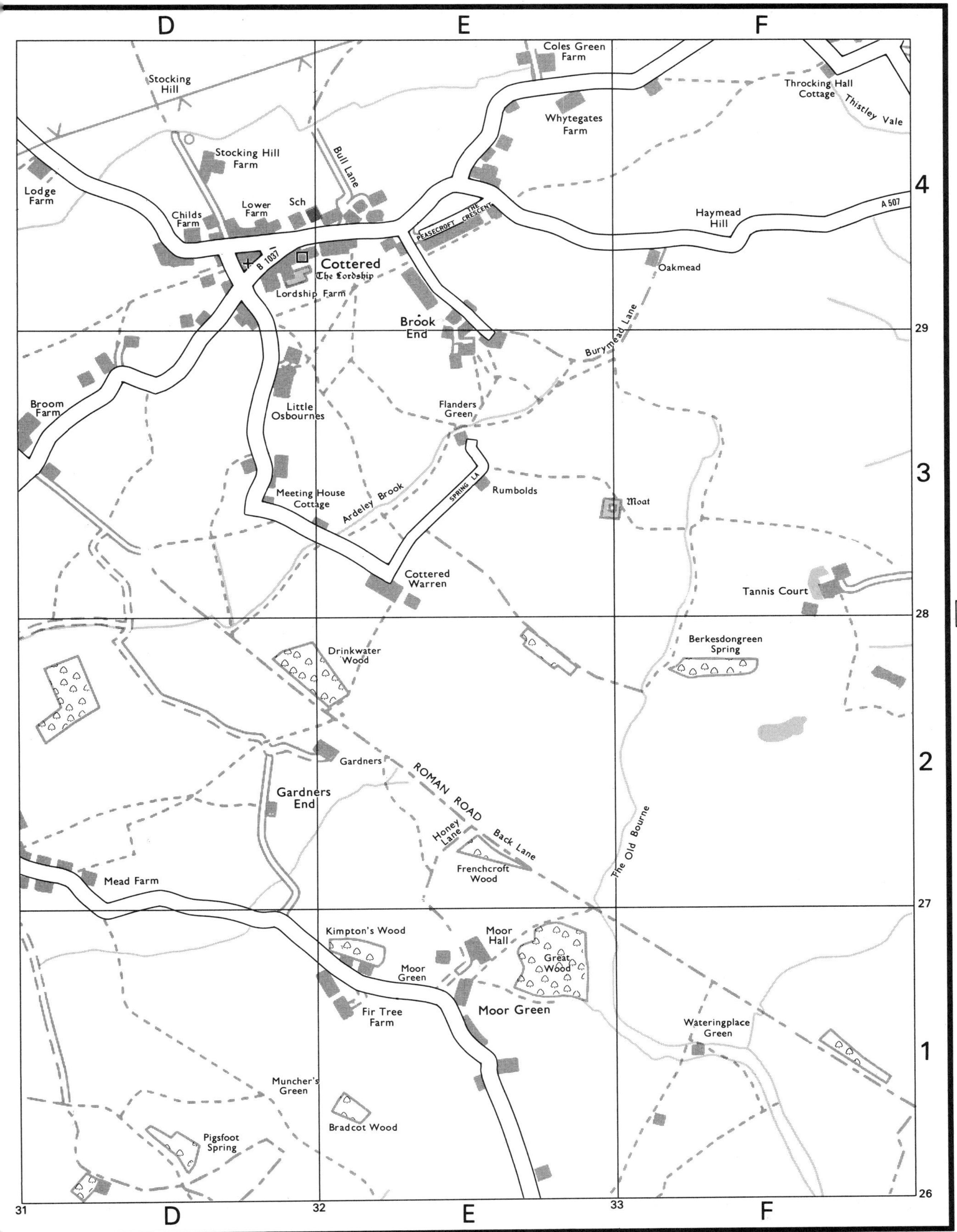
D
E
F
Coles Green
Farm
Stocking
Hill
Throcking Hall
Cottage
Thistley Vale
Whytegates
Farm
Stocking Hill
Farm
Bull Lane
4
Lodge
Farm
Childs
Farm
Lower
Farm
Sch
THE
CRESCENT
PEASECROFT
Haymead
Hill
A 507
B 1037
Cottered
The Lordship
Oakmead
Lordship Farm
Brook
End
29
Burymead Lane
Broom
Farm
Little
Osbournes
Flanders
Green
3
Meeting House
Cottage
Ardeley Brook
SPRING LA
Rumbolds
Moat
Cottered
Warren
Tannis Court
28
Drinkwater
Wood
Berkesdongreen
Spring
2
Gardners
ROMAN ROAD
Gardners
End
Honey
Lane
Back Lane
The Old Bourne
Frenchcroft
Wood
Mead Farm
27
Kimpton's Wood
Moor
Hall
Great
Wood
Moor
Green
Moor Green
Fir Tree
Farm
Wateringplace
Green
1
Muncher's
Green
Bradcot Wood
Pigsfoot
Spring
26
31
32
33
D
E
F

40

53

27

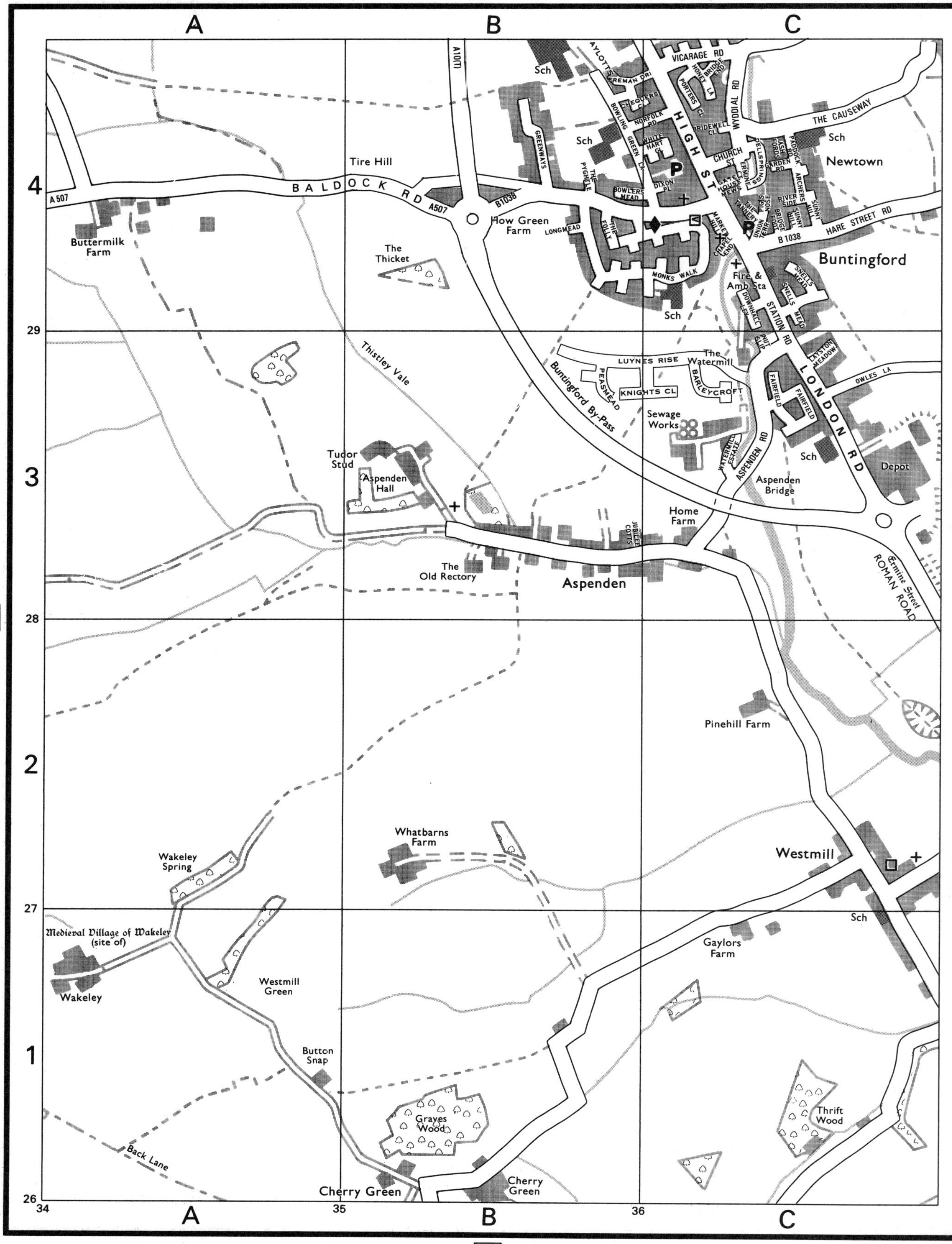

A
B
C
4
3
2
1
29
28
27
26
34
35
36
A10(T)
BALDOCK RD
A507
B1038
Tire Hill
Buttermilk Farm
How Green Farm
The Thicket
LONGMEAD
THE FOLLY
BOWLERS MEAD
DIXON PL
MONKS WALK
THE PYGHLE
GREENWAYS
BOWLING GREEN LA
CHEQUERS CL
NORFOLK RD
WHITE HART CL
FREMAN DR
AYLOTTS
Sch
HIGH ST
VICARAGE RD
HONEY LA
BRIDGE END
PORTERS CL
BRIDEWELL CL
WYDDIAL RD
THE CAUSEWAY
CHURCH ST
CASTLE HOUSE MEWS
ERMINE
WELLSPRING
THE TANNERY
UNION TERR
PADDOCK
ARCHERS
GARDEN RD
RIVER SIDE
SUNNY HILL
HARE STREET RD
B1038
CHAPEL END
MARKET HILL
Newtown
Buntingford
Fire & Amb Sta
SNELLS MEAD
STATION RD
DOWNHALL LEY
LAYSTON MEADOW
OWLES LA
LONDON RD
LUYNES RISE
The Watermill
PEASMEAD
KNIGHTS CL
BARLEYCROFT
FAIRFIELD
Sewage Works
WATERMILL ESTATE
ASPENDEN RD
Buntingford By-Pass
Thistley Vale
Tudor Stud
Aspenden Hall
Home Farm
JUBILEE COTTS
Aspenden Bridge
Depot
The Old Rectory
Aspenden
Ermine Street
ROMAN ROAD
Pinehill Farm
Whatbarns Farm
Wakeley Spring
Westmill
Medieval Village of Wakeley (site of)
Wakeley
Westmill Green
Gaylors Farm
Button Snap
Graves Wood
Thrift Wood
Back Lane
Cherry Green
Cherry Green

39

54

28

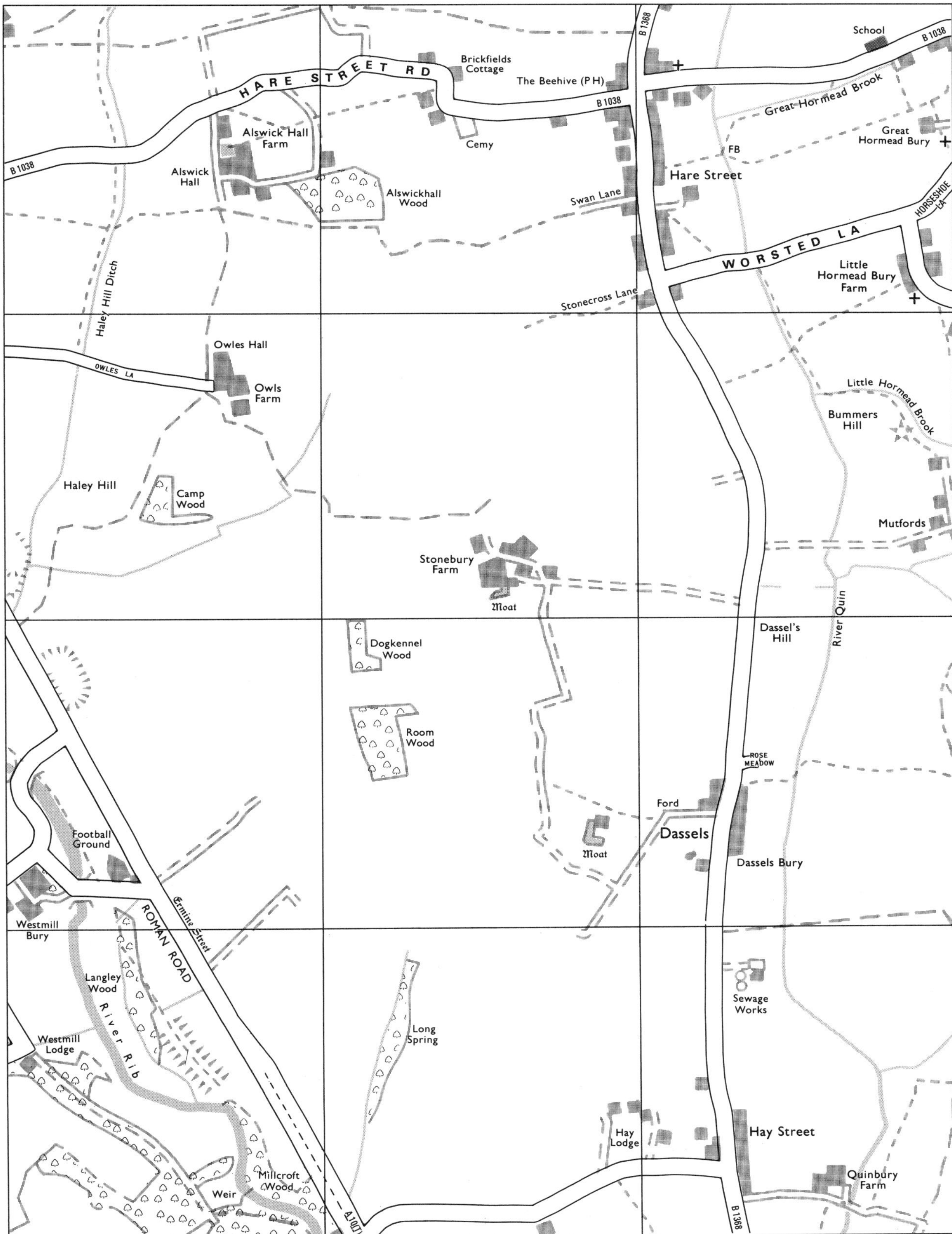
D
E
F
HARE STREET RD
B 1038
B 1368
Brickfields Cottage
The Beehive (PH)
School
Great Hormead Brook
Great Hormead Bury
FB
Alswick Hall Farm
Alswick Hall
Cemy
Alswickhall Wood
Swan Lane
Hare Street
HORSESHOE LA
WORSTED LA
Little Hormead Bury Farm
Stonecross Lane
Haley Hill Ditch
Owles Hall
OWLES LA
Owls Farm
Little Hormead Brook
Bummers Hill
Haley Hill
Camp Wood
Mutfords
Stonebury Farm
Moat
Dassel's Hill
River Quin
Dogkennel Wood
Room Wood
ROSE MEADOW
Ford
Dassels
Moat
Dassels Bury
Football Ground
Westmill Bury
ROMAN ROAD
Ermine Street
Langley Wood
River Rib
Sewage Works
Long Spring
Westmill Lodge
Hay Lodge
Hay Street
Quinbury Farm
Millcroft Wood
Weir
A10(T)
B 1368
4
3
2
1
29
28
27
26
37
38
39
D
E
F

42

55

29

41

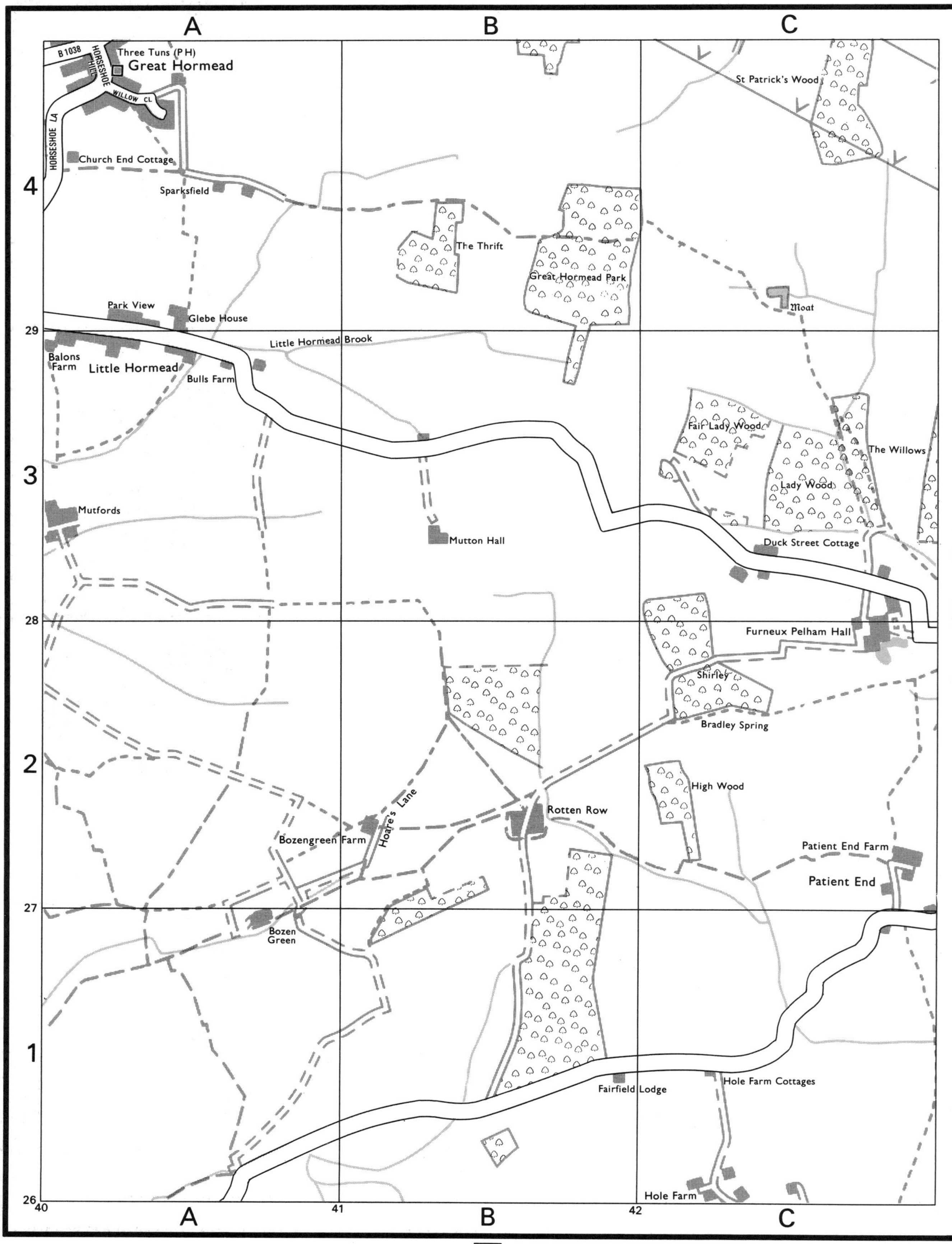
A
B
C
4
3
2
1
29
28
27
26
40
41
42
B1038
HORSESHOE HILL
HORSESHOE LA
WILLOW CL
Three Tuns (PH)
Great Hormead
Church End Cottage
Sparksfield
Park View
Glebe House
Balons Farm
Little Hormead
Bulls Farm
Little Hormead Brook
The Thrift
Great Hormead Park
St Patrick's Wood
Moat
Fair Lady Wood
The Willows
Lady Wood
Duck Street Cottage
Mutfords
Mutton Hall
Furneux Pelham Hall
Shirley
Bradley Spring
High Wood
Rotten Row
Hoare's Lane
Bozengreen Farm
Bozen Green
Patient End Farm
Patient End
Fairfield Lodge
Hole Farm Cottages
Hole Farm

56

30

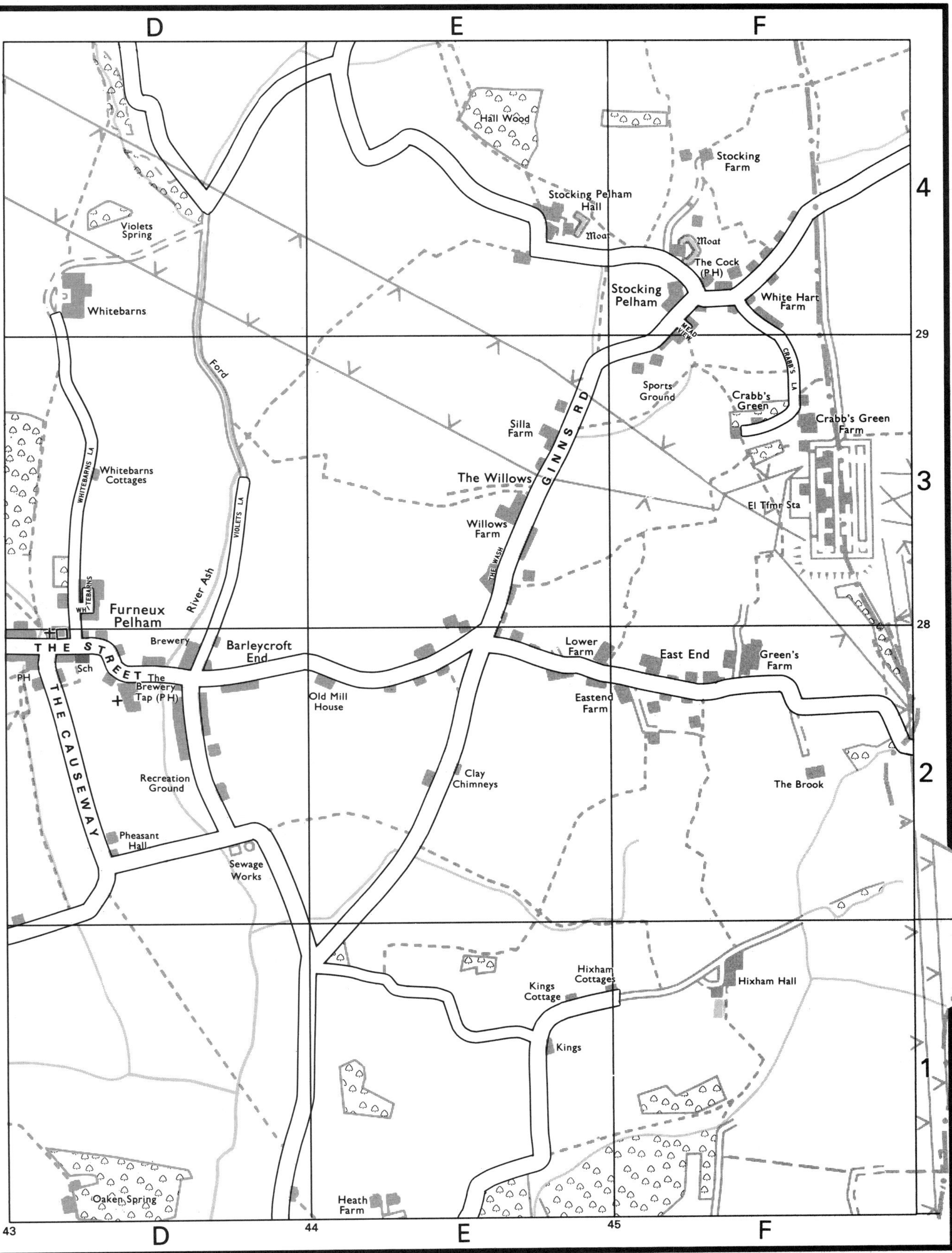

not continued, see key diagram

57

not continued, see key diagram

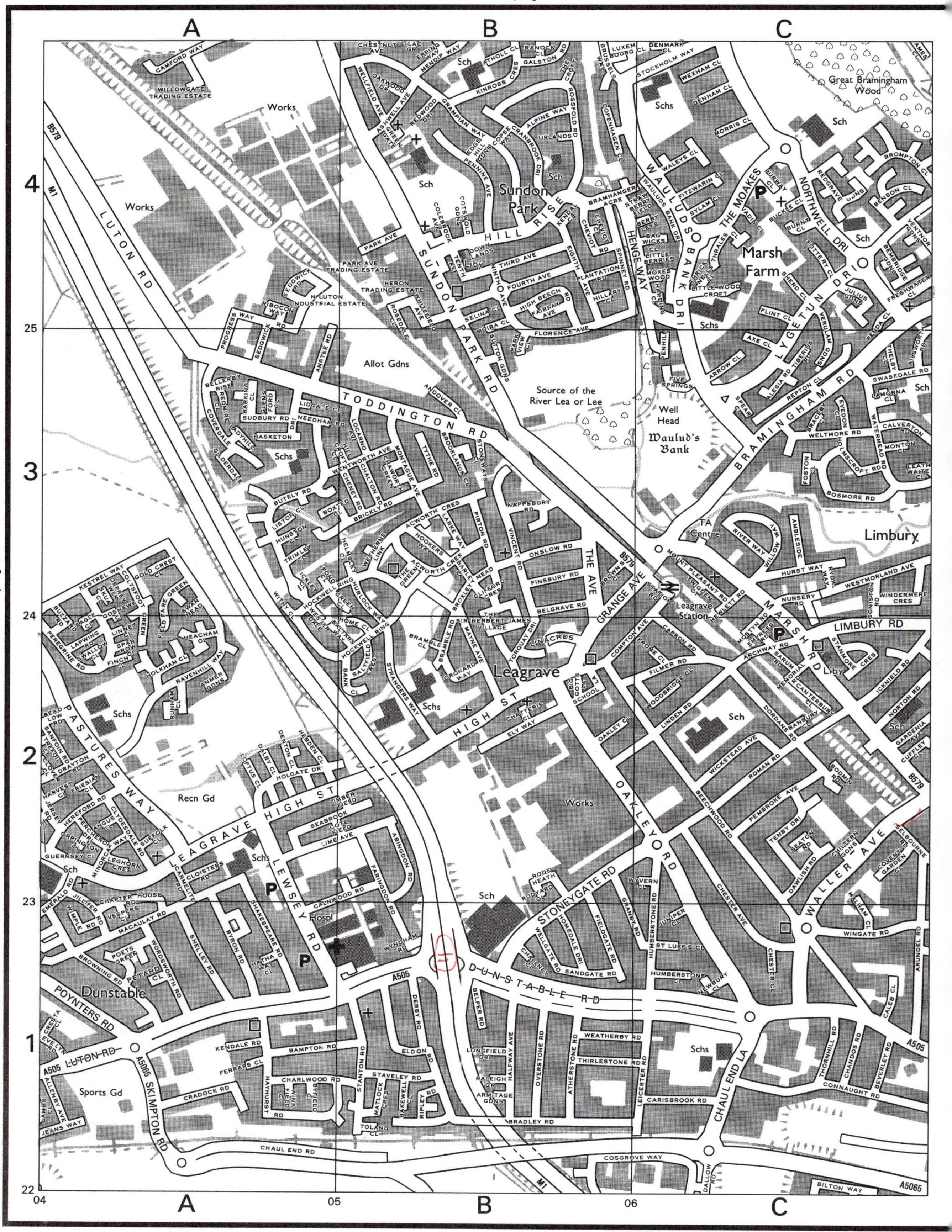

31

D
E
F
4
3
2
1
25
24
23
22
07
08
09
Warden Hill
Golf Course
Common Farm
Stopsley Common
Stopsley Common
Caravan Park
Little Bramingham Wood
Playing Field
LUTON
Biscot
Round Green
Museum & Art Gallery
Wardown Park
People's Park
River Lea or Lee
College
College
School
School
Schs
Schs
Sch
F Sta
FB
BRAMINGHAM RD
WHITEHORSE VALE
ICKNIELD WAY
GRASMERE RD
LABURNUM GR
BIRDSFOOT LA
BARTON RD
CROMER WAY
NEW BEDFORD RD
OLD BEDFORD RD
BARNFIELD AVE
KINGSDOWN AVE
RIDDY LA
AUSTIN RD
BUSHMEAD RD
STOCKINGSTONE RD
MONTROSE AVE
ST MARGARETS AVE
BISHOPSCOTE RD
NUNNERY LA
BANCROFT RD
BLUNDELL RD
NEVILLE RD
LIMBURY RD
TRINITY RD
LEAGRAVE RD
BISCOT RD
DUNSTABLE RD
KINGSWAY
HIGH TOWN RD
HITCHIN RD
ST THOMAS'S RD
BRADGERS HILL RD
LORRIMER CL
ELVEDEN CL
THETFORD GDNS
ROOKERY DRI
MARLBOROUGH RD
LANSDOWNE RD
SELBOURNE RD
SHERWOOD RD
MARYPORT RD
WINGATE RD
CONNAUGHT RD
A6
A505
A5065
B579

46

63

32

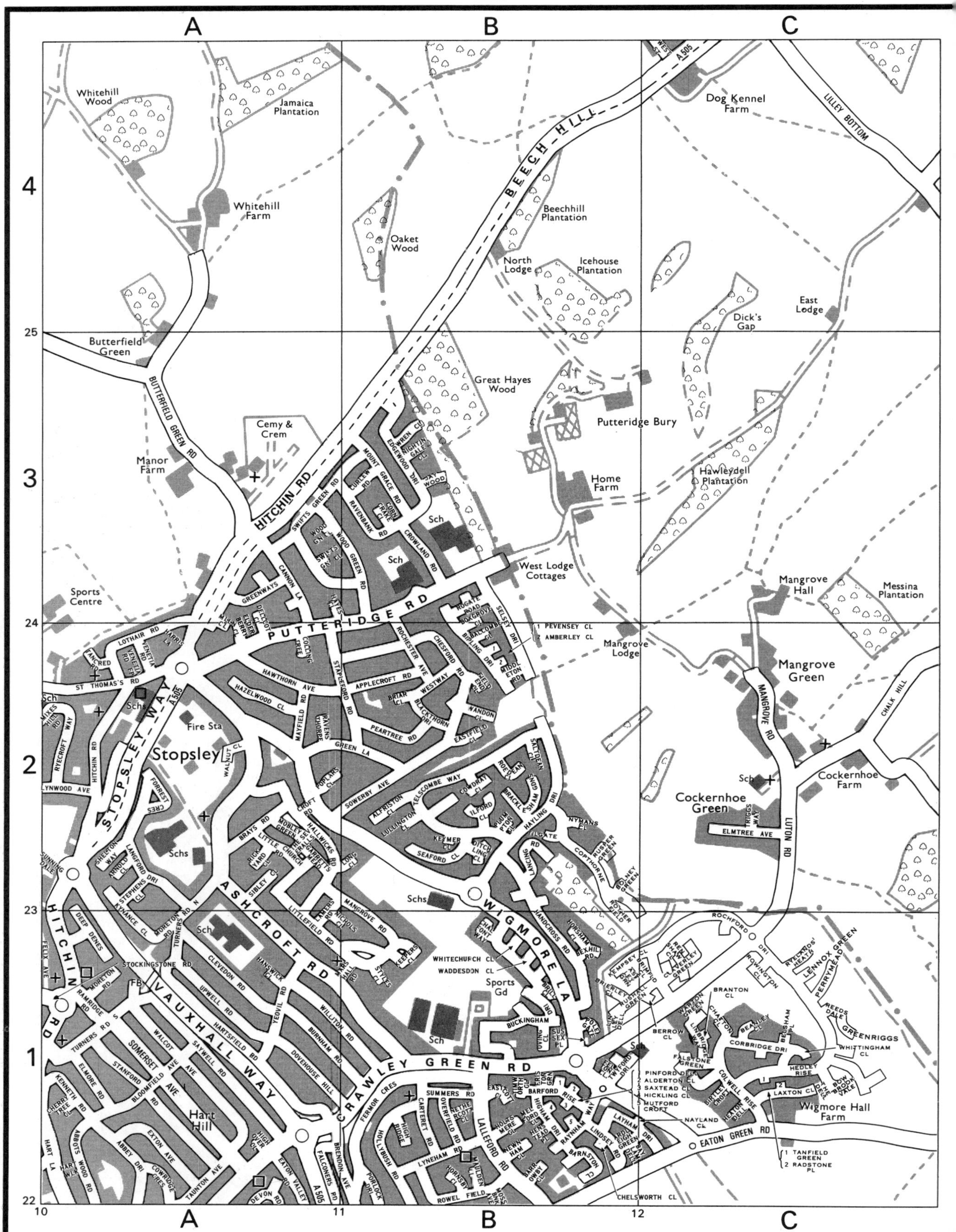

A
B
C
Whitehill Wood
Jamaica Plantation
Whitehill Farm
Dog Kennel Farm
LILLEY BOTTOM
BEECH HILL
A505
Beechhill Plantation
Oaket Wood
North Lodge
Icehouse Plantation
East Lodge
Dick's Gap
Butterfield Green
BUTTERFIELD GREEN RD
Great Hayes Wood
Putteridge Bury
Cemy & Crem
Manor Farm
Home Farm
Hawleydell Plantation
HITCHIN RD
Sch
West Lodge Cottages
Mangrove Hall
Messina Plantation
Sports Centre
PUTTERIDGE RD
1 PEVENSEY CL
2 AMBERLEY CL
Mangrove Lodge
Mangrove Green
MANGROVE RD
CHALK HILL
ST THOMAS'S RD
STOPSLEY WAY
Fire Sta
Stopsley
Cockernhoe Farm
Cockernhoe Green
ELMTREE AVE
LUTON RD
Schs
ASHCROFT RD
WIGMORE LA
VAUXHALL WAY
HITCHIN RD
ROCHFORD DRI
LENNOX GREEN
PERRYMEAD
WHITECHURCH CL
WADDESDON CL
Sports Gd
BRANTON CL
GREENRIGGS
WHITTINGHAM CL
CRAWLEY GREEN RD
1 PINFORD DRI
2 ALDERTON CL
3 SAXTEAD CL
4 HICKLING CL
5 MUTFORD CROFT
NAYLAND CL
Wigmore Hall Farm
EATON GREEN RD
1 TANFIELD GREEN
2 RADSTONE PL
Hart Hill
CHELSWORTH CL
4
3
2
1
25
24
23
22
10
11
12

45

64

33

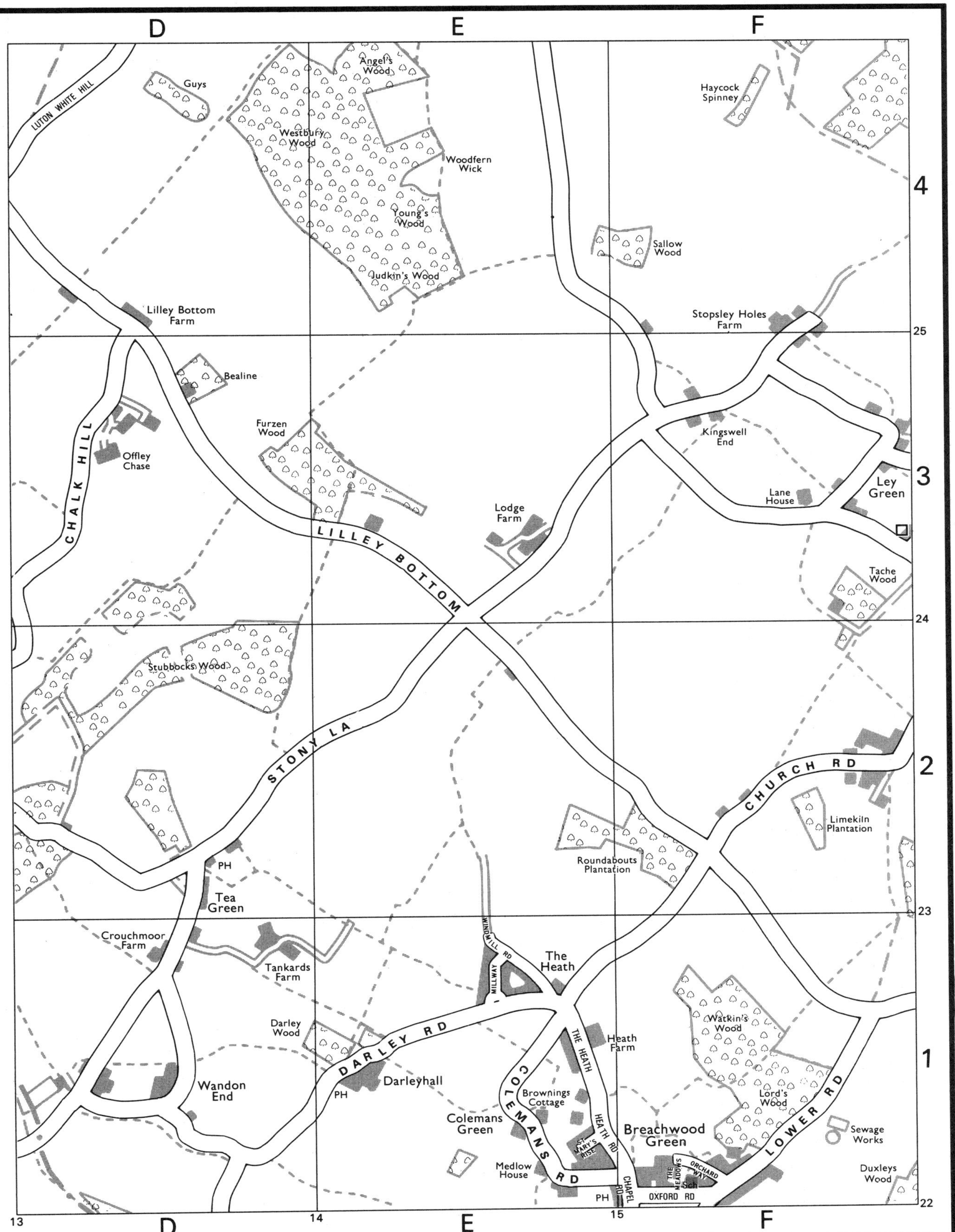
D
E
F
Guys
LUTON WHITE HILL
Angel's Wood
Westbury Wood
Woodfern Wick
Young's Wood
Judkin's Wood
Haycock Spinney
Sallow Wood
4
Lilley Bottom Farm
Stopsley Holes Farm
25
Bealine
CHALK HILL
Offley Chase
Furzen Wood
Kingswell End
Lane House
Ley Green
3
Lodge Farm
LILLEY BOTTOM
Tache Wood
24
Stubbocks Wood
STONY LA
CHURCH RD
2
Limekiln Plantation
Roundabouts Plantation
PH
Tea Green
23
Crouchmoor Farm
Tankards Farm
WINDMILL RD
MILLWAY
The Heath
Darley Wood
DARLEY RD
THE HEATH
Heath Farm
Watkin's Wood
1
Wandon End
Darleyhall
PH
COLEMANS RD
Brownings Cottage
Colemans Green
HEATH RD
ST MARY'S RISE
Breachwood Green
Lord's Wood
LOWER RD
Sewage Works
Medlow House
THE MEADOWS
ORCHARD WAY
Sch
Duxleys Wood
PH
CHAPEL RD
OXFORD RD
22
13
14
15
D
E
F

48

65

34

47

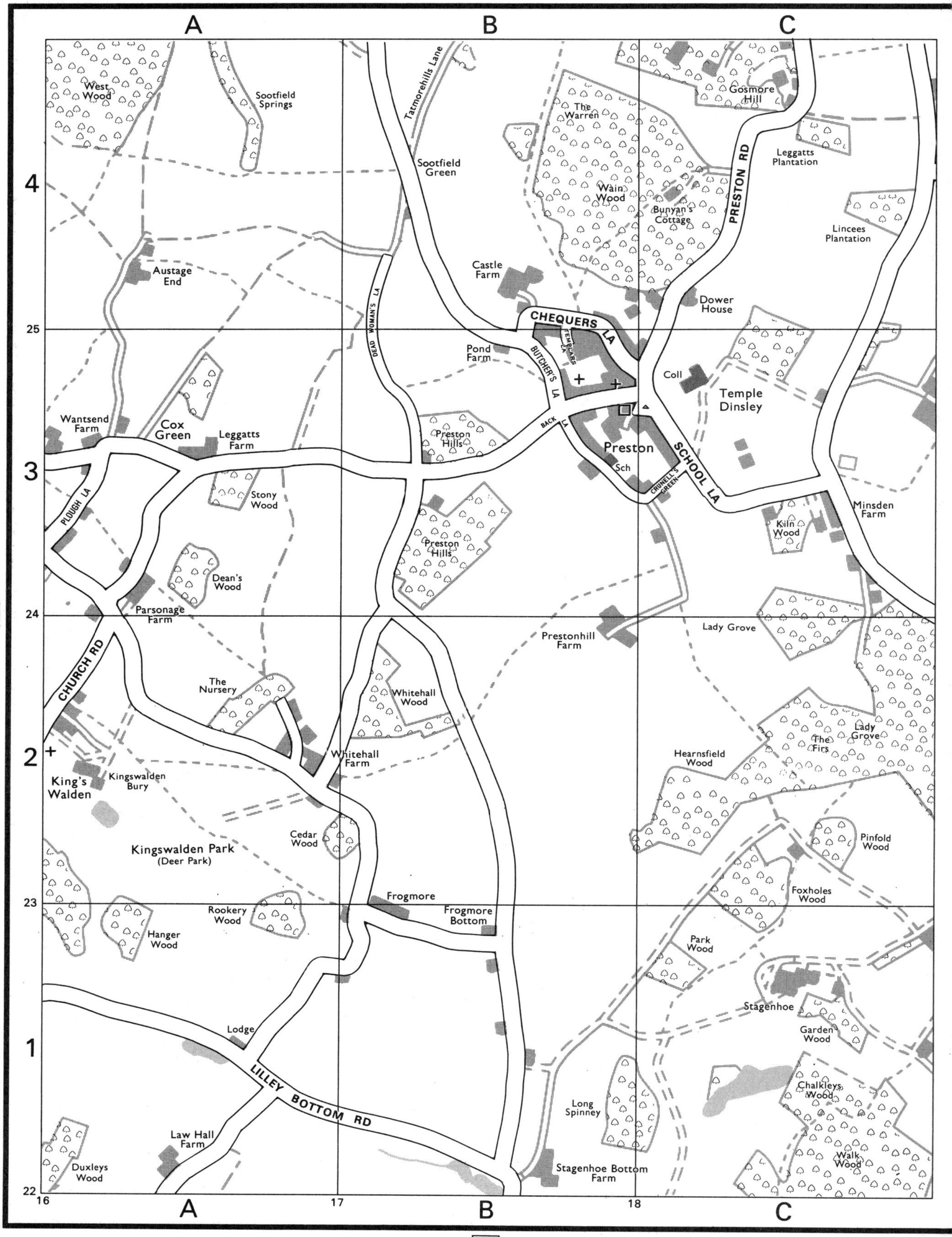
A
B
C
4
3
2
1
25
24
23
22
16
17
18
West Wood
Sootfield Springs
Tatmorehills Lane
Sootfield Green
The Warren
Gosmore Hill
Leggatts Plantation
PRESTON RD
Wain Wood
Bunyan's Cottage
Lincees Plantation
Austage End
Castle Farm
Dower House
DEAD WOMAN'S LA
CHEQUERS LA
TEMPLARS LA
Pond Farm
BUTCHER'S LA
Coll
Temple Dinsley
Wantsend Farm
Cox Green
Leggatts Farm
BACK LA
Preston Hills
Preston
Sch
SCHOOL LA
CRUNELL'S GREEN
Stony Wood
PLOUGH LA
Minsden Farm
Kiln Wood
Preston Hills
Dean's Wood
Parsonage Farm
Lady Grove
Prestonhill Farm
CHURCH RD
The Nursery
Whitehall Wood
Lady Grove
The Firs
Hearnsfield Wood
Whitehall Farm
King's Walden
Kingswalden Bury
Cedar Wood
Pinfold Wood
Kingswalden Park
(Deer Park)
Foxholes Wood
Frogmore
Rookery Wood
Frogmore Bottom
Hanger Wood
Park Wood
Stagenhoe
Lodge
Garden Wood
LILLEY BOTTOM RD
Chalkleys Wood
Long Spinney
Law Hall Farm
Walk Wood
Duxleys Wood
Stagenhoe Bottom Farm

66

35

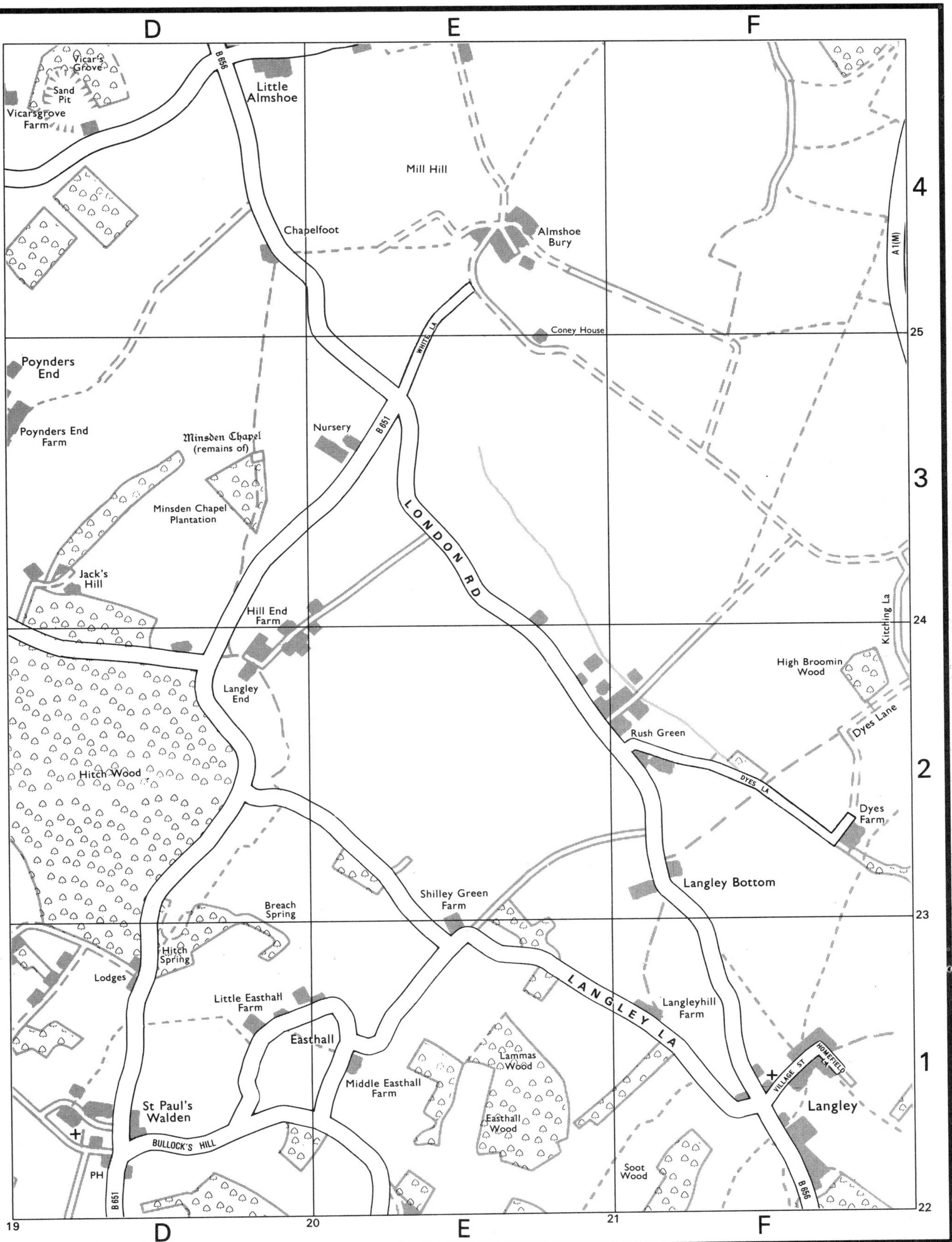

D
E
F
Vicar's Grove
Sand Pit
Vicarsgrove Farm
B656
Little Almshoe
Mill Hill
Chapelfoot
Almshoe Bury
A1(M)
4
White La
Coney House
25
Poynders End
Poynders End Farm
Minsden Chapel (remains of)
Nursery
B651
Minsden Chapel Plantation
London Rd
3
Jack's Hill
Hill End Farm
Kitching La
24
Langley End
High Broomin Wood
Dyes Lane
Rush Green
Hitch Wood
Dyes La
2
Dyes Farm
Langley Bottom
Shilley Green Farm
Breach Spring
23
Hitch Spring
Lodges
Langley La
Little Easthall Farm
Langleyhill Farm
Easthall
Lammas Wood
1
Village St
Homefield
Middle Easthall Farm
St Paul's Walden
Langley
Easthall Wood
Bullock's Hill
PH
Soot Wood
B656
B651
22
19
20
21

50

67

36

49

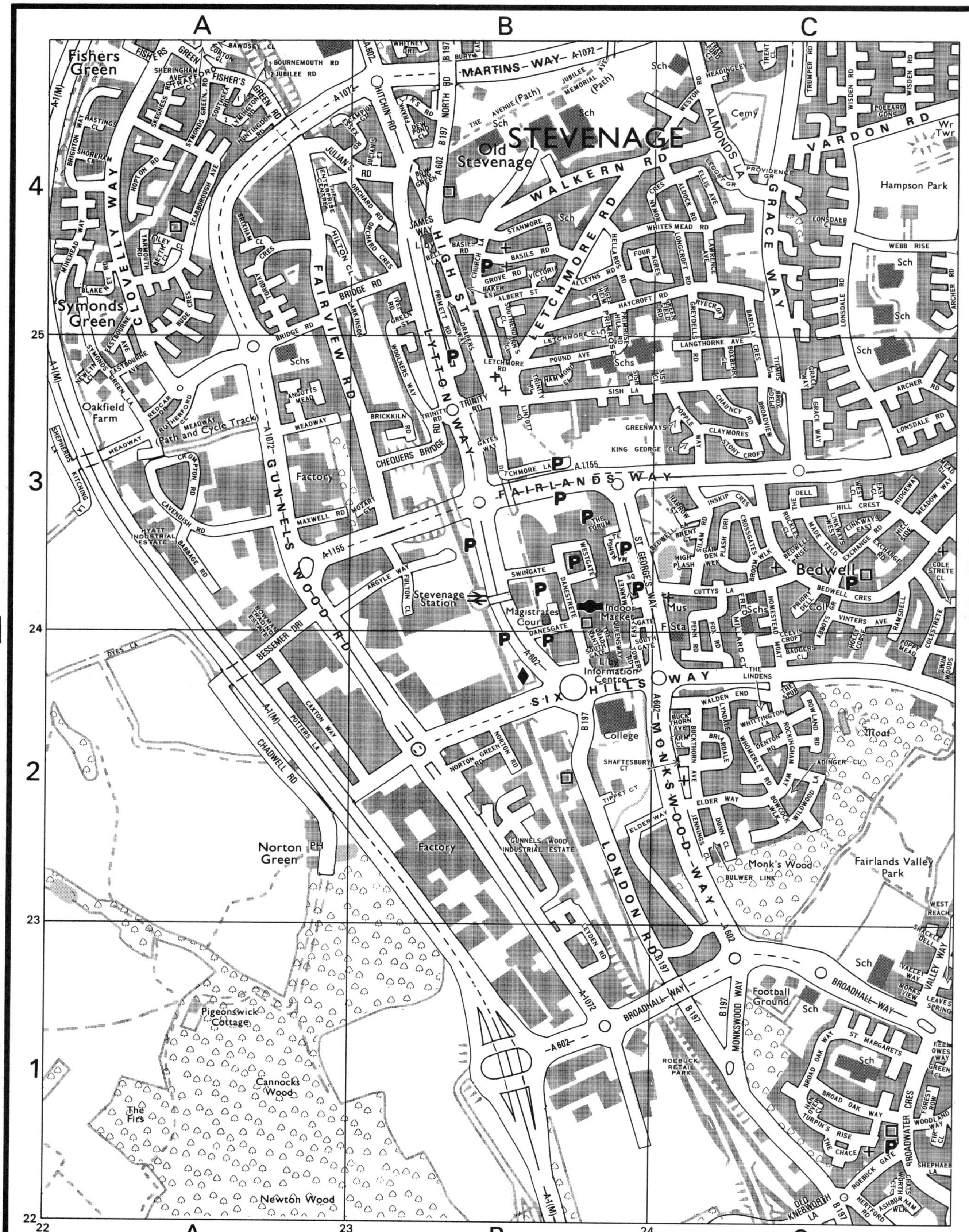
A
B
C
4
3
2
1
25
24
23
22
STEVENAGE
Old Stevenage
Fishers Green
Symonds Green
Oakfield Farm
Hampson Park
Bedwell
Stevenage Station
Magistrates Court
Indoor Market
Information Centre
College
Factory
Norton Green
Pigeonswick Cottage
Cannocks Wood
The Firs
Newton Wood
Monk's Wood
Fairlands Valley Park
Football Ground
Roebuck Retail Park
Gunnels Wood Industrial Estate
Hyatt Industrial Estate
Cemy
Moat
MARTINS WAY
A1072
NORTH RD
B197
HIGH ST
LYTTON WAY
WALKERN RD
LETCHMORE RD
GRACE WAY
VARDON RD
ALMONDS LA
FAIRVIEW RD
GUNNELS WOOD RD
FAIRLANDS WAY
A1155
SIX HILLS WAY
ST GEORGE'S WAY
MONKSWOOD WAY
LONDON RD
BROADHALL WAY
A602
CHADWELL RD
CLOVELLY WAY
A1(M)
BROADWATER CRES
MONKSWOOD WAY
VALLEY WAY
BROAD OAK WAY
KING GEORGE CL
SISH LA
CHEQUERS BRIDGE
BESSEMER DRI
DYES LA
SHEPHERDS LA
KITCHING LA
CAXTON WAY
POTTERS LA
NORTON GREEN RD
ELDER WAY
SHAFTESBURY CT
TIPPET CT
LEYDEN RD
OLD KNEBWORTH LA
HERTFORD RD
ROEBUCK GATE
WEBB RISE
LONSDALE RD
ARCHER RD
BRIDGE RD
ARGYLE WAY
FULTON CL
MAXWELL RD
MEADWAY
DANESTRETE
SWINGATE
WESTGATE
QUEENSWAY
CUTTYS LA
INSKIP CRES
WALDEN END
WHITTINGTON LA
ROWLAND RD
ADINGER CL
BULWER LINK
JENNINGS CL
DUNN CL
RAMSDELL
COLESTRETE
VINTERS AVE
POPPY MEAD
BEDWELL CRES
RIDGEWAY
HILL CREST
MEADOW WAY
WALKERN RD
STANMORE RD
BASILS RD
ALBERT ST
HAYCROFT RD
LANGTHORNE AVE
POUND AVE
CHAUNCY RD
CLAYMORES
STONY CROFT
GREENWAYS
BROADVIEW
FOUR ACRES
WHITES MEAD RD
ALDOCK RD
ELLIS AVE
LONGCROFT RD
HEADINGLEY CL
WISDEN RD
TRUMPER RD
POLLARD GDNS
LONSDALE
FAIRVIEW RD
ORCHARD RD
HILTON CL
JULIAN'S RD
BRIXHAM CRES
TORQUAY CRES
BRIDGE RD
ANGOTTS MEAD
BRICKKILN RD
WOOLNERS WAY
TRINITY RD
GATES WAY
LINTOTT CL
CROMPTON RD
CAVENDISH RD
BABBAGE RD
REDCAR DRI
RUTHERFORD WAY
MEADWAY (Path and Cycle Track)
BRIGHTON WAY
HASTINGS CL
SHOREHAM CL
MINEHEAD WAY
HOPTON RD
SCARBOROUGH AVE
BUDE CRES
EASTBOURNE AVE
SYMONDS GREEN LA
NEWLYN CL
BOURNEMOUTH RD
JUBILEE RD
BAWDSEY CL
FISHERS GREEN
FISHER'S GREEN RD
SKEGNESS RD
TRAFFORD CL
LYMINGTON RD
HUNTINGDON RD
THE AVENUE (Path)
JUBILEE MEMORIAL AVE (Path)
Sch
Schs
P
Mus
Lib
F Sta
PH
ST MARGARETS
TURPIN'S RISE
THE CHACE
WOODLAND WAY
FOREST ROW
SHEPHALL LA
ASHBURNAM WLK
THE LINDENS
THE SPUR
BOWCOCK WLK
WILDWOOD LA
ROCKINGHAM WAY
DENTON RD
WHOMERLEY RD
BRIARDALE
BUCKTHORN AVE
HOMESTEAD MOAT
FOX RD
PENN RD
PRIORY DELL
ABBOTS GROVE
BADGERS CL
CRONSGATES
PLASH DRI
HIGH PLASH
BRENT CT
BEDWELL CL
LINKWAYS EAST
LINKWAYS WEST
EXCHANGE RD
MADE FELD
RUCKLES CL
WEST REACH
SHACKLEDELL
VALLEY WAY
MONKS VIEW
LEAVES SPRING
FEATHER DELL

68

37

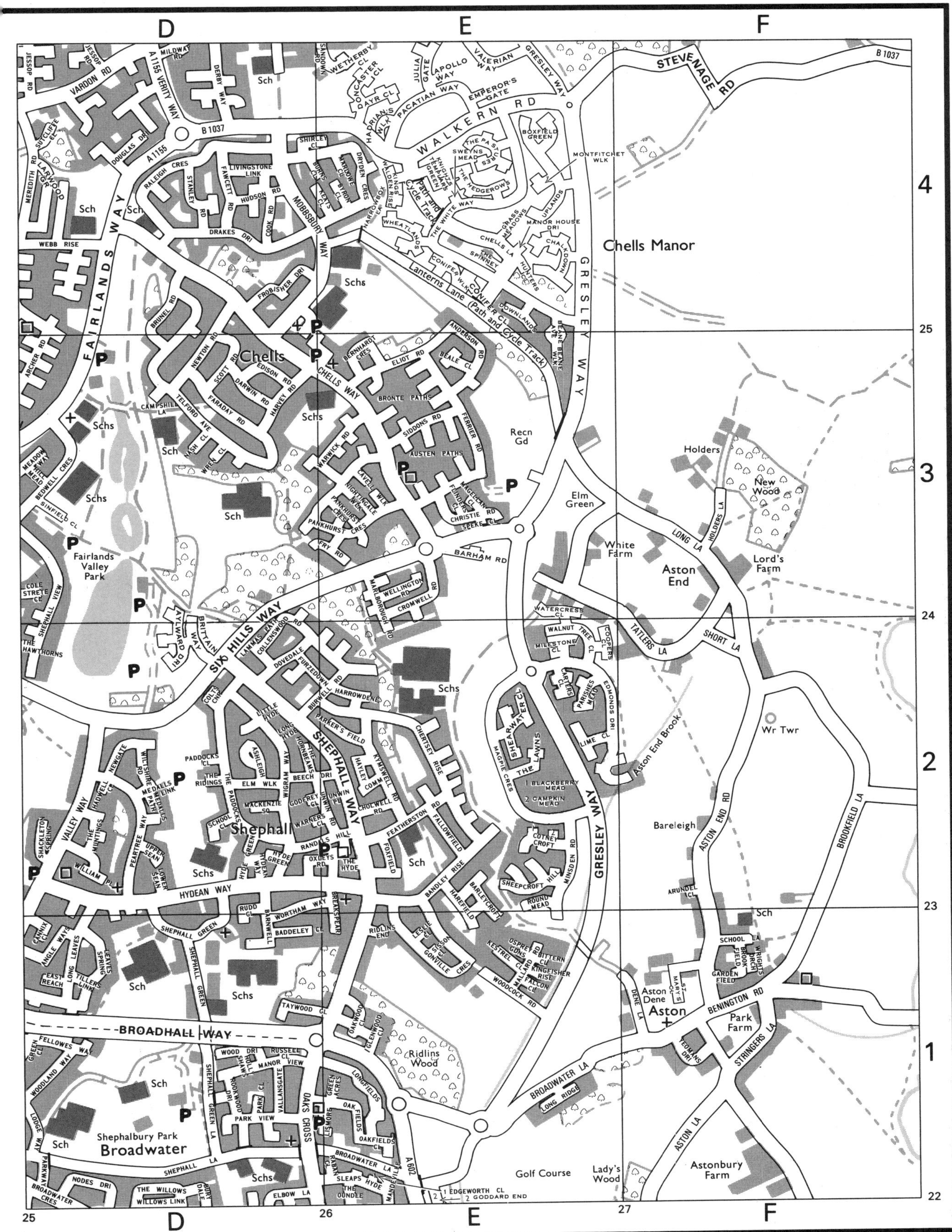
D
E
F
4
3
2
1
25
24
23
22
26
27
B 1037
STEVENAGE RD
JESSOP RD
VARDON RD
A1155 VERITY WAY
MILDWAY RD
DERBY WAY
Sch
SANDOWN RD
WETHERBY CL
DONCASTER CL
DAYR CL
JULIA GATE
APOLLO WAY
VALERIAN WAY
GRESLEY WAY
PACATIAN WAY
EMPEROR'S GATE
HADRIAN'S WLK
WALKERN RD
BOXFIELD GREEN
MONTFITCHET WLK
THE PASTURES
SWEYNS MEAD
THE HEDGEROWS
KNIGHTS TEMPLARS GREEN
SUTCLIFFE CL
MEREDITH RD
LARWOOD GR
DOUGLAS DR
A1155
B 1037
SHIRLEY CL
RALEIGH CRES
LIVINGSTONE LINK
STANLEY RD
FAWCETT RD
HUDSON RD
COOK RD
MOBBSBURY WAY
BURNS CL
KEATS CL
MARLOWE CL
BYRON CL
DRYDEN CRES
WALDEN RISE
KINGS
HARROWBOX CL
Path and Cycle Track
THE WHITE WAY
UPLANDS
GRASS MEADOWS
MANOR HOUSE DRI
WHEATLANDS
CHELLS LA
THE SPINNEY
HUNTERS
CHALKDOWN
Chells Manor
Sch
Sch
DRAKES DRI
WEBB RISE
FAIRLANDS WAY
Schs
FROBISHER DRI
Lanterns Lane (Path and Cycle Track)
CONIFER WLK
CONIFER CL
DOWNLANDS
BEANE AVE
BEANE WLK
BRUNEL RD
NEWTON RD
Chells
SCOTT RD
EDISON RD
DARWIN RD
FARADAY RD
HARVEY RD
TELFORD AVE
NASH CL
WREN CL
CAMPSHILL LA
P
P
P
CHELLS WAY
BERNHARDT CRES
ELIOT RD
ANDERSON RD
BEALE CL
BRONTE PATHS
SIDDONS RD
FERRIER RD
AUSTEN PATHS
Recn Gd
ARCHER RD
Schs
Sch
Schs
Sch
MEADOW WAY
WHITE MEAD
BEDWELL CRES
SINFIELD CL
WARWICK RD
LAVELL WLK
NIGHTINGALE WLK
PANKHURST CRES
FRY RD
MAGELLAN CL
FUNDY CL
CHRISTIE RD
SEEKE CL
P
Elm Green
Holders
New Wood
LONG LA
HOLDERS LA
White Farm
Aston End
Lord's Farm
Fairlands Valley Park
BARHAM RD
COLE GREEN STREET CL
SHEPHALL VIEW
THE HAWTHORNS
P
P
AYLWARD DRI
BRITTAIN WAY
SIX HILLS WAY
LAMMAS PATH
COLLENSWOOD RD
WELLINGTON RD
MARLBOROUGH RD
CROMWELL RD
WATERCRESS CL
WALNUT TREE CL
COOPERS CL
MILESTONE CL
TATLERS LA
SHORT LA
DOVEDALE
FURZEDOWN RD
HARROWDENE
BURWELL RD
Schs
COLTS CNR
LITTLE HYDE
LONG HYDE
PARKER'S FIELD
CHERTSEY RISE
SHEARWATER CL
CARTERS CL
PARISHES MEAD
EDMONDS DRI
LIME CL
Aston End Brook
Wr Twr
NEWGATE
WILTSHIRE RD
MEDALLS LINK
MEDALLS PATH
PADDOCKS CL
THE RIDINGS
THE PADDOCKS
ASHLEIGH
WIGRAM WAY
HORNBEAMS
BEECH DRI
ELM WLK
SHEPHALL WAY
HATLEY CL
AYMSWELL RD
THE LAWNS
MAGPIE CRES
1 BLACKBERRY MEAD
2 CAMPKIN MEAD
GRESLEY WAY
VALLEY WAY
HADWELL CL
THE MINTINGS
MACKENZIE SQ
GODFREY CL
UNWIN PL
CHOLWELL RD
FEATHERSTON RD
FALLOWFIELD
ASTON END RD
BROOKFIELD LA
Bareleigh
SHACKLETON SPRING
SCHOOL LA
Shephall
WARGERS CL
RANDALLS HILL
OXEYES RD
THE HYDE
FOXFIELD
COTNEY CROFT
MINSDEN RD
PEARTREE WAY
UPPER SEAN
LOWER SEAN
HYDE GREEN
HYDEAN GREEN
Schs
Sch
WILLIAM PL
HYDEAN WAY
BANDLEY RISE
HAREFIELD
BARLEYCROFT
SHEEPCROFT HILL
ROUND MEAD
ARUNDEL CL
Sch
RUDD CL
BARNWELL
WORTHAM WAY
BADDELEY CL
BREAKSPEAR
RIDLINS END
LESLIE CL
GIBSON CL
GONVILLE CRES
OSPREY GDNS
BITTERN CL
KINGFISHER RISE
KESTREL CL
MALLARD RD
FALCON CL
WOODCOCK RD
SCHOOL LA
BROOKFIELD
WRIGHTS ORCH
GARDEN FIELD
CANNIX CL
ANGLE WAYS
LONG LEAVES
LEAVES SPRING
TILLERS LINK
EAST REACH
SHEPHALL GREEN
Sch
Schs
TAYWOOD CL
DENE LA
Aston Dene
ST MARY'S CL
Aston
BENINGTON RD
Park Farm
BROADHALL WAY
FELLOWES WAY
GREEN CL
WOODLAND WAY
WOOD DRI
RUSSELL CL
MANOR
VIEW
ROOKWOOD DRI
OAKWOOD CL
GLENWOOD CL
Ridlins Wood
LONGFIELDS
YEOMANS DRI
STRINGERS LA
Sch
P
PARK VIEW
PARK CL
VALLANSGATE
GREEN ACRES
OAK FIELDS
OAKFIELDS CL
LISMORE
BROADWATER LA
LONG RIDGE
ASTON LA
LODGE WAY
Shephalbury Park
Sch
Broadwater
SHEPHALL GREEN LA
OAKS CROSS
SHEPHALL LA
BROADWATER LA
A 602
Golf Course
Lady's Wood
Astonbury Farm
NODES DRI
THE WILLOWS
WILLOWS LINK
BURYDALE
Schs
SLEAPS HYDE
RABAN
THE OUNDLE
MANDEVILLE
1 EDGEWORTH CL
2 GODDARD END
ELBOW LA
BROADWATER CRES
PARKWAY

52

69

38

51

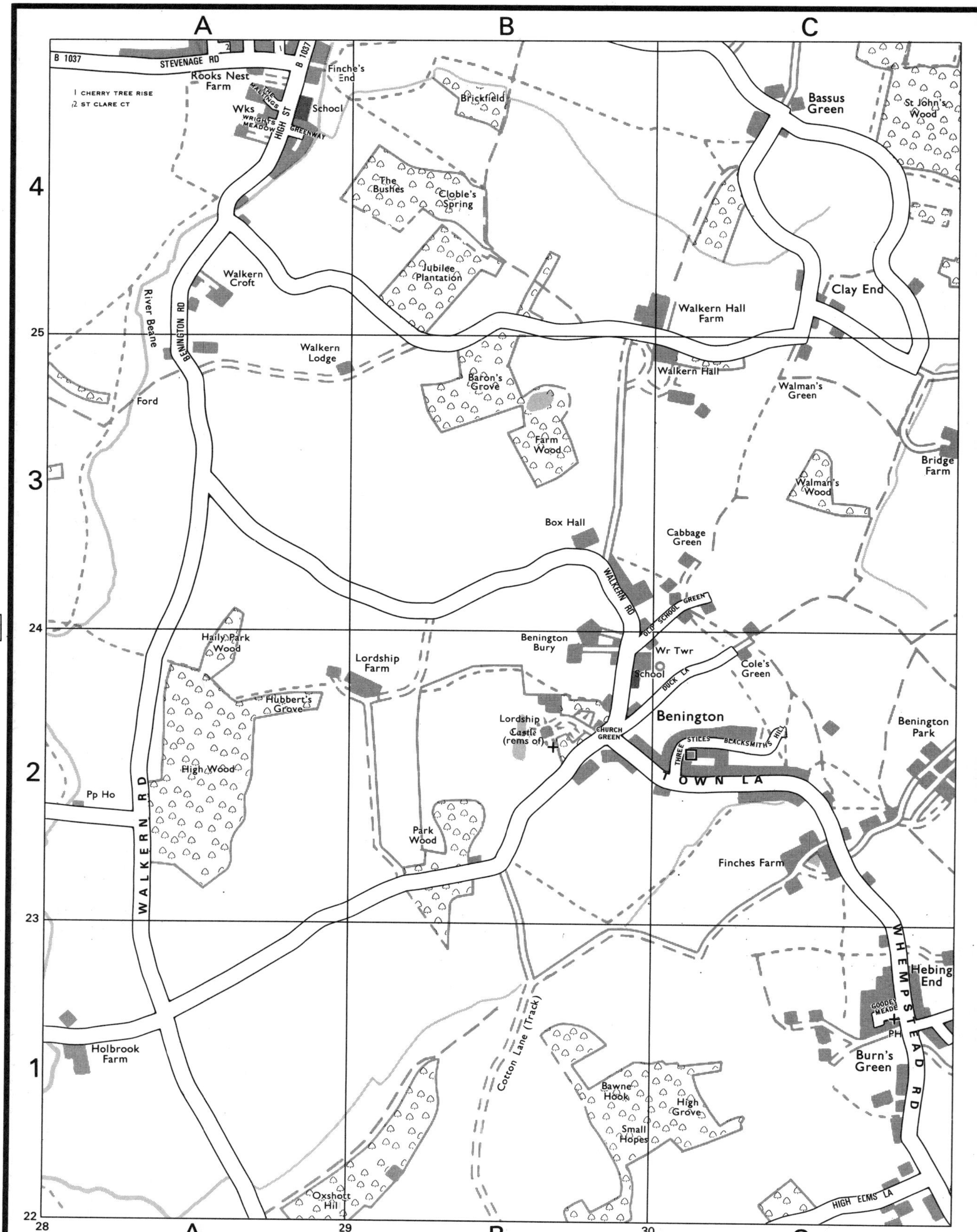
A
B
C
B 1037
STEVENAGE RD
B 1037
Rooks Nest Farm
Finche's End
1 CHERRY TREE RISE
2 ST CLARE CT
THE MALTINGS
Wks
WRIGHTS MEADOW
HIGH ST
School
GREENWAY
Brickfield
Bassus Green
St John's Wood
4
The Bushes
Cloble's Spring
Walkern Croft
Jubilee Plantation
Clay End
River Beane
BENINGTON RD
Walkern Hall Farm
25
Walkern Lodge
Walkern Hall
Baron's Grove
Walman's Green
Ford
Farm Wood
Bridge Farm
3
Walman's Wood
Box Hall
Cabbage Green
WALKERN RD
OLD SCHOOL GREEN
24
Haily Park Wood
Benington Bury
Wr Twr
Lordship Farm
School
Cole's Green
DUCK LA
Hubbert's Grove
Benington
Benington Park
Lordship Castle (rems of)
CHURCH GREEN
THREE STILES
BLACKSMITHS HILL
2
High Wood
TOWN LA
Pp Ho
Park Wood
Finches Farm
WALKERN RD
23
WHEMPSTEAD RD
Hebing End
GOODEY MEADE
PH
Holbrook Farm
Burn's Green
1
Cotton Lane (Track)
Bawne Hook
High Grove
Small Hopes
Oxshott Hil
HIGH ELMS LA
22
28
29
30
A
B
C

70

39

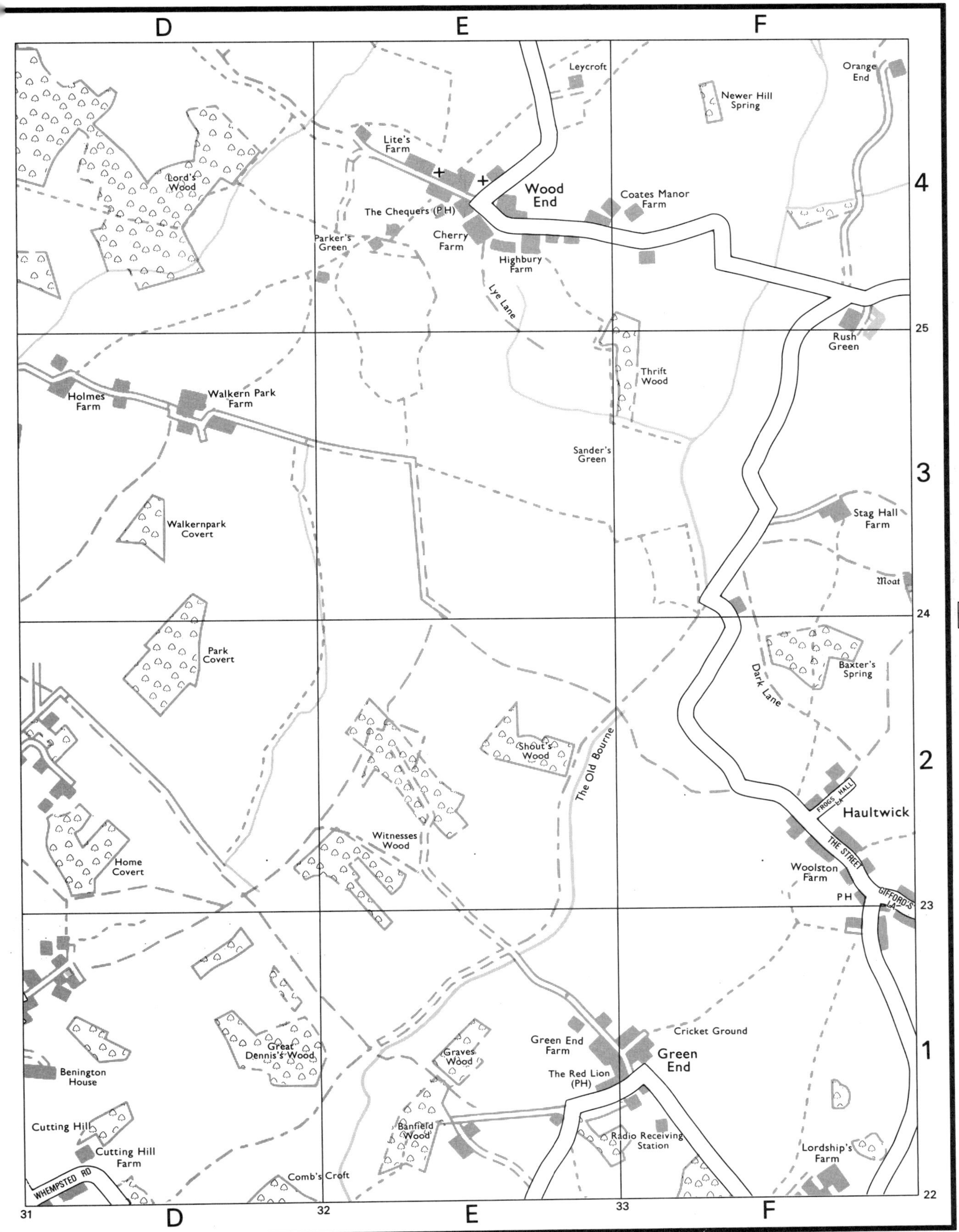
D
E
F
Leycroft
Orange End
Newer Hill Spring
Lite's Farm
Lord's Wood
Wood End
Coates Manor Farm
The Chequers (PH)
Parker's Green
Cherry Farm
Highbury Farm
Lye Lane
Rush Green
Thrift Wood
Holmes Farm
Walkern Park Farm
Sander's Green
Stag Hall Farm
Walkernpark Covert
Moat
Park Covert
Baxter's Spring
Dark Lane
Shout's Wood
The Old Bourne
FROGS HALL LA
Haultwick
THE STREET
Witnesses Wood
Home Covert
Woolston Farm
PH
GIFFORD'S LA
Cricket Ground
Green End Farm
Green End
Graves Wood
Great Dennis's Wood
The Red Lion (PH)
Benington House
Banfield Wood
Radio Receiving Station
Cutting Hill
Cutting Hill Farm
Lordship's Farm
WHEMPSTED RD
Comb's Croft
4
3
2
1
25
24
23
22
31
32
33
D
E
F

54

71

40

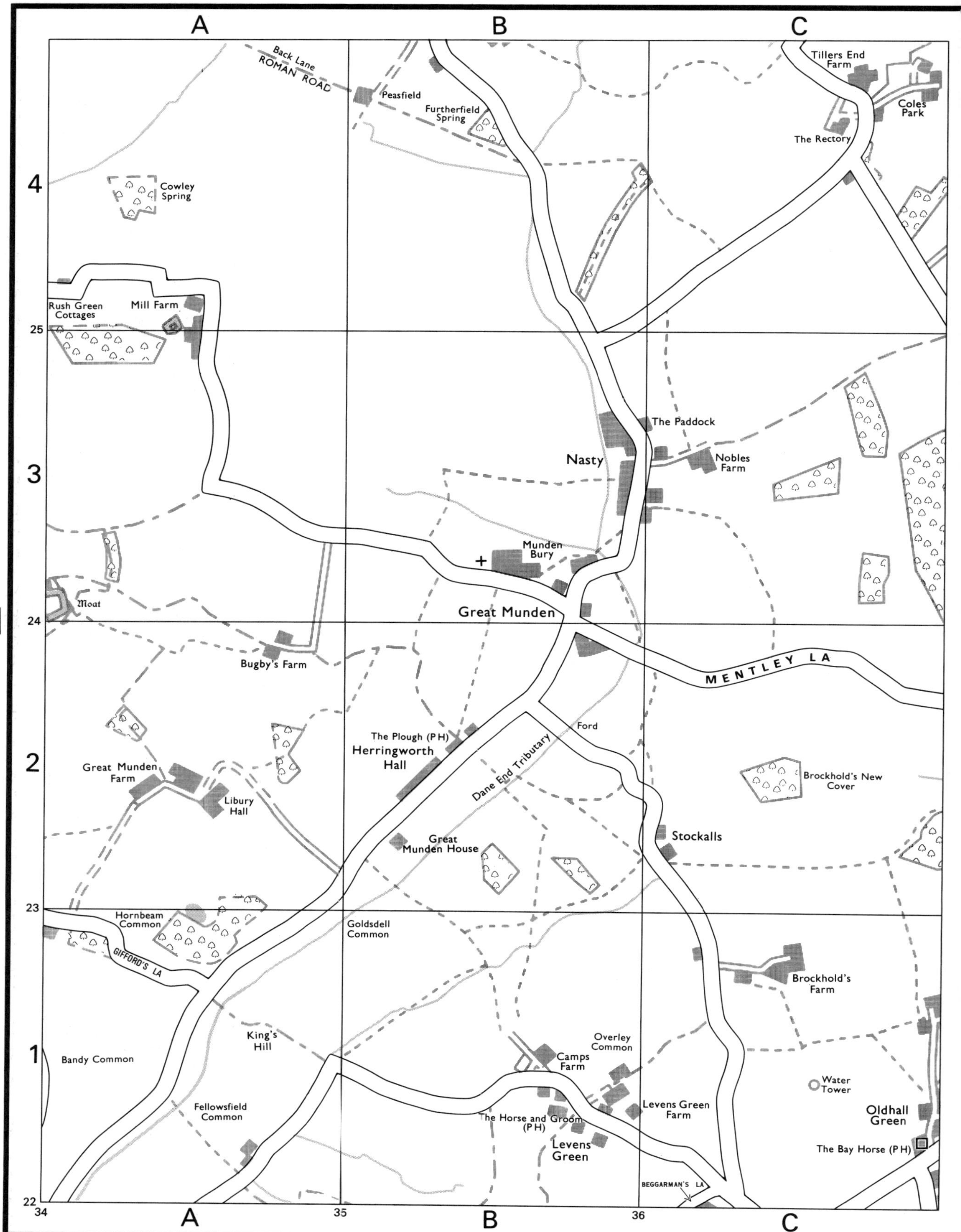
A
B
C
4
3
2
1
25
24
23
22
34
35
36
Back Lane
ROMAN ROAD
Peasfield
Furtherfield Spring
Tillers End Farm
Coles Park
The Rectory
Cowley Spring
Rush Green Cottages
Mill Farm
The Paddock
Nasty
Nobles Farm
Munden Bury
Moat
Great Munden
MENTLEY LA
Bugby's Farm
Ford
The Plough (PH)
Herringworth Hall
Dane End Tributary
Brockhold's New Cover
Great Munden Farm
Libury Hall
Stockalls
Great Munden House
Hornbeam Common
Goldsdell Common
GIFFORD'S LA
Brockhold's Farm
King's Hill
Overley Common
Camps Farm
Bandy Common
Water Tower
Fellowsfield Common
Levens Green Farm
The Horse and Groom (PH)
Oldhall Green
Levens Green
The Bay Horse (PH)
BEGGARMAN'S LA

53

72

41

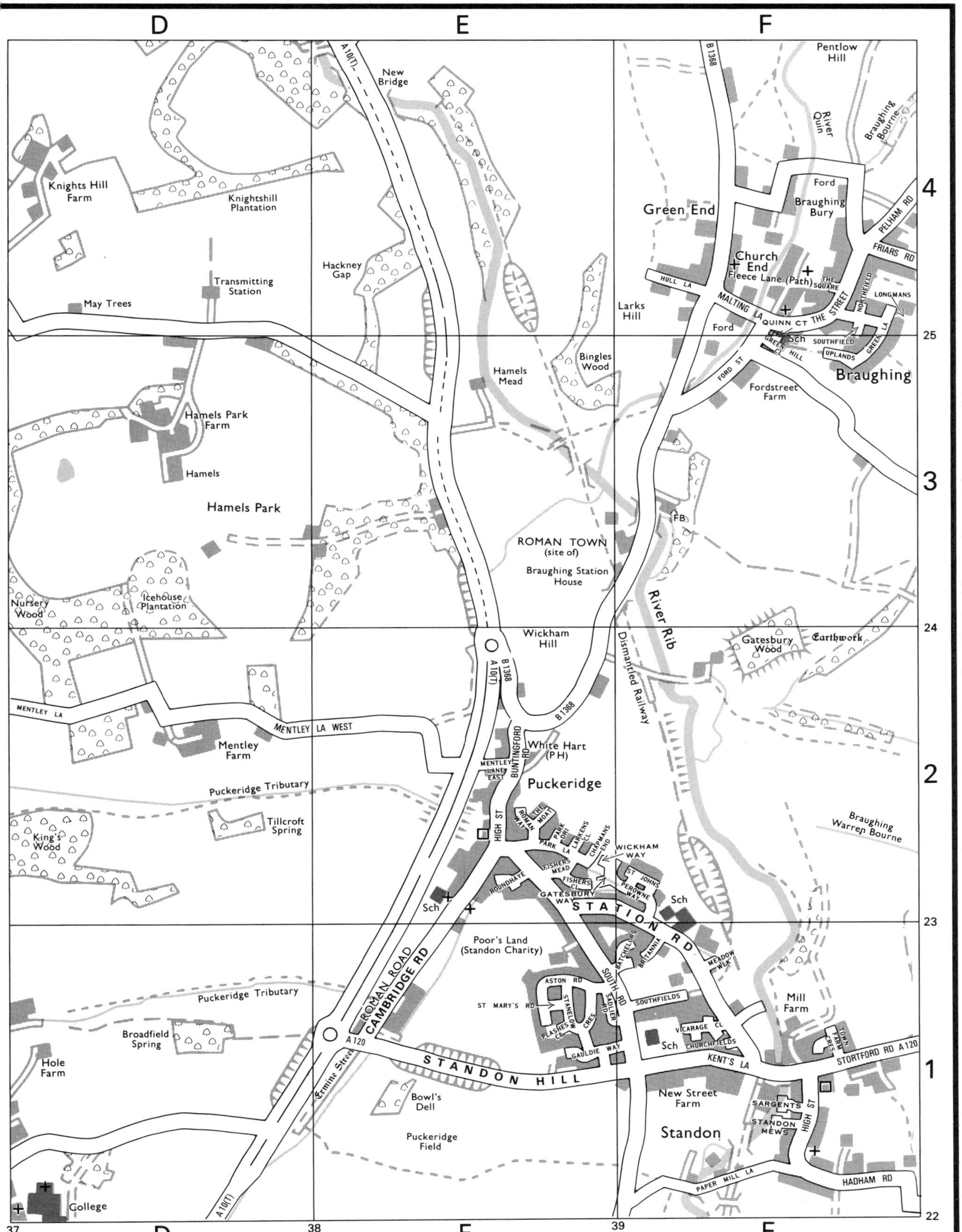
D
E
F
4
3
2
1
25
24
23
22
37
38
39
Pentlow Hill
River Quin
Braughing Bourne
New Bridge
A 10(T)
B 1368
Knights Hill Farm
Knightshill Plantation
Ford
Braughing Bury
Green End
PELHAM RD
FRIARS RD
Church End
Fleece Lane (Path)
THE SQUARE
HULL LA
NORTHFIELD
LONGMANS
Hackney Gap
Transmitting Station
May Trees
Larks Hill
MALTING LA
QUINN CT
THE STREET
Ford
Sch
SOUTHFIELD
GREEN LA
GREEN CL
HILL
UPLANDS
Braughing
FORD ST
Fordstreet Farm
Hamels Mead
Bingles Wood
Hamels Park Farm
Hamels
Hamels Park
FB
ROMAN TOWN (site of)
Braughing Station House
Nursery Wood
Icehouse Plantation
River Rib
Wickham Hill
Dismantled Railway
Gatesbury Wood
Earthwork
MENTLEY LA
MENTLEY LA WEST
Mentley Farm
B 1368
BUNTINGFORD RD
White Hart (PH)
MENTLEY LANE EAST
Puckeridge
Puckeridge Tributary
Tillcroft Spring
King's Wood
Braughing Warren Bourne
HIGH ST
ROMAN WAY
THE MOAT
PARK DRI
PARK LA
LARKENS CL
CHAPMANS END
WICKHAM WAY
FISHERS MEAD
FISHERS CL
ST JOHNS
PEROWNE WAY
ROUNDHAYE
GATESBURY WAY
Sch
Sch
STATION RD
Poor's Land (Standon Charity)
BATCHELORS
BRITANNIA
MEADOW WLK
ROMAN ROAD
CAMBRIDGE RD
Puckeridge Tributary
ASTON RD
SOUTH RD
ST MARY'S RD
STANELOW CRES
SADLIER RD
SOUTHFIELDS
Mill Farm
Broadfield Spring
PLASHES CL
VICARAGE CL
TOWN FARM CRES
A 120
GAULDIE WAY
Sch
CHURCHFIELDS
STORTFORD RD A 120
Hole Farm
STANDON HILL
KENT'S LA
Ermine Street
Bowl's Dell
New Street Farm
SARGENTS
HIGH ST
STANDON MEWS
Standon
Puckeridge Field
PAPER MILL LA
HADHAM RD
College
A 10(T)

56

73

42

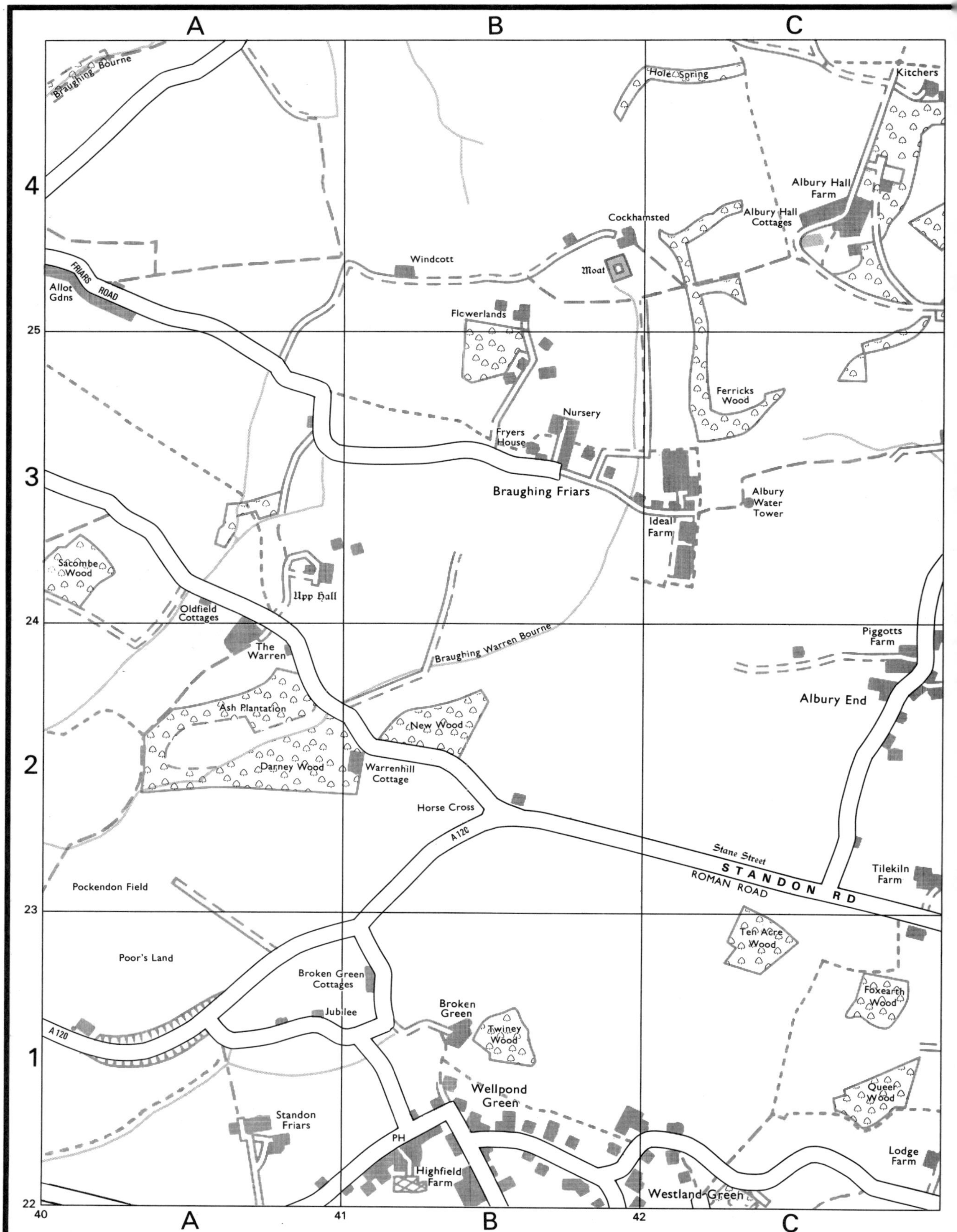
A
B
C
4
3
2
1
25
24
23
22
40
41
42
Braughing Bourne
Hole Spring
Kitchers
Albury Hall Farm
Cockhamsted
Albury Hall Cottages
Windcott
Moat
Allot Gdns
FRIARS ROAD
Flowerlands
Ferricks Wood
Nursery
Fryers House
Braughing Friars
Albury Water Tower
Ideal Farm
Sacombe Wood
Upp Hall
Oldfield Cottages
The Warren
Braughing Warren Bourne
Piggotts Farm
Albury End
Ash Plantation
New Wood
Darney Wood
Warrenhill Cottage
Horse Cross
A120
Stane Street
STANDON RD
ROMAN ROAD
Tilekiln Farm
Pockendon Field
Ten Acre Wood
Poor's Land
Broken Green Cottages
Foxearth Wood
Jubilee
Broken Green
Twiney Wood
A120
Wellpond Green
Queer Wood
Standon Friars
PH
Highfield Farm
Lodge Farm
Westland Green

55

74

43

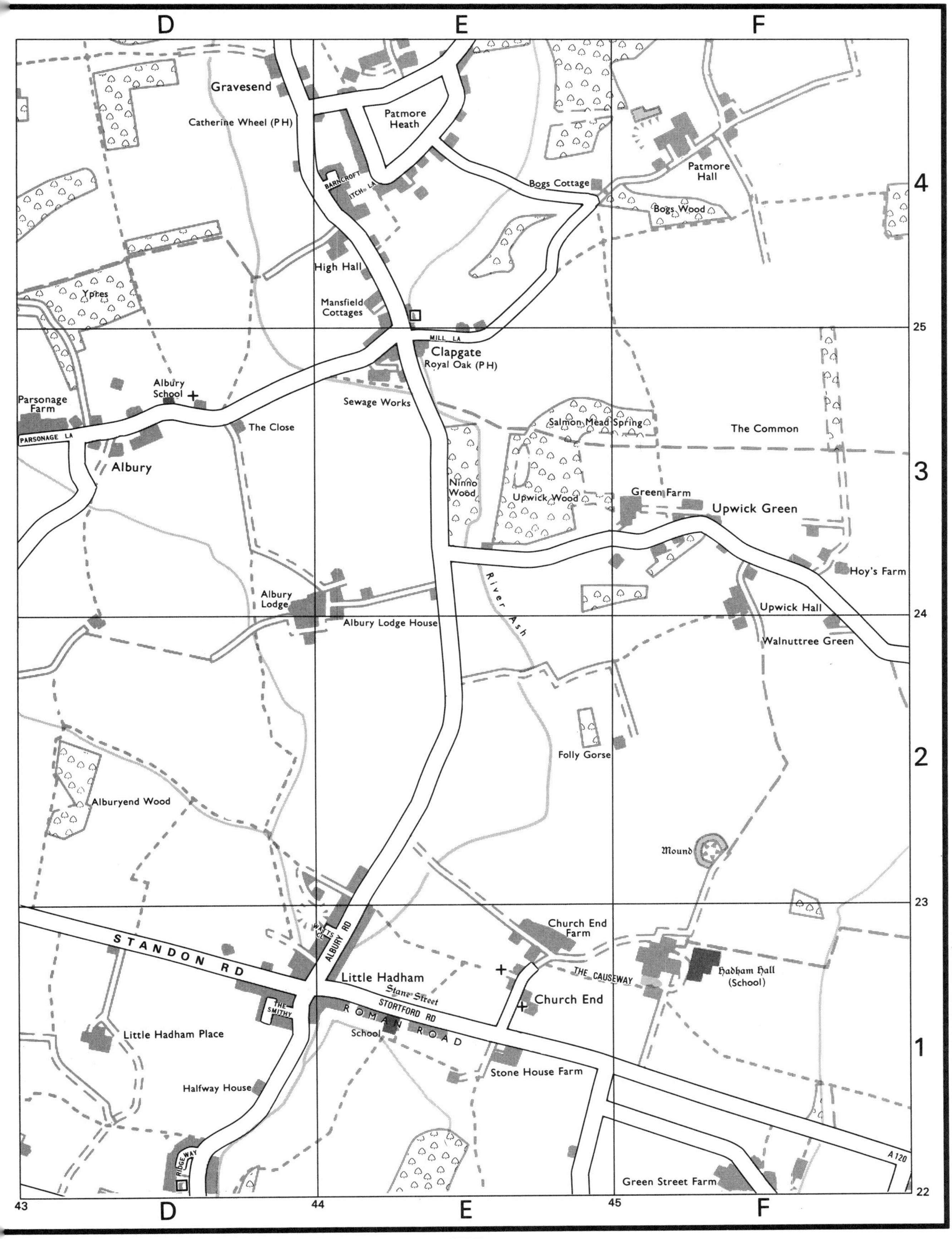
D
E
F
Gravesend
Catherine Wheel (PH)
Patmore Heath
Patmore Hall
Bogs Cottage
Bogs Wood
BARNCROFT
ITCH LA
High Hall
Ypres
Mansfield Cottages
MILL LA
Clapgate
Royal Oak (PH)
Albury School
Parsonage Farm
PARSONAGE LA
Sewage Works
The Close
Salmon Mead Spring
The Common
Albury
Ninno Wood
Upwick Wood
Green Farm
Upwick Green
Hoy's Farm
River Ash
Albury Lodge
Albury Lodge House
Upwick Hall
Walnuttree Green
Folly Gorse
Alburyend Wood
Mound
Church End Farm
STANDON RD
ALBURY RD
Little Hadham
Stane Street
THE CAUSEWAY
Hadham Hall (School)
Church End
THE SMITHY
STORTFORD RD
ROMAN ROAD
School
Little Hadham Place
Stone House Farm
Halfway House
RIDGEWAY
A120
Green Street Farm
43
44
45
25
24
23
22
4
3
2
1

58

75

not continued, see key diagram

57

76

not continued, see key diagram

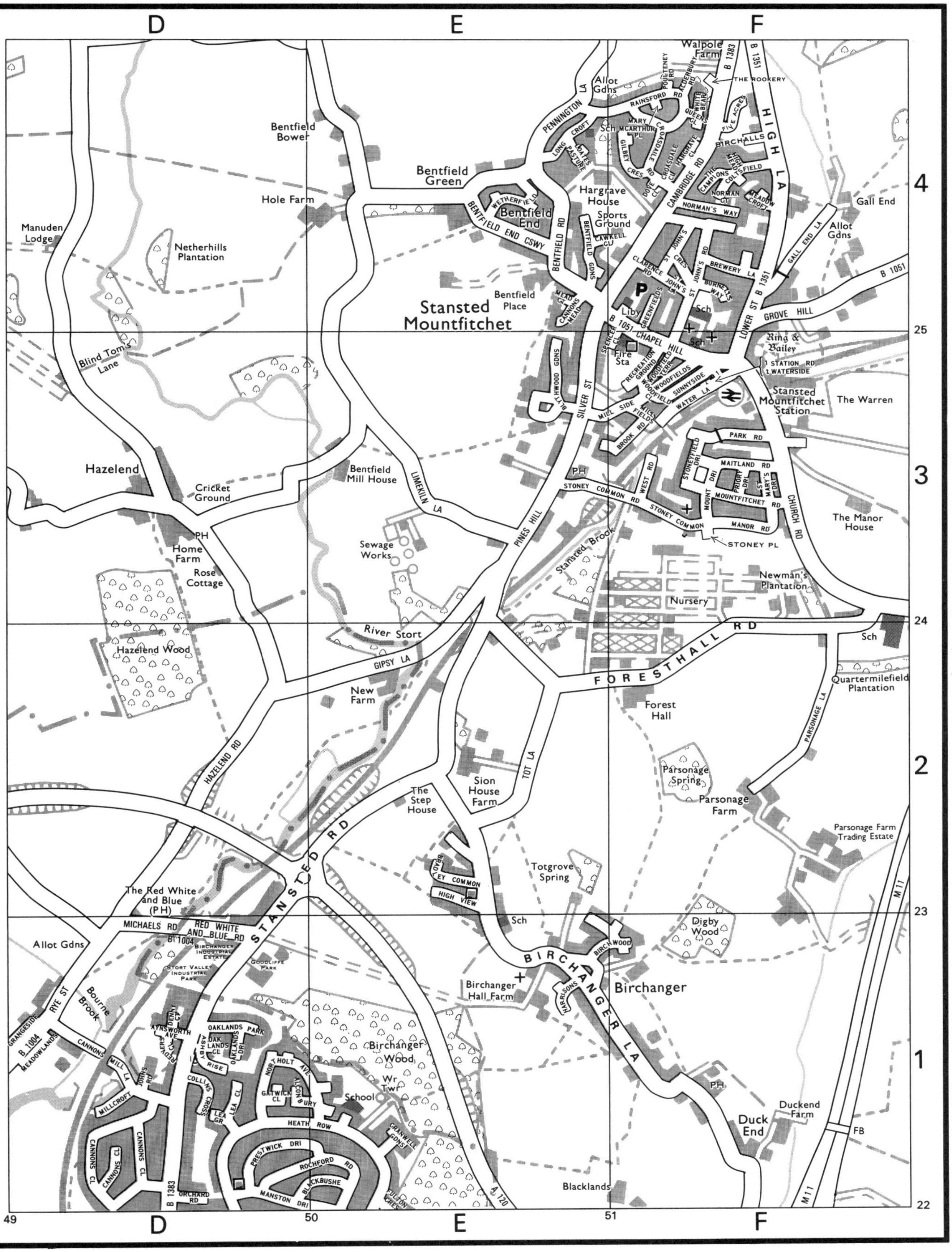

not continued, see key diagram

77

not continued, see key diagram

not continued, see key diagram

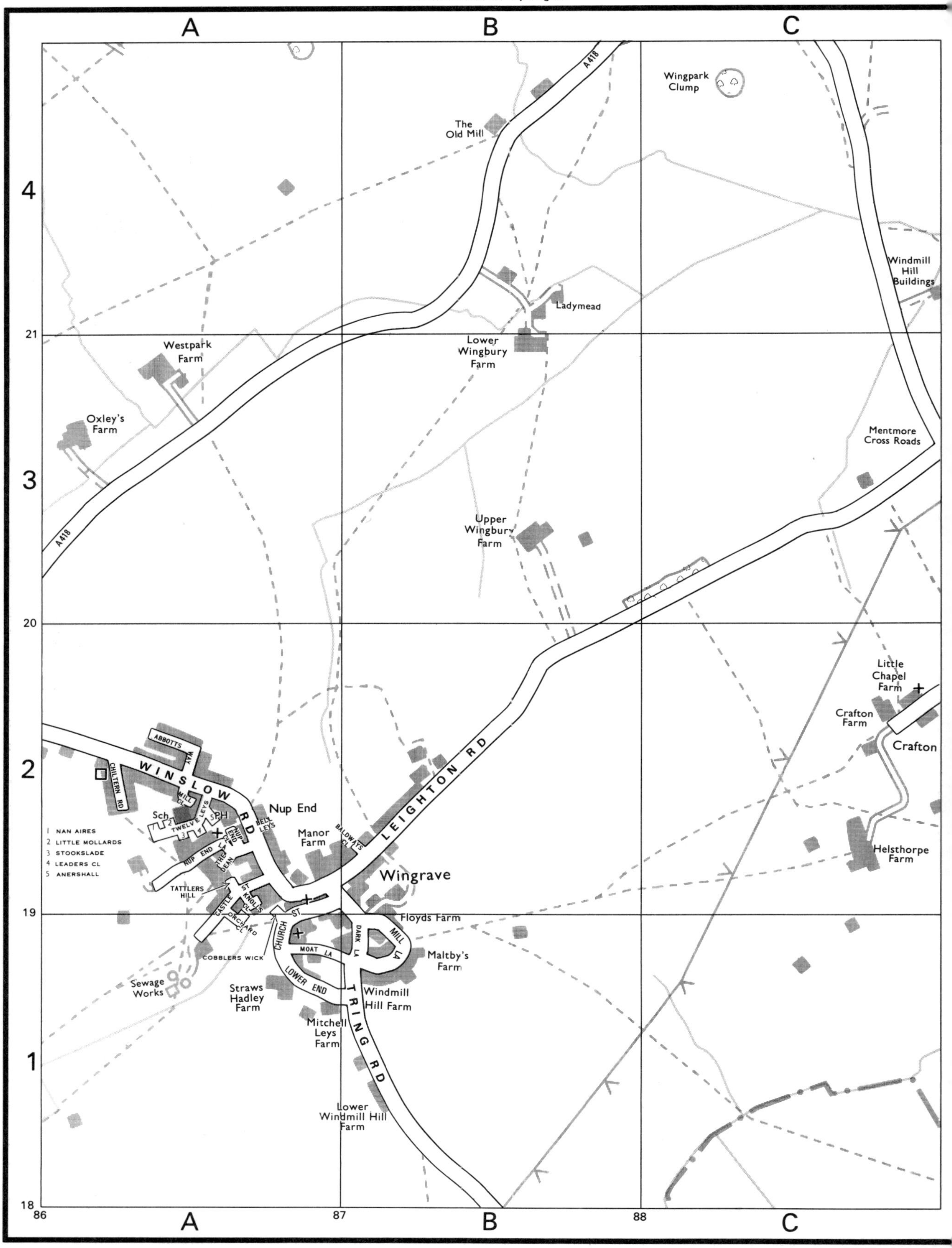

78

not continued, see key diagram

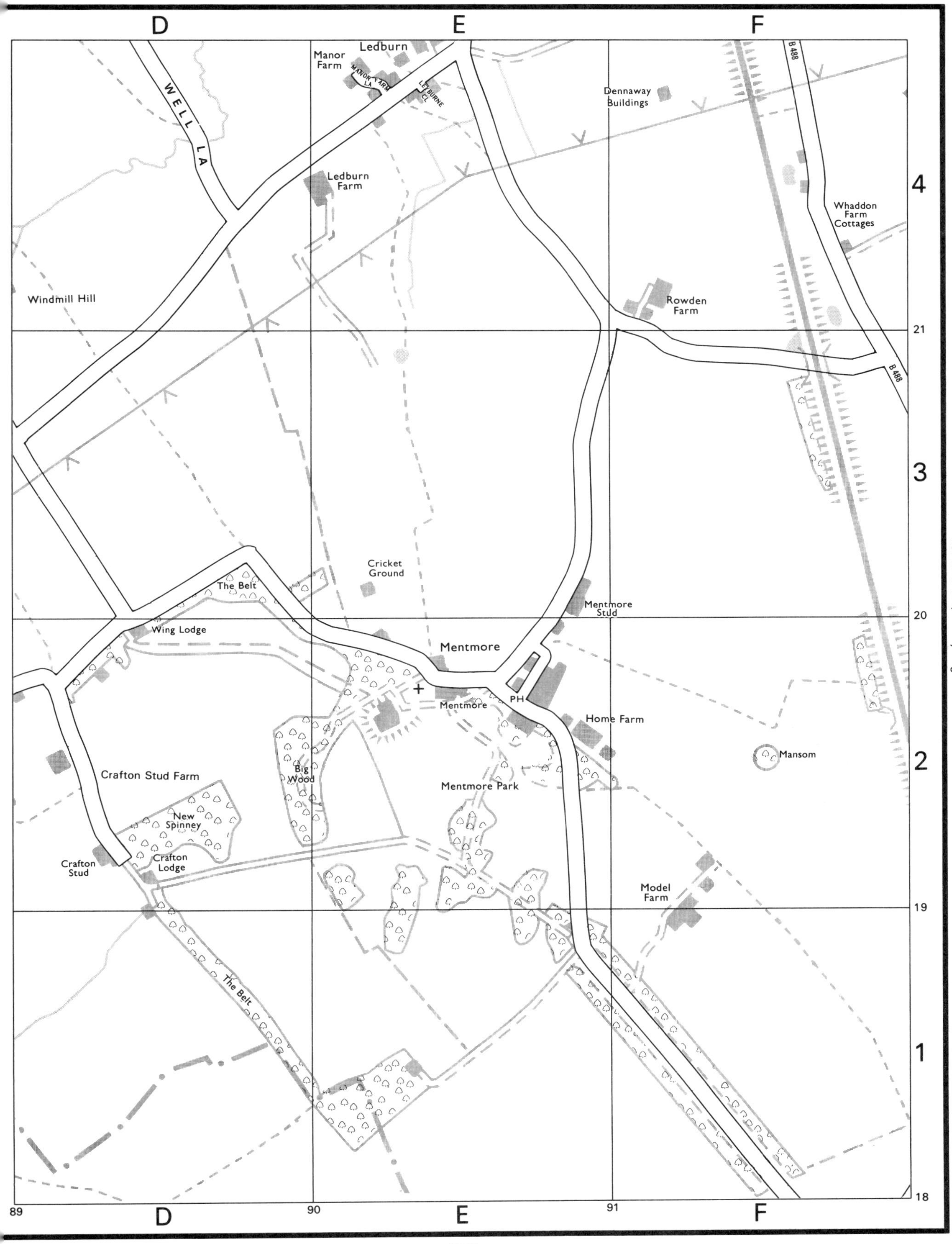

not continued, see key diagram

79

44

not continued, see key diagram

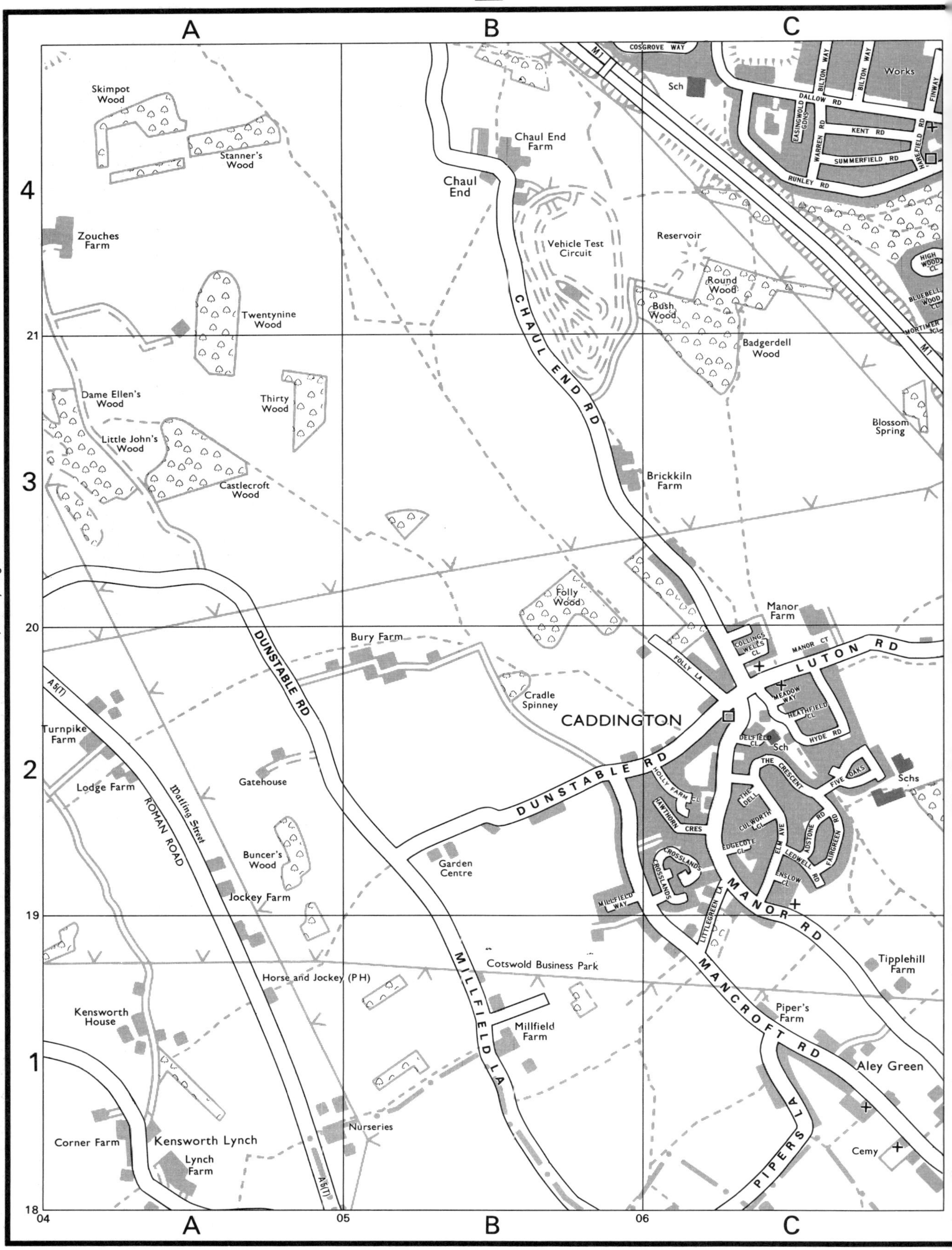

83

45

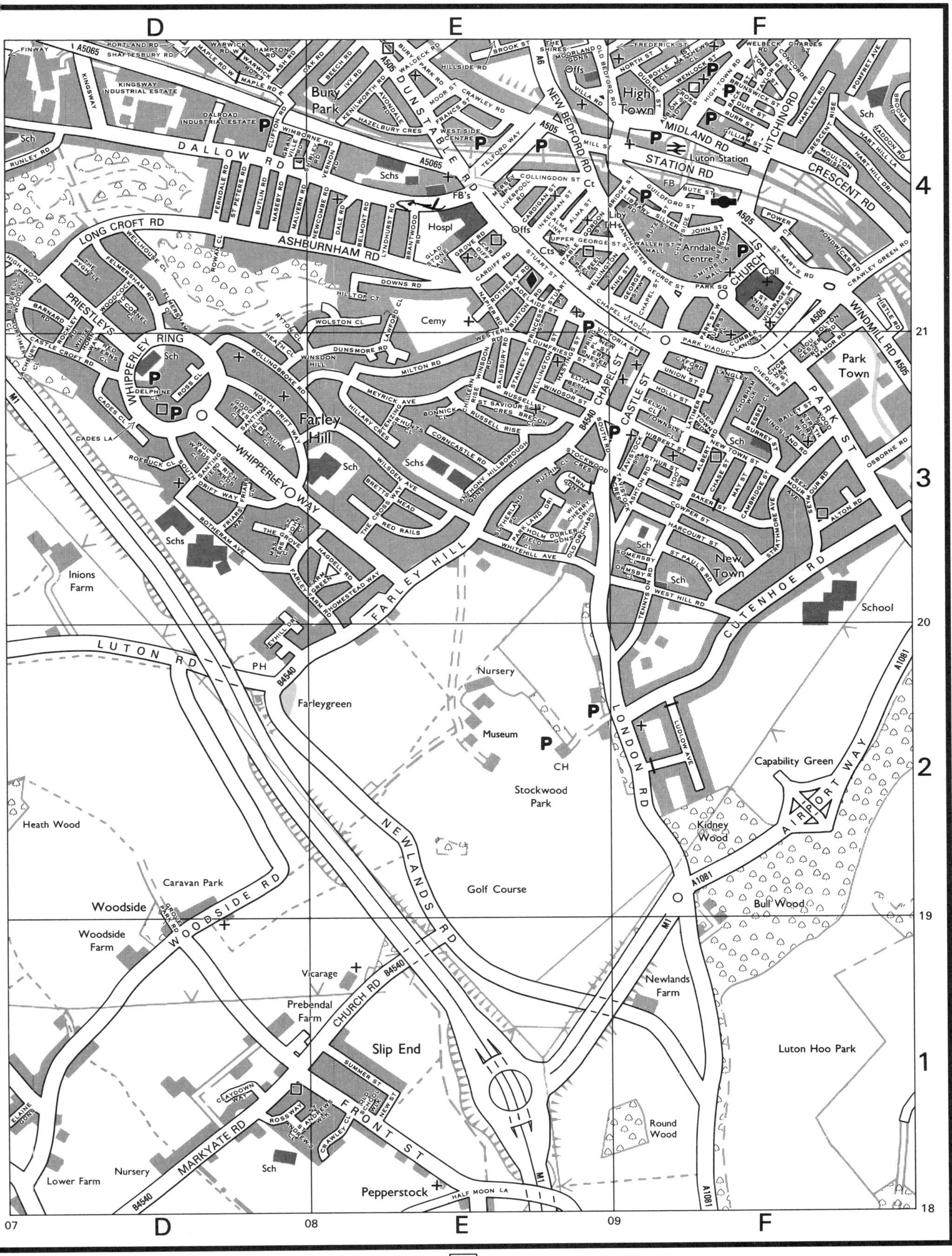

D
E
F
4
3
2
1
21
20
19
18
07
08
09
Bury Park
High Town
Luton Station
STATION RD
MIDLAND RD
CRESCENT RD
DALLOW RD
DUNSTABLE RD
NEW BEDFORD RD
HITCHIN RD
Kingsway Industrial Estate
Dalroad Industrial Estate
LONG CROFT RD
ASHBURNHAM RD
Hospl
Schs
Sch
Cemy
Arndale Centre
CHURCH ST
Coll
PARK ST
WINDMILL RD
Park Town
PRIESTLEYS
WHIPPERLEY RING
WHIPPERLEY WAY
Farley Hill
FARLEY HILL
CHAPEL ST
CASTLE ST
New Town
CUTENHOE RD
School
LUTON RD
PH
Farleygreen
Inions Farm
Nursery
Museum
CH
Stockwood Park
LONDON RD
Capability Green
AIRPORT WAY
Kidney Wood
Heath Wood
Caravan Park
Woodside
Woodside Farm
WOODSIDE RD
NEWLANDS RD
Golf Course
Bull Wood
Newlands Farm
Vicarage
Prebendal Farm
CHURCH RD
Slip End
Luton Hoo Park
Round Wood
MARKYATE RD
FRONT ST
Nursery
Lower Farm
Pepperstock
HALF MOON LA
M1
A1081
A505
A5065
B4540
A6

64

84

46

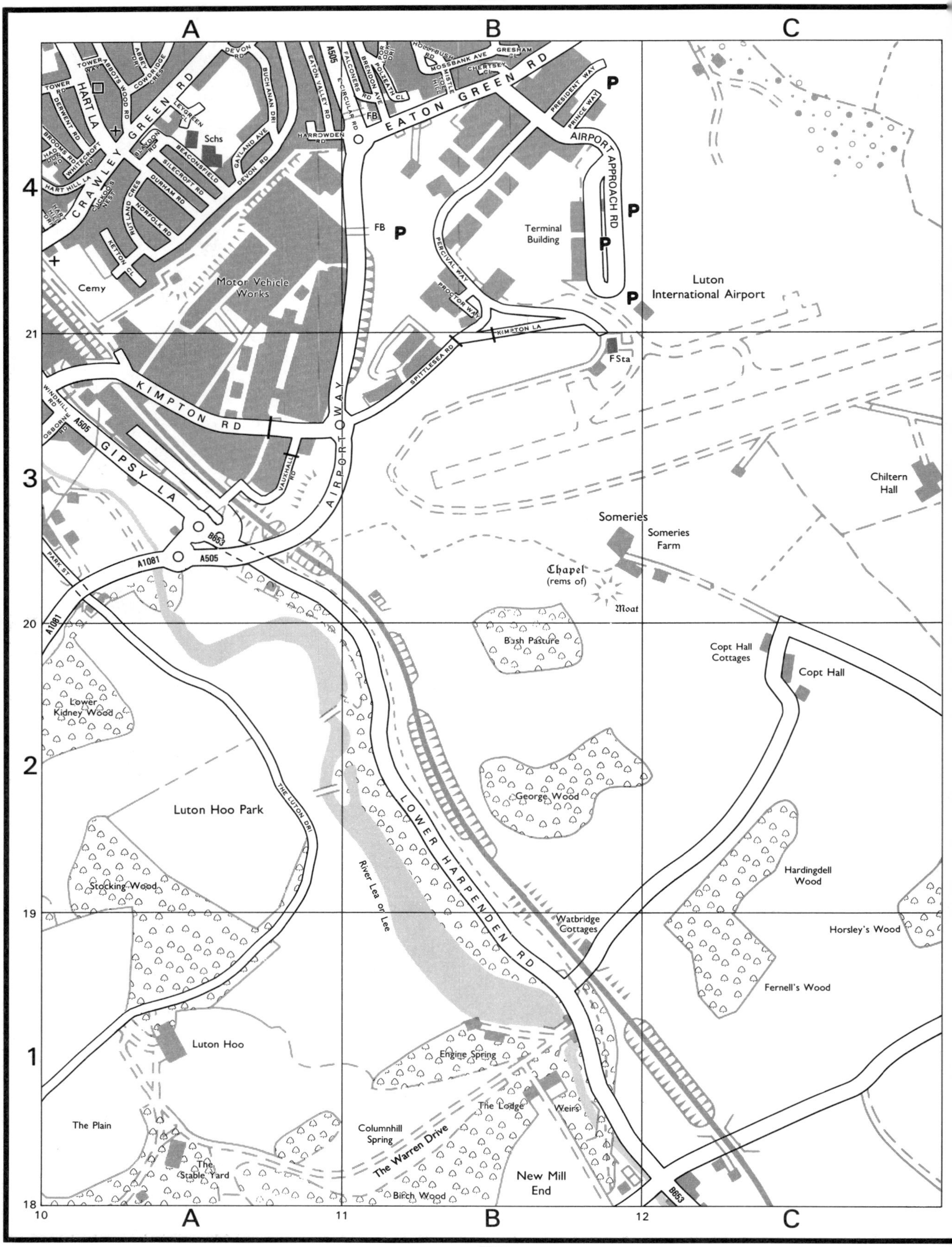
A
B
C
4
3
2
1
21
20
19
18
10
11
12
CRAWLEY GREEN RD
HART LA
EATON GREEN RD
AIRPORT APPROACH RD
AIRPORT WAY
KIMPTON RD
KIMPTON LA
GIPSY LA
LOWER HARPENDEN RD
THE LUTON DRI
A505
A1081
B653
Schs
Cemy
Motor Vehicle Works
FB
P
Terminal Building
Luton International Airport
FSta
PERCIVAL WAY
PROCTOR WAY
SPITTLESEA RD
VAUXHALL RD
WINDMILL RD
OSBORNE RD
PARK ST
DEVON RD
BUCHANAN DRI
EATON VALLEY RD
E-CIRCULAR RD
FALCONERS RD
BRENDON AVE
POLZEATH CL
MOSSBANK AVE
GRESHAM
CHERTSEY CL
PRESIDENT WAY
PRINCE WAY
HARROWDEN RD
GAYLAND AVE
BEACONSFIELD
SILECROFT RD
DURHAM RD
NORFOLK RD
RUTLAND CRES
KETTON CL
CUCKOO'S NEST
LEYGREEN CL
BLADON RD
COWDRIDGE CRES
ABBEY
TOWER WAY
TOWER RD
ABBOTS WOOD RD
DERWENT RD
BROOMS RD
WHITECROFT RD
HART HILL LA
Chiltern Hall
Someries
Someries Farm
Chapel (rems of)
Moat
Bush Pasture
Copt Hall Cottages
Copt Hall
Lower Kidney Wood
George Wood
Luton Hoo Park
Hardingdell Wood
Stocking Wood
River Lea or Lee
Watbridge Cottages
Horsley's Wood
Fernell's Wood
Luton Hoo
Engine Spring
The Lodge
Weirs
The Plain
Columnhill Spring
The Warren Drive
The Stable Yard
New Mill End
Birch Wood

63

85

47

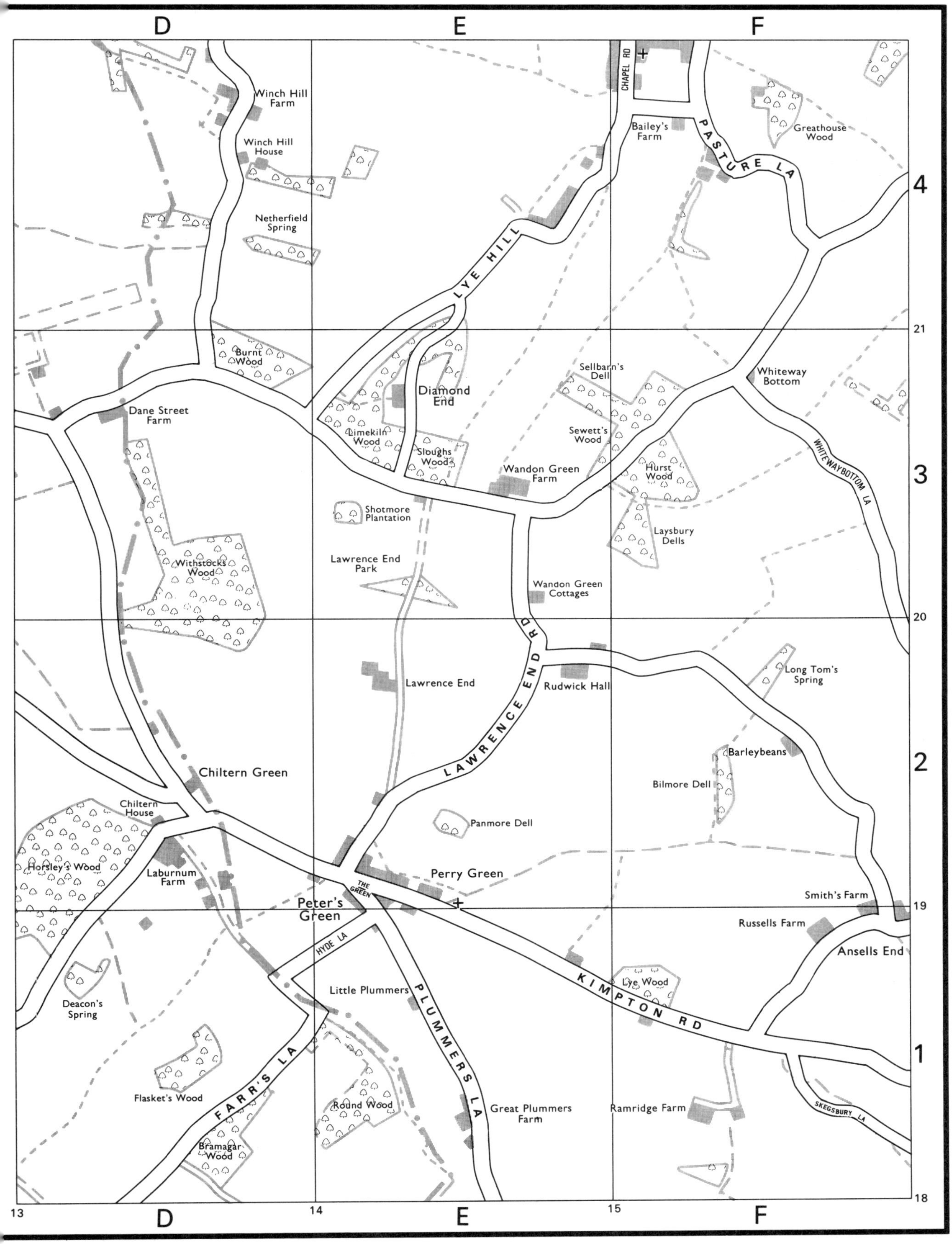
D
E
F
Winch Hill Farm
Winch Hill House
Netherfield Spring
CHAPEL RD
Bailey's Farm
PASTURE LA
Greathouse Wood
LYE HILL
Burnt Wood
Diamond End
Sellbarn's Dell
Whiteway Bottom
Dane Street Farm
Limekiln Wood
Sloughs Wood
Sewett's Wood
Wandon Green Farm
Hurst Wood
WHITEWAYBOTTOM LA
Shotmore Plantation
Laysbury Dells
Withstocks Wood
Lawrence End Park
Wandon Green Cottages
Long Tom's Spring
Lawrence End
Rudwick Hall
LAWRENCE END RD
Barleybeans
Chiltern Green
Bilmore Dell
Chiltern House
Panmore Dell
Horsley's Wood
Laburnum Farm
Perry Green
THE GREEN
Peter's Green
Smith's Farm
Russells Farm
Ansells End
HYDE LA
Little Plummers
Lye Wood
KIMPTON RD
Deacon's Spring
PLUMMERS LA
FARR'S LA
Flasket's Wood
Round Wood
Great Plummers Farm
Ramridge Farm
SKEGSBURY LA
Bramagar Wood
4
21
3
20
2
19
1
18
13
14
15

66

86

48

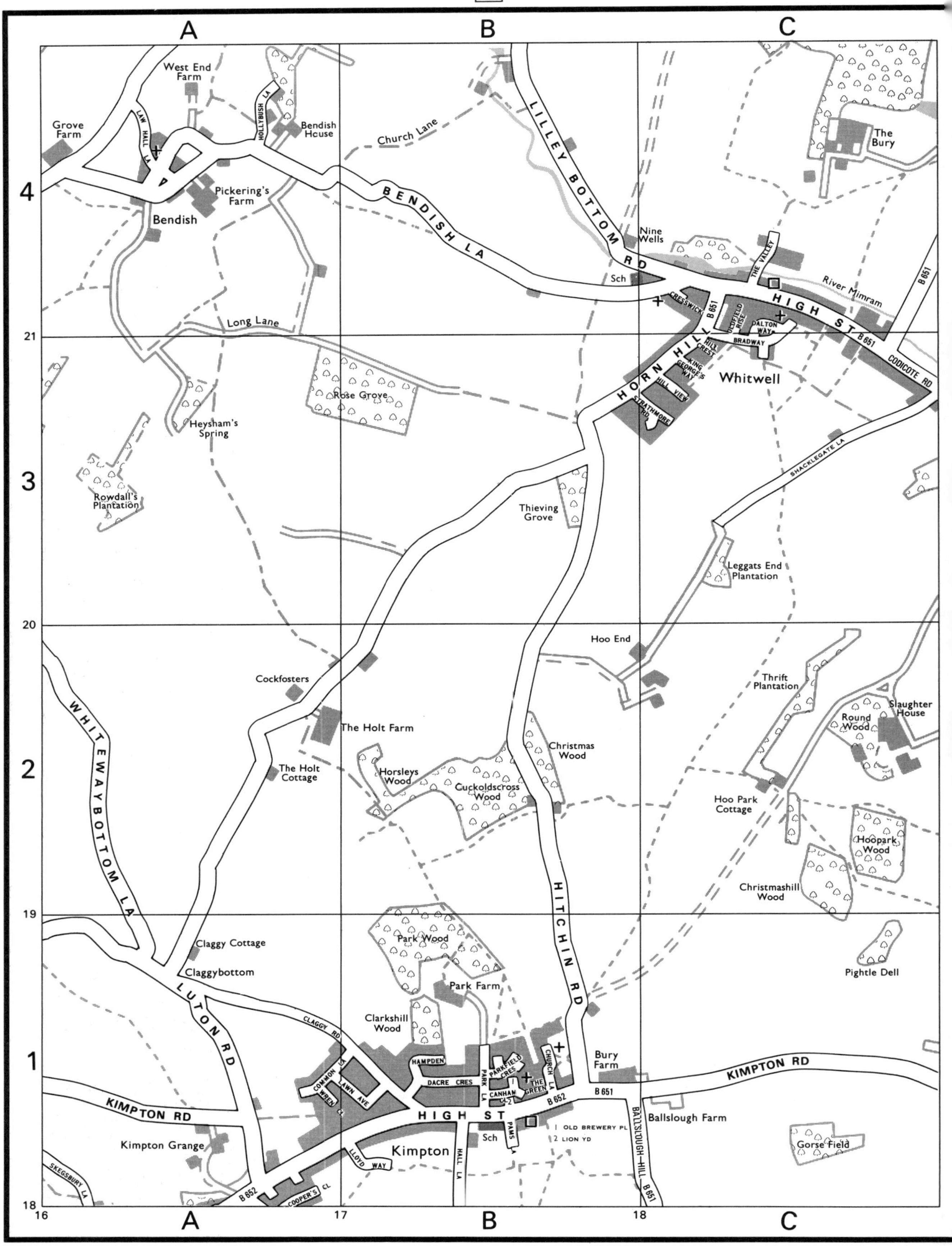
A
B
C
4
3
2
1
21
20
19
18
16
17
18
West End Farm
Grove Farm
LAW HALL LA
HOLLYBUSH LA
Bendish House
Pickering's Farm
Bendish
Church Lane
LILLEY BOTTOM RD
BENDISH LA
Nine Wells
Sch
THE VALLEY
The Bury
River Mimram
B 651
HIGH ST
CRESSWICK
FIELD RISE
DALTON WAY
BRADWAY
HILL CREST
KING GEORGE'S WAY
HILL VIEW
STRATHMORE RD
HORN HILL
Whitwell
CODICOTE RD
Long Lane
Rose Grove
Heysham's Spring
Rowdall's Plantation
Thieving Grove
SHACKLEGATE LA
Leggats End Plantation
Hoo End
Cockfosters
The Holt Farm
The Holt Cottage
WHITEWAYBOTTOM LA
Horsleys Wood
Cuckoldscross Wood
Christmas Wood
Thrift Plantation
Round Wood
Slaughter House
Hoo Park Cottage
Hoopark Wood
Christmashill Wood
HITCHIN RD
Park Wood
Claggy Cottage
Claggybottom
Park Farm
LUTON RD
CLAGGY RD
Clarkshill Wood
Pightle Dell
HAMPDEN
PARKFIELD CRES
CHURCH LA
THE GREEN
DACRE CRES
PARK LA
CANHAM CL
COMMON LA
LAWN AVE
WREN CL
Bury Farm
KIMPTON RD
HIGH ST
B 652
B 651
1 OLD BREWERY PL
2 LION YD
PAMS LA
Sch
BALLSLOUGH HILL
Ballslough Farm
Kimpton Grange
Kimpton
HALL LA
LLOYD WAY
SKEGSBURY LA
COOPER'S CL
Gorse Field

65

87

49

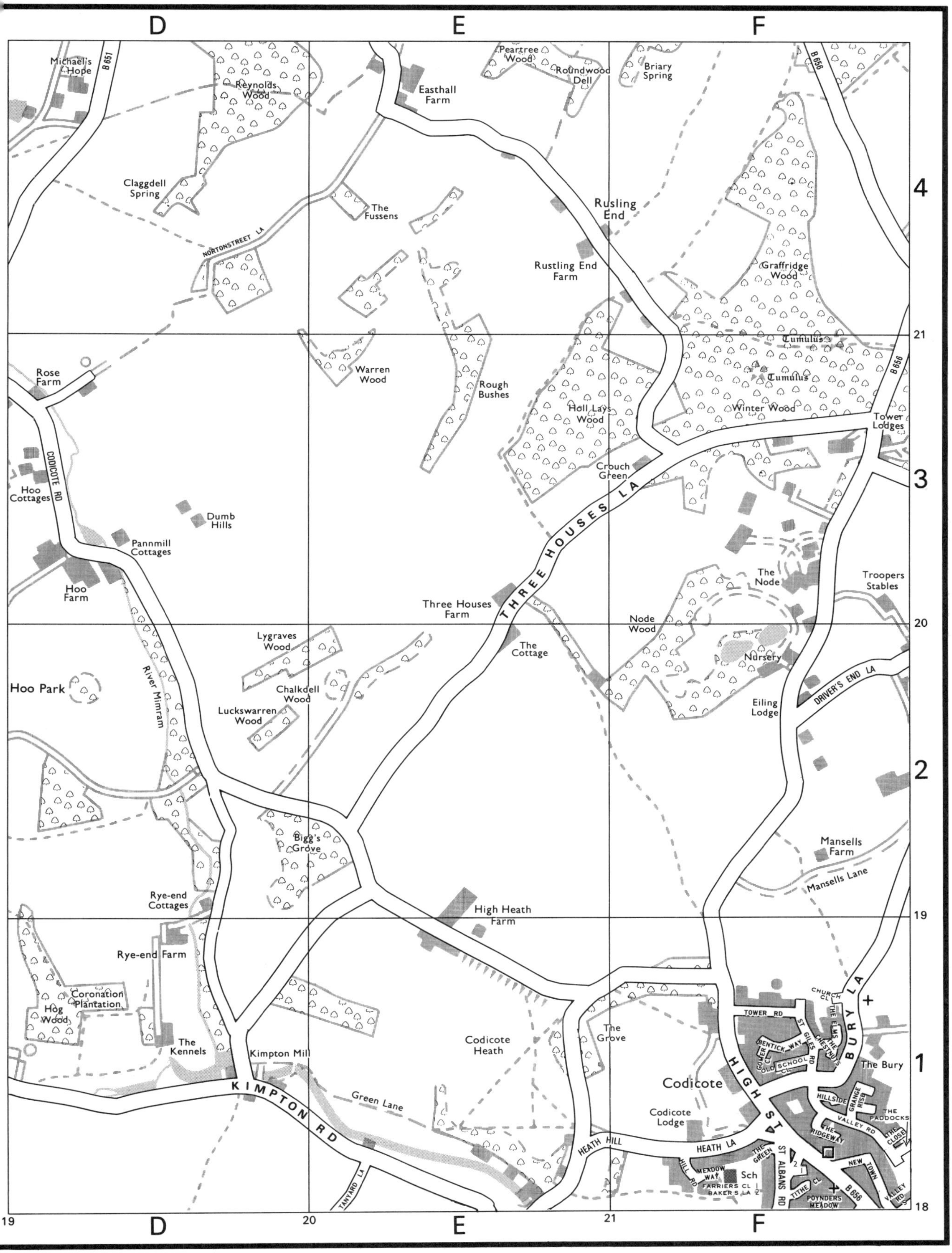
D
E
F
Michael's Hope
B 651
Reynolds Wood
Peartree Wood
Roundwood Dell
Briary Spring
B 656
Easthall Farm
Claggdell Spring
The Fussens
Rusling End
NORTONSTREET LA
Rustling End Farm
Graffridge Wood
4
21
Tumulus
Tumulus
Rose Farm
Warren Wood
Rough Bushes
Holl Lays Wood
Winter Wood
Tower Lodges
B 656
CODICOTE RD
Crouch Green
3
Hoo Cottages
Dumb Hills
THREE HOUSES LA
Pannmill Cottages
The Node
Troopers Stables
Hoo Farm
Three Houses Farm
Node Wood
20
Lygraves Wood
The Cottage
Nursery
Hoo Park
River Mimram
Chalkdell Wood
DRIVER'S END LA
Luckswarren Wood
Eiling Lodge
2
Bigg's Grove
Mansells Farm
Mansells Lane
Rye-end Cottages
High Heath Farm
19
Rye-end Farm
CHURCH CL
BURY LA
TOWER RD
Coronation Plantation
Hog Wood
Codicote Heath
The Grove
THE ELMS
BENTICK WAY
ST GILES RD
THE CHESTNUTS
The Kennels
Kimpton Mill
GOLDCL
OLD SCHOOL CL
The Bury
1
KIMPTON RD
Codicote
HIGH ST
HILLSIDE
GRANGE RISE
Green Lane
Codicote Lodge
THE PADDOCKS
VALLEY RD
THE RIDGEWAY
THE CLOSE
HEATH HILL
HEATH LA
THE GREEN
HILL RD
MEADOW WAY
Sch
FARRIERS CL
BAKERS LA
ST ALBANS RD
TITHE CL
NEW TOWN
B 656
POYNDERS MEADOW
VALLEY RD
TANYARD LA
18
19
D
20
E
21
F

68

88

50

67

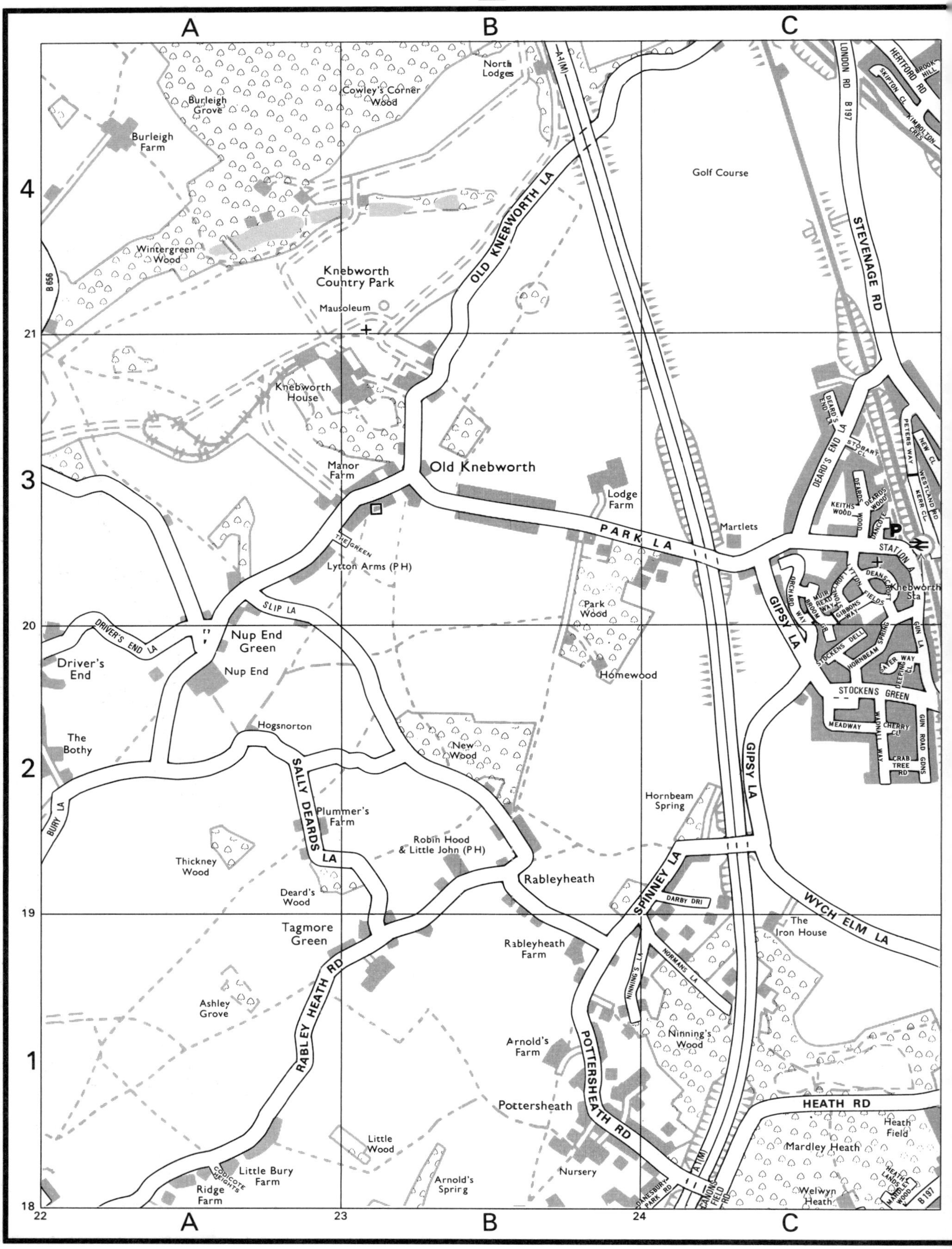
A
B
C
4
3
2
1
21
20
19
18
22
23
24
North Lodges
A1(M)
Cowley's Corner Wood
Burleigh Grove
Burleigh Farm
Golf Course
LONDON RD B197
HERTFORD RD
BROOK HILL
SKIPTON CL
KIMBOLTON CRES
STEVENAGE RD
Wintergreen Wood
B656
Knebworth Country Park
Mausoleum
OLD KNEBWORTH LA
Knebworth House
Manor Farm
Old Knebworth
Lodge Farm
THE GREEN
Lytton Arms (PH)
PARK LA
Martlets
DEARD'S END LA
STOBART CL
PETERS WAY
NEW CL
WESTLAND RD
KERR CL
KEITHS WOOD
DEARDS WOOD
OAKCOTE
STATION A
Knebworth Sta
ORCHARD WAY
GIPSY LA
DEANSCROFT
LYTTON FIELDS
GIBBONS WAY
STOCKENS DELL
HORNBEAM SPRING
SAYER WAY
GUN LA
DEEPING CL
STOCKENS GREEN
MEADWAY
WADNALL WAY
CHERRY CL
CRAB TREE RD
GUN ROAD GDNS
SLIP LA
Park Wood
DRIVER'S END LA
Driver's End
Nup End Green
Nup End
Homewood
The Bothy
Hogsnorton
New Wood
SALLY DEARDS LA
Plummer's Farm
Hornbeam Spring
BURY LA
Robin Hood & Little John (PH)
Thickney Wood
Rableyheath
SPINNEY LA
DARBY DRI
Deard's Wood
Tagmore Green
The Iron House
WYCH ELM LA
Rableyheath Farm
NINNING'S LA
NORMANS LA
RABLEY HEATH RD
Ashley Grove
Ninning's Wood
Arnold's Farm
POTTERSHEATH RD
HEATH RD
Pottersheath
Heath Field
Little Wood
Mardley Heath
Little Bury Farm
CODICOTE HEIGHTS
Ridge Farm
Arnold's Spring
Nursery
DANESBURY PARK RD
CANONS FIELD RD
A1(M)
Welwyn Heath
HEATH LANDS
MARDLEY WOOD
B197

89

51

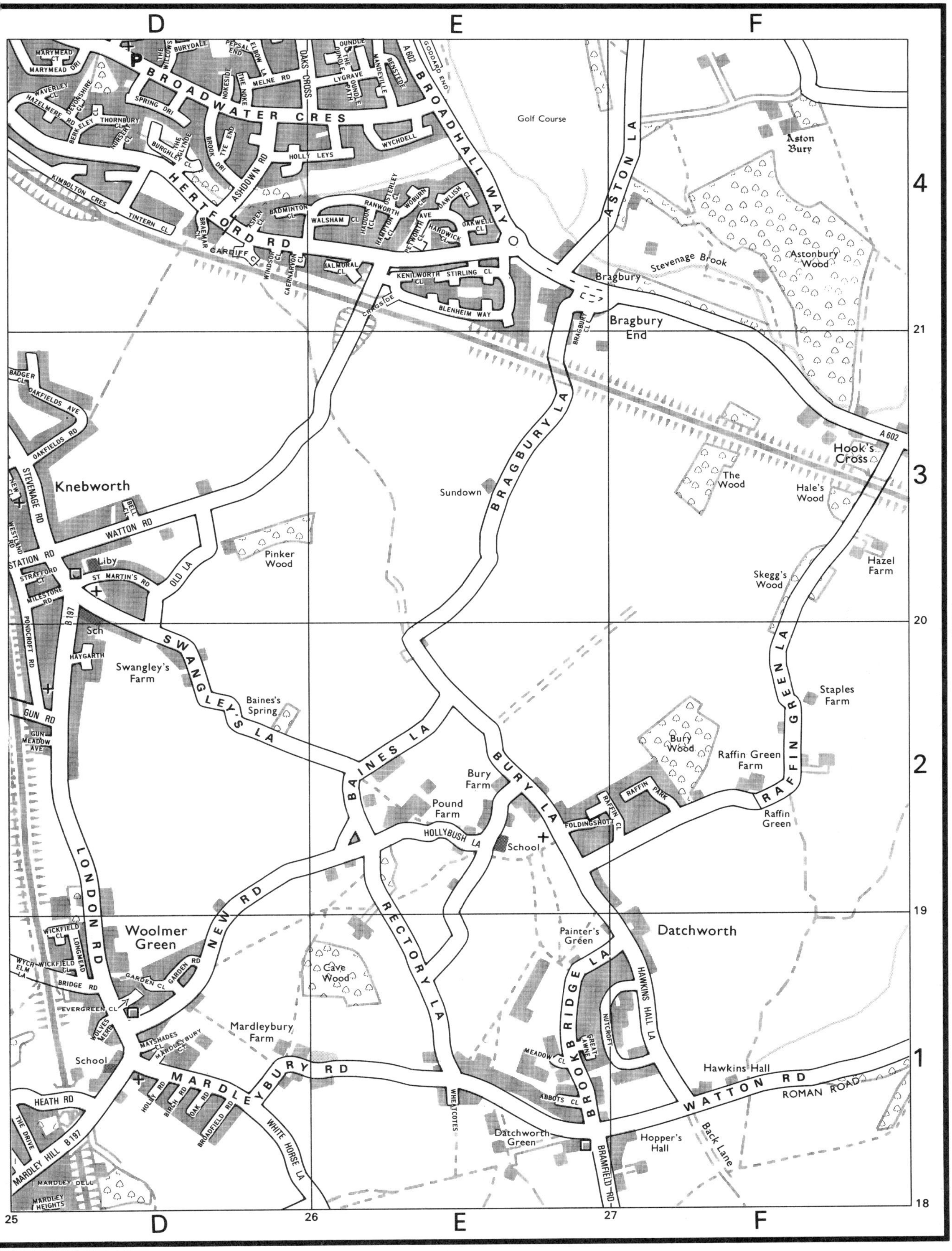
D
E
F
4
3
2
1
21
20
19
18
25
26
27
BROADWATER CRES
BROADHALL WAY
A 602
HERTFORD RD
KIMBOLTON CRES
TINTERN CL
MARYMEAD CT
MARYMEAD DRI
WAVERLEY CL
DEVONSHIRE CL
HAZELMERE RD
BERKELEY CL
THORNBURY CL
NURSERY CL
BURGHLEY CL
THE GLYNDE
SPRING DRI
BROOK DRI
TYE END
ASHDOWN RD
HOLLY LEYS
WYCHDELL
THE WILLOWS
BURYDALE
PEPSAL END
ELBOW LA
NOKESIDE
THE NOKE
MELNE RD
OAKS CROSS
OUNDLE
LYGRAVE
MANDEVILLE
BENSTEDE
GODDARD END
ASPEN CL
BRAEMAR CL
CARDIFF CL
WINDSOR CL
CAERNARVON CL
BADMINTON CL
WALSHAM CL
BALMORAL CL
RANWORTH CL
HADDON CL
HAMPTON CL
OSTERLEY CL
WOBURN CL
PETWORTH CL
HARDWICK CL
DAWLISH CL
OAKWELL CL
KENILWORTH CL
STIRLING CL
CRAGSIDE
BLENHEIM WAY
Golf Course
ASTON LA
Aston Bury
Astonbury Wood
Stevenage Brook
Bragbury
Bragbury End
BRAGBURY CL
BRAGBURY LA
A 602
Hook's Cross
The Wood
Hale's Wood
Hazel Farm
Skegg's Wood
Sundown
BADGER CL
OAKFIELDS AVE
OAKFIELDS RD
Knebworth
STEVENAGE RD
WESTLAND RD
BELL CL
WATTON RD
Pinker Wood
STATION RD
Liby
STRAFFORD CT
ST MARTIN'S RD
OLD LA
MILESTONE RD
B 197
PONDCROFT RD
Sch
HAYGARTH
SWANGLEY'S LA
Swangley's Farm
Baines's Spring
GUN RD
GUN MEADOW AVE
BAINES LA
BURY LA
Bury Farm
Pound Farm
HOLLYBUSH LA
School
Bury Wood
Raffin Green Farm
RAFFIN GREEN LA
Staples Farm
RAFFIN PARK
RAFFIN CL
FOLDINGSHOTT
Raffin Green
LONDON RD
NEW RD
RECTORY LA
Woolmer Green
WICKFIELD CL
LONGMEAD
WYCH ELM
WICKFIELD CL
BRIDGE RD
GARDEN CL
GARDEN RD
EVERGREEN CL
WOLVES MERE
MAYSHADES
MARDLEYBURY CT
Mardleybury Farm
Cave Wood
Painter's Green
Datchworth
BROOKBRIDGE LA
HAWKINS HALL LA
NUTCROFT
GREAT LAWNE
MEADOW CL
ABBOTS CL
School
MARDLEYBURY RD
HOLLY RD
BIRCH RD
OAK RD
BROADFIELD RD
WHITE HORSE LA
WHEATCOTES
HEATH RD
THE DRIVE
MARDLEY HILL B 197
MARDLEY DELL
MARDLEY HEIGHTS
Datchworth Green
BRAMFIELD RD
Hopper's Hall
Hawkins Hall
WATTON RD
ROMAN ROAD
Back Lane

70

90

52

69

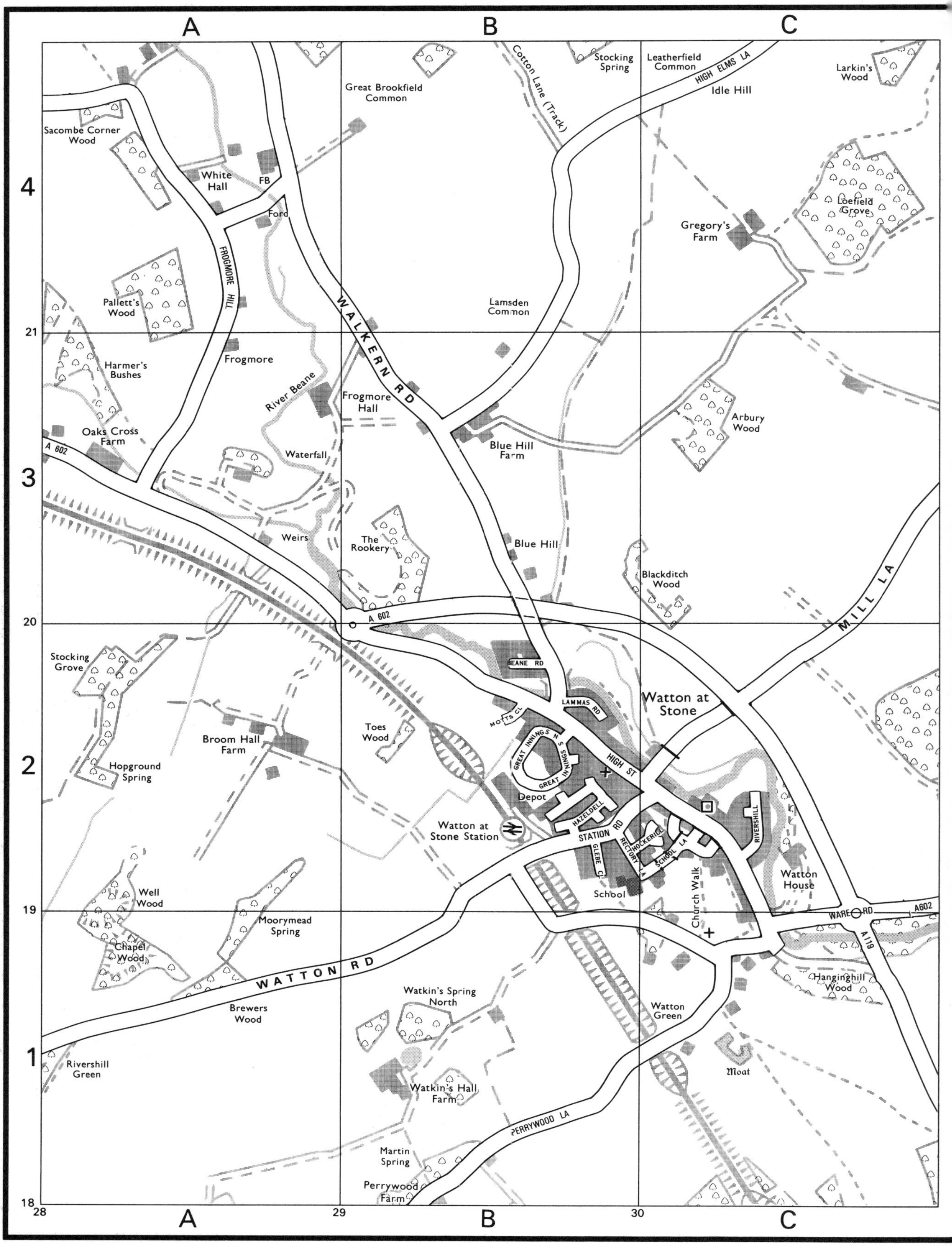
A
B
C
4
3
2
1
21
20
19
18
28
29
30
Sacombe Corner Wood
White Hall
FB
Ford
Great Brookfield Common
Cotton Lane (Track)
Stocking Spring
Leatherfield Common
HIGH ELMS LA
Idle Hill
Larkin's Wood
Loefield Grove
Gregory's Farm
FROGMORE HILL
Pallett's Wood
WALKERN RD
Lamsden Common
Harmer's Bushes
Frogmore
River Beane
Frogmore Hall
Arbury Wood
Oaks Cross Farm
A 602
Blue Hill Farm
Waterfall
Weirs
The Rookery
Blue Hill
Blackditch Wood
MILL LA
A 602
Stocking Grove
BEANE RD
LAMMAS RD
Watton at Stone
MOTTS CL
GREAT INNINGS N
GREAT INNINGS S
Toes Wood
Broom Hall Farm
HIGH ST
Hopground Spring
Depot
HAZELDELL
RIVERSHILL
Watton at Stone Station
STATION RD
HOCKERILL
GLEBE CL
RECTORY LA
SCHOOL LA
Church Walk
Watton House
School
WARE RD
A602
A119
Well Wood
Moorymead Spring
Chapel Wood
WATTON RD
Hanginghill Wood
Watkin's Spring North
Brewers Wood
Watton Green
Rivershill Green
Moat
Watkin's Hall Farm
PERRYWOOD LA
Martin Spring
Perrywood Farm

91

53

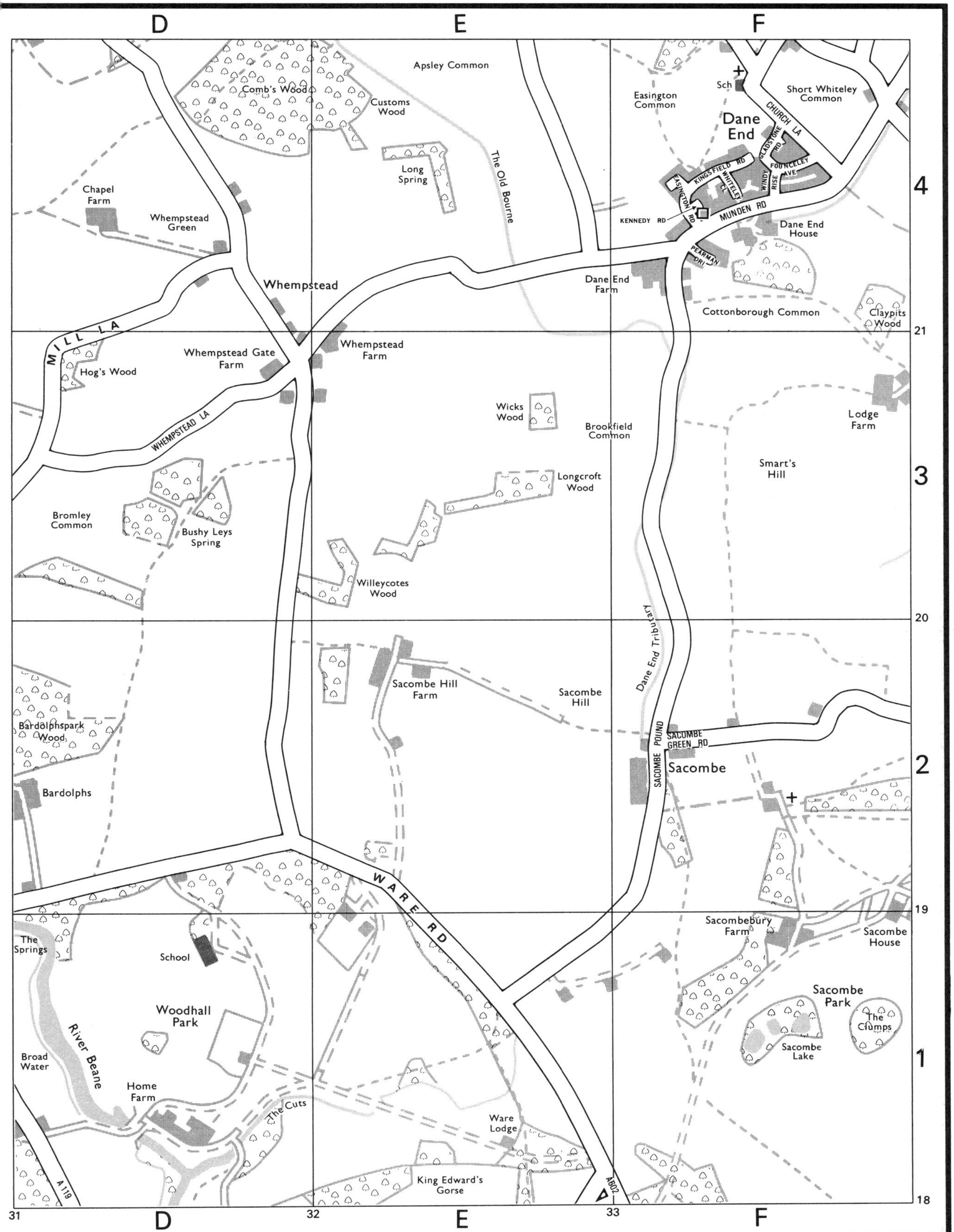
D
E
F
Apsley Common
Comb's Wood
Customs Wood
Long Spring
The Old Bourne
Easington Common
Sch
Dane End
Short Whiteley Common
CHURCH LA
GLADSTONE RD
KINGSFIELD RD
WHITELEY CL
WINDY RISE
FOURCELEY AVE
EASINGTON RD
KENNEDY RD
MUNDEN RD
PEARMAN DRI
Dane End House
Chapel Farm
Whempstead Green
Whempstead
Dane End Farm
Cottonborough Common
Claypits Wood
MILL LA
Hog's Wood
Whempstead Gate Farm
Whempstead Farm
Wicks Wood
Brookfield Common
Lodge Farm
WHEMPSTEAD LA
Smart's Hill
Longcroft Wood
Bromley Common
Bushy Leys Spring
Willeycotes Wood
Dane End Tributary
Sacombe Hill Farm
Sacombe Hill
Bardolphspark Wood
SACOMBE POUND
SACOMBE GREEN RD
Sacombe
Bardolphs
WARE RD
Sacombebury Farm
Sacombe House
The Springs
School
Woodhall Park
Sacombe Park
The Clumps
Sacombe Lake
River Beane
Broad Water
Home Farm
The Cuts
Ware Lodge
King Edward's Gorse
A119
A602
4
3
2
1
21
20
19
18
31
32
33

72

54

71

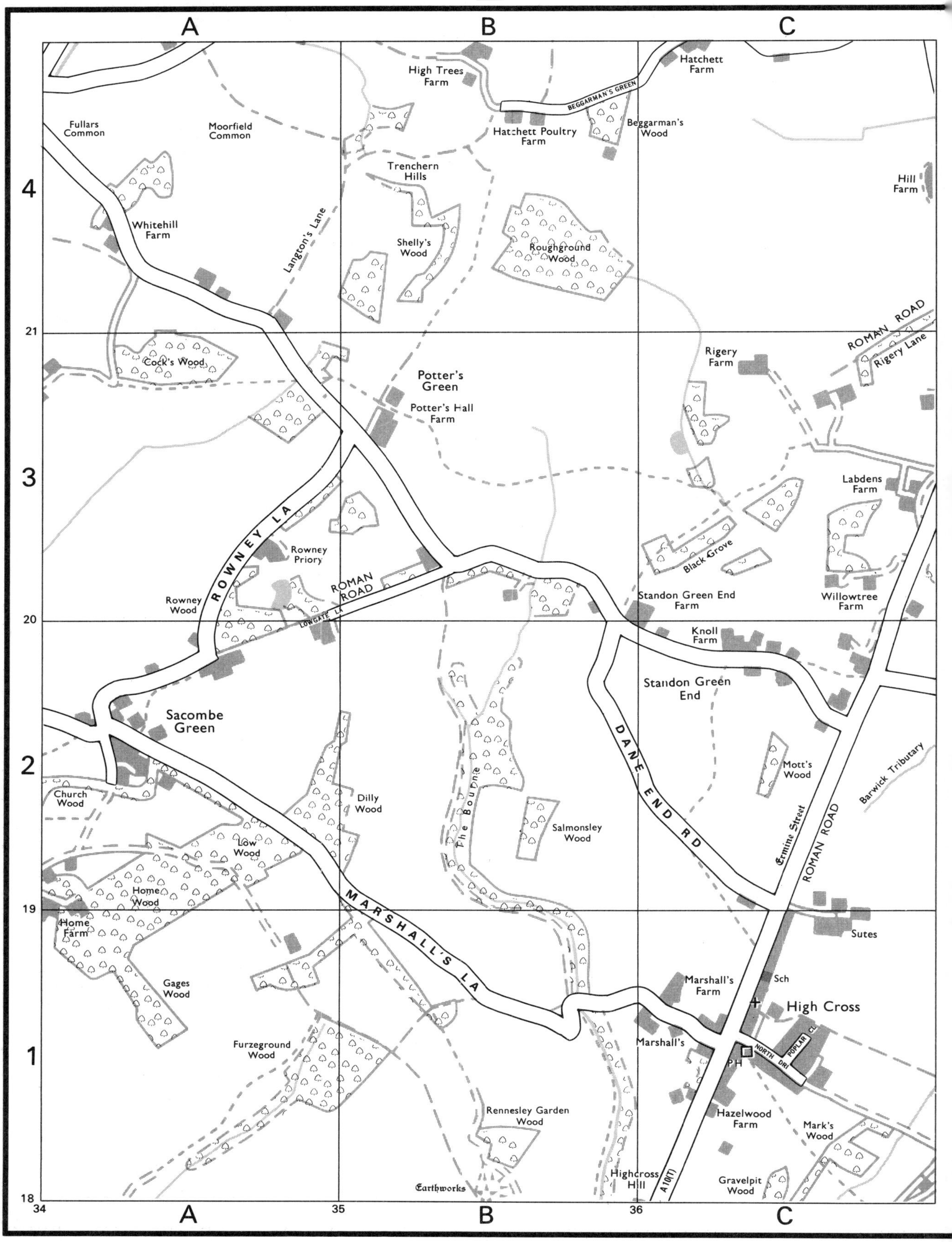
A
B
C
1
2
3
4
18
19
20
21
34
35
36
Fullars Common
Moorfield Common
High Trees Farm
Hatchett Poultry Farm
Hatchett Farm
BEGGARMAN'S GREEN
Beggarman's Wood
Trenchern Hills
Hill Farm
Whitehill Farm
Langton's Lane
Shelly's Wood
Roughground Wood
ROMAN ROAD
Rigery Lane
Rigery Farm
Cock's Wood
Potter's Green
Potter's Hall Farm
Labdens Farm
Black Grove
ROWNEY LA
Rowney Priory
ROMAN ROAD
Rowney Wood
LOWGATE LA
Standon Green End Farm
Willowtree Farm
Knoll Farm
Standon Green End
Sacombe Green
DANE END RD
Mott's Wood
Barwick Tributary
Church Wood
Dilly Wood
The Bourne
Salmonsley Wood
Ermine Street
ROMAN ROAD
Low Wood
Home Wood
MARSHALL'S LA
Home Farm
Sutes
Gages Wood
Marshall's Farm
Sch
High Cross
Marshall's
PH
NORTH DRI
POPLAR CL
Furzeground Wood
Rennesley Garden Wood
Hazelwood Farm
Mark's Wood
Highcross Hill
A10(T)
Gravelpit Wood
Earthworks

93

55

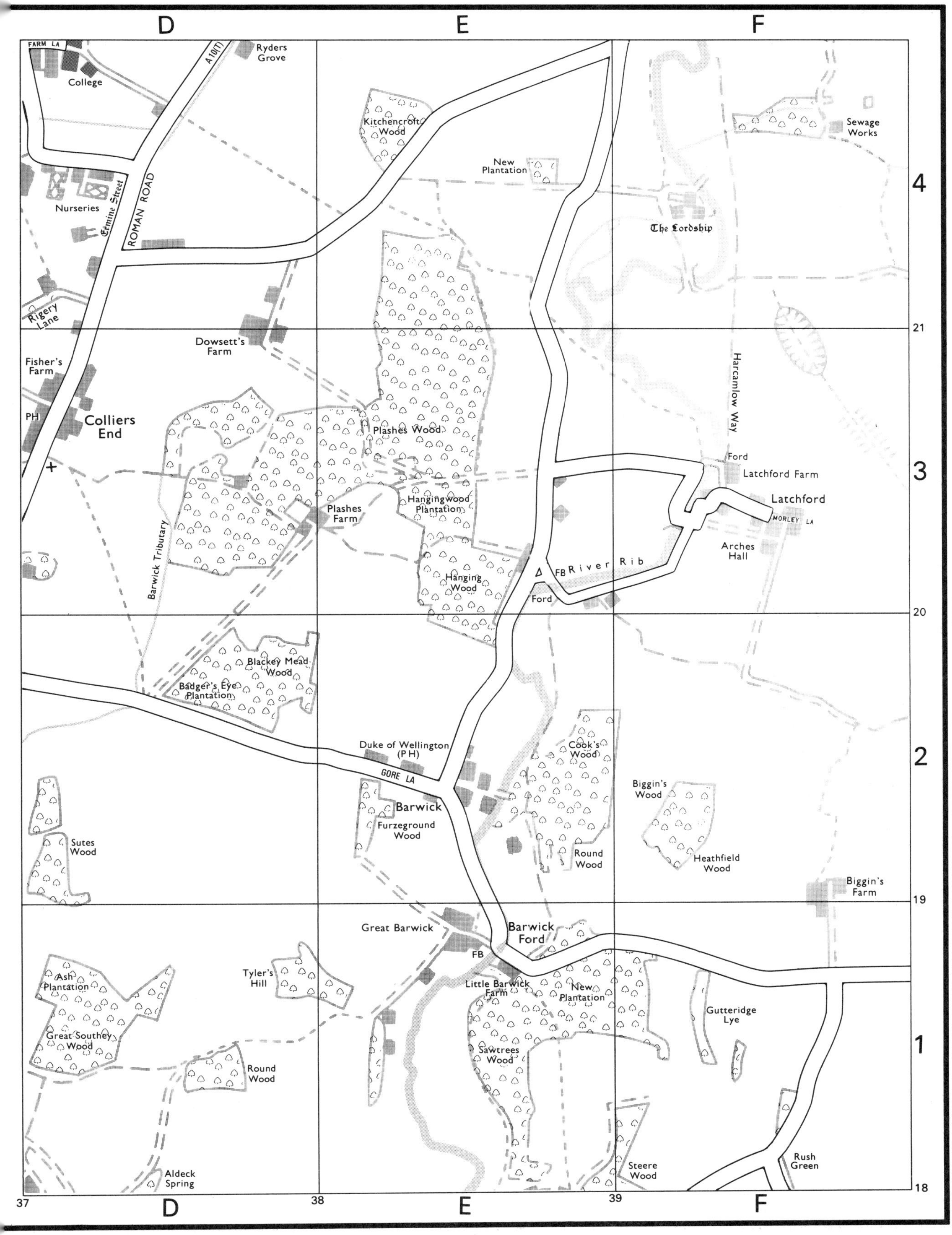
D
E
F
FARM LA
College
Ryders Grove
A 10(T)
Kitchencroft Wood
Sewage Works
New Plantation
4
Nurseries
Ermine Street
ROMAN ROAD
The Lordship
Rigery Lane
21
Dowsett's Farm
Fisher's Farm
Harcamlow Way
PH
Colliers End
Plashes Wood
Ford
Latchford Farm
3
Plashes Farm
Hangingwood Plantation
Latchford
MORLEY LA
Barwick Tributary
Arches Hall
Hanging Wood
FB
River Rib
Ford
20
Blackey Mead Wood
Badger's Eye Plantation
Cook's Wood
Duke of Wellington (PH)
2
Biggin's Wood
GORE LA
Barwick
Furzeground Wood
Sutes Wood
Round Wood
Heathfield Wood
Biggin's Farm
19
Great Barwick
Barwick Ford
FB
Tyler's Hill
Ash Plantation
Little Barwick Farm
New Plantation
Gutteridge Lye
1
Great Southey Wood
Sawtrees Wood
Round Wood
Steere Wood
Rush Green
Aldeck Spring
18
37
38
39

74

94

56

73

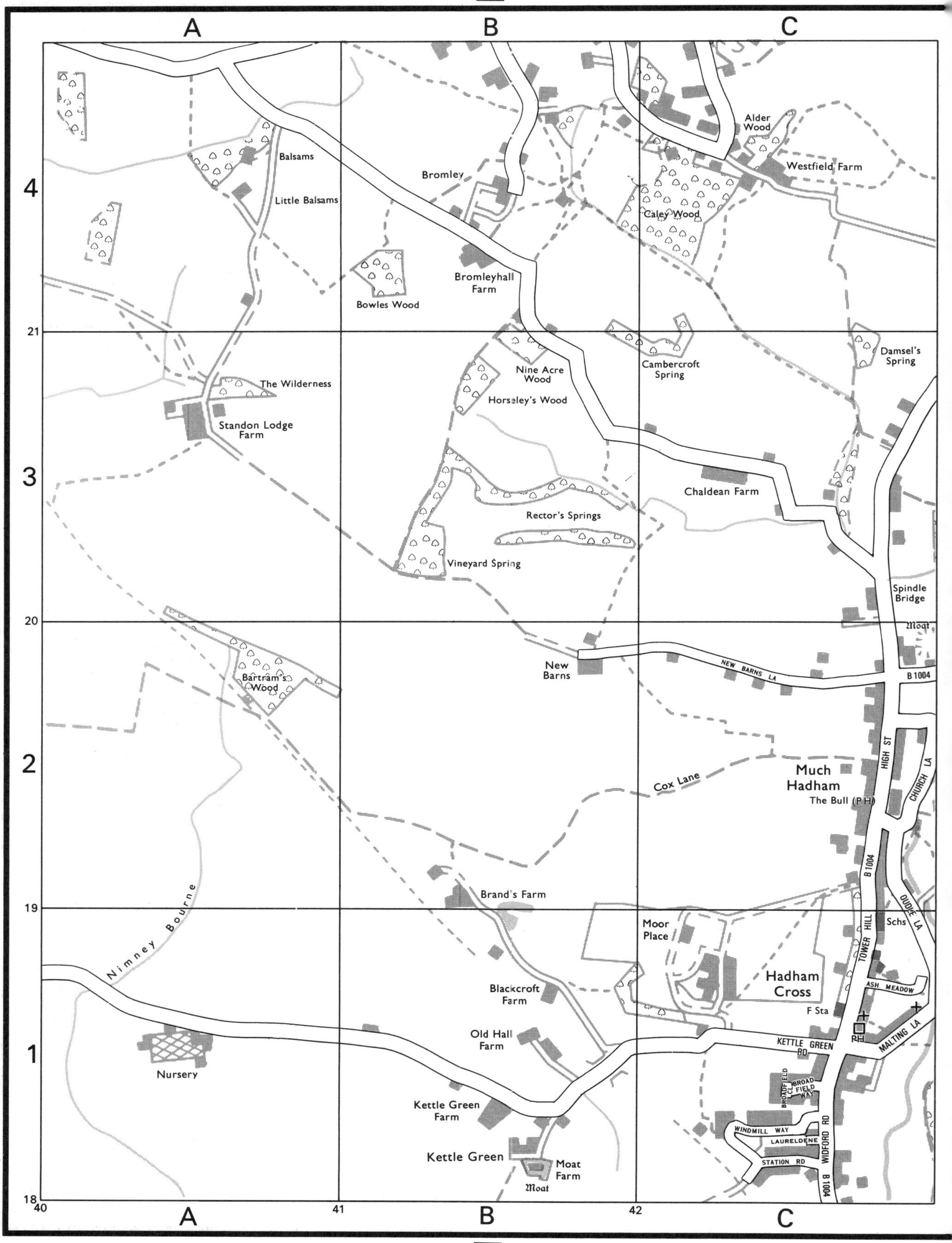
A
B
C
4
3
2
1
21
20
19
18
40
41
42
Balsams
Little Balsams
Bromley
Bromleyhall Farm
Bowles Wood
Alder Wood
Westfield Farm
Caley Wood
Cambercroft Spring
Damsel's Spring
Nine Acre Wood
Horseley's Wood
The Wilderness
Standon Lodge Farm
Chaldean Farm
Rector's Springs
Vineyard Spring
Spindle Bridge
Moat
New Barns
NEW BARNS LA
B 1004
Bartram's Wood
Much Hadham
HIGH ST
CHURCH LA
The Bull (PH)
Cox Lane
B 1004
Brand's Farm
Nimney Bourne
Moor Place
TOWER HILL
Schs
OUDLE LA
Hadham Cross
ASH MEADOW
F Sta
Blackcroft Farm
Old Hall Farm
KETTLE GREEN RD
MALTING LA
PH
Nursery
BROADFIELD CL
BROAD FIELD WAY
Kettle Green Farm
WINDMILL WAY
LAURELDENE
WIDFORD RD
STATION RD
Kettle Green
Moat Farm
Moat
B 1004

95

57

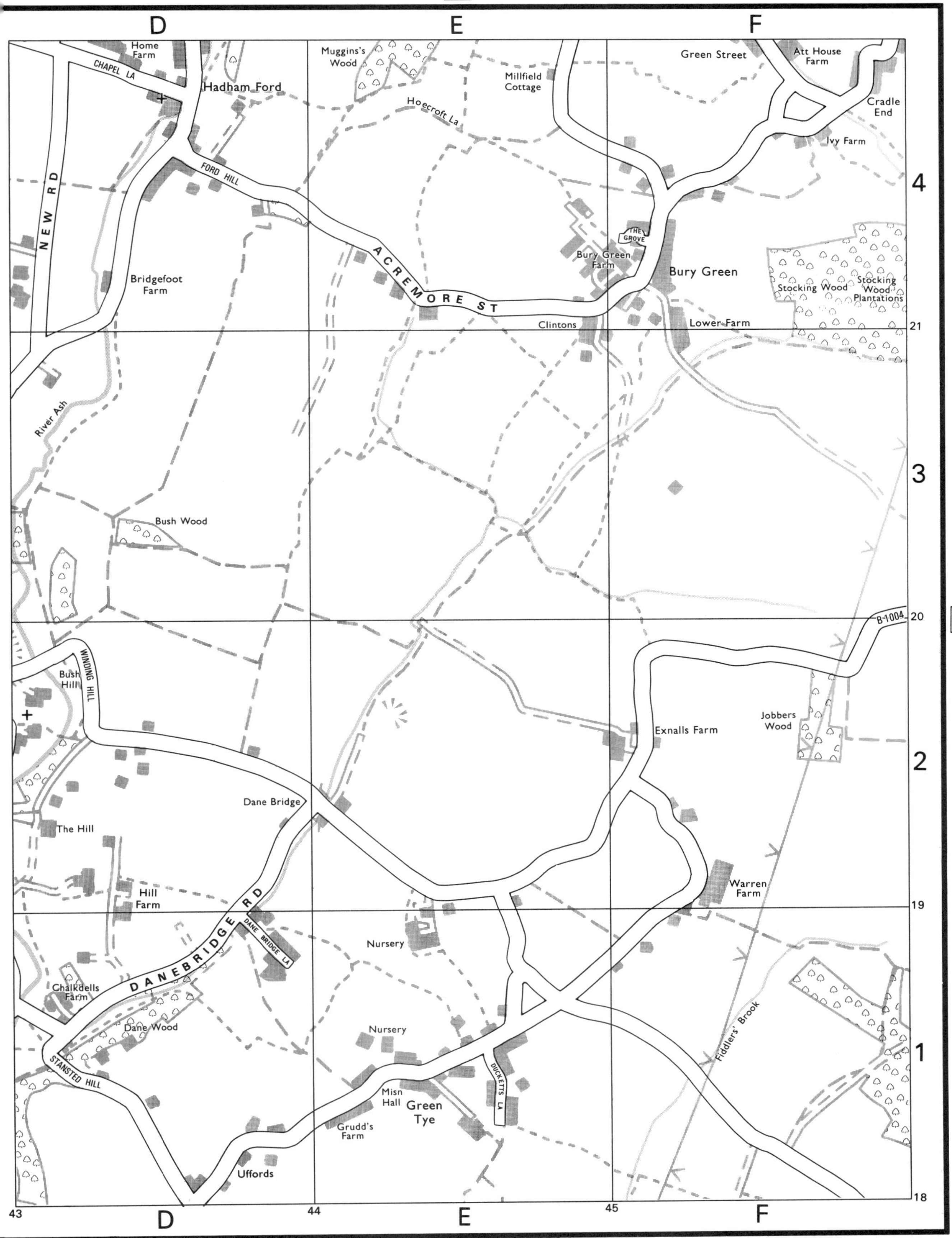
D
E
F
Home Farm
CHAPEL LA
Hadham Ford
Muggins's Wood
Hoecroft La
Millfield Cottage
Green Street
Att House Farm
Cradle End
Ivy Farm
NEW RD
FORD HILL
ACREMORE ST
THE GROVE
Bury Green Farm
Bury Green
Stocking Wood
Stocking Wood Plantations
Bridgefoot Farm
Clintons
Lower Farm
River Ash
Bush Wood
B1004
WINDING HILL
Bush Hill
Jobbers Wood
Exnalls Farm
Dane Bridge
The Hill
Warren Farm
Hill Farm
DANEBRIDGE RD
DANE BRIDGE LA
Nursery
Chalkdells Farm
Dane Wood
Fiddlers' Brook
STANSTED HILL
DUCKETTS LA
Misn Hall
Green Tye
Grudd's Farm
Uffords
4
3
2
1
21
20
19
18
43
44
45

76

96

58

75

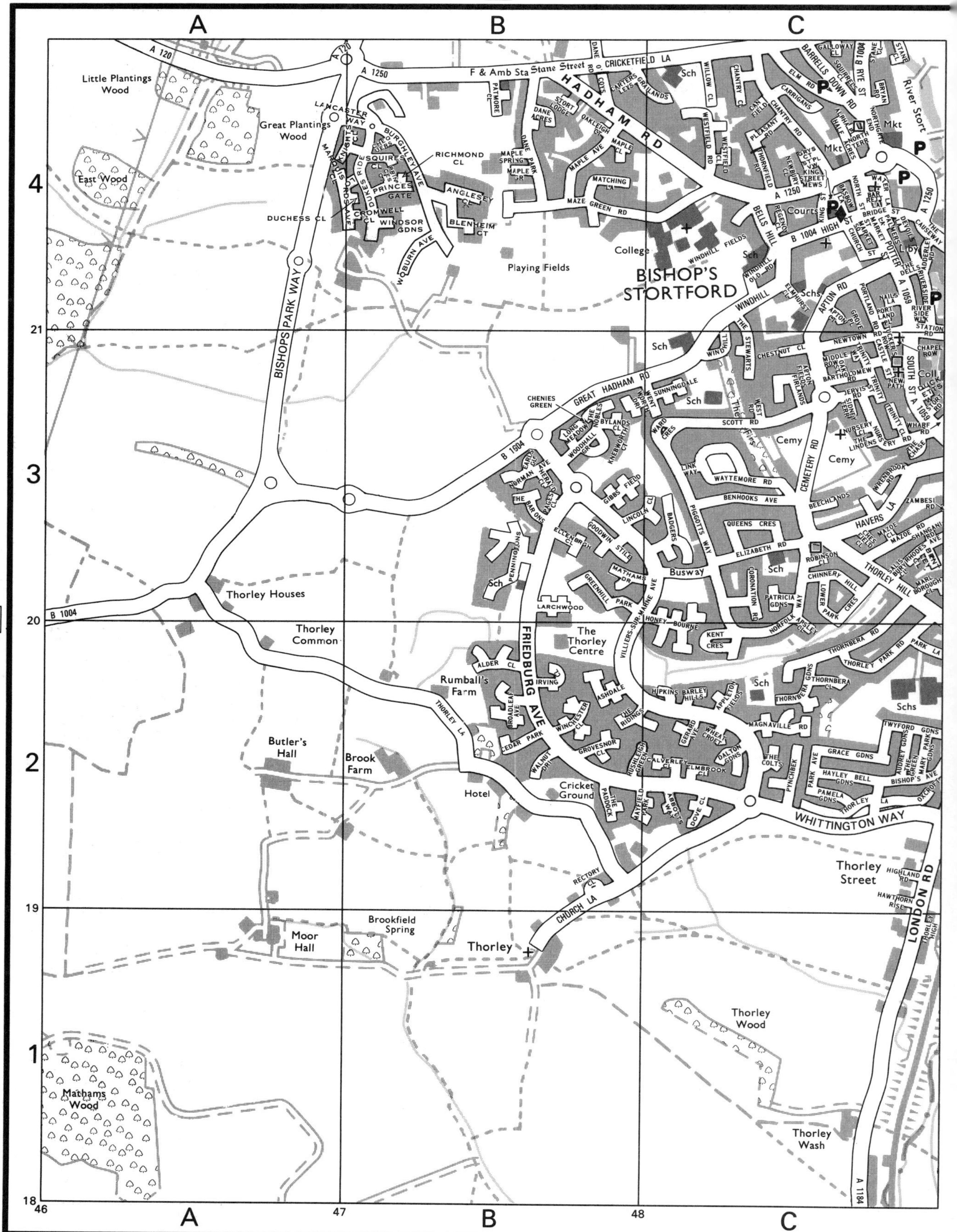
A
B
C
4
3
2
1
21
20
19
18
46
47
48
Little Plantings Wood
Great Plantings Wood
East Wood
A 120
A 1250
F & Amb Sta
Stane Street
CRICKETFIELD LA
HADHAM RD
BISHOP'S STORTFORD
BISHOPS PARK WAY
Playing Fields
College
Courts
Mkt
River Stort
Sch
Schs
Cemy
Busway
GREAT HADHAM RD
B 1004
B 1004 HIGH ST
A 1059
A 1184
Thorley Houses
Thorley Common
The Thorley Centre
FRIEDBURG AVE
Rumball's Farm
THORLEY LA
Butler's Hall
Brook Farm
Hotel
Cricket Ground
WHITTINGTON WAY
Thorley Street
LONDON RD
CHURCH LA
Moor Hall
Brookfield Spring
Thorley
Thorley Wood
Thorley Wash
Mathams Wood
MAZE GREEN RD
WINDHILL
CEMETERY RD
THORLEY HILL
PIGGOTTS WAY
VILLIERS-SUR-MARNE AVE
LARCHWOOD
BENHOOKS AVE
WAYTEMORE RD
QUEENS CRES
ELIZABETH RD
SCOTT RD
HAVERS LA
THORLEY PARK RD
MAGNAVILLE RD
GRACE GDNS

97

59

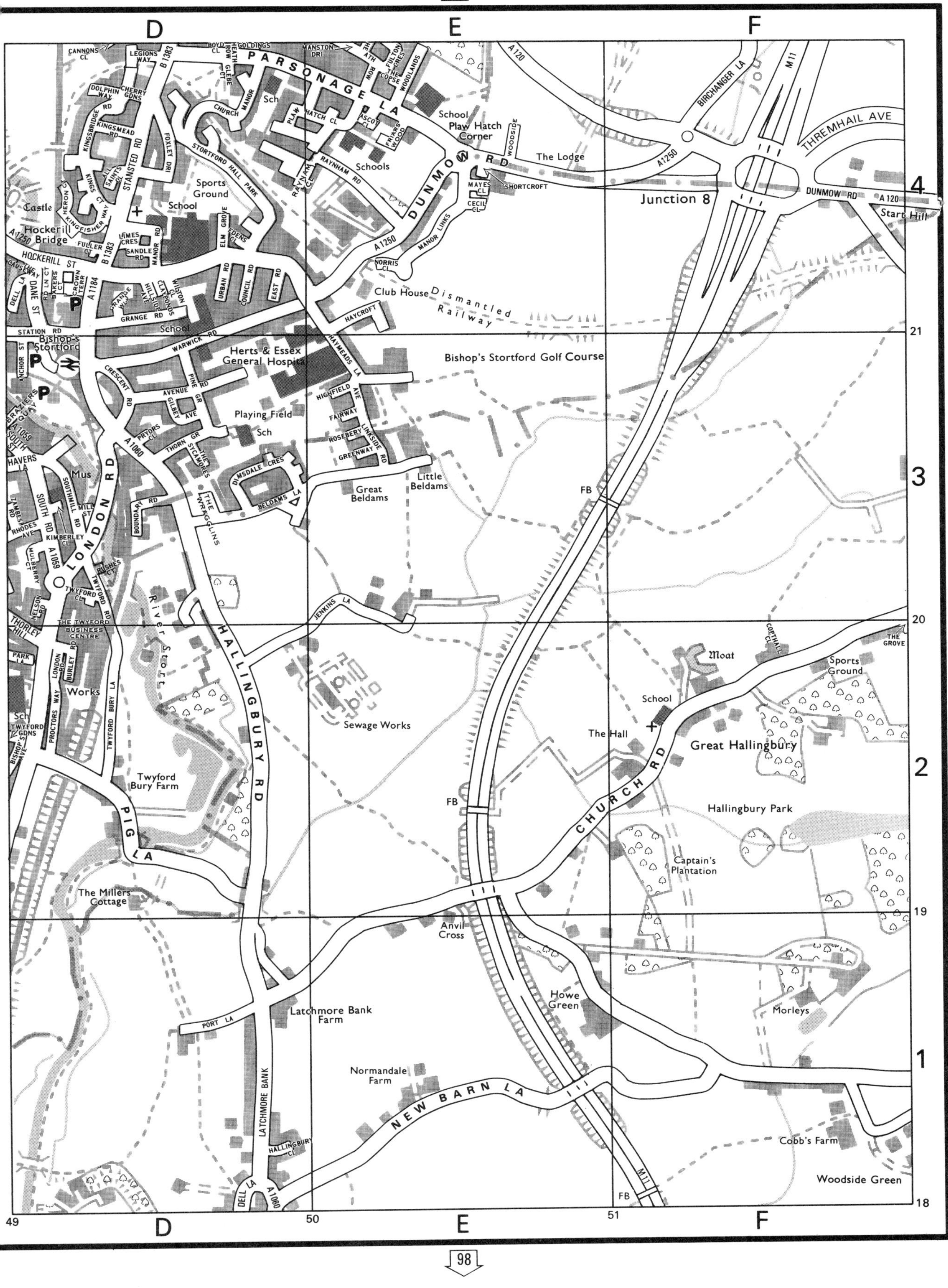
D
E
F
PARSONAGE LA
School
Plaw Hatch Corner
DUNMOW RD
The Lodge
Schools
Sports Ground
School
Castle
Hockerill Bridge
HOCKERILL ST
STANSTED RD
Junction 8
DUNMOW RD
A120
Start Hill
THREMHAIL AVE
BIRCHANGER LA
M11
A1250
Club House
Dismantled Railway
HAYCROFT
Bishop's Stortford
STATION RD
Herts & Essex General Hospital
Bishop's Stortford Golf Course
Playing Field
Sch
Mus
LONDON RD
Great Beldams
Little Beldams
FB
JENKINS LA
HALLINGBURY RD
River Stort
Sewage Works
Moat
School
The Hall
Great Hallingbury
Sports Ground
CHURCH RD
Hallingbury Park
Captain's Plantation
Works
Twyford Bury Farm
PIG LA
The Millers Cottage
Anvil Cross
Howe Green
Morleys
Latchmore Bank Farm
PORT LA
Normandale Farm
NEW BARN LA
LATCHMORE BANK
Cobb's Farm
Woodside Green
DELL LA
A1060
4
3
2
1
21
20
19
18
49
50
51
not continued, see key diagram

98

60

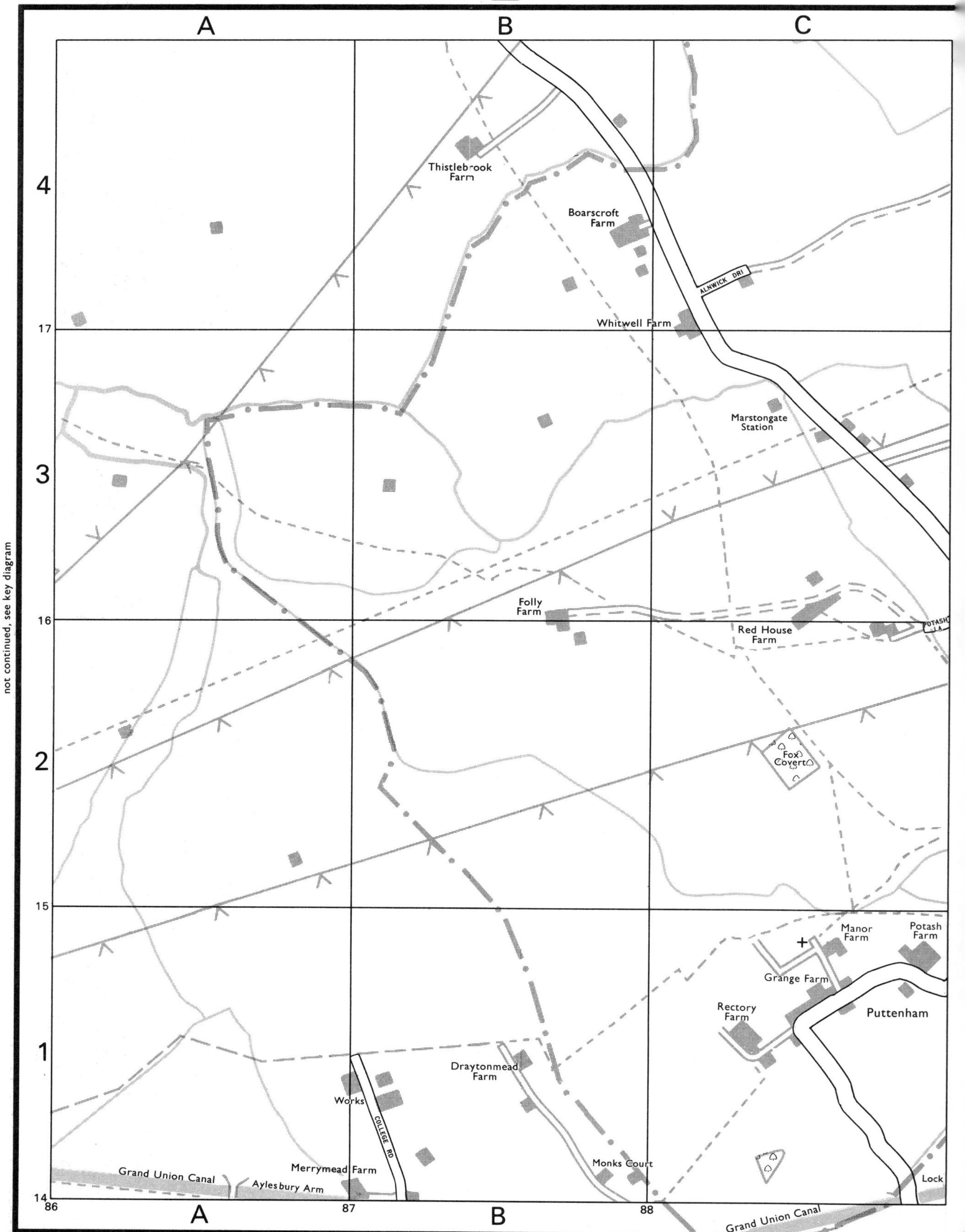

not continued, see key diagram

not continued, see key diagram

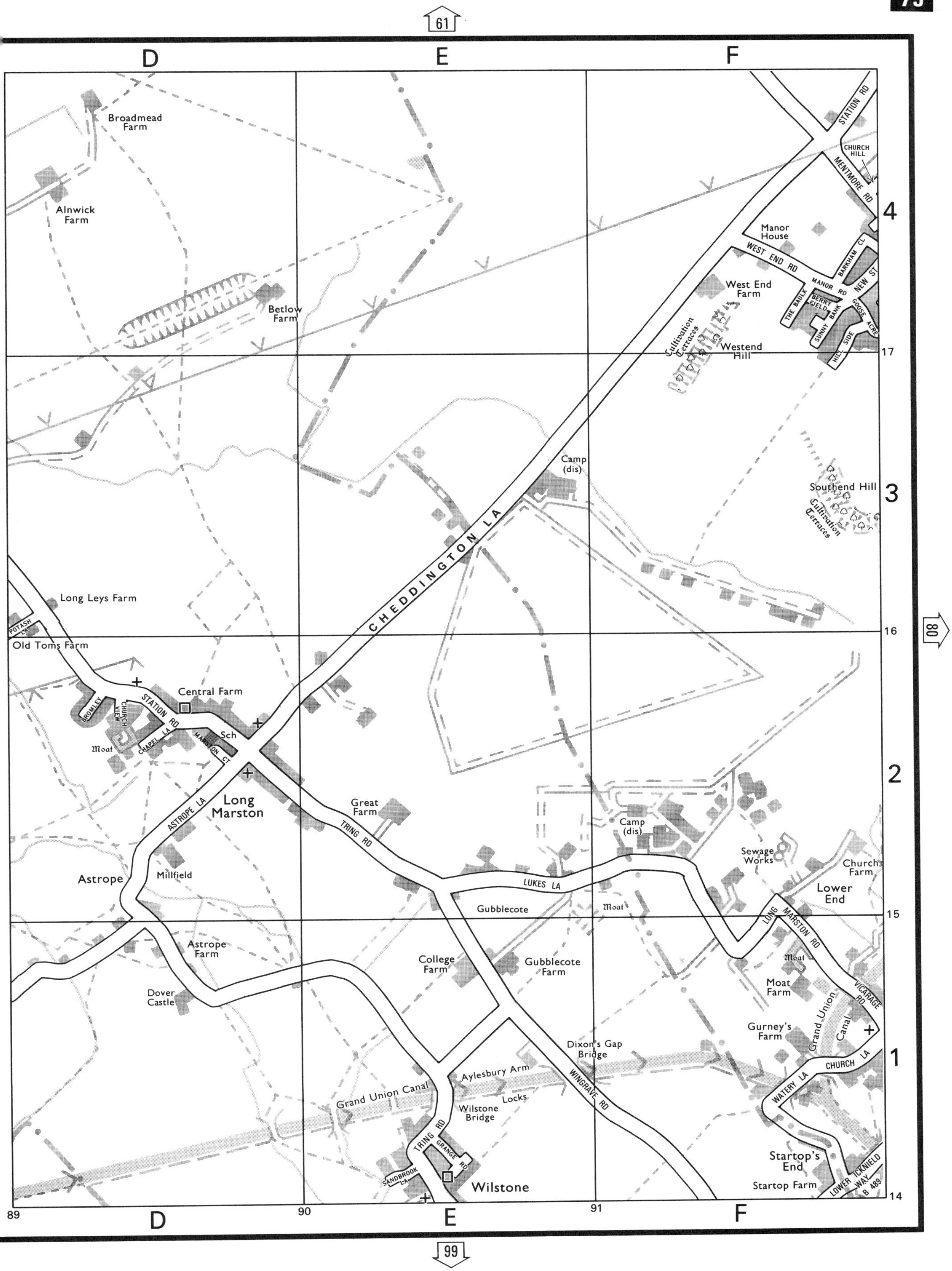

61
D
E
F
Broadmead Farm
Alnwick Farm
Betlow Farm
STATION RD
CHURCH HILL
MENTMORE RD
Manor House
WEST END RD
BARKHAM CL
MANOR RD
NEW ST
West End Farm
THE BAULK
BERRY FIELD
SUNNY BANK
GOOSE ACRE
HILL SIDE
Cultivation Terraces
Westend Hill
Camp (dis)
Southend Hill
Cultivation Terraces
CHEDDINGTON LA
Long Leys Farm
POTASH LA
Old Toms Farm
Central Farm
BROMLEY
CHURCH VIEW
STATION RD
CHAPEL LA
MARSTON CT
Sch
Moat
Long Marston
ASTROPE LA
Great Farm
TRING RD
Camp (dis)
Sewage Works
Church Farm
Lower End
Astrope
Millfield
LUKES LA
Gubblecote
Moat
LONG MARSTON RD
Astrope Farm
College Farm
Gubblecote Farm
Moat
Moat Farm
VICARAGE RD
Dover Castle
Gurney's Farm
Grand Union Canal
Dixon's Gap Bridge
CHURCH LA
Aylesbury Arm
WINGRAVE RD
Locks
Grand Union Canal
Wilstone Bridge
WATERY LA
TRING RD
GRANGE RD
SANDBROOK LA
Wilstone
Startop's End
Startop Farm
LOWER ICKNIELD WAY B 489
4
3
2
1
17
16
15
14
89
90
91
80
99

not continued, see key diagram

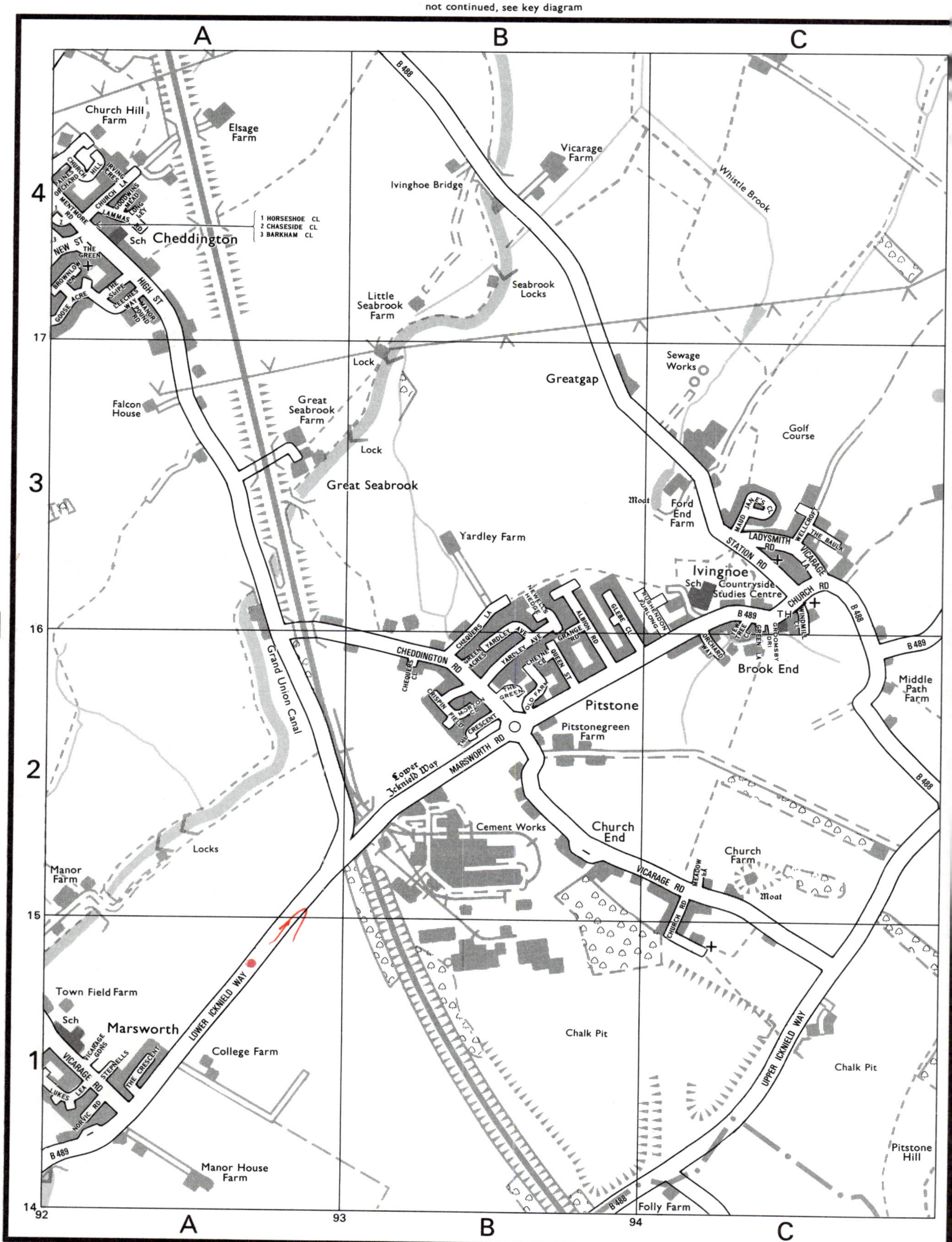

79

100

not continued, see key diagram

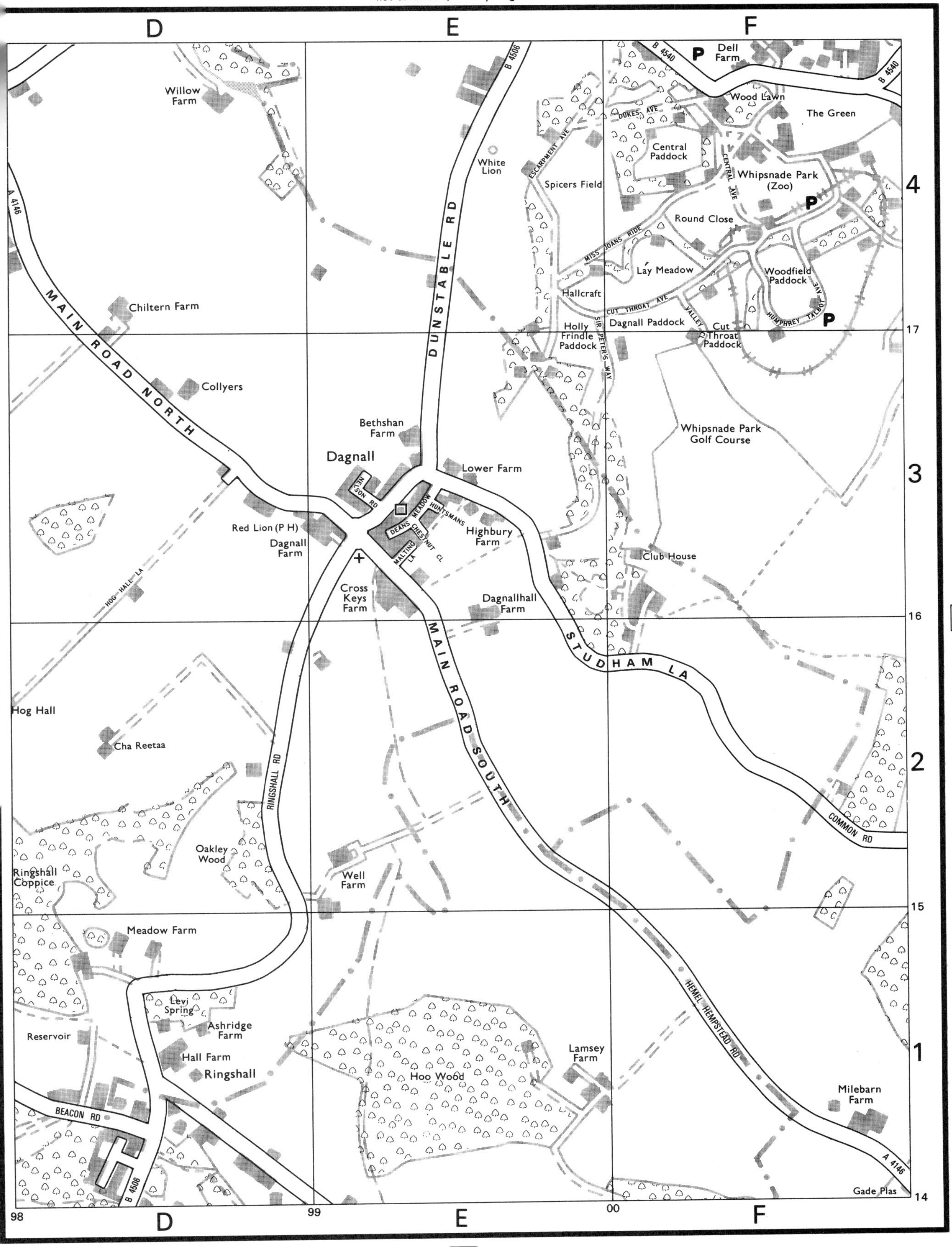

102

not continued, see key diagram

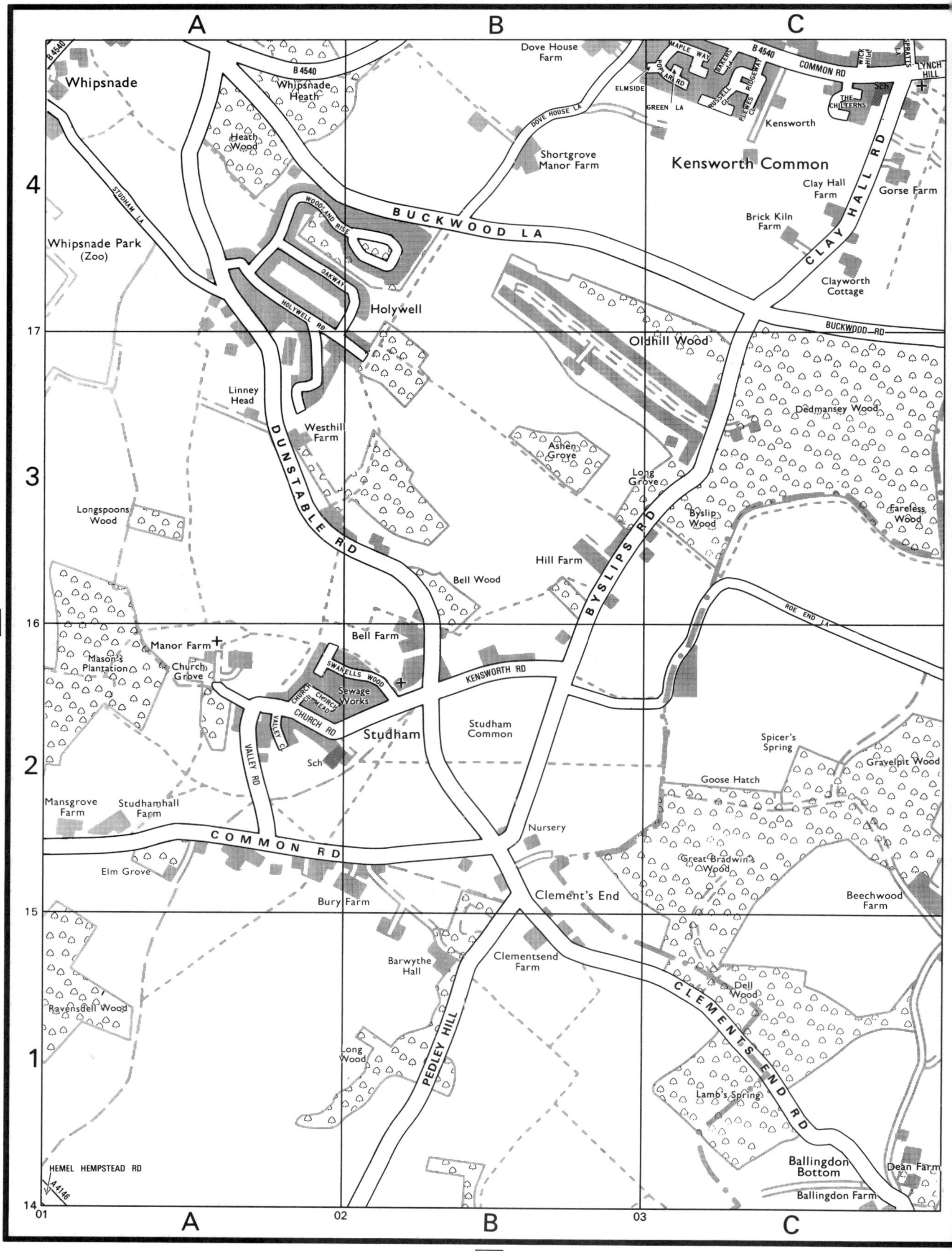

103

62

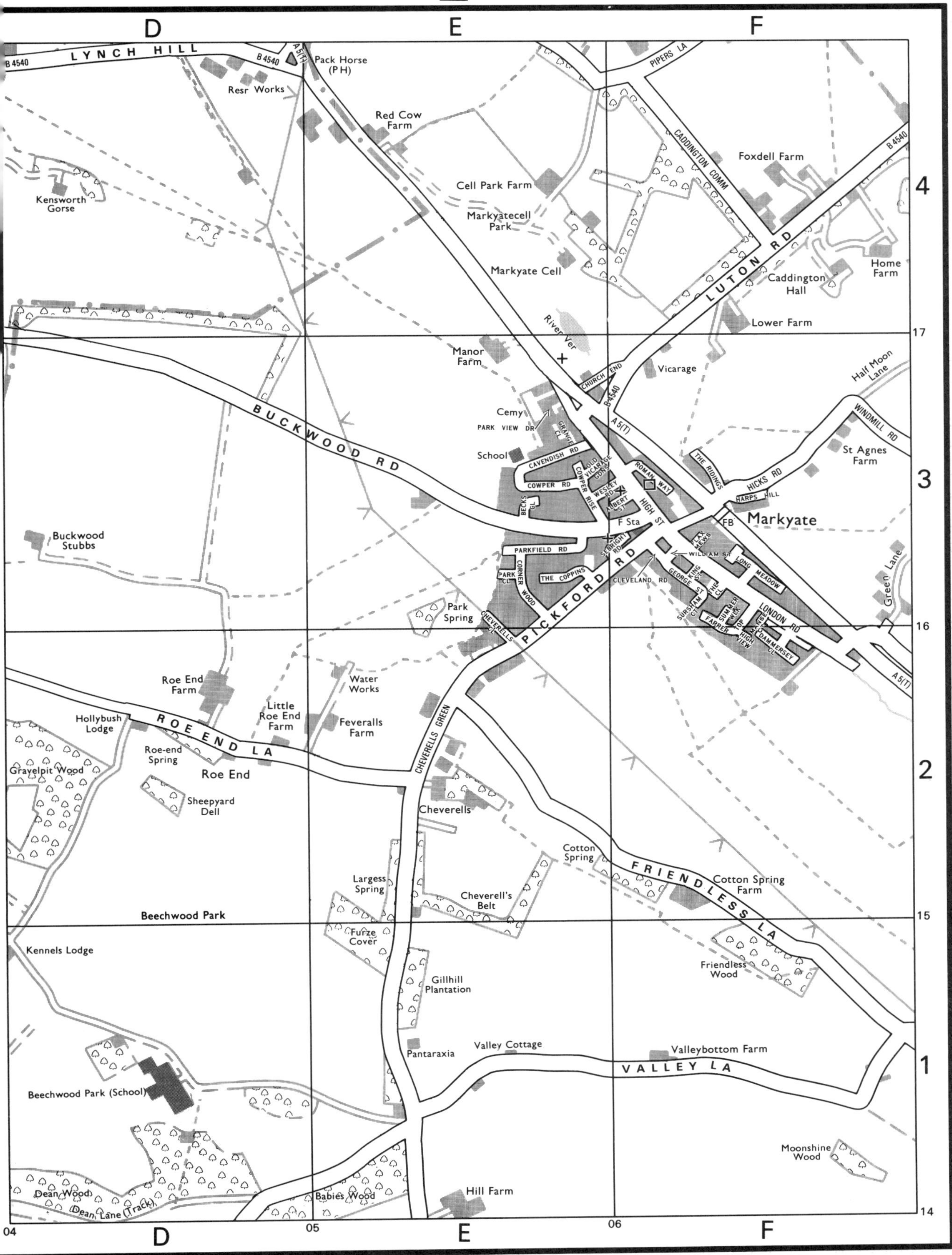

D
E
F
LYNCH HILL
B 4540
A 5(T)
Pack Horse (PH)
Resr Works
Red Cow Farm
PIPERS LA
CADDINGTON COMM
Foxdell Farm
Cell Park Farm
Markyatecell Park
Markyate Cell
Kensworth Gorse
LUTON RD
Caddington Hall
Home Farm
Lower Farm
River Ver
Manor Farm
CHURCH END
Vicarage
Half Moon Lane
WINDMILL RD
BUCKWOOD RD
Cemy
PARK VIEW DR
GRANGE CL
School
CAVENDISH RD
COWPER RD
COWPER RISE
OLD VICARAGE GDNS
WESLEY RD
ALBERT ST
ROMAN WAY
HIGH ST
THE RIDINGS
HICKS RD
HARPS HILL
St Agnes Farm
BECKS CL
F Sta
FB
Markyate
Buckwood Stubbs
PARKFIELD RD
SEBRIGHT RD
FLAX MEWS
WILLIAM ST
LONG MEADOW
Green Lane
PARK CL
CORNER WOOD
THE COPPINS
CLEVELAND RD
GEORGE ST
KING ST
SURSHAM CT
THE CL
SUMMER TOP
FARRER TOP
HIGH VIEW
LONDON RD
MANSE CT
DAMMERSEY CL
PICKFORD RD
Park Spring
CHEVERELLS CL
Roe End Farm
Water Works
Little Roe End Farm
Feveralls Farm
Hollybush Lodge
ROE END LA
CHEVERELLS GREEN
Roe-end Spring
Gravelpit Wood
Roe End
Sheepyard Dell
Cheverells
Cotton Spring
FRIENDLESS LA
Cotton Spring Farm
Largess Spring
Cheverell's Belt
Beechwood Park
Furze Cover
Kennels Lodge
Friendless Wood
Gillhill Plantation
Pantaraxia
Valley Cottage
Valleybottom Farm
VALLEY LA
Beechwood Park (School)
Moonshine Wood
Dean Wood
Dean Lane (Track)
Babies Wood
Hill Farm
4
3
2
1
17
16
15
14
04
05
06

84

104

63

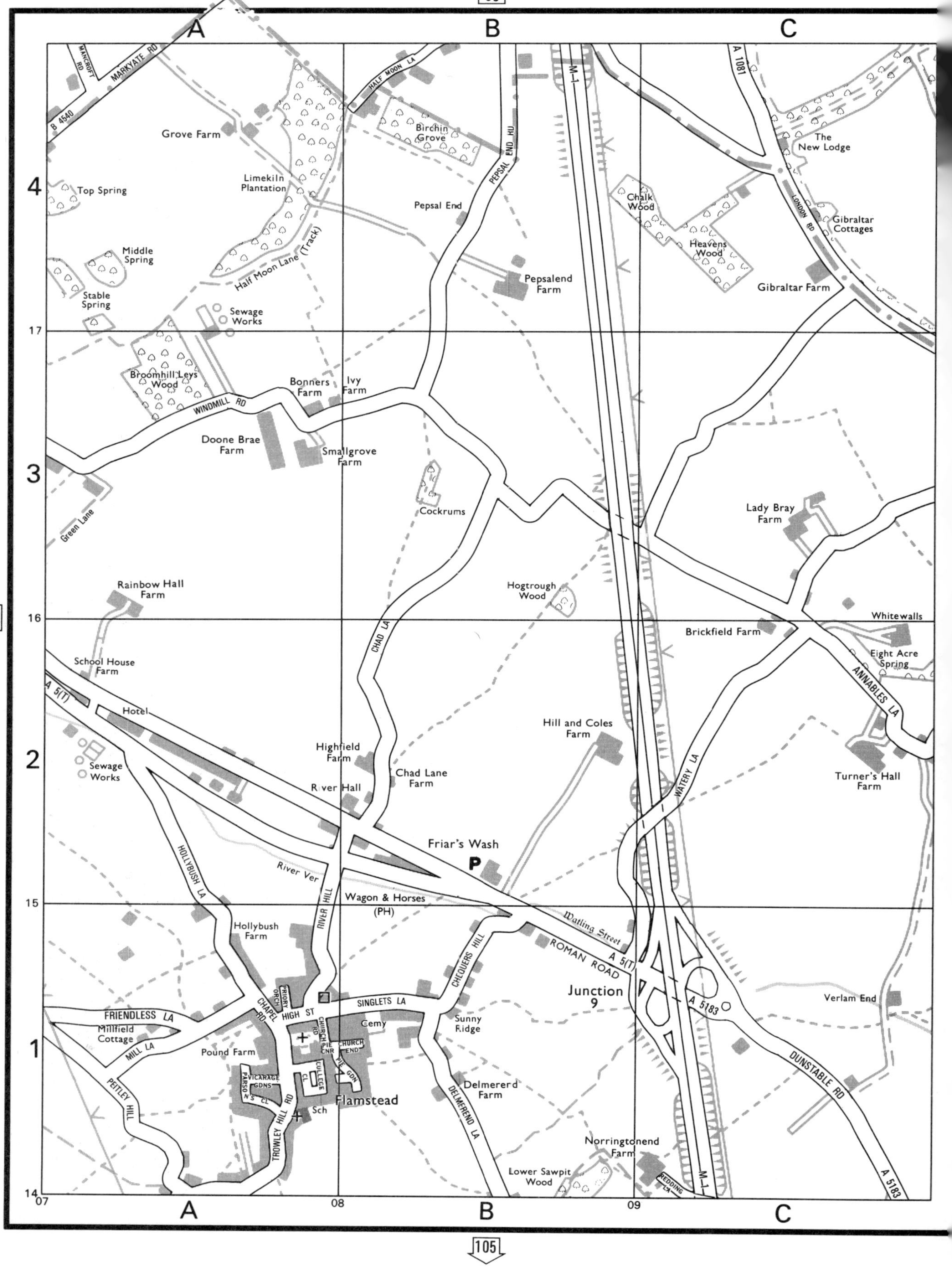

A
B
C
4
3
2
1
17
16
15
14
07
08
09
MANCROFT RD
MARKYATE RD
B 4540
Grove Farm
Top Spring
Limekiln Plantation
Middle Spring
Stable Spring
Half Moon Lane (Track)
Sewage Works
HALF MOON LA
Birchin Grove
PEPSAL END HU
Pepsal End
Pepsalend Farm
M-1
A 1081
The New Lodge
Chalk Wood
Heavens Wood
LONDON RD
Gibraltar Cottages
Gibraltar Farm
Broomhill Leys Wood
WINDMILL RD
Bonners Farm
Ivy Farm
Doone Brae Farm
Smallgrove Farm
Cockrums
Green Lane
Lady Bray Farm
Rainbow Hall Farm
Hogtrough Wood
Whitewalls
Brickfield Farm
Eight Acre Spring
School House Farm
A 5(T)
Hotel
CHAD LA
ANNABLES LA
Hill and Coles Farm
Sewage Works
Highfield Farm
Chad Lane Farm
River Hall
Turner's Hall Farm
WATERY LA
HOLLYBUSH LA
Friar's Wash
P
River Ver
RIVER HILL
Wagon & Horses (PH)
Watling Street
ROMAN ROAD
A 5(T)
Hollybush Farm
CHEQUERS HILL
Junction 9
A 5183
Verlam End
PRIORY ORCH
CHAPEL RD
HIGH ST
SINGLETS LA
FRIENDLESS LA
Millfield Cottage
MILL LA
Cemy
CHURCH RD
PIE CNR
CHURCH END
Sunny Ridge
Pound Farm
VICARAGE GDNS
PARSONS CL
COLLEGE CL
PIE GDN
DUNSTABLE RD
PEITLEY HILL
TROWLEY HILL RD
Flamstead
Sch
Delmererd Farm
DELMEREND LA
Norringtonend Farm
Lower Sawpit Wood
REDDING LA
M-1
A 5183

83

105

64

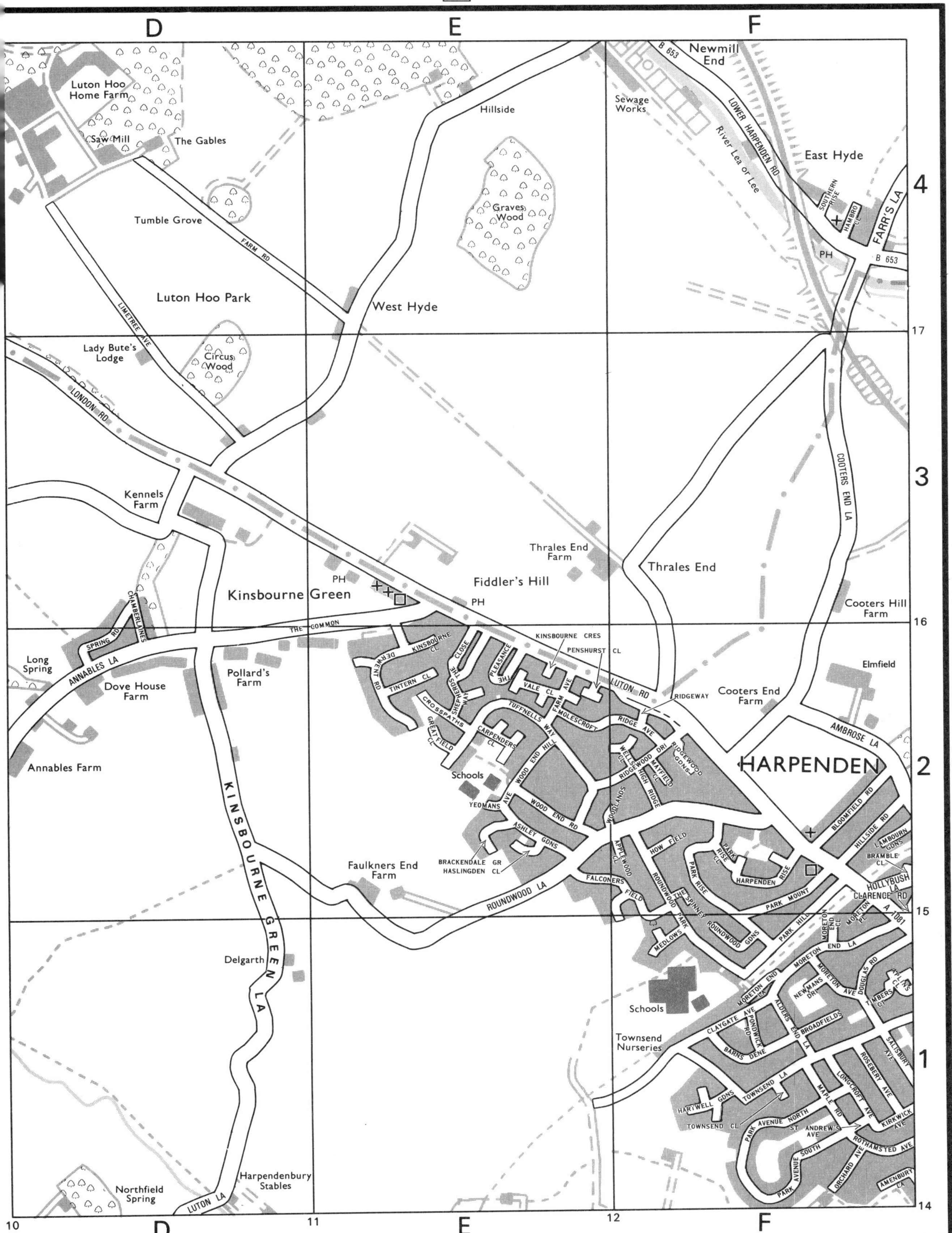
D
E
F
Newmill End
B 653
Luton Hoo Home Farm
Saw Mill
The Gables
Hillside
Sewage Works
LOWER HARPENDEN RD
River Lea or Lee
East Hyde
SOUTHERN RISE
HAMBRO CL
FARR'S LA
PH
B 653
4
Tumble Grove
FARM RD
Graves Wood
Luton Hoo Park
LIMETREE AVE
West Hyde
17
Lady Bute's Lodge
Circus Wood
LONDON RD
COOTERS END LA
3
Kennels Farm
Thrales End Farm
Thrales End
PH
Fiddler's Hill
Kinsbourne Green
PH
Cooters Hill Farm
16
CHAMBERLAINES
SPRING RD
THE COMMON
KINSBOURNE CRES
PENSHURST CL
Long Spring
ANNABLES LA
Dove House Farm
Pollard's Farm
DERWENT RD
KINSBOURNE CL
CLOSE
THE PLEASANCE
TINTERN CL
VALE CL
FARM AVE
LUTON RD
RIDGEWAY
Cooters End Farm
Elmfield
CROSSPATHS
THE SHEPHERDS WAY
TUFFNELLS WAY
MOLESCROFT
RIDGE AVE
AMBROSE LA
GREAT FIELD CL
CARPENDERS CL
WOOD END HILL
WELLCROFT CL
RIDGEWOOD DRI
RIDGEWOOD GDNS
HARPENDEN
2
Annables Farm
Schools
MAYFIELD CL
HIGH RIDGE
BLOOMFIELD RD
KINSBOURNE GREEN LA
YEOMANS AVE
WOOD END RD
WOODLANDS
HILLSIDE RD
LAMBOURN GDNS
ASHLEY GDNS
APPLEWOOD CL
HOW FIELD
PARK RISE CL
BRAMBLE CL
BRACKENDALE GR
HASLINGDEN CL
Faulkners End Farm
FALCONERS FIELD
ROUNDWOOD PARK
PARK RISE
HARPENDEN RISE
HOLLYBUSH LA
CLARENCE RD
ROUNDWOOD LA
THE SPINNEY
PARK MOUNT
A 1081
15
MEDLOWS
ROUNDWOOD GDNS
PARK HILL
MORETON END CL
MORETON PL
MORETON END LA
Delgarth
NEWMANS DRI
MORETON AVE
DOUGLAS RD
TIMBERS CL
Schools
MORETON END
CLAYGATE AVE
PONDWICK RD
ALDERS END LA
BROADFIELDS
SALISBURY AVE
Townsend Nurseries
BARNS DENE
ROSEBERY AVE
1
HARTWELL GDNS
TOWNSEND LA
MAPLE RD
LONGCROFT AVE
KIRKWICK AVE
TOWNSEND CL
PARK AVENUE NORTH
ST ANDREW'S AVE
ROTHAMSTED AVE
PARK AVENUE SOUTH
ORCHARD AVE
AMENBURY LA
Northfield Spring
Harpendenbury Stables
LUTON LA
14
10
D
11
E
12
F

86

106

65

85

A
B
C
4
3
2
1
17
16
15
14
13
14
15
FARR'S LA
Garden Wood
Hyde Home Farm
The Hyde
Home Wood
East Hyde Park
Little Cutts Farm
PLUMMERS LA
Hill Farm
Bishey Wood
Tallents Farm (Research Farm)
Dane Farm
Animal Welfare Centre
KIMPTON BOTTOM
Great Cutts Farm
Ladies Spring
Dane Spring
B 653
LOWER HARPENDEN RD
Poultry Farm
HOLLY LA
Hyde Mill Farm
Broadlands
Wall Wood
BOWER HEATH LA
Bower Heath
Holly Oak Nursery
SAUNCEY WOOD LA
THE SLYPE
COMMON LA
Turnershall Farm
The Osiers
B 652
Riding School
B 653
SAUNCEY WOOD
Westfield Wood
Hospital (private)
Cemy
Sch
LINDLEY CL
Highfield Oval
WESTFIELD RD
LOWER LUTON RD
Mackerye End
Mackery End Farm
Mackerye End
Batford Farm
HOLLYBUSH LA
AMBROSE LA
Schs
THE BUNGALOWS
River Lea or Lee
Batford
Batford Mill
HARPENDEN
Harpenden Memorial Hospital
STATION RD
MANOR RD
MARSHALLS WAY
B653
Sch
HIGH ST
A1081
Harpenden Central Station
Sewage Works
PIGGOTTSHILL LA
Piggottshill Wood
LEASEY BRIDGE LA
F Sta
Schs
Sch

107

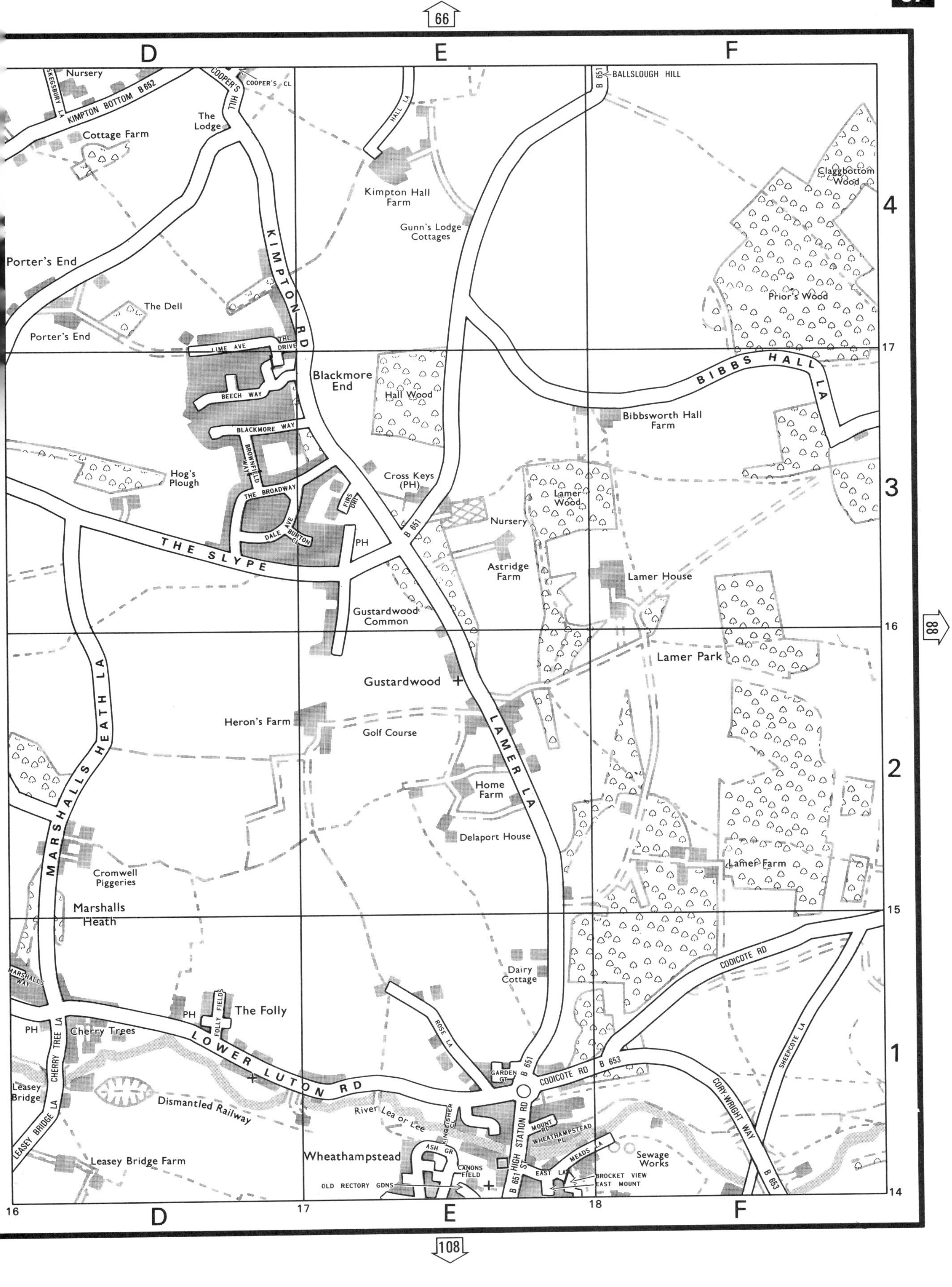

66
D
E
F
Nursery
KIMPTON BOTTOM B652
COOPER'S HILL
COOPER'S CL
B 651
BALLSLOUGH HILL
HALL LA
The Lodge
Cottage Farm
Kimpton Hall Farm
Claggbottom Wood
4
Gunn's Lodge Cottages
Porter's End
KIMPTON RD
Prior's Wood
The Dell
Porter's End
LIME AVE
THE DRIVE
17
BIBBS HALL LA
Blackmore End
BEECH WAY
Hall Wood
Bibbsworth Hall Farm
BLACKMORE WAY
BROWNFIELD WAY
Hog's Plough
Cross Keys (PH)
3
THE BROADWAY
FIRS DRI
Lamer Wood
Nursery
DALE AVE
BURTON CL
PH
THE SLYPE
Astridge Farm
Lamer House
Gustardwood Common
16
88
Lamer Park
Gustardwood
Heron's Farm
Golf Course
LAMER LA
MARSHALLS HEATH LA
2
Home Farm
Delaport House
Lamer Farm
Cromwell Piggeries
Marshalls Heath
15
CODICOTE RD
Dairy Cottage
MARSHALLS WAY
FOLLY FIELDS
The Folly
PH
PH
Cherry Trees
SHEEPCOTE LA
ROSE LA
1
CHERRY TREE LA
LOWER LUTON RD
GARDEN CT
CODICOTE RD B 653
Leasey Bridge
Dismantled Railway
CORY-WRIGHT WAY
River Lea or Lee
KINGFISHER CL
HIGH STATION RD
MOUNT RD
WHEATHAMPSTEAD PL
LEASEY BRIDGE LA
ASH GR
MEADS LA
Sewage Works
Wheathampstead
Leasey Bridge Farm
CANONS FIELD
EAST LA
BROCKET VIEW
EAST MOUNT
HIGH ST
OLD RECTORY GDNS
B 651
B 653
14
16
17
18
D
E
F
108

67

87

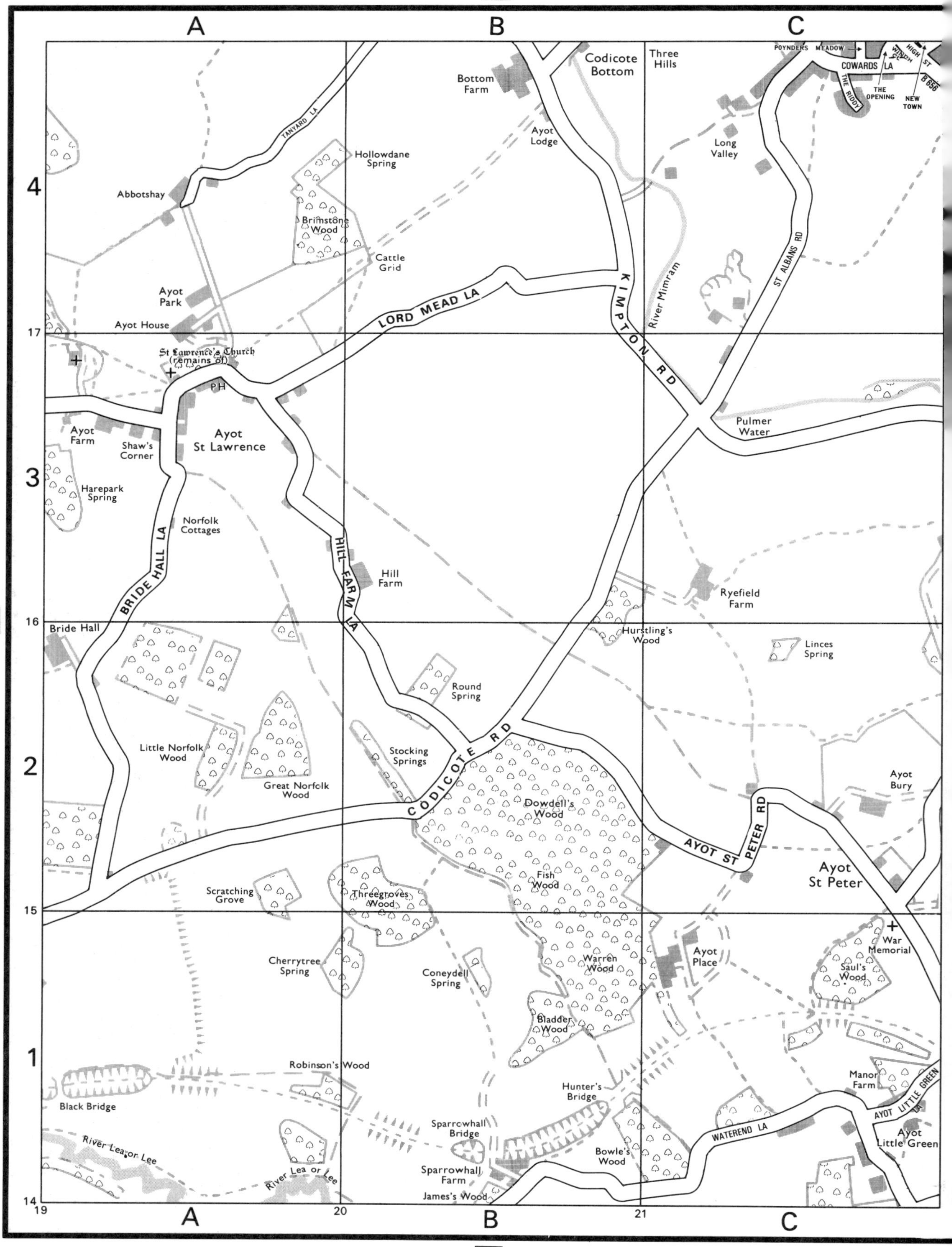
A
B
C
4
3
2
1
17
16
15
14
19
20
21
POYNDERS MEADOW
COWARDS LA
HIGH ST
B 656
THE RIDDY
THE OPENING
NEW TOWN
Codicote Bottom
Three Hills
Bottom Farm
Ayot Lodge
Long Valley
TANYARD LA
Hollowdane Spring
Abbotshay
Brimstone Wood
Cattle Grid
ST ALBANS RD
River Mimram
KIMPTON RD
LORD MEAD LA
Ayot Park
Ayot House
St Lawrence's Church (remains of)
PH
Ayot Farm
Shaw's Corner
Ayot St Lawrence
Pulmer Water
Harepark Spring
Norfolk Cottages
HILL FARM LA
Hill Farm
BRIDE HALL LA
Ryefield Farm
Bride Hall
Hurstling's Wood
Linces Spring
Round Spring
Little Norfolk Wood
Great Norfolk Wood
Stocking Springs
CODICOTE RD
Dowdell's Wood
Ayot Bury
AYOT ST PETER RD
Fish Wood
Ayot St Peter
Scratching Grove
Threegroves Wood
War Memorial
Cherrytree Spring
Coneydell Spring
Warren Wood
Ayot Place
Saul's Wood
Bladder Wood
Robinson's Wood
Hunter's Bridge
Manor Farm
AYOT LITTLE GREEN LA
Black Bridge
Sparrowhall Bridge
WATEREND LA
Ayot Little Green
River Lea or Lee
Bowle's Wood
Sparrowhall Farm
James's Wood

109

68

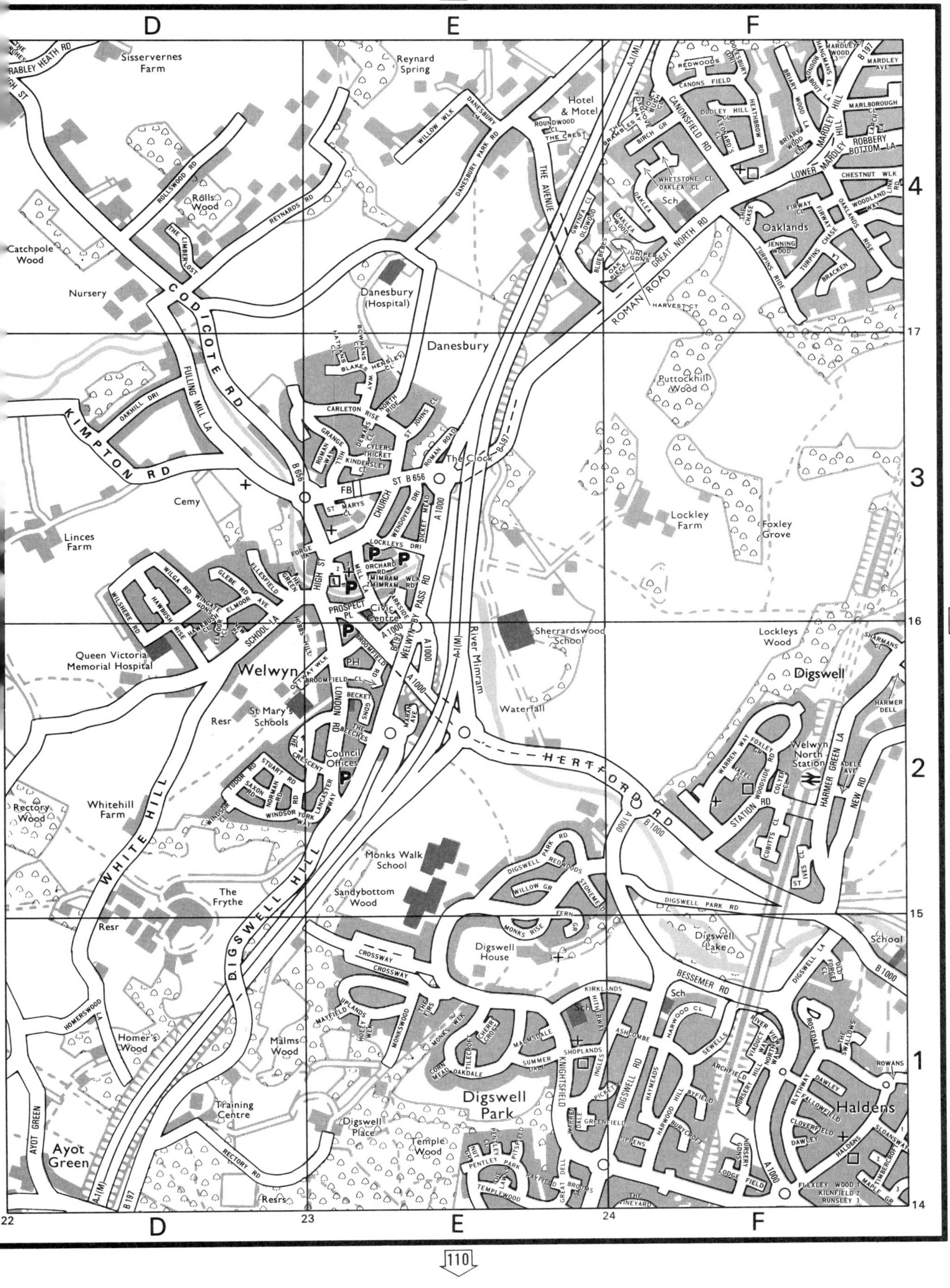
D
E
F
Sisservernes Farm
Reynard Spring
Hotel & Motel
Rolls Wood
Catchpole Wood
Nursery
Danesbury (Hospital)
Danesbury
CODICOTE RD
KIMPTON RD
FULLING MILL LA
OAKHILL DRI
ROLLSWOOD RD
REYNARDS RD
THE LIMBERLOST
WILLOW WLK
DANESBURY PARK RD
THE AVENUE
ROUNDWOOD CL
THE CREST
GREAT NORTH RD
ROMAN ROAD
CANONSFIELD RD
CANONS FIELD
REDWOODS
DUDLEY HILL CL
HEATHBROW RD
BIRCH GR
WHETSTONE CL
OAKLEA CL
Sch
Oaklands
LOWER MARDLEY HILL
MARDLEY HILL
MARLBOROUGH
ROBBERY BOTTOM LA
CHESTNUT WLK
WOODLAND WAY
FIRWAY CL
FIRWAY
OAKLANDS RISE
TURPINS CHASE
TURPINS RIDE
JENNING WOOD
BRACKEN
THE CHASE
HARVEST CT
Puttockhill Wood
Lockley Farm
Foxley Grove
Lockleys Wood
Digswell
The Clock
Cemy
Lince Farm
CHURCH ST B656
ST MARYS CL
WENDOVER DRI
DICKET MEAD
LOCKLEYS DRI
ORCHARD RD
MIMRAM RD
MIMRAM WLK
HIGH ST
PROSPECT PL
Civic Centre
BY PASS RD
WELWYN BY PASS RD
A1000
A1(M)
River Mimram
Sherrardswood School
Waterfall
Queen Victoria Memorial Hospital
Welwyn
WILGA RD
GLEBE RD
WINGATE GDNS
ELMOOR AVE
HAWBUSH RISE
WILSHERE RD
SCHOOL LA
BROOMFIELD CL
BROOMFIELD RD
BECKET GDNS
THE BEECHES
LONDON RD
Resr
St Mary's Schools
Council Offices
THE CRESCENT
STUART RD
TUDOR RD
SAXON RD
NORMAN RD
LANCASTER WAY
WINDSOR RD
YORK WAY
HERTFORD RD
B1000
Welwyn North Station
WARREN WAY
FOXLEY GR
STATION RD
WOODSIDE RD
COLYER CL
CUBITTS CL
ST IVES CL
HARMER GREEN LA
NEW RD
HARMER DELL
SHARMANS CL
Rectory Wood
Whitehill Farm
WHITE HILL
DIGSWELL HILL
Monks Walk School
Sandybottom Wood
The Frythe
DIGSWELL PARK RD
REDWOODS
WILLOW GR
STONEMEAD
FERN GR
MONKS RISE
Digswell House
Digswell Lake
School
BESSEMER RD
DIGSWELL LA
OLD FORGE CL
B1000
CROSSWAY
KIRKLANDS
HITHERWAY
HARWOOD CL
ROSEDALE
THE SWALLOWS
ROWANS
MAYFIELD
UPLANDS
MONKSWOOD
THE FIRS
MONKS WLK
TILECROFT
CHERRY CROFT
MALMSDALE
SUMMER DALE
SHOPLANDS
KNIGHTSFIELD
INGLES
ASHCOMBE
DIGSWELL RD
HAYMEADS
HARWOOD HILL
SEWELLS
ARCHFIELD
BYFIELD
BURYCROFT
VIADUCT WAY
NORTHWAY
RIVER VIEW
NURSERY HILL
BLYTHWAY
DAWLEY
FALLOWFIELD
CLOVERFIELD
Haldens
HALDENS
SLOANSWAY
TIMBERCROFT
MAPLE GR
FLEXLEY WOOD
KILNFIELD
RUNSLEY
Resr
HOMERSWOOD LA
Homer's Wood
Malms Wood
Training Centre
Digswell Park
Digswell Place
Temple Wood
CORN MEAD
OAKDALE
PENTLEY PARK
PITSFIELD
THE LAWNS
TEMPLEWOOD
HAYFIELD
GREAT DELL
BROOKS CL
GREENFIELD
PIPPENS
PICKETTS
NURSERY GDNS
LODGE FIELD
THE VINEYARD
A1000
RECTORY RD
Resrs
AYOT GREEN
Ayot Green
A1(M)
B197
17
16
15
14
4
3
2
1
22
23
24

90

110

69

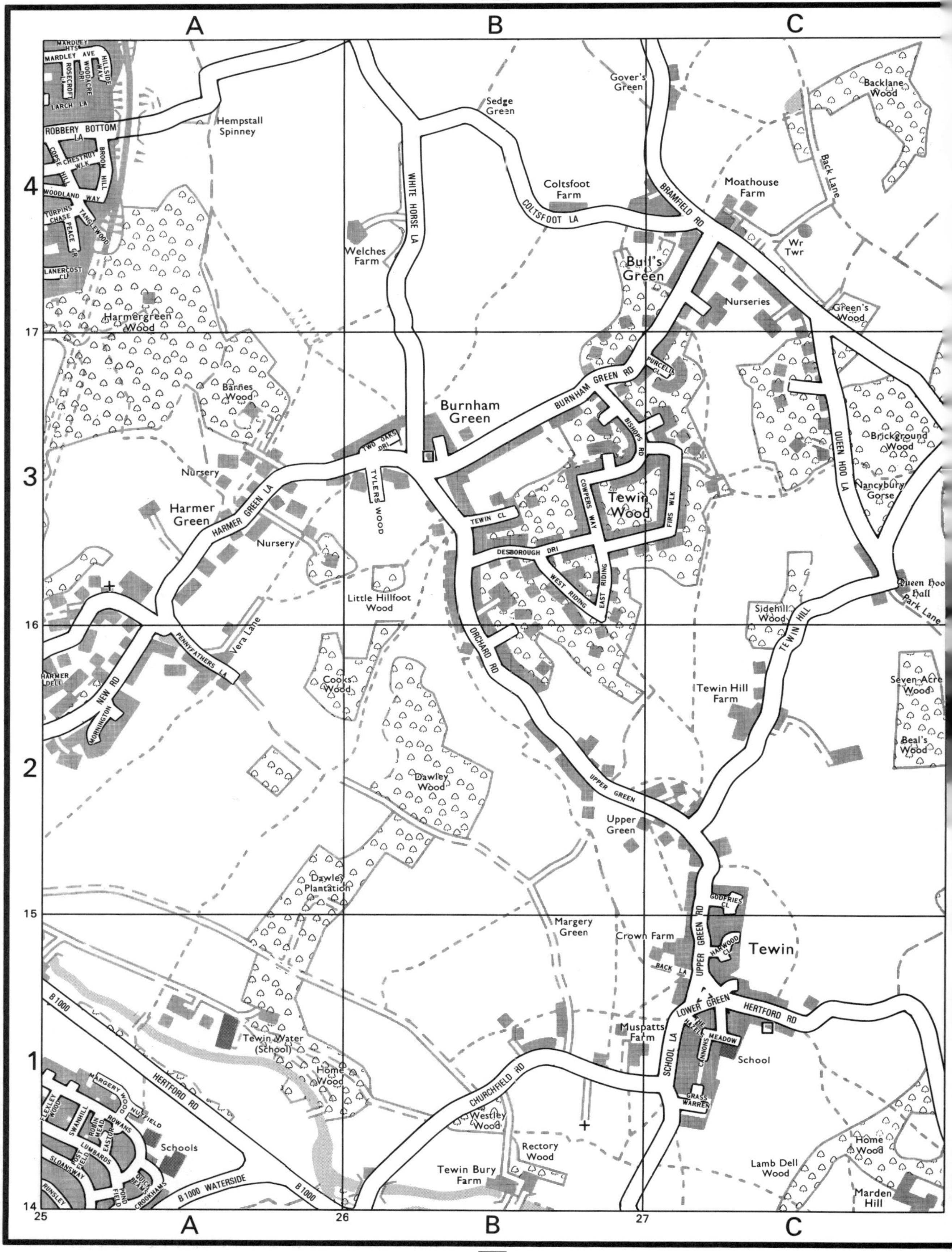
A
B
C
4
3
2
1
17
16
15
14
25
26
27
Mardley Hts
Mardley Ave
Woodacre Dri
Rosecroft La
Hillside Way
Larch La
Robbery Bottom La
Copse Hill
Chestnut Wlk
Broom Hill
Woodland Way
Turpins Chase
Peace Gr
Tanglewood
Lanercost Cl
Hempstall Spinney
Sedge Green
Gover's Green
Backlane Wood
Back Lane
White Horse La
Coltsfoot Farm
Coltsfoot La
Bramfield Rd
Moathouse Farm
Wr Twr
Welches Farm
Bull's Green
Nurseries
Green's Wood
Harmergreen Wood
Barnes Wood
Burnham Green
Burnham Green Rd
Purcell Cl
Bishops Rd
Queen Hoo La
Brickground Wood
Nancybury Gorse
Two Oaks Dri
Tylers Wood
Nursery
Harmer Green
Harmer Green La
Tewin Cl
Cowpers Way
Tewin Wood
Firs Wlk
Desborough Dri
West Riding
East Riding
Queen Hoo Hall
Park Lane
Little Hillfoot Wood
Sidehill Wood
Tewin Hill
Vera Lane
Pennyfathers La
Harmer Dell
New Rd
Mornington
Orchard Rd
Cooks Wood
Tewin Hill Farm
Seven Acre Wood
Beal's Wood
Dawley Wood
Upper Green
Dawley Plantation
Godfries Cl
Margery Green
Crown Farm
Upper Green Rd
Harwood Cl
Tewin
Back La
B 1000
Lower Green
Hertford Rd
Tewin Water (School)
Muspatts Farm
School La
The Hollies
Cannons Meadow
School
Home Wood
Margery Wood
Nuffield
Lexley Wood
Swanhill
Robin Mead
Rowans
Eastor
Lumbards
Sloansway
Rest Field
Schools
Beams
Pond Field
Crookhams
Runsley
B 1000 Waterside
Churchfield Rd
Westley Wood
Rectory Wood
Grass Warren
Lamb Dell Wood
Tewin Bury Farm
Marden Hill

89

111

70

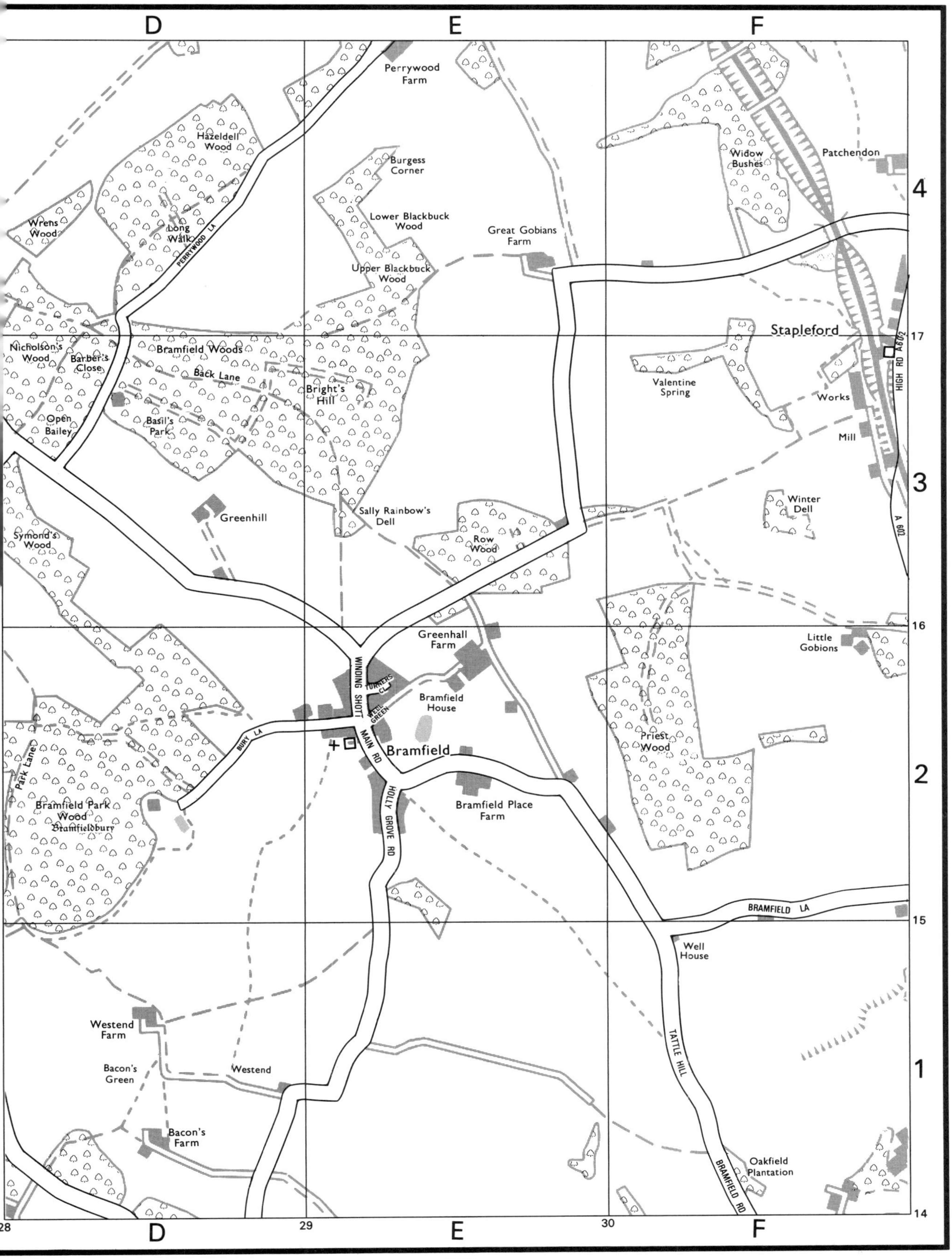
D
E
F
Perrywood Farm
Hazeldell Wood
Burgess Corner
Patchendon
Widow Bushes
Wrens Wood
Long Walk
PERRYWOOD LA
Lower Blackbuck Wood
Great Gobians Farm
Upper Blackbuck Wood
Stapleford
Nicholson's Wood
Barber's Close
Bramfield Woods
Back Lane
Bright's Hill
Valentine Spring
Works
HIGH RD A602
Mill
Open Bailey
Basil's Park
Winter Dell
Greenhill
Sally Rainbow's Dell
Row Wood
A 602
Symond's Wood
Greenhall Farm
Little Gobions
WINDING SHOTT
TURNERS CL
WELL GREEN
Bramfield House
BURY LA
MAIN RD
Bramfield
Priest Wood
Park Lane
HOLLY GROVE RD
Bramfield Park Wood
Bramfieldbury
Bramfield Place Farm
BRAMFIELD LA
Well House
Westend Farm
TATTLE HILL
Bacon's Green
Westend
Bacon's Farm
Oakfield Plantation
BRAMFIELD RD
4
3
2
1
17
16
15
14
28
29
30

92

112

71

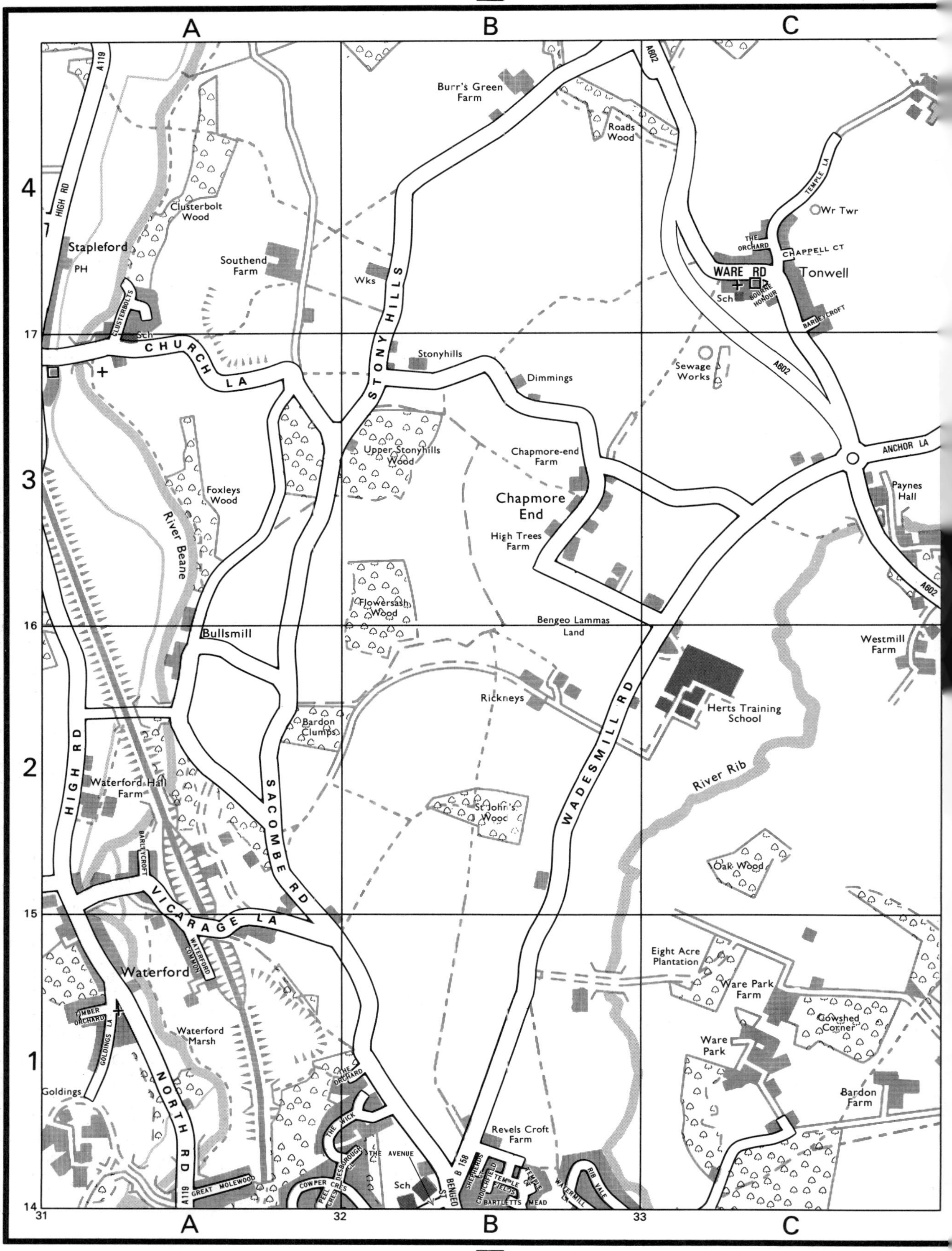
A
B
C
4
3
2
1
17
16
15
14
31
32
33
Burr's Green Farm
Roads Wood
Clusterbolt Wood
Stapleford
PH
Southend Farm
Wks
STONY HILLS
HIGH RD
A119
A602
TEMPLE LA
Wr Twr
THE ORCHARD
CHAPPELL CT
WARE RD
Tonwell
Sch
BOURNE HONOUR
BARLEYCROFT
CLUSTERBOLTS
CHURCH LA
Stonyhills
Dimmings
Sewage Works
Upper Stonyhills Wood
Chapmore-end Farm
ANCHOR LA
Paynes Hall
Foxleys Wood
River Beane
Chapmore End
High Trees Farm
Flowersash Wood
Bengeo Lammas Land
Westmill Farm
Bullsmill
Rickneys
Herts Training School
Bardon Clumps
WADESMILL RD
River Rib
Waterford Hall Farm
SACOMBE RD
St John's Wood
Oak Wood
VICARAGE LA
WATERFORD COMMON
Eight Acre Plantation
Waterford
Ware Park Farm
Cowshed Corner
Waterford Marsh
NORTH RD
GOLDINGS LA
Ware Park
Goldings
Bardon Farm
THE ORCHARD
THE WICK
Revels Croft Farm
THE AVENUE
B 158
GREAT MOLEWOOD
COWPER CRES
PEEL CRES
Sch
BENGEO ST
CROUCHFIELD
TEMPLE FIELDS
BARTLETTS MEAD
WATERMILL LA
RIB VALE

91

113

72

D
E
F
4
3
2
1
17
16
15
14
34
35
36
Chelsing Farm
Lord's Wood
Bourne Wood
Chelsing Cottages
Youngsbury
Wadesmill
Rennesley Farm
Upper Millfield Wood
Wade's Wood
Moat
Church
Sch
Thundridge
OLD CHURCH LA
Thundridgehill
ANCHOR LA
River Rib
Chelsing Lodge
COLD CHRISTMAS LA
B158
B 158
A10(T)
Sow & Pigs (PH)
Cowards
HANBURY MEWS
HANBURY DRI
POLES LA
Hanbury Manor
Mole's Wood
Moles Farm
A10(T)
A1170
Jubilee Plantation
South Lodge
Leisure Centre
Round House
Little Fanhams
Great Cozens
WESTMILL RD
GENTLEMENS FIELD
A602
FANHAMS HALL RD
Cemy
WADESMILL RD
WATTON RD
KINGS WAY
FANHAMS RD
WARE
Schs
F Sta
B 1001
PARK RD
Works
College
BALDOCK ST
HIGH ST
The Priory
Liby
FB
Monastery
River Lea or Lee
Sch
STAR ST
VICARAGE RD
KING EDWARD'S RD
B 1004
WIDBURY HILL
Drill Hall
HERTFORD RD
A10(T)

94

114

73

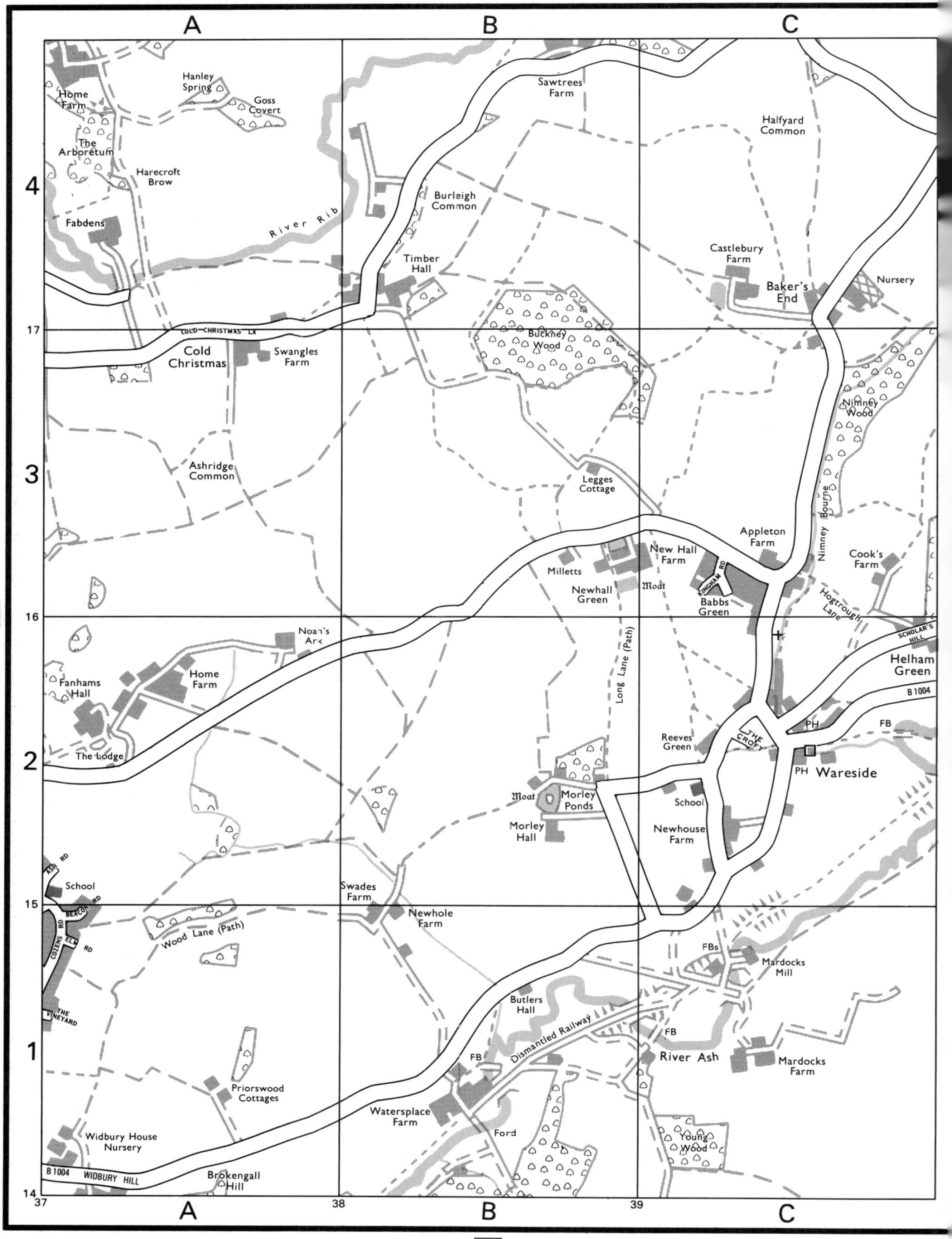
A
B
C
4
3
2
1
17
16
15
14
37
38
39
Home Farm
Hanley Spring
Goss Covert
The Arboretum
Harecroft Brow
Fabdens
River Rib
Sawtrees Farm
Halfyard Common
Burleigh Common
Timber Hall
Castlebury Farm
Baker's End
Nursery
COLD CHRISTMAS LA
Cold Christmas
Swangles Farm
Buckney Wood
Nimney Wood
Ashridge Common
Legges Cottage
Nimney Bourne
Appleton Farm
New Hall Farm
Cook's Farm
Milletts
Newhall Green
Moat
KINGHAM RD
Babbs Green
Hogtrough Lane
Noah's Ark
SCHOLAR'S HILL
Helham Green
Fanhams Hall
Home Farm
Long Lane (Path)
B 1004
PH
FB
The Lodge
Reeves Green
THE CROFT
Wareside
Moat
Morley Ponds
School
Morley Hall
Newhouse Farm
ASH RD
School
BEACON RD
Swades Farm
Newhole Farm
COZENS RD
ELM RD
Wood Lane (Path)
FBs
Mardocks Mill
THE VINEYARD
Butlers Hall
Dismantled Railway
FB
River Ash
Mardocks Farm
Priorswood Cottages
Watersplace Farm
Ford
Young Wood
Widbury House Nursery
B 1004
WIDBURY HILL
Brokengall Hill

93

115

74

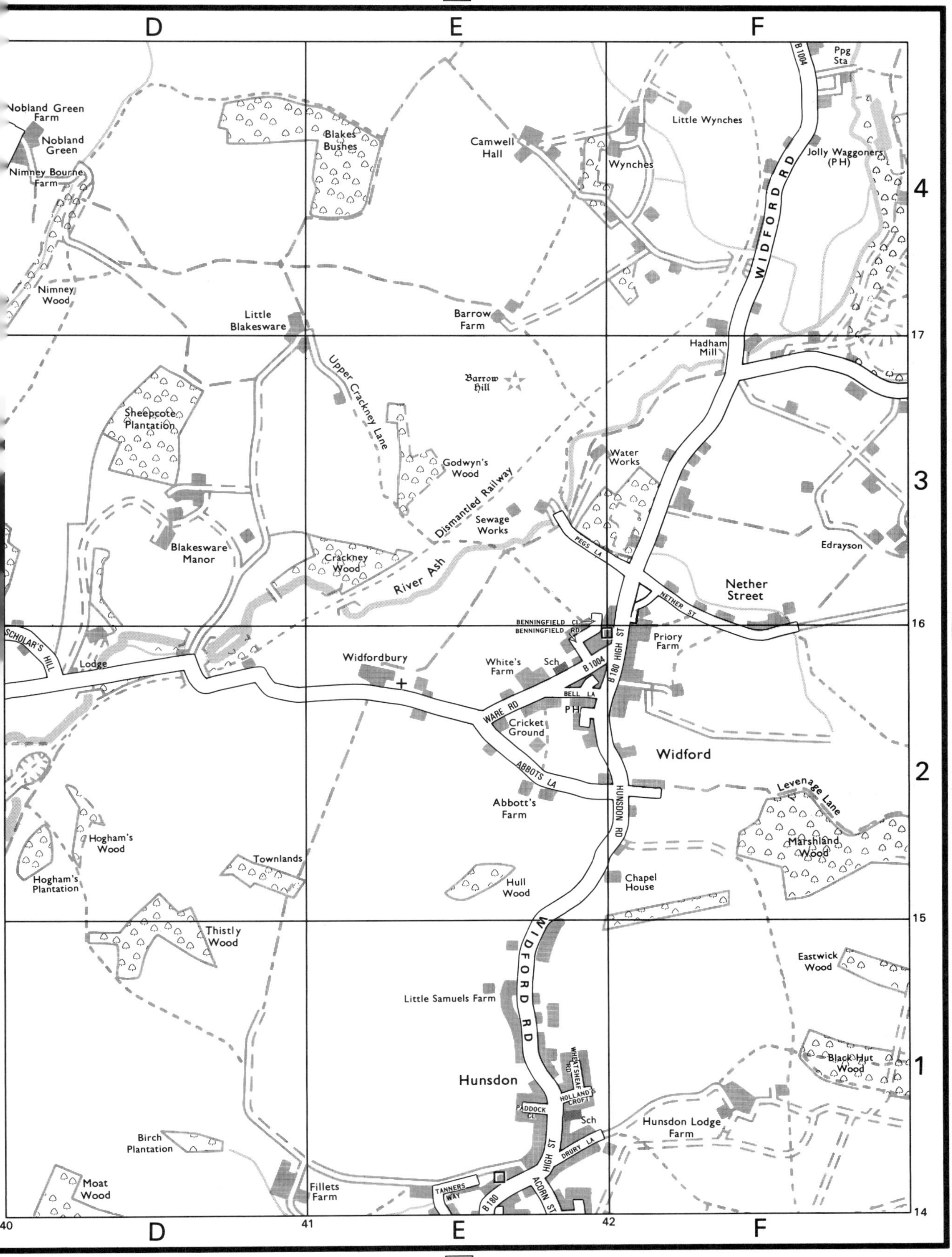
D
E
F
4
3
2
1
17
16
15
14
40
41
42
Nobland Green Farm
Nobland Green
Nimney Bourne Farm
Nimney Wood
Blakes Bushes
Camwell Hall
Little Wynches
Wynches
Ppg Sta
B 1004
WIDFORD RD
Jolly Waggoners (PH)
Little Blakesware
Barrow Farm
Hadham Mill
Upper Crackney Lane
Barrow Hill
Sheepcote Plantation
Godwyn's Wood
Water Works
Dismantled Railway
Sewage Works
Blakesware Manor
Crackney Wood
River Ash
PEGS LA
Edrayson
Nether Street
NETHER ST
BENNINGFIELD CL
BENNINGFIELD RD
SCHOLAR'S HILL
Lodge
Widfordbury
White's Farm
Sch
B 1004
B 180 HIGH ST
Priory Farm
BELL LA
WARE RD
PH
Cricket Ground
Widford
ABBOTS LA
HUNSDON RD
Abbott's Farm
Levenage Lane
Marshland Wood
Hogham's Wood
Hogham's Plantation
Townlands
Hull Wood
Chapel House
Thistly Wood
WIDFORD RD
Eastwick Wood
Little Samuels Farm
WHEATSHEAF RD
HOLLAND'S CROFT
Black Hut Wood
Hunsdon
PADDOCK CL
Sch
Hunsdon Lodge Farm
Birch Plantation
DRURY LA
HIGH ST
Moat Wood
Fillets Farm
TANNERS WAY
B 180
ACORN ST

96

116

75

95

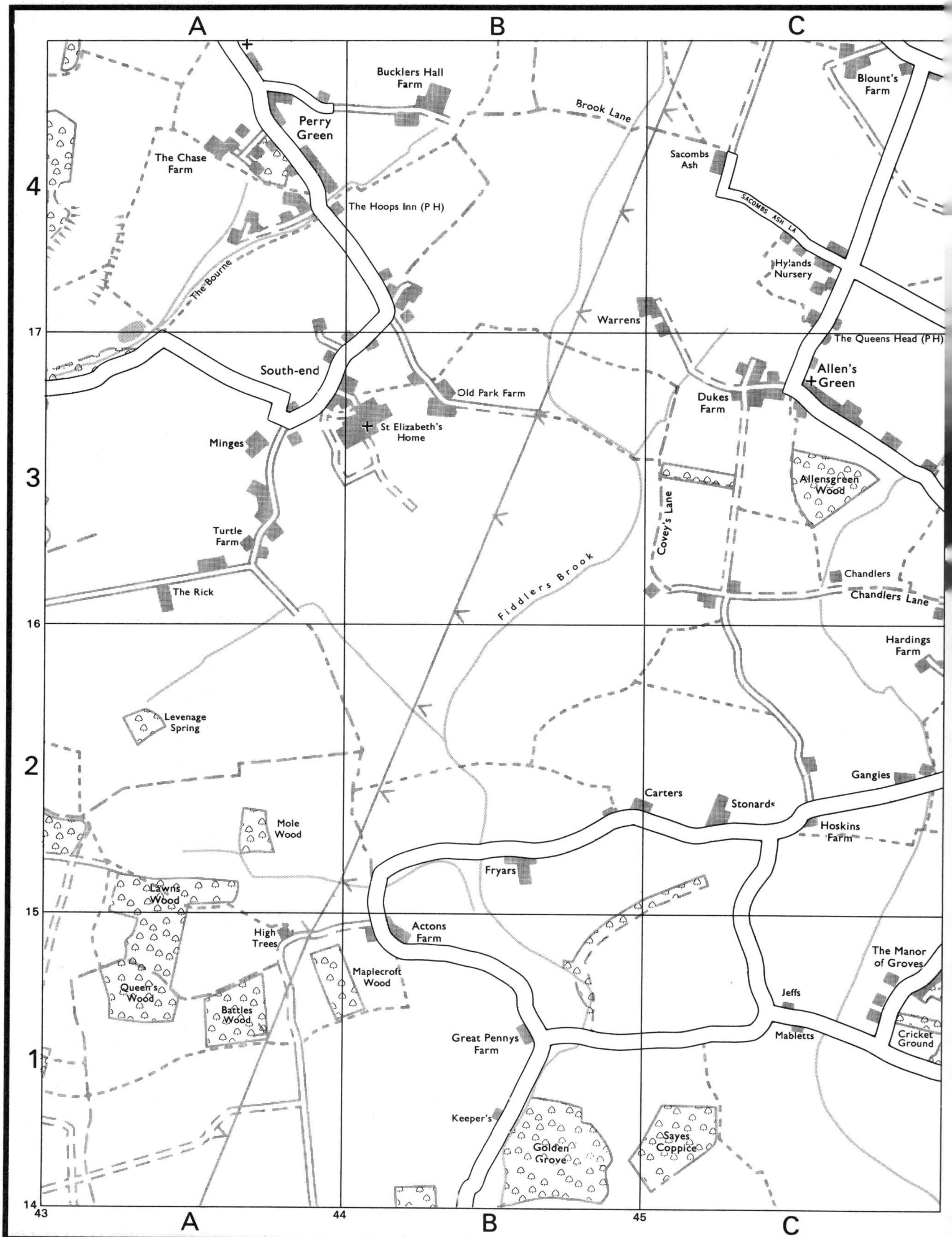
A
B
C
4
3
2
1
17
16
15
14
43
44
45
Bucklers Hall Farm
Brook Lane
Perry Green
The Chase Farm
Sacombs Ash
SACOMBS ASH LA
Blount's Farm
The Hoops Inn (P H)
Hylands Nursery
The Bourne
Warrens
The Queens Head (P H)
South-end
Allen's Green
Old Park Farm
Dukes Farm
St Elizabeth's Home
Minges
Allensgreen Wood
Covey's Lane
Turtle Farm
Fiddlers Brook
Chandlers
The Rick
Chandlers Lane
Hardings Farm
Levenage Spring
Gangies
Carters
Stonards
Mole Wood
Hoskins Farm
Fryars
Lawns Wood
High Trees
Actons Farm
The Manor of Groves
Maplecroft Wood
Queen's Wood
Jeffs
Battles Wood
Great Pennys Farm
Mabletts
Cricket Ground
Keeper's
Golden Grove
Sayes Coppice

117

76

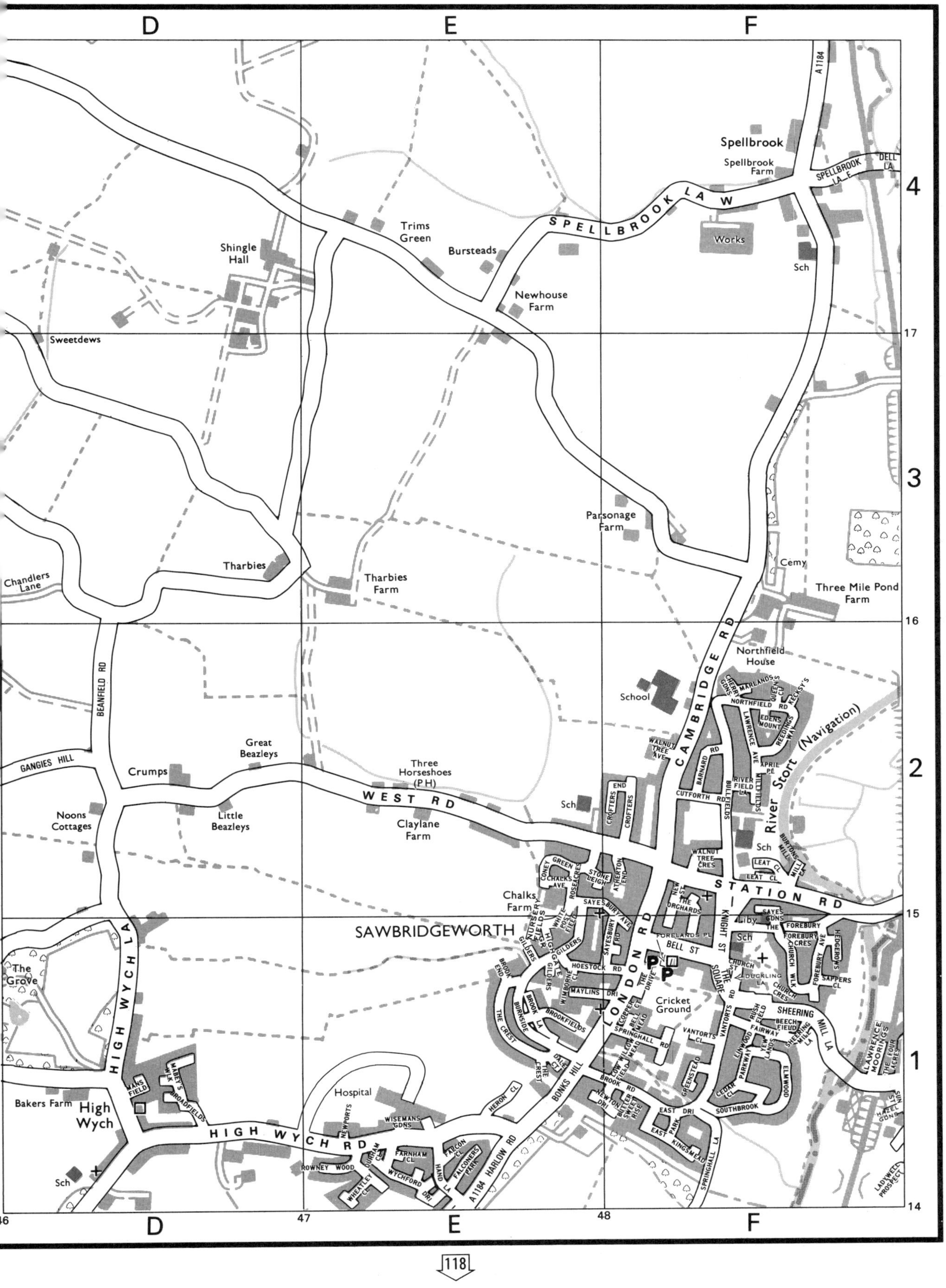

D
E
F
4
3
2
1
17
16
15
14
46
47
48
A1184
Spellbrook
Spellbrook Farm
SPELLBROOK LA W
SPELLBROOK LA E
DELL LA
Works
Sch
Shingle Hall
Trims Green
Bursteads
Newhouse Farm
Sweetdews
Parsonage Farm
Tharbies
Chandlers Lane
Tharbies Farm
Cemy
Three Mile Pond Farm
Northfield House
School
CAMBRIDGE RD
BEANFIELD RD
GANGIES HILL
Great Beazleys
Crumps
Three Horseshoes (P.H)
WEST RD
Noons Cottages
Little Beazleys
Claylane Farm
Sch
River Stort (Navigation)
STATION RD
Chalks Farm
SAWBRIDGEWORTH
The Grove
HIGH WYCH LA
LONDON RD
BELL ST
KNIGHT ST
Cricket Ground
SHEERING MILL LA
LAWRENCE MOORINGS
Hospital
Bakers Farm
High Wych
HIGH WYCH RD
HARLOW RD
BONKS HILL
Sch
ROWNEY WOOD
WHEATLEY CL
WYCHFORD DRI
FALCONERS PARK
SOUTHBROOK
SPRINGHALL LA
KINGSMEAD
EAST DRI
LADYWELL PROSPECT

98

118

77

97

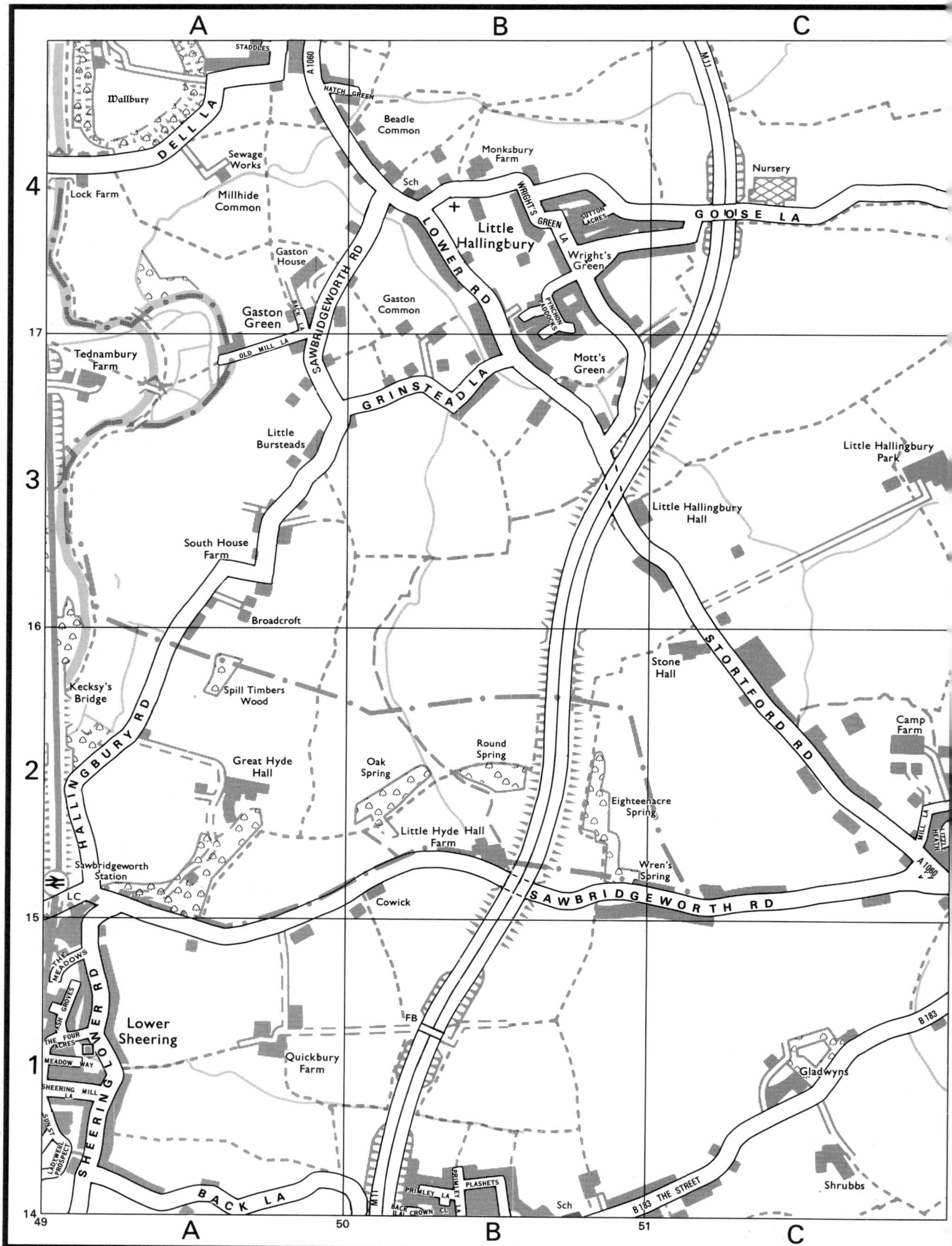

not continued, see key diagram

79

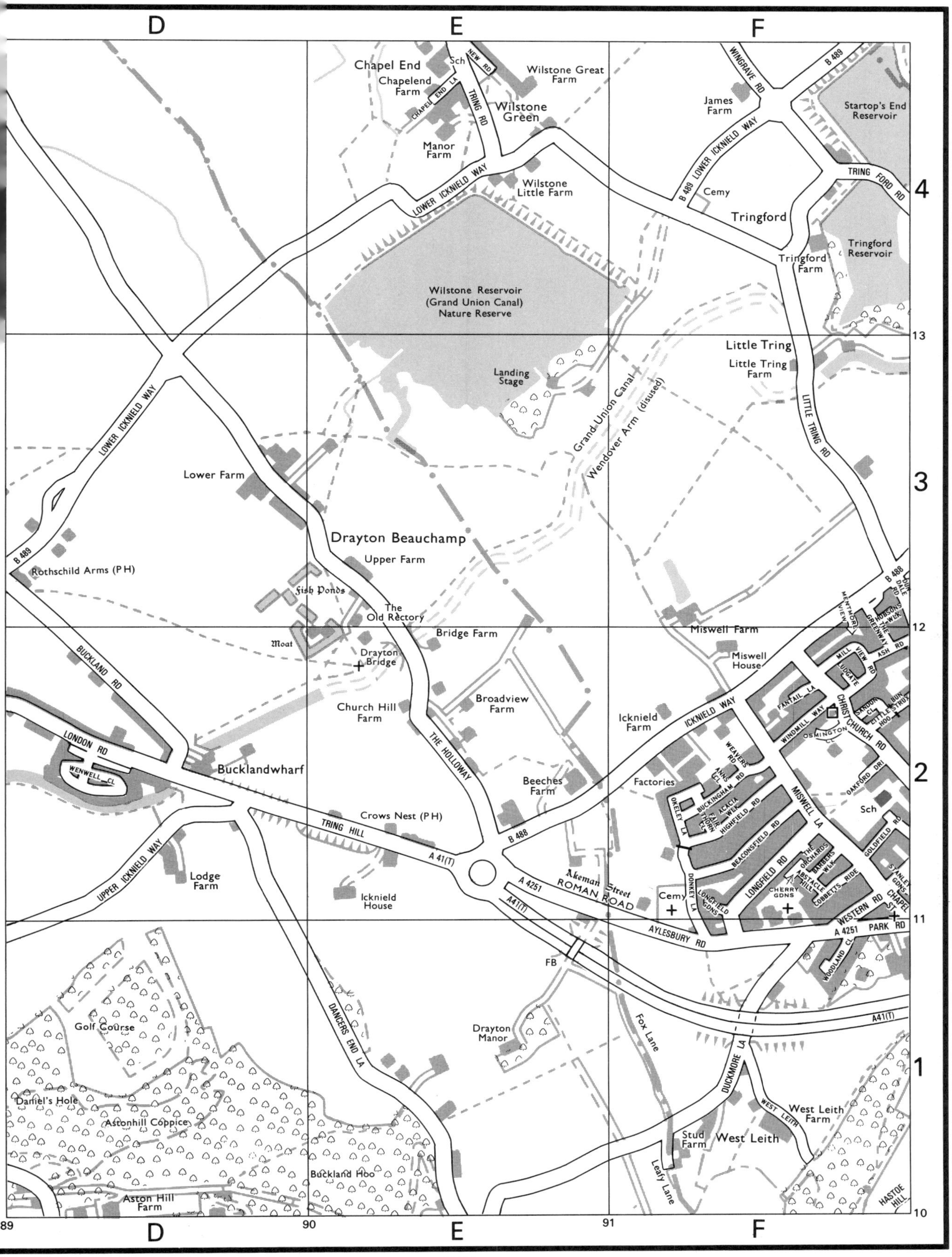

D
E
F
Chapel End
Chapelend Farm
Sch
NEW RD
TRING RD
CHAPEL END LA
Wilstone Great Farm
Wilstone Green
Manor Farm
Wilstone Little Farm
LOWER ICKNIELD WAY
WINGRAVE RD
B 489
James Farm
Startop's End Reservoir
B 489 LOWER ICKNIELD WAY
Cemy
Tringford
TRING FORD RD
Tringford Reservoir
Tringford Farm
Wilstone Reservoir
(Grand Union Canal)
Nature Reserve
Little Tring
Little Tring Farm
LITTLE TRING RD
Landing Stage
Grand Union Canal
Wendover Arm (disused)
Lower Farm
Drayton Beauchamp
Upper Farm
B 489
Rothschild Arms (PH)
Fish Ponds
The Old Rectory
Moat
Bridge Farm
Miswell Farm
Miswell House
Drayton Bridge
BUCKLAND RD
Broadview Farm
Church Hill Farm
Icknield Farm
ICKNIELD WAY
THE HOLLOWAY
LONDON RD
WENWELL CL
Bucklandwharf
Beeches Farm
Factories
Sch
Crows Nest (PH)
TRING HILL
B 488
A 41(T)
UPPER ICKNIELD WAY
Lodge Farm
Icknield House
A 4251
Akeman Street
ROMAN ROAD
Cemy
A41(T)
AYLESBURY RD
A 4251
PARK RD
WESTERN RD
CHAPEL ST
FB
MISWELL LA
LONGFIELD RD
BEACONSFIELD RD
HIGHFIELD RD
BUCKINGHAM RD
OKELEY LA
DONKEY LA
LONGFIELD GDNS
CHERRY GDNS
COBBETTS RIDE
THE ORCHARDS
BARBERS WLK
ABSTACLE HILL
WEAVERS RD
FANTAIL LA
WINDMILL WAY
OSMINGTON CL
CHRISTCHURCH RD
MILL VIEW RD
LUDGATE
ASH RD
B 488
MENTMORE VIEW
THE GREENWAY
HOBSONS WLK
OAKFORD DR
GOLDFIELD RD
STANLEY GDNS
WOODLAND CL
A41(T)
Golf Course
DANCERS END LA
Drayton Manor
Fox Lane
DUCKMORE LA
WEST LEITH
West Leith Farm
Daniel's Hole
Astonhill Coppice
Stud Farm
West Leith
Buckland Hoo
Leafy Lane
Aston Hill Farm
HASTOE HILL
4
3
2
1
13
12
11
10
89
90
91
D
E
F

100

119

80

99

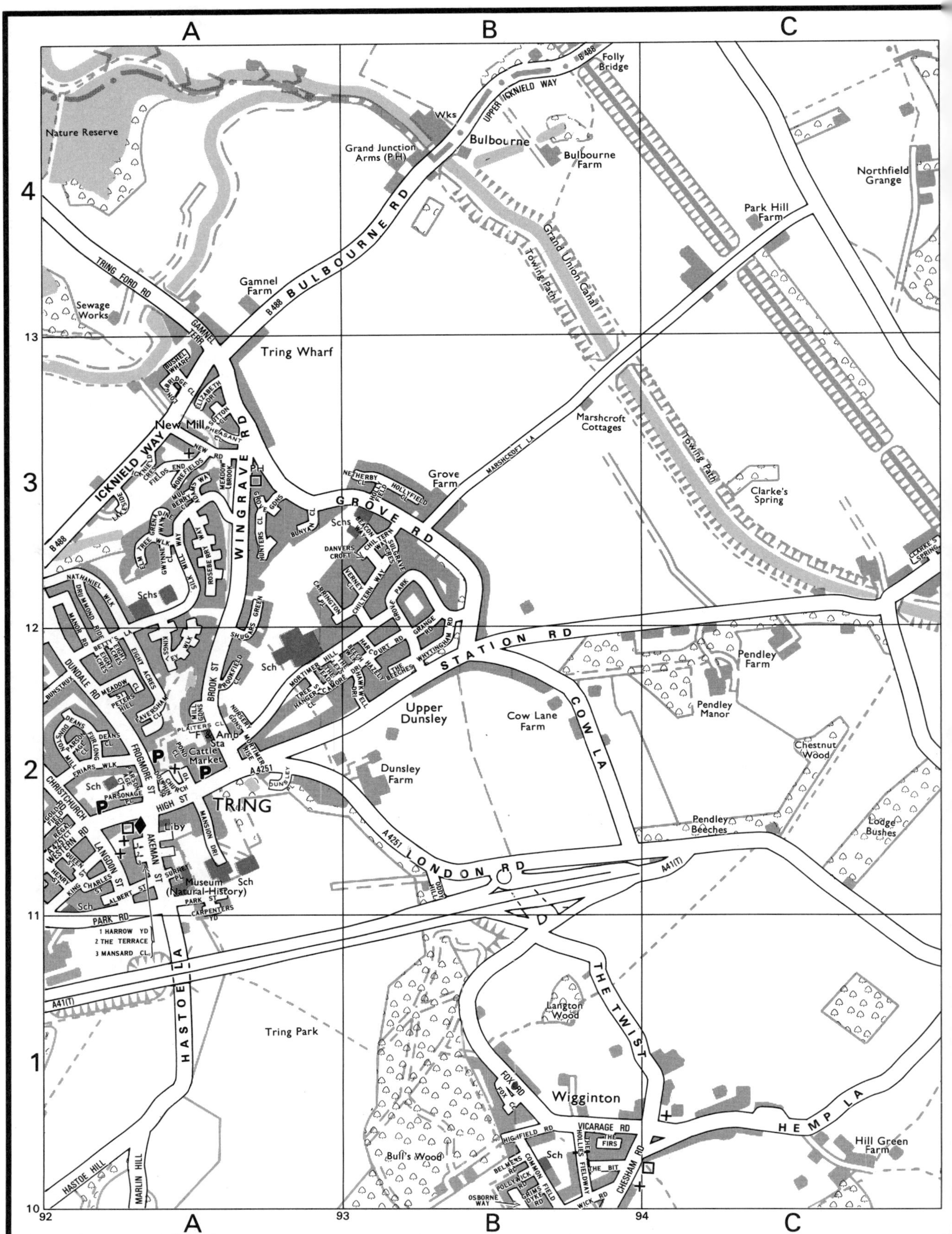
A
B
C
4
3
2
1
13
12
11
10
92
93
94
Nature Reserve
Folly Bridge
UPPER ICKNIELD WAY
B488
Wks
Grand Junction Arms (P.H)
Bulbourne
Bulbourne Farm
Northfield Grange
Park Hill Farm
BULBOURNE RD
Grand Union Canal
Towing Path
TRING FORD RD
Gamnel Farm
Sewage Works
GAMNEL TERR
Tring Wharf
BUSHEL WHARF
CARTRIDGE CL
ELIZABETH DRI
New Mill
SUTTON
PHEASANT
NEW RD
ICKNIELD WAY
WINGRAVE RD
PH
Marshcroft Cottages
MARSHCROFT LA
Grove Farm
NETHERBY CL
HOLLYFIELD
GROVE RD
Schs
BUNYAN CL
HUNTERS CL
BEACON WAY
DANVERS CROFT
CHILTERN WAY
SULGRAVE
Clarke's Spring
CLARKE'S SPRING
Towing Path
NATHANIEL WLK
DRUMMOND RIDE
MANOR RD
Schs
SILK MILL WAY
ROSEBERY WAY
GWYNNE CL
ELM TREE WLK
CARRINGTON PL
VERNEY CL
CHILTERN WAY
GROVE PARK
GRANGE RD
WHYTTINGHAM RD
STATION RD
BETTY'S LA
EIGHT ACRES
DUNDALE RD
BROOK ST
BROOKFIELD CL
Sch
HARCOURT RD
THE BEECHES
MORTIMER HILL
CADMORE
Pendley Farm
Pendley Manor
BUNSTRUX
MEADOW CL
ST PETERS HILL
FAVERSHAM CL
MILL GDNS
NURSERY GDNS
MORTIMER RISE
Upper Dunsley
Cow Lane Farm
COW LA
DEANS FURLONG
DEANS CL
PLAITERS CL
F & Amb Sta
Cattle Market
P
FROGMORE ST
Chestnut Wood
FRIARS WLK
A4251
DUNSLEY PL
Dunsley Farm
CHRISTCHURCH
Sch
PARSONAGE PL
HIGH ST
TRING
Liby
MANSION DRI
Pendley Beeches
Lodge Bushes
WESTERN RD
LANGDON ST
AKEMAN ST
SURREY PL
A4251 LONDON RD
ODDY HILL
A41(T)
KING CHARLES ST
ALBERT ST
Museum (Natural History)
Sch
PARK ST
CARPENTERS YD
PARK RD
1 HARROW YD
2 THE TERRACE
3 MANSARD CL
HASTOE LA
A41(T)
THE TWIST
Langton Wood
Tring Park
FOX RD
FOX CL
Wigginton
HEMP LA
VICARAGE RD
HIGHFIELD RD
THE FIRS
Hill Green Farm
Sch
Bull's Wood
COMMON FIELD
FIELDWAY
THE BIT
CHESHAM RD
BELMERS RD
POLLYWICK RD
GRIMS DYKE RD
OSBORNE WAY
WICK RD
HASTOE HILL
MARLIN HILL

120

not continued, see key diagram

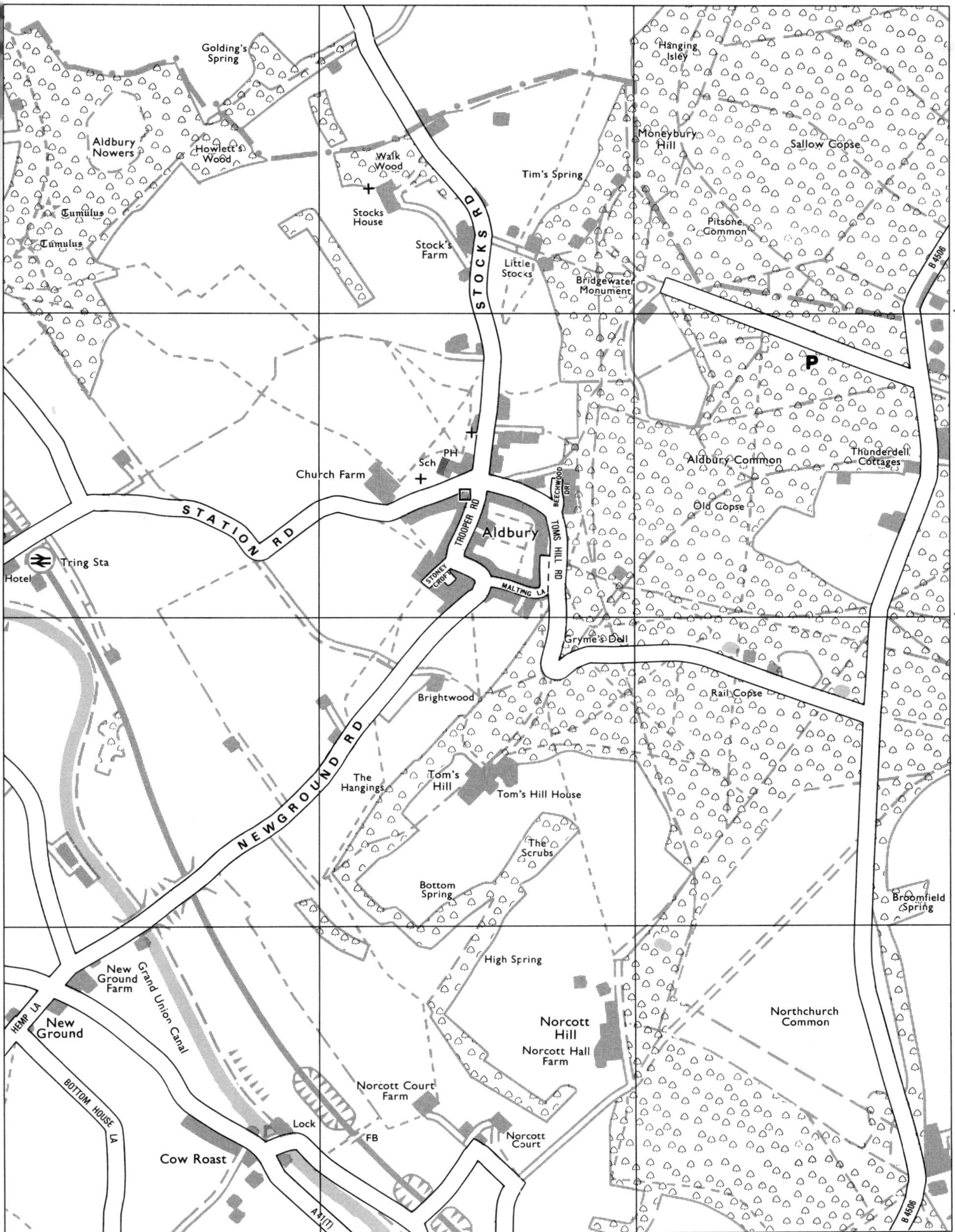

102

121

81

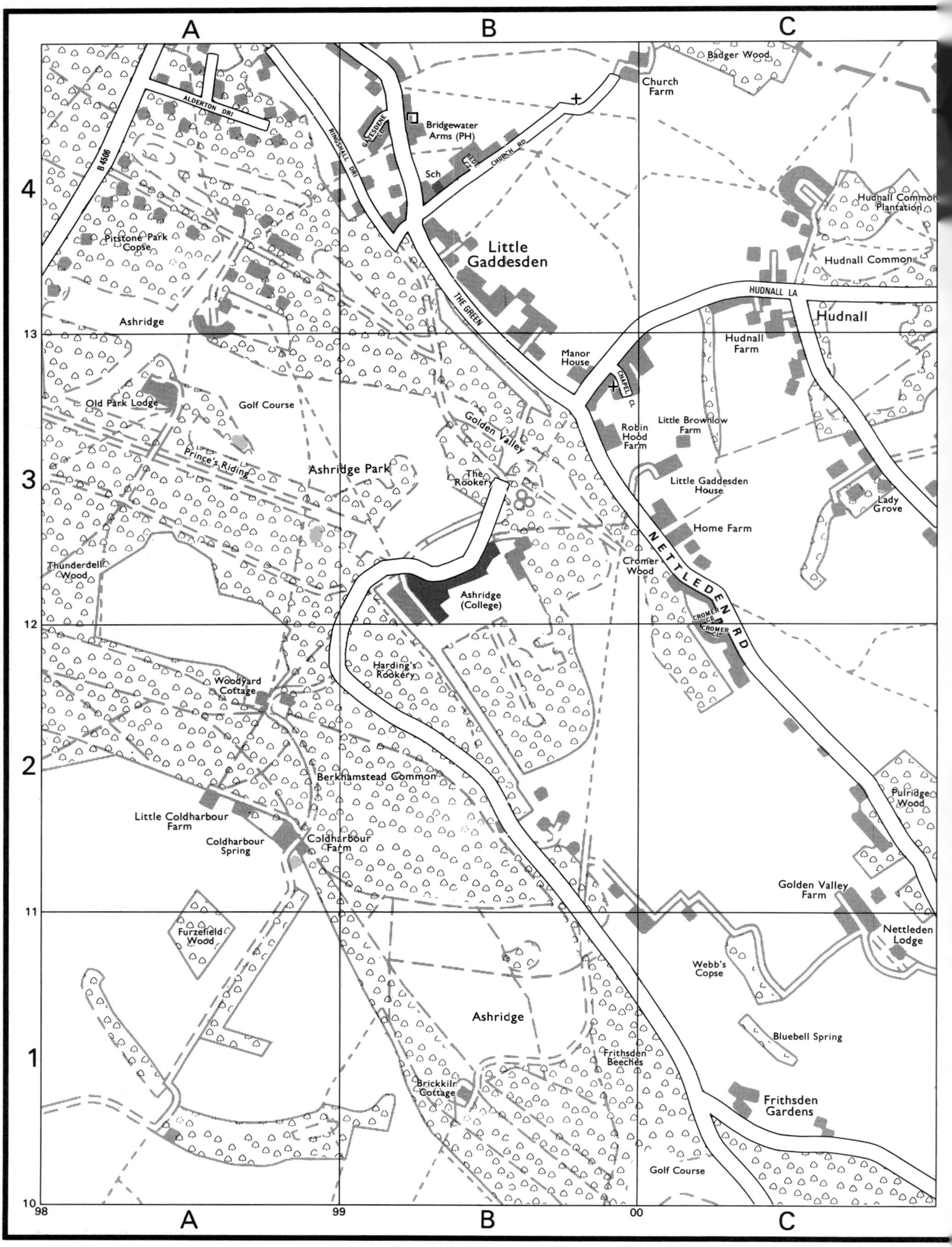
A
B
C
4
3
2
1
13
12
11
10
98
99
00
Badger Wood
Church Farm
ALDERTON DRI
B 4506
RINGSHALL DRI
GATESDENE CL
Bridgewater Arms (PH)
BEDE CT
CHURCH RD
Sch
Hudnall Common Plantation
Pitstone Park Copse
Little Gaddesden
Hudnall Common
THE GREEN
HUDNALL LA
Hudnall
Ashridge
Hudnall Farm
Manor House
CHAPEL CL
Old Park Lodge
Golf Course
Little Brownlow Farm
Robin Hood Farm
Golden Valley
Prince's Riding
Ashridge Park
The Rookery
Little Gaddesden House
Lady Grove
Home Farm
NETTLEDEN RD
Thunderdell Wood
Cromer Wood
Ashridge (College)
CROMER CL
Harding's Rookery
Woodyard Cottage
Berkhamstead Common
Pulridge Wood
Little Coldharbour Farm
Coldharbour Spring
Coldharbour Farm
Golden Valley Farm
Furzefield Wood
Nettleden Lodge
Webb's Copse
Ashridge
Bluebell Spring
Frithsden Beeches
Brickkiln Cottage
Frithsden Gardens
Golf Course

101

122

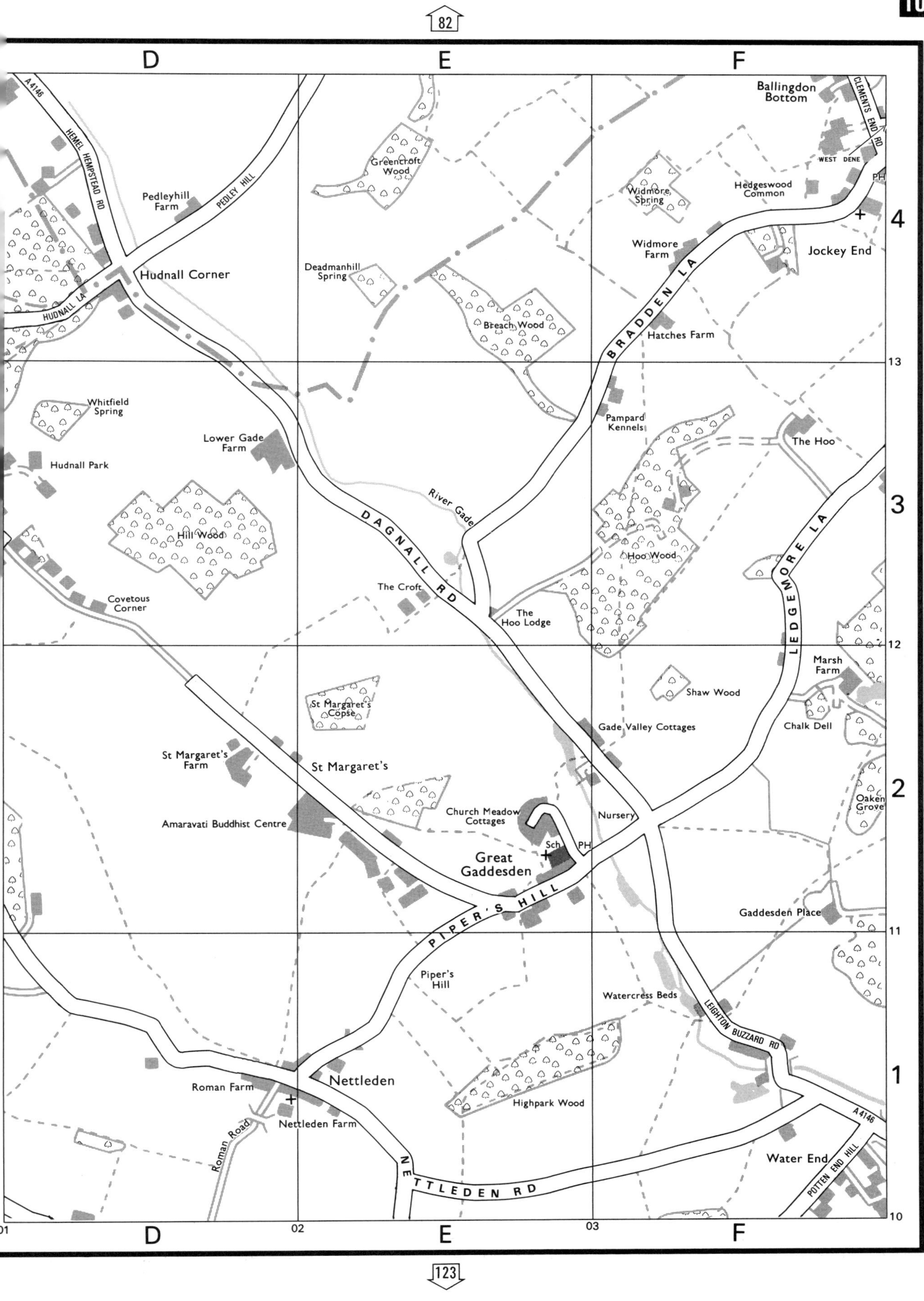
82
D
E
F
A4146
HEMEL HEMPSTEAD RD
Pedleyhill Farm
PEDLEY HILL
Hudnall Corner
HUDNALL LA
Greencroft Wood
Deadmanhill Spring
Breach Wood
Ballingdon Bottom
CLEMENTS END RD
WEST DENE
PH
Hedgeswood Common
Widmore Spring
Widmore Farm
Jockey End
BRADDEN LA
Hatches Farm
4
13
Whitfield Spring
Lower Gade Farm
Hudnall Park
Hill Wood
Pampard Kennels
The Hoo
River Gade
DAGNALL RD
Hoo Wood
LEDGEMORE LA
3
The Croft
Covetous Corner
The Hoo Lodge
12
104
Marsh Farm
Shaw Wood
St Margaret's Copse
Gade Valley Cottages
Chalk Dell
St Margaret's Farm
St Margaret's
2
Oaken Grove
Church Meadow Cottages
Nursery
Amaravati Buddhist Centre
Sch
PH
Great Gaddesden
PIPER'S HILL
Gaddesden Place
11
Piper's Hill
Watercress Beds
LEIGHTON BUZZARD RD
1
Roman Farm
Nettleden
Highpark Wood
A4146
Nettleden Farm
Roman Road
NETTLEDEN RD
Water End
POTTEN END HILL
10
01
02
03
123

83

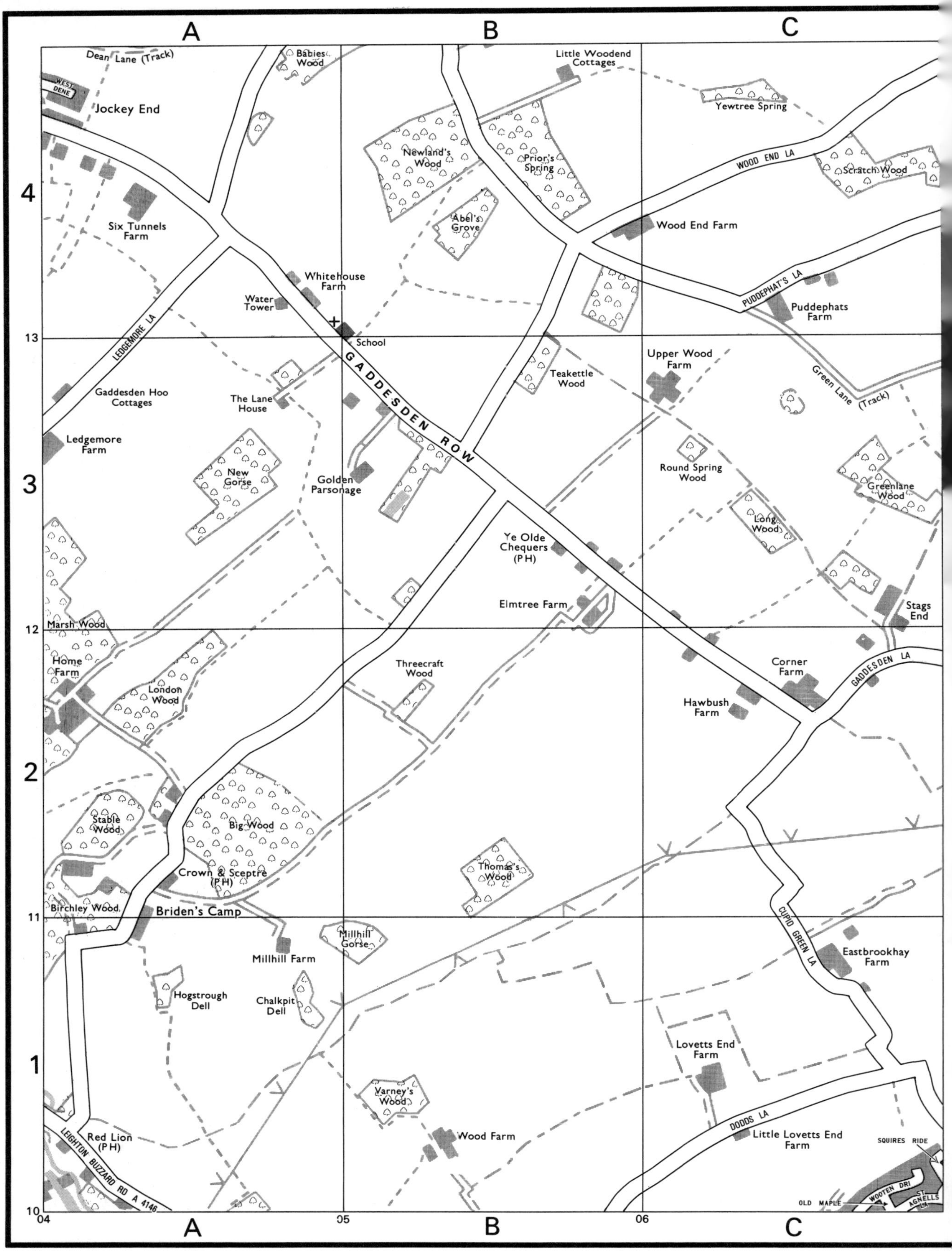
A
B
C
Dean Lane (Track)
Babies Wood
Little Woodend Cottages
West Dene
Jockey End
Yewtree Spring
Newland's Wood
Prior's Spring
Wood End La
Scratch Wood
Abel's Grove
Six Tunnels Farm
Wood End Farm
Whitehouse Farm
Water Tower
Puddephat's La
Puddephats Farm
School
Ledgemore La
Gaddesden Row
Teakettle Wood
Upper Wood Farm
Green Lane (Track)
Gaddesden Hoo Cottages
The Lane House
Ledgemore Farm
Round Spring Wood
New Gorse
Golden Parsonage
Greenlane Wood
Long Wood
Ye Olde Chequers (PH)
Elmtree Farm
Stags End
Marsh Wood
Home Farm
London Wood
Threecraft Wood
Corner Farm
Gaddesden La
Hawbush Farm
Stable Wood
Big Wood
Thomas's Wood
Crown & Sceptre (PH)
Birchley Wood
Briden's Camp
Cupid Green La
Millhill Gorse
Millhill Farm
Eastbrookhay Farm
Hogstrough Dell
Chalkpit Dell
Lovetts End Farm
Varney's Wood
Dodds La
Red Lion (PH)
Wood Farm
Little Lovetts End Farm
Squires Ride
Leighton Buzzard Rd A 4146
Wooten Dri
Old Maple
St Agnells La
4
13
3
12
2
11
1
10
04
05
06

103

124

84

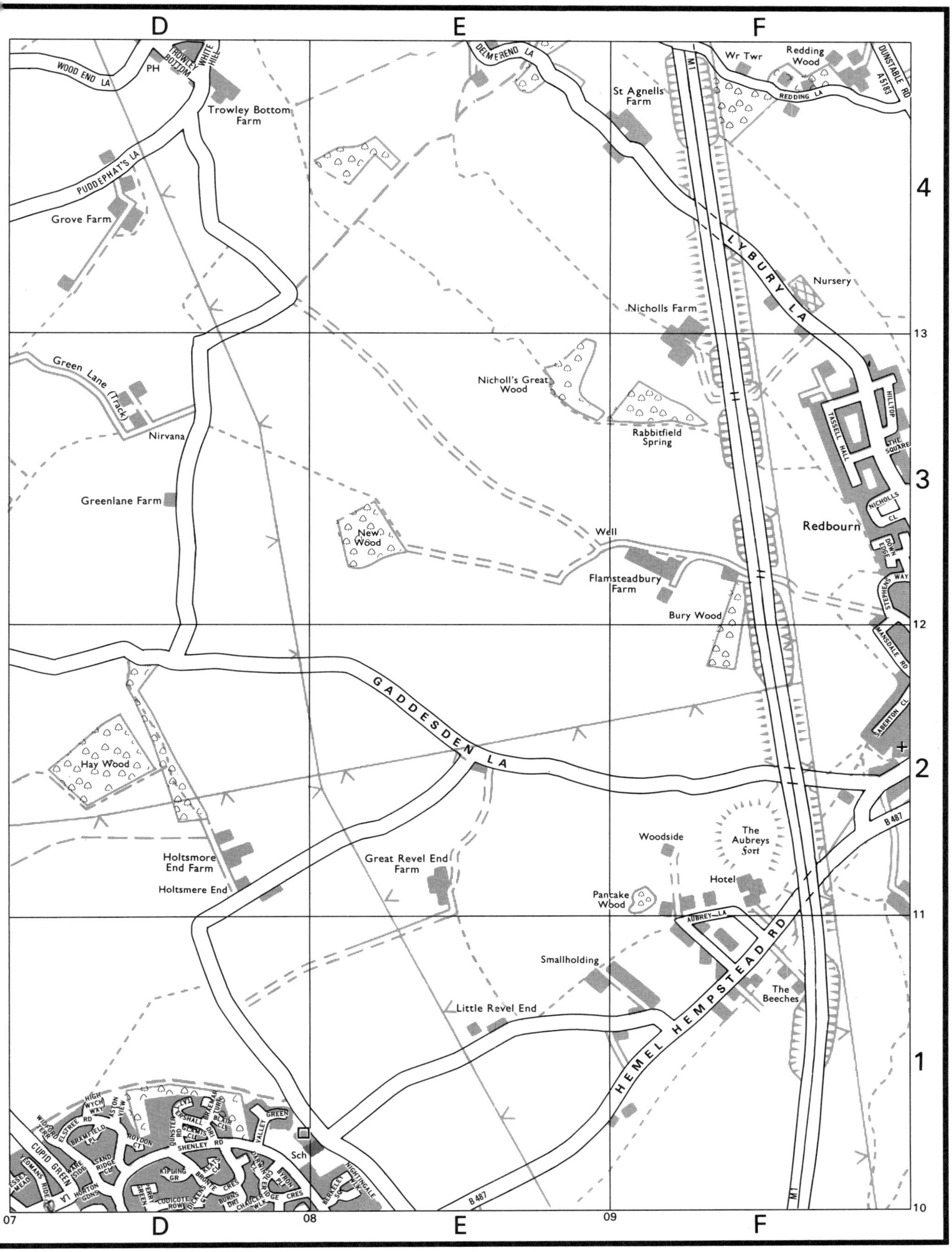
D
E
F
WOOD END LA
PH
TROWLEY BOTTOM
WHITE HILL
Trowley Bottom Farm
DELMEREND LA
St Agnells Farm
M1
Wr Twr
Redding Wood
REDDING LA
DUNSTABLE RD
A5183
PUDDEPHAT'S LA
Grove Farm
4
LYBURY LA
Nursery
Nicholls Farm
13
Green Lane (Track)
Nirvana
Nicholl's Great Wood
Rabbitfield Spring
TASSELL HALL
HILLTOP
THE SQUARE
3
Greenlane Farm
New Wood
Well
NICHOLLS CL
Redbourn
DOWN EDGE
Flamsteadbury Farm
STEPHENS WAY
Bury Wood
12
MANSDALE RD
GADDESDEN LA
SABERTON CL
Hay Wood
2
B 487
Woodside
The Aubreys Fort
Holtsmore End Farm
Great Revel End Farm
Holtsmere End
Pancake Wood
Hotel
11
AUBREY LA
HEMEL HEMPSTEAD RD
Smallholding
The Beeches
Little Revel End
1
HIGH WYCH WAY
ASTON VIEW
WIDFORD TERR
ELSTREE RD
BRAMFIELD PL
ROYDON CT
DUNSTER RD
BRAEMAR
BLAIR CL
GLAMIS CL
VALLEY GREEN
SHENLEY RD
Sch
CUPID GREEN LA
YEOMANS RIDE
ESSEX MEAD
WAKE SIDE
SAND RIDGE CL
HORTON GDNS
KIPLING GR
PERRY GREEN
CUDICOTE ROW
BRONTE CRES
KEATS CL
DICKENS GT
BURNS DRI
CHAUCER WLK
RIDGE CRES
BYRON PL
DARWIN CL
BERKELEY SQ
NIGHTINGALE WLK
B 487
M1
10
07
08
09

106

125

85

105

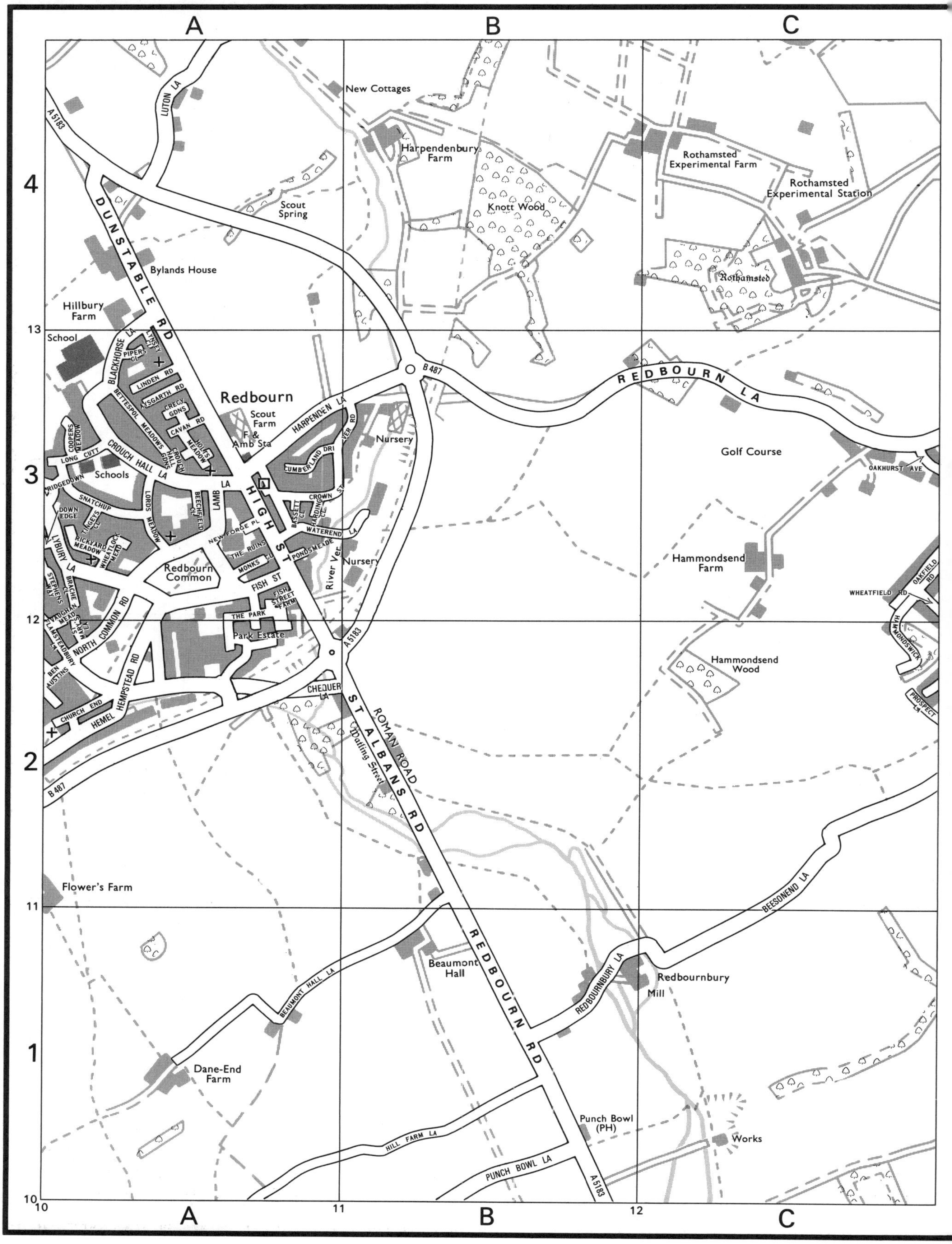
A
B
C
4
3
2
1
13
12
11
10
10
11
12
New Cottages
Harpendenbury Farm
Knott Wood
Rothamsted Experimental Farm
Rothamsted Experimental Station
Rothamsted
Scout Spring
Bylands House
Hillbury Farm
School
Redbourn
Scout Farm
F & Amb Sta
Nursery
Schools
Redbourn Common
Park Estate
Golf Course
Hammondsend Farm
Hammondsend Wood
Flower's Farm
Beaumont Hall
Redbournbury
Mill
Dane-End Farm
Punch Bowl (PH)
Works
LUTON LA
A 5183
DUNSTABLE RD
B 487
REDBOURN LA
HARPENDEN LA
HIGH ST
CROUCH HALL LA
BLACKHORSE LA
PIPERS CL
LINDEN RD
AYSGARTH RD
CRECY GDNS
CAVAN RD
BETTESPOL MEADOWS
CROUCH HALL GDNS
HOLTS MEADOW
COOPERS MEADOW
LONG CUTT
RIDGEDOWN
SNATCHUP
DOWN EDGE
TINGEYS CL
LORDS MEADOW
BEECHFIELD CL
LAMB LA
CUMBERLAND DRI
CROWN ST
BASSETT CL
HARDING CL
WATEREND LA
NEW FORGE PL
THE RUINS
PONDSMEADE
MONKS CL
FISH ST
FISH STREET FARM
THE PARK
River Ver
LYBURY LA
RICKYARD MEADOW
WHEATLOCK MEAD
STEPHENS WAY
BRACHE CL
VAUGHAN MEAD
FLAMSTEADBURY LA
NORTH COMMON RD
BEN AUSTINS
CHURCH END
HEMEL HEMPSTEAD RD
CHEQUER LA
ST ALBANS RD
ROMAN ROAD
Watling Street
OAKHURST AVE
WHEATFIELD RD
OAKFIELD RD
HAMMONDSWICK
PROSPECT LA
BEESONEND LA
REDBOURN RD
REDBOURNBURY LA
BEAUMONT HALL LA
HILL FARM LA
PUNCH BOWL LA
A
B
C

126

86

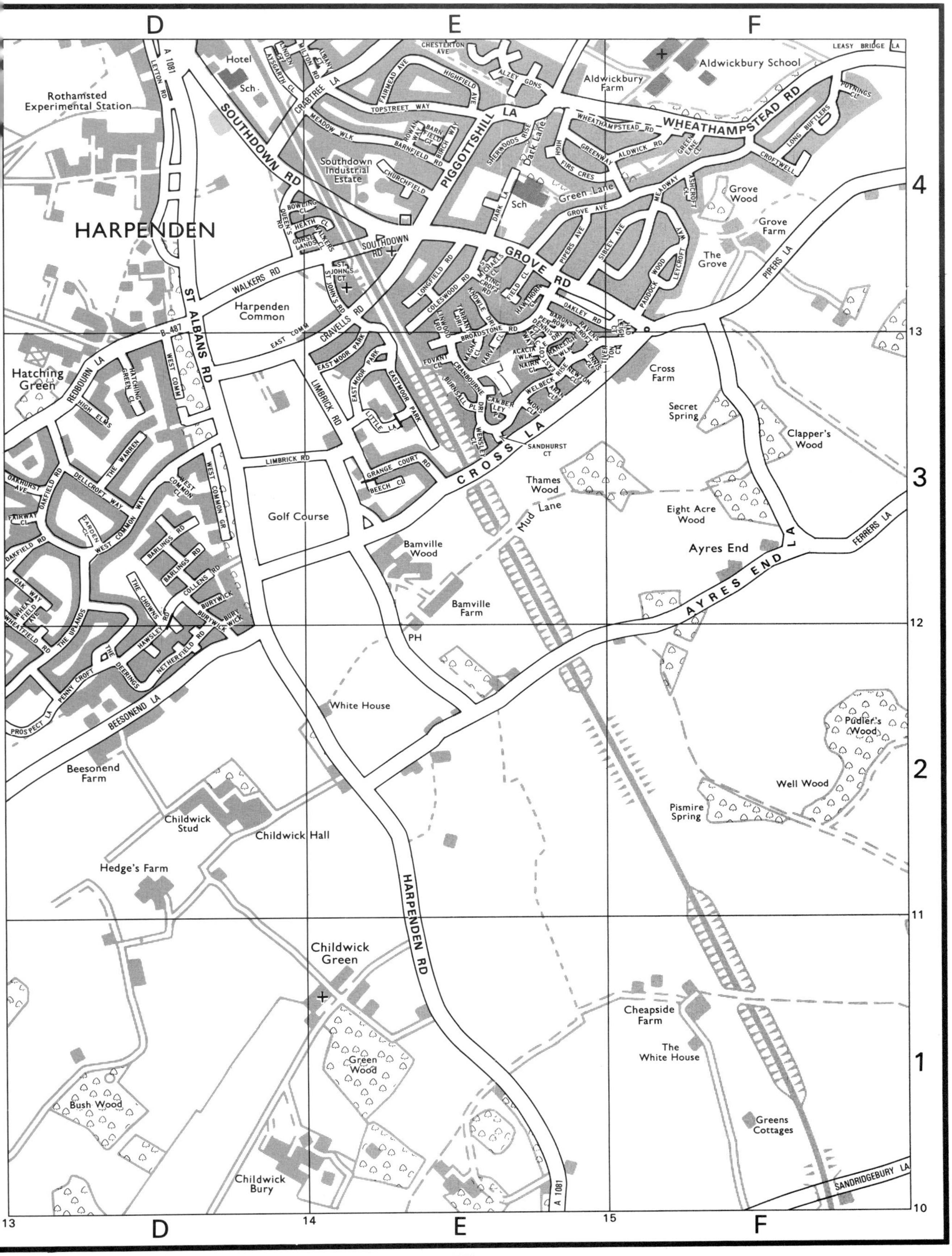

D
E
F
HARPENDEN
Rothamsted Experimental Station
Hotel
Sch.
Hatching Green
Harpenden Common
Golf Course
Southdown Industrial Estate
Aldwickbury School
Aldwickbury Farm
Grove Wood
Grove Farm
The Grove
Cross Farm
Secret Spring
Clapper's Wood
Thames Wood
Eight Acre Wood
Ayres End
Bamville Wood
Bamville Farm
PH
White House
Beesonend Farm
Childwick Stud
Childwick Hall
Hedge's Farm
Pudler's Wood
Well Wood
Pismire Spring
Childwick Green
Green Wood
Bush Wood
Childwick Bury
Cheapside Farm
The White House
Greens Cottages
Sch
Dark Lane
Green Lane
Mud Lane
SOUTHDOWN RD
PIGGOTTSHILL LA
WHEATHAMPSTEAD RD
GROVE RD
ST ALBANS RD
WALKERS RD
CROSS LA
AYRES END LA
HARPENDEN RD
BEESONEND LA
REDBOURN LA
LIMBRICK RD
FERRERS LA
PIPERS LA
SANDRIDGEBURY LA
LEASY BRIDGE LA
A 1081
B 487
4
3
2
1
13
12
11
10
14
15

108

127

87

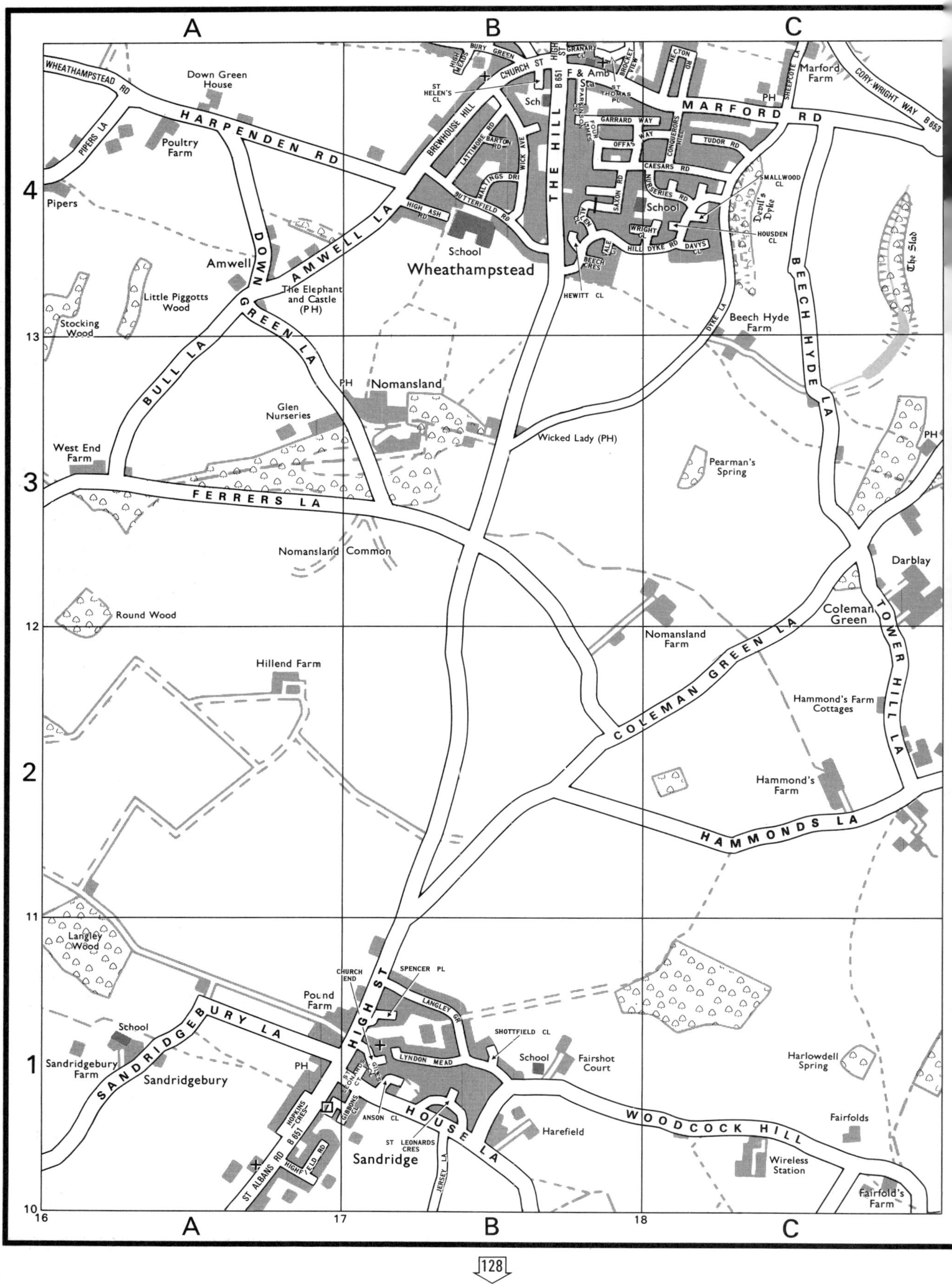

A
B
C
4
13
3
12
2
11
1
10
16
17
18
WHEATHAMPSTEAD RD
Down Green House
HARPENDEN RD
PIPERS LA
Poultry Farm
Pipers
Amwell
DOWN GREEN LA
AMWELL LA
HIGH ASH RD
BUTTERFIELD RD
MALTINGS DRI
LATTIMORE RD
BARTON RD
WICK AVE
BREWHOUSE HILL
CHURCH ST
ST HELEN'S CL
HIGH MEADS
BURY GREEN
HIGH ST
GRANARY CL
BROCKET VIEW
NECTON RD
F & Amb Sta
ST THOMAS PL
Sch
B 651
THE HILL
PARKINSON CL
FOUR LIMES
GARRARD WAY
OFFA'S WAY
CONQUERORS HILL
CAESARS RD
NURSERIES RD
SAXON RD
TUDOR RD
MARFORD RD
SHEEPCOTE LA
Marford Farm
CORY-WRIGHT WAY
B 653
PH
SMALLWOOD CL
HOUSDEN CL
School
WRIGHT CL
HILL DYKE RD
DAVYS CL
VALE CT
BEECH CRES
HEWITT CL
School
Wheathampstead
Devil's Dyke
The Slad
Little Piggotts Wood
Stocking Wood
The Elephant and Castle (PH)
BEECH HYDE LA
DYKE LA
Beech Hyde Farm
BULL LA
PH
Nomansland
Glen Nurseries
Wicked Lady (PH)
West End Farm
Pearman's Spring
FERRERS LA
Nomansland Common
Darblay
Round Wood
Nomansland Farm
Coleman Green
TOWER HILL LA
COLEMAN GREEN LA
Hillend Farm
Hammond's Farm Cottages
Hammond's Farm
HAMMONDS LA
Langley Wood
CHURCH END
SPENCER PL
LANGLEY GR
Pound Farm
SHOTTFIELD CL
School
School
Fairshot Court
SANDRIDGEBURY LA
Sandridgebury Farm
Sandridgebury
PH
HIGH ST
LYNDON MEAD
ST LEONARDS CT
ST GILES
GIBBONS CL
ANSON CL
HOUSE LA
ST LEONARDS CRES
HOPKINS CRES
B 651
HIGHFIELD RD
ST ALBANS RD
Sandridge
JERSEY LA
Harefield
WOODCOCK HILL
Harlowdell Spring
Fairfolds
Wireless Station
Fairfold's Farm

107

128

88

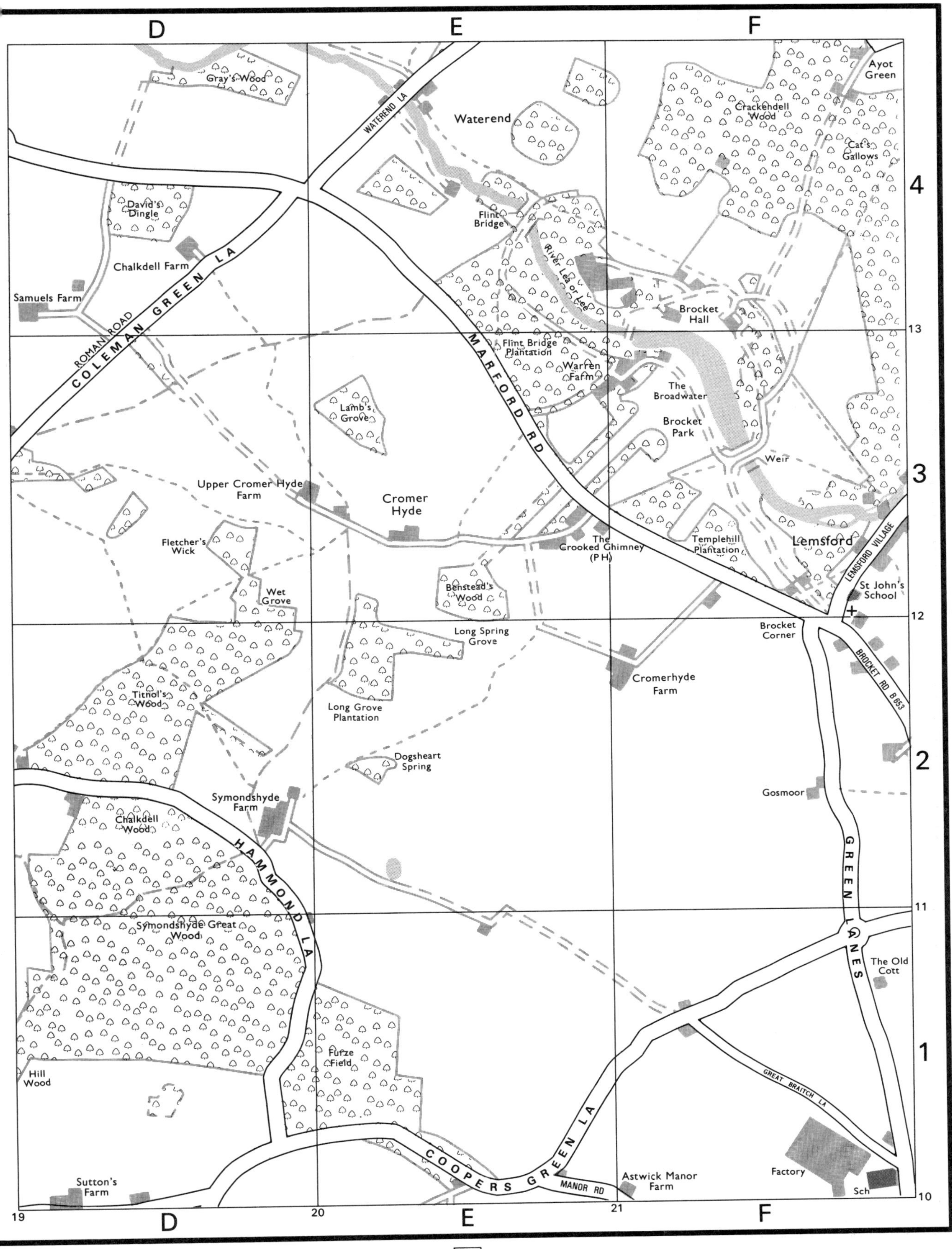
D
E
F
Gray's Wood
WATEREND LA
Waterend
Ayot Green
Crackendell Wood
Cat's Gallows
4
David's Dingle
Flint Bridge
River Lea or Lee
Chalkdell Farm
COLEMAN GREEN LA
Samuels Farm
ROMAN ROAD
Brocket Hall
13
MARFORD RD
Flint Bridge Plantation
Warren Farm
The Broadwater
Lamb's Grove
Brocket Park
Weir
3
Upper Cromer Hyde Farm
Cromer Hyde
Fletcher's Wick
The Crooked Chimney (PH)
Templehill Plantation
Lemsford
LEMSFORD VILLAGE
Wet Grove
Benstead's Wood
St John's School
12
Long Spring Grove
Brocket Corner
BROCKET RD B653
Titnol's Wood
Cromerhyde Farm
Long Grove Plantation
Dogsheart Spring
2
Gosmoor
Symondshyde Farm
Chalkdell Wood
HAMMOND LA
GREEN LANES
11
Symondshyde Great Wood
The Old Cott
1
Furze Field
Hill Wood
GREAT BRAITCH LA
COOPERS GREEN LA
Factory
Sutton's Farm
Astwick Manor Farm
MANOR RD
Sch
10
19
20
21
D
E
F

110

129

89

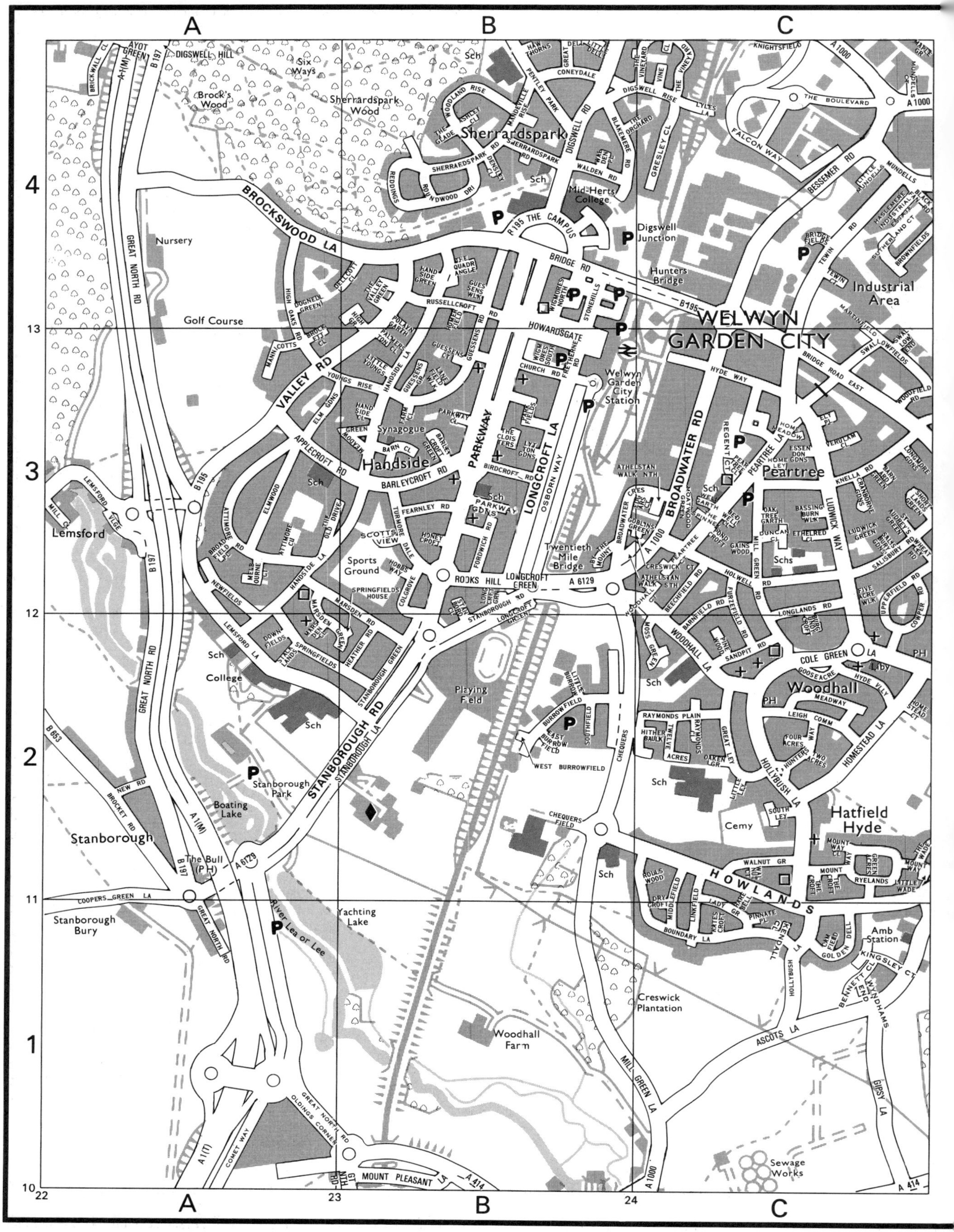
A
B
C
4
3
2
1
13
12
11
10
22
23
24
Six Ways
Brock's Wood
Sherrardspark Wood
Sherrardspark
BROCKSWOOD LA
Nursery
Golf Course
GREAT NORTH RD
DIGSWELL HILL
AYOT GREEN
BRICKWALL CL
B 197
Sch
Mid-Herts College
B195 THE CAMPUS
Digswell Junction
Hunters Bridge
BRIDGE RD
WELWYN GARDEN CITY
Industrial Area
THE BOULEVARD
A 1000
FALCON WAY
BESSEMER RD
KNIGHTSFIELD
CONEYDALE
DIGSWELL RISE
DIGSWELL RD
WALDEN RD
BLAKEMERE RD
GRESLEY CL
SHERRARDSPARK RD
ROUNDWOOD DRI
REDDINGS
RUSSELLCROFT
HOWARDSGATE
CHURCH RD
STONEHILLS
VALLEY RD
YOUNGS RISE
ELM GDNS
Synagogue
APPLECROFT RD
Handside
BARLEYCROFT RD
PARKWAY
LONGCROFT LA
OSBORN WAY
BIRDCROFT RD
FEARNLEY RD
Welwyn Garden City Station
HYDE WAY
BROADWATER RD
Peartree
PEARTREE LA
LUDWICK WAY
KNELLA RD
Lemsford
B 195
ELMWOOD
ATTIMORE RD
Sch
Scotts View
Sports Ground
SPRINGFIELDS HOUSE
ROOKS HILL
LONGCROFT GREEN
A 6129
Twentieth Mile Bridge
ATHELSTAN WALK NTH
A 1000
Schs
HOLWELL RD
LONGLANDS RD
COLE GREEN LA
Woodhall
WOODHALL LA
NEWFIELDS
LEMSFORD LA
SPRINGFIELDS
HEATHER RD
STANBOROUGH GREEN
STANBOROUGH RD
STANBOROUGH LA
College
Playing Field
BURROWFIELD
WEST BURROWFIELD
CHEQUERS
HOLLYBUSH LA
HOMESTEAD LA
Hatfield Hyde
Cemy
B 653
NEW RD
BROCKET RD
Stanborough
Stanborough Park
Boating Lake
The Bull (PH)
A1(M)
A 6129
COOPERS GREEN LA
Stanborough Bury
River Lea or Lee
Yachting Lake
HOWLANDS
WALNUT GR
RYELANDS
BOUNDARY LA
GOLDEN DELL
KINGSLEY CT
Amb Station
Creswick Plantation
ASCOTS LA
Woodhall Farm
MILL GREEN LA
GIPSY LA
A 1(T)
COMET WAY
OLDINGS CORNER
MOUNT PLEASANT LA
A 414
Sewage Works
A 1000

109

130

90

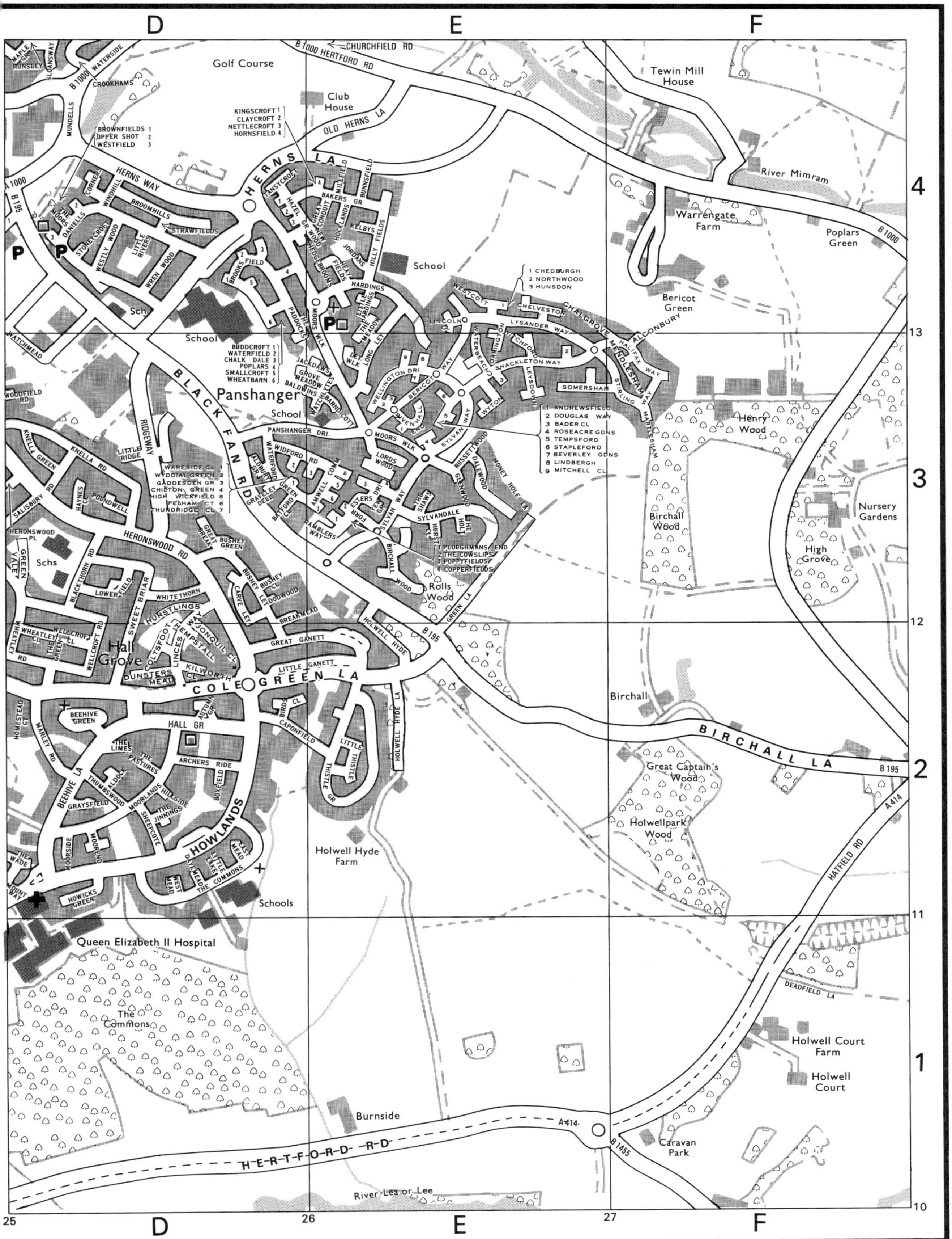
D
E
F
Golf Course
Club House
Tewin Mill House
River Mimram
Warrengate Farm
Poplars Green
School
Bericot Green
Sch
School
Panshanger
School
Henry Wood
Nursery Gardens
Birchall Wood
High Grove
Schs
Rolls Wood
Hall Grove
Birchall
BIRCHALL LA
Great Captain's Wood
Holwellpark Wood
Holwell Hyde Farm
Schools
Queen Elizabeth II Hospital
The Commons
Holwell Court Farm
Holwell Court
Burnside
Caravan Park
HERTFORD RD
River Lea or Lee
HATFIELD RD
DEADFIELD LA
HERNS LA
BLACK FAN RD
COLE GREEN LA
HOWLANDS
B 1000 HERTFORD RD
CHURCHFIELD RD
OLD HERNS LA
HERNS WAY
KINGSCROFT 1
CLAYCROFT 2
NETTLECROFT 3
HORNSFIELD 4
BROWNFIELDS 1
UPPER SHOT 2
WESTFIELD 3
1 CHEDBURGH
2 NORTHWOOD
3 HUNSDON
BUDDCROFT 1
WATERFIELD 2
CHALK DALE 3
POPLARS 4
SMALLCROFT 5
WHEATBARN 6
1 ANDREWSFIELD
2 DOUGLAS WAY
3 BADER CL
4 ROSEACRE GDNS
5 TEMPSFORD
6 STAPLEFORD
7 BEVERLEY GDNS
8 LINDBERGH
9 MITCHELL CL
WARESIDE CL 1
WYDDIAL GREEN 2
GADDESDEN GR 3
CHILTON GREEN 4
HIGH WICKFIELD 5
PEDHAM CT 6
THUNDRIDGE CL 7
1 PLOUGHMANS END
2 THE COWSLIPS
3 POPPYFIELDS
4 COPPERFIELDS
4
3
2
1
13
12
11
10
25
26
27
B 1000
B 195
A 414
B 1455
A 1000

112

131

91

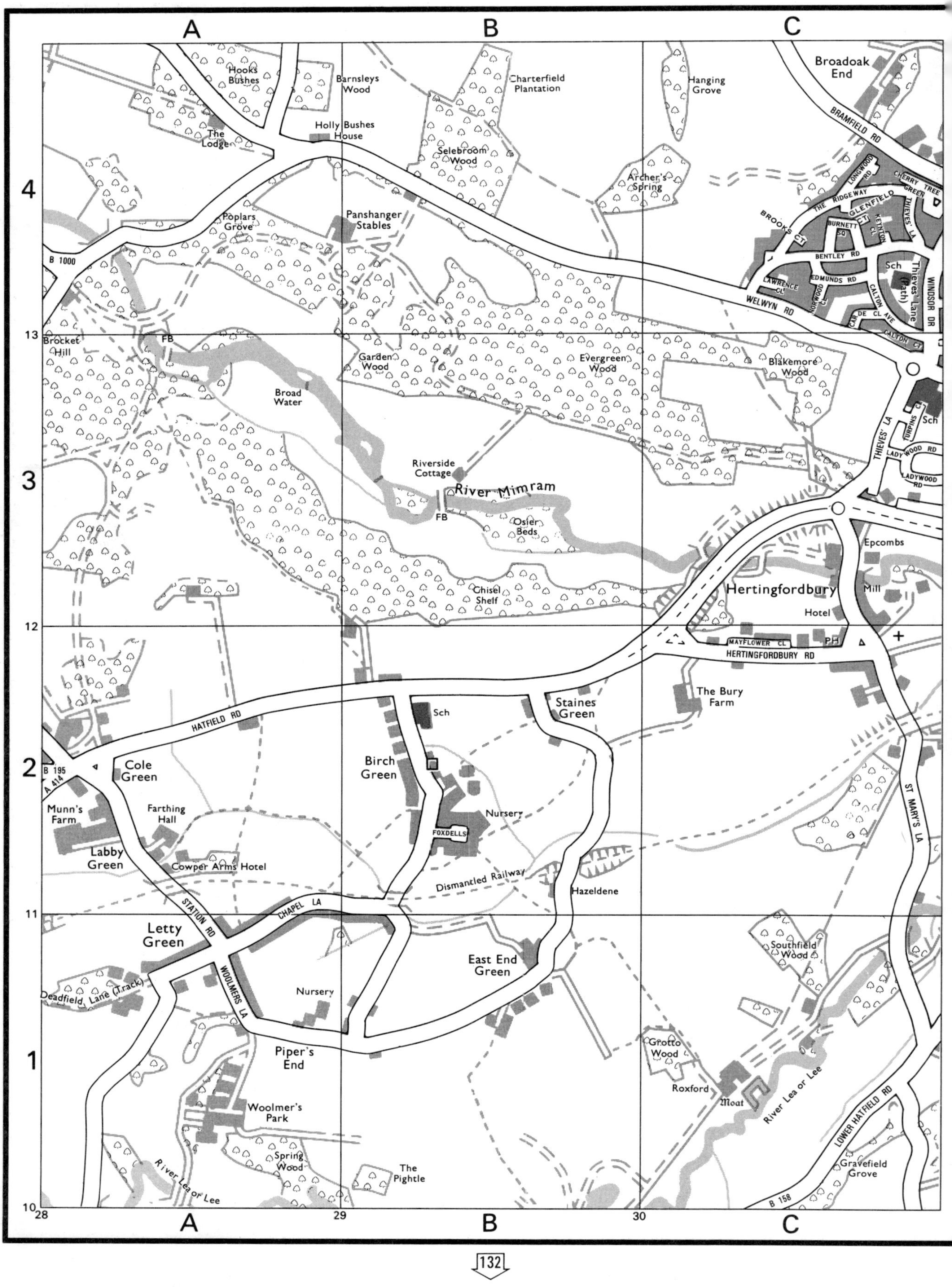
A
B
C
4
3
2
1
13
12
11
10
28
29
30
Hooks Bushes
Barnsleys Wood
Charterfield Plantation
Hanging Grove
Broadoak End
BRAMFIELD RD
Holly Bushes House
The Lodge
Selebroom Wood
Archer's Spring
LONGWOOD RD
CHERRY TREE GREEN
THE RIDGEWAY
GLENFIELD CT
BROOKS CT
BURNETT SQ
KEYNTON CL
THIEVES LA
Panshanger Stables
Poplars Grove
BENTLEY RD
B 1000
LAWRENCE CL
EDMUNDS RD
NORWOOD CL
Sch
Thieves Lane (Path)
WINDSOR DR
CALTON AVE
CAR DE CL
CALTON CT
WELWYN RD
Brocket Hill
FB
Garden Wood
Evergreen Wood
Blakemore Wood
Broad Water
TURPINS CL
Sch
THIEVES' LA
LADY WOOD RD
LADYWOOD RD
Riverside Cottage
River Mimram
FB
Osier Beds
Epcombs
Hertingfordbury
Mill
Chisel Shelf
Hotel
MAYFLOWER CL
PH
HERTINGFORDBURY RD
The Bury Farm
HATFIELD RD
Sch
Staines Green
B 195
A 414
Cole Green
Birch Green
ST MARY'S LA
Munn's Farm
Farthing Hall
Nursery
FOXDELLS
Labby Green
Cowper Arms Hotel
Dismantled Railway
Hazeldene
STATION RD
CHAPEL LA
Letty Green
Southfield Wood
WOOLMERS LA
East End Green
Deadfield Lane (Track)
Nursery
Piper's End
Grotto Wood
Roxford
Moat
River Lea or Lee
LOWER HATFIELD RD
Woolmer's Park
River Lea or Lee
Spring Wood
The Pightle
Gravefield Grove
B 158

111

132

92

D
E
F
HERTFORD
Bengeo
Bengeo Hall
Hertford North Station
Hertford East Station
Hertford County Hospital
County Hall
Crown Court
Cattle Market
Balls Park (University)
Cemy
River Beane
River Mimram
River Lea or Lee
River Lee Navigation
Terrace Wood
Nursery
School
Schools
Dunkirks Farm
Swallow Grove Farm
Ducketts Cottages
Home Farm
Brickendonbury
Brickendon Brook
Thrift Cottages
Sailor's Grove
Bayford Brook
Bayfordbury Park Farm
Bayfordbury (Polytechnic)
NORTH RD
WELWYN RD
BRAMFIELD RD
HERTINGFORDBURY RD
LONDON RD
WARE RD
MANGROVE RD
MANGROVE LA
BRICKENDON LA
LOWER HATFIELD RD
BENGEO ST
PORT HILL
BEANE RD
MEAD LA
GASCOYNE WAY
BULLOCK'S LA
HIGHFIELD RD
FORE ST
A119
A414
B158
B1000
B1197
B1502
4
3
2
1
13
12
11
10
31
32
33

114

133

93

113

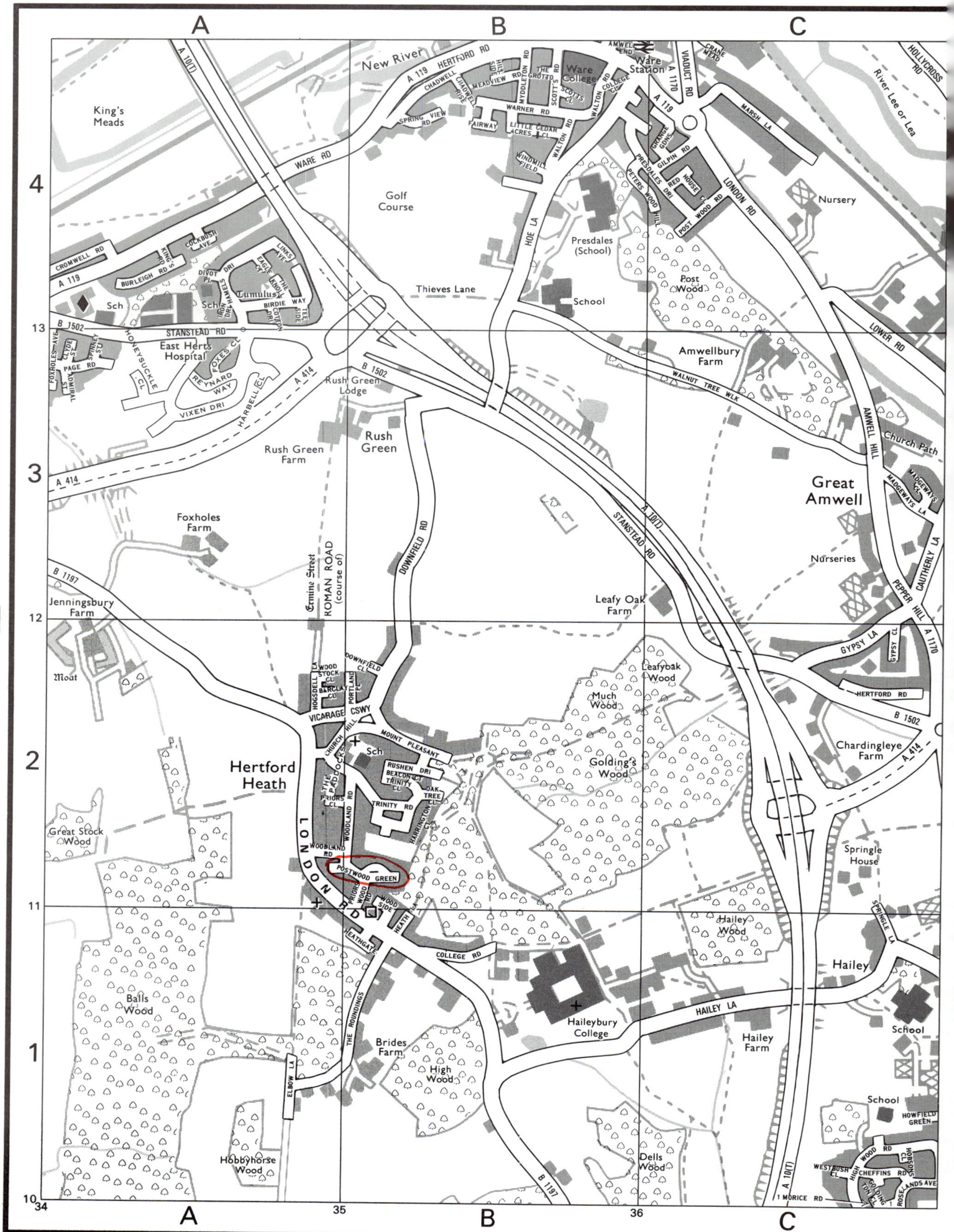
A
B
C
4
3
2
1
13
12
11
10
34
35
36
New River
King's Meads
WARE RD
A 119
A 10(T)
HERTFORD RD
CHADWELL
SPRING VIEW RD
MEADVIEW RD
MYDDLETON RD
THE GROTTO
Ware College
SCOTT'S RD
SCOTTS CL
WARNER RD
FAIRWAY
LITTLE ACRES
CEDAR CL
WINDMILL FIELD
WALTON RD
COLLEGE CL
Ware Station
AMWELL END
VIADUCT RD
A 1170
CRANE MEAD
MARSH LA
HOLLYCROSS RD
River Lee or Lea
GRANGE GDNS
GILPIN RD
RED HOUSE CL
PRESDALES DRI
PETERS WOOD HILL
POST WOOD RD
LONDON RD
Nursery
Golf Course
HOE LA
Presdales (School)
School
Post Wood
Thieves Lane
CROMWELL RD
KING'S RD
COCKBUSH AVE
LINKS AVE
BURLEIGH RD
DIVOT PL
HAMELS DRI
EAGLE CL
THE KNOLL
Tumulus
IRON DRI
BIRDIE CL
COTTON DRI
WAY TEE SIDE
Sch
Sch
B 1502
STANSTEAD RD
FOXHOLES AVE
CLYDE ST
SPINNEY ST
PAGE RD
ADMIRAL ST
HONEYSUCKLE CL
East Herts Hospital
FOXES CL
REYNARD WAY
VIXEN DRI
HARBELL CL
A 414
Rush Green Lodge
Rush Green
Rush Green Farm
Amwellbury Farm
WALNUT TREE WLK
LOWER RD
AMWELL HILL
Church Path
Great Amwell
MADGEWAYS CL
MADGEWAYS LA
Nurseries
CAUTHERLY LA
PEPPER HILL
Foxholes Farm
Ermine Street
ROMAN ROAD (course of)
DOWNFIELD RD
STANSTEAD RD
Leafy Oak Farm
B 1197
Jenningsbury Farm
Moat
GYPSY LA
GYPSY CL
A 1170
HERTFORD RD
B 1502
Leafyoak Wood
Much Wood
DOWNFIELD CL
HOGSDELL LA
WOOD STOCK CL
BARCLAY CL
PORTLAND PL
VICARAGE CSWY
CHURCH HILL
MOUNT PLEASANT
Sch
Hertford Heath
THE PADDOCKS
RUSHEN DRI
BEACON CL
TRINITY CL
OAK TREE CL
TRINITY RD
PRIORS CL
WOODLAND RD
HARRINGTON CL
Golding's Wood
Chardingleye Farm
A 414
Great Stock Wood
WOODLAND RD
POSTWOOD GREEN
LONDON RD
PRIORS WOOD RD
WOOD SIDE
HEATH LA
HEATHGATE
COLLEGE RD
Springle House
Hailey Wood
SPRINGLE LA
Hailey
Balls Wood
THE ROUNDINGS
Haileybury College
HAILEY LA
School
Brides Farm
High Wood
Hailey Farm
ELBOW LA
School
HOWFIELD GREEN
Hobbyhorse Wood
B 1197
Dells Wood
A 10(T)
WESTBUSH CL
HIGH WOOD RD
CHEFFINS RD
HOBSONS CL
GOLDINGTON CL
ROSE ANDS AVE
MORICE RD

134

94

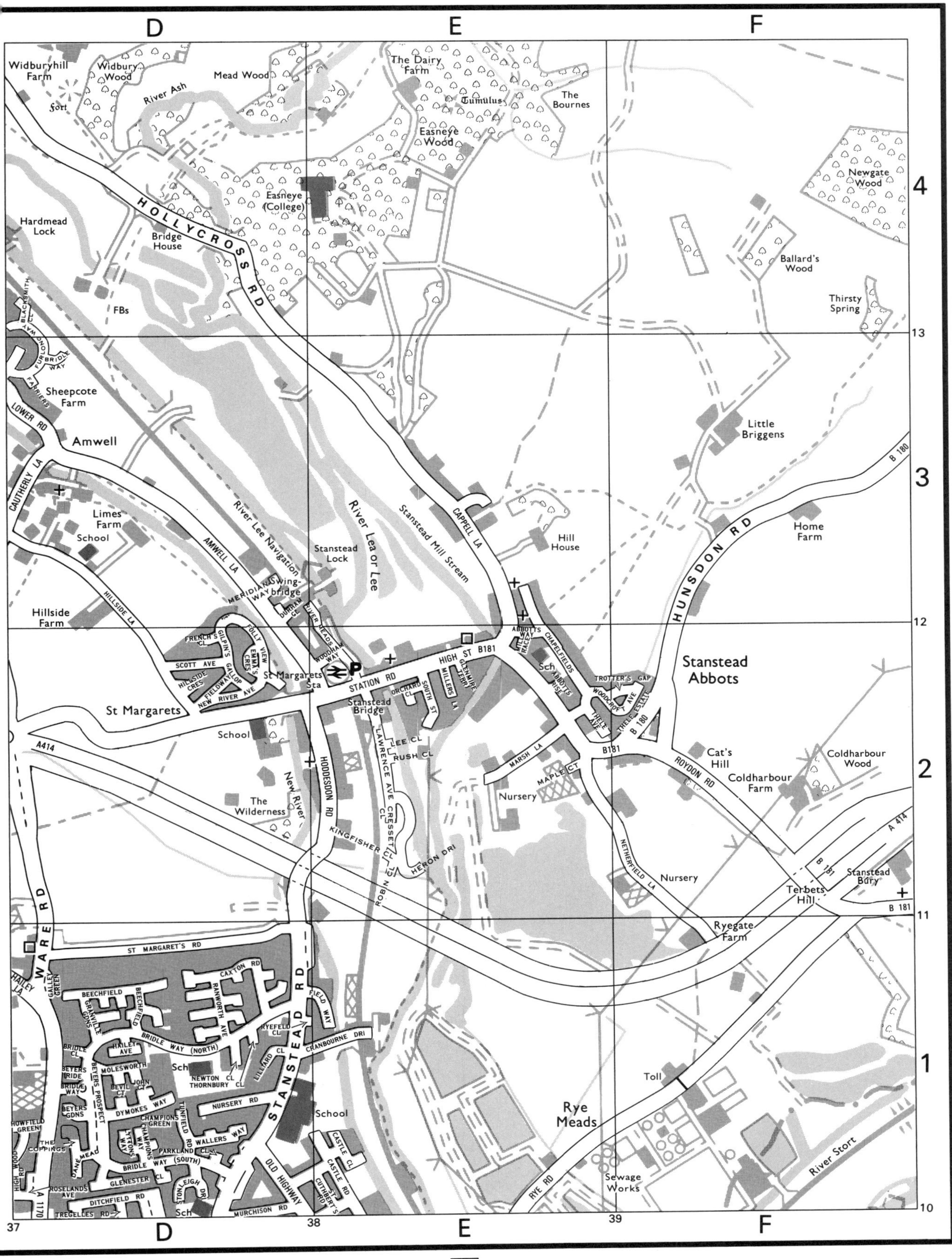
D
E
F
Widburyhill Farm
Widbury Wood
Mead Wood
River Ash
Fort
The Dairy Farm
Tumulus
The Bournes
Easneye Wood
Newgate Wood
4
Easneye (College)
Hardmead Lock
HOLLYCROSS RD
Bridge House
Ballard's Wood
Thirsty Spring
FBs
BLACKSMITH CL
FURLONG WAY
BRIDLE WAY
13
Sheepcote Farm
FARRIERS
LOWER RD
Amwell
Little Briggens
B 180
3
CAUTHERLY LA
Limes Farm
School
River Lee Navigation
River Lea or Lee
Stanstead Mill Stream
CAPPELL LA
Home Farm
HUNSDON RD
Hill House
AMWELL LA
Stanstead Lock
MERIDIAN WAY
Swing-bridge
DURHAM CL
RIVER MEADS
Hillside Farm
HILLSIDE LA
12
ABBOTTS WAY
CHAPELFIELDS
Stanstead Abbots
FRENCH'S CL
GILPIN'S GALLOP
FOLLY VIEW
EMMA'S CRES
SCOTT AVE
HILLSIDE CRES
FIELDWAY
NEW RIVER AVE
St Margarets Sta
WOODHAM WAY
STATION RD
HIGH ST B181
GLENMIRE TERR
MILLERS LA
ORCHARD CL
SOUTH ST
Sch
ABBOTTS RISE
TROTTER'S GAP
WOODCROFT AVE
THELE ESTATE
THELE AVE
B 180
St Margarets
School
Stanstead Bridge
LEE CL
RUSH CL
LAWRENCE AVE
A414
MARSH LA
B181
Cat's Hill
ROYDON RD
Coldharbour Wood
Coldharbour Farm
2
MAPLE CT
Nursery
HODDESDON RD
New River
The Wilderness
KINGFISHER
CRESSET CL
HERON DRI
ROBIN CL
NETHERFIELD LA
Nursery
A 414
B 181
Stanstead Bury
Terbets Hill
B 181
11
WARE RD
ST MARGARET'S RD
Ryegate Farm
HAILEY LA
GALLEY GREEN
CAXTON RD
BEECHFIELD
GRANVILLE GDNS
RANWORTH AVE
STANSTEAD RD
FIELD WAY
RYEFELD CL
HAILEY AVE
BRIDLE WAY (NORTH)
CRANBOURNE DRI
BRIDLE CL
BEYERS RIDE
MOLESWORTH
JOHN CL
LILLIARD CL
Sch
NEWTON CL
THORNBURY CL
1
BRIDLE WAY
BEVIL CT
BEYERS PROSPECT
Toll
BEYERS GDNS
DYMOKES WAY
NURSERY RD
School
Rye Meads
CHAMPIONS GREEN
TUNFIELD RD
HOWFIELD GREEN
THE COPPINGS
WALLERS WAY
PARKLAND CL
CASTLE CL
River Stort
DANE MEAD
BRIDLE WAY (SOUTH)
HIGH WOOD RD
ROSELANDS AVE
GLENESTER CL
OLD HIGHWAY
STONLEIGH DRI
ST CUTHBERT'S RD
RYE RD
Sewage Works
A 1170
DITCHFIELD RD
TREGELLES RD
Sch
MURCHISON RD
10
37
38
39

116

135

95

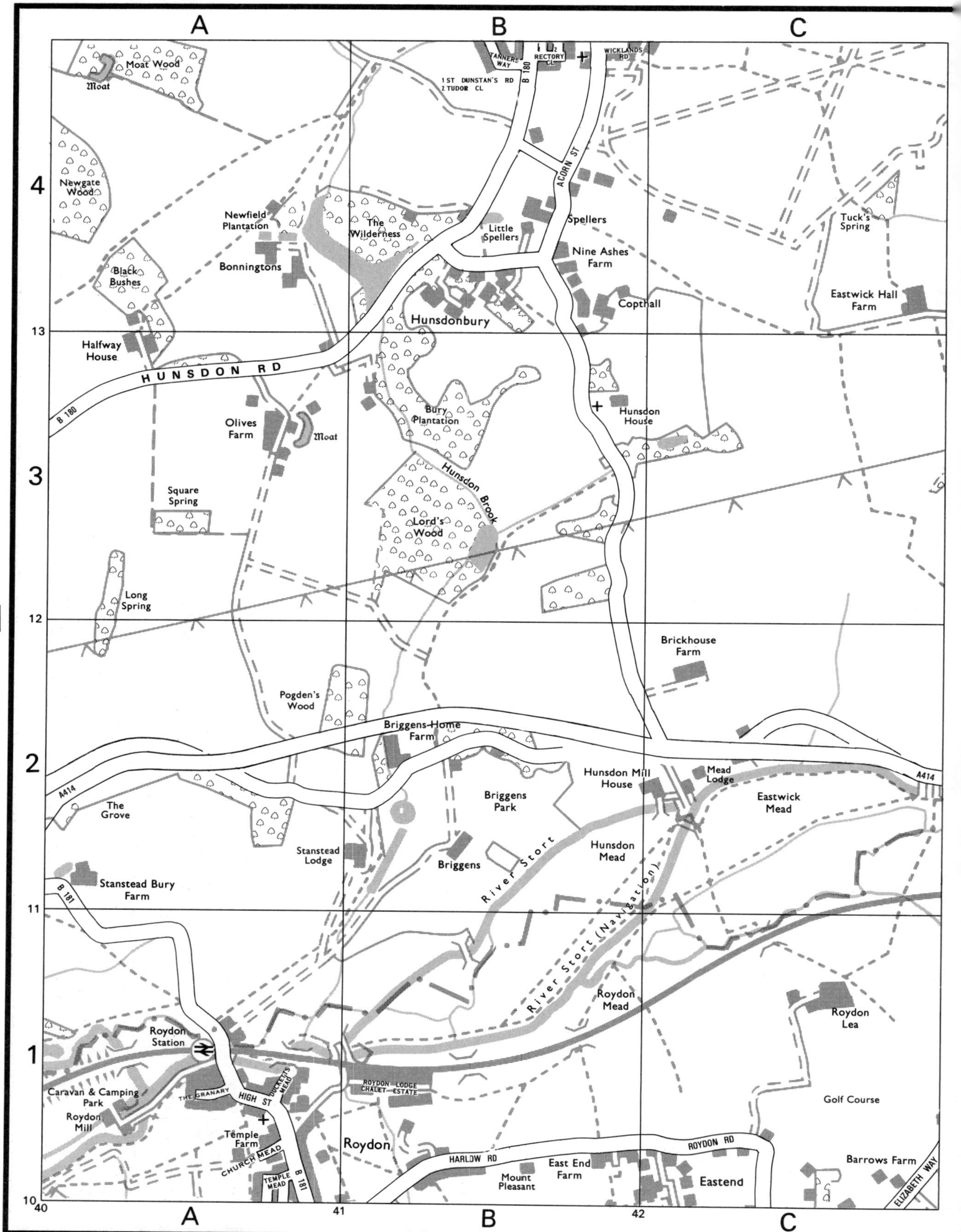

115

not continued, see key diagram

96

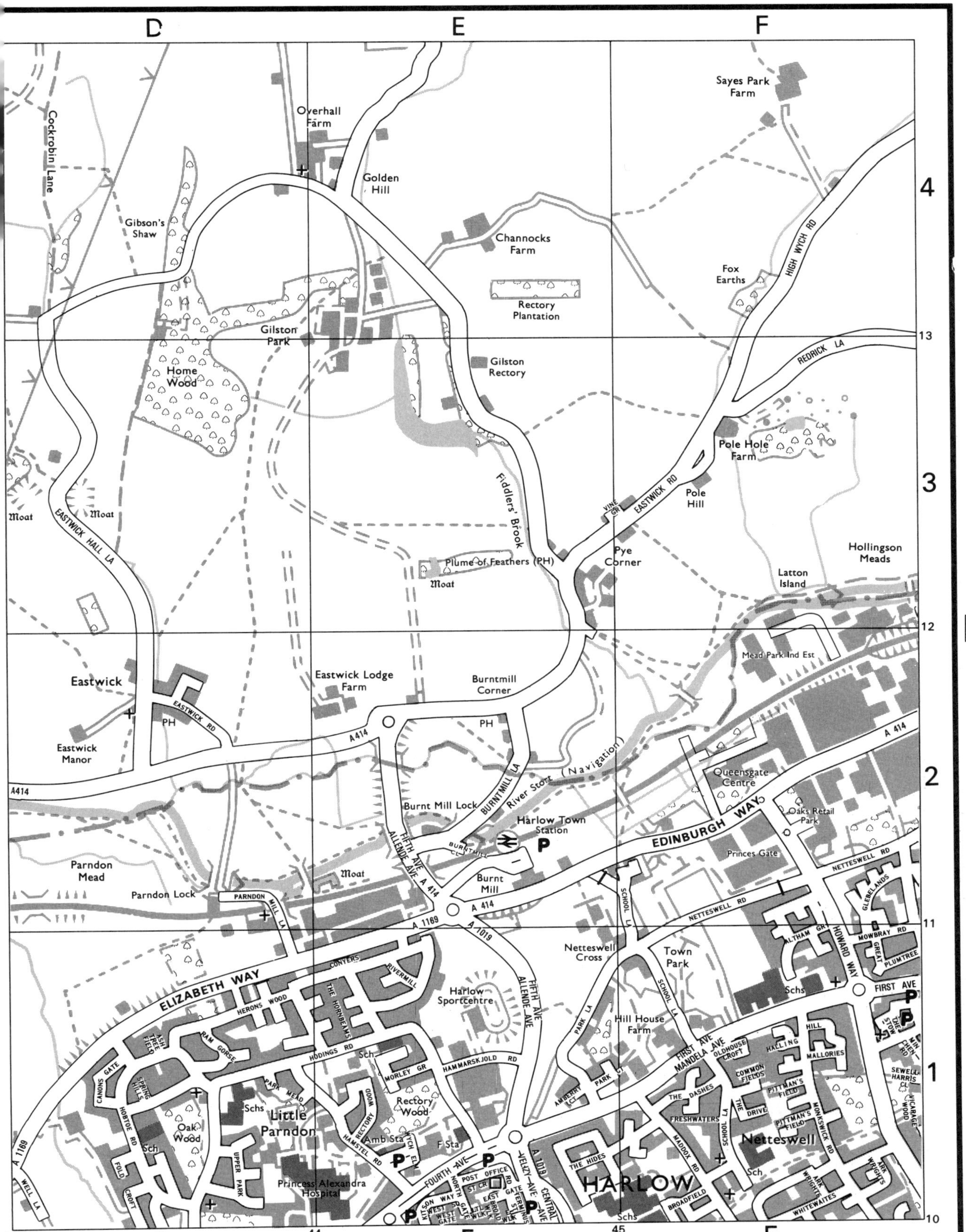
D
E
F
4
3
2
1
13
12
11
10
43
44
45
Cockrobin Lane
Overhall Farm
Golden Hill
Sayes Park Farm
Gibson's Shaw
Channocks Farm
Fox Earths
HIGH WYCH RD
Rectory Plantation
Gilston Park
Home Wood
Gilston Rectory
REDRICK LA
Pole Hole Farm
Pole Hill
Moat
EASTWICK HALL LA
Fiddlers' Brook
EASTWICK RD
VINE GR
Pye Corner
Hollingson Meads
Latton Island
Plume of Feathers (PH)
Mead Park Ind Est
Eastwick
Eastwick Lodge Farm
Burntmill Corner
PH
Eastwick Manor
A414
A 414
Queensgate Centre
River Stort (Navigation)
BURNTMILL LA
Burnt Mill Lock
Harlow Town Station
P
EDINBURGH WAY
Oaks Retail Park
Princes Gate
Parndon Mead
Burnt Mill
FIFTH AVE
ALLENDE AVE
Parndon Lock
PARNDON MILL LA
SCHOOL LA
NETTESWELL RD
GLEBELANDS
A 1169
A 1019
Netteswell Cross
Town Park
ALTHAM GR
HOWARD WAY
MOWBRAY RD
GREAT PLUMTREE
ELIZABETH WAY
CONTERS
RIVERMILL
HERONS WOOD
THE HORNBEAMS
Harlow Sportcentre
PARK LA
Hill House Farm
Schs
FIRST AVE
ASH TREE FIELD
RAM GORSE
HODINGS RD
Sch
HAMMARSKJOLD RD
MANDELA AVE
OLDHOUSE CROFT
HALLING HILL
MALLORIES
COMMON FIELDS
PITTMAN'S FIELD
SEWELL-HARRIS CL
CANONS GATE
SPRING HILLS
PARK MEAD
MORLEY GR
Rectory Wood
AMBERRY CT
THE DASHES
FRESHWATERS
THE DRIVE
MONKSWICK RD
VICARAGE WOOD
HOBTOE RD
Oak Wood
Little Parndon
RECTORY WOOD
Amb Sta
F Sta
HAMSTEL RD
FOURTH AVE
VELIZY AVE
CENTRAL AVE
MADDOX RD
Netteswell
THE HIDES
FOLD CROFT
UPPER PARK
Princess Alexandra Hospital
POST OFFICE RD
HARLOW
BROADFIELD
WRIGHTS
WHITEWAITES
WELL LA
WEST GATE
EAST GATE
TERMINUS ST

118

97

117

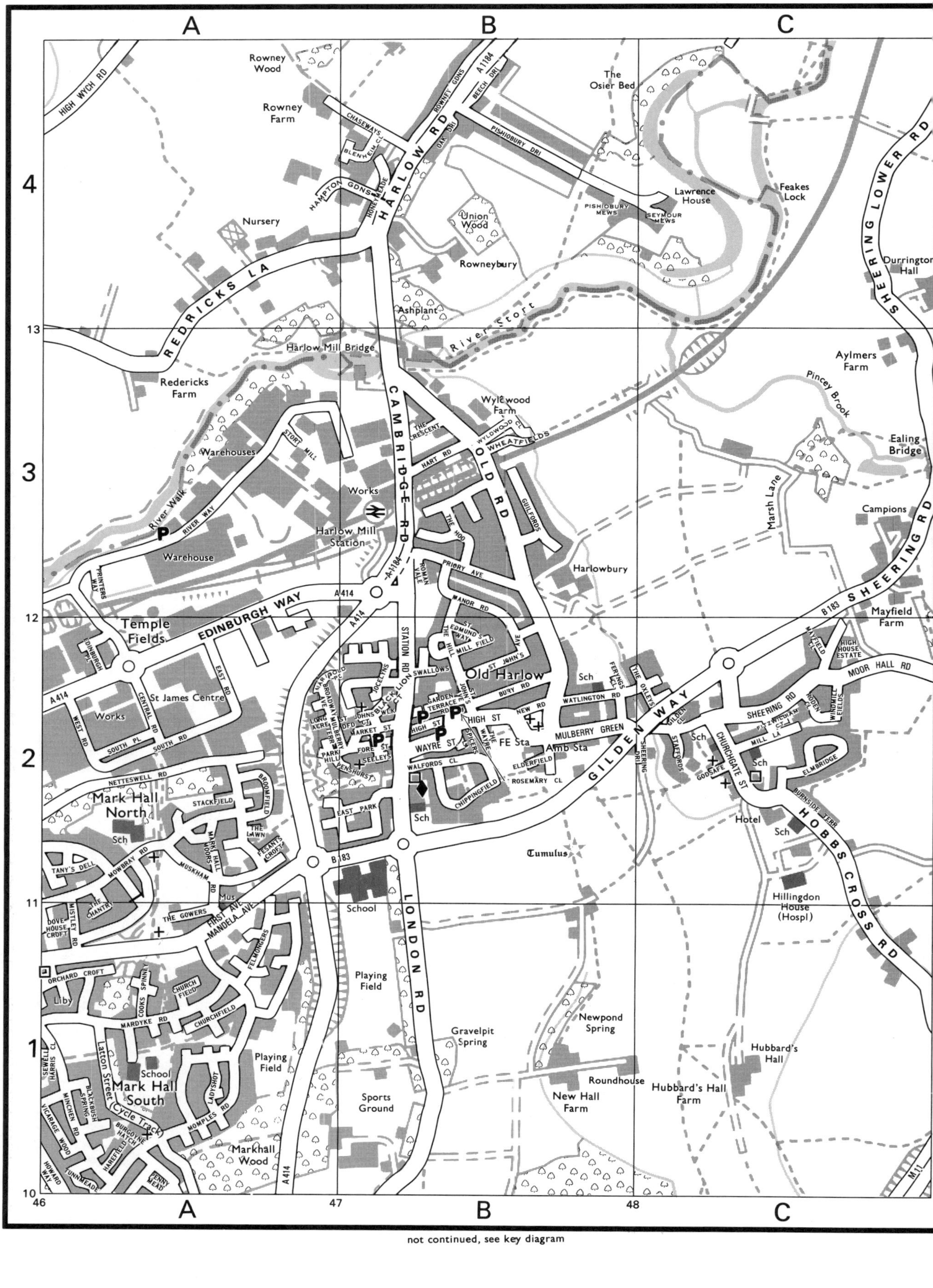
A
B
C
Rowney Wood
Rowney Farm
The Osier Bed
HIGH WYCH RD
HARLOW RD
PISHIOBURY DRI
Lawrence House
Feakes Lock
SHEERING LOWER RD
Nursery
Union Wood
Rowneybury
Durrington Hall
REDERICKS LA
Ashplant
River Stort
Harlow Mill Bridge
Redericks Farm
Aylmers Farm
Pincey Brook
Wylewood Farm
CAMBRIDGE RD
OLD RD
WHEATFIELDS
Warehouses
Works
Harlow Mill Station
Warehouse
River Walk
RIVER WAY
Marsh Lane
Ealing Bridge
Campions
Harlowbury
SHEERING RD
Mayfield Farm
EDINBURGH WAY
Temple Fields
A414
B183
MOOR HALL RD
Old Harlow
St James Centre
Works
HIGH ST
MULBERRY GREEN
GILDEN WAY
FE Sta
Amb Sta
Sch
Hotel
HOBBS CROSS RD
NETTESWELL RD
Mark Hall North
Cumulus
Hillingdon House (Hospl)
School
LONDON RD
Playing Field
Liby
Newpond Spring
Gravelpit Spring
Hubbard's Hall
Roundhouse
Hubbard's Hall Farm
New Hall Farm
Mark Hall South
Sports Ground
Markhall Wood
Latton Street (Cycle Track)
M11
46
47
48
13
12
11
10
4
3
2
1

99

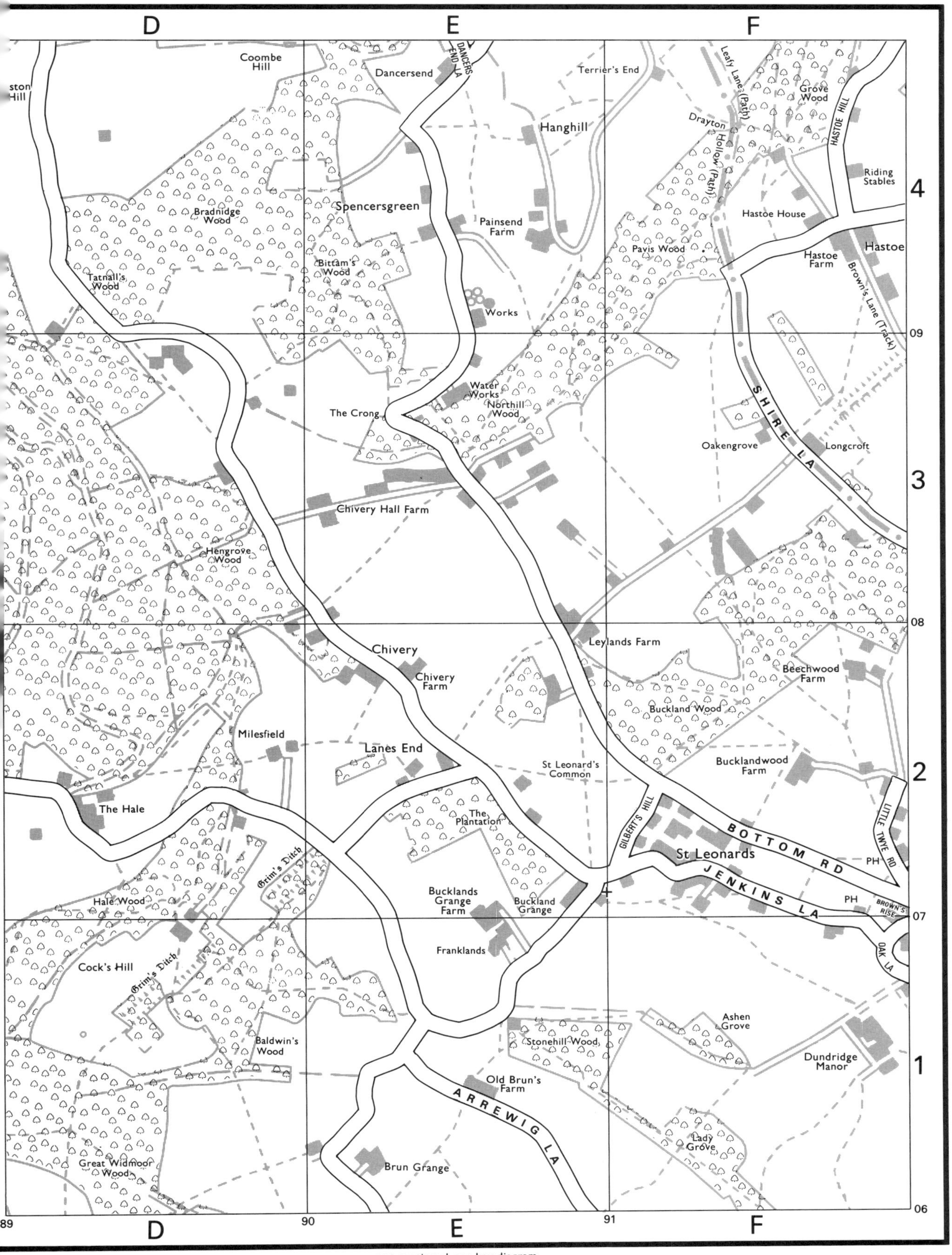

120

not continued, see key diagram

100

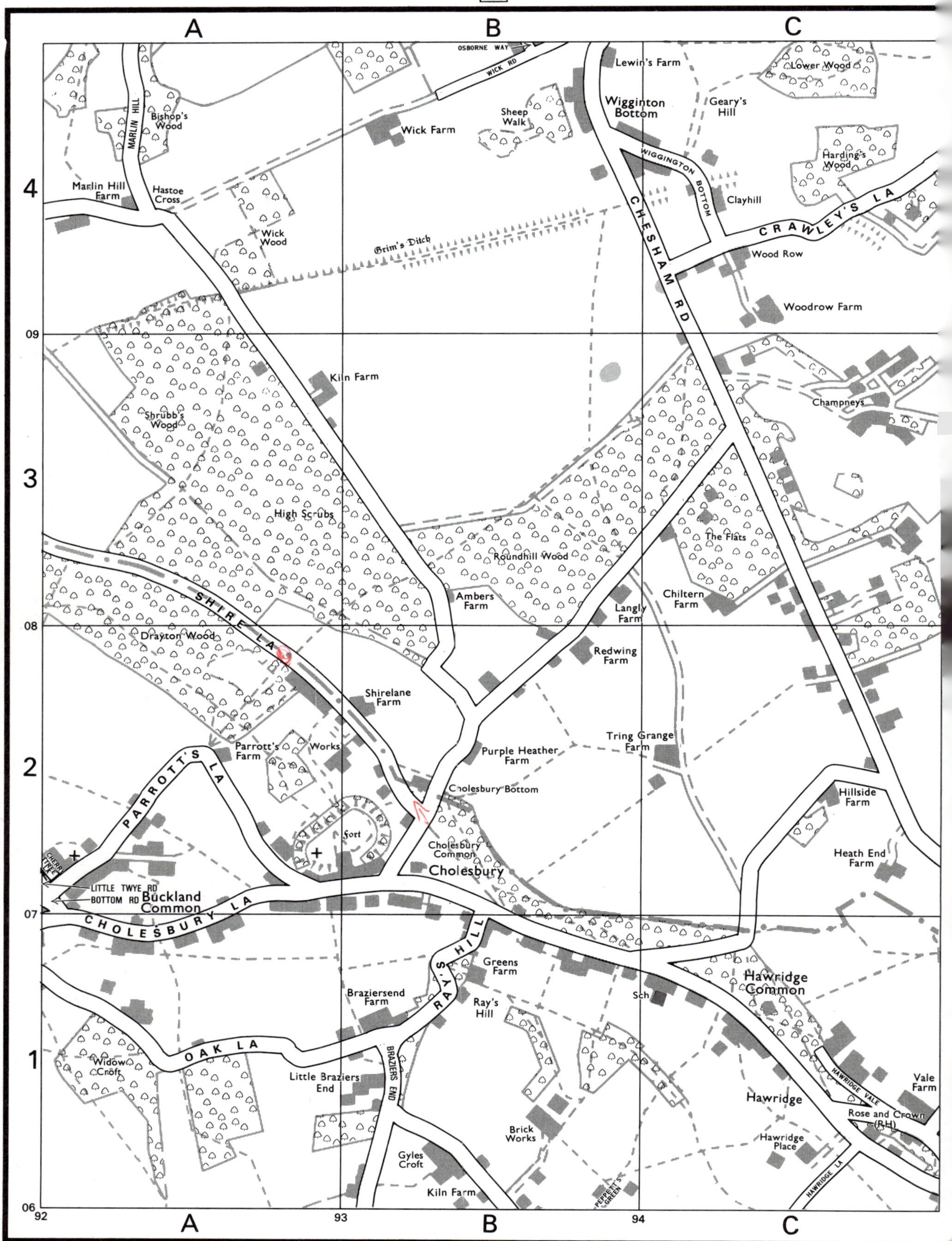

119

not continued, see key diagram

101

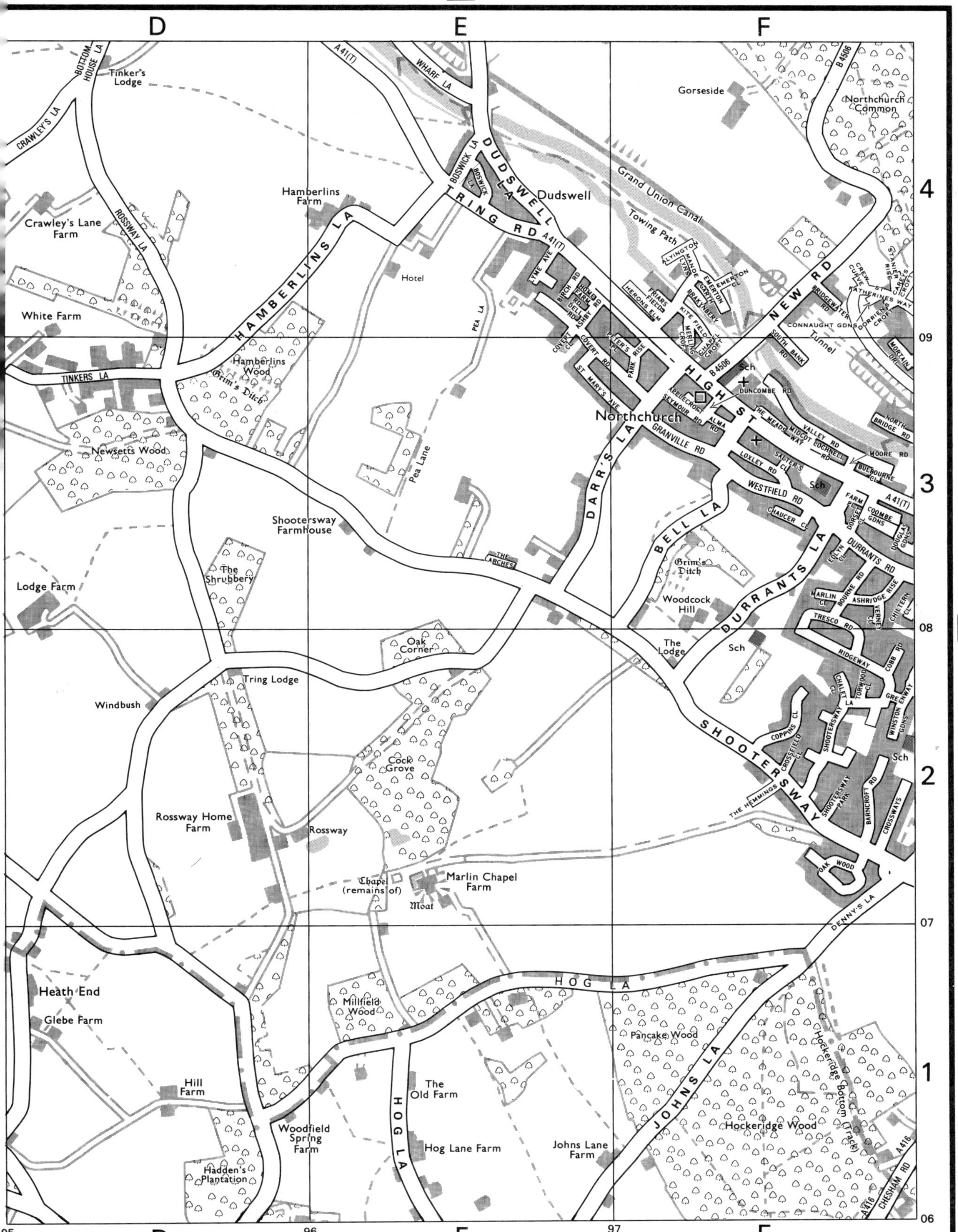

122

not continued, see key diagram

102

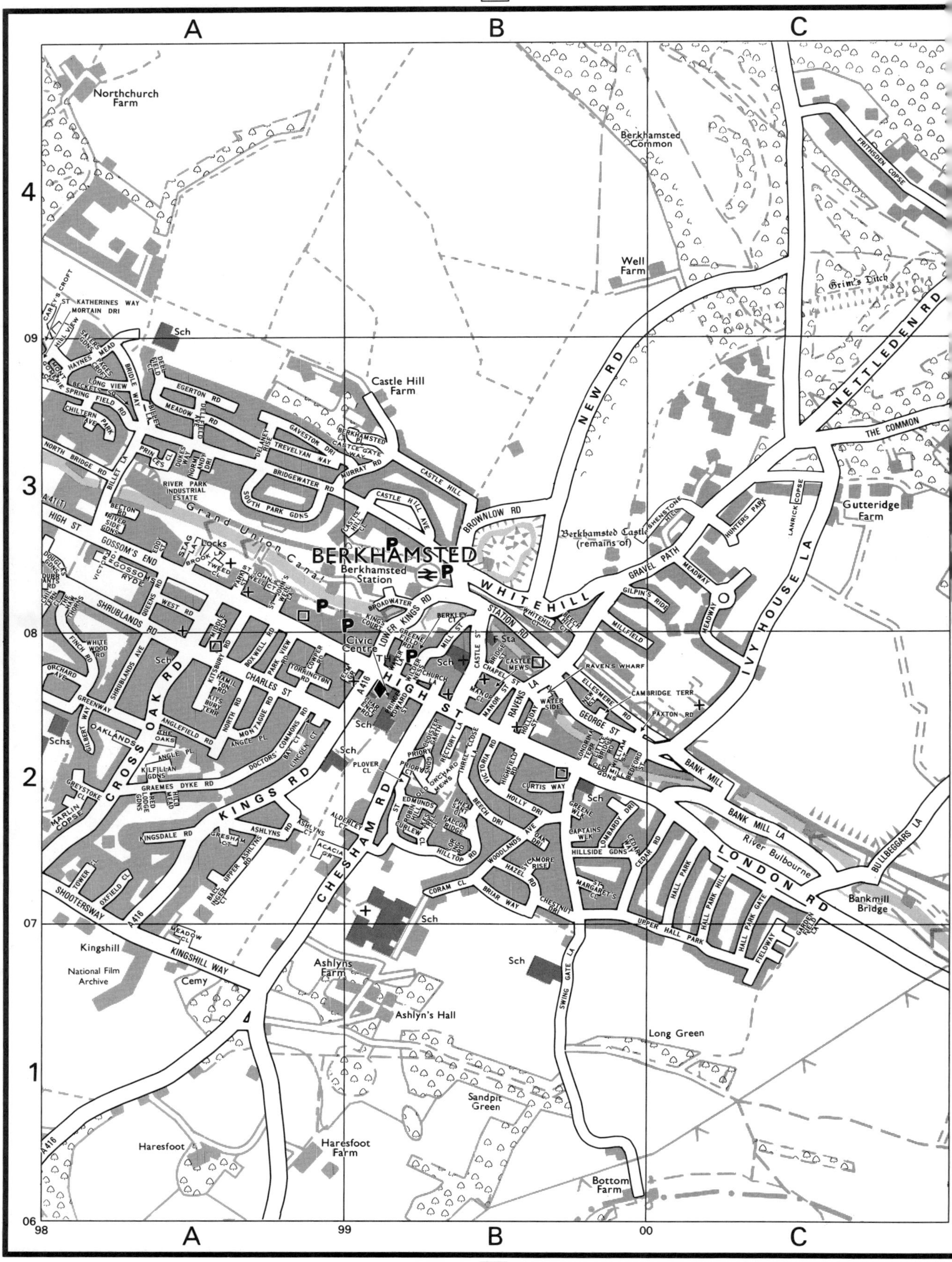
A
B
C
4
3
2
1
09
08
07
06
98
99
00
Northchurch Farm
Berkhamsted Common
Well Farm
Grim's Ditch
NETTLEDEN RD
FRITHSDEN COPSE
THE COMMON
Gutteridge Farm
Castle Hill Farm
NEW RD
BERKHAMSTED
Berkhamsted Station
Berkhamsted Castle (remains of)
Grand Union Canal
Locks
WHITEHILL
GRAVEL PATH
IVY HOUSE LA
HUNTERS PARK
LANRICK COPSE
SHENSTONE HILL
MEADWAY
HEADWAY
GILPIN'S RIDE
MILLFIELD
BEECH CL
STATION RD
BROWNLOW RD
CASTLE HILL
CASTLE HILL AVE
CASTLE HILL CL
MURRAY RD
GAVESTON DRI
TREVELYAN WAY
CASTLE GATE WAY
BRIDGEWATER RD
SOUTH PARK GDNS
DELANEY RISE
EGERTON RD
MEADOW RD
DELLFIELD
BRIDLE WAY
BILLET LA
BILLET LA
PRINCES CL
DUKES WAY
NORMANDY DRI
RIVER PARK INDUSTRIAL ESTATE
NORTH BRIDGE RD
CHILTERN PARK AVE
SPRING FIELD RD
BECKETS SQ
LONG VIEW
HAYNES MEAD
SAYERS GDNS
ST KATHERINES WAY
MORTAIN DRI
CAREY'S CROFT
HILL VIEW
Sch
A 41(T)
HIGH ST
GOSSOM'S END
GOSSOMS RYDE
BELTON RD
RIVERSIDE GDNS
EDDY ST
STAG LA
BROOK ST
TWEED
ST JOHN'S WELL LA
ST JOHN'S WELL CT
SHRUBLANDS RD
QUEENS RD
WEST RD
MIDDLE RD
BOXWELL RD
PARK VIEW
TORRINGTON RD
COWPER RD
KITSBURY RD
HAMILTON RD
KITSBURY TERR
CHARLES ST
NORTH RD
MONTAGUE RD
ANGLE PL
DOCTORS COMMONS RD
BAY CT
LINCOLN CT
BROADWATER
KINGS COURT
LOWER KINGS RD
BERKLEY CT
GREENE FIELD
Civic Centre
TH
WATER LA
MILL ST
CASTLE ST
F Sta
BRIDGE ST
CHAPEL ST
CASTLE MEWS
RAVENS WHARF
CAMBRIDGE TERR
PAXTON RD
ELLESMERE RD
GEORGE ST
WATER SIDE
RAVENS LA
HOLLIDAY ST
MANOR ST
MANOR CL
CHURCH LA
HIGH ST
PRINCE EDWARD ST
CLARENCE RD
A 416
FINCH RD
WHITE WOOD RD
ORCHARD AVE
SHRUBLANDS AVE
GREENWAY
GILBERT WAY
OAKLANDS
CROSS OAK RD
ANGLEFIELD RD
THE OAKS
ANGLE PL
KILFILLAN GDNS
GRAEMES DYKE RD
HILLSIDE MEAD
LODGE GDNS
GREYSTOKE CL
MARLIN COPSE
Schs
KINGS RD
KINGSDALE RD
ASHLYNS RD
GRESHAM CT
ASHLYNS CT
UPPER ASHLYNS RD
BALLINGER CT
TOWER CL
OXFIELD CL
SHOOTERSWAY
MEADOW CL
KINGSHILL WAY
Kingshill
National Film Archive
Cemy
PLOVER CL
ALDERLEY CT
ACACIA GR
CHESHAM RD
ST EDMUNDS
PRIORY GDNS
PRIORY
CLOISTER GARTH
RECTORY LA
THREE CLOSE LA
ORCHARD MEWS
PHEASANT CL
FALCON RIDGE
CURLEW CL
HILLTOP RD
BEECH DRI
VICTORIA RD
HIGHFIELD RD
HOLLY DRI
CURTIS WAY
WOODLANDS AVE
OAK DRI
HAZEL RD
SYCAMORE RISE
CORAM CL
BRIAR WAY
CHESTNUT DRI
ST MARGARET'S CL
GREENE WLK
CAPTAINS WLK
LOMBARDY DRI
HILLSIDE GDNS
CEDAR WAY
CEDAR RD
HALL PARK
HALL PARK HILL
HALL PARK GATE
UPPER HALL PARK
FIELDWAY
GARDEN FIELD LA
LONDON RD
BANK MILL
BANK MILL LA
River Bulbourne
BULLBEGGARS LA
Bankmill Bridge
LONDRINA TERR
LITTLE BRIDGE RD
OLD MILL GDNS
WILLIAM ST
BEDFORD ST
SWING GATE LA
Ashlyns Farm
Ashlyn's Hall
Long Green
Sandpit Green
Haresfoot
Haresfoot Farm
Bottom Farm
A416

121

136

103

D
E
F
Holly Bush Farm
Frithsden Vines (Vineyard)
Frithsden
Little Frithsden Copse
Crossways Farm
Heizdin's Wood
Strathgade Farm
Bingham's Park Farm
Bingham's Park
NETTLEDEN RD
POTTEN END HILL
Brown's Spring
Rumblers Farm
Hollybush Wood
HOLLYBUSH CL
Catstail Wood
WATER END RD
Woodcroft Farm
Pottenend Farm
VICARAGE RD
THE HAMLET
BROWNS SPR
OLIVER'S CL
HEDGESIDE
BRIAR CL
THE FRONT
THE BACK
HOME FIELD
PLOUGH LA
VICARAGE GDNS
COMMON GREEN
CHURCH RD
Sch
RAMBLING WAY
SCHOOL GDNS
CHESTNUT CL
THE LAURELS
THE COMMON
HEMPSTEAD LA
Potten End
Amersfort
Boxted Farm
BERKHAMSTED RD
FENNYCROFT RD
HOWARDS DRI
CHASDEN RD
School
Little Heath
Little Heath Farm
Boxted House
POLEHANGER LA
School
Gutteridge Wood
BULLBEGGARS LA
FIELDS END LA
LYNE WAY
ROBE END
SOMERIES RD
GALLEY HILL
SPRING LA
SACOMBE RD
THE AVENUE
BOXTED RD
Littleheath Great Farm
Lower Little Heath Farm
Fields End Farm
Fields End
THE COPSE
THE LAWNS
PULLEYS LA
Sch
MARTINDALE RD
HITCHENS CL
HARDINS CL
THE GLADES
THE SHRUBBERY
Sch
Warners End
HOLLYBUSH LA
HAREPARK CL
MICKLEM DRI
GOOSE CROFT
PULLEYS CL
Bullbeggars Wood
LITTLE HEATH LA
POUCHEN END LA
ROSEWOOD CT
BRIARCLIFF
HAWTHORN LA
RIPLEY WAY
ROSEHEATH
FLINT
YOUNGFIELD RD
NEWLANDS RD
MYRTLE GREEN
JUNIPER GREEN
MERROW DRI
GREAT STURGESS RD
VARNEY RD
PARKWOOD DRI
GREEN END LA
STONEY CROFT
LONG CHAULDEN
PADDOCK WAY
SIDFORD CL
VALLEY SIDE
LEGGFIELD TERR
MIDDLEHILL
LUCKS HILL
JOCKETTS HILL
Shrub Hill Common
ST NICHOLAS MOUNT
WESTRIDGE CL
RIDGE LEA
WHITE HILL
ROWCROFT
JOCKETTS RD
SHRUB HILL RD
Pouchen End Hall
Pouchen End Farm
HONEYCROSS RD
SCHOOL ROW
Sch
DAMASK GREEN
SHEPHERDS GREEN
Pix Farm
Pouchen End
LINDLINGS
CUTTSFIELD TERR
CHAULDEN TERR
NORTHRIDGE WAY
UPPER SALES
LONDON RD
OLDFIELD RD
HAZELDELL RD
Sch
PIXIES HILL CRES
LOWER SALES
BENCHLEYS RD
Broadway Farm
PIX FARM LA
Chaulden
THISTLE CL
THE COLTSFOOT
CHAULDEN HOUSE GDNS
Grand Union Canal
CHAULDEN LA
SHARPES LA
Cress Farm
Winkwell
WINKWELL
River Bulbourne
MOORLAND RD
Broadway Orchard
Motel
LONDON RD
Bourne End Farm
OLD FISHERY LA
SUGAR LA
Bourne End
BOURNE END LA
A41(T)
Saw Mill
Moorend Farm
4
3
2
1
09
08
07
06
01
02
03
D
E
F

124

137

104

123

A
B
C
4
3
2
1
09
08
07
06
04
05
06
Grist House Farm
Thrift Wood
Gaddesden Hall
DODDS LA
PICCOTTS END
Piccotts End
Dell Wood
Warnersend Wood
Boar's Head (P H)
Marchmont Farm
Marchmont Arms (Hotel)
Howe Grove
Grovehill
Highfield
Dismantled Railway
Gadebridge
Photographic Training Centre
Gadebridge Park
River Gade
LEIGHTON BUZZARD RD
GALLEY HILL
GADEBRIDGE RD
WARNERS END RD
HIGH ST
QUEENSWAY
ADEYFIELD RD
Hemel Hempstead General Hospital
Hammerfield
Counters End
Green End
Northridge Park
Lockers Park
MARLOWES
HEATH LA
Paradise
ST ALBANS RD
HEMEL HEMPSTEAD
Jarman Fields
Bennetts End Hospital
ST JOHN'S RD
Boxmoor
STATION RD
Grand Union Canal
LONDON RD
A41(T)
A414
A4146
A4147
B487
PICCOTTS END LA
FLETCHER WAY
JUPITER DRI
LEYS RD
ST AGNELLS LA
Sports Centre

138

105

D
E
F
4
3
2
1
09
08
07
06
REDBOURN RD
CHERRYTREE LA
Wood End Farm
Reservoir
BIRCH LEYS
LOWER EMMS
HALF MOON MEADOW
CRACKLEY MEADOW
HUNTERS OAK
THE MELINGS
MEDWICK MEWS
ST AGNELLS LA
ST AGNELLS CT
SHENLEY CT
SHENLEY RD
CHALFONT CL
CHENIES CT
DATCHET CT
ARKLEY CT
ARKLEY RD
LATIMER CL
BOTLEY RD
SARRATT AVE
DENHAM CL
EPPING GREEN
NORTHAW CL
CATHERINE CL
PARK CRES
BOLEYN CL
ARAGON CL
CLEVES RD
KIMPTON CL
SHENLEY RD
CUFFLEY CT
BAYFORD CL
B 487
A 4147
Sch
Schs
FINWAY RD
THREE CHERRY TREES LA
Eaton Lodge
PUNCH BOWL LA
M-1
Works
EASTMAN WAY
SWALLOWDALE LA
REDBOURN RD
SATURN WAY
DEIMOS DRI
QUEENSWAY
SAINFOIN END
EATON RD
MAXTED RD
BOUNDARY WAY
CHERRYTREE LA
HOGG END LA
MAXTED CL
GROVELANDS
SPRING WAY
CLEVELAND WAY
CLEVELAND RD
MARK RD
HIGH STREET GREEN
HIGHFIELD LA
WIDMORE
CONNAUGHT
ELLINGHAM CL
ELLINGHAM RD
BUNCEFIELD LA
GREEN LA
Woodwell's Farm
WOOD LANE END
MAYLANDS AVE
UNDERACRES CL
BRIERY WAY
BRANKSOME CL
HOBLETTS RD
Schs
EASTWOOD CT
SARACENS HEAD
SOUTHERNWOOD CL
ADEYFIELD RD
TEDDER RD
MONTGOMERY AVE
HILLARY RD
EVEREST WAY
TENZING RD
MALUS CL
WELLSWOOD CL
HALESWOOD RD
LEVERSTOCK GREEN RD
NEWFORD CL
MASONS RD
ARUNDEL CL
NEW PARK DRI
THE FLAGS
DUXONS TURN
HALES PARK
CREST PARK
HALES PARK CL
Breakspears
Junction 8
BREAKSPEAR WAY
A 4147
Motel
WELLBURY TERR
GREENWAY
MADDOX RD
A 414
Adeyfield
Sch
LONGLANDS
VAUXHALL RD
RANELAGH RD
FARLAND RD
FIELD RD
HIGHLAND DRI
CROSSWAYS
LEVERSTOCK GREEN WAY
TEWIN RD
HARLEY CROFT
WOOLMER DRI
DATCHWORTH TURN
ST MARGARETS WAY
CLINTON END
MICKLEFIELD RD
HILL END
BALDOCK WAY
PELHAM CT
CAMBRIDGE
POYNDERS HILL
RYECROFT CT
LINK RD
PAYMORE
CHELSING RISE
BURLEIGH RD
GRAVELEY CT
HARTSBOURNE WAY
Westwick Farm
Sch
WINDMILL RD
WHITE HART RD
HOMEFIELD RD
GRANGE
EASTWICK ROW
MARINER WAY
SANDMERE CL
ST ALBANS RD
ST ALBANS RD
RITCROFT DRI
RITCROFT ST
RITCROFT CL
HYBURN CL
ASHMORE GDNS
BRICKMAKERS LA
KILN CT
BRICKFIELD AVE
THE WAYSIDE
Leverstock Green
LOMBARDY
PANCAKE LA
EDENHALL CL
WESTWICK CL
DELMAR AVE
GREENACRES
TRINITY MEWS
ST DAVID'S CL
WESTWICK ROW
Westwick Row Farm
M 10
M-1
BELSIZE RD
KEITHS RD
ACORN RD
SYLVAN CL
MARSTON CL
HADDON CL
MEADOW
FIR TREE CL
TILE KILN LA
KENDALE
THE DELLS
THE CROFTS
WINDERMERE
CONISTON CL
CROSSETT GREEN
LEVERSTOCK GREEN RD
CHURCH RD
BARTEL CL
THORNCROFT
KILNCROFT
LONGFIELD
GRASMERE
ULLSWATER
DERWENT RD
ESKDALE
MALMES CROFT
MISSDEN DRI
THE HORSESHOE
ANTHONYS AVE
ST MICHAELS AVE
CROFTS PATH
CARD
KINDERSCOUT
BENNETTS END RD
THREE CORNERS
KILN GROUND
FLATFIELD RD
ROBINS NEST
GOLDCROFT
PEASCROFT RD
RUMBALLS RD
MILLFIELD WLK
HOWE RD
KIMPS WAY
LEYS RD
REDDINGS
Schs
Sch
COLONSAY
STORNOWAY
TARANSEY
NORTHEND
ORONSAY
WESTRAY
MANAN CL
ARRAN CL
LISMORE
STRONSAY
TIREE CL
RATHLIN
AUTUMN GLADES
CHAMBERSBURY LA
WOODFIELD DRI
WOODFIELD GDNS
BEDMOND RD
HEMEL HEMPSTEAD RD
BLACKWATER LA
Corner Farm
A 414

126

139

106

125

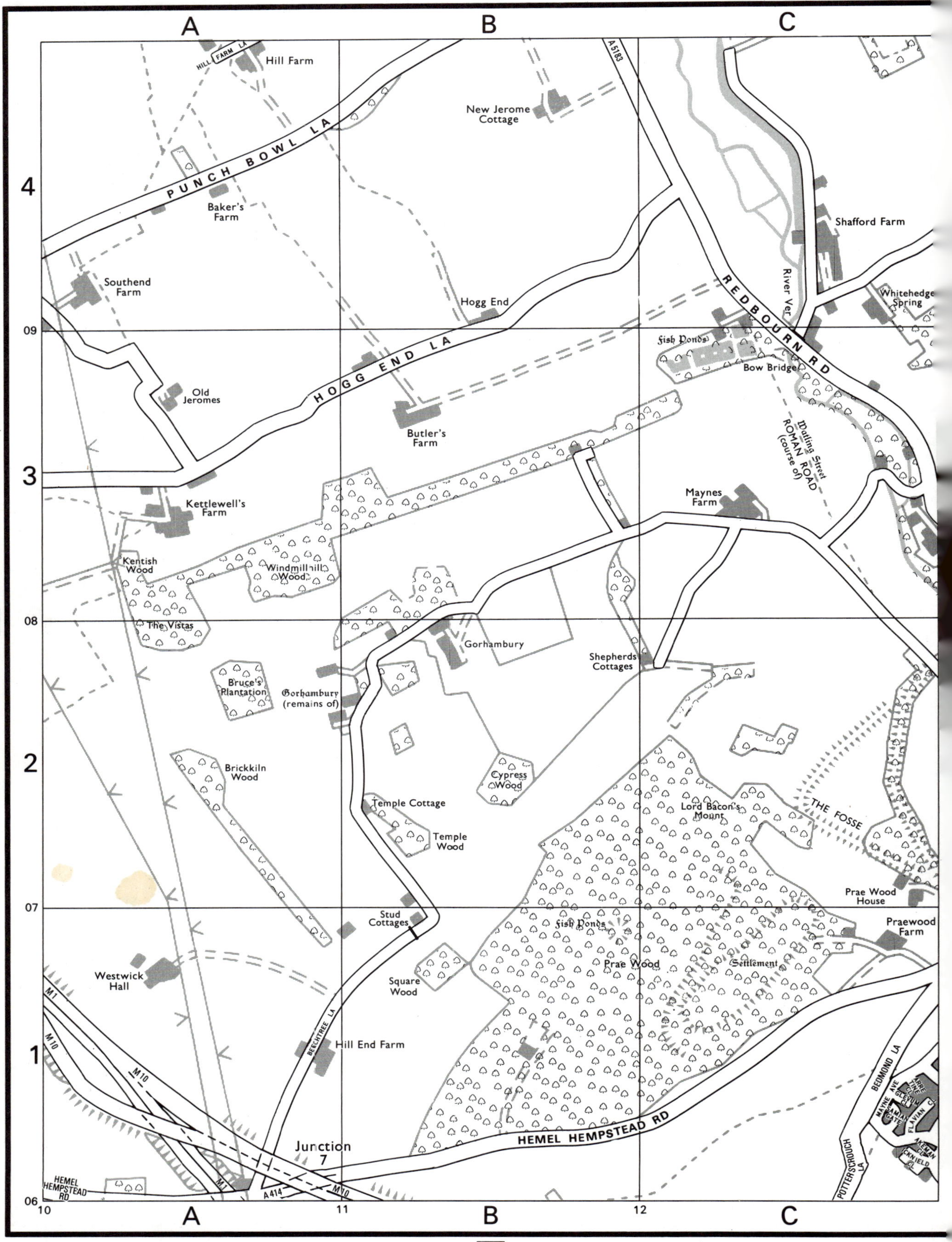
A
B
C
4
3
2
1
09
08
07
06
10
11
12
HILL FARM LA
Hill Farm
A5183
New Jerome Cottage
PUNCH BOWL LA
Baker's Farm
Shafford Farm
Southend Farm
Hogg End
River Ver
Whitehedge Spring
REDBOURN RD
HOGG END LA
Fish Ponds
Bow Bridge
Old Jeromes
Butler's Farm
Watling Street
ROMAN ROAD
(course of)
Kettlewell's Farm
Maynes Farm
Kentish Wood
Windmillhill Wood
The Vistas
Gorhambury
Shepherds Cottages
Bruce's Plantation
Gorhambury (remains of)
Brickkiln Wood
Cypress Wood
Temple Cottage
Lord Bacon's Mount
THE FOSSE
Temple Wood
Prae Wood House
Stud Cottages
Fish Ponds
Praewood Farm
Westwick Hall
Square Wood
Prae Wood
Settlement
M1
M10
BEECHTREE LA
Hill End Farm
BEDMOND LA
HEMEL HEMPSTEAD RD
Junction 7
HEMEL HEMPSTEAD RD
A414
POTTERSCROUGH LA
FLAVIAN CL

140

107

D
E
F
4
3
2
1
09
08
07
06
13
14
15
The Plantation
Ladygrove
Ladies Grove Wood
Whitehedge Spring
Batch Wood
Batchwood Hall (CH)
Golf Course
Playing Field
School
SPARROWSWICK RIDE
CAVAN DRI
FLINT WAY
HENDERSON CL
BLUNDELL CL
CARNEGIE RD
HIGH OAKS
Schools
WOOLLAM CRES
PARTRIDGE RD
NEW GREENS AVE
BLUEBERRY
TAMARISK
SANDRIDGEBURY LA
A1081
Long Spring
Works
PORTERS WOOD
SOOTHOUSE SPRING
Ditch
School
DARWIN CL
VALLEY RD
MELBOURNE
CANBERRA CL
TOULMIN DRI
LAWRANCE CL
BLENKIN CL
MAPLE AVE
New Greens
GREEN LA
THERFIELD RD
NICHOLAS CL
BIRCHMEAD CL
FRANCIS AVE
HARPENDEN RD
OLD HARPENDEN RD
TUDOR RD
Beech Bottom
FIRBANK RD
BEECH RD
ST ALBANS RD
B651
MARSHALS WICK LA
HOBART WALK
MARSHALL AVE
MARSHAL'S DRI
ALVERTON
BATCHWOOD GDNS
BEECH PLACE
BEECH BOTTOM
School
Townsend
Schs
GRIMTHORPE CL
BECKETT'S AVE
CONNAUGHT RD
EVERLASTING LA
LANGLEY CRES
LITTLE ACRE
SHEPPARDS CL
School
Bernard's Heath
Youth Centre
F & Amb Sta
SEYMOUR RD
WATSON AVE
FONTMELL CL
BRIDLE CL
SANDRIDGE RD
BATTLEFIELD RD
LANCASTER RD
GURNEY COURT RD
BATCHWOOD DRI
WAVERLEY RD
BATCHWOOD VIEW
Convent
ELEANOR AVE
ALBAN AVE
TOWNSEND DRI
HEYDONS CL
MAY CL
DORMIE CL
LADIES GR
LINKS VIEW
WHITE HEDGE DRI
EVERLASTING LA
MARGARET AVE
EDMUND BEAUFORT DRI
HEATH FARM LA
THE LIMES
SPENCER GATE
STONECROSS CL
School
CULVER RD
BOUNDARY
HEATH RD
WARWICK RD
WALTON ST
CANTERBURY CT
REDBOURN RD
St Albans City Hospital
KIMBERLEY RD
NORMANDY RD
LADY SLOTH
FOLLY AVE
ASHWELL ST
DICKENS
DALTON ST
BERNARD ST
GRANGE ST
CHURCH ST
PALFREY CL
CARLISLE AVE
HEATH CL
ST BERNARD'S
HOLMES
STONECROSS RD
SANDPIT LA
HEATHFIELD CT
AVENUE RD
JAMESON CT
CRANMORE CT
EASTBURY CT
BLENHEIM RD
CLARENCE RD
JENNINGS RD
GAINSBOROUGH AVE
DOWNEDGE
A414
CUMBERLAND CT
THORNTON ST
CANNON ST
Sch
RAYMER CL
BOWGATE
HILLSIDE RD
ALTHORP RD
MURTON CT
THIRLESTANE
LEMSFORD RD
CORRINGHAM CT
YORK RD
CAMLET WAY
BRANCH RD
KINGSBURY AVE
VERULAM RD
FOLLY LA
St Albans City Hospital
GOMBARDS
WORLEY RD
CATHERINE ST
ST PETER'S ST
TOWNSEND AVE
HALL PLACE GDNS
ESSEX RD
MANOR RD
ST PETER'S RD
CLIFTON ST
College
Mus
Coll
ST ALBANS
Clarence Park
BLACKSMITH'S LA
PRAE CL
Museum
Sch
ST MICHAEL'S ST
KING'S RD
MOUNT PLEASANT
PORTLAND ST
HILL ST
NEW ENGLAND ST
RUSSELL AVE
DROVERS WAY
WADDINGTON RD
HATFIELD RD
AVONDALE ST
CHALFONT RD
LATTIMORE RD
BEDFORD PARK RD
College
CAVENDISH RD
ROMAN THEATRE
Hotel
Museum
FISHPOOL ST
LOWER DAGNALL ST
SPENCER ST
UPPER DAGNALL ST
CROSS ST
City Hall
Cts
BRICKET RD
UPPER MARLBOROUGH RD
MARLBOROUGH GATE
LIVERPOOL RD
BEACONSFIELD RD
St Albans City Station
GRANVILLE RD
STANHOPE RD
CAMP RD
ALBION RD
CECIL RD
VERVLAMIVM ROMAN TOWN
HEMEL HEMPSTEAD RD
ROMELAND HILL
Abbey Gate
School
GEORGE ST
CHRISTOPHER PL
HIGH ST
CHEQUER ST
B691
THE MALTINGS
NEW KENT RD
MARLBOROUGH RD
VICTORIA ST
The Lake
CATH
SUMPTER YD
A5183
A1081
DOLPHIN YD
HART RD
PAGEANT RD
ALBERT ST
ALEXANDRA RD
BEDFORD RD
INKERMAN RD
ALMA RD
OSWALD RD
RIDGMONT RD
CLARE
GRIMSTON RD
EDWARD CL
FLORA GR
BREAKSPEAR AVE
VANDA CRES
SHIRLEY RD
BLUEHOUSE HILL
ROMAN WALL (course of)
ABBEY MILL LA
ORCHARD ST
LADY SPENCER'S GR
School
ABBEY MILL END
MALTHOUSE CT
BARDWELL CT
SOPWELL LA
KEYFIELD TERR
WATSON'S WALK
ALMA CUT
TELFORD CT
GATE (remains of)
River Ver
PONDWICKS CL
GROVE RD
BELMONT HILL
THORPE RD
Works
BARDWELL RD
COTTONMILL CRES
PAXTON RD
OLD LONDON RD
BLACK CUT
LONDON RD
GROSVENOR RD
BEDMOND LA
MAYNE AVE
ANTONINE GATE
ERMINE CL
CLAUDIAN PL
AUGUSTUS CL
KING HARRY LA
THE RAMPARTS
GATE
School
Sch
LOWER PAXTON RD
ABBEY FIELDS
RAMSBURY RD
RIVERSIDE RD
CORNWALL RD
APPROACH RD
School
Cottonmill Bridge
ASPASIA CL
ORCHARD
KENTON GDNS
COLINDALE AVE
HORDLE GDNS
CUNNINGHAM AVE
DELLFIELD
Westminster Lodge
Abbey Theatre
HOLYWELL HILL
PROSPECT RD
NUNNERY STABLES
OLD SOPWELL GDNS
COTTONMILL LA
LINDUM PL
CORINIUM
HADRIAN CL
DEVA CL
DUBRAE CL
WESTFIELDS
ROWLATT DRI
WINDRIDGE CL
Playing Field
CARDINAL AVE
CATHEDRAL
School
College
Coll
WESTMINSTER CT
Abbey Station
ST JULIAN'S RD
LEYLAND AVE
NUNNERY
MENTMORE RD
SADLIER RD
CUNNINGHAM HILL RD
Hotel
MAYNE AVE
JEROME DRI
MEAUTYS
ABBEY AVE
ST STEPHEN'S AVE
WATFORD RD
B4630
A5183
HAVERCROFT CL
ST STEPHEN'S HILL
EYWOOD RD
EVERARD CL
MERCERS ROW
WILSHERE AVE
DOGGETTS WAY
WATLING ST
St Stephens
Works
GRAHAM CL
BERNERS DRI
ABBOTS PARK
A1081

128

141

108

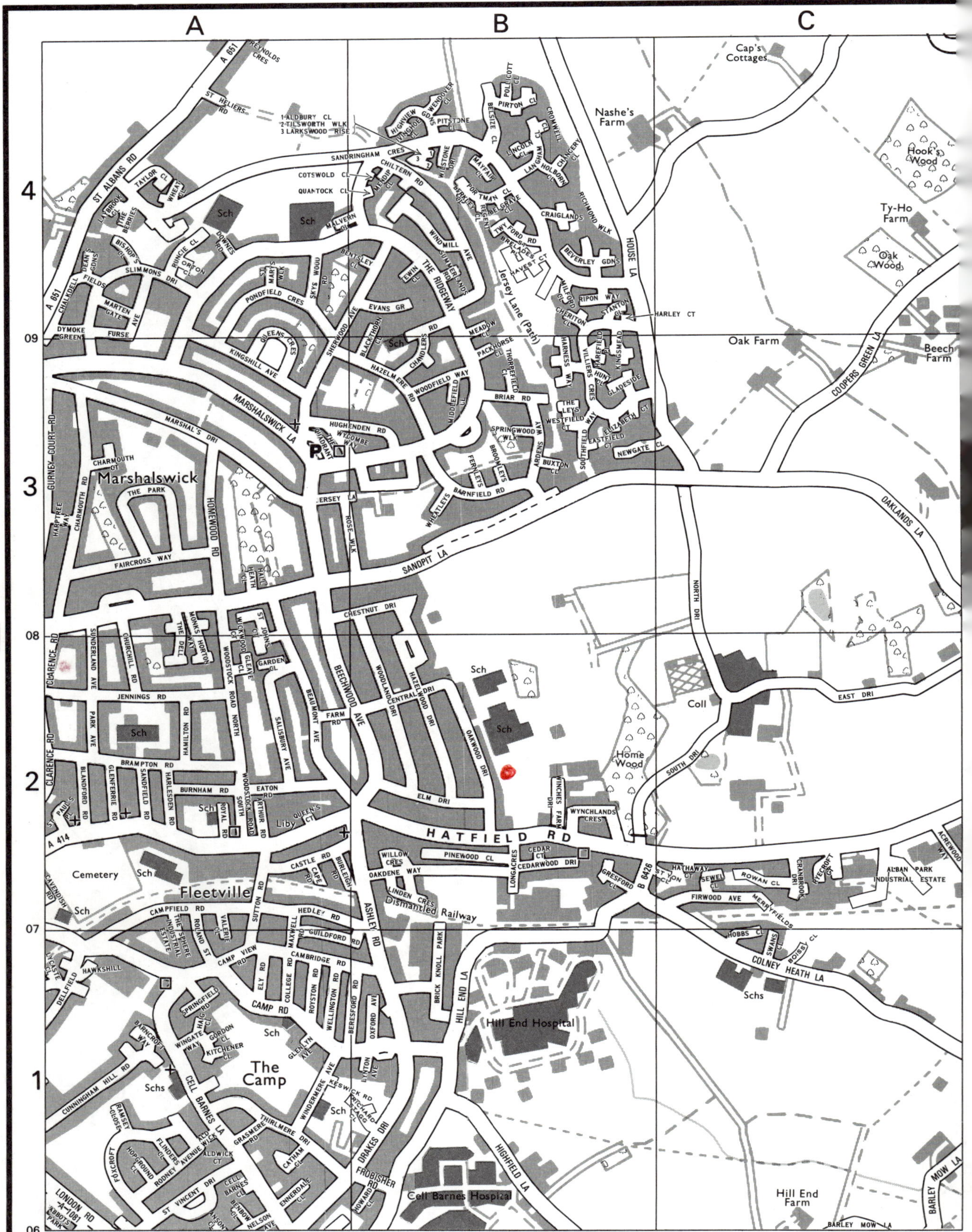

A
B
C
4
3
2
1
09
08
07
06
16
17
18
Cap's Cottages
Nashe's Farm
Hook's Wood
Ty-Ho Farm
Oak Wood
Oak Farm
Beech Farm
COOPERS GREEN LA
OAKLANDS LA
HOUSE LA
Jersey Lane (Path)
HARLEY CT
1 ALDBURY CL
2 TILSWORTH WLK
3 LARKSWOOD RISE
REYNOLDS CRES
ST HELIERS RD
A 651
ST ALBANS RD
TAYLOR CL
SANDRINGHAM CRES
COTSWOLD CL
QUANTOCK CL
CHILTERN RD
PITSTONE
PIRTON CL
CROMWELL
LANGHAM
HOLBORN
CHANCERY
CRAIGLANDS
RICHMOND WLK
BEVERLEY GDNS
RIPON WAY
STANTON
CHERITON
HAVEST CT
Sch
SLIMMONS DRI
MARTEN GATE
DYMOKE GREEN
FURSE AVE
CHALKDELL FIELDS
POND FIELD CRES
QUEENS CRES
KINGSHILL AVE
EVANS GR
SHERWOOD AVE
BLACKTHORN
THE RIDGEWAY
WINDMILL AVE
MEADOW
PACKHORSE
THORPEFIELD
HARNESS WAY
VILLIERS CRES
KINGSMEAD
GLADESIDE
HAZELMERE RD
WOODFIELD WAY
MIDDLEFIELD
BRIAR RD
MARSHALSWICK LA
MARSHAL'S DRI
HUGHENDEN RD
WYCOMBE WAY
SPRINGWOOD WLK
BROOMLEYS
FERNLEYS
ARDENS WAY
BUXTON CL
WESTFIELD
SOUTHFIELD WAY
ELIZABETH CT
EASTFIELD
NEWGATE CL
BARNFIELD RD
WHEATLEYS
Marshalswick
CHARMOUTH CT
THE PARK
GURNEY COURT RD
HARPTREE WAY
HOMEWOOD RD
FAIRCROSS WAY
JERSEY LA
ROSE WLK
SANDPIT LA
NORTH DRI
CHESTNUT DRI
SUNDERLAND AVE
CHURCHILL RD
THE DELL
MONKS HORTON WAY
WOODSTOCK ROAD NORTH
WICKWOOD
GLEAVE
ST JOHNS
GARDEN CL
BEECHWOOD AVE
WOODLANDS DRI
HAZELWOOD DRI
CENTRAL DRI
OAKWOOD DRI
Sch
Coll
EAST DRI
SOUTH DRI
Home Wood
CLARENCE RD
JENNINGS RD
PARK AVE
HAMILTON RD
BEAUMONT AVE
FARM RD
SALISBURY AVE
BRAMPTON RD
BLANDFORD RD
GLENFERRIE RD
SANDFIELD RD
HARLESDEN RD
BURNHAM RD
EATON RD
ARTHUR RD
QUEEN'S CT
ELM DRI
WINCHES FARM DRI
WYNCHLANDS CRES
HATFIELD RD
A 414
B 6426
Liby
Cemetery
CAVENDISH RD
Fleetville
CASTLE RD
BURLEIGH RD
WILLOW CRES
PINEWOOD CL
CEDAR CT
CEDARWOOD DRI
LONGACRES
GRESFORD CL
HATHAWAY CT
SEWELL CL
ROWAN CL
CRANBROOK DRI
HYECROFT
ACREWOOD WAY
ALBAN PARK INDUSTRIAL ESTATE
FIRWOOD AVE
MERRYFIELDS
OAKDENE WAY
LINDEN CRES
Dismantled Railway
CAMPFIELD RD
THE SPHERE INDUSTRIAL ESTATE
ROLAND ST
VALERIE CL
SUTTON RD
HEDLEY RD
GUILDFORD RD
MAXWELL RD
CAMBRIDGE RD
ASHLEY RD
CAMP VIEW RD
ELY RD
COLLEGE RD
ROYSTON RD
WELLINGTON RD
BERESFORD RD
OXFORD AVE
BRICK KNOLL PARK
HILL END LA
HOBBS CL
SWANS CL
BOISSY CL
COLNEY HEATH LA
Schs
HAWKSHILL
DELLFIELD
CAMP RD
SPRINGFIELD
HAIG CL
GORDON CL
WINGATE WAY
KITCHENER CL
BARNCROFT WAY
GLENLYN AVE
LYNTON AVE
Hill End Hospital
CUNNINGHAM HILL RD
CELL BARNES LA
The Camp
WINDERMERE AVE
KESWICK RD
RICHARD STAGG CL
THIRLMERE DRI
GRASMERE RD
CATHAM CL
DRAKES DRI
FROBISHER RD
HOWARD CL
ENNERDALE CL
HIGHFIELD LA
Cell Barnes Hospital
RAMSEY CLOSE
FOXCROFT
HOPGROUND CL
FLINDERS CL
RODNEY AVENUE
ALDWICK CT
ST VINCENT DRI
CELL BARNES CL
BENBOW CL
NELSON AVE
LONDON RD
A 1081
Hill End Farm
BARLEY MOW LA

127

142

109

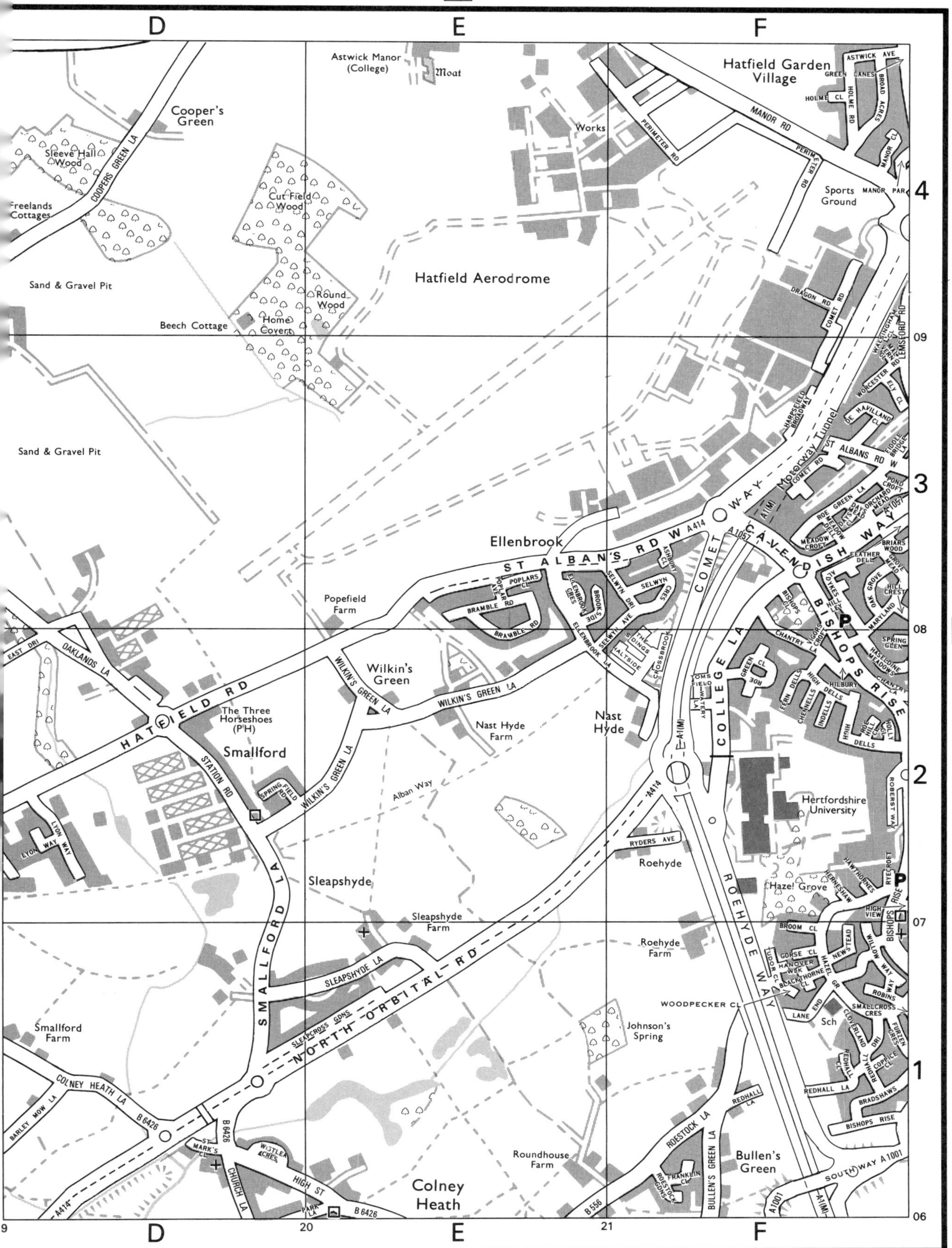
D
E
F
Astwick Manor (College)
Moat
Hatfield Garden Village
ASTWICK AVE
GREEN LANES
HOLME CL
HOLME RD
BROAD ACRES
MANOR RD
MANOR CL
Cooper's Green
Works
PERIMETER RD
Sleeve Hall Wood
COOPERS GREEN LA
Cut Field Wood
Sports Ground
MANOR PAR
4
Freelands Cottages
Sand & Gravel Pit
Hatfield Aerodrome
Round Wood
DRAGON RD
COMET RD
Beech Cottage
Home Covert
09
LEMSFORD RD
WORCESTER RD
ELY CL
DE HAVILLAND CL
HARPSFIELD BROADWAY
Motorway Tunnel
ST ALBANS RD W
Sand & Gravel Pit
3
W-A-Y
A1(M)
ROE GREEN LA
ORCHARD MEAD
MEADOW CROFT
A1057
Ellenbrook
ST ALBANS RD W A414
A1057
CAVENDISH WAY
BRIARS WOOD
FEATHER DELL
POPLARS CL
POPLARS AVE
ELLENBROOK CRES
BROOKSIDE
SELWYN DRI
SELWYN CRES
ASHBURY CL
COMET
HILL CREST
Popefield Farm
BRAMBLE RD
BISHOPS RISE
P
MARYLAND
EAST DRI
OAKLANDS LA
BRAMBLE RD
SELWYN AVE
ELLENBROOK LA
THE SIDINGS
CROSSBROOK
HALTSIDE
COLLEGE LA
CHANTRY
ROE GREEN CL
SPRING GLEN
08
Wilkin's Green
WILKIN'S GREEN LA
FERN DELLS
HIGH DELLS
HILBURY
CHENNELLS
INDELLS
HATFIELD RD
The Three Horseshoes (P H)
Nast Hyde
Nast Hyde Farm
TOMS FIELD
WATERY LA
A1(M)
Smallford
STATION RD
SPRING FIELD RD
WILKIN'S GREEN LA
A414
Alban Way
2
ROBERTS WAY
Hertfordshire University
LYON WAY
RYDERS AVE
Roehyde
HAWTHORNES
RYECROFT
HERNESHAW
Sleapshyde
Haze! Grove
BISHOPS RISE
HIGH VIEW
07
SMALLFORD LA
Sleapshyde Farm
ROEHYDE WAY
BROOM CL
Roehyde Farm
GORSE CL
HANOVER WLK
TUDOR CL
BLACKTHORNE CL
NEWSTEAD
HAZEL GR
WILLOW WAY
ROBINS WAY
SLEAPSHYDE LA
NORTH ORBITAL RD
WOODPECKER CL
SMALLCROSS CRES
LANE END
Sch
Smallford Farm
SLEAPCROSS GDNS
Johnson's Spring
CLOVERLAND
REDHALL DRI
FURZEN CRES
COPPICE CL
REDHALL CL
1
COLNEY HEATH LA
REDHALL LA
REDHALL LA
BRADSHAWS
BISHOPS RISE
BARLEY MOW LA
B 6426
B 6426
ST MARK'S CL
WISTLEA CRES
ROESTOCK LA
Roundhouse Farm
BULLEN'S GREEN LA
Bullen's Green
FRANKLIN CL
ROESTOCK GDNS
SOUTHWAY A1001
A1001
A414
CHURCH LA
HIGH ST
PARK LA
B 6426
Colney Heath
B 556
A1(M)
06
19
20
21
D
E
F

130

143

110

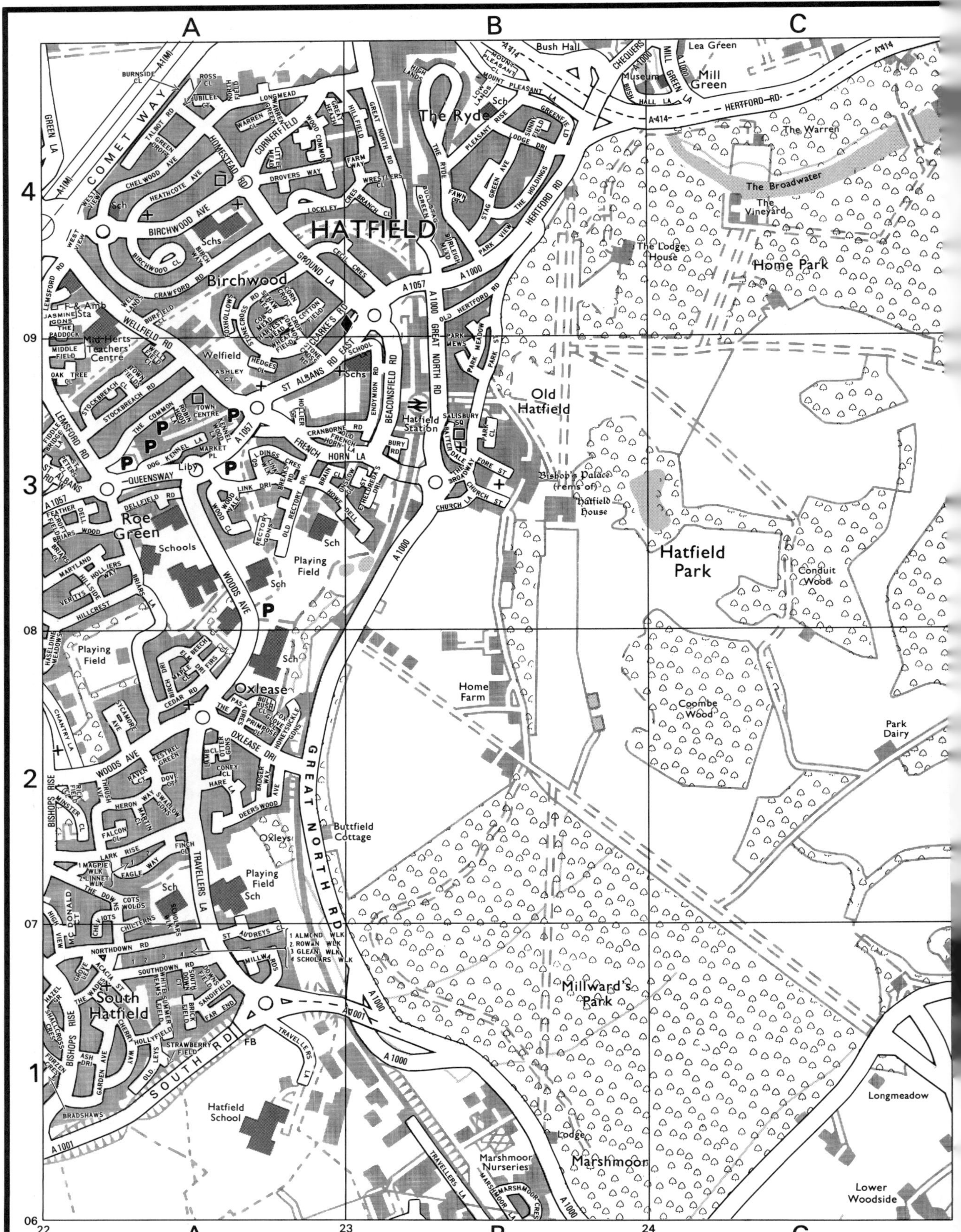
A
B
C
HATFIELD
The Ryde
Bush Hall
Lea Green
Mill Green
Museum
The Warren
The Broadwater
The Vineyard
The Lodge House
Home Park
Birchwood
Welfield
Mid-Herts Teachers' Centre
F & Amb Sta
Old Hatfield
Hatfield Station
Bishop's Palace (rems of)
Hatfield House
Hatfield Park
Conduit Wood
Roe Green
Schools
Playing Field
Oxlease
Home Farm
Coombe Wood
Park Dairy
Buttfield Cottage
Oxleys
South Hatfield
Millward's Park
Hatfield School
Marshmoor Nurseries
Marshmoor
Lodge
Longmeadow
Lower Woodside
GREAT NORTH RD
COMET WAY
HERTFORD RD
BIRCHWOOD AVE
WOODS AVE
TRAVELLERS LA
SOUTH RD
QUEENSWAY
ST ALBANS RD EAST
BEACONSFIELD RD
A1000
A1057
A414
A1001
A1(M)
1 ALMOND WLK
2 ROWAN WLK
3 GLEAN WLK
4 SCHOLARS WLK
4
3
2
1
09
08
07
06
22
23
24

129

144

111

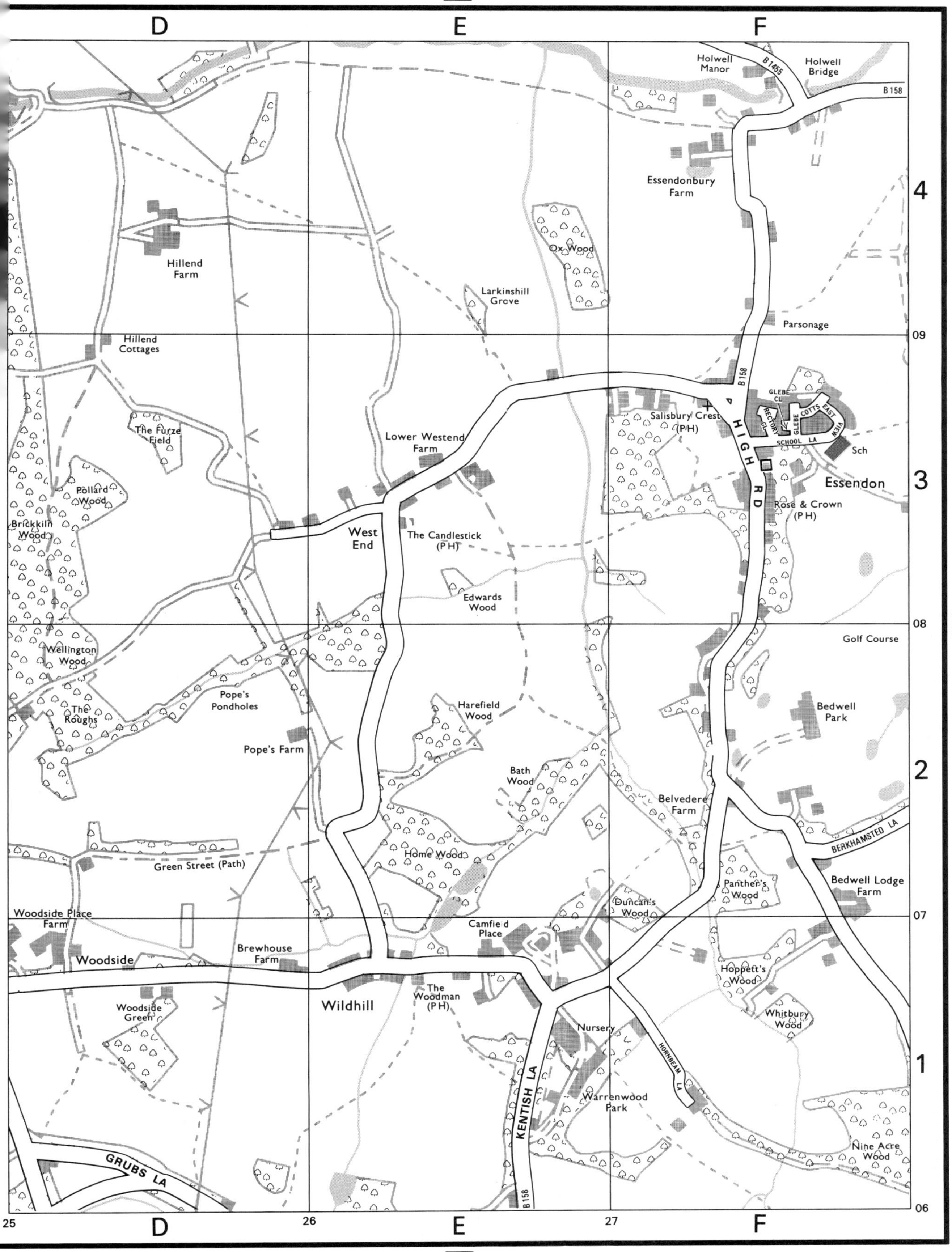
D
E
F
Holwell Manor
B1455
Holwell Bridge
B158
4
Essendonbury Farm
Ox Wood
Hillend Farm
Larkinshill Grove
Parsonage
Hillend Cottages
09
B158
GLEBE CL
RECTORY CL
GLEBE COTTS
EAST VIEW
Salisbury Crest (PH)
HIGH RD
SCHOOL LA
Sch
The Furze Field
Lower Westend Farm
Essendon
3
Pollard Wood
Rose & Crown (PH)
Brickkiln Wood
West End
The Candlestick (PH)
Edwards Wood
08
Golf Course
Wellington Wood
Pope's Pondholes
The Roughs
Harefield Wood
Bedwell Park
Pope's Farm
2
Bath Wood
Belvedere Farm
BERKHAMSTED LA
Home Wood
Green Street (Path)
Panther's Wood
Bedwell Lodge Farm
Duncan's Wood
Woodside Place Farm
07
Camfield Place
Brewhouse Farm
Woodside
Hoppett's Wood
The Woodman (PH)
Wildhill
Woodside Green
Whitbury Wood
Nursery
HORNBEAM LA
1
KENTISH LA
Warrenwood Park
Nine Acre Wood
GRUBS LA
B158
06
25
26
27

132

145

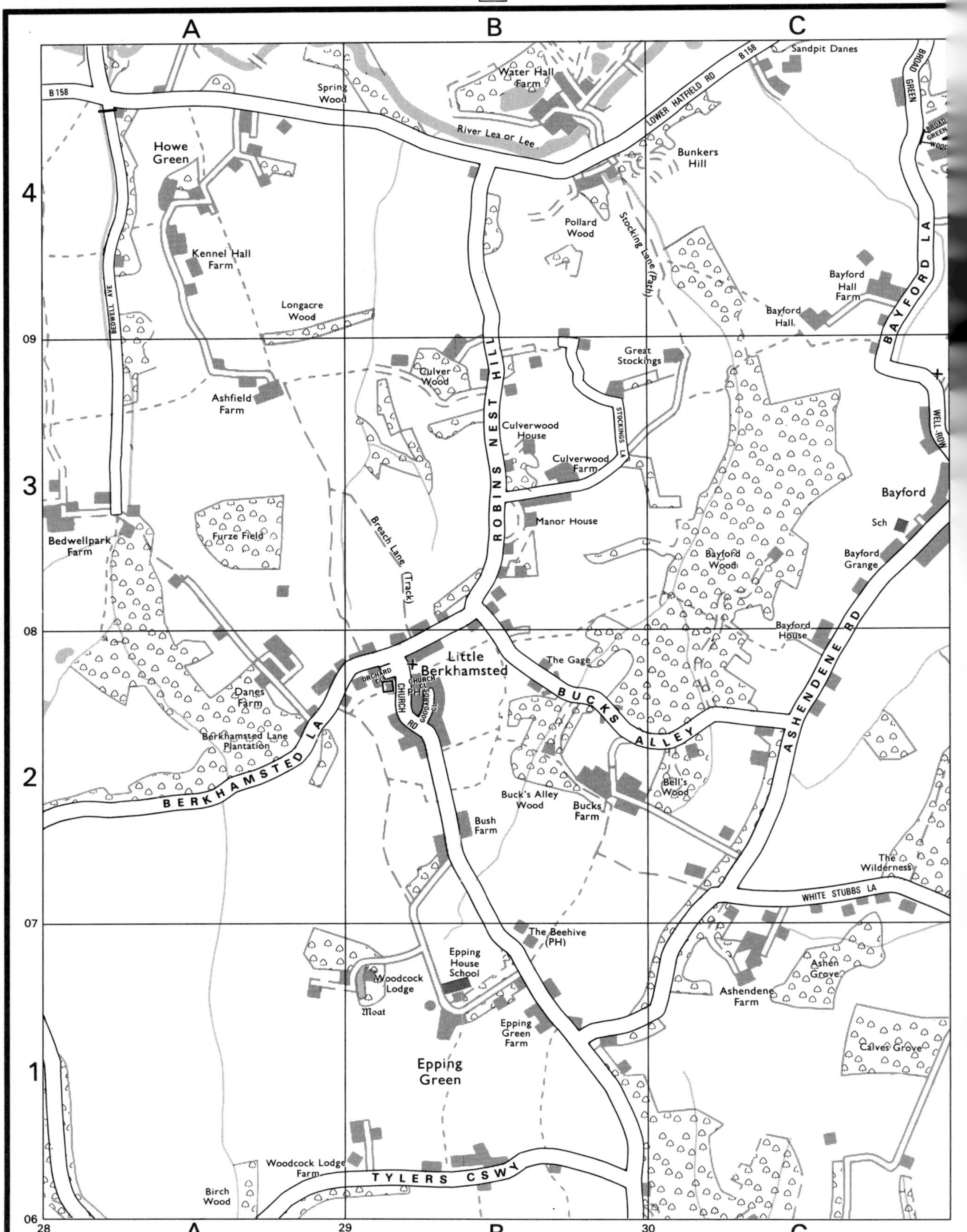
112
146
131
A
B
C
4
3
2
1
09
08
07
06
28
29
30
B 158
Spring Wood
Water Hall Farm
Sandpit Danes
LOWER HATFIELD RD
BROAD GREEN
River Lea or Lee
Howe Green
Bunkers Hill
Pollard Wood
Stocking Lane (Path)
Kennel Hall Farm
BEDWELL AVE
Longacre Wood
Bayford Hall Farm
Bayford Hall
BAYFORD LA
Great Stockings
Culver Wood
Ashfield Farm
STOCKINGS LA
Culverwood House
Culverwood Farm
ROBINS NEST HILL
WELL ROW
Bayford
Sch
Bedwellpark Farm
Furze Field
Breach Lane (Track)
Manor House
Bayford Wood
Bayford Grange
Bayford House
ASHENDENE RD
Little Berkhamsted
The Gage
ORCHARD CL
CHURCH RD
CHURCH CL
GODDARDS CL
PH
Danes Farm
Berkhamsted Lane Plantation
BERKHAMSTED LA
BUCKS ALLEY
Bell's Wood
Buck's Alley Wood
Bucks Farm
Bush Farm
The Wilderness
WHITE STUBBS LA
The Beehive (PH)
Epping House School
Woodcock Lodge
Moat
Epping Green Farm
Ashen Grove
Ashendene Farm
Calves Grove
Epping Green
Woodcock Lodge Farm
TYLERS CSWY
Birch Wood

113

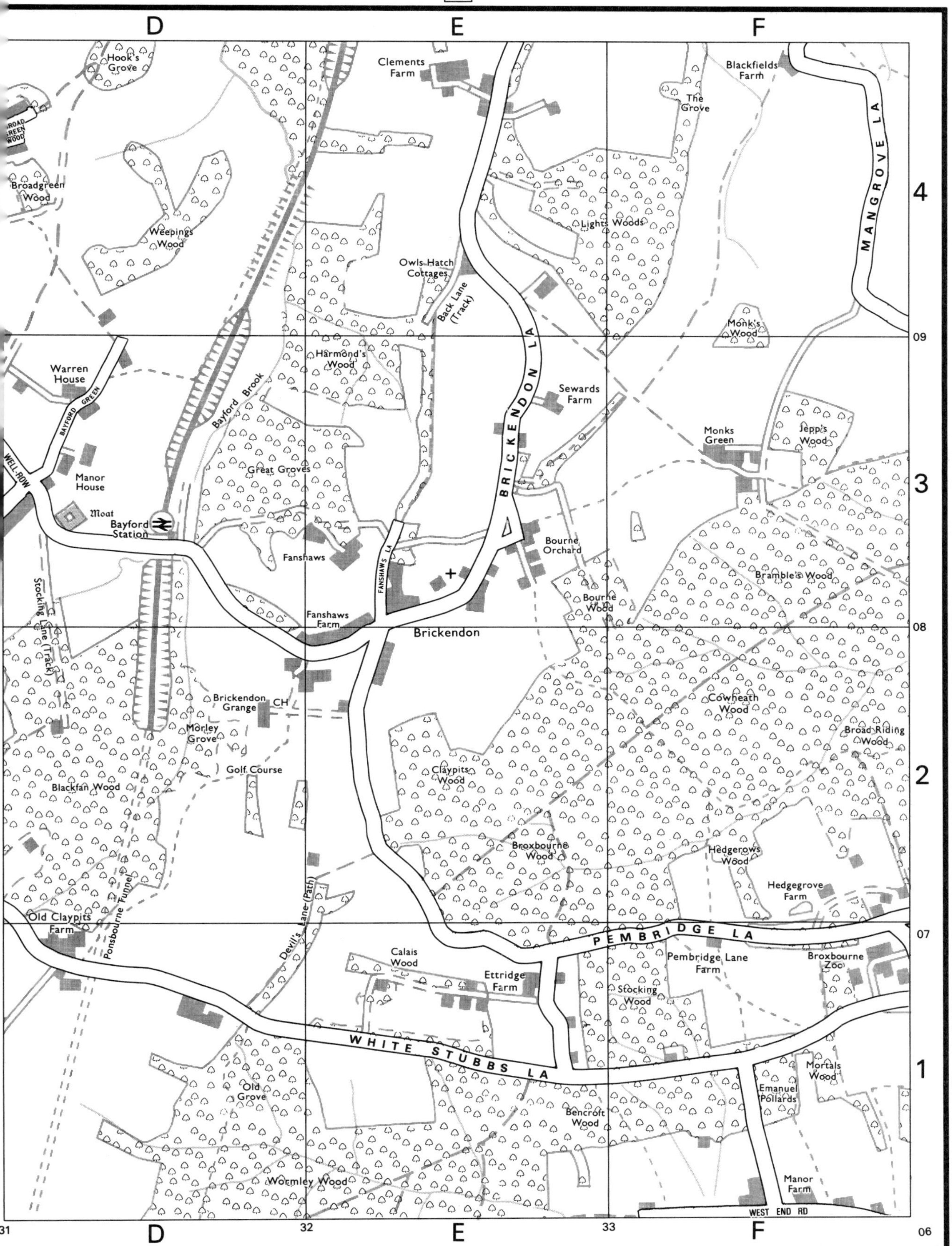
D
E
F
Hook's Grove
Clements Farm
Blackfields Farm
The Grove
BROAD GREEN WOOD
MANGROVE LA
Broadgreen Wood
Weepings Wood
Lights Woods
Owls Hatch Cottages
Back Lane (Track)
Monk's Wood
4
09
Warren House
BAYFORD GREEN
Harmond's Wood
Bayford Brook
BRICKENDON LA
Sewards Farm
Monks Green
Jepp's Wood
WELL ROW
Manor House
Great Groves
3
Moat
Bayford Station
Fanshaws
FANSHAWS LA
Bourne Orchard
Bramble's Wood
Stocking Lane (Track)
Bourne Wood
Fanshaws Farm
Brickendon
08
134
Brickendon Grange
CH
Cowheath Wood
Morley Grove
Broad Riding Wood
Golf Course
Claypits Wood
2
Blackfan Wood
Broxbourne Wood
Hedgerows Wood
Hedgegrove Farm
Old Claypits Farm
Ponsbourne Tunnel
Devil's Lane (Path)
PEMBRIDGE LA
07
Calais Wood
Pembridge Lane Farm
Broxbourne Zoo
Ettridge Farm
Stocking Wood
WHITE STUBBS LA
1
Mortals Wood
Old Grove
Emanuel Pollards
Bencroft Wood
Wormley Wood
Manor Farm
WEST END RD
31
32
33
06

147

114

133

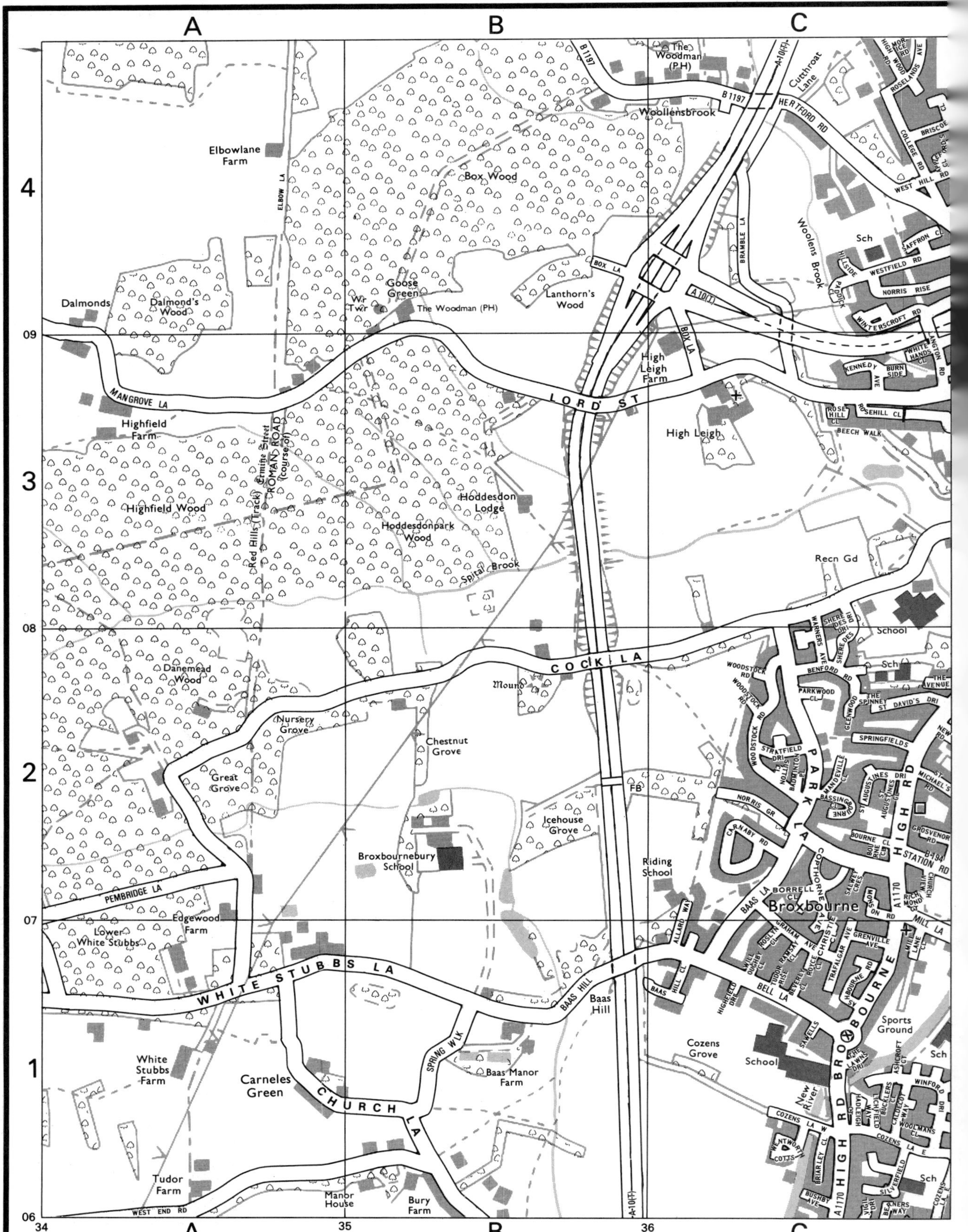
A
B
C
4
3
2
1
09
08
07
06
34
35
36
The Woodman (PH)
B1197
Cutthroat Lane
HERTFORD RD
Woollensbrook
Elbowlane Farm
ELBOW LA
Box Wood
BOX LA
Lanthorn's Wood
A10(T)
BRAMBLE LA
Woolens Brook
Sch
WESTFIELD RD
NORRIS RISE
WINTERSCROFT RD
KENNEDY AVE
BURN SIDE
WHITE HANDS CL
ROSE HILL
ROSEHILL CL
BEECH WALK
COLLEGE RD
BRISCOE CL
WEST HILL RD
ROSELANDS AVE
HILLSIDE
PADDICK CL
SAFFRON CL
Dalmonds
Dalmond's Wood
Goose Green
Wr Twr
The Woodman (PH)
High Leigh Farm
MANGROVE LA
LORD ST
High Leigh
Highfield Farm
Ermine Street
ROMAN ROAD (course of)
Red Hills (Track)
Highfield Wood
Hoddesdon Lodge
Hoddesdonpark Wood
Spital Brook
Recn Gd
School
WARNERS AVE
SHERE DES DRI
Danemead Wood
COCK LA
Mound
WOODSTOCK RD
BENFORD RD
THE AVENUE
PARKWOOD CL
GLENWOOD
THE SPINNEY
ST DAVID'S DRI
Nursery Grove
Chestnut Grove
SPRINGFIELDS
STRATFIELD DRI
PARK LA
MANDEVILLE CL
Great Grove
FB
NORRIS GR
BASSINGBOURNE CL
ST AUGUSTINES DRI
HIGH RD
ST MICHAEL'S
GROSVENOR RD
Icehouse Grove
CARNABY RD
BOURNE CL
Broxbournebury School
Riding School
STATION RD
B194
BAAS LA
BORRELL CL
COPTHORNE AVE
Broxbourne
CHURCH FIELDS
PEMBRIDGE LA
Lower White Stubbs
Edgewood Farm
ALLARD WAY
GRAHAM AVE
CHRISTIE
TRAFALGAR AVE
GRENVILLE AVE
MILL LA
A1170
ROYCE CL
TUDOR RAMSAY CL
HARBOURNE RD
WHITE STUBBS LA
BAAS HILL
Baas Hill
BAAS HILL CL
BELL LA
HIGHFIELD DRI
BOURNE
Sports Ground
SAWELLS
White Stubbs Farm
SPRING WLK
Baas Manor Farm
Cozens Grove
School
New River
Sch
Carneles Green
CHURCH LA
COZENS LA W
WENTWORTH COTTS
COZENS LA E
WINFORD DRI
LICHFIELD WAY
CALVERT CL
WOOLMANS CL
Tudor Farm
BRIARLEY CL
BUSHBY AVE
SILVERFIELD
Sch
WEST END RD
Manor House
Bury Farm
A1170 HIGH RD BROXBOURNE
A10(T)

148

115

not continued, see key diagram

149

122

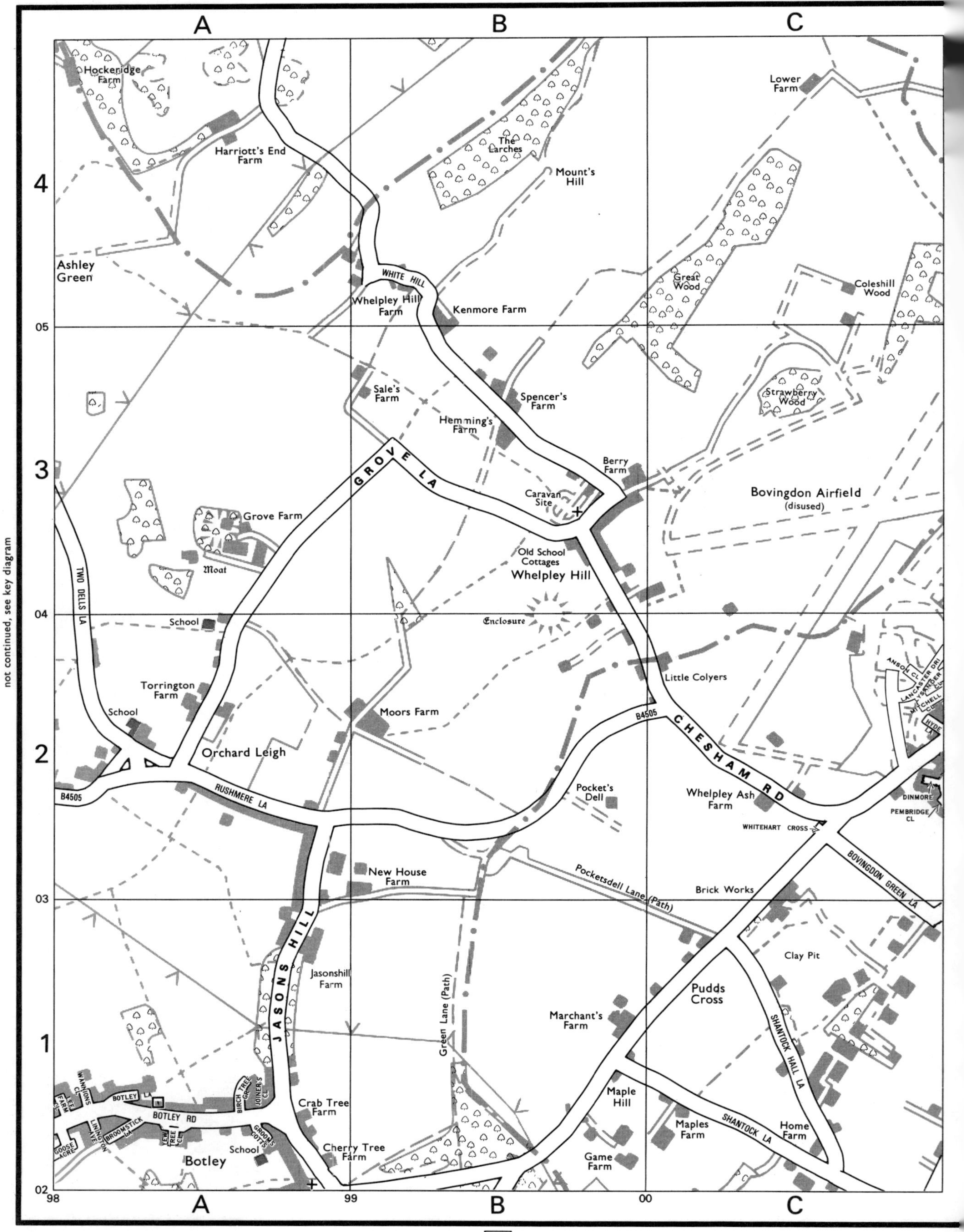
A
B
C
4
3
2
1
05
04
03
02
98
99
00
Hockeridge Farm
Harriott's End Farm
The Larches
Mount's Hill
Lower Farm
Ashley Green
WHITE HILL
Whelpley Hill Farm
Kenmore Farm
Great Wood
Coleshill Wood
Sale's Farm
Spencer's Farm
Strawberry Wood
Hemming's Farm
GROVE LA
Berry Farm
Caravan Site
Bovingdon Airfield
(disused)
Grove Farm
Old School Cottages
Whelpley Hill
Moat
TWO DELLS LA
School
Enclosure
Torrington Farm
Little Colyers
ANSON CL
LANCASTER DR
LYSANDER CL
MITCHELL CL
HYDE
School
Moors Farm
B4505
CHESHAM RD
Orchard Leigh
B4505
RUSHMERE LA
Pocket's Dell
Whelpley Ash Farm
DINMORE
PEMBRIDGE CL
WHITEHART CROSS
New House Farm
Pocketsdell Lane (Path)
Brick Works
BOVINGDON GREEN LA
JASONS HILL
Jasonshill Farm
Clay Pit
Pudds Cross
Marchant's Farm
Green Lane (Path)
SHANTOCK HALL LA
WANNIONS CL
LEE FARM CL
BOTLEY LA
BIRCH TREE GRO
JOINER'S CL
BOTLEY RD
LINTINGTON AVE
BROOMSTICK LA
YEW TREE CT
GROOMS COTTS
GOOSE ACRE
Maple Hill
Crab Tree Farm
Maples Farm
SHANTOCK LA
Home Farm
School
Cherry Tree Farm
Game Farm
Botley
not continued, see key diagram

150

123

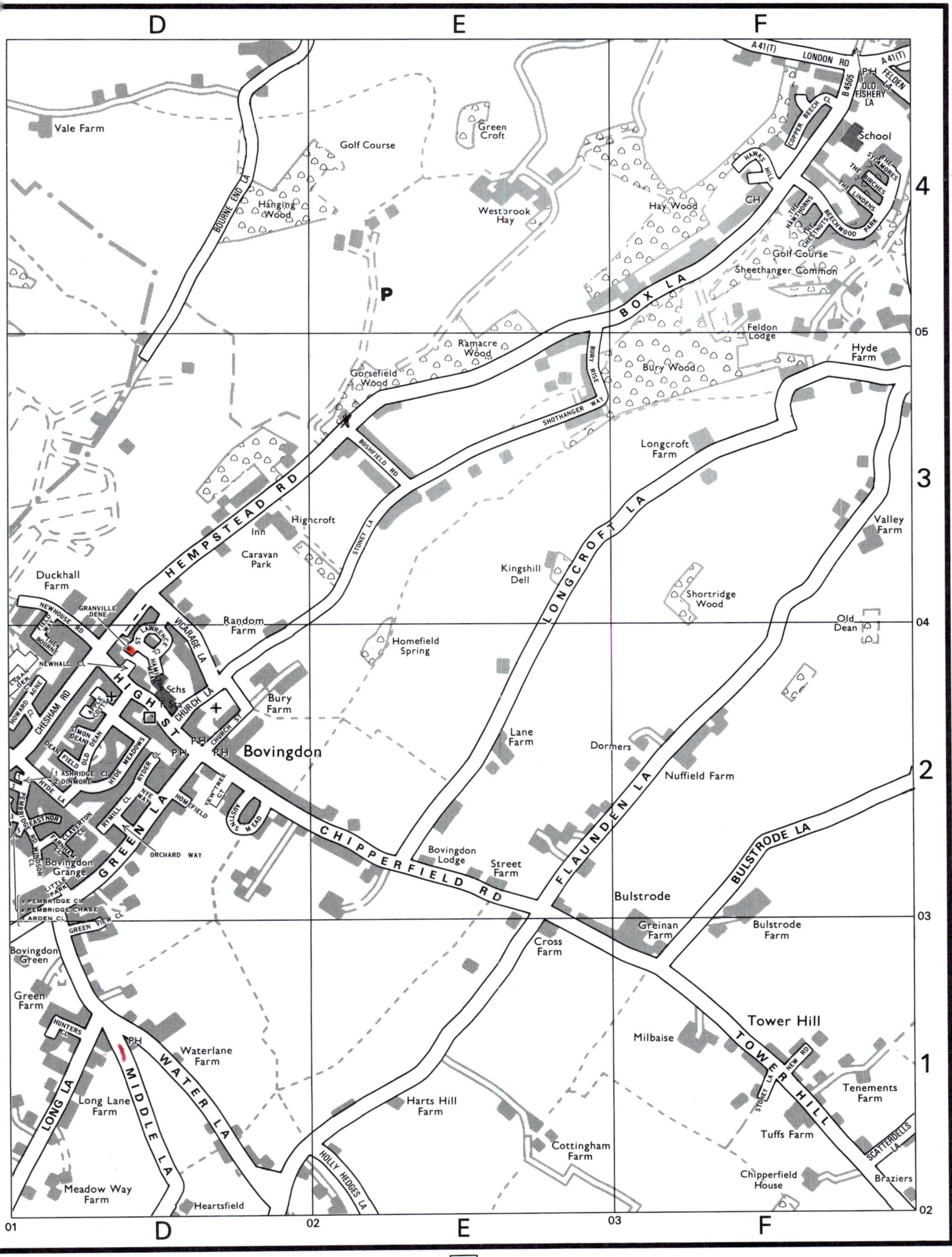
D
E
F
A 41(T)
LONDON RD
A 41(T)
FELDEN LA
B 4505
PH
OLD FISHERY LA
School
COPPER BEECH CL
Vale Farm
Golf Course
Green Croft
BOURNE END LA
Hanging Wood
Westbrook Hay
Hay Wood
HAWKS HILL
CH
THE SYCAMORES
THE BIRCHES
THE LINDENS
THE HAWTHORNS
THE CHESTNUTS
BEECHWOOD PARK
Golf Course
Sheethanger Common
P
BOX LA
Felden Lodge
Hyde Farm
Ramacre Wood
BURY RISE
Bury Wood
Gorsefield Wood
SHOTHANGER WAY
BUSHFIELD RD
Longcroft Farm
HEMPSTEAD RD
Inn
Highcroft
Caravan Park
STONEY LA
Valley Farm
Kingshill Dell
LONGCROFT LA
Shortridge Wood
Duckhall Farm
NEWHOUSE RD
GRANVILLE DENE
Random Farm
VICARAGE LA
ST LAWRENCE CL
Homefield Spring
Old Dean
THE BOURNE
NEWHALL CL
HAMILTON MEAD
Schs
F Sta
CHURCH LA
HIGH ST
Bury Farm
CHESHAM RD
HOWARD AGNE
CHURCH ST
PH
Bovingdon
Lane Farm
Dormers
SIMON DEAN
OLD DEAN
DEAN FIELD
HYDE MEADOWS
RYDER CL
1 ASHRIDGE CL
2 DINMORE
HYDE LA
Nuffield Farm
NYE WAY
HOMEFIELD
YEWTREE CT
AUSTINS MEAD
RYMILL CL
PEMBRIDGE RD
EASTNOR
LAVERTON CL
FARNHAM CL
WINDSOR CL
GREEN LA
ORCHARD WAY
FLAUNDEN LA
BULSTRODE LA
CHIPPERFIELD RD
Bovingdon Grange
Bovingdon Lodge
Street Farm
Bulstrode
LITTLE PARK
3 PEMBRIDGE CL
4 PEMBRIDGE CHASE
5 ARDEN CL
GREEN VIEW CL
Greinan Farm
Bulstrode Farm
Cross Farm
Bovingdon Green
Green Farm
HUNTERS CL
PH
Tower Hill
Milbaise
TOWER HILL
NEW RD
Waterlane Farm
WATER LA
MIDDLE LA
LONG LA
Long Lane Farm
Harts Hill Farm
Tenements Farm
STONEY LA
Tuffs Farm
Cottingham Farm
SCATTERDELLS LA
Meadow Way Farm
HOLLY HEDGES LA
Chipperfield House
Braziers
Heartsfield
4
05
3
04
2
03
1
02
01
02
03
D
E
F

138

151

124

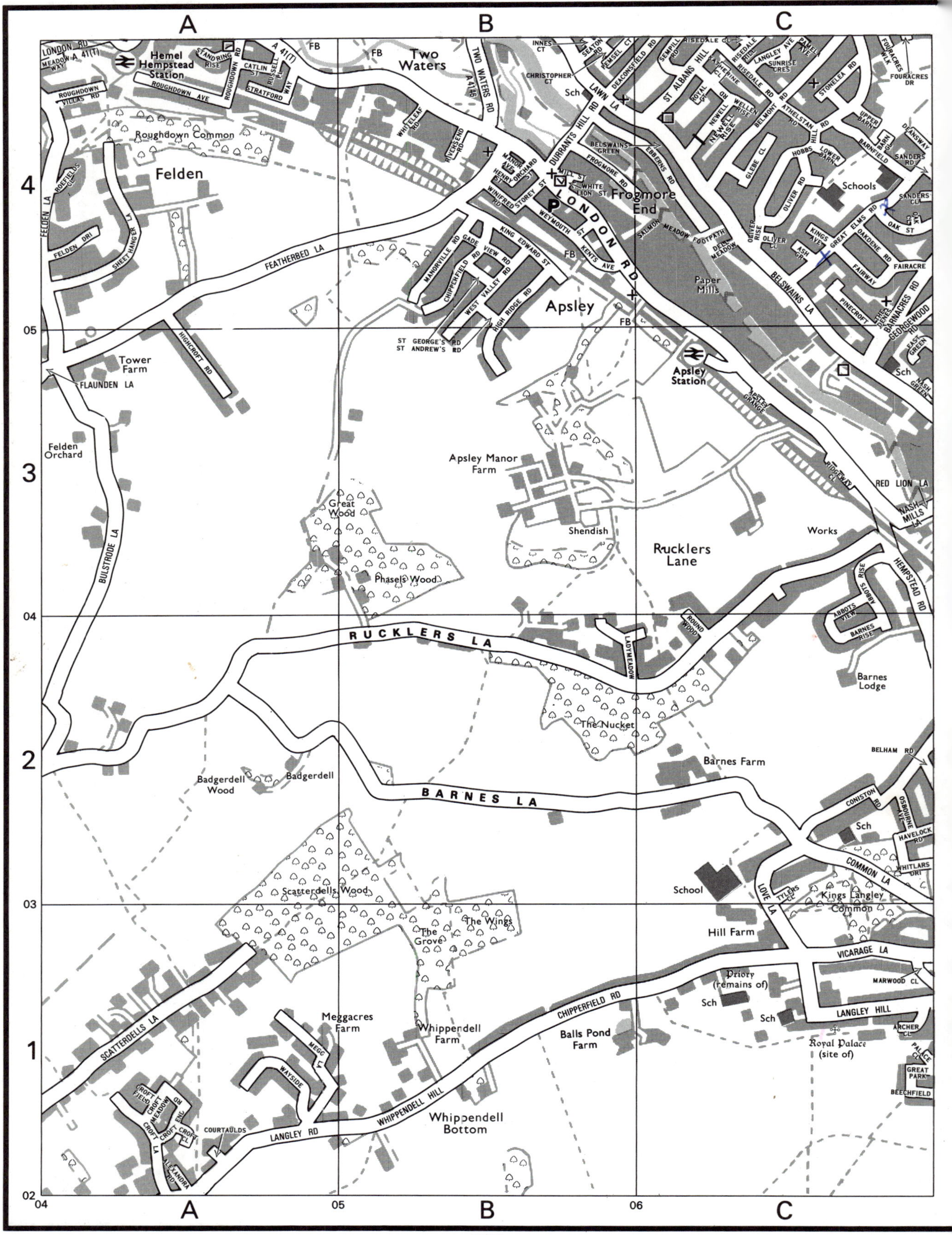
A
B
C
A
B
C
4
3
2
1
05
04
03
02
04
05
06
Hemel Hempstead Station
Two Waters
Roughdown Common
Felden
Frogmore End
Apsley
Paper Mills
Apsley Station
Tower Farm
Felden Orchard
Apsley Manor Farm
Great Wood
Shendish
Rucklers Lane
Works
Phasels Wood
RUCKLERS LA
The Nucket
Barnes Lodge
Barnes Farm
Badgerdell Wood
Badgerdell
BARNES LA
Scatterdells Wood
The Wings
The Grove
School
Kings Langley Common
Hill Farm
Priory (remains of)
Sch
Meggacres Farm
Whippendell Farm
Balls Pond Farm
Royal Palace (site of)
Whippendell Bottom
FEATHERBED LA
FLAUNDEN LA
BULSTRODE LA
HIGHCROFT RD
SCATTERDELLS LA
CHIPPERFIELD RD
WHIPPENDELL HILL
LANGLEY RD
LONDON RD
BELSWAINS LA
HEMPSTEAD RD
COMMON LA
VICARAGE LA
LANGLEY HILL
LOVE LA
RED LION LA
Schools
FB

137

152

125

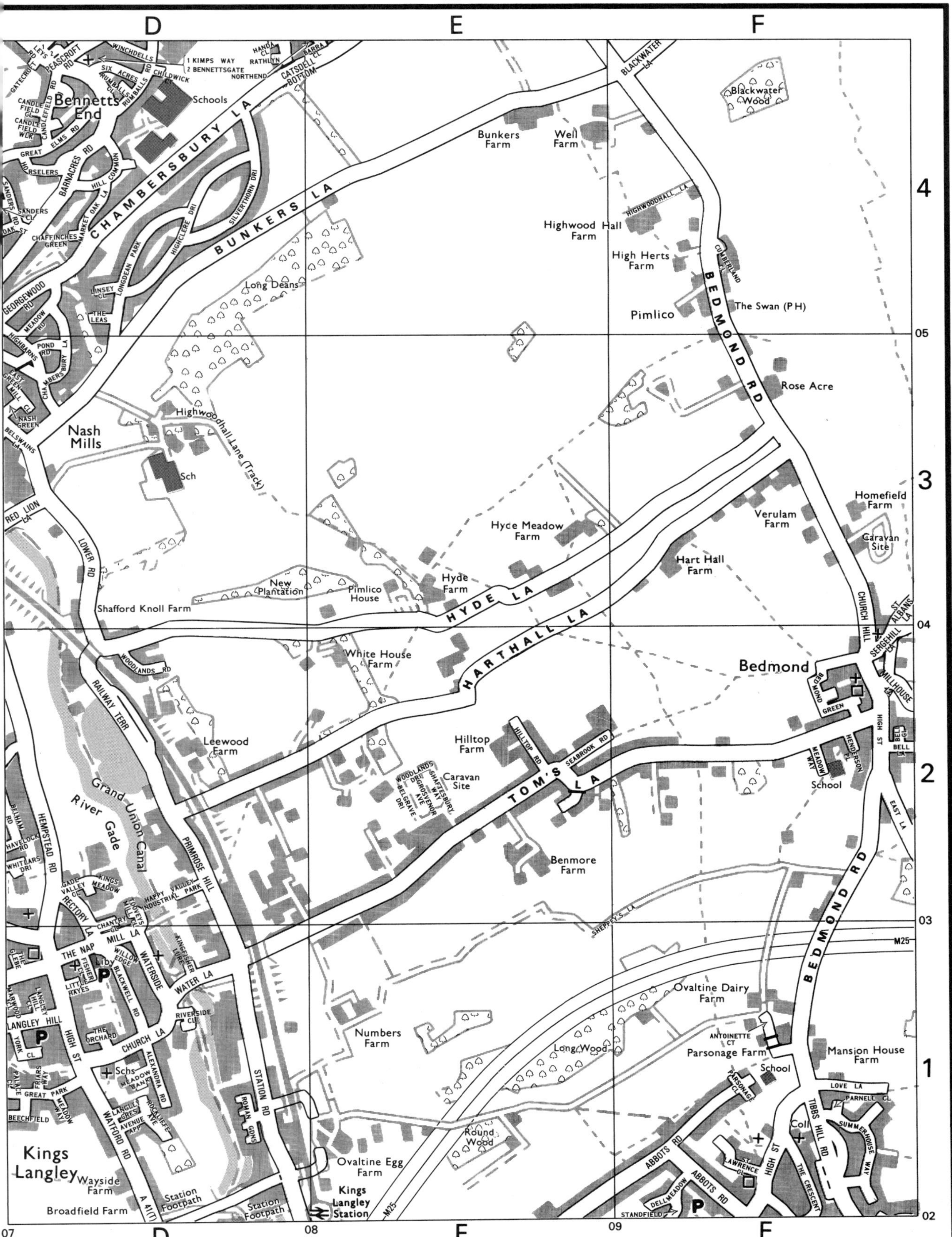
D
E
F
Bennetts End
Schools
Chambersbury La
Bunkers La
Bunkers Farm
Well Farm
Blackwater Wood
Blackwater La
Highwoodhall La
Highwood Hall Farm
High Herts Farm
Cumberland
Bedmond Rd
The Swan (PH)
Pimlico
Long Deans
Rose Acre
Nash Mills
Highwoodhall Lane (Track)
Sch
Red Lion La
Lower Rd
Hyce Meadow Farm
Verulam Farm
Homefield Farm
Caravan Site
Hart Hall Farm
New Plantation
Pimlico House
Hyde Farm
Hyde La
Shafford Knoll Farm
Harthall La
Church Hill
St Albans La
Sergehill La
White House Farm
Bedmond
Bedmond Green
Millhouse La
Woodlands Rd
Railway Terr
Leewood Farm
Hilltop Farm
Hilltop Rd
Seabrook Rd
Caravan Site
Tom's La
Meadow Way
Henderson Pl
School
High St
Bell La
East La
Grand Union Canal
River Gade
Primrose Hill
Hempstead Rd
Benmore Farm
Happy Valley Industrial Park
Sheppey's La
M25
Mill La
Water La
Waterside
Ovaltine Dairy Farm
Numbers Farm
Long Wood
Antoinette Ct
Parsonage Farm
School
Mansion House Farm
Love La
Parnell Cl
Langley Hill
High St
Church La
Schs
Station Rd
Roman Gdns
Round Wood
Abbots Rd
Tibbs Hill Rd
Summerhouse Way
The Crescent
Coll
St Lawrence Cl
Dellmeadow
Standfield
Kings Langley
Wayside Farm
Broadfield Farm
Watford Rd
A 41(T)
Station Footpath
Ovaltine Egg Farm
Kings Langley Station
4
3
2
1
05
04
03
02
07
08
09

140

153

126

139

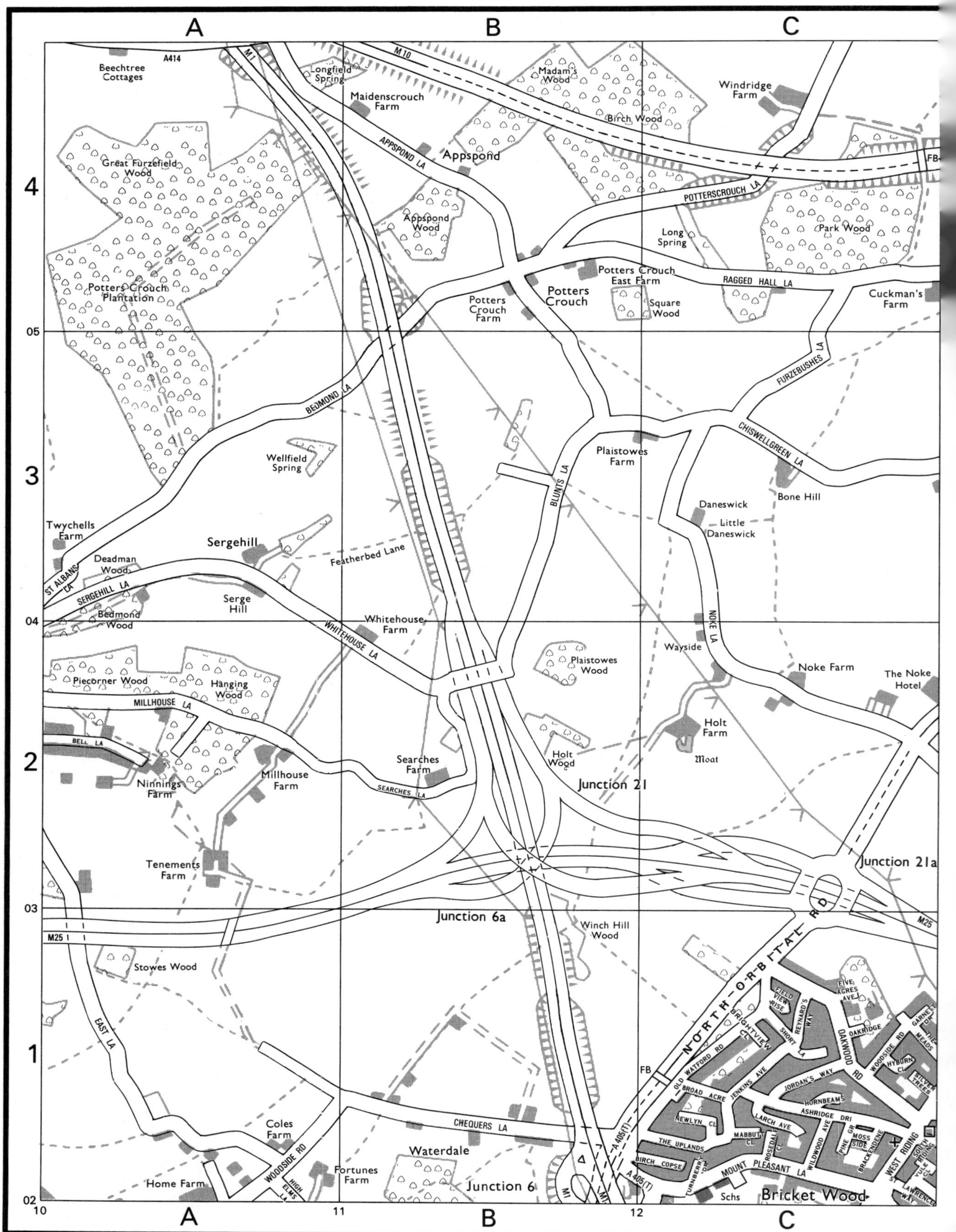
A
B
C
4
3
2
1
05
04
03
02
10
11
12
A414
M1
M10
Beechtree Cottages
Longfield Spring
Maidenscrouch Farm
Madam's Wood
Birch Wood
Windridge Farm
FB
APPSPOND LA
Appspond
Great Furzefield Wood
Appspond Wood
POTTERSCROUCH LA
Long Spring
Park Wood
Potters Crouch Plantation
Potters Crouch East Farm
RAGGED HALL LA
Potters Crouch Farm
Potters Crouch
Square Wood
Cuckman's Farm
BEDMOND LA
FURZEBUSHES LA
CHISWELLGREEN LA
Plaistowes Farm
Wellfield Spring
BLUNTS LA
Bone Hill
Daneswick
Little Daneswick
Twychells Farm
Sergehill
Featherbed Lane
Deadman Wood
ST ALBANS LA
SERGEHILL LA
Serge Hill
Bedmond Wood
Whitehouse Farm
WHITEHOUSE LA
NOKE LA
Wayside
Noke Farm
The Noke Hotel
Plaistowes Wood
Piecorner Wood
Hanging Wood
MILLHOUSE LA
BELL LA
Holt Farm
Moat
Searches Farm
Holt Wood
Ninnings Farm
Millhouse Farm
SEARCHES LA
Junction 21
Junction 21a
Tenements Farm
Junction 6a
Winch Hill Wood
NORTH ORBITAL RD
M25
Stowes Wood
FIELD VIEW RISE
FIVE ACRES AVE
BRIGHTVIEW CL
SHORT LA
REYNARD'S WAY
OAKWOOD RD
OAKRIDGE
GARNETT DR
THE MEADS
EAST LA
WATFORD RD
WOODSIDE RD
HYBURN CL
SILVER TREES
OLD WATFORD RD
BROAD ACRE
JENKINS AVE
JORDAN'S WAY
HORNBEAMS
ASHRIDGE DRI
NEWLYN CL
LARCH AVE
CHEQUERS LA
A405(T)
MABBUTT CL
ROSEDALE CL
WILDWOOD AVE
PINE GR
MOSS SIDE
BRACKENDENE
WEST RIDING
SOUTH RIDING
Coles Farm
THE UPLANDS
Waterdale
BIRCH COPSE
TURNBERRY DR
MOUNT PLEASANT LA
YULE CL
Home Farm
WOODSIDE RD
HIGH ELMS LA
Fortunes Farm
Junction 6
Schs
Bricket Wood
LAWRENCE AVE

154

127

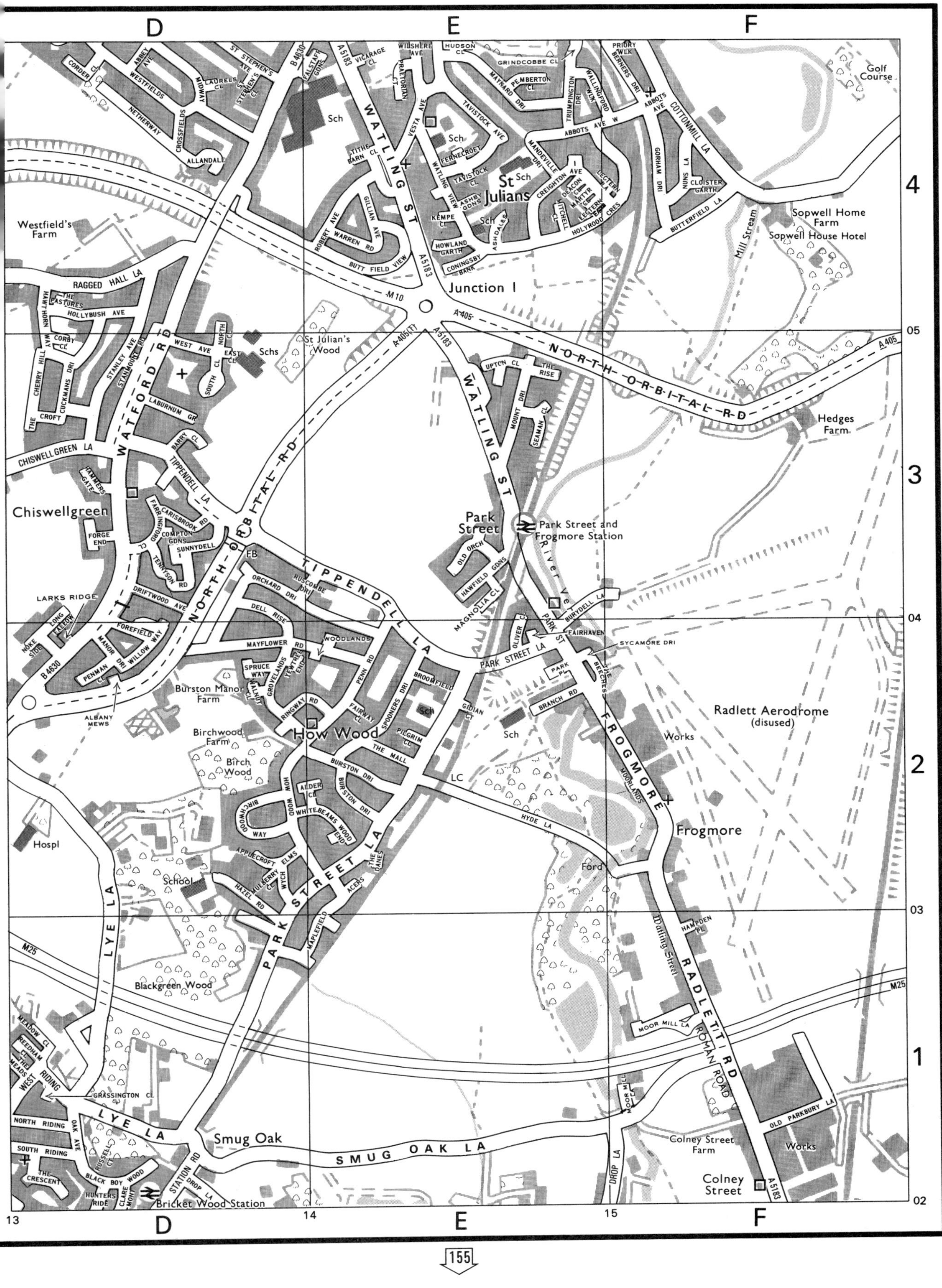

D
E
F
4
3
2
1
05
04
03
02
13
14
15
Sch
St Julians
Junction 1
Westfield's Farm
Chiswellgreen
St Julian's Wood
Schs
Park Street
Park Street and Frogmore Station
Burston Manor Farm
Birchwood Farm
Birch Wood
How Wood
Hospl
School
Blackgreen Wood
Smug Oak
Bricket Wood Station
Colney Street Farm
Colney Street
Works
Frogmore
Ford
Radlett Aerodrome (disused)
Hedges Farm
Sopwell Home Farm
Sopwell House Hotel
Golf Course
Mill Stream
River Ver
WATLING ST
NORTH ORBITAL RD
WATFORD RD
TIPPENDELL LA
PARK STREET LA
FROGMORE
RADLETT RD
ROMAN ROAD
SMUG OAK LA
LYE LA
HYDE LA
CHISWELL GREEN LA
RAGGED HALL LA
M10
M25
A405
A5183
B4630

142

155

128

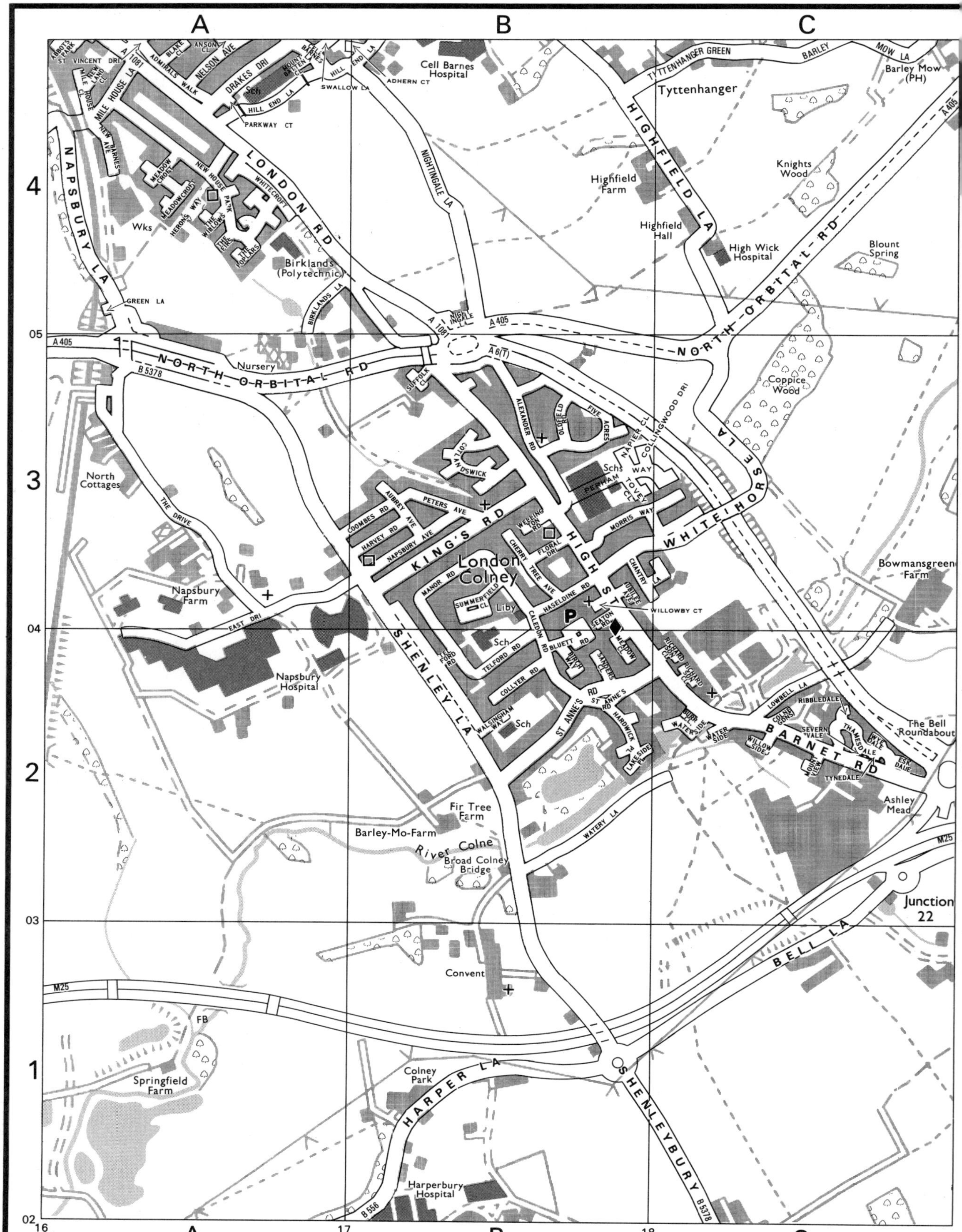
A
B
C
4
3
2
1
05
04
03
02
16
17
18
Tyttenhanger
Tyttenhanger Green
Barley Mow La
Barley Mow (PH)
Cell Barnes Hospital
Highfield Farm
Highfield Hall
High Wick Hospital
Knights Wood
Blount Spring
Birklands (Polytechnic)
London Rd
Napsbury La
Nightingale La
Highfield La
North Orbital Rd
Nursery
Coppice Wood
North Cottages
The Drive
Napsbury Farm
Napsbury Hospital
London Colney
King's Rd
High St
Shenley La
White Horse La
Bowmansgreen Farm
The Bell Roundabout
Barnet Rd
Ashley Mead
Fir Tree Farm
Barley-Mo-Farm
River Colne
Broad Colney Bridge
Watery La
Junction 22
Bell La
Convent
M25
FB
Springfield Farm
Colney Park
Harper La
Shenleybury
Harperbury Hospital
A 405
A 1081
A 6(T)
B 5378
B 556
Sch
Schs
Liby
Wks
Green La
East Dri
Willowby Ct
Hill End La
Swallow La
Adhern Ct
Parkway Ct
Drakes Dri
Nelson Ave
Admirals Walk
Mile House La
St Vincent Dri
Whitecroft
Meadowcroft
Herons Way
The Willows
The Firs
The Poplars
Birklands La
Suffolk Cl
Alexander Rd
Oldfield Rd
Five Acres
Napier Cl
Collingwood Dri
Perham Way
Tovey Cl
Morris Way
Cotlandswick
Peters Ave
Aubrey Ave
Coombes Rd
Harvey Rd
Napsbury Ave
Manor Rd
Summerfield Cl
Cherry Tree Ave
Floral Dri
Haseldine Rd
Caledon Rd
Telford Rd
Collyer Rd
Bluett Rd
St Anne's Rd
Walsingham Way
Hardwick Pl
Lakeside Pl
Chantry La
Jubilee Ave
Seaton Rd
Meadow
Richard Stagg Cl
Waterside
Willowside
Lowbell La
Ribbledale
Colne Gdns
Severn Vale
Thamesdale
Wye Dale
Esk Dale
Tynedale
Vouje View

141

156

129

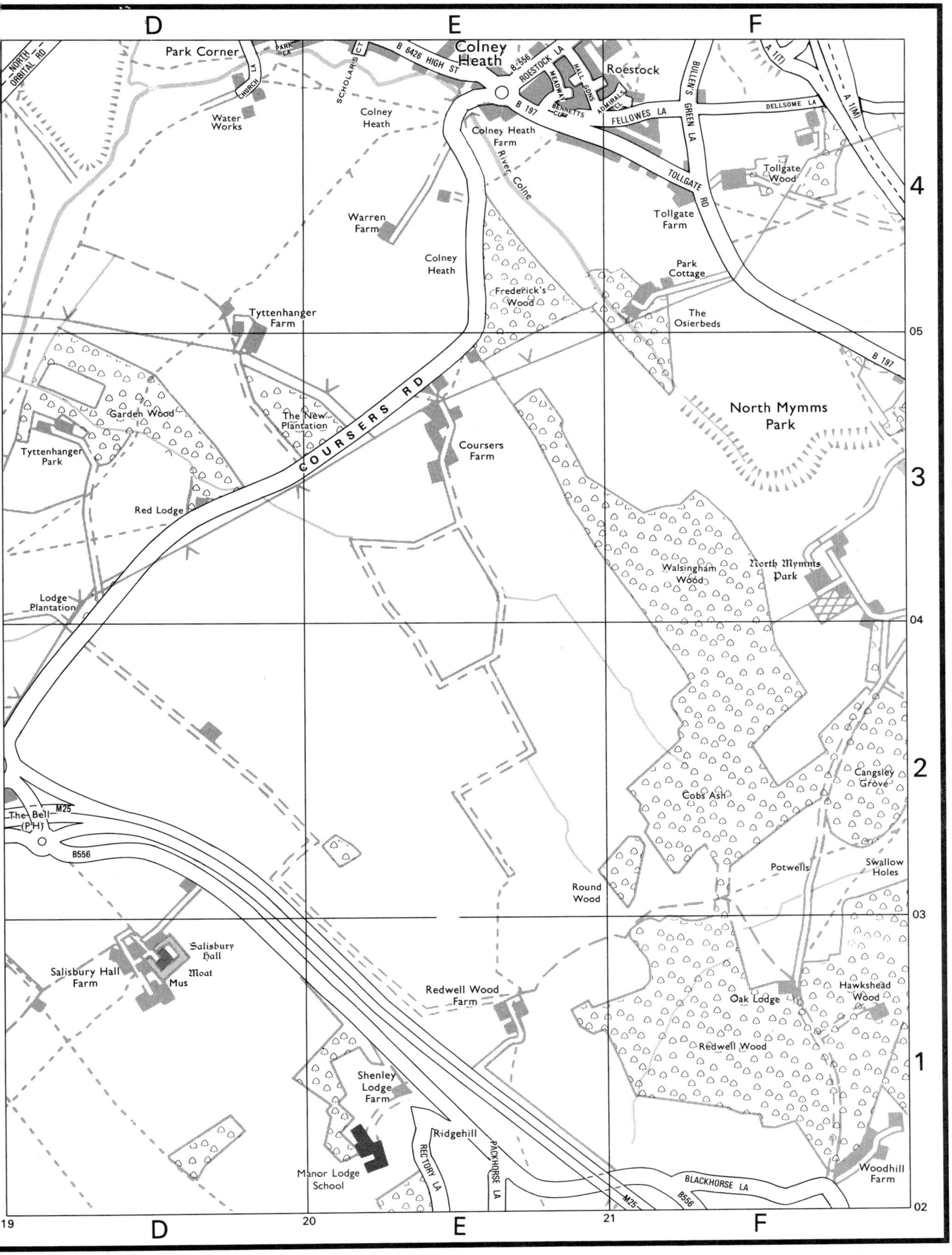
D
E
F
Park Corner
NORTH ORBITAL RD
PARK LA
CHURCH LA
Water Works
SCHOLARS CT
B 6426 HIGH ST
Colney Heath
B 556
ROESTOCK LA
MEADWAY
HALL GDNS
Roestock
BENNETTS CL
ADMIRALS CL
B 197
FELLOWES LA
BULLEN'S GREEN LA
DELLSOME LA
A 1(T)
A 1(M)
Colney Heath
Colney Heath Farm
River Colne
TOLLGATE RD
Tollgate Wood
Tollgate Farm
Warren Farm
Colney Heath
Park Cottage
Frederick's Wood
The Osierbeds
Tyttenhanger Farm
B 197
North Mymms Park
Garden Wood
The New Plantation
COURSERS RD
Coursers Farm
Tyttenhanger Park
Red Lodge
Walsingham Wood
North Mymms Park
Lodge Plantation
Cangsley Grove
Cobs Ash
The Bell (PH)
M25
B556
Potwells
Swallow Holes
Round Wood
Salisbury Hall
Salisbury Hall Farm
Moat
Mus
Redwell Wood Farm
Oak Lodge
Hawkshead Wood
Redwell Wood
Shenley Lodge Farm
Ridgehill
RECTORY LA
PACKHORSE LA
Manor Lodge School
BLACKHORSE LA
M25
B556
Woodhill Farm
19
20
21
D
E
F
05
04
03
02
4
3
2
1

144

157

130

143

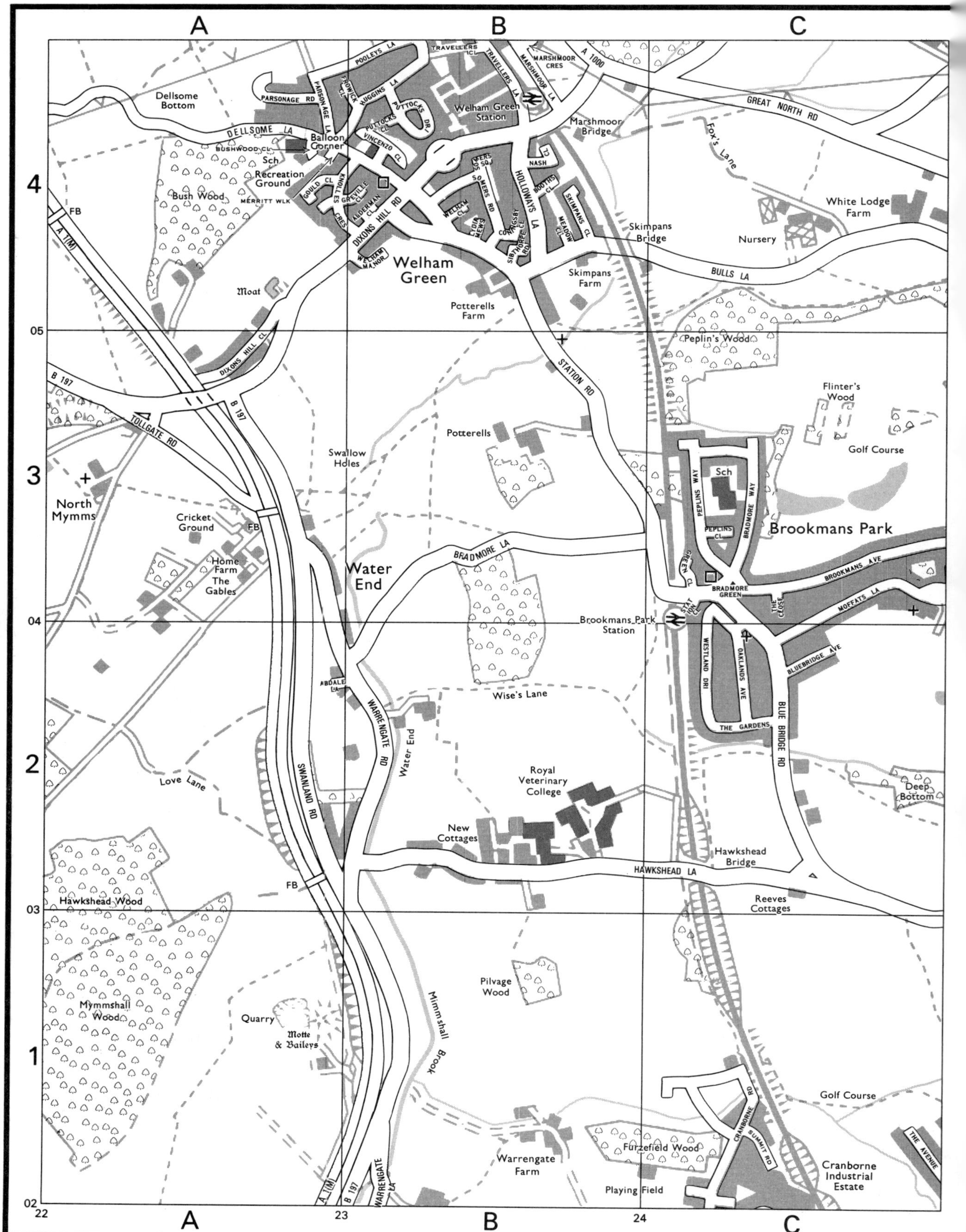
A
B
C
4
3
2
1
05
04
03
02
22
23
24
Dellsome Bottom
PARSONAGE RD
PARSONAGE LA
POOLEYS LA
FROWICK CL
HUGGINS LA
TRAVELLERS CL
TRAVELLERS LA
MARSHMOOR CRES
MARSHMOOR LA
A 1000
GREAT NORTH RD
PUTTOCKS DR
PUTTOCKS CL
Welham Green Station
DELLSOME LA
BUSHWOOD CL
Balloon Corner
VINCENZO CL
NASH
Marshmoor Bridge
Fox's Lane
Sch
Recreation Ground
Bush Wood
MERRITT WLK
GOULD CL
KNOLL CRES
GREVILLE CL
ALDERMAN CL
DIXONS HILL RD
HOLLOWAYS LA
BOOTHS CL
SKIMPANS CL
MEADOW CL
WELHAM CL
LYDIA MEWS
CONINGSBY
SIBTHORPE RD
WELHAM MANOR
White Lodge Farm
Skimpans Bridge
Nursery
FB
A 1(M)
Welham Green
Skimpans Farm
BULLS LA
Moat
Potterells Farm
Peplin's Wood
DIXONS HILL CL
STATION RD
B 197
TOLLGATE RD
Flinter's Wood
Potterells
Golf Course
Swallow Holes
North Mymms
Sch
PEPLINS WAY
BRADMORE WAY
PEPLINS CL
Cricket Ground
Brookmans Park
BRADMORE LA
Home Farm
The Gables
Water End
GREEN CL
BRADMORE GREEN
BROOKMANS AVE
THE CLOSE
MOFFATS LA
Brookmans Park Station
STATION CL
WESTLAND DRI
OAKLANDS AVE
BLUEBRIDGE AVE
ABDALE LA
Wise's Lane
WARRENGATE RD
Water End
THE GARDENS
BLUE BRIDGE RD
SWANLAND RD
Love Lane
Royal Veterinary College
Deep Bottom
New Cottages
Hawkshead Bridge
HAWKSHEAD LA
Reeves Cottages
Hawkshead Wood
Pilvage Wood
Mymmshall Wood
Quarry
Motte & Baileys
Mimmshall Brook
Golf Course
CRANBORNE RD
SUMMIT RD
THE AVENUE
Furzefield Wood
Warrengate Farm
Playing Field
Cranborne Industrial Estate
WARRENGATE LA

158

131

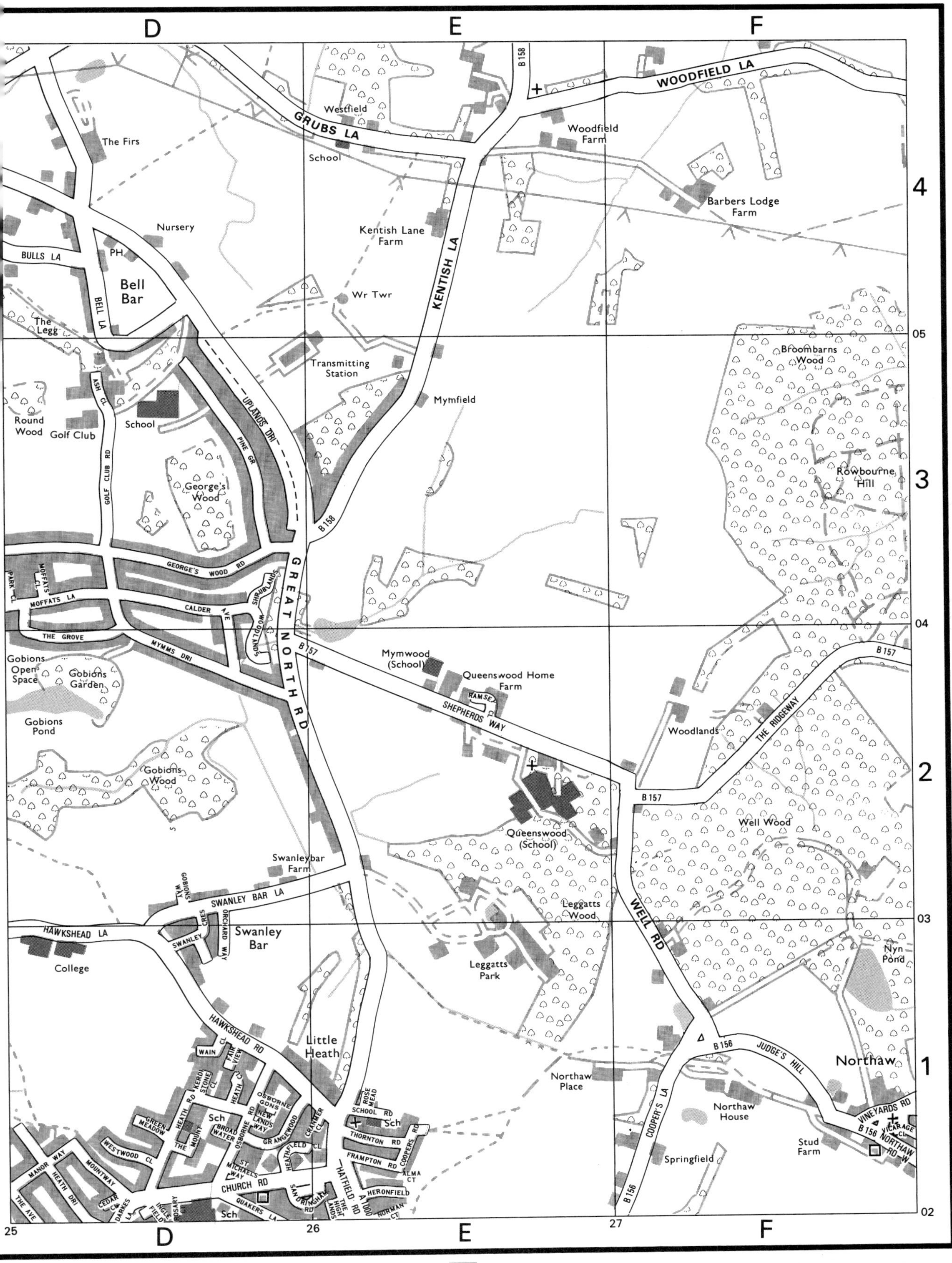
D
E
F
D
E
F
4
3
2
1
05
04
03
02
25
26
27
WOODFIELD LA
B 158
GRUBS LA
Westfield
School
The Firs
Woodfield Farm
Barbers Lodge Farm
Nursery
Kentish Lane Farm
KENTISH LA
BULLS LA
PH
Bell Bar
BELL LA
Wr Twr
The Legg
Transmitting Station
Broombarns Wood
Mymfield
ASH CL
UPLANDS DRI
Round Wood
Golf Club
School
PINE GR
GOLF CLUB RD
George's Wood
Rowbourne Hill
B 158
GEORGE'S WOOD RD
GREAT NORTH RD
MOFFATS CL
PARK CL
MOFFATS LA
SHRUBLANDS
CALDER AVE
WOODLANDS
THE GROVE
MYMMS DRI
B 157
Mymwood (School)
Queenswood Home Farm
RAMSEY
SHEPHERDS WAY
B 157
THE RIDGEWAY
Gobions Open Space
Gobions Garden
Gobions Pond
Woodlands
Gobions Wood
B 157
Well Wood
Queenswood (School)
Swanleybar Farm
GOBIONS WAY
SWANLEY BAR LA
Leggatts Wood
WELL RD
HAWKSHEAD LA
SWANLEY CRES
ORCHARD WAY
Swanley Bar
Nyn Pond
College
Leggatts Park
HAWKSHEAD RD
Little Heath
B 156
JUDGE'S HILL
Northaw
WAIN CL
FAIR VIEW
KEROL STONE CL
Northaw Place
HEATH CL
OSBORNE GDNS
ROSE MEAD
COOPER'S LA
Northaw House
VINEYARDS RD
VICARAGE CL
HEATH RD
NEW LANDS WAY
Sch
SCHOOL RD
Sch
GREEN MEADOW
THE MOUNT
BROAD WATER
OSBORNE RD
GRANGEWOOD
CHANTRY CL
B 156
NORTHAW RD W
THORNTON RD
COOPERS RD
Stud Farm
WESTWOOD CL
ST MICHAELS WAY
HEATHFIELD CL
FRAMPTON RD
ALMA CT
Springfield
MANOR WAY
MOUNTWAY
HEATH DRI
CHURCH RD
SANDRINGHAM RD
HATFIELD RD
HERONFIELD
THE AVE
CEDAR CL
DARKES LA
INGLE FIELD
ROSARY
QUAKERS LA
Sch
THE HIGHLANDS
NORMAN CT
B 156

146

159

132

145

A
B
C
4
3
2
1
05
04
03
02
28
29
30
Birchwood Cottages
Moat
TYLERS CSWY
WOODFIELD LA
Coldharbour Farm
Hell Wood
Coldharbour Plantation
Ponsfall Farm
The Warren
Ponsbourne Park Cottages
Home Farm
Ponsbourne Park
Newgate Street
Coll
NEWGATE ST
Sch
New Park
NEW PARK RD
Home Farm
NEWGATE STREET VILLAGE
TOLMERS MEWS
Tolmers Park Farm
Newgate Street Bridge
Justice Hill
Great Wood (Country Park)
Grimes Bottom
Postern Gate
Postern Bridge
CARBONE HILL
County School Camp
Tolmers
Grimes Brook
P
The Cottage
Tolmers Road
B 157
Home Wood
THE RIDGEWAY
HOMEWOOD LA
Carbone Bottom
BROOKSIDE CRES
HOMEWOOD AVE
BRADGATE
FARM CL
RIDGE HIGH
COULTER CL
WARWICK AVE
WARWICK CL
WOOD VIEW
HANYARDS END
BRADGATE CL
HIGHFIELDS
HILL LEYS
HANYARDS LA
ROBIN WAY
TOLMERS AVE
TOLMERS RD
THRUSH LA
STARLING LA
Nyn Manor Farm
HANDPOST HILL
SUTHERLAND AVE
SUTHERLAND WAY
HILL RISE
ORCHARD CL
Cuffley
THE DRIVEWAY
Thornton's Farm
KINGSMEAD
THE MEADWAY
VINEYARDS RD
EAST RIDGEWAY
ACORN BA
OAK LA
High Willows
Cuffley Hills Farm
CRANFIELD CRES
BACONS DRI
PLOUGH HILL B 157
TOLMERS GDNS
MAYNARD
Vineyard Bridge
Liby
B 156
STATION RD
KING JAMES AVE
CHURCH CL
LAMBS CL
Cuffley Sta
SOPERS RD
The Vineyard
VINEYARD HILL
Hemps Hill
Sch
Works
KINGSWELL RIDE
BURLEIGH WAY
KINGS WAY
THEOBALD'S RD
THEOBALD'S
CHURCH
COLESDALE
NORTHAW RD E
SOUTH DRI
Ppg Sta
GREEN FIELDS
Waterworks Cottages
Sch
B 156
NORTHAW RD W
PARK RD
Hook Lane
Wells Farm

160

133
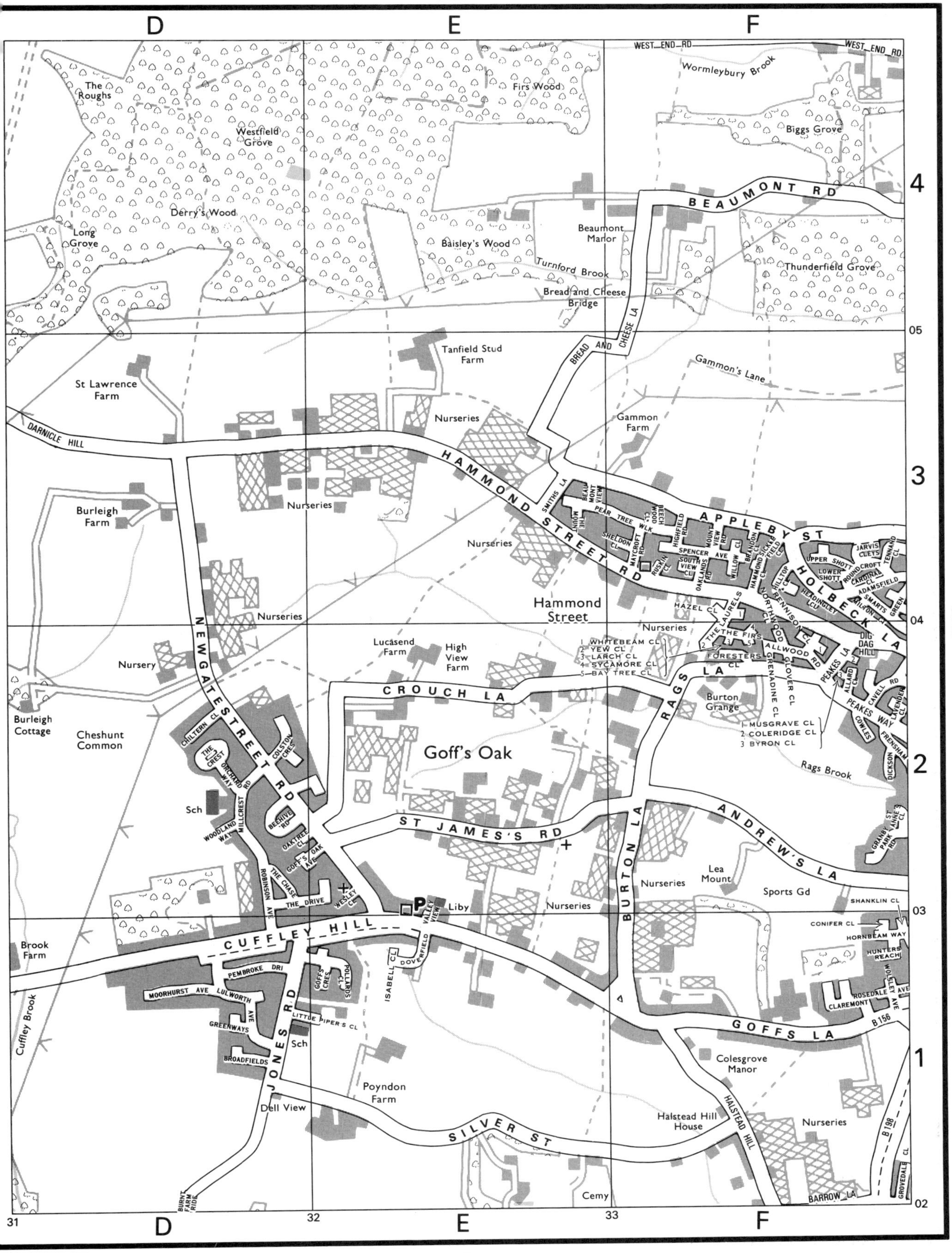
D
E
F
WEST END RD
Wormleybury Brook
The Roughs
Westfield Grove
Firs Wood
Biggs Grove
Derry's Wood
Long Grove
Baisley's Wood
Beaumont Manor
BEAUMONT RD
Turnford Brook
Thunderfield Grove
Bread and Cheese Bridge
BREAD AND CHEESE LA
Tanfield Stud Farm
St Lawrence Farm
Gammon's Lane
DARNICLE HILL
Nurseries
Gammon Farm
HAMMOND STREET RD
Burleigh Farm
APPLEBY ST
SMITHS LA
THE MOUNT
BEAUMONT VIEW
PEAR TREE WLK
BEECH WOOD CL
SHELDON CL
MAYCROFT RD
HIGHFIELD RD
SPENCER AVE
SOUTH VIEW CL
OAKLANDS RD
WILLOW CL
BRANDON CL
HAMMOND CL
SICKLEFIELD CL
RUSKIN CL
HOLBECK LA
UPPER SHOTT
LOWER SHOTT
JARVIS CLEYS
TENNAND CL
ROUNDCROFT
CARDINAL CL
ADAMSFIELD
SMARTS GREEN
MILTON CL
HEADINGLEY CL
HILLTOP CL
HAZEL CL
THE LAURELS
NORTHWOOD
RENNISON CL
Hammond Street
Nursery
Lucasend Farm
High View Farm
1 WHITEBEAM CL
2 YEW CL
3 LARCH CL
4 SYCAMORE CL
5 BAY TREE CL
THE FIRS
ALLWOOD RD
FORESTERS CL
DIG DAG HILL
PEAKES LA
PEAKES WAY
ALLARD CL
CAVELL RD
LAVENDER CL
COWLES
CROUCH LA
RAGS LA
Burton Grange
GRENADINE CL
GLOVER CL
1 MUSGRAVE CL
2 COLERIDGE CL
3 BYRON CL
FRENSHAM
DICKSON
Burleigh Cottage
Cheshunt Common
NEWGATESTREET RD
CHILTERN CL
THE CREST
ORCHARD WAY
COLSTON CRES
Goff's Oak
Rags Brook
Sch
MILLCREST RD
WOODLAND WAY
BEEHIVE RD
ST JAMES'S RD
ANDREW'S LA
GRANBY PARK
ST ANNE'S CL
OAKTREE CL
GOFF'S OAK AVE
THE CHASE
ROBINSON AVE
THE DRIVE
WESLEY CL
BURTON LA
Lea Mount
Sports Gd
P
Liby
VALLEY VIEW
SHANKLIN CL
CONIFER CL
HORNBEAM WAY
HUNTERS REACH
Brook Farm
CUFFLEY HILL
DOVERFIELD
ISABELL CL
PEMBROKE DRI
GOFFS CRES
POLLARDS CL
MOORHURST AVE
LULWORTH AVE
ROSEDALE AVE
CLAREMONT
WOLSLEY AVE
GOFFS LA
B156
Cuffley Brook
GREENWAYS
LITTLE PIPER'S CL
JONES RD
Colesgrove Manor
BROADFIELDS
Poyndon Farm
Dell View
SILVER ST
Halstead Hill House
HALSTEAD HILL
Nurseries
B198
GROVEDALE CL
BURNT FARM RIDE
Cemy
BARROW LA
4
05
3
04
2
03
1
02
31
32
33
148
161

134

147

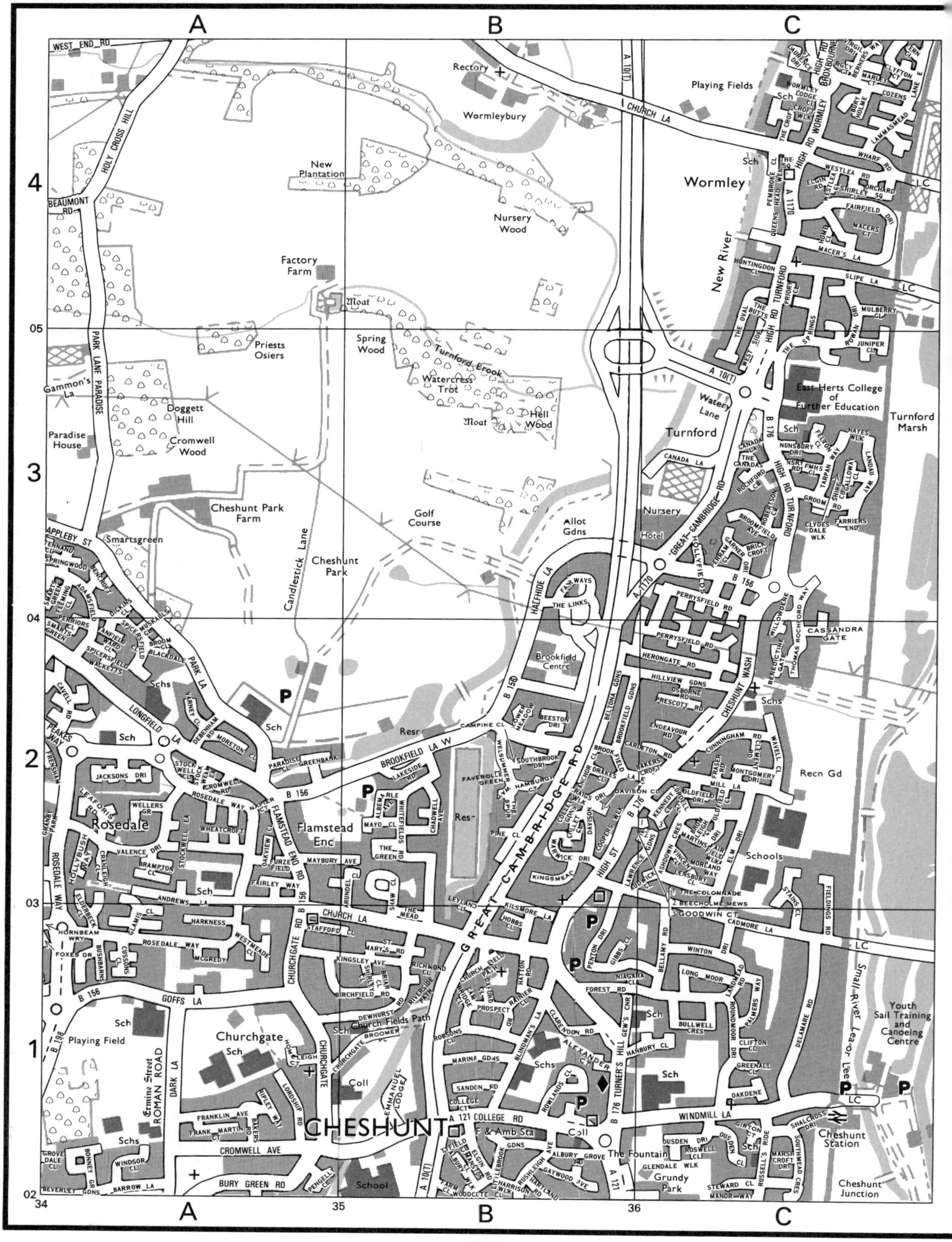
A
B
C
4
3
2
1
05
04
03
02
34
35
36
WEST END RD
Rectory
Wormleybury
CHURCH LA
A 10(T)
Playing Fields
Sch
Wormley
New River
HOLY CROSS HILL
BEAUMONT RD
New Plantation
Nursery Wood
Factory Farm
Moat
Priests Osiers
Spring Wood
Turnford Brook
Watercress Trot
Hell Wood
PARK LANE PARADISE
Gammon's La
Doggett Hill
Cromwell Wood
Paradise House
Cheshunt Park Farm
Golf Course
Allot Gdns
Nursery
Hotel
Turnford
Watery Lane
East Herts College of Further Education
Turnford Marsh
HIGH RD TURNFORD
GREAT CAMBRIDGE RD
APPLEBY ST
Smartsgreen
Candlestick Lane
Cheshunt Park
HALFHIDE LA
Brookfield Centre
CHESHUNT WASH
CASSANDRA GATE
PARK LA
LONGFIELD LA
Schs
Resr
BROOKFIELD LA W
B 156
Res
Recn Gd
Rosedale
Flamstead End
FLAMSTEAD END RD
ROSEDALE WAY
CHURCH LA
HIGH ST
Schools
CADMORE LA
LC
GOFFS LA
Playing Field
Churchgate
CHURCHGATE
Coll
Ermine Street
ROMAN ROAD
DARK LA
CHESHUNT
A 121 COLLEGE RD
F & Amb Sta
The Fountain
WINDMILL LA
Youth Sail Training and Canoeing Centre
Small River Lea or Lee
Cheshunt Station
CROMWELL AVE
BURY GREEN RD
School
Grundy Park
Cheshunt Junction
DELAMARE RD

162

135

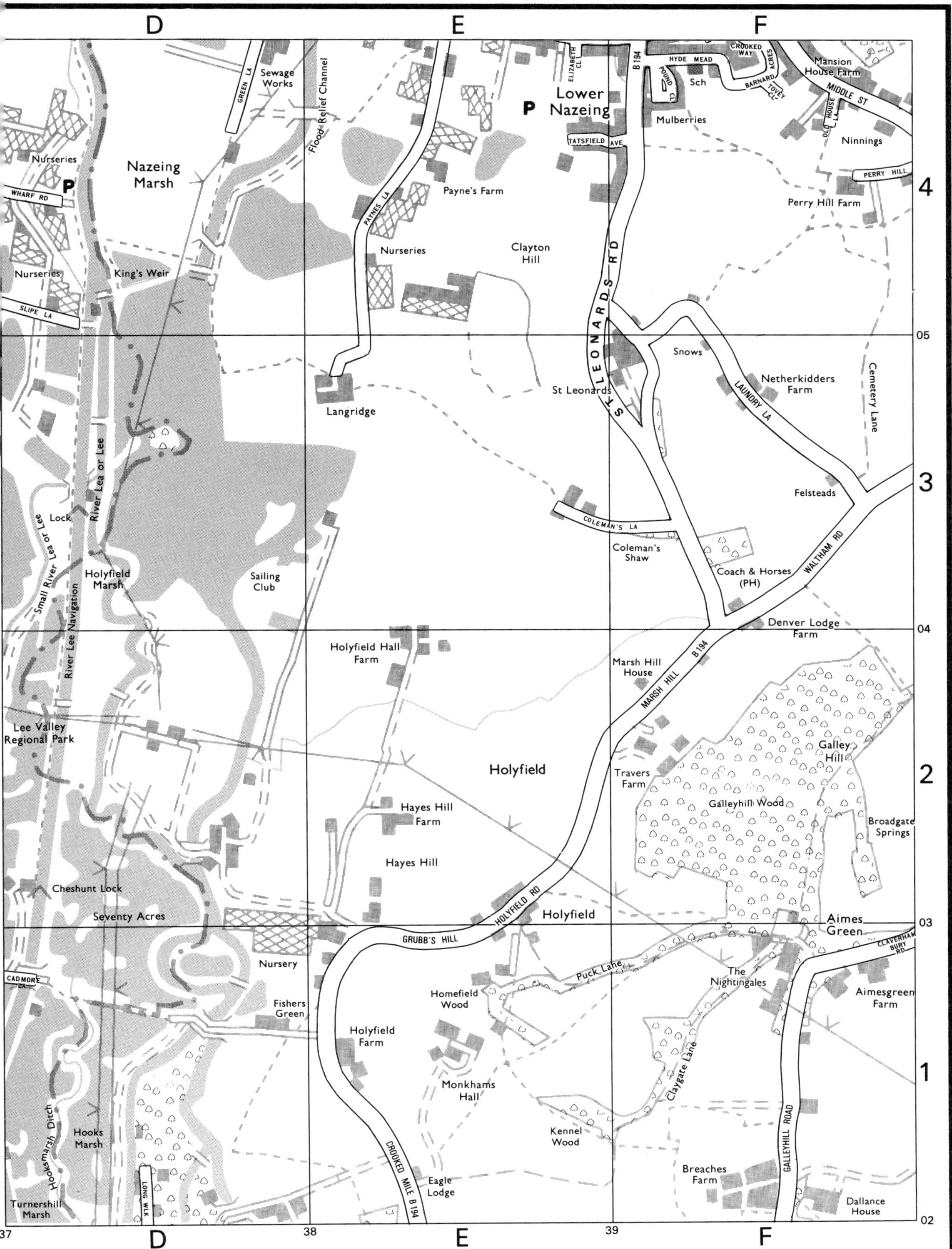
D
E
F
Sewage Works
Flood Relief Channel
GREEN LA
Lower Nazeing
P
Nurseries
Nazeing Marsh
WHARF RD
Nurseries
King's Weir
SLIPE LA
Payne's Farm
PAYNES LA
Nurseries
Clayton Hill
Langridge
ELIZABETH CL
B 194
HYDE MEAD
CROOKED WAY
ACRES
BARNARD
TOVEY CL
POUND CL
Sch
Mulberries
TATSFIELD AVE
Mansion House Farm
MIDDLE ST
OLD HOUSE LA
Ninnings
PERRY HILL
Perry Hill Farm
ST LEONARDS RD
Snows
St Leonards
Netherkidders Farm
LAUNDRY LA
Cemetery Lane
Felsteads
COLEMAN'S LA
Coleman's Shaw
Coach & Horses (PH)
WALTHAM RD
Denver Lodge Farm
Lock
River Lea or Lee
Small River Lea or Lee
River Lee Navigation
Holyfield Marsh
Sailing Club
Holyfield Hall Farm
Marsh Hill House
MARSH HILL
B 194
Lee Valley Regional Park
Holyfield
Travers Farm
Galley Hill
Galleyhill Wood
Broadgate Springs
Hayes Hill Farm
Hayes Hill
Cheshunt Lock
Seventy Acres
HOLYFIELD RD
Holyfield
Aimes Green
CLAVERHAM BURY RD
GRUBB'S HILL
Nursery
CADMORE LA
Puck Lane
The Nightingales
Aimesgreen Farm
Homefield Wood
Fishers Green
Holyfield Farm
Monkhams Hall
Claygate Lane
Kennel Wood
GALLEYHILL ROAD
Hooksmarsh Ditch
Hooks Marsh
Turnershill Marsh
LONG WLK
CROOKED MILE B 194
Eagle Lodge
Breaches Farm
Dallance House
4
3
2
1
05
04
03
02
37
38
39
not continued, see key diagram

163

136

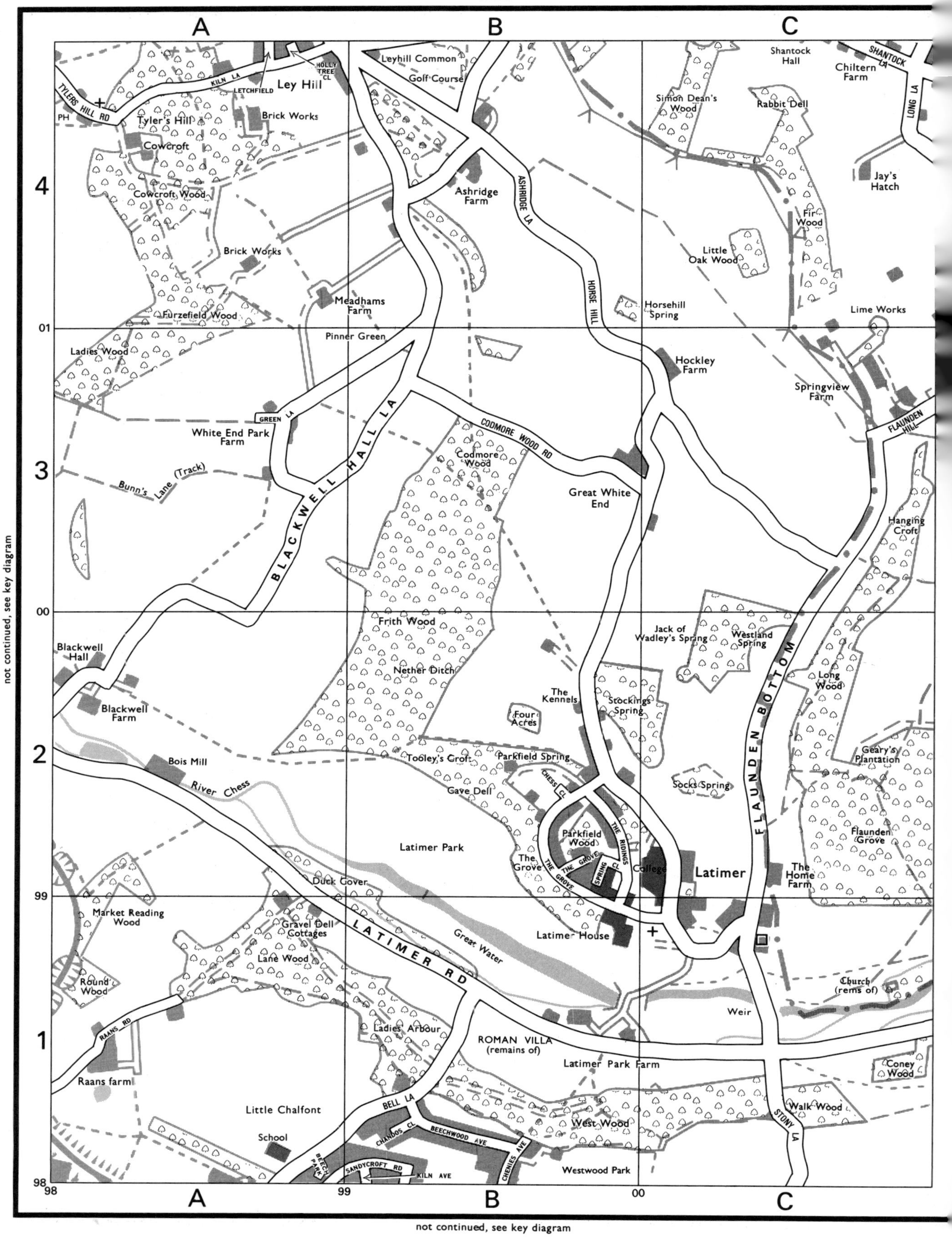

not continued, see key diagram

not continued, see key diagram

137

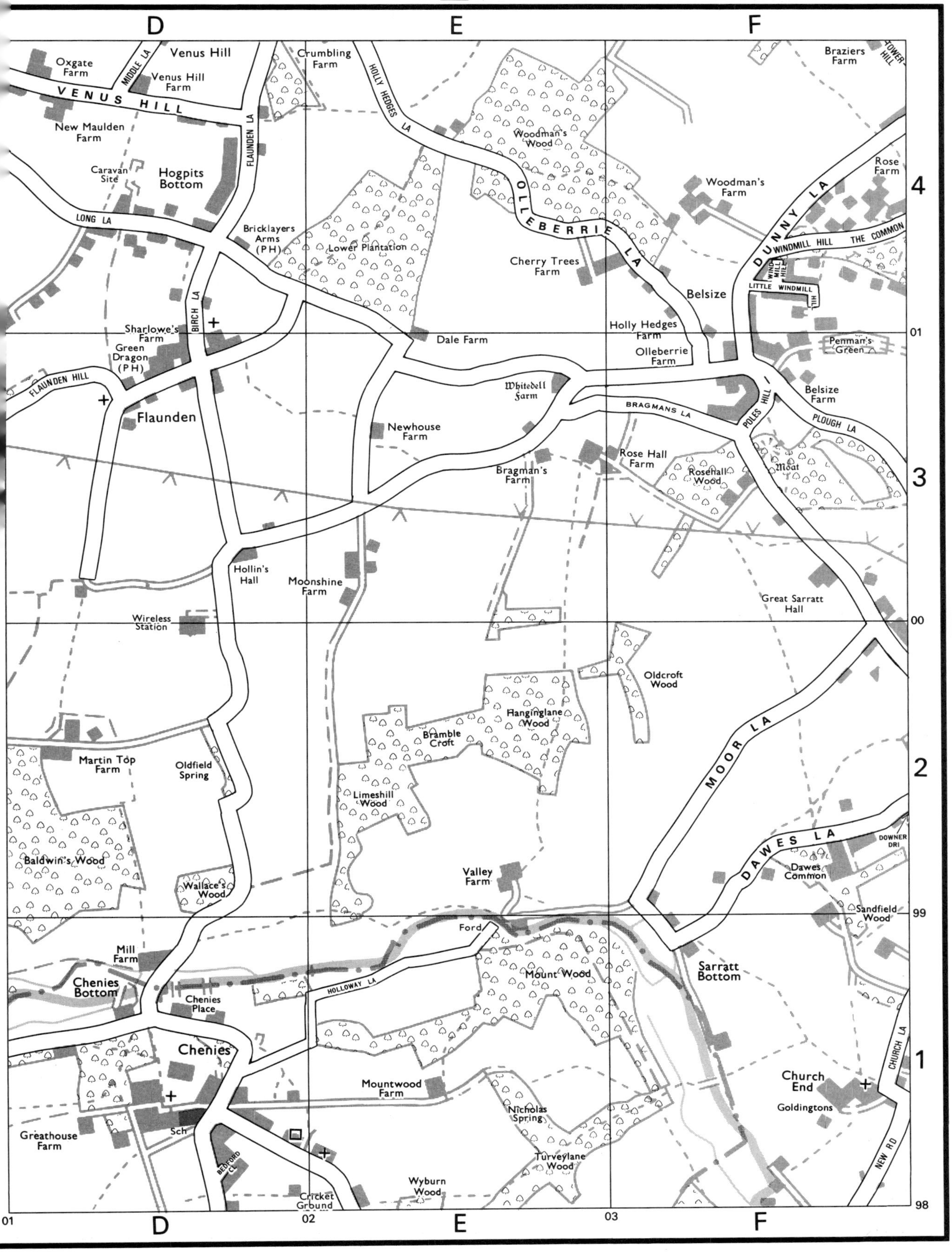
D
E
F
Oxgate Farm
Venus Hill
Venus Hill Farm
MIDDLE LA
VENUS HILL
Crumbling Farm
HOLLY HEDGES LA
Braziers Farm
TOWER HILL
New Maulden Farm
FLAUNDEN LA
Woodman's Wood
Caravan Site
Hogpits Bottom
Rose Farm
Woodman's Farm
4
OLLEBERRIE LA
DUNNY LA
LONG LA
Bricklayers Arms (PH)
Lower Plantation
WINDMILL HILL
THE COMMON
Cherry Trees Farm
WINDMILL HILL
LITTLE WINDMILL HILL
Belsize
BIRCH LA
Sharlowe's Farm
Holly Hedges Farm
01
Dale Farm
Penman's Green
Green Dragon (PH)
Olleberrie Farm
FLAUNDEN HILL
Whitedell Farm
Belsize Farm
Flaunden
BRAGMANS LA
POLES HILL
PLOUGH LA
Newhouse Farm
Rose Hall Farm
Bragman's Farm
Rosehall Wood
Moat
3
Hollin's Hall
Moonshine Farm
Great Sarratt Hall
Wireless Station
00
Oldcroft Wood
Hanginglane Wood
Bramble Croft
MOOR LA
Martin Top Farm
Oldfield Spring
2
Limeshill Wood
DAWES LA
DOWNER DRI
Baldwin's Wood
Valley Farm
Dawes Common
Wallace's Wood
Sandfield Wood
99
Ford
Mill Farm
Mount Wood
Sarratt Bottom
Chenies Bottom
HOLLOWAY LA
Chenies Place
Chenies
CHURCH LA
1
Mountwood Farm
Church End
Goldingtons
Nicholas Spring
Greathouse Farm
Sch
BEDFORD CL
Turveylane Wood
NEW RD
Wyburn Wood
Cricket Ground
98
01
02
03
D
E
F

152

164

138

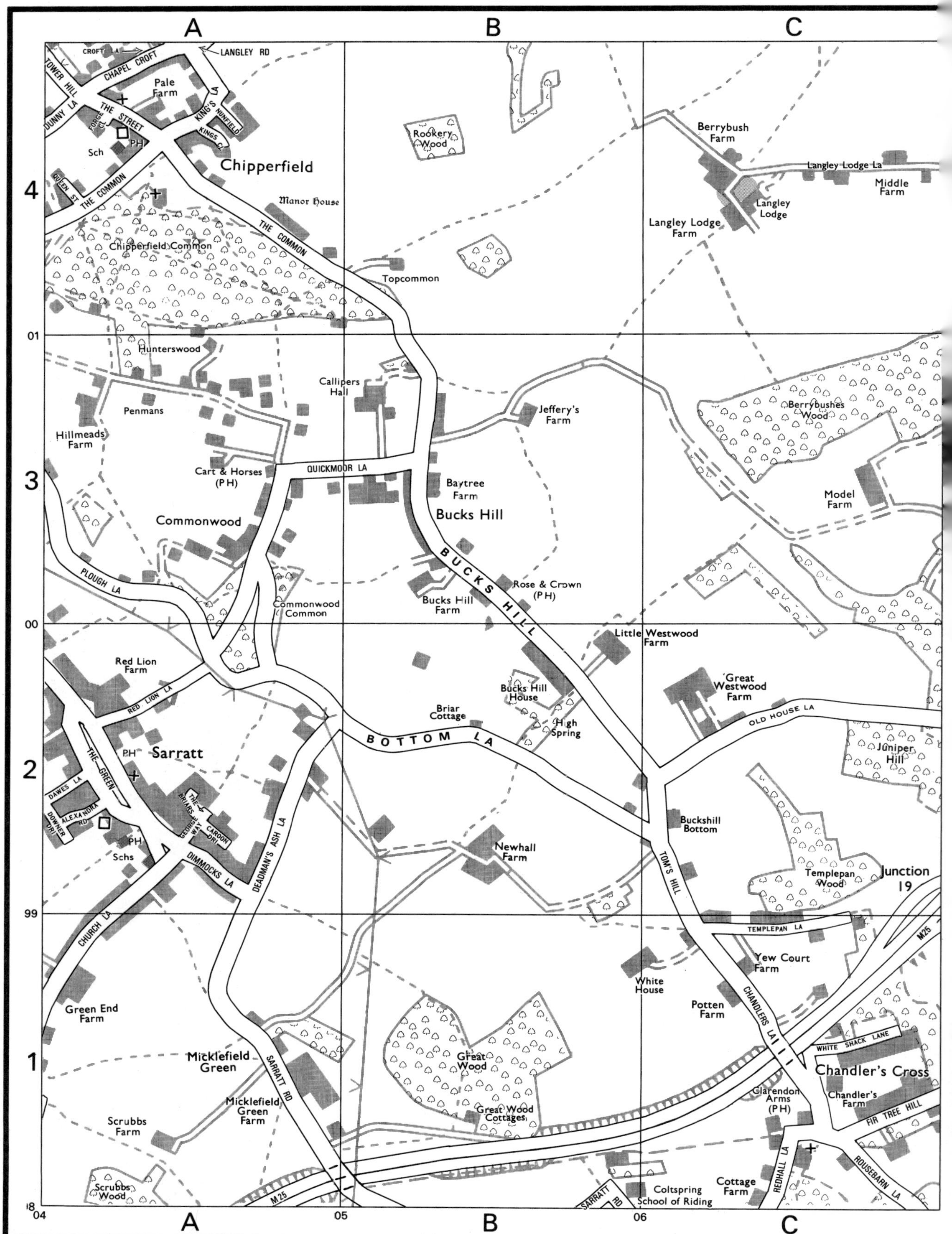
A
B
C
4
3
2
1
01
00
99
98
04
05
06
CROFT LA
LANGLEY RD
TOWER HILL
CHAPEL CROFT
Pale Farm
KING'S LA
NUNFIELD
KINGS C
DUNNY LA
FORGE CL
THE STREET
PH
Sch
Chipperfield
QUEEN ST
THE COMMON
Manor House
Chipperfield Common
THE COMMON
Topcommon
Rookery Wood
Berrybush Farm
Langley Lodge La
Middle Farm
Langley Lodge
Langley Lodge Farm
Hunterswood
Callipers Hall
Penmans
Hillmeads Farm
Jeffery's Farm
Berrybushes Wood
Cart & Horses (PH)
QUICKMOOR LA
Baytree Farm
Bucks Hill
Model Farm
Commonwood
PLOUGH LA
BUCKS HILL
Rose & Crown (PH)
Bucks Hill Farm
Commonwood Common
Little Westwood Farm
Red Lion Farm
RED LION LA
Great Westwood Farm
Bucks Hill House
OLD HOUSE LA
Briar Cottage
High Spring
Juniper Hill
BOTTOM LA
PH
Sarratt
THE GREEN
DAWES LA
ALEXANDRA RD
DOWNER DRI
THE BRIARS
GEORGE WAY
CARGON DRI
PH
Schs
DIMMOCKS LA
DEADMAN'S ASH LA
Buckshill Bottom
Newhall Farm
TOM'S HILL
Templepan Wood
Junction 19
CHURCH LA
TEMPLEPAN LA
M25
Yew Court Farm
White House
Potten Farm
Green End Farm
CHANDLERS LA
WHITE SHACK LANE
Micklefield Green
SARRATT RD
Great Wood
Chandler's Cross
Clarendon Arms (PH)
Chandler's Farm
FIR TREE HILL
Micklefield Green Farm
Scrubbs Farm
Great Wood Cottages
REDHALL LA
ROUSEBARN LA
Scrubbs Wood
M25
SARRATT RD
Coltspring School of Riding
Cottage Farm

151

165

139

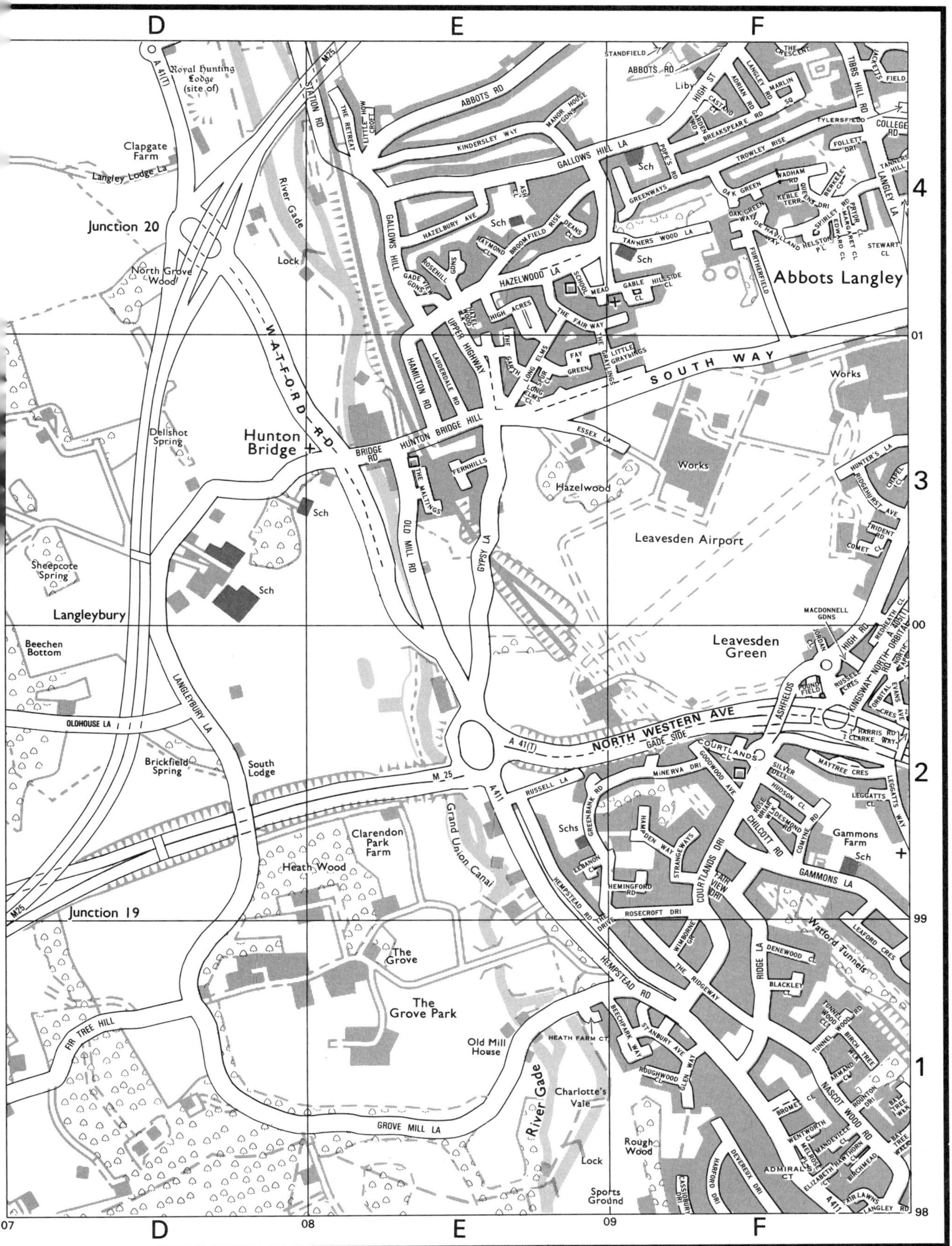
D
E
F
Royal Hunting Lodge (site of)
Clapgate Farm
Langley Lodge La
Junction 20
North Grove Wood
Lock
River Gade
STATION RD
M25
A 41(T)
ABBOTS RD
THE RETREAT
LITTLE CROFT
KINDERSLEY WAY
MANOR HOUSE GDNS
GALLOWS HILL LA
GALLOWS HILL
HAZELBURY AVE
Sch
ASH CL
BROOMFIELD RISE
DEANS CL
RAYMOND CL
ROSEHILL GDNS
GADE VIEW GDNS
HAZELWOOD LA
SCHOOL MEAD
GABLE CL
HILLSIDE CL
HIGH ACRES
THE FAIR WAY
UPPER HIGHWAY
HAMILTON RD
LAUDERDALE RD
THE GARTH
LONG ELMS
LONG ELMS CL
SPUR CL
FAY GREEN
THE GRAILINGS
LITTLE GRAYLINGS
SOUTH WAY
STANDFIELD
ABBOTS RD
Liby
HIGH ST
CASTANO CT
GARDEN RD
ADRIAN RD
LANGLEY RD
MARLIN SQ
THE CRESCENT
BREAKSPEARE RD
TIBBS HILL RD
JACKETTS FIELD
TYLERSFIELD
COLLEGE RD
FOLLETT DRI
TROWLEY RISE
POPE'S RD
GREENWAYS
OAK GREEN
WADHAM RD
KEBLE TERR
QUEENS DRI
BERKELEY CL
TANNERS HILL
LANGLEY LA
OAK GREEN WAY
DE HAVILLAND WAY
HELSTON PL
SPIRLEY CL
EDWARD CL
MARGARET CL
PRYOR CL
STEWART CL
TANNERS WOOD LA
FURTHERFIELD
Abbots Langley
4
01
Works
WATFORD RD
Dellshot Spring
Hunton Bridge
BRIDGE RD
HUNTON BRIDGE HILL
THE MALTINGS
FERNHILLS
ESSEX LA
Works
Hazelwood
HUNTER'S LA
RIDGEHURST AVE
CHAPEL CL
TRIDENT RD
COMET CL
3
Leavesden Airport
OLD MILL RD
GYPSY LA
Sheepcote Spring
Langleybury
Beechen Bottom
MACDONNELL GDNS
JORDAN CL
HIGH RD
REDHEATH CL
Leavesden Green
00
ASHFIELDS
POUND FIELD
RUSSELL CRES
KINGSWAY
NORTH ORBITAL RD
ORBITAL CRES
EVANS AVE
HARRIS RD
CLARKE WAY
LANGLEYBURY LA
OLDHOUSE LA
Brickfield Spring
South Lodge
NORTH WESTERN AVE
A 41(T)
GADE SIDE
COURTLANDS CL
MINERVA DRI
GOODWOOD AVE
SILVER DELL
MAYTREE CRES
2
LEGGATTS CL
LEGGATTS WAY
M 25
A 411
RUSSELL LA
GREENBANK RD
Grand Union Canal
Clarendon Park Farm
Heath Wood
Schs
HAMPDEN WAY
STRANGEWAYS
HUDSON CL
ROSE WLK
BRIAR WLK
DESMOND RD
COMYNE RD
CHILCOTT RD
Gammons Farm
Sch
LEBANON CL
HEMINGFORD RD
COURTLANDS DRI
FAIR VIEW DRI
GAMMONS LA
HEMPSTEAD RD
THE DRIVE
ROSECROFT DRI
Junction 19
M25
99
Watford Tunnels
LEAFORD CRES
WIMBORNE GR
THE RIDGEWAY
RIDGE LA
DENEWOOD CL
The Grove
HEMPSTEAD RD
BLACKLEY CL
The Grove Park
TUNNEL WOOD CL
TUNNEL WOOD RD
FIR TREE HILL
Old Mill House
HEATH FARM CT
BEECHPARK WAY
STANBURY AVE
BIRCH TREE WLK
ARMAND CL
1
ROUGHWOOD CL
GLEN WAY
River Gade
Charlotte's Vale
BROMET CL
NASCOT WOOD RD
ROUNTON DRI
BAY TREE WLK
GROVE MILL LA
Rough Wood
Lock
WENTWORTH CL
MELROSE PL
MANDEVILLE CL
HAWTHORN CL
BIRCHMEAD
ELIZABETH CT
DEVEREUX DRI
HARFORD DRI
CASSIOBURY DRI
ADMIRAL'S CT
Sports Ground
A 411
FAIR LAWNS
LANGLEY RD
98
07
08
09
D
E
F

154

166

140

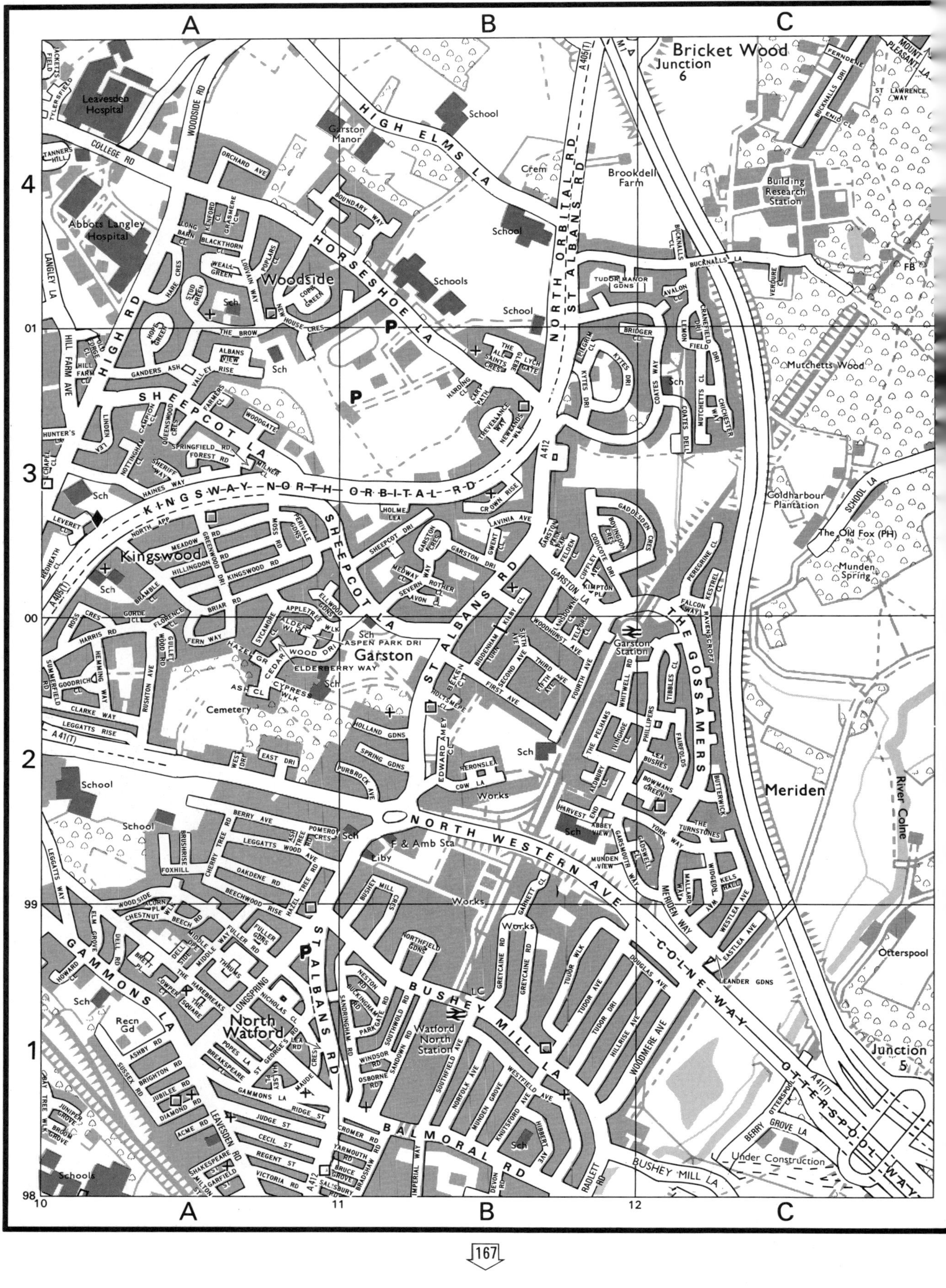

A
B
C
4
3
2
1
01
00
99
98
10
11
12
Bricket Wood
Junction 6
Leavesden Hospital
Abbots Langley Hospital
Garston Manor
School
Schools
Crem
Brookdell Farm
Building Research Station
Woodside
Sch
Mutchetts Wood
Coldharbour Plantation
The Old Fox (PH)
Munden Spring
Kingswood
Garston
Garston Station
Cemetery
Meriden
River Colne
Works
F & Amb Sta
Liby
Otterspool
Junction 5
North Watford
Watford North Station
Recn Gd
Under Construction
FB
HIGH ELMS LA
HORSESHOE LA
NORTH ORBITAL RD
ST ALBANS RD
KINGSWAY-NORTH ORBITAL RD
SHEEPCOT LA
HIGH RD
COLLEGE RD
WOODSIDE RD
ORCHARD AVE
BOUNDARY WAY
BUCKNALLS LA
BUCKNALLS DRI
TUDOR MANOR GDNS
AVALON CL
BRIDGER CL
KYTES DRI
COATES WAY
COATES DELL
MUTCHETTS CL
CHICHESTER
LEMON FIELD DRI
CRANEFIELD DRI
PILGRIM CL
ALL SAINTS CRES
LYCH GATE
GLEBE
HARDING CL
CARTH PATH
TREVELYAN WAY
NEWLANDS WLK
CROWN RISE
HOLME LEA
SHEEPCOT DRI
GARSTON CRES
GARSTON DRI
GWENT CL
LAVINIA AVE
MEDWAY CL
SEVERN WAY
ROTHER CL
AVON CL
GADDESDEN CRES
BOVINGDON CRES
CODICOTE DRI
CUFFLEY AVE
KIMPTON PL
FELDEN CL
GARSTON LA
LANSDOWNE
TELFORD CL
WOODHURST AVE
KILBY CL
BIDDENHAM TURN
SIXTH AVE
THIRD AVE
FIFTH AVE
FIRST AVE
SECOND AVE
FOURTH AVE
PEREGRINE CL
KESTREL CL
FALCON WAY
RAVENSCROFT
THE GOSSAMERS
TIBBLES CL
WHITWELL RD
THE PELHAMS
IVINGHOE CL
PHILLIPERS
FAIRFOLDS
LEA BUSHES
BOWMANS GREEN
BUTTERWICK
THE TURNSTONES
YORK WAY
GADSWELL CL
GARSMOUTH WAY
MUNDEN VIEW
ABBEY VIEW
HARVEST END
ALDBURY CL
MERIDEN WAY
MALLARD WAY
WIDGEON WAY
KELS HALL
WESTLEA AVE
EASTLEA AVE
LEANDER GDNS
NORTH WESTERN AVE
COLNE WAY
OTTERSPOOL WAY
BERRY GROVE LA
OTTERSPOOL LA
BUSHEY MILL LA
RADLETT RD
WOODMERE AVE
HILLRISE AVE
TUDOR DRI
TUDOR AVE
TUDOR WLK
DOUGLAS AVE
GREYCAINE RD
GARNETT CL
HIBBERT AVE
KNUTSFORD AVE
WESTFIELD AVE
MUNDEN GROVE
NORFOLK AVE
SOUTHFIELD AVE
BALMORAL RD
DEVON RD
IMPERIAL WAY
NORTHFIELD GDNS
BUSHEY MILL CRES
NESTON RD
BUCKINGHAM RD
SANDRINGHAM RD
PARKGATE RD
SOUTHWOLD RD
SANDOWN RD
WINDSOR RD
OSBORNE RD
CROMER RD
YARMOUTH RD
BRUCE GROVE
BRADSHAW RD
SALISBURY
EDWARD AMEY CL
HERONSLEA
COW LA
HOLLYSMERE
BEKEN CL
HOLLAND GDNS
SPRING GDNS
PURBROCK AVE
EAST DRI
WEST DRI
POMEROY CRES
BERRY AVE
ASH TREE RD
LEGGATTS WOOD AVE
OAKDENE RD
BEECHWOOD RISE
HAZEL TREE RD
CHERRY TREE RD
BRUSHRISE
FOXHILL
LEGGATTS WAY
LEGGATTS RISE
A41(T)
A405(T)
A412
CLARKE WAY
GOODRICH CL
HEMMING WAY
SUMMERFIELD RD
HARRIS RD
ROSS CRES
GORDE CL
FLORENCE CL
GULLET WOOD RD
RUSHTON AVE
FERN WAY
BRIAR RD
SYCAMORE
APPLETREE WLK
ALDER WLK
ELLWOOD GDNS
ASPEN PARK DRI
WOOD DRI
ELDERBERRY WAY
CEDAR
HAZEL GR
CYPRESS WLK
ASH CL
KINGSWOOD RD
HILLINGDON RD
GREENWOOD DRI
MEADOW RD
NORTH APP
MOSS RD
PERIVALE GDNS
BRAMBLE CL
REDHEATH CL
LEVERET CL
HAINES WAY
SHERIFF WAY
FOREST RD
SPRINGFIELD RD
MILNER CL
NOTTINGHAM CL
QUEENSWOOD CRES
CAMPION CL
LINDEN LEA
FARMERS CL
WOODGATE
GANDERS ASH
VALLEY RISE
ALBANS VIEW
THE BROW
NEW HOUSE CRES
COPSE GREEN
LOUVAIN WAY
POPLARS CL
STUD GREEN
HOPE GREEN
HARE CRES
WEALL GREEN
BLACKTHORN CL
LONG BARN CL
KENFORD CL
GRASMERE CL
HILL FARM AVE
HILL FARM CL
HUNTER'S LA
CHAPEL LA
LANGLEY LA
TANNERS HILL
JACKETTS FIELD
TYLERSFIELD
ST LAWRENCE WAY
MOUNT PLEASANT LA
FERNDENE
BUCKNALLS ENID CL
VERDURE CL
SCHOOL LA
GAMMONS LA
WOODSIDE
ACORN PL
CHESTNUT
ELM GROVE
DELL RD
BEECH RD
MIDDLE WAY
FULLER RD
FULLER GDNS
HOWARD CL
BRETT PL
THE HAREBREAKS
COWPER RD
THE SQUARE
THRUMS
LONGSPRING
NICHOLAS CL
LEA CL
ST GEORGE'S RD
MAUDE CRES
HALSEY PL
POPES LA
BREAKSPEARE
ASHBY RD
BRIGHTON RD
JUBILEE RD
DIAMOND RD
SUSSEX RD
ACME RD
LEAVESDEN RD
JUDGE ST
CECIL ST
REGENT ST
VICTORIA RD
RIDGE ST
GAMMONS LA
SHAKESPEARE ST
GARFIELD ST
CRAY TREE WLK
JUNIPER GROVE
BROOM GROVE

153

167

141

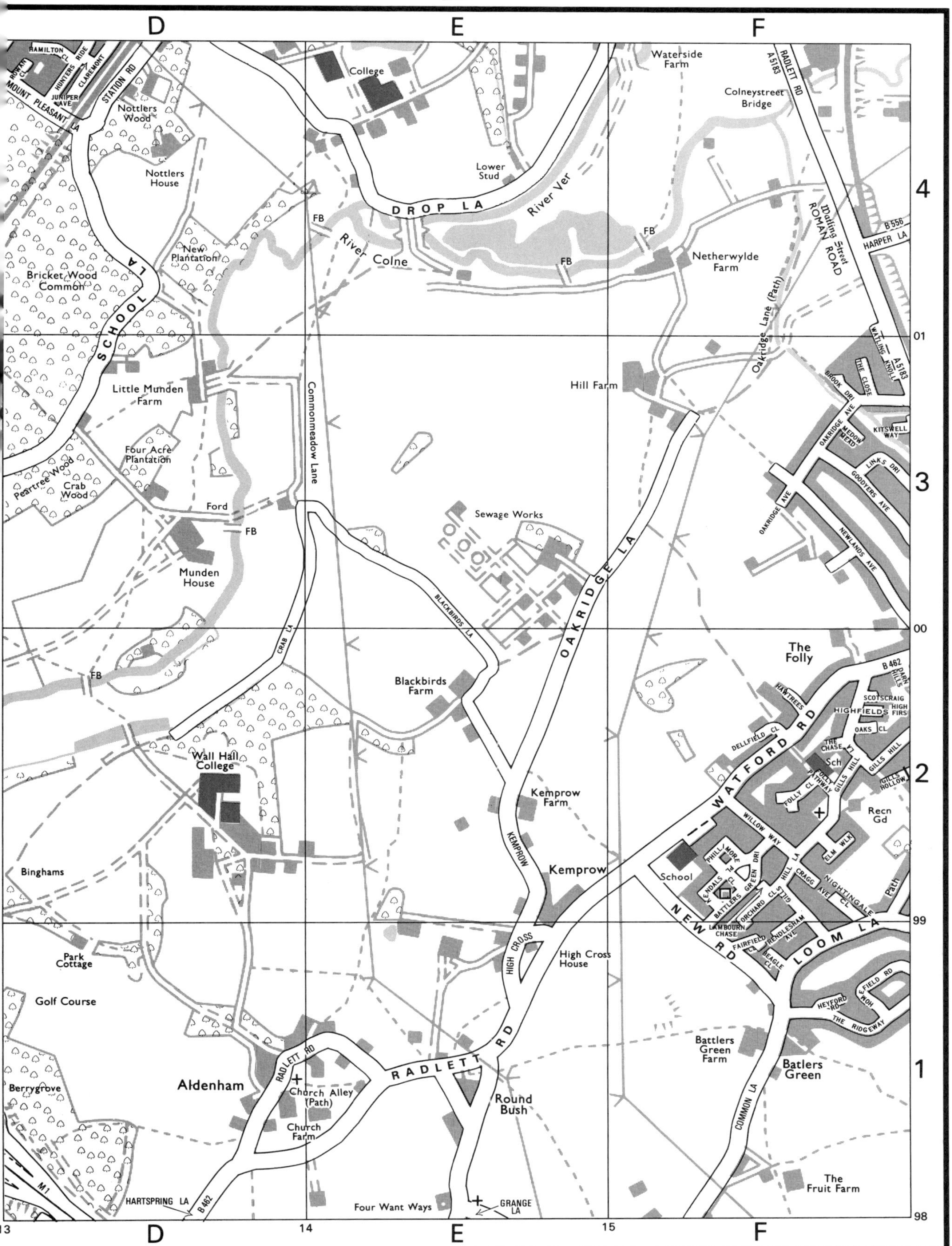
D
E
F
HAMILTON CL
ROWAN CL
HUNTERS RIDE
CLAREMONT
JUNIPER AVE
MOUNT PLEASANT LA
STATION RD
Nottlers Wood
Nottlers House
College
Lower Stud
DROP LA
River Ver
Waterside Farm
Colneystreet Bridge
A5183
RADLETT RD
Watling Street ROMAN ROAD
B 556
HARPER LA
FB
River Colne
New Plantation
Bricket Wood Common
SCHOOL LA
Netherwylde Farm
Oakridge Lane (Path)
WATLING KNOLL
A5183
BROOK DRI
THE CLOSE
Little Munden Farm
Commonmeadow Lane
Hill Farm
OAKRIDGE AVE
MEDOW MEAD
KITSWELL WAY
LINKS DRI
GOODYERS AVE
Four Acre Plantation
Peartree Wood
Crab Wood
Ford
FB
Sewage Works
OAKRIDGE AVE
NEWLANDS AVE
Munden House
OAKRIDGE LA
BLACKBIRDS LA
CRAB LA
FB
The Folly
B 462
PARK HILLS
Blackbirds Farm
HAWTREES
SCOTSCRAIG
HIGHFIELDS
HIGH FIRS
OAKS CL
DELLFIELD CL
THE CHASE
Sch
GILLS HILL
Wall Hall College
FOLLY PATHWAY
GILLS HOLLOW
FOLLY CL
Kemprow Farm
WATFORD RD
Recn Gd
WILLOW WAY
ELM WLK
KEMPROW
Kemprow
Binghams
School
PHILLIMORE PL
KENDALS CL
BATTLERS GREEN DRI
HILL LA
CRAGG AVE
NIGHTINGALE CL
Path
ORCHARD CL
LAMBOURN CHASE
FRENDLESHAM AVE
NEW RD
LOOM LA
FAIRFIELD CL
BEAGLE CL
Park Cottage
HIGH CROSS
High Cross House
Golf Course
HEYFORD RD
HOMEFIELD RD
THE RIDGEWAY
RADLETT RD
Battlers Green Farm
Batlers Green
RADLETT RD
Berrygrove
Aldenham
Church Alley (Path)
Round Bush
Church Farm
COMMON LA
M1
The Fruit Farm
HARTSPRING LA
B 462
Four Want Ways
GRANGE LA
4
3
2
1
01
00
99
98
13
14
15

156

168

142

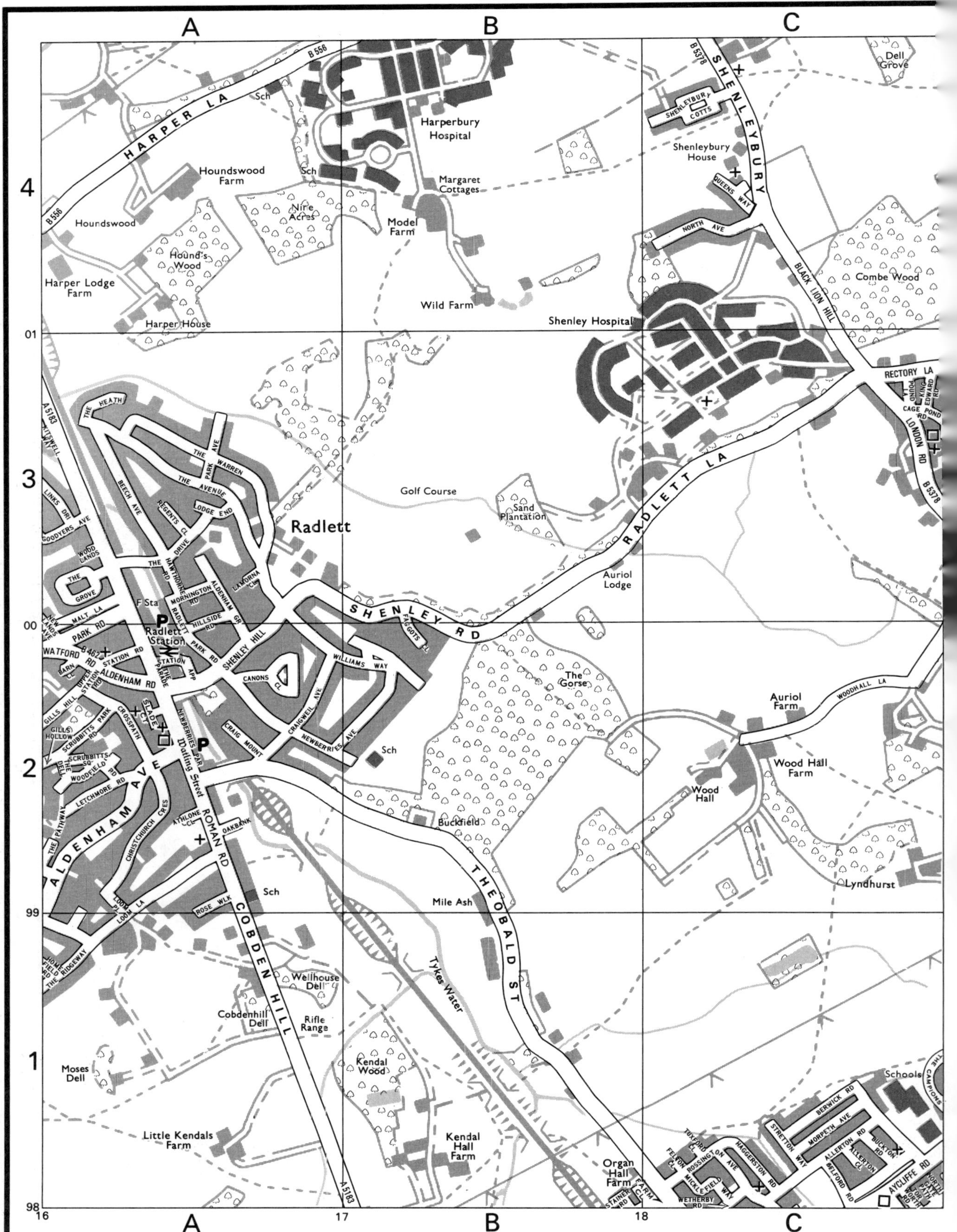
A
B
C
4
3
2
1
01
00
99
98
16
17
18
HARPER LA
B 556
Sch
Harperbury Hospital
Houndswood Farm
Margaret Cottages
Nine Acres
Model Farm
Houndswood
Hound's Wood
Harper Lodge Farm
Harper House
Wild Farm
B 5378
SHENLEYBURY
SHENLEYBURY COTTS
Shenleybury House
QUEENS WAY
NORTH AVE
BLACK LION HILL
Dell Grove
Combe Wood
Shenley Hospital
RECTORY LA
LONDON RD
B 5378
RADLETT LA
Golf Course
Sand Plantation
Radlett
Auriol Lodge
SHENLEY RD
A 5183
THE HEATH
THE PARK
WARREN
THE AVENUE
BEECH AVE
REGENTS CL
LODGE END
LINKS DR
GOODYERS AVE
WOODLANDS
THE GROVE
THE HAWTHORNE DRIVE
MORNINGTON RD
ALDENHAM GR
LAMORNA CL
F Sta
MALT LA
PARK RD
Radlett Station
HILLSIDE RD
SHENLEY HILL
FAGGOTS CL
WILLIAMS WAY
CANONS CL
WATFORD RD
B 462
STATION RD
ALDENHAM RD
THE PARADE
CRAGWEIL AVE
NEWBERRIES AVE
CRAIG MOUNT
GILLS HILL
GILLS HOLLOW
SCRUBBITTS PARK
SCRUBBITTS SQ
CROSSPATH
SLADE CT
Watling Street
NEWBERRIES PAR
Sch
The Gorse
WOODHALL LA
Auriol Farm
Wood Hall Farm
Wood Hall
Buckfield
WOODFIELD RD
LETCHMORE RD
ALDENHAM AVE
THE PATHWAY
CHRISTCHURCH CRES
ATHLONE CL
OAKBANK
ROMAN RD
Sch
ROSE WLK
LOOM LA
COBDEN HILL
Mile Ash
THEOBALD ST
Lyndhurst
THE RIDGEWAY
Wellhouse Dell
Tykes Water
Cobdenhill Dell
Rifle Range
Moses Dell
Kendal Wood
Little Kendals Farm
Kendal Hall Farm
A 5183
Organ Hall Farm
FARM CL
STAINER RD
Schools
BERWICK RD
MORPETH AVE
STRETTON WAY
BUCKTON RD
ALLERTON RD
ALLERTON CL
TUXFORD CL
HAGGERSTON RD
FELTON CL
ROSSINGTON AVE
MICKLEFIELD WAY
WETHERBY RD
BELFORD RD
AYCLIFFE RD

155

169

143

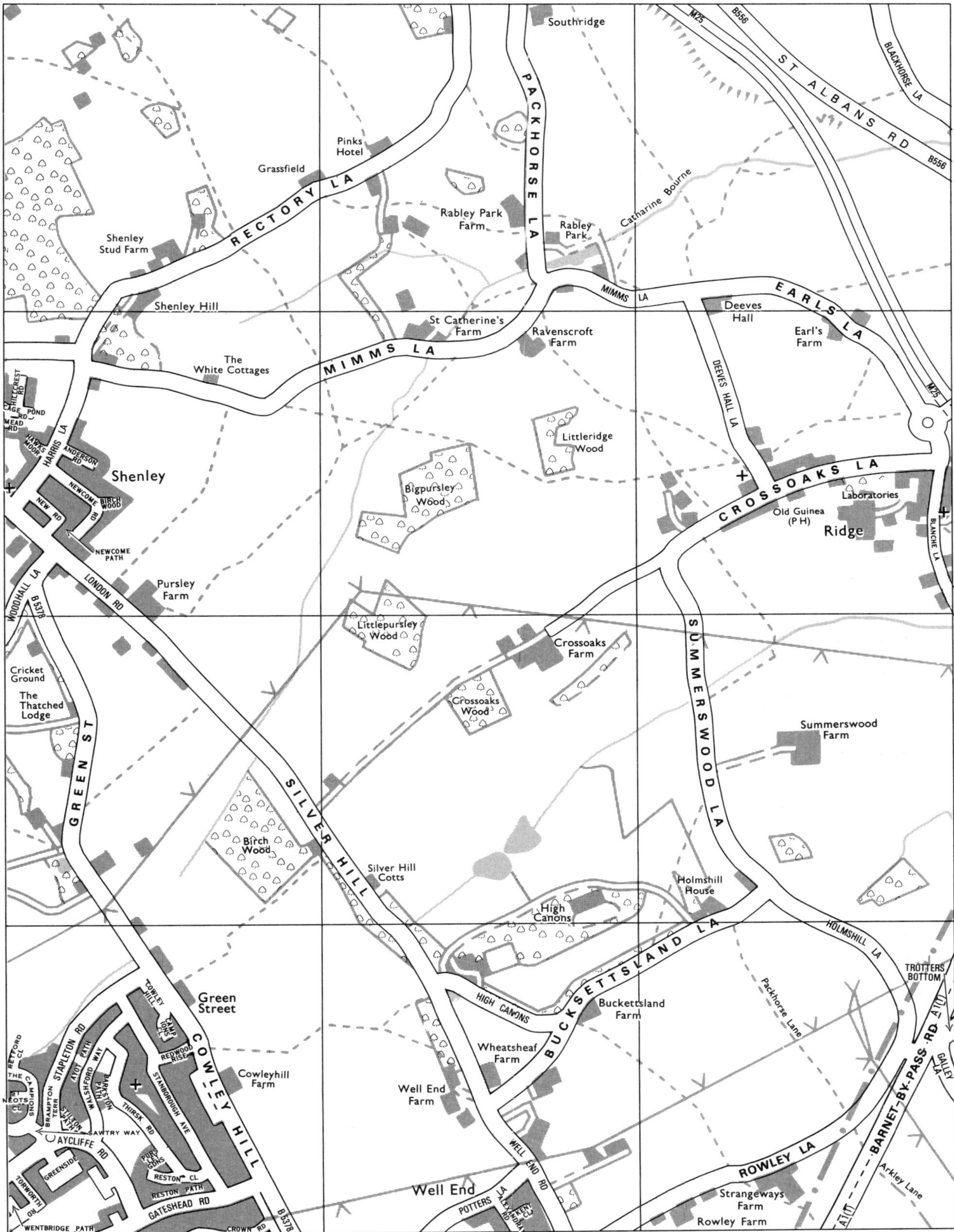
D
E
F
Southridge
PACKHORSE LA
ST ALBANS RD
B556
M25
BLACKHORSE LA
Pinks Hotel
Grassfield
RECTORY LA
Rabley Park Farm
Rabley Park
Catharine Bourne
Shenley Stud Farm
Shenley Hill
MIMMS LA
EARLS LA
Deeves Hall
Earl's Farm
St Catherine's Farm
Ravenscroft Farm
The White Cottages
DEEVES HALL LA
Littleridge Wood
Shenley
HARRIS LA
ANDERSON RD
NEWCOME RD
BIRCH WOOD
NEW RD
NEWCOME PATH
CROSSOAKS LA
Bigpursley Wood
Laboratories
Old Guinea (PH)
Ridge
BLANCHE LA
Pursley Farm
WOODHALL LA
B5378
LONDON RD
Littlepursley Wood
Crossoaks Farm
SUMMERSWOOD LA
Cricket Ground
The Thatched Lodge
Crossoaks Wood
Summerswood Farm
GREEN ST
SILVER HILL
Birch Wood
Silver Hill Cotts
Holmshill House
High Canons
HOLMSHILL LA
TROTTERS BOTTOM
BUCKETTSLAND LA
HIGH CANONS
Buckettsland Farm
Green Street
COWLEY HILL
Packhorse Lane
Wheatsheaf Farm
Cowleyhill Farm
Well End Farm
BARNET-BY-PASS RD
A1(T)
GALLEY LA
STAPLETON RD
AYOT PATH
WALSHFORD WAY
BARKSTON PATH
STANBOROUGH AVE
THIRSK RD
REDWOOD RISE
CAMPIONS
AYCLIFFE RD
SAWTRY WAY
GREENSIDE
RESTON CL
RESTON PATH
GATESHEAD RD
WELL END RD
ROWLEY LA
Arkley Lane
Well End
POTTERS LA
Strangeways Farm
Rowley Farm
WENTBRIDGE PATH
CROWN RD
TORWORTH RD
4
3
2
1
01
00
99
98
19
20
21

158

170

144

157

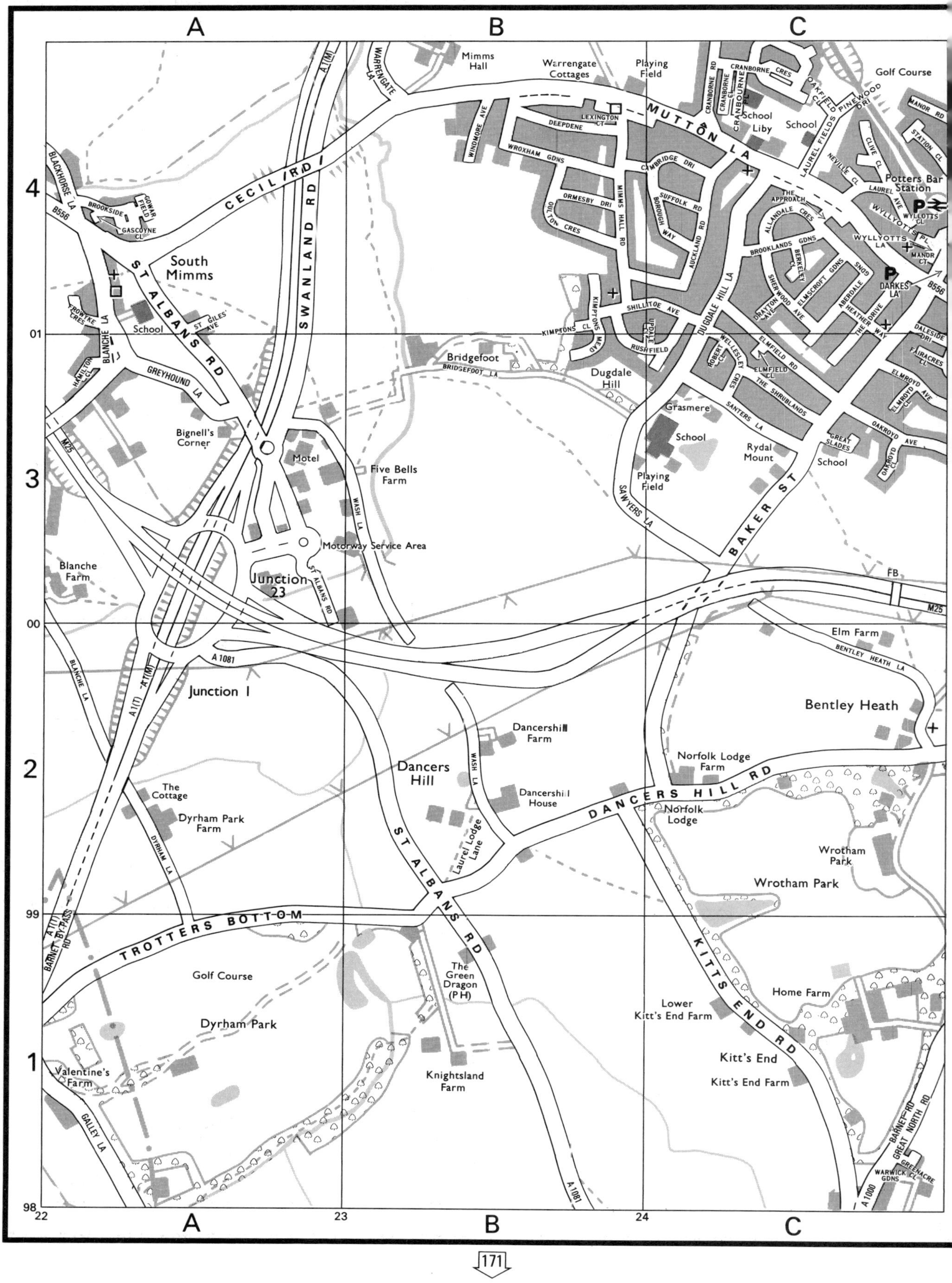
A
B
C
4
3
2
1
01
00
99
98
22
23
24
Mimms Hall
Warrengate Cottages
Playing Field
Golf Course
WARRENGATE LA
A1(M)
MUTTON LA
CECIL RD
SWANLAND RD
ST ALBANS RD
BLACKHORSE LA
B556
BROOKSIDE
GOWAR FIELD
GASCOYNE CL
South Mimms
School
FROWYKE CRES
BLANCHE LA
ST GILES' AVE
HAMILTON CL
GREYHOUND LA
LEXINGTON CT
DEEPDENE
WINDMORE AVE
WROXHAM GDNS
CAMBRIDGE DRI
ORMESBY DRI
OULTON CRES
MIMMS HALL RD
BOROUGH WAY
SUFFOLK RD
AUCKLAND RD
CRANBORNE RD
CRANBORNE CL
CRANBORNE PL
CRANBORNE CRES
School
Liby
OAKFIELD CL
LAUREL FIELDS
PINEWOOD DRI
MANOR RD
STATION CL
CLIVE CL
NEVILLE CL
Potters Bar Station
LAUREL AVE
THE APPROACH
ALLANDALE CRES
WYLLYOTTS CL
WYLLYOTTS PL
WYLLYOTTS LA
MANOR CT
BROOKLANDS GDNS
BERKELEY
ELMSCROFT GDNS
SHERWOOD AVE
DRAYTON AVE
ABERDALE GDNS
HEATHER WAY
THE DRIVE
DARKES LA
B556
DALESIDE DRI
FAIRACRES
KIMPTONS CL
KIMPTONS MEAD
SHILLITOE AVE
UPDALE CL
RUSHFIELD
DUGDALE HILL LA
ROBERT CL
WELLESLEY CRES
ELMFIELD RD
ELMFIELD CL
THE SHRUBLANDS
ELMROYD AVE
ELMROYD CL
OAKROYD AVE
OAKROYD CL
GREAT SLADES
Bridgefoot
BRIDGEFOOT LA
Dugdale Hill
Grasmere
SANTERS LA
School
Rydal Mount
School
Playing Field
SAWYERS LA
BAKER ST
M25
Bignell's Corner
Motel
Five Bells Farm
WASH LA
Motorway Service Area
Blanche Farm
Junction 23
ST ALBANS RD
FB
M25
A 1081
Elm Farm
BENTLEY HEATH LA
Junction 1
BLANCHE LA
A1(T)
A1(M)
Bentley Heath
Dancershill Farm
Dancers Hill
Norfolk Lodge Farm
DANCERS HILL RD
Dancershill House
Norfolk Lodge
The Cottage
Dyrham Park Farm
DYRHAM LA
Laurel Lodge Lane
Wrotham Park
Wrotham Park
TROTTERS BOTTOM
BARNET BY-PASS
A1(T) RD
Golf Course
The Green Dragon (PH)
KITTS END RD
Lower Kitt's End Farm
Home Farm
Dyrham Park
Kitt's End
Kitt's End Farm
Valentine's Farm
Knightsland Farm
GALLEY LA
BARNET RD
GREAT NORTH RD
GREENACRE CL
WARWICK GDNS
A1000
A 1081

171

145

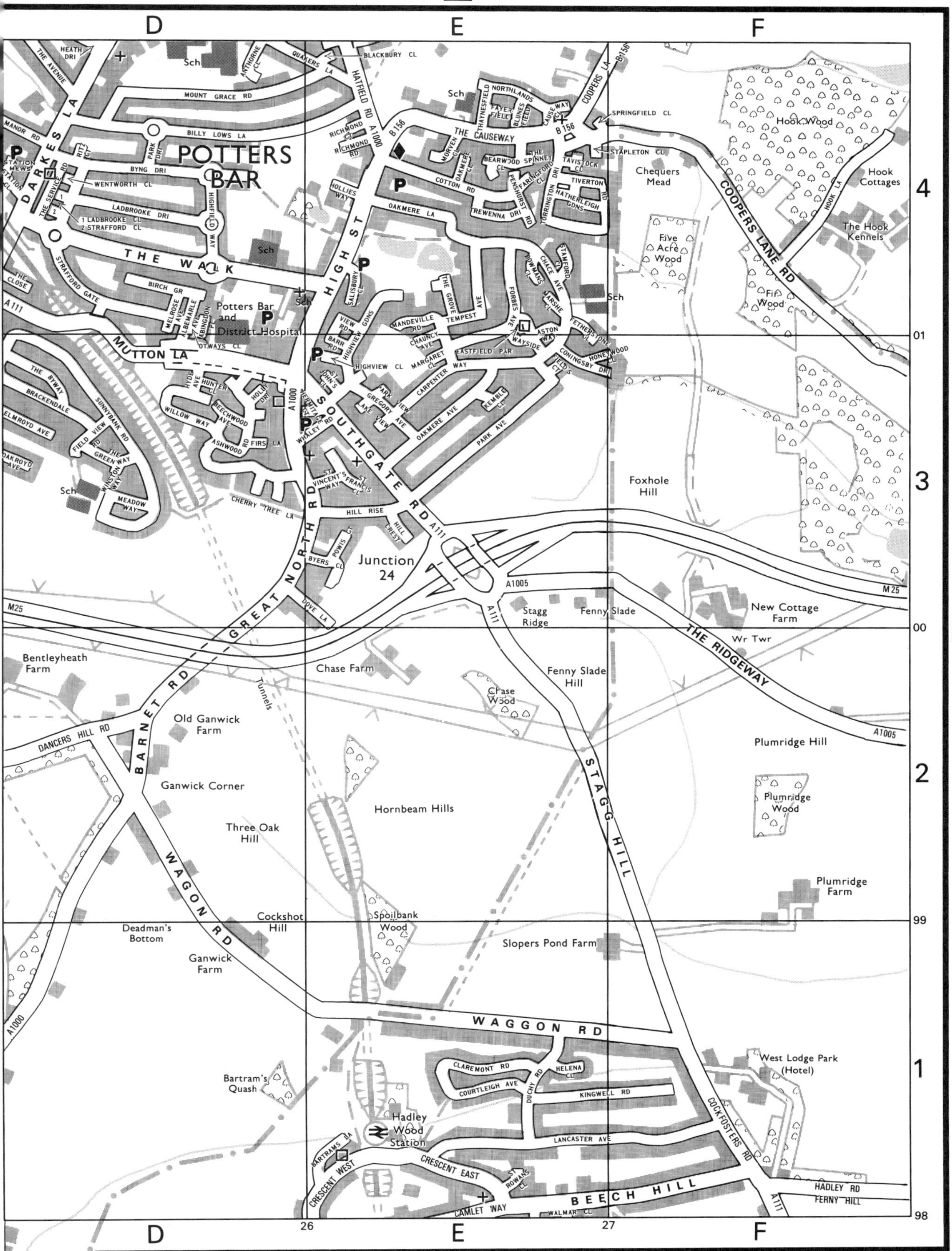

160

not continued, see key diagram

146

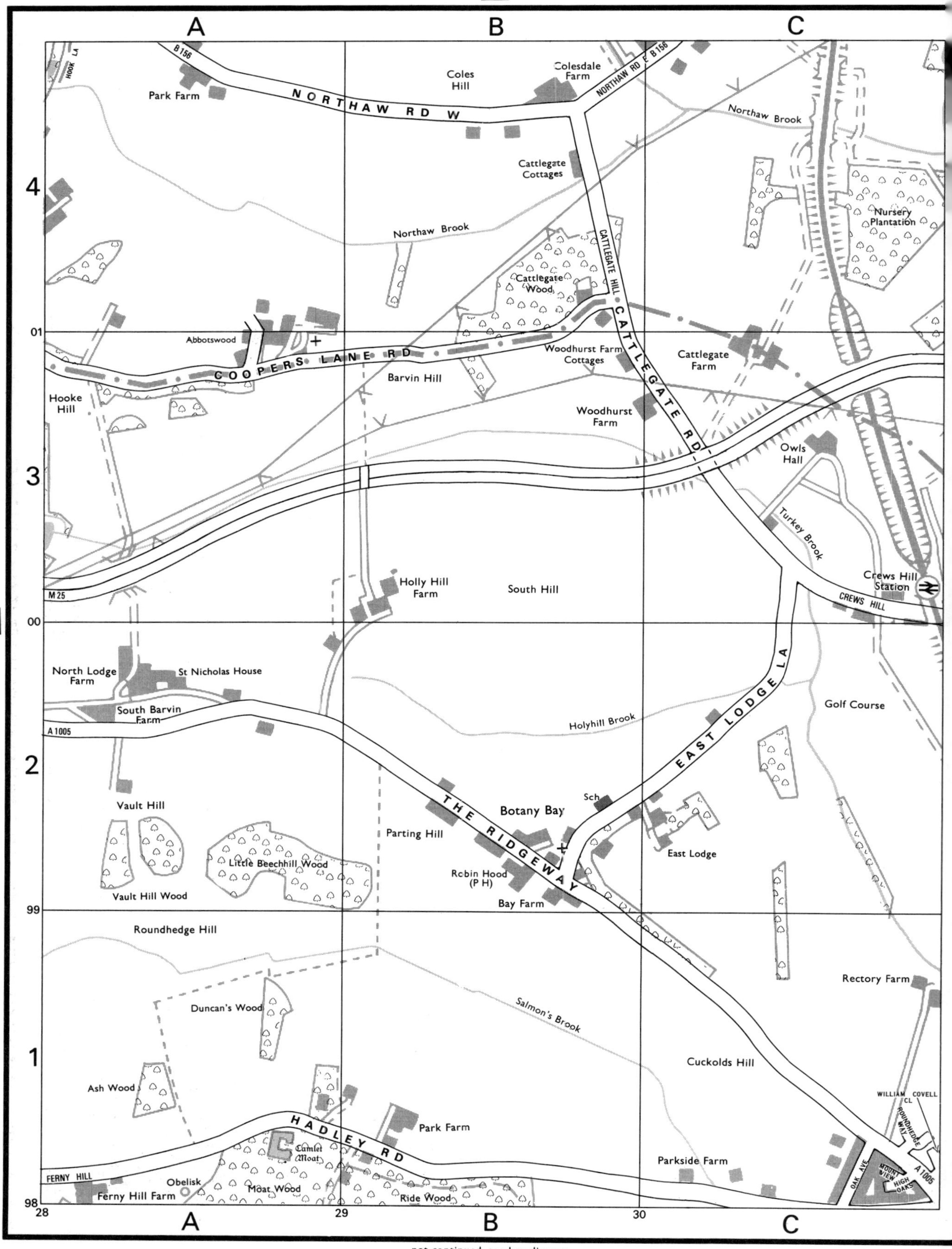

159

not continued, see key diagram

147

D
E
F
Woodgreen Farm
Burnt Farm
Broadfield Farm
BARROW LA
B 198
Theobalds
4
Burnt Farm Cottage
BURNTFARM RIDE
Cattlins
Dysons Osiers
OLDPARK RIDE
Home Wood
Hanging Plantation
01
Spring Farm
Theobalds Manor
Home Plantation
Tilekiln Osiers
Gunsite Stud
The Paddocks
South Osiers
3
Crews Hill Piggeries
Nurseries
Glasgow Stud
Cemy
Sander's Corner
Sloemans Farm
Whitewebbs Farm
CATTLEGATE RD
M25
00
Crews Hill
WHITEWEBBS RD
WHITEWEBBS LA
Mus
BEECH AVE
ASHE RIDE
ROSEWOOD DRI
WROXHAM GDNS
GOLF RIDE
CYPRESS AVE
Nurseries
Whitewebbs Wood
King & Tinker (PH)
THEOBALDS PARK RD
Water Garden Centre
White Webbs
2
Nurseries
FB
Whitewebbs Park
New River (Old Course)
Turkey Brook
FLASH LA
Cuffley Brook
King's Oak Plain
Sch
STRAYFIELD RD
99
Brayside Farm
Queenswood Farm
The Red House
PH
Clay Hill
Hospital
ST JOHN'S TERR
CLAY HILL
STRATTON AVE
Forty Hall Farm
P
PARK BROOK GDNS
HILLSIDE CRES
Forty Hall
1
Turkey Brook
Allot Gdns
E.M. GDNS
Chase Farm Hospital
Hilly Fields Park
VINTON DRI
Allot Gdns
BROWNING RD
MORLEY HILL
WOODBINE GR
CONWAY GDNS
PH
FORTY HILL
Sch
COOK'S HOLE RD
PHIPPS HATCH LA
ST LUKE'S AVE
MYRTLE GR
GOAT LA
LAME TREE WLK
CEDAR
PARK RD
VIOLET AVE
BIRKBECK RD
BURNHAM CL
ADELAIDE CL
OLD FORGE RD
ST GEORGE'S RD
Cemy
CEDAR RD
CHANTRY CL
YORK TERR
BRIGADIER HILL
GLOUCESTER RD
BRODIE RD
ACACIA
LAVENDER
RD 1
RD 2
BAKER ST
MYDDLETON AVE
HALLSIDE RD
RUSSELL RD
BRIDGENHALL RD
SPRING COURT RD
GLENVILLE AVE
RIDLER RD
GARNAULT RD
Amb Sta
RENDLESHAM RD
BLOSSOM LA
RIPLEY RD
BEDALE RD
WETHERBY RD
MERTON RD
WOODLANDS RD
HAWTHORN GR
KENILWORTH CRES
CARTER HATCH LA
LAYARD RD
LAVENDER GDNS
TUDOR CRES
BRIGADIER AVE
STERLING RD
Sch
31
32
33
98

162

148

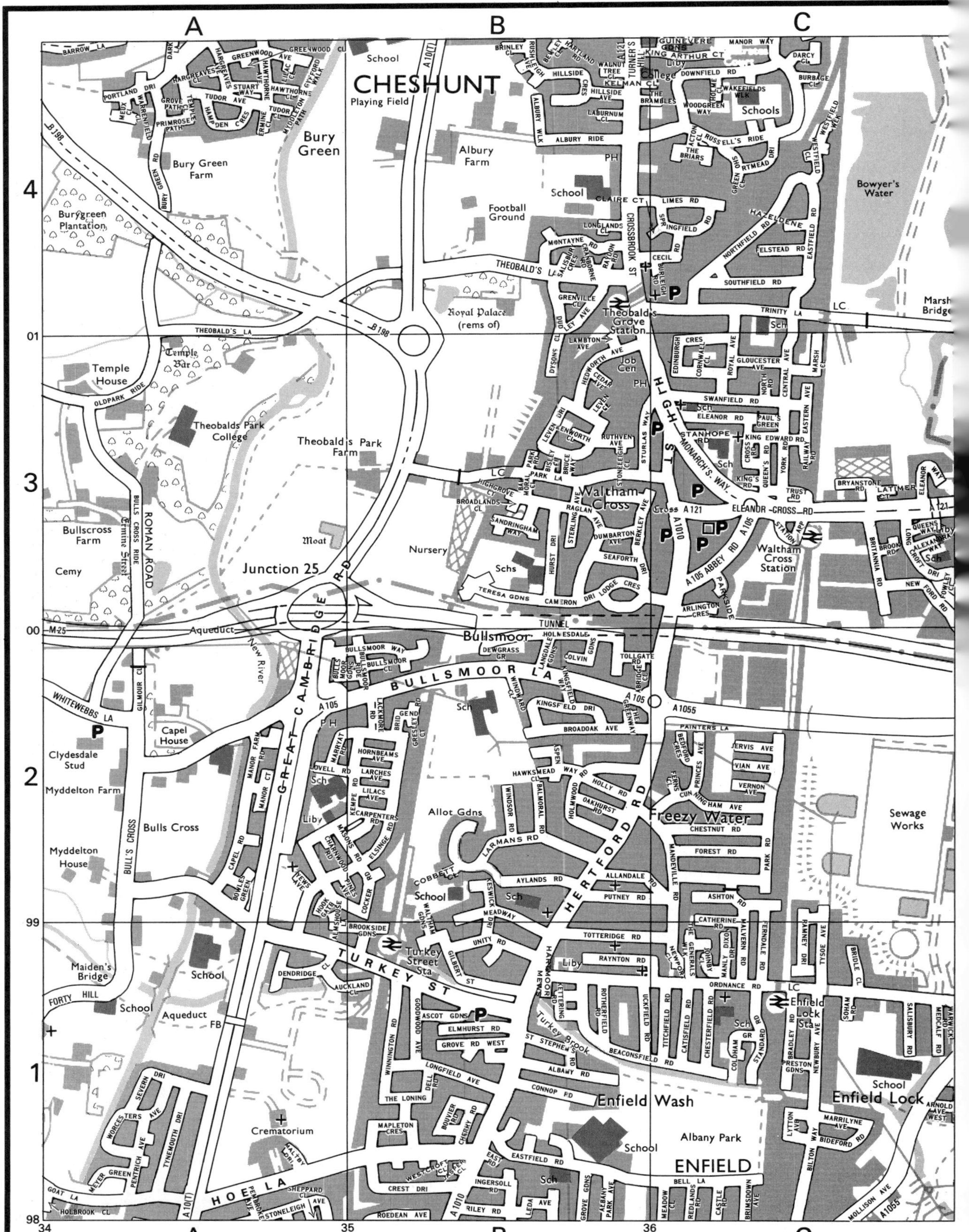

A
B
C
CHESHUNT
School
Playing Field
Bury Green
Bury Green Farm
Burygreen Plantation
Albury Farm
Football Ground
Schools
Bowyer's Water
Royal Palace (rems of)
Theobald's Grove Station
Temple House
Temple Bar
Theobalds Park College
Theobald's Park Farm
Waltham Cross
Waltham Cross Station
Bullscross Farm
Cemy
Moat
Nursery
Junction 25
Schs
Bullsmoor
Aqueduct
New River
TUNNEL
M25
Capel House
Clydesdale Stud
Myddelton Farm
Bulls Cross
Myddelton House
Allot Gdns
Freezy Water
Sewage Works
Maiden's Bridge
Turkey Street Sta
Enfield Lock Sta
Enfield Wash
Enfield Lock
Albany Park
ENFIELD
Crematorium
Marsh Bridge
ROMAN ROAD
Ermine Street
GREAT CAMBRIDGE RD
HERTFORD RD
HIGH ST
TURKEY ST
HOE LA
BULLSMOOR LA
THEOBALD'S LA
ELEANOR CROSS RD
WHITEWEBBS LA
FORTY HILL
BULL'S CROSS
A10(T)
A105
A121
A1010
A1055
B198
4
3
2
1
01
00
99
98
34
35
36

161

149

not continued, see key diagram

not continued, see key diagram

151

not continued, see key diagram

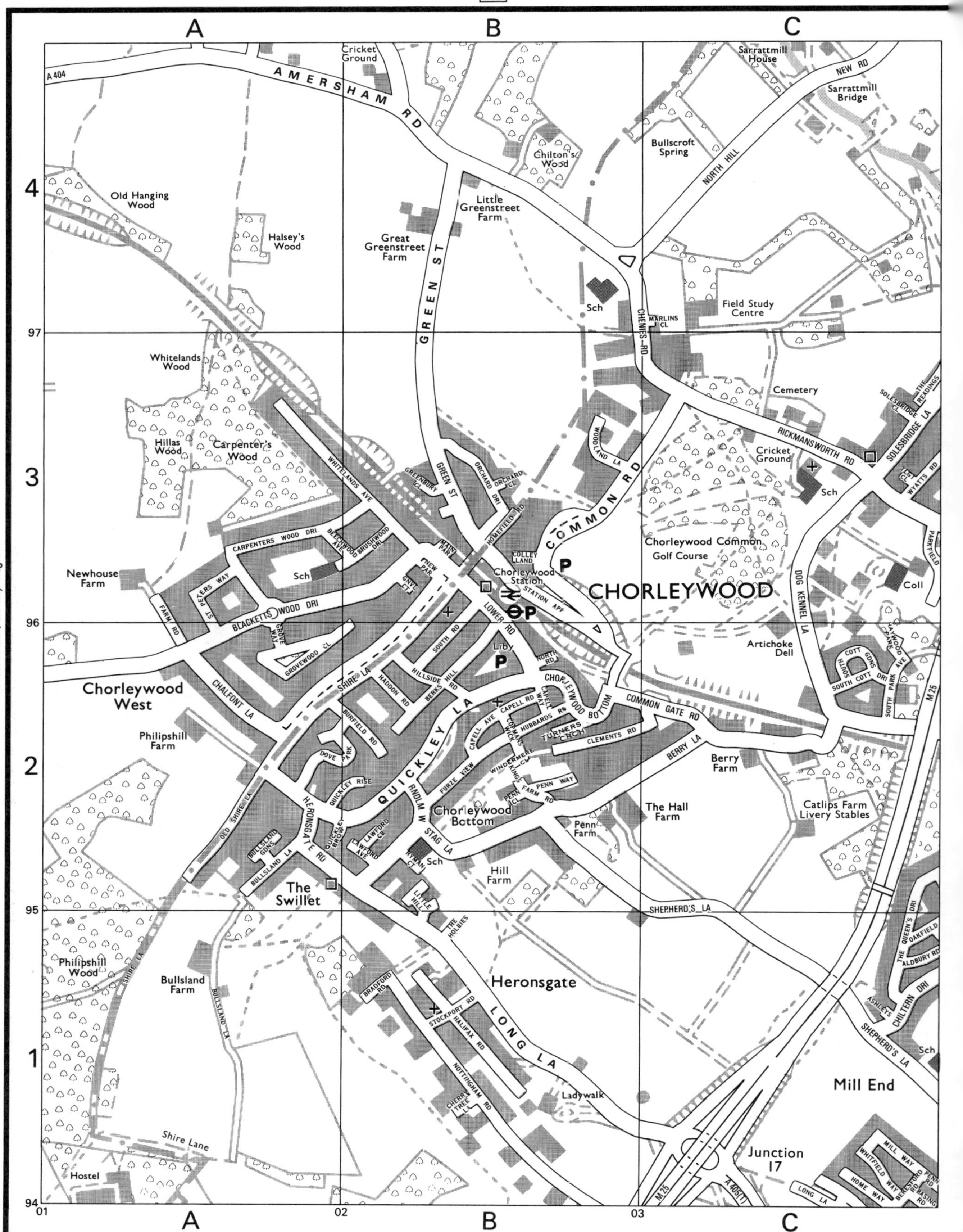

172

152

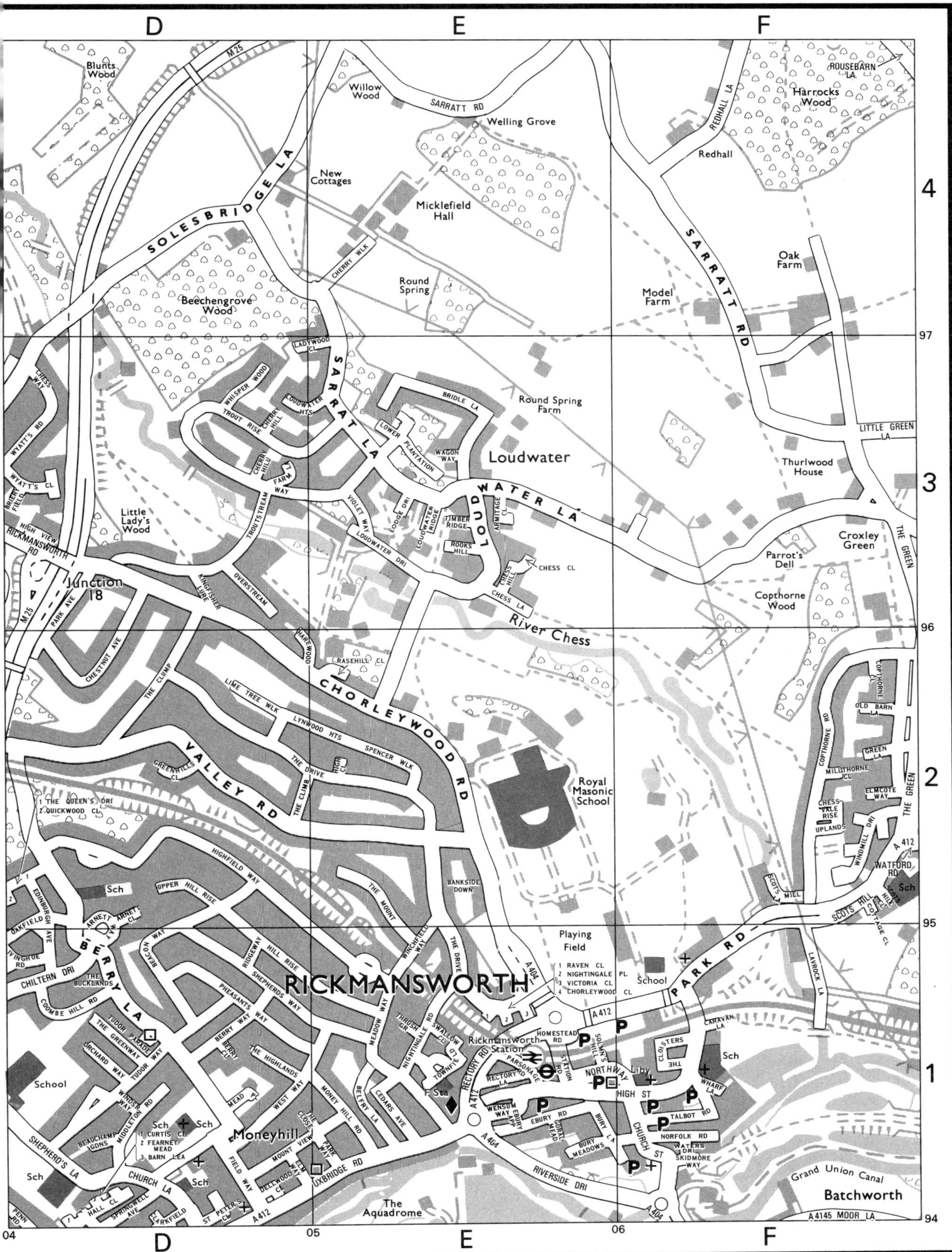
D
E
F
Blunts Wood
Willow Wood
SARRATT RD
Welling Grove
ROUSEBARN LA
Harrocks Wood
REDHALL LA
Redhall
M25
SOLESBRIDGE LA
New Cottages
Micklefield Hall
SARRATT RD
Oak Farm
CHERRY WLK
Round Spring
Beechengrove Wood
Model Farm
LADYWOOD CL
SARRAT LA
CHESS WAY
WHISPER WOOD
BRIDLE LA
Round Spring Farm
LITTLE GREEN LA
WYATT'S RD
TROUT RISE
CHERRY HILL
LOUDWATER HTS
LOWER PLANTATION
WAGON WAY
Loudwater
Thurlwood House
WYATT'S CL
FARM WAY
LOUDWATER LA
BRIERFIELD
Little Lady's Wood
TROUTSTREAM
VIOLET WAY
LODGE DRI
LOUDWATER RIDGE
TIMBER RIDGE
ARMITAGE CL
Croxley Green
HIGH VIEW
RICKMANSWORTH RD
LOUDWATER DRI
ROOKS HILL
Parrot's Dell
THE GREEN
CHESS HILL
CHESS CL
Junction 18
KINGFISHER LURE
OVERSTREAM
CHESS LA
Copthorne Wood
PARK AVE
River Chess
HAREWOOD
CHESTNUT AVE
RASEHILL CL
THE CLUMP
CHORLEYWOOD RD
COPTHORNE CL
LIME TREE WLK
LYNWOOD HTS
OLD BARN LA
SPENCER WLK
GREEN LA
COPTHORNE RD
GREENHILLS CL
VALLEY RD
THE DRIVE
HIGH CL
Royal Masonic School
MILLTHORNE CL
ELMCOTE WAY
1 THE QUEEN'S DRI
2 QUICKWOOD CL
THE CLIMB
CHESS VALE RISE
UPLANDS
WINDMILL DRI
A 412
HIGHFIELD WAY
WATFORD RD
Sch
UPPER HILL RISE
THE MOUNT
BANKSIDE DOWN
SCOTS LA
SCOTS MILL
SCOTS HILL
SCOTS HILL CL
EDINBURGH AVE
ARNETT WAY
ARNETT CL
OAKFIELD AVE
BEACON WAY
RIDGEWAY
HILL RISE
WINCHFIELD WAY
THE DRIVE
Playing Field
COTTAGE CL
IVINGHOE CL
BERRY LA
SHEPHERDS WAY
A 404
1 RAVEN CL
2 NIGHTINGALE PL
3 VICTORIA CL
4 CHORLEYWOOD CL
PARK RD
CHILTERN DRI
THE BUCKLANDS
PHEASANTS WAY
RICKMANSWORTH
School
LAYROCK LA
COOMBE HILL RD
MEADOW WAY
THRUSH GR
NIGHTINGALE RD
SWALLOW CL
A 412
CARAVAN LA
TUDOR PARADE
THE GREENWAY
BERRY WAY
BERRY CL
Rickmansworth Station
HOMESTEAD RD
SOLMNS HILLS
THE CLOISTERS
ORCHARD WAY
TUDOR WAY
THE HIGHLANDS
TOWNFIELD
RECTORY RD
PARSONAGE RD
STATION RD
NORTHWAY
Liby
Sch
School
WEST WAY
MONEY HILL RD
BELFRY LA
CEDARS AVE
RECTORY LA
HIGH ST
WHARF LA
WINDSOR WAY
MIDDLETON RD
MEAD PL
THE CLOSE
F Sta
A 412
WENSUM WAY
EBURY APP
EBURY RD
CURTIS MEAD
BURY LA
CHURCH ST
TALBOT RD
Sch
Sch
1 CURTIS CL
2 FEARNEY MEAD
3 BARN LEA
BEAUCHAMP GDNS
Moneyhill
MOUNT VIEW
PARK WAY
A 404
NORFOLK RD
BURY MEADOWS
WATERSDRI
SKIDMORE WAY
SHEPHERD'S LA
Sch
ELM WAY
CHURCH LA
Sch
FIELD WAY
DELLWOOD CL
UXBRIDGE RD
RIVERSIDE DRI
Grand Union Canal
Batchworth
PENN RD
HALL CL
SPRINGWELL AVE
LARKFIELD
ST PETER'S CL
A 412
The Aquadrome
A 404
A 4145 MOOR LA
04
05
06
D
E
F
4
3
2
1
97
96
95
94

166

173

153

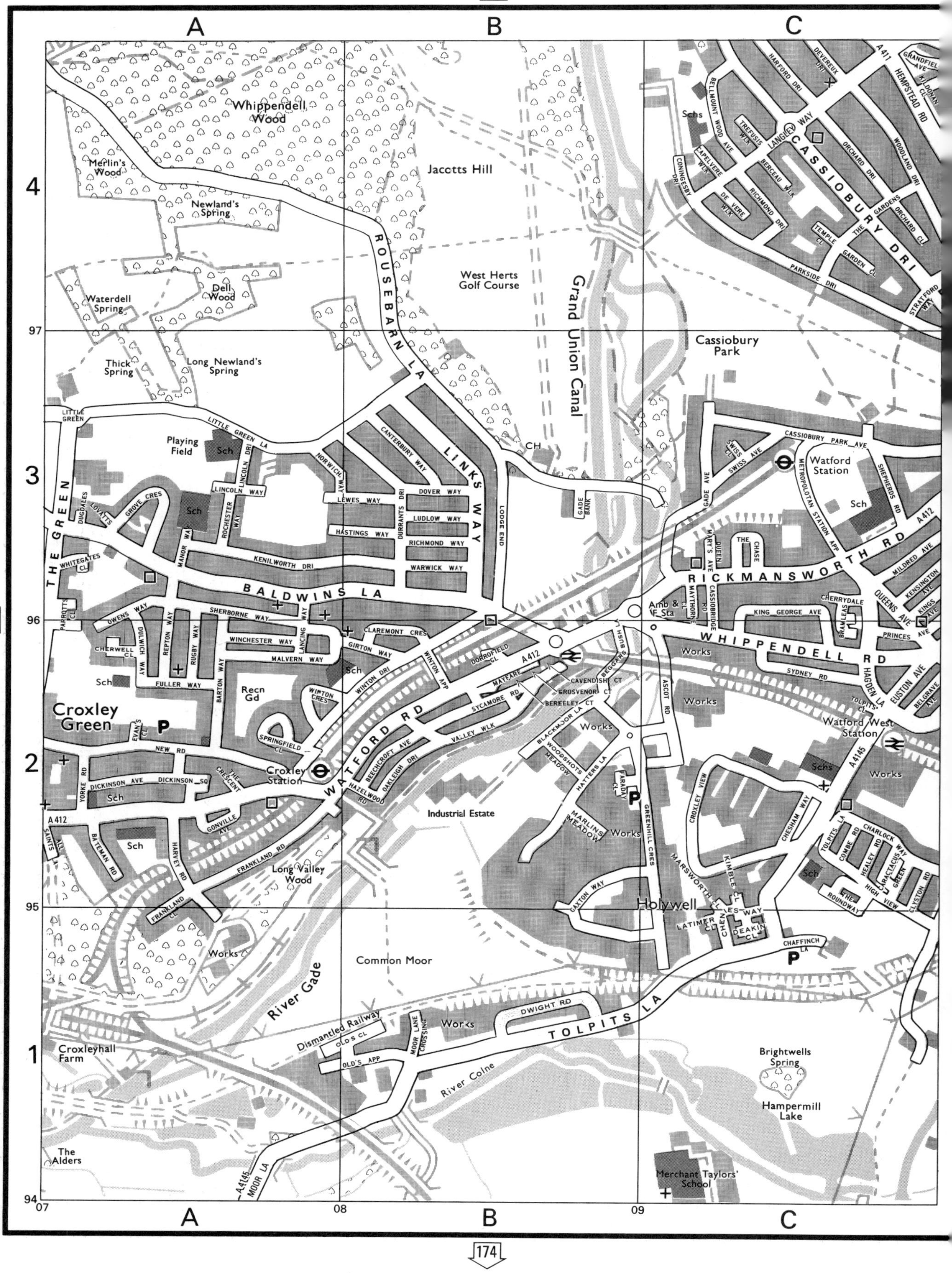
A
B
C
4
3
2
1
97
96
95
94
07
08
09
Whippendell Wood
Merlin's Wood
Newland's Spring
Jacotts Hill
Dell Wood
Waterdell Spring
West Herts Golf Course
Grand Union Canal
Thick Spring
Long Newland's Spring
ROUSEBARN LA
Cassiobury Park
LITTLE GREEN
LITTLE GREEN LA
Playing Field
Sch
LINKS WAY
CH
THE GREEN
BALDWINS LA
Croxley Green
Recn Gd
Croxley Station
WATFORD RD
Industrial Estate
Watford Station
RICKMANSWORTH RD
WHIPPENDELL RD
Works
Watford West Station
Amb & F Sta
Holywell
Long Valley Wood
Common Moor
River Gade
Dismantled Railway
TOLPITS LA
River Colne
Croxleyhall Farm
Brightwells Spring
Hampermill Lake
The Alders
Merchant Taylors' School
MOOR LA
A4145
A412
A411
CASSIOBURY DRI
HEMPSTEAD RD
LANGLEY WAY
PARKSIDE DRI
CASSIOBURY PARK AVE
DOVER WAY
LUDLOW WAY
RICHMOND WAY
WARWICK WAY
HASTINGS WAY
LEWES WAY
KENILWORTH DRI
SHERBORNE WAY
WINCHESTER WAY
MALVERN WAY
FULLER WAY
NEW RD
DICKINSON AVE
DICKINSON SQ
YORKE RD
BATEMAN RD
HARVEY RD
FRANKLAND RD
GAXTON WAY
DWIGHT RD
OLD'S CL
OLD'S APP
CHAFFINCH LA
Schs
P

165

174

154

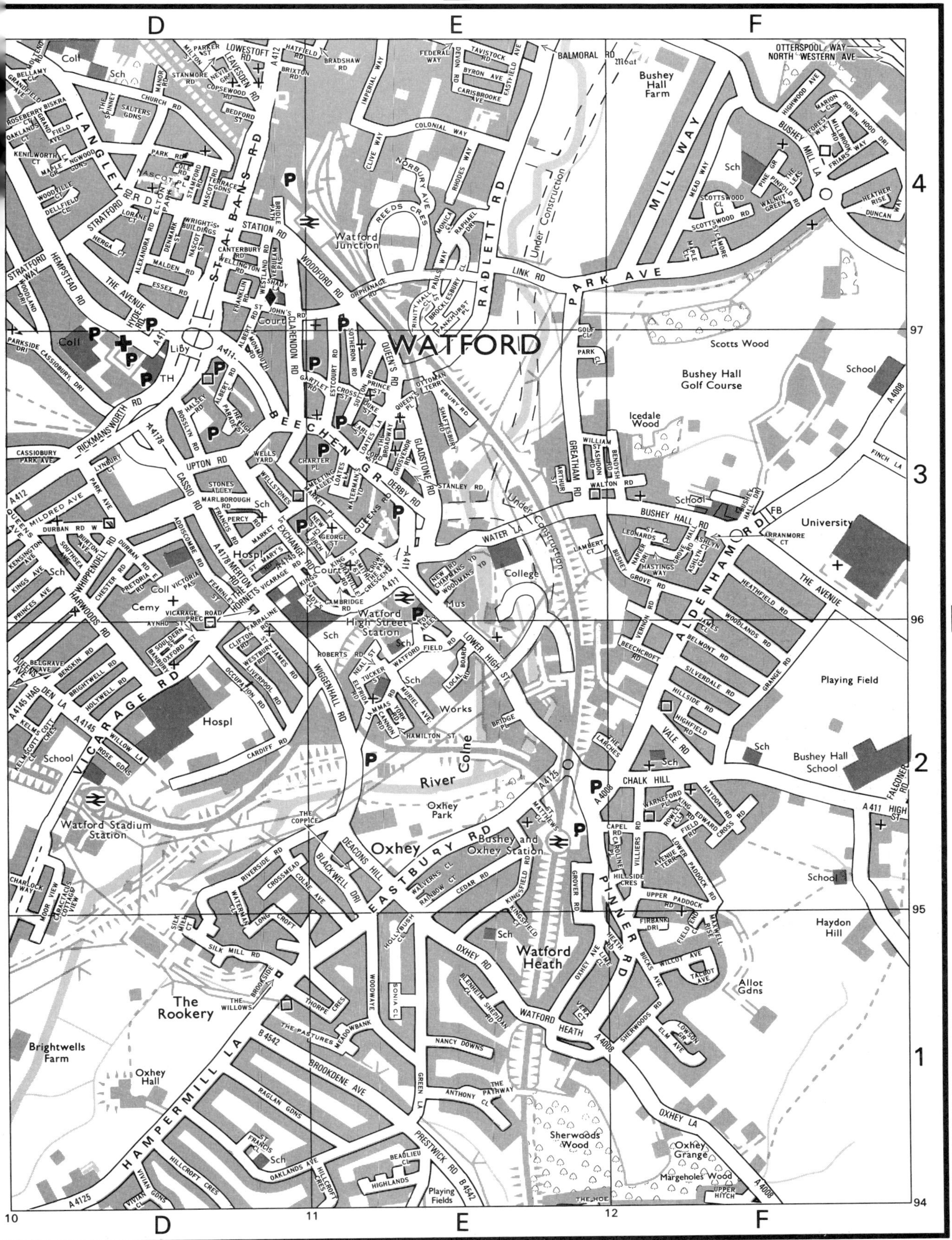
D
E
F
WATFORD
Watford Junction
Watford High Street Station
Watford Stadium Station
Bushey and Oxhey Station
Bushey Hall Farm
Scotts Wood
Bushey Hall Golf Course
Icedale Wood
University
Playing Field
Bushey Hall School
Haydon Hill
Allot Gdns
Oxhey
Oxhey Park
River Colne
Watford Heath
The Rookery
Brightwells Farm
Oxhey Hall
Sherwoods Wood
Oxhey Grange
Margeholes Wood
Playing Fields
Hospl
Cemy
College
Mus
Works
School
Sch
Coll
LANGLEY RD
ST ALBANS RD
STATION RD
WOODFORD RD
RADLETT RD
PARK AVE
LINK RD
MILL WAY
BUSHEY MILL LA
BEECHEN GR
RICKMANSWORTH RD
VICARAGE RD
WIGGENHALL RD
LOWER HIGH ST
BUSHEY HALL RD
ALDENHAM RD
THE AVENUE
CHALK HILL
EASTBURY RD
PINNER RD
OXHEY RD
WATFORD HEATH
HAMPERMILL LA
BROOKDENE AVE
PRESTWICK RD
OXHEY LA
HEMPSTEAD RD
WATER LA
Under Construction
97
96
95
94
4
3
2
1
10
11
12

168

175

155

167

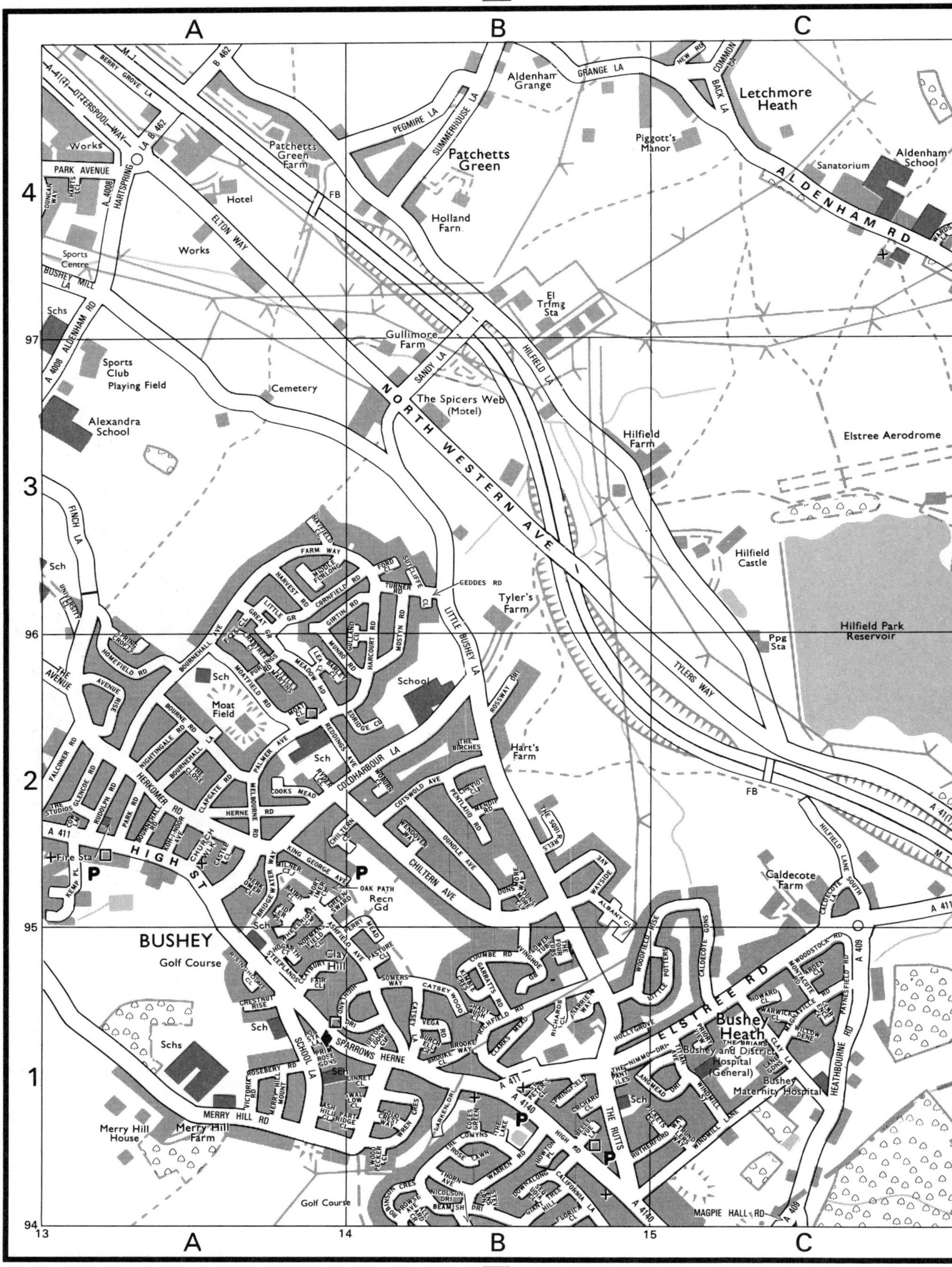
A
B
C
Aldenham Grange
GRANGE LA
Letchmore Heath
Piggott's Manor
Patchetts Green Farm
Patchetts Green
Holland Farn
PEGMIRE LA
SUMMERHOUSE LA
Works
PARK AVENUE
Hotel
ELTON WAY
FB
Sanatorium
Aldenham School
ALDENHAM RD
Sports Centre
BUSHEY MILL LA
Works
El Trfmg Sta
Schs
97
ALDENHAM RD
Sports Club
Playing Field
Gullimore Farm
SANDY LA
HILFIELD LA
Cemetery
The Spicers Web (Motel)
NORTH WESTERN AVE
Alexandra School
Hilfield Farm
Elstree Aerodrome
3
FINCH LA
Sch
Hilfield Castle
Tyler's Farm
GEDDES RD
LITTLE BUSHEY LA
96
Hilfield Park Reservoir
Ppg Sta
TYLERS WAY
School
Sch
Moat Field
Hart's Farm
2
Sch
COLDHARBOUR LA
HERKOMER RD
FB
HIGH ST
Fire Sta
CHILTERN AVE
Recn Gd
Caldecote Farm
A 411
M 1
95
BUSHEY
Golf Course
Clay Hill
ELSTREE RD
Sch
Bushey Heath
Schs
SPARROWS HERNE
Bushey and District Hospital (General)
Bushey Maternity Hospital
1
Sch
MERRY HILL RD
Merry Hill House
Merry Hill Farm
THE RUTTS
HIGH RD
HEATHBOURNE RD
Golf Course
MAGPIE HALL RD
94
13
14
15
A
B
C

176

156

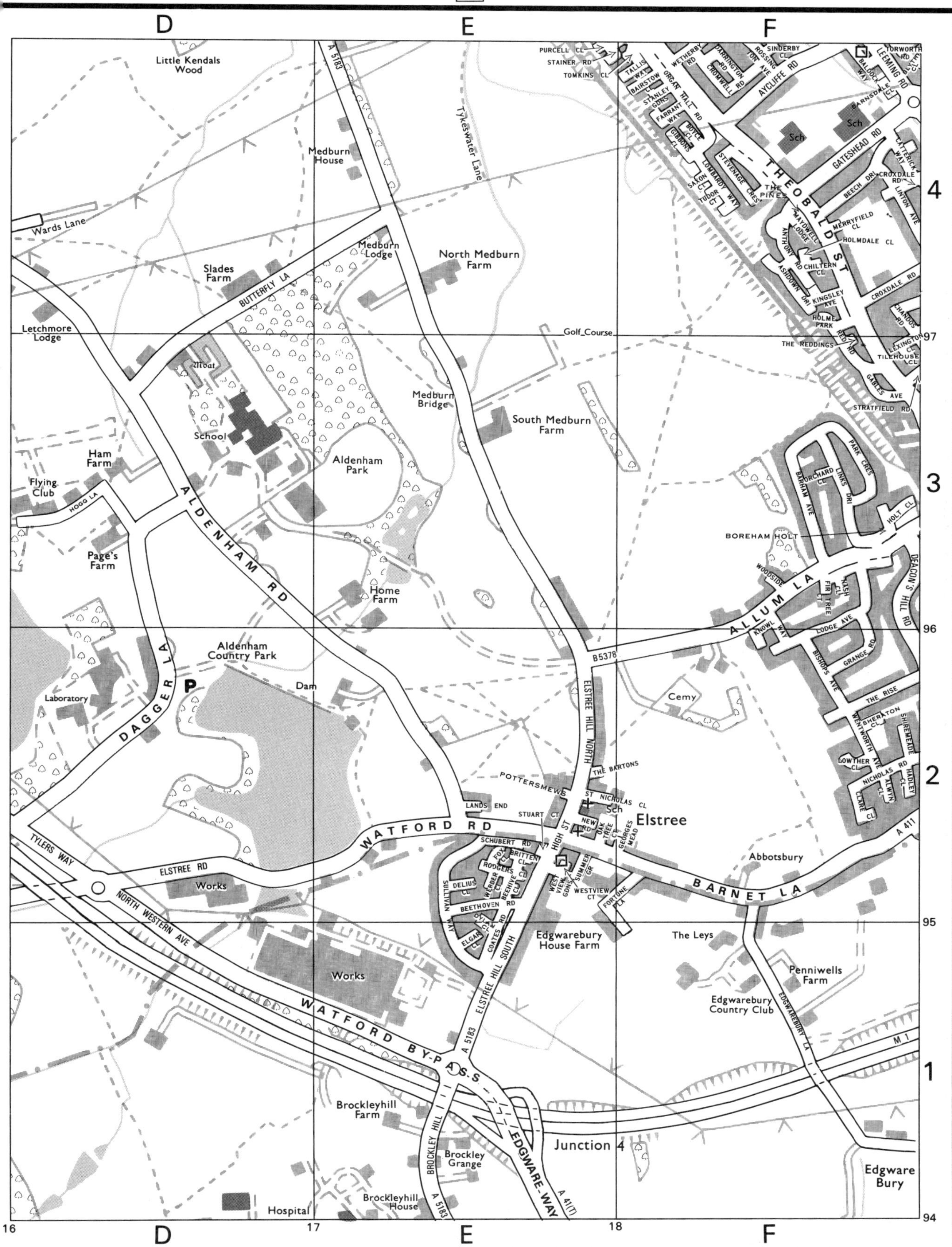
D
E
F
Little Kendals Wood
Medburn House
Tykeswater Lane
Wards Lane
Slades Farm
Butterfly La
Medburn Lodge
North Medburn Farm
Letchmore Lodge
Golf Course
Moat
School
Medburn Bridge
South Medburn Farm
Ham Farm
Flying Club
Hogg La
Aldenham Park
Aldenham Rd
Page's Farm
Home Farm
Aldenham Country Park
Dagger La
Laboratory
Dam
B5378
Elstree Hill North
Cemy
Allum La
Boreham Holt
Woodside
Fir Tree Ct
Nash Cl
Knowl Way
Lodge Ave
Bishops Ave
Grange Rd
The Rise
Deacon's Hill Rd
Sheraton Cl
Shirehead
Wentworth Ave
Lowther Cl
Nicholas Rd
Alwyn Cl
Hadley Cl
Clare Cl
A 411
Potters Mews
The Bartons
St Nicholas Cl
Sch
Elstree
Lands End
Stuart Ct
Watford Rd
High St
New Rd
Oak Tree Ct
Georges Mead
Schubert Rd
Fox Cl
Britten Cl
Rodgers Cl
Delius Cl
Sullivan Way
Webber Cl
Beehive Cl
Beethoven Rd
Elgar Cl
Coates Rd
Summer Gr
West View Gdns
Westview Ct
Fortune La
Barnet La
Abbotsbury
Tylers Way
Elstree Rd
Works
North Western Ave
Edgwarebury House Farm
The Leys
Penniwells Farm
Edgwarebury Country Club
Edgwarebury La
Watford By-Pass
A 5183
Elstree Hill South
M 1
Brockleyhill Farm
Brockley Hill
Brockley Grange
Edgware-Way
A 41(T)
Junction 4
Edgware Bury
Hospital
Brockleyhill House
A 5183
Purcell Cl
Stainer Rd
Tomkins Cl
Tallis Way
Bairstow Cl
Stanley Gdns
Farrant Way
Gibbons Cl
Saxon Cl
Tudor Ct
Lombardy Way
Stevenage Cres
Boyle Cl
Organ Hall Rd
Wetherby Rd
Darrington Rd
Cromwell Rd
Rossington Ave
Sinderby Cl
Aycliffe Rd
Torworth Rd
Leeming Rd
Baldock Way
Barnsdale Cl
Sch
Sch
Gateshead Rd
Catterick Way
Croxdale Rd
Linton Ave
Beech Dri
The Pines
Theobald St
Maydwell Lodge
Merryfield Cl
Holmdale Cl
Anthony Rd
Chiltern Cl
Ashdown Dri
Kingsley Ave
Holme Park
Croxdale Rd
Chandos Rd
Lexington Cl
Tilehouse Cl
The Reddings
Red Rd
Gables Ave
Stratfield Rd
Park Cres
Orchard Cl
Barham Ave
Links Dri
Holt Cl
4
3
2
1
97
96
95
94
16
17
18

170

157

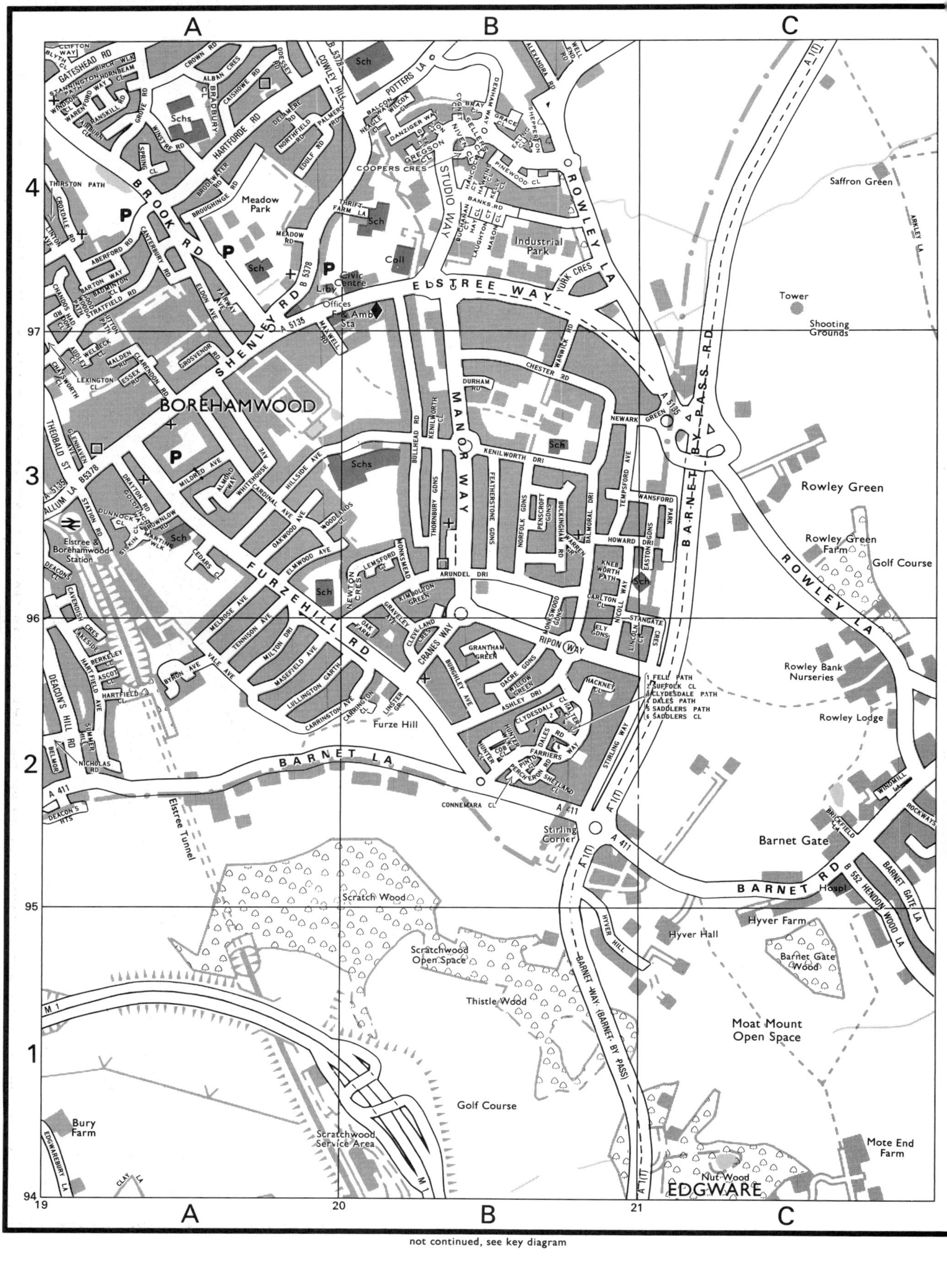
A
B
C
4
3
2
1
97
96
95
94
19
20
21
BOREHAMWOOD
EDGWARE
Meadow Park
Industrial Park
Civic Centre
Liby
Offices
F & Amb Sta
Sch
Schs
Coll
Elstree & Borehamwood Station
Saffron Green
Tower
Shooting Grounds
Rowley Green
Rowley Green Farm
Golf Course
Rowley Bank Nurseries
Rowley Lodge
Barnet Gate
Hospl
Hyver Farm
Hyver Hall
Barnet Gate Wood
Moat Mount Open Space
Mote End Farm
Nut Wood
Stirling Corner
Furze Hill
Elstree Tunnel
Scratch Wood
Scratchwood Open Space
Thistle Wood
Scratchwood Service Area
Bury Farm
ELSTREE WAY
SHENLEY RD
BROOK RD
MANOR WAY
ROWLEY LA
BARNET BY-PASS RD
BARNET LA
BARNET RD
FURZEHILL RD
BARNET WAY (BARNET BY PASS)
STUDIO WAY
THEOBALD ST
ALLUM LA
STATION RD
DEACON'S HILL RD
HENDON WOOD LA
BARNET GATE LA
EDGWAREBURY LA
CLAY LA
HYVER HILL
STIRLING WAY
KENILWORTH DRI
CHESTER RD
ARUNDEL DRI
RIPON WAY
COWLEY HILL
HARTFORDE RD
A 5135
A 411
A 1(T)
B 5378
B 552
M 1
1 FELL PATH
2 SUFFOLK CL
3 CLYDESDALE PATH
4 DALES PATH
5 SADDLERS PATH
6 SADDLERS CL
CONNEMARA CL

169

158

not continued, see key diagram

not continued, see key diagram

164

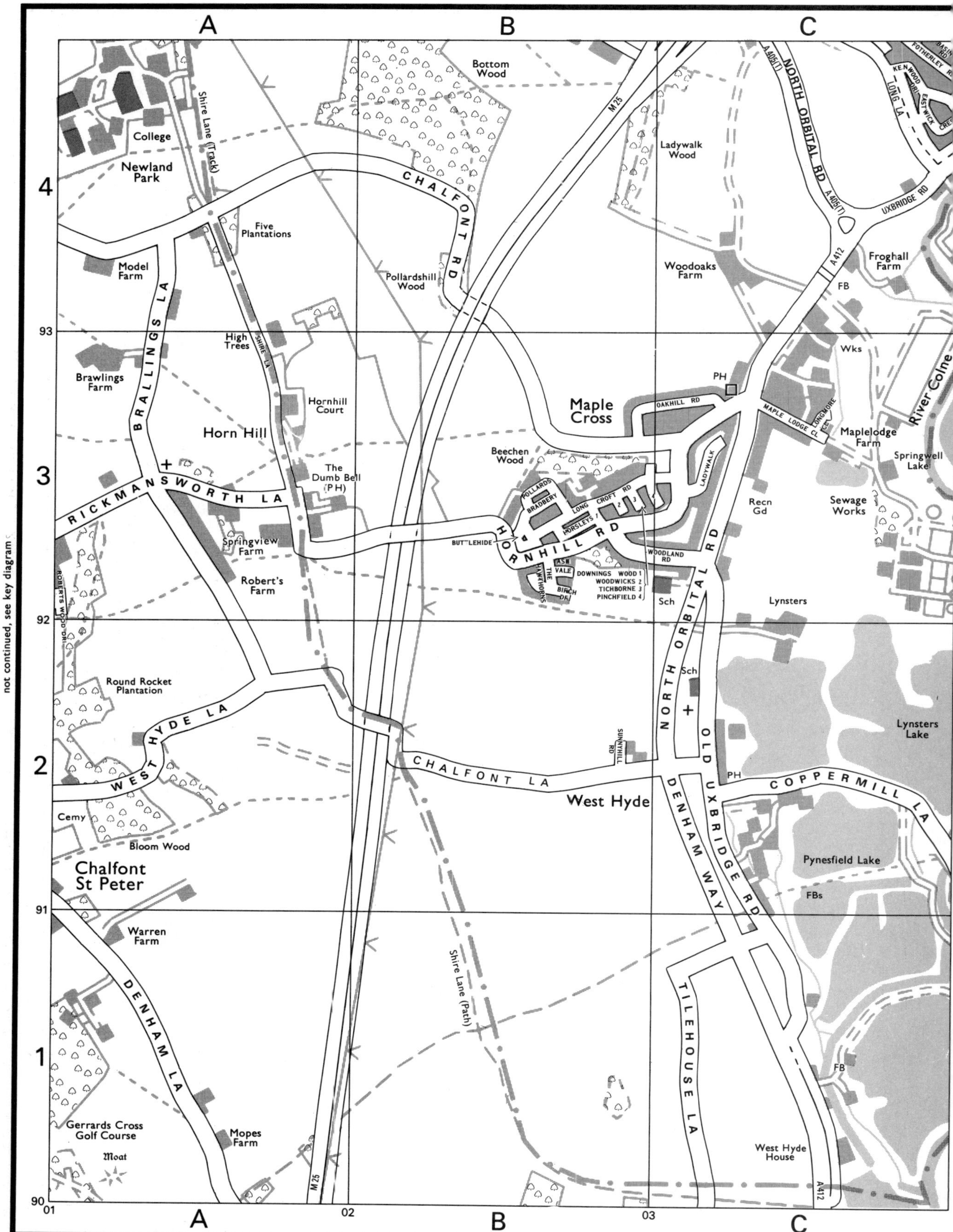

not continued, see key diagram

not continued, see key diagram

165

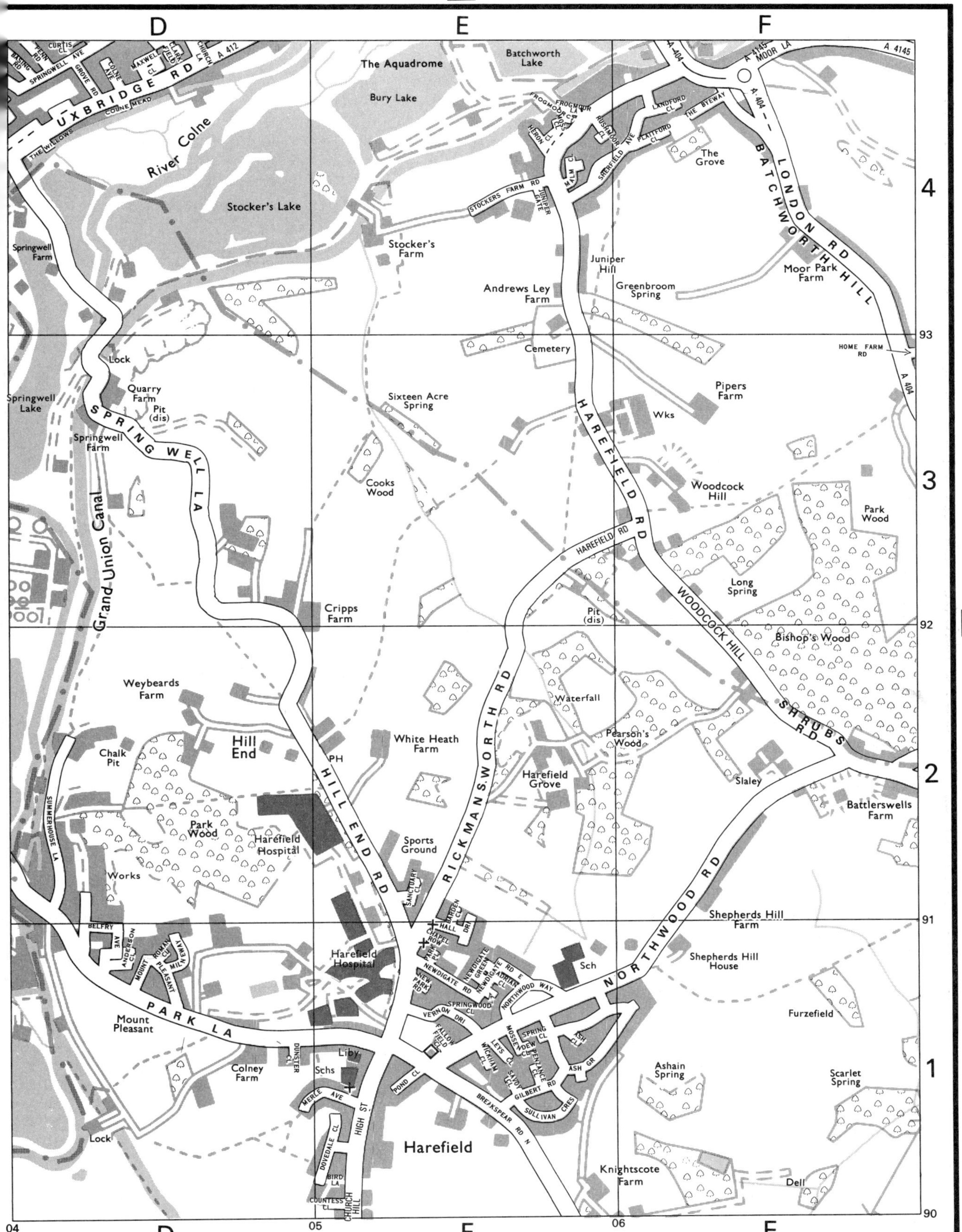

174

not continued, see key diagram

166

173

not continued, see key diagram

167

D
E
F
Oxhey Warren
Big Wood
Playing Fields
Warren Dell
Carpenders Park
Carpenders Park Station
Married Quarters
Capenders Park Farm
HILLCROFT CRES
HAYLING RD
GOSFORTH LA
Schools
Young Hangings
South Oxhey
Old Hangings
OXHEY DRI
The Plantation
Oxhey Woods
Cemetery
LITTLE OXHEY LA
HMS Warrior
PRESTWICK RD
School
Nanscot Wood
Reservoir
Pinnerwood House
Pinnerwood Farm
Hatch End
Golf Course
POTTER STREET HILL
HILLSIDE RD
NORTHWOOD WAY
Pinnerwood Park
THE BROADWAY
UXBRIDGE RD
Northwood, Pinner and District Hospital
Liby
School
PINNER RD
Grim's Ditch
Pinner Green
RICKMANSWORTH RD
Northwood Hills Station
WAXWELL LA
PINNER
MOSS LA
GEORGE V. AVE
River Pinn
4
3
2
1
93
92
91
90
10
11
12

176

168

175

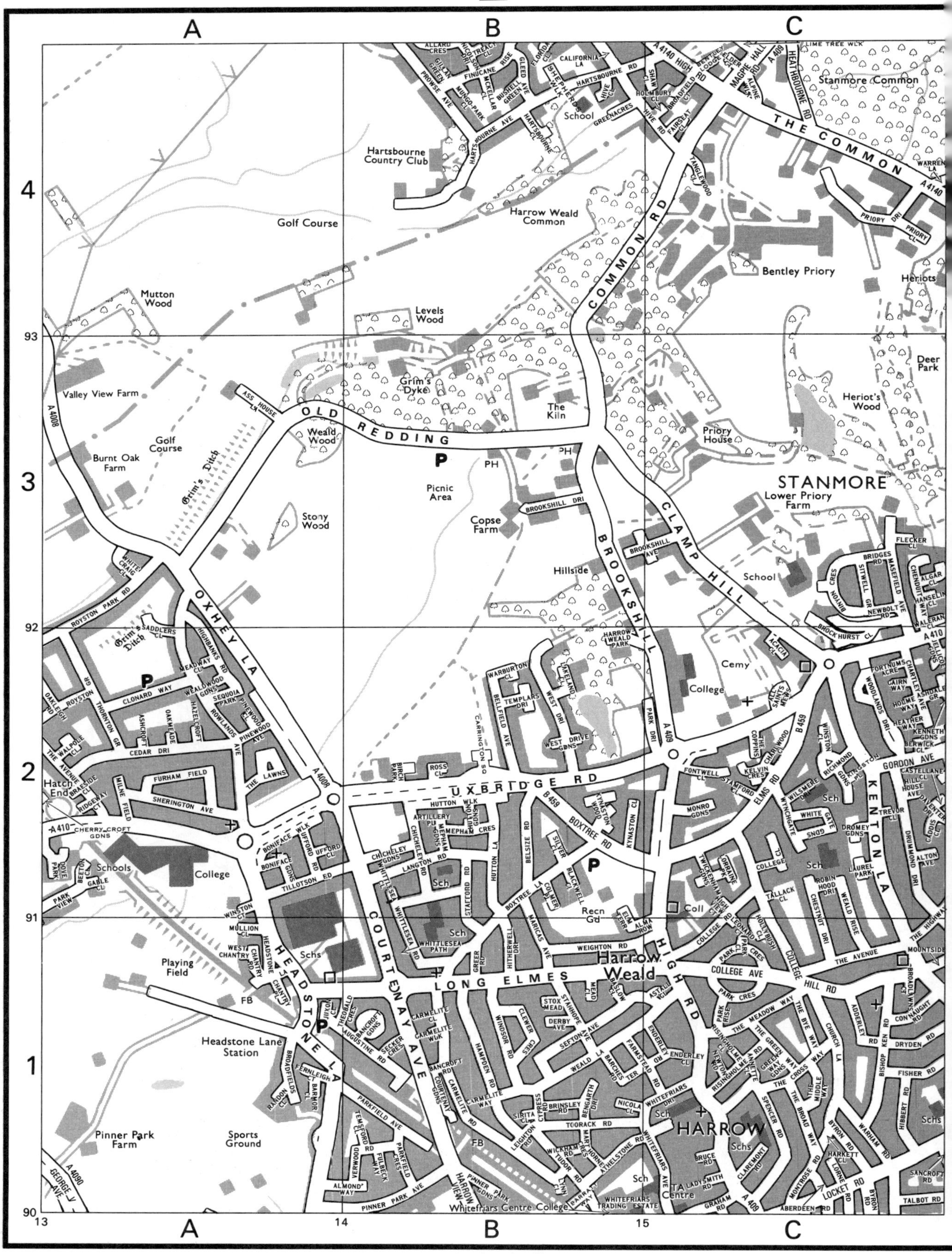

not continued, see key diagram

INDEX

EXPLANATION OF THE STREET INDEX REFERENCE SYSTEM

Street names are listed alphabetically and show the locality, the map page number and a reference to the square in which the name falls on the map page.

Example:	Ordnance Rd. Enf..*162* C1
Ordnance Rd	This is the full street name, which may have been abbreviated on the map.
Enf	This is the abbreviation for the town, village or locality in which the street falls. Postal codes have been used for street names in the London Postal District.
162	This is the page number of the map on which the street name appears.
C1	The letter and figure indicate the square on the map in which the centre of the street falls. The square can be found at the junction of the vertical column carrying the appropriate letter and the horizontal row carrying the appropriate figure.

ABBREVIATIONS USED IN THE INDEX

Road Names

Approach	App
Avenue	Ave
Broadway	Bwy
By-Pass	By-Ps
Causeway	Cswy
Common	Comm
Corner	Cnr
Cottages	Cotts
Court	Ct
Crescent	Cres
Drive	Dri
Drove	Dro
East	E
Gardens	Gdns
Grove	Gr
Heights	Hts
Lane	La
North	N
Orchard	Orch
Parade	Par
Passage	Pas
Place	Pl
Pleasant	Plea
Precinct	Prec
Promenade	Prom
Road	Rd
South	S
Square	Sq
Street, Saint	St
Terrace	Terr
Walk	Wlk
West	W
Yard	Yd

Abbots Langley	Abb L	153	F4
Albury	Alb	57	D3
Aldbury	Ald	101	E3
Aldenham	Aldhm	155	D1
Anstey	Ans	29	D3
Apsley End	Aps En	19	F4
Ardeley	Ard	38	C2
Arlesey	Arl	11	D3
Ashley Green	Ash Gr	136	A4
Ashwell	Ashw	4	B2
Aspenden	Asp	40	B3
Aston	Ast	51	F1
Aston End	Ast En	51	F3
Ayot St Lawrence	A St L	88	A3
Ayot St Peter	A St P	88	C2
Baldock	Bal	23	F4
Barkway	Bark	17	E2
Barley	Bar	8	C1
Barnet	Barn	171	F2
Bayford	Bay	132	C3
Bedmond	Bed	139	F2
Benington	Benn	52	C2
Berkhamsted	Berk	122	B3
Birchanger	Birhr	59	F1
Birch Green	Bir Gr	112	B2
Bird Green	Brd Gr	30	C4
Bishop's Stortford	Bis St	76	C4
Blackmore End	Bla En	87	E3
Borehamwood	Bor	170	A3
Botley	Bot	136	A1
Bourne End	Bor En	123	D1
Bovingdon	Bov	137	D2
Bramfield	Bram	91	E2
Braughing	Brag	55	F3
Breachwood Green	Bre Gr	47	F1
Brent Pelham	Bre P	30	A1
Brickendon	Bric	133	E2
Bricket Wood	Bri Wd	140	C1
Brookmans Park	Bro Pk	144	C3
Buckland	Buck	27	E4
Buckland Common	Buc Co	120	A2
Bull's Green	Bul Gr	90	C4
Buntingford	Bun	40	C4
Burnham Green	Brn Gr	90	B3
Bury Green	Bry Gr	75	F4
Bushey	Bus	170	A1
Bygrave	Byg	13	E3
Caddington	Cad	62	C2
Caldecote	Cal	3	E1
Chalfont St Peter	C St P	172	A2
Chandler's Cross	Cha Cr	152	C1
Chapmore End	Cha En	92	B3
Cheddington	Ched	80	A4
Chenies	Chen	151	D1
Cheshunt	Ches	148	B1
Chipperfield	Chipf	152	A4
Chipping	Chipp	27	E3
Chiswellgreen	Chis	141	D3
Cholesbury	Chol	120	B2
Chorleywood	Chor	164	B3
Church End	Ch En	11	D4
Clapgate	Clap	57	E3
Clothall	Clo	24	C2
Cockernhoe Green	Cok Gr	46	C2
Codicote	Cod	67	F1
Colliers End	Col En	73	D3
Colney Heath	Coln H	143	E4
Colney Street	Col St	141	F1
Cottered	Cotrd	39	E4
Crafton	Cra	60	C2
Cromer	Cro	38	B3
Croxley Green	Cro Gr	166	A2
Cuffley	Cuf	146	C2
Dagnall	Dagn	81	E3
Dane End	Dan En	71	F4
Datchworth	Dat	69	F1
Digswell	Digs	89	F2
Drayton Beauchamp	Dra B	99	E3
Dunstable	Dun	44	A1
Eastwick	East	117	D2
Edgware	Edg	170	C1
Edworth	Edw	3	D3
Elstree	Elst	169	F2
Enfield	Enf	162	C1
Epping Green	Ep Gr	132	B1
Essendon	Ess	131	F3
Farnham	Far	58	B3
Felden	Fel	138	A4
Flamstead	Fla	84	A1
Flaunden	Flau	151	D3
Ford End	Fo En	30	C2
Frogmore	Fro	141	F2
Furneux Pelham	Fur P	43	D3
Goff's Oak	Gofs O	147	E2
Gosmore	Gos	34	C2
Graveley	Gra	36	B2
Gravesend	Gravnd	57	D4
Great Amwell	Gt Am	114	C3
Great Chiswell	Gt Ch	9	F1
Great Gaddesden	Gt Ga	103	E2
Great Hallingbury	Gt Ha	77	F2
Great Hormead	Gt Ho	42	A4
Great Munden	Gt Mu	54	B3
Great Offley	Gt Of	33	E1
Great Wymondley	Gt Wy	35	F3
Green End	Gr En	26	B4
Green End, (Braughing)	Gr En	75	E1
Green Tye	Gr Ty	75	E1
Guilden Morden	Gu M	1	C3
Hadham Cross	Had Cr	74	C1
Hall's Green	Hal Gr	37	F3
Hammond Street	Ham St	147	E3
Harefield	Hare	173	E1
Hare Street, (Ardeley)	H St A	38	C3
Hare Street, (Hormead)	H St H	41	F4
Harlow	Harl	117	F1
Harmer Green	Har Gr	90	A3
Harpenden	Harp	86	A1
Harrow	Har	176	C1
Harrow Weald	Har W	176	B1
Hastoe	Has	119	F4
Hatfield	Hat	130	B4
Haultwick	Hault	53	F2
Hay Street	Hay St	41	F1
Hebing End	Heb En	52	C1
Hemel Hempstead	Heml H	124	C1
Henlow	Henlw	10	B4
Heronsgate	Heron	164	B1
Hertford	Hert	114	A2
Hertingfordbury	Hertng	112	C3
Hexton	Hex	19	D1
High Cross	H Cr	72	C1
Higham Gobion	H Gobn	19	D3
High Wych	H Wy	97	D1
Hinxworth	Hin	3	E3
Hitchin	Hit	34	C4
Hoddesdon	Hod	135	D3
Holwell	Hol	21	D4
Horn Hill	Hrn H	172	A3
Hunsdon	Hun	95	E1
Ickleford	Ick	21	F2
Ivinghoe	Ivin	80	C4
Kelsall	Kel	15	E3
Kensworth Common	Ken Co	82	C4
Kimpton	Kim	66	B1
Kings Langley	Kin L	139	D1
Kings Walden	Kin Wd	48	A2
Kinsbourne Green	Kin Gr	85	D3
Knebworth	Kneb	69	D3
Kneesworth	Knee	2	A3
Langley	Lan	49	F1
Latimer	Lat	150	C2
Lemsford	Lem	110	A3
Letchmore Heath	Let H	168	C4
Letchworth	Letw	22	C4
Letty Green	Let Gr	112	A1
Levens Green	Lev Gr	54	B1
Lilley	Lily	32	B1
Little Almshoe	L Alm	49	D1
Little Berkhamsted	L Berk	132	B2
Little Chalfont	L Chal	150	A1
Little Chishill	L Chis	18	C4
Little Gaddesden	L Gad	102	B4
Little Hadham	L Had	57	E1
Little Hallingbury	L Hal	98	B4
Little Hormead	L Hor	42	A3
Little Wymondley	L Wym	35	F2
London Colney	Lon C	142	B3
Long Marston	Lon M	79	D2
Lower Nazeing	Lo Naz	149	E4
Luffenhall	Luf	38	B4
Luton	Luton	45	E2
Mangrove Green	Man Gr	46	C2
Maple Cross	Map Cr	172	B3
Markyate	Mark	83	F3
Marsworth	Mars	80	A1
Meesden	Mee	29	F3
Mentmore	Men	61	E2
Mill End	Mil En	26	C3
Much Hadham	Muc H	74	C2
Nettleden	Net	103	E1
Newgate Street	New St	146	C4
Newmill End	Nwml E	85	F4
Newnham	Newn	12	C4
Newsells	News	17	E4
Northaw	Nort	145	F1
Northchurch	Nthch	121	F3
North Mymms	N Mym	144	A3
Northwood	Norwd	174	C2
Norton	Nor	12	A1
Nuthampstead	Nut	18	A1
Odsey	Odsey	5	E1
Oldhall Green	Odh Gr	54	C1
Old Knebworth	Old K	68	B3
Park Street	Pk St	141	E3
Patchetts Green	Pat Gr	168	B4
Pegsdon	Pegs	19	E1
Peter's Green	Pet Gr	65	E2
Piccotts End	Pic En	124	B4
Pirton	Pirt	20	B2
Pitstone	Pit	80	B2
Pinner	Pnr	175	F1
Potten End	Pot En	123	D3
Potters Bar	Pot B	159	D4
Preston	Pres	48	B3
Puckeridge	Puc	55	E2
Puttenham	Put	78	C1
Radlett	Radl	156	A3
Radwell	Radw	12	B2
Redbourn	Red	106	A3
Reed	Reed	16	C3
Rickmansworth	Ric	165	E1
Ridge	Ridge	157	F3
Ringshall	Rin	81	D1
Roast Green	Rst Gr	30	C3
Roe Green	Ro Gr	26	A4
Roydon	Roy	116	B1
Royston	Royst	7	E3
Rushden	Rus	25	F2
St Albans	St Alb	127	F2
St Ippolitts	St Ipp	35	D2
St Leonards	St Le	119	F2
St Pauls Walden	St P W	49	D1
Sacombe	Sac	71	F2
Sacombe Green	Sac Gr	72	A2
Sandon	San	15	D1
Sandridge	Sand	108	B1
Sarratt	Sar	152	A2
Sawbridgeworth	Saw	97	F1
Shenley	Shen	157	D3
Smallford	Sal	129	D2
Southern Green	Stn Gr	26	A2
South Oxhey	Sth Ox	175	E4
Spellbrook	Spel	97	F4
Stanborough	Stanb	110	A2
Standon	Stand	55	F1
Stanmore	Stan	176	C3
Stanstead Abbotts	Sta Ab	115	F2
Stanstead Mountfitchet	Sta M	59	E4
Stapleford	Stap	92	A4
Starlings Green	Sta Gr	30	C2
Steeple Morden	Ste Mo	5	D4
Stevenage	Stev	50	B4
Stocking Pelham	Sto P	43	F4
Stotford	Stot	11	F4
Streatley	Str	31	D3
Studham	Stu	82	B2
Tea Green	T Gr	47	D2
Tewin	Tewin	90	C1
Therfield	Ther	15	F4
Thorley	Thor	76	B1
Throcking	Tho	26	C1
Thundridge	Thun	93	F4
Tonwell	Tonw	92	C4
Tring	Tri	100	A2
Tyttenhanger	Tyt	142	C4
Wadesmill	Wad	93	E4
Wallington	Wal	25	E4
Walkern	Wal	38	A1
Waltham Abbey	Wa Aby	163	E3
Waltham Cross	Wa Cr	162	B3
Ware	Ware	93	F1
Wareside	Wars	94	C2
Warren's Green	Wa Gr	37	E3
Water End	Wa En	144	B3
Waterford	Wat	92	A1
Watford	Watf	167	E3
Watton at Stone	Wat St	70	C2
Welham Green	Wel Gr	144	B4
Wellpond Green	Wep Gr	56	B1
Welwyn	Welw	89	D2
Welwyn Garden City	WelGC	110	C3
Westland Green	Wes Gr	56	C1
Westmill	West	40	C2
Weston	Wes	24	B1
Wheathampstead	Whea	108	B4
Whitwell	Whit	66	C3
Widford	Widf	95	F2
Wigginton	Wigg	100	B1
Wildhill	Wild	131	E1
Willian	Will	23	D1
Wilstone	Wils	79	E1
Wingrave	Wing	60	B2
Wood End	Wd En	53	E4
Woolmer Green	Wl Gr	69	D1
Wyddial	Wyd	28	A2

Abbey Ave. St Alb 127 D1
Abbey Ct. Wa Aby 163 D3
Abbey Dri. Luton 46 A1
Abbey Mill End. St Alb 127 E1
Abbey Mill La. St Alb 127 E1
Abbey Rd. Ches 162 C3
Abbey View Rd. St Alb 127 E2
Abbey View. Watf 154 B2
Abbeyfields. St Alb 127 F1
Abbeyview. Wa Aby 163 E3
Abbis Orch. Ick 21 F3
Abbots Ave W. St Alb 141 E4
Abbots Ave. St Alb 141 F4
Abbots Cl. Dat 69 E1
Abbots Gr. Stev 50 C3
Abbots Park. St Alb 128 A1
Abbots Rd. Abb L 153 E4
Abbots Rise. Kin L 138 C3
Abbots View. Kin L 138 C2
Abbots Wood Rd. Luton 46 A1
Abbotsford Lodge. Norwd 174 C3
Abbotts La. Widf 95 E2
Abbotts Rd. Letw 22 B3
Abbotts Rise. Sta Ab 115 E2
Abbotts Way. Bis St 76 C2
Abbotts Way. Sta Ab 115 E2
Abbotts Way. Wing 60 A2
Abdale La. Wa En 144 A2
Abel Cl. Heml H 125 D2
Aberdale Gdns. Pot B 158 C4
Aberdeen Rd. Har 176 C1
Aberford Rd. Bor 170 A4
Abigail Cl. Luton 45 E2
Abingdon Pl. Pot B 159 D4
Abingdon Rd. Luton 44 B2
Abridge Cl. Enf 162 B2
Abstacle Hill. Tri 99 F2
Acacia Cl. Stan 176 B2
Acacia Gr. Berk 122 A2
Acacia Rd. Enf 161 E1
Acacia St. Hat 130 A1
Acacia Wlk. Harp 107 E3
Acacia Wlk. Tri 99 F2
Acers. Chis 141 E2
Achilles Cl. Heml H 124 C3
Ackroyd Rd. Roystn 7 F4
Acme Rd. Watf 154 A1
Acorn La. Cuf 146 C1
Acorn Pl. Watf 154 A1
Acorn Rd. Heml H 125 D1
Acorn St. Hun 116 B4
Acre Way. Norwd 174 C1
Acre Wood. Heml H 124 C1
Acremore St. Bry Gr 75 E4
Acrewood Way. St Alb 128 C2
Acton Cl. Ches 162 C4
Acworth Cres. Luton 44 B3
Adam's Yard. Hert 113 E3
Adams Way. Tri 100 A3
Adamsfield. Ham St 148 A3
Adderley Rd. Bis St 76 C4
Adderley Rd. Har 176 C1
Addiscombe Rd. Watf 167 D3
Addison Cl. Norwd 175 D1
Addison Way. Norwd 174 C1
Adelaide Cl. Enf 161 F1
Adelaide St. Luton 63 E4
Adelaide St. St Alb 127 E2
Adele Ave. Har Gr 89 F2
Adeyfield Gdns. Heml H 124 C2
Adeyfield Rd. Heml H 124 C2
Adhara Rd. Norwd 175 D3
Adhern Ct. St Alb 142 B4
Adinger Cl. Stev 50 C2
Admiral St. Hert 114 A3
Admiral's Ct. Watf 153 F2
Admirals Cl. Coln H 143 F4
Admirals Wlk. Hod 135 D2
Admirals Wlk. St Alb 142 A4
Adrian Cl. Hare 173 E1
Adrian Rd. Abb L 153 F4
Adstone Rd. Cad 62 C2
Ailsworth Rd. Luton 45 D4
Ainsdale Rd. Sth Ox 175 E4
Aintree Rd. Roystn 7 F3
Airedale. Heml H 124 C3
Airport Approach Rd. Luton 64 B4
Airport Way. Luton 64 A4
Airport Way. Nwml E 64 A3
Aitken Rd. Barn 171 E2
Akeman St. Tri 100 A2
Alan Dri. Barn 171 F2
Alandale Dri. Pnr 175 D1
Alban Ave. St Alb 127 E3
Alban Cres. Bor 170 A4
Alban Park Ind Est. St 128 C2
Alban Rd. Letw 23 E2
Albans View. Watf 154 A3
Albany Cl. Bus 168 B2
Albany Ct. Harp 107 E4
Albany Mews. Chis 141 D2
Albany Park Ave. Enf 162 B1
Albany Rd. Enf 162 B1
Albemarle Ave. Ches 148 B2
Albemarle Ave. Pot B 159 D4
Albert Rd N. Watf 167 D3
Albert Rd S. Watf 167 D3
Albert Rd. Arl 11 D2
Albert Rd. Luton 63 F3
Albert St. Mark 83 F3
Albert St. St Alb 127 E1
Albert St. Stev 50 B4
Albert St. Tri 100 A2
Albion Cl. Hert 113 F4
Albion Hill. Heml H 124 B1
Albion Rd. Luton 63 F4
Albion Rd. Pit 80 B3
Albion Rd. St Alb 127 F2
Albury Cl. Luton 31 D1
Albury Dri. Pnr 175 E2
Albury Grove Rd. Ches 148 B1
Albury Rd. L Had 57 E1
Albury Ride. Ches 162 B4
Albury Wlk. Ches 162 B4
Alconbury. Bis St 59 D1
Alconbury. Wel G C 111 D2
Aldbury Cl. St Alb 128 B4
Aldbury Cl. Watf 154 B2
Aldbury Gr. Wel GC 111 D3
Aldbury Rd. Ric 164 C1
Aldeburgh Cl. Stev 36 A1
Aldenham Gr. Radl 156 A3
Aldenham Rd. Bus 167 F3
Aldenham Rd. Elst 169 D3
Aldenham Rd. Radl 156 A2
Alder Cl. Bal 23 F4
Alder Cl. Bis St 76 B2
Alder Cl. Chis 141 E2
Alder Cres. Luton 45 D2
Alder Ct. Luton 45 D2
Alder Wlk. Watf 154 A2
Alderbury Rd. Sta Mo 59 F4
Alderley Ct. Berk 122 B2
Alderman Cl. Wel Gr 144 B4
Alders End La. Harp 85 F1
Aldersgrove. Wa Aby 163 F3
Alderton Cl. Luton 46 B1
Alderton Dri. Rin 102 A4
Aldhouse Cl. Luton 45 D3
Aldock Rd. Stev 50 C4
Aldock. Wel GC 111 D2
Aldridge Ave. Enf 163 D1
Aldwick Ct. St Alb 128 A1
Aldwick Rd. Harp 107 F4
Aldwick. St Alb 128 A1
Aldwickbury Cres. Harp 86 B1
Aldwyck Ct. Heml H 124 B2
Aldwyke Rise. Ware 93 E2
Aldykes. Hat 129 F3
Alesia Rd. Luton 44 C3
Alexander Ct. Ches 148 B1
Alexander Rd. Hertng 113 D3
Alexander Rd. Lon C 142 B3
Alexander Rd. Stot 11 F3
Alexandra Ave. Luton 45 E1
Alexandra Rd. Bor 170 B4
Alexandra Rd. Chipf 138 A1
Alexandra Rd. Heml H 124 B2
Alexandra Rd. Hit 21 F1
Alexandra Rd. Kin L 139 D1
Alexandra Rd. St Alb 127 F2
Alexandra Rd. Watf 167 D4
Alexandra Way. Ches 162 C3
Aleyn Way. Clo 13 D1
Alfriston Cl. Luton 46 B2
Algar Cl. Stan 176 C3
Alington La. Letw 22 C2
All Saints Cl. Bis St 77 D4
All Saints Cres. Watf 154 B3
All Saints La. Cro Gr 166 A2
All Saints Mews. Har 176 B2
Allandale Cres. Pot B 158 C4
Allandale Rd. Enf 162 B2
Allandale. Heml H 124 C3
Allandale. St Alb 141 D4
Allard Cl. Ham St 147 F2
Allard Cres. Bus 176 B4
Allard Way. Hod 134 C1
Alldicks Rd. Heml H 124 C1
Allen Cl. Whea 108 B4
Allenby Ave. Dun 44 A1
Allendale. Luton 31 D1
Allende Ave. Harl 117 E1
Allerton Cl. Bor 156 C1
Allerton Rd. Bor 156 C1
Alleyns Rd. Stev 50 B4
Allison. Letw 23 E3
Allton Rd. Henlw 10 A2
Allum La. Elst 169 F3
Allwood Rd. Ham St 147 F2
Alma Ct. Pot B 145 E1
Alma Cut. St Alb 127 F1
Alma Link. Luton 63 E4
Alma Rd. Nthch 121 F3
Alma Rd. St Alb 127 F1
Alma Row. Har 176 B1
Alma St. Luton 63 E4
almes Croft. Heml H 125 E1
Almond Cl. Luton 45 D2
Almond Way. Bor 170 A3
Almond Way. Har 176 B1
Almond Wlk. Hat 130 A1
Almonds La. Stev 50 C4
Alms La. Ashw 4 B2
Almshouse La. Enf 162 A1
Alnwick Dri. Lon M 78 C4
Alpha Pl. Bis St 76 C4
Alpine Cl. Hit 35 D3
Alpine Way. Luton 44 B4
Alpine Wlk. Bus 176 C4
Alston Ct. Barn 171 F3
Alston Rd. Barn 171 F3
Alston Rd. Heml H 124 A1
Altair Way. Norwd 174 C3
Altham Gr. Harl 117 F1
Altham Rd. Pnr 175 F2
Althorp Rd. Luton 45 E1
Althorp Rd. St Alb 127 F2
Alton Ave. Stan 176 C2
Alton Rd. Luton 63 F3
Altwood. Harp 86 B1
Alva Way. Watf 175 E4
Alverton. St Alb 141 E3
Alwyn Cl. Elst 169 F2
Alwyn Cl. Luton 45 F1
Alyington. Nthch 121 F4
Alzey Gdns. Harp 107 E4
Amberley Cl. Harp 86 A1
Amberley Cl. Luton 46 B2
Amberley Green. Ware 93 E2
Amberry Ct. Harl 117 E1
Ambleside. Harp 86 B1
Ambleside. Luton 44 C3
Ambrose La. Harp 85 F2
Amenbury La. Harp 86 A1
Amersham Rd. Chen 164 A4
Ames Cl. Luton 44 C4
Amor Way. Letw 23 D3
Amwell Comm. Wel GC 111 E3
Amwell Ct. Hod 135 D4
Amwell Ct. Wa Aby 163 F3
Amwell End. Ware 93 E1
Amwell Hill. Hert H 114 C3
Amwell La. Sta Ab 115 D3
Amwell La. Whea 108 A4
Amwell St. Hod 135 D4
Anchor Cl. Ches 148 B2
Anchor La. Heml H 124 A1
Anchor La. Wad 93 E4
Anchor Rd. Bal 23 F4
Anchor St. Bis St 77 D3
Anderson Cl. Hare 173 D1
Anderson Rd. Shen 157 D3
Anderson Rd. Stev 51 E3
Anderson's La. Gt Ho 29 D1
Andover Cl. Luton 44 B3
Andrew's La. Ham St 147 F2
Andrews La. Ches 148 A2
Andrewsfield. Wel GC 111 E3
Anershall. Wing 60 A2
Angel Pavement. Royston 7 E3
Angell's Meadow. Ashw 4 B2
Angle Pl. Berk 122 A2
Angle Ways. Stev 51 D1
Anglefield Rd. Berk 122 A2
Anglesey Cl. Bis St 76 B4
Anglesey Rd. Sth Ox 175 E3
Angotts Mead. Stev 50 A3
Angus Cl. Luton 44 A2
Anmer Gdns. Luton 44 A2
Annables La. Kin Gr 85 D2
Annette Cl. Har 176 C1
Anns Cl. Tri 99 F2
Anselm Rd. Pnr 175 F2
Anson Cl. Bov 136 B2
Anson Cl. Sand 108 B1
Anson Cl. St Alb 142 A4
Anson Wlk. Norwd 174 B3
Anstee Rd. Luton 44 A3
Anthony Cl. Watf 167 E1
Anthony Gdns. Luton 63 E3
Anthony Rd. Bor 169 F4
Anthorne Cl. Pot B 159 D4
Anthus Mews. Norwd 174 C2
Antoinette Ct. Abb L 139 F1
Antoneys Cl. Pnr 175 E1
Antonine Gate. St Alb 127 D1
Aplins Cl. Harp 86 A1
Apollo Ave. Norwd 175 D3
Apollo Way. Heml H 124 C3
Apollo Way. Stev 51 E4
Apple Cotts. Bov 137 D2
Apple Orch The. Hem H 124 C3
Appleby St. Ham St 147 F3
Applecroft Rd. Luton 46 B2
Applecroft Rd. Wel GC 110 A3
Applecroft. Chis 141 D2
Applecroft. Henlw 10 A2
Applecroft. Nthch 121 F3
Appleford's Cl. Hod 134 C4
Appleton Fields. Bis St 76 C2
Appletree Wlk. Watf 154 A2
Applewood Cl. Harp 85 F2
Approach Rd. St Alb 127 F1
Approach The. Pot B 158 C4
Appspond La. Chis 140 B4
April Pl. Saw 97 F2
Apsley Cl. Bis St 76 C2
Apsley End Rd. Aps Er 19 F3
Apsley Grange. Heml H 138 C3
Apton Ct. Bis St 76 C4
Apton Fields. Bis St 76 C3
Apton Rd. Bis St 76 C4
Aquarius Way. Norwd 175 D3
Aquila Cl. Norwd 175 D3
Aragon Cl. Heml H 125 E4
Aran Cl. Harp 107 E3
Arbour Cl. Luton 31 D1
Arbour The. Hert 113 E2
Arbroath Green. Sth Ox 175 D4
Arcade The. Letw 22 C3
Arcade Wlk. Hit 34 C4
Arch Rd. Gt Wy 35 F3
Archer Cl. Kin L 138 C1
Archer Rd. Stev 51 D3
Archers Cl. Hert 113 E4
Archers Ride. Wel GC 111 D2
Archers Way. Letw 22 B3
Archers. Bun 40 C4
Arches The. Letw 23 D4
Archfield. Wel GC 89 F1
Archway Ct. Heml H 124 B3
Archway Rd. Luton 44 C2
Arden Cl. Bov 137 D2
Arden Cl. Bus 168 C1
Arden Gr. Harp 86 A1
Arden Pl. Luton 45 F1
Arden Press Way. Letw 23 D4
Ardens Way. St Alb 128 B3
Ardleigh Green. Luton 46 C1
Ardross Ave. Norwd 174 C3
Arena Par. Letw 22 C3
Argyle Rd. Barn 171 E3
Argyle Way. Stev 50 B3
Argyll Ave. Luton 45 E1
Argyll Rd. Heml H 124 C4
Arkley Ct. Heml H 125 D4
Arkley Dri. Barn 171 D2
Arkley La. Barn 171 D3
Arkley Rd. Heml H 125 D4
Arkley View. Barn 171 D3
Arkwrights. Harl 117 F1
Arlesey Rd. Henlw 10 C4
Arlesey Rd. Hit 21 F3
Arlesey Rd. Ick 21 F2
Arlesey Rd. Stot 11 F3
Arlington Cres. Ches 162 C3
Armand Cl. Watf 153 F1
Armitage Cl. Chor 165 E3
Armitage Gdns. Luton 44 B1
Armour Rise. Hit 22 A1
Armstrong Pl. Heml H 124 B2
Arncliffe Cres. Luton 45 F1
Arnett Cl. Chor 165 D2
Arnett Way. Chor 165 D2
Arnold Ave East. Enf 163 D1
Arnold Ave West. Enf 162 C1
Arnold Cl. Luton 46 A2
Arnold Cl. Stev 36 B1
Arnolds La. Hin 3 E3
Arran Cl. Heml H 125 E1
Arranmore Ct. Bus 167 F3
Arretine Cl. St Alb 126 C1
Arrewig La. St Le 119 E1
Arrow Cl. Luton 44 C3
Arthur Rd. St Alb 128 A2
Arthur St. Bus 167 E3
Arthur St. Luton 63 F3
Artillery Pl. Har 176 B2
Arundel Cl. Ches 148 B2
Arundel Cl. Heml H 125 D2
Arundel Cl. Stev 51 F2
Arundel Dri. Bor 170 B3
Arundel Rd. Luton 44 C1
Ascot Cl. Bis St 77 E4
Ascot Cl. Elst 170 A2
Ascot Cres. Stev 37 D1
Ascot Gdns. Enf 162 B1
Ascot Rd. Luton 45 D1
Ascot Rd. Roystn 7 F3
Ascot Rd. Watf 166 C2
Ascots La. Wel GC 110 C1
Ash Cl. Abb L 153 E4
Ash Cl. Bro Pk 145 D3
Ash Cl. Hare 173 E1
Ash Cl. Watf 154 A2
Ash Dri. Hat 130 A1
Ash Dri. Hit 35 D2
Ash Dri. Lon M 79 D2
Ash Gr. Hare 173 E1
Ash Gr. Heml H 138 C4
Ash Gr. Whea 87 E1
Ash Groves. Saw 98 A1
Ash Hill Cl. Bus 168 A1
Ash Hill. Bark 17 E2
Ash Meadow. Muc H 74 C1
Ash Rd. Luton 63 D4
Ash Rd. Tri 99 F2
Ash Rd. Ware 94 A2
Ash Ride. Enf 161 D2
Ash Tree Field. Harl 117 D1
Ash Tree Rd. Watf 154 A2
Ash Vale. Map Cr 172 B3
Ash Way. Roystn 7 F3
Ashanger La. Clo 24 B2
Ashbourne Cl. Letw 23 D2
Ashbourne Rd. Hod 134 C1
Ashbourne Sq. Norwd 174 C2
Ashbrook La. St Ipp 35 D2
Ashburnam Wlk. Stev 50 C1
Ashburnham Cl. Sth Ox 175 D4
Ashburnham Dr. Sth Ox 175 D4
Ashburnham Rd. Luton 63 E4
Ashbury Cl. Hat 129 F3
Ashby Gdns. St Alb 141 E4
Ashby Rd. Nthch 121 E4
Ashby Rd. Watf 154 A1
Ashby Rise. Bis St 59 D1
Ashcombe. Wel GC 89 F1
Ashcroft Cl. Harp 107 F4
Ashcroft Ct. Hod 134 C1
Ashcroft Rd. Luton 46 A1
Ashcroft. Pnr 176 A2
Ashdale Gdns. Luton 31 D1
Ashdale Gr. Stan 176 C2
Ashdale. Bis St 76 B2
Ashdales. St Alb 141 E4
Ashdon Rd. Bus 167 E3
Ashdown Cres. Ches 148 C2
Ashdown Dri. Bor 169 F4
Ashdown Rd. Stev 69 D4
Ashdown. Letw 11 F1
Ashendene Rd. Bay 132 C2
Ashendene. Bay 133 D3
Ashfield Ave. Bus 168 B1
Ashfield Way. Luton 45 D3
Ashfields. Watf 153 F2
Ashford Green. Sth Ox 175 E3
Ashfords. Bun 40 C4
Ashleigh. Stev 51 D2
Ashley Cl. Pnr 175 D1
Ashley Cl. Wel GC 110 B4
Ashley Ct. Hat 130 A3
Ashley Dri. Bor 170 B2
Ashley Gdns. Harp 85 E2
Ashley Rd. Hertng 113 D3
Ashley Rd. St Alb 128 B1
Ashleys. Ric 164 C1
Ashlyn Cl. Bus 167 F3
Ashlyn Ct. Bus 167 F3
Ashlyns Ct. Berk 122 A2
Ashlyns Rd. Berk 122 A2
Ashmore Gdns. Heml H 125 D1
Ashridge Cl. Bov 137 D2
Ashridge Dri. Bri Wd 140 C1
Ashridge Dri. Sth Ox 175 E3
Ashridge La. Bot 150 B4
Ashridge Rise. Berk 121 F3
Ashton Rd. Enf 162 C2
Ashton Rd. Luton 63 F3
Ashton's La. Bal 23 F3
Ashtree Way. Heml H 124 A1
Ashurst Cl. Norwd 174 C2
Ashville Way. Bal 13 D1
Ashwell Ave. Luton 44 B4
Ashwell Cl. Gra 36 A2
Ashwell Common. Gra 36 A2
Ashwell Park. Harp 86 B1
Ashwell Rd. Byg 13 E2
Ashwell Rd. Gu M 1 C1
Ashwell Rd. Hin 3 F3
Ashwell Rd. Newn 12 C4
Ashwell Rd. Ste Mo 5 D4
Ashwell St. Ashw 4 B2
Ashwell St. Knee 2 A2
Ashwell St. St Alb 127 E2
Ashwood Rd. Pot B 159 D3
Askew Rd. Norwd 174 B4
Aspasia Cl. St Alb 127 F1
Aspen Cl. Stev 69 D4
Aspen Park Dri. Watf 154 A2
Aspen Way. Enf 162 B2
Aspenden Rd. Bun 40 C3
Aspens The. Hit 35 D3
Aspfield Row. Heml H 124 A3
Ass House La. Har 176 A3
Astall Cl. Har 176 B1
Astley Green. Luton 46 B1
Astley Rd. Heml H 124 B2
Aston End Rd. Ast 51 F2
Aston La. Ast 69 F4
Aston Rd. Stand 55 E1
Aston Rise. Hit 35 D3
Aston View. Heml H 105 D1
Aston Way. Pot B 159 E4
Astons Rd. Norwd 174 B3
Astra Ct. Luton 45 F1
Astral Cl. Henlw 10 A2
Astrope La. Lon M 79 D2
Astwick Ave. Hat 129 F4
Astwick Rd. Stot 3 D1
Astwick Rd. Stot 11 F4
Athelstan Rd. Heml H 138 C4
Athelstan Wlk N. Wel GC 110 C3
Athelstan Wlk S. Wel GC 110 B3
Athelstone Rd. Har 176 B1
Athena Pl. Norwd 174 C1
Atherstone Rd. Luton 44 B1
Atherton End. Saw 97 F2
Athlone Cl. Radl 156 A2
Athol Cl. Pnr 175 D1
Athol Gdns. Pnr 175 D1
Atholl Cl. Luton 44 B4
Atria Rd. Norwd 175 D3
Attimore Cl. Wel GC 110 A3
Attimore Rd. Wel GC 110 A3
Aubrey La. Red 105 F1
Aubrey Rd. Lon C 142 B3
Aubreys Rd. Heml H 123 F2
Aubreys. Letw 23 D1
Aubries. Wal 38 A1
Auckland Cl. Enf 162 B1
Auckland Rd. Pot B 158 C4
Audley Cl. Bor 170 A3
Audley Ct. Pnr 175 E1
Audley Gdns. Wa Aby 163 E3
Audrey Gdns. Bis St 76 C2
Audwick Cl. Ches 148 C2
Augustine Rd. Har 176 B1
Augustus Cl. St Alb 127 D1
Austen Paths. Stev 51 E3

stin Rd. Luton 45 E2
stins Mead. Bov 137 D2
stins Pl. Heml H 124 B2
umn Glades. Heml H 125 E1
umn Gr. Wel GC 111 D2
alon Cl. Watf 154 C4
e Grimaldi. Luton 45 D2
e The. Luton 44 B3
ebury Ave. Luton 45 E2
enue App. Kin L 139 D1
enue One. Letw 23 E3
enue Rd. Bis St 77 D3
enue Rd. Pnr 175 F1
enue Rd. Roy 135 E3
enue Rd. St Alb 127 F2
enue Rise. Bus 168 A2
enue St Nicholas. Harp 86 A1
enue Terr. Watf 167 F2
enue The. Barn 171 F3
enue The. Bus 167 F3
enue The. Har 176 C1
venue The. Heml H 123 F3
enue The. Hert 113 D4
enue The. Hit 35 D4
venue The. Norwd 174 B2
venue The. Pnr 175 F2
venue The. Pot B 159 D4
venue The. Radl 156 A3
venue The. Stev 50 B4
venue The. Stot 11 F3
venue The. Watf 167 D4
venue The. Wl Gr 89 E4
vey La. Wa Aby 163 F1
vior Dri. Norwd 174 C3
vocet. Letw 11 F1
von Cl. Watf 154 B3
von Mews. Pnr 175 F2
von Rd. Henlw 10 B2
von Sq. Heml H 124 C4
vondale Ct. St Alb 127 F2
vondale Rd. Luton 63 E4
xe Cl. Luton 44 C3
ycliffe Dri. Heml H 124 C4
ycliffe Rd. Bor 156 C1
ydon Rd. Luton 45 D3
ylands Rd. Enf 162 B2
ylesbury Rd. Tri 99 F1
ylotts. Bun 40 B4
ylsham Rd. Hod 135 E4
ylward Dri. Stev 51 D2
ynho St. Watf 167 D2
ynsworth Ave. Bis St 59 D1
Ayot Green. A St P 89 D1
Ayot Little Green La. A St P 88 C1
Ayot Path. Bor 157 D1
Ayot St Peter Rd. A St P 88 C2
Ayr Cl. Stev 51 E4
Ayres End La. Harp 107 F3
Aysgarth Cl. Harp 107 D4
Aysgarth Rd. Red 106 A3

Baas Hill Cl. Hod 134 C1
Baas Hill. Hod 134 B1
Baas La. Hod 134 C2
Babbage Rd. Stev 50 A3
Back La. Aldhm 168 C4
Back La. Buck 27 E4
Back La. Hal 98 A4
Back La. Letw 23 E4
Back La. Pres 48 B3
Back La. Saw 98 A1
Back La. Tewin 90 C1
Back St. Ashw 4 B2
Back St. Luton 63 F4
Back The. Pot En 123 D4
Bacon's Yd. Ashw 4 B2
Bacons Dri. Cuf 146 C1
Badburgham Ct. Wa Aby 163 F3
Baddeley Cl. Stev 51 D1
Bader Cl. Stev 36 C1
Bader Cl. Wel GC 111 E3
Badger Cl. Kneb 69 D3
Badger Way. Hat 130 A2
Badgers Cl. Bor 169 F4
Badgers Cl. Stev 50 C2
Badgers Croft. N20 171 F1
Badgers. Bis St 76 C3
Badminton Cl. Bor 170 A4
Badminton Cl. Stev 69 D4
Badminton Pl. Hod 134 C2
Bagwicks Cl. Luton 44 C4
Bailey St. Luton 63 F3
Baines La. Dat 69 E2
Baird Cl. Bus 168 A2
Bairstow Cl. Bor 169 F4
Baker St. Enf 161 F1
Baker St. Hert 113 F3
Baker St. Luton 63 F3
Baker St. Pot B 158 C3
Baker St. Stev 50 B4
Baker's La. Bar 8 C1
Baker's La. Cod 67 F1
Bakers Ct. Bis St 77 D4
Bakers Gr. Wel GC 111 E4
Bakers La. Ken Co 82 C4
Bakers Rd. Ches 148 A1
Bakerscroft. Ches 148 C2
Bakewell Cl. Luton 44 B1
Balcombe Cl. Luton 46 B2
Balcon Way. Bor 170 B4
Baldock La. Letw 23 E2
Baldock La. Will 23 D1
Baldock Rd. Bun 40 B4
Baldock Rd. Letw 23 D3
Baldock Rd. Roystn 7 D3
Baldock Rd. Ste Mo 6 B2
Baldock Rd. Stot 12 A3
Baldock St. Roystn 7 E3
Baldock St. Ware 93 E1
Baldock Way. Bor 169 F4
Baldways Cl. Wing 60 B2
Baldwins La. Cro Gr 166 A3
Baldwins. Wel GC 111 E3
Balfour St. Hert 113 E4
Baliol Rd. Hit 34 C4
Ballater Cl. Sth Ox 175 E3
Ballinger Ct. Berk 122 A2
Ballslough Hill. Kim 66 C1
Balmoral Cl. Ches 162 B3
Balmoral Cl. Stev 69 E4
Balmoral Dri. Bor 170 B3
Balmoral Rd. Enf 162 B2
Balmoral Rd. Hit 21 F1
Balmoral Rd. Watf 154 B1
Balsams Cl. Hert 113 E2
Bampton Rd. Luton 44 A1
Banbury Cl. Luton 44 C2
Banbury St. Watf 167 D2
Bancroft Ct. Hit 34 C4
Bancroft Gdns. Har 176 B1
Bancroft Rd. Har 176 B1
Bancroft Rd. Luton 45 D3
Bancroft. Hit 34 C4
Bandley Rise. Stev 51 E2
Banes Down. Lo Naz 135 F1
Bank Cl. Luton 44 B2
Bank Ct. Heml H 124 B1
Bank Mill La. Berk 122 B2
Bank Mill La. Pot En 122 B2
Bank Mill. Berk 122 B2
Banks Rd. Bor 170 B4
Bankside Down. Ric 165 E2
Baracroft Way. St Alb 128 A1
Barbel Cl. Ches 163 D3
Barberry Rd. Heml H 124 A2
Barbers Wlk. Tri 99 F2
Barchester Rd. Har 176 B1
Barclay Cl. Hert H 114 A2
Barclay Cres. Stev 50 C4
Barclay Ct. Hod 135 D3
Barden Cl. Hare 173 E2
Bardwell Ct. St Alb 127 E1
Bardwell Rd. St Alb 127 E1
Barford Rise. Luton 46 B1
Bargrove Ave. Heml H 124 A1
Barham Ave. Elst 169 F3
Barham Rd. Stev 51 E3
Barkham Cl. Ched 79 F4
Barking Cl. Luton 44 A3
Barkston Path. Bor 157 D1
Barkway Hill. Bark 17 F3
Barkway Rd. Roystn 7 F3
Barkway St. Roystn 7 E3
Barley Cl. Bus 168 A2
Barley Croft. Heml H 125 E2
Barley Croft. Hert 113 E4
Barley Hills. Bis St 76 C2
Barley La. Luton 44 B3
Barley Mow La. Tyt 128 C1
Barley Ponds Cl. Ware 93 F1
Barley Ponds Rd. Ware 93 F1
Barley Rd. Gt Ch 9 D4
Barley Rd. Gt Ch 9 E1
Barley Rise. Bal 24 A4
Barleycroft Green. Wel GC 110 B3
Barleycroft Rd. Wel GC 110 B3
Barleycroft. Bun 40 C3
Barleycroft. Stev 51 E2
Barleycroft. Tonw 92 C4
Barleycroft. Wat 92 A2
Barleyvale. Luton 45 D4
Barlings Rd. Harp 107 D3
Barmor Cl. Har 176 A1
Barn Cl. Heml H 138 C4
Barn Cl. Radl 156 A2
Barn Cl. Wel GC 110 B3
Barn Lea. Ric 165 D1
Barnacres Rd. Heml H 139 D4
Barnard Acres. Lo Naz 149 F4
Barnard Green. Wel GC 110 C3
Barnard Rd. Luton 63 D4
Barnard Rd. Saw 97 F2
Barnard Way. Heml H 124 C1
Barncroft Rd. Berk 121 F2
Barncroft. Gravnd 57 E4
Barndell Cl. Stot 11 F3
Barndicott. Wel GC 111 E3
Barnes La. Chipf 138 B2
Barnes Rise. Kin L 138 C2
Barnet By-Ps Rd. Barn 170 C3
Barnet Gate La. Barn 170 C2
Barnet Hill. Barn 171 F3
Barnet La. Bor 170 B2
Barnet La. Elst 169 F2
Barnet La. N20 171 F1
Barnet Rd. Barn 171 D2
Barnet Rd. Lon C 142 C2
Barnet Rd. Pot B 159 D2
Barnet Stall Market. Barn 171 F3
Barnet Trad Est. Barn 171 F3
Barnet Way. NW7 170 B1
Barnfield Ave. Luton 45 E3
Barnfield Cl. Hod 135 D4
Barnfield Cl. Lo Naz 135 F1
Barnfield Ct. Harp 107 E4
Barnfield Rd. Harp 107 E4
Barnfield Rd. St Alb 128 B3
Barnfield Rd. Wel GC 110 C2
Barnfield. Heml H 138 C4
Barnhurst Path. Sth Ox 175 E3
Barns Dene. Harp 85 F1
Barnsdale Cl. Bor 169 F4
Barnside Ct. Wel GC 110 B3
Barnston Cl. Luton 46 B1
Barnwell. Stev 51 D1
Baron Ct. Stev 36 A1
Barons Row. Harp 107 E4
Barons The. Bis St 76 B3
Barr Rd. Pot B 159 E3
Barra Cl. Heml H 139 E4
Barracks La. Barn 171 F3
Barratt Way. Har 176 B1
Barrells Down Rd. Bis St 58 C1
Barrett La. Bis St 76 C4
Barrington Rd. Letw 22 C2
Barrow La. Ches 147 F1
Barrow Point Ave. Pnr 175 F1
Barrow Point La. Pnr 175 F1
Barrowby Cl. Luton 46 B1
Barrowdene Cl. Pnr 175 F1
Barry Cl. Chis 141 D3
Bartel Cl. Heml H 125 E1
Bartholomew Rd. Bis St 76 C3
Bartletts Mead. Hert 92 B1
Barton Cl. Harp 86 B2
Barton Rd. Hex 19 D1
Barton Rd. Luton 45 E4
Barton Rd. Whea 108 B4
Barton Way. Bor 170 A4
Barton Way. Cro Gr 166 A2
Bartons The. Elst 169 E2
Bartrams La. Barn 159 E1
Basbow La. Bis St 76 C4
Basildon Sq. Heml H 124 C4
Basils Rd. Stev 50 B4
Basing Rd. Ric 173 D4
Baslow Cl. Har 176 B1
Bassett Cl. Red 106 A3
Bassil Rd. Heml H 124 B1
Bassingbourne Cl. Hod 134 C2
Bassingburn Wlk. Wel GC 110 C3
Batchelors. Stand 55 F1
Batchwood Dri. St Alb 127 E3
Batchwood Gdns. St Alb 127 E3
Batchwood View. St Alb 127 E3
Batchworth Heath Hill. Ric 174 A3
Batchworth Hill. Ric 173 F4
Batchworth La. Norwd 174 B3
Bateman Rd. Cro Gr 166 A2
Batford Cl. Wel GC 111 D3
Batford Rd. Harp 86 B2
Bath Rd. Luton 45 E1
Bathurst Rd. Heml H 124 C3
Batterdale. Hat 130 B3
Battlefield Rd. St Alb 127 F3
Battlers Green Dri. Radl 155 F2
Baulk The. Ched 79 F4
Baulk The. Ivin 80 C3
Baulk The. Lily 32 B1
Bawdsey Cl. Stev 50 A4
Bay Ct. Berk 122 A2
Bay Tree Wlk. Watf 154 A1
Bayford Cl. Heml H 125 E4
Bayford Cl. Hert 113 E2
Bayford Green. Bay 133 D3
Bayford La. Bay 132 C4
Bayhurst Dri. Norwd 174 C2
Bayworth. Letw 23 D3
Beacon Ct. Hert H 114 B2
Beacon Rd. Rin 81 D1
Beacon Rd. Ware 94 A1
Beacon Way. Ric 165 D1
Beacon Way. Tri 100 B3
Beaconsfield Rd. Enf 162 C1
Beaconsfield Rd. Hat 130 B3
Beaconsfield Rd. St Alb 127 F2
Beaconsfield Rd. Tri 99 F2
Beaconsfield. Luton 64 A4
Beadlow Rd. Luton 44 A2
Beagle Cl. Radl 155 F1
Beale Cl. Stev 51 E3
Beamish Dri. Bus 168 B1
Beane Ave. Stev 51 E3
Beane Rd. Hert 113 D4
Beane Rd. Wat St 70 B2
Beane River View. Hert 113 E3
Beane Wlk. Stev 51 E3
Beanfield Rd. H Wy 97 D2
Beanley Cl. Luton 46 C1
Bear La. Ashw 4 B2
Bearton Ave. Hit 34 C4
Bearton Green. Hit 21 F1
Bearton Rd. Hit 21 F1
Bearwood Cl. Pot B 159 E4
Beauchamp Gdns. Ric 165 D1
Beaulieu Cl. Watf 167 E1
Beaumayes Cl. Heml H 124 A1
Beaumont Ave. St Alb 128 A2
Beaumont Cl. Hit 34 B4
Beaumont Hall La. Red 106 A1
Beaumont Pl. Barn 171 F4
Beaumont Rd. Ham St 147 F4
Beaumont Rd. Luton 45 D1
Beaumont View. Ham St 147 E3
Becket Gdns. Welw 89 E2
Beckets Sq. Berk 122 A3
Beckett's Ave. St Alb 127 E3
Becketts. Hertng 113 D3
Beckfield La. Gr En 26 B4
Beckham Cl. Luton 45 E4
Becks Cl. Mark 83 E3
Bedale Rd. Enf 161 E1
Bede Cl. Pnr 175 E1
Bede Ct. L Gad 102 B4
Bedford Ave. Barn 171 F3
Bedford Cl. Chen 151 D1
Bedford Cres. Enf 162 C2
Bedford Park Rd. St Alb 127 F2
Bedford Rd. Henlw 10 A2
Bedford Rd. Hit 21 E1
Bedford Rd. Hol 21 E4
Bedford Rd. Ick 21 E2
Bedford Rd. Letw 22 B4
Bedford Rd. Norwd 174 B3
Bedford Rd. St Alb 127 F1
Bedford St. Berk 122 B2
Bedford St. Hit 34 B4
Bedford St. Watf 167 D4
Bedmond Green. Bed 139 F2
Bedmond La. Abb L 139 F1
Bedmond La. Bed 140 A3
Bedmond La. Chis 140 B4
Bedmond La. St Alb 126 C1
Bedmond Rd. Bed 139 F3
Bedwell Ave. L Berk 132 A4
Bedwell Cl. Wel GC 110 C3
Bedwell Cres. Stev 50 C3
Bedwell La. Stev 50 C3
Bedwell Rise. Stev 50 C3
Beech Ave. Enf 161 D2
Beech Ave. Radl 156 A3
Beech Bottom. St Alb 127 E3
Beech Cl. Harp 107 E3
Beech Cl. Hat 130 A2
Beech Dri. Berk 122 B2
Beech Dri. Bor 169 F4
Beech Dri. Saw 118 B4
Beech Dri. Stev 51 D2
Beech Hill Ct. Berk 122 B3
Beech Hill. Barn 159 F1
Beech Hill. Letw 22 B4
Beech Hill. Lily 46 B4
Beech Hyde La. Sand 108 C3
Beech Hyde La. Whea 108 C4
Beech Park. L Chal 150 A1
Beech Pl. St Alb 127 E3
Beech Rd. Luton 63 E4
Beech Rd. St Alb 127 F3
Beech Rd. Watf 154 A1
Beech Way. Bla En 87 D3
Beech Wlk. Hod 134 C3
Beech Wlk. Tri 100 B2
Beechcroft Ave. Cro Gr 166 B2
Beechcroft Rd. Bus 167 F2
Beechen Gr. Watf 167 E3
Beeches The. Hit 35 D3
Beeches The. Pk St 141 E2
Beeches The. Tri 100 B2
Beeches The. Welw 89 E2
Beechfield Cl. Red 106 A3
Beechfield Rd. Heml H 124 A1
Beechfield Rd. Ware 93 F1
Beechfield Rd. Wel GC 110 C3
Beechfield Wlk. Wa Aby 163 E2
Beechfield. Hod 115 D1
Beechfield. Kin L 139 D1
Beechfield. Saw 97 F1
Beeching Cl. Harp 86 A2
Beechlands. Bis St 76 C3
Beecholme Mews. Ches 148 C2
Beechpark Way. Watf 153 F1
Beechtree La. St Alb 126 A1
Beechwood Ave. Chor 164 A3
Beechwood Ave. L Chal 150 B1
Beechwood Ave. Po B 159 D3
Beechwood Ave. St Alb 128 A2
Beechwood Cl. Bal 23 F3
Beechwood Cl. Ham St 147 F3
Beechwood Cl. Hert 113 F3
Beechwood Dri. Ald 101 E3
Beechwood Park. Fel 137 F4
Beechwood Rd. Luton 44 C2
Beechwood Rise. Watf 154 A1
Beecroft La. Wal 38 B1
Beehive Cl. Elst 169 E2
Beehive Green. Wel GC 111 D2
Beehive La. Wel GC 111 D2
Beehive Rd. Gofs O 147 D2
Beesonend La. Harp 106 C2
Beeston Cl. Sth Ox 175 E3
Beeston Dri. Ches 148 B2
Beethoven Rd. Elst 169 E2
Beeton Cl. Pnr 176 A2
Beggarman's La. Lev Gr 72 B4
Beggars Bush La. Watf 166 B2
Beken Ct. Watf 154 B2
Belcher Rd. Hod 135 D4
Beldam Ave. Roystn 7 E3
Beldams La. Bis St 77 D3
Belfairs Green. Sth Ox 175 E3
Belford Rd. Bor 156 C1
Belfry Ave. Hare 173 D2
Belfry La. Ric 165 E1
Belgrave Ave. Watf 166 C2
Belgrave Cl. St Alb 128 B4
Belgrave Dri. Bed 139 E2
Belgrave Rd. Luton 44 B3
Belham Rd. Bed 139 D2
Bell Acre Gdns. Letw 23 D2
Bell Acre. Letw 23 D2
Bell Cl. Bed 139 F2
Bell Cl. Hit 35 D3
Bell Cl. Kneb 69 D3
Bell Cl. Pnr 175 E1
Bell La. Bed 140 A2
Bell La. Bro Pk 144 C4
Bell La. Enf 162 C1
Bell La. Hert 113 E3
Bell La. Hod 134 C1
Bell La. Hod 135 D3
Bell La. L Chal 150 B1
Bell La. Lon C 142 C1
Bell La. Nthch 121 F3
Bell La. Stev 50 B4
Bell La. Widf 95 E2
Bell Leys. Wing 60 A2
Bell Mead. Saw 97 F1
Bell St. Saw 97 F1
Bellamy Cl. Watf 167 D4
Bellamy Rd. Ches 148 C1
Belle Vue La. Bus 168 B1
Belle Vue Rd. Ware 93 F1
Bellerby Rise. Luton 44 A3
Bellfield Ave. Har 176 B2
Bellgate. Heml H 124 C3
Bellmount Wood Ave. Watf 166 C4
Bells Hill. Barn 171 E3
Bells Hill. Bis St 76 C4
Belmers Rd. Wigg 100 B2
Belmont Hill. St Alb 127 E1
Belmont Rd. Bus 167 F2
Belmont Rd. Heml H 138 C4
Belmont Rd. Luton 63 E4
Belmor. Elst 170 A2
Belper Rd. Luton 44 B1
Belsham Pl. Luton 46 C1
Belsize Cl. Heml H 125 D1
Belsize Cl. St Alb 128 B4
Belsize Rd. Har 176 B2
Belsize Rd. Heml H 125 D1
Belswains Green. Heml H 138 C4
Belswains La. Heml H 138 C4
Belton Rd. Berk 122 A3
Beltona Gdns. Ches 148 B2
Belvedere Rd. Luton 45 D3
Bembridge Gdns. Luton 44 C4
Ben Austins. Red 106 A2
Benbow Cl. St Alb 128 A1
Benchley Hill. Hit 35 E4
Benchleys Rd. Heml H 123 F1
Bencroft. Ham St 148 A3
Bendish La. Whit 66 B4
Bendysh Rd. Bus 167 F3
Benedictine Gate. Ches 148 C2
Benford Rd. Hod 134 C2
Bengarth Dri. Har 176 B1
Bengeo St. Hert 113 E4
Benhooks Ave. Bis St 76 C3
Benington Cl. Luton 45 F3
Benington Rd. Ast 51 F1
Benington Rd. Wal 52 A3
Bennett Cl. Norwd 174 C2
Bennett Cl. Wel G C 110 C1
Bennett Ct. Letw 23 D3
Bennetts Cl. Coln H 143 E4
Bennetts End Cl. Heml H 124 C1
Bennetts End Rd. Heml H 125 D1
Bennettsgate. Heml H 139 D4
Benningfield Cl. Widf 95 E3
Benningfield Rd. Widf 95 E2
Benskin Rd. Watf 167 D2
Benslow La. Hit 35 D4
Benslow Rise. Hit 35 D4
Benson Cl. Luton 44 C4
Benstede. Stev 69 E4
Bentfield End Cswy. Sta Mo 59 E4
Bentfield Gdns. Sta Mo 59 E4
Bentfield Rd. Sta Mo 59 E4
Bentick Way. Cod 67 F1
Bentley Cl. Bis St 76 C3
Bentley Heath La. Pot B 158 C2
Bentley Lodge. Bus 176 C4
Bentley Rd. Hertng 112 C4
Benton Rd. Sth Ox 175 E3
Bentsley Cl. St Alb 128 B4
Berceau Wlk. Watf 166 C4
Berefield. Heml H 124 B3
Beresford Rd. Luton 45 D1
Beresford Rd. Ric 164 C1
Beresford Rd. St Alb 128 B1
Bericot Way. Wel GC 111 E3
Berkeley Cl. Abb L 153 F4
Berkeley Cl. Elst 170 A2
Berkeley Cl. Hit 34 B4
Berkeley Cl. Pot B 158 C4
Berkeley Cl. Stev 69 D4
Berkeley Cl. Ware 93 E1
Berkeley Cl. Cro Gr 166 B2
Berkeley Ct. Harp 86 A1
Berkeley Sq. Red 105 E1

Berkeley. Letw 23 D2
Berkhamsted La. L Berk 132 A2
Berkhamsted Pl. Berk 122 A3
Berkhamsted Rd. Heml H 123 E3
Berkley Ave. Ches 162 B3
Berkley Cl. St Alb 128 B4
Berkley Ct. Berk 122 B2
Berks Hill. Chor 164 B2
Bernard St. St Alb 127 E2
Berners Dri. St Alm 141 F4
Berners Way. Hod 148 C4
Bernhardt Cres. Stev 51 E3
Berries The. St Alb 128 A4
Berrow Cl. Luton 46 C1
Berry Ave. Watf 154 A2
Berry Cl. Ric 165 D1
Berry Grove La. Bus 154 C1
Berry Grove La. Bus 168 A4
Berry La. Chor 164 C2
Berry La. Ric 165 D1
Berry Leys. Luton 44 C4
Berry Way. Ric 165 D1
Berryfield. Ched 79 F4
Berrymead. Heml H 124 C3
Berwick Cl. Ches 163 D3
Berwick Cl. Stan 176 C2
Berwick Rd. Bor 156 C1
Bessemer Dri. Stev 50 A2
Bessemer Rd. Wel GC 89 F1
Bethune Cl. Luton 63 D3
Betony Vale. Roystn 7 F3
Bettespol Meadows. Red 106 A3
Betty's La. Tri 100 A2
Bevan Cl. Heml H 124 C1
Beverley Cl. Roystn 7 D4
Beverley Gdns. Ches 148 A1
Beverley Gdns. St Alb 128 B4
Beverley Gdns. Wel GC 111 E3
Beverley Rd. Luton 44 C1
Beverley Rd. Stev 37 D1
Beverly Cl. Hod 134 C1
Bevil Ct. Hod 115 D1
Bewley Cl. Ches 162 B4
Bexhill Rd. Luton 46 B1
Beyers Gdns. Hod 115 D1
Beyers Prospect. Hod 115 D1
Beyers Ride. Hod 115 D1
Bibbs Hall La. A St L 87 F3
Biddenham Turn. Watf 154 B2
Bideford Gdns. Luton 45 E2
Bideford Rd. Enf 162 C1
Bidwell Cl. Letw 23 D3
Biggin Hill. Ans 28 B4
Biggin La. Hit 34 C4
Billet La. Berk 122 A3
Billy Lows La. Pot B 159 D4
Bilton Rd. Hit 21 F1
Bilton Way. Enf 162 C1
Bilton Way. Luton 62 C4
Bingen Rd. Hit 21 E1
Bingley Rd. Hod 135 E3
Binham Cl. Luton 45 E4
Binyon Cres. Stan 176 C3
Birch Copse. Bri Wd 140 C1
Birch Ct. Norwd 174 B2
Birch Dri. Hat 130 A2
Birch Dri. Map Cr 172 B3
Birch Gr. Luton 45 F2
Birch Gr. Pot B 159 D4
Birch Gr. Wl Gr 89 F4
Birch Green. Heml H 123 F3
Birch La. Flau 151 D4
Birch Leys. Heml H 125 E4
Birch Link. Luton 45 E1
Birch Park. Har 176 B2
Birch Rd. Nthch 121 E4
Birch Rd. Wl Gr 69 D1
Birch Tree Gr. Bot 136 A1
Birch Tree Wlk. Watf 153 F1
Birch Way. Harp 107 E4
Birch Way. Lon C 142 B2
Birch Wlk. Bor 170 A4
Birchall La. Wel GC 111 F2
Birchall Wood. Wel GC 111 E3
Birchalls. Sta M 59 F3
Birchanger La. Birhr 59 F1
Bircherley Ct. Hert 113 E3
Bircherley St. Hert 113 E3
Birches The. Bus 168 B2
Birches The. Fel 137 F4
Birches The. Letw 22 C4
Birchfield Rd. Ches 148 B1
Birchmead Cl. St Alb 127 E3
Birchmead. Watf 153 F1
Birchway. Hat 130 A4
Birchwood Ave. Hat 130 A4
Birchwood Cl. Hat 130 A4
Birchwood Way. Chis 141 D2
Birchwood. Birhr 59 E1
Birchwood. Shen 157 D3
Birchwood. Wa Aby 163 F3
Bird La. Hare 173 E1
Birdcroft Rd. Wel GC 110 B3
Birdie Way. Hert 114 A4
Birds Cl. Wel GC 111 D2
Birds Hill. Letw 23 D3
Birdsfoot La. Luton 45 D3
Birkbeck Rd. Enf 161 E1
Birkdale Gdns. Sth Ox 175 E4
Birklands La. St Alb 142 A4
Birling Dri. Luton 46 B2
Birstall Green. Sth Ox 175 E3
Birtley Croft. Luton 46 C1
Biscot Rd. Luton 45 E1
Bishop Ken Rd. Har 176 C1
Bishop's Ave. Bis St 76 C2
Bishop's Cl. St Alb 128 A4
Bishops Ave. Elst 169 F2
Bishops Ave. Norwd 174 C4
Bishops Cl. Barn 171 E2
Bishops Cl. Hat 129 F3
Bishops Mead. Heml H 124 A1
Bishops Park Way. Bis St 76 A4
Bishops Rd. Tewin 90 B3
Bishops Rise. Hat 129 F2
Bishopscote Rd. Luton 45 D2
Biskra. Watf 167 D4
Bisley Cl. Ches 162 B3
Bit The. Wigg 100 B1
Bittern Cl. Stev 51 E1
Bittern Way. Letw 11 F1
Black Boy Wood. Bri Wd 141 D1
Black Cut. St Alb 127 F1
Black Ditch Rd. Wa Aby 163 E2
Black Fan Rd. Wel GC 110 C4
Black Fan Rd. Wel GC 111 D3
Black Lion Ct. Saw 118 B2
Black Lion Hill. Shen 156 C4
Black Swan La. Luton 45 D3
Blackberry Mead. Stev 51 E2
Blackbirds La. Aldhm 155 E3
Blackbury Cl. P Bar 159 E4
Blackbush Spring. Harl 118 A1
Blackbushe. Bis St 59 E1
Blackdale. Ham St 148 A2
Blackendale Gr. Luton 45 D3
Blacketts Wood Dri. Chor 164 A3
Blackford Rd. Sth Ox 175 E3
Blackhorn Dri. Luton 46 B2
Blackhorse Cl. Hit 35 D3
Blackhorse La. Hit 35 D3
Blackhorse La. Pot B 157 F4
Blackhorse La. Red 106 A3
Blackhorse La. Ridge 143 F1
Blackhorse Rd. Letw 23 E4
Blackley Cl. Watf 153 F1
Blackmoor La. Watf 166 B2
Blackmore Way. Bla En 87 D3
Blackmore. Letw 23 D2
Blacksmith Cl. Gt Am 115 D4
Blacksmith's La. Reed 16 B3
Blacksmith's St. St Alb 127 D2
Blacksmiths Hill. Benn 52 C2
Blackthorn Cl. St Alb 128 B3
Blackthorn Cl. Watf 154 A4
Blackthorn Rd. Wel GC 111 D3
Blackthorne Cl. Hat 129 F1
Blackwater La. Heml H 125 F1
Blackwell Cl. Har 176 B2
Blackwell Dri. Watf 167 E2
Blackwell Hall La. Lat 150 B3
Blackwell Rd. Kin L 139 D1
Bladon Cl. L Wym 35 F2
Blair Cl. Heml H 105 D1
Blairhead Dr. Sth Ox 175 D4
Blake Cl. St Alb 142 A4
Blakemere Rd. Wel GC 110 B4
Blakeney Dri. Luton 45 E4
Blakeney Rd. Stev 50 A4
Blakes Way. Welw 89 E3
Blanche La. Pot B 158 A3
Blandford Ave. Luton 45 E3
Blandford Rd. St Alb 128 A2
Blanes The. Ware 93 E2
Blaydon Rd. Luton 64 A4
Blenheim Cl. Saw 118 B4
Blenheim Cl. Watf 167 E1
Blenheim Cres. Luton 45 E1
Blenheim Ct. Bis St 77 B4
Blenheim Rd. Barn 171 E3
Blenheim Rd. St Alb 127 F2
Blenheim Way. Stev 69 E4
Blenkin Cl. St Alb 127 E4
Blind La. h St A 38 C3
Blindman's La. Ches 148 B1
Bloomfield Ave. Luton 46 A1
Bloomfield Rd. Harp 85 F2
Blossom La. Enf 161 E1
Blue Bridge Rd. Bro Pk 144 C2
Bluebell Wood Cl. Luton 62 C4
Bluebells. Wl Gr 89 F4
Blueberry Cl. St Alb 127 E4
Bluebridge Ave. Bro Pk 144 C2
Bluecoat Yard. Ware 93 E1
Bluecoats Ave. Hert 113 E3
Bluecoats Ct. Hert 113 E3
Bluehouse Hill. St Alb 127 D2
Bluett Rd. Lon C 142 B2
Blundell Cl. St Alb 127 E4
Blundell Rd. Luton 45 D2
Blunesfield. P Bar 159 E4
Blunts La. Chis 140 B3
Blyth Cl. Bor 170 A4
Blyth Cl. Stev 50 A4
Blythe Rd. Roy 135 E3
Blythway. Wel GC 89 F1
Blythwood Gdns. Sta Mo 59 E3
Blythwood Rd. Pnr 175 E1
Bockings. Wal 38 B1
Bodmin Rd. Luton 44 C2
Bodwell Cl. Heml H 124 A2
Boech Cres. Whea 108 B4
Bogmoor Rd. Bar 18 A4
Bognor Gdns. Sth Ox 175 E3
Bohemia. Heml H 124 C2
Boissy Cl. St Alb 128 C1
Boleyn Cl. Heml H 125 E4
Bollingbroke Rd. Luton 63 D3
Bolney Green. Luton 46 B2
Bolton Rd. Luton 63 F4
Boniface Gdns. Har 176 A2
Boniface Wlk. Har 176 A2
Bonks Hill. Saw 97 E1
Bonney Gr. Ches 148 A1
Bonnick Cl. Luton 63 E3
Booths Cl. Wel Gr 144 B4
Boreham Holt. Elst 169 F3
Borough Way. Pot B 158 C4
Borrell Cl. Hod 134 C2
Borrowdale Ct. Heml H 124 C3
Borton Ave. Henlw 10 A2
Bosanquet Rd. Hod 135 E4
Boscombe Ct. Letw 23 D3
Bosmore Rd. Luton 44 C3
Boswell Dri. Ick 21 F2
Boswell Gdns. Stev 36 B1
Boswick La. Nthch 121 E4
Botley La. Bot 136 A1
Botley Rd. Bot 136 A1
Botley Rd. Heml H 125 D4
Bottom House La. Wigg 101 D1
Bottom La. Sar 152 B2
Bottom Rd. St Le 119 F2
Boulevard The. Wel GC 110 C4
Boulton Rd. Stev 37 E1
Bounce The. Heml H 124 B3
Boundary Dri. Hert 113 E4
Boundary La. Wel GC 110 C1
Boundary Rd. Bis St 77 D3
Boundary Rd. St Alb 127 F3
Boundary Way. Heml H 125 E3
Boundary Way. Watf 154 B4
Bourne Cl. Hod 134 C2
Bourne Cl. Ware 93 E1
Bourne End La. Heml H 137 D4
Bourne End Rd. Norwd 174 C3
Bourne Honour. Tonw 92 C4
Bourne Rd. Berk 121 F3
Bourne Rd. Bus 168 A2
Bourne The. Bov 137 D2
Bourne The. Ware 93 E1
Bournehall Ave. Bus 168 A2
Bournehall La. Bus 168 A2
Bournehall Rd. Bus 168 A2
Bournemouth Rd. Stev 50 A4
Bouvier Rd. Enf 162 B1
Bovingdon Cres. Watf 154 B3
Bovingdon Green La. Bov 136 B2
Bowbrook Vale. Luton 46 C1
Bowcock Wlk. Stev 50 C2
Bower Heath La. Harp 86 B3
Bowers Way. Harp 86 A1
Bowershott. Letw 23 D2
Bowgate. St Alb 127 F2
Bowlers Mead. Bun 40 B4
Bowles Green. Enf 162 A2
Bowling Cl. Harp 107 E4
Bowling Green La. Bun 40 B4
Bowling Green La. Luton 45 F1
Bowling Green. Stev 50 B4
Bowling Rd. Ware 93 F1
Bowman Trad Est. Stev 50 A3
Bowmans Ave. Hit 35 D4
Bowmans Cl. Pot B 159 E4
Bowmans Cl. Welw 89 E3
Bowmans Ct. Heml H 124 C3
Bowmans Green. Watf 154 C2
Bowring Green. Sth Ox 175 E3
Bowyer's Cl. Hit 21 E1
Bowyers. Heml H 124 B3
Box La. Fel 137 F4
Box La. Hod 134 C3
Boxberry Cl. Stev 50 C3
Boxfield Green. Stev 51 E4
Boxfield. Wel GC 111 D2
Boxgrove Cl. Luton 46 B3
Boxhill. Heml H 124 B3
Boxted Cl. Luton 44 B3
Boxted Rd. Heml H 123 F3
Boxtree La. Har 176 B2
Boxtree Rd. Har 176 B2
Boxwell Rd. Berk 122 A2
Boyce Cl. Bor 169 F4
Boyd Cl. Bis St 77 D4
Boyle Cl. Luton 63 F4
Braceby Cl. Luton 44 C3
Brache Cl. Red 106 A3
Bracken La. Wl Gr 89 F4
Brackendale Gr. Harp 85 E2
Brackendale. Pot B 159 D3
Brackendene. Bri Wd 140 C1
Brackens The. Heml H 124 B2
Bracklesham Gdns. Luton 46 B2
Bracknell Pl. Heml H 124 C4
Bradbery. Map Cr 172 B3
Bradbury Cl. Bor 170 A4
Bradden La. Gt Ga 103 F4
Bradford Rd. Heron 164 B1
Bradgate Cl. Cuf 146 B2
Bradgate. Cuf 146 B2
Bradgers Hill Rd. Luton 45 F2
Bradley Common. Birhr 59 E2
Bradley Rd. Enf 162 C1
Bradley Rd. Luton 44 B1
Bradleys Cnr. Hit 35 E4
Bradman Way. Stev 37 D1
Bradmore Green. Bro Pk 144 C3
Bradmore La. Wa En 144 B3
Bradmore Way. Bro Pk 144 C3
Bradshaw Rd. Watf 154 B1
Bradshaws. Hat 129 F1
Bradway. Whit 66 C3
Braemar Cl. Stev 69 D4
Braemar Turn. Heml H 105 D1
Braeside Cl. Pnr 176 A2
Bragbury Cl. Stev 69 E4
Bragbury La. Dat 69 E3
Bragmans La. Chipf 151 F3
Brain Cl. Hat 130 A3
Brakynbery. Nthch 121 F4
Brallings La. C St P 172 A3
Bramble Cl. atf 154 A3
Bramble Cl. Harp 85 F2
Bramble Cl. Luton 44 B2
Bramble La. Hod 134 C4
Bramble Rd. Hat 129 E3
Bramble Rd. Luton 44 B2
Brambles The. Ches 162 C4
Brambles The. Roystn 7 F3
Brambles The. Stev 36 B1
Brambles The. Ware 93 E2
Brambles The. Wl Gr 89 F4
Brambling Rise. Heml H 124 C4
Bramfield La. Wat 91 F2
Bramfield Pl. Heml H 105 D1
Bramfield Rd. Dat 90 C4
Bramfield Rd. Hertng 112 C4
Bramfield. Hit 35 D3
Bramham Ct. Norwd 174 C2
Bramhanger Acre. Luton 44 B4
Bramingham Busn Park. Luton 45 D4
Bramingham Rd. Luton 44 C3
Bramleas. Watf 166 C3
Bramley Cl. Bal 12 C1
Bramley Gdns. Sth Ox 175 E3
Bramley Shaw. Wa Aby 163 F3
Brampton Cl. Ches 148 A2
Brampton Cl. Harp 86 B1
Brampton Park Rd. Hit 21 F1
Brampton Rd. Roystn 7 F3
Brampton Rd. St Alb 128 A2
Brampton Rd. Sth Ox 175 D4
Brampton Terr. Bor 157 D1
Bramshaw Gdns. Sth Ox 175 E3
Bramshot Way. Sth Ox 175 D4
Bramshott Cl. Hit 34 C3
Branch Cl. Hat 130 B4
Branch Rd. Fro 141 E2
Branch Rd. St Alb 127 D2
Brand St. Hit 34 C4
Brandles Rd. Letw 23 D2
Branksome Cl. Heml H 125 D2
Branton Cl. Luton 46 C1
Brantwood Rd. Luton 63 E4
Braunds Alley. Hit 34 C4
Bray Cl. Bor 170 B4
Brayes Manor. Stot 11 F3
Brays Rd. Luton 46 A2
Brays Springs. Wa Aby 163 F3
Brazier's Field. Hert 113 F3
Braziers End. Chol 120 B1
Braziers Quay. Bis St 77 D3
Bread and Cheese La. Ham St 147 F4
Breadcroft La. Harp 86 A1
Breakmead. Wel GC 111 D3
Breaks Rd. Hat 130 A3
Breakspear Ave. St Alb 127 F1
Breakspear Rd N. Hare 173 E1
Breakspear Way. Heml H 125 E2
Breakspear Way. St Alb 125 F2
Breakspear. Stev 51 E2
Breakspeare Cl. Watf 154 A1
Breakspeare Rd. Abb L 153 F4
Brecon Cl. Luton 63 E3
Breeze Terr. Ches 148 B2
Brendon Ave. Luton 46 B1
Brent Ct. Stev 50 C3
Brent Pl. Barn 171 F2
Brereton Ct. Heml H 124 C1
Brett Pl. Watf 154 A1
Brett Rd. Barn 171 E2
Bretts Mead. Luton 63 E3
Brewery La. Bal 12 C1
Brewery La. Sta Mo 59 F4
Brewery Rd. Hod 135 D3
Brewhouse Hill. Whea 108 B4
Brewhouse La. Hert 113 E3
Briants Cl. Pnr 175 F1
Briar Cl. Ches 148 B1
Briar Cl. Luton 46 B2
Briar Cl. Pot En 123 D4
Briar Patch La. Letw 22 B2
Briar Rd. St Alb 128 B3
Briar Rd. Watf 154 A3
Briar Way. Berk 122 B2
Briarcliff. Heml H 123 F2
Briardale. Stev 50 C2
Briardale. Ware 93 E2
Briarley Cl. Hod 134 C1
Briars Cl. Hat 130 A3
Briars La. Hat 130
Briars The. Bus 168
Briars The. Ches 162
Briars Wood. Hat 129
Briarwood Dri. Norwd 175
Briary La. Roystn 7
Briary Wood End. Wl Gr 89
Briary Wood La. Wl Gr 89
Brick Kiln La. Hit 34
Brick Knoll Park. St Alb 128
Brickcroft. Ches 148
Brickenden Ct. Wa Aby 163
Brickendon La. Bric 133
Brickendon La. Hert 113
Bricket Rd. St Alb 127
Brickfield Ave. Heml H 125
Brickfield La. Barn 170
Brickfield. Hat 130
Brickfields The. Ware 93
Brickkiln Rd. Stev 50
Brickly Rd. Luton 44
Brickmakers La. Heml H 125
Brickwall Cl. A St P 110
Brickyard La. Reed 16
Bride Hall La. A St L 88
Bridewell Cl. Bun 40
Bridge End. Bun 40
Bridge Foot. Ware 93
Bridge Pl. Watf 167
Bridge Rd E. Wel GC 110
Bridge Rd. Abb L 153
Bridge Rd. Letw 22
Bridge Rd. Stev 50
Bridge Rd. Wel GC 110
Bridge Rd. Wl Gr 69
Bridge St. Berk 122
Bridge St. Bis St 76
Bridge St. Heml H 124
Bridge St. Hit 34
Bridge St. Knee 2
Bridge St. Luton 63
Bridgefields. Wel GC 110
Bridgefoot La. Pot B 158
Bridgefoot. Bun 40
Bridgend Rd. Enf 162
Bridgenhall Rd. Enf 161
Bridger Cl. Watf 154
Bridges Ct. Hert 113
Bridges Rd. Stan 176
Bridgewater Rd. Berk 122 A3
Bridgewater Rd. Nthch 121 F4
Bridgewater Way. Bus 168 A2
Bridle Cl. Enf 162 C1
Bridle Cl. Hod 115 D1
Bridle Cl. St Alb 127 F3
Bridle La. Chor 165 E3
Bridle Path. Watf 167 D4
Bridle Way (N). Hod 115 D1
Bridle Way (S). Hod 115 D1
Bridle Way. Berk 122 A3
Bridle Way. Gt Am 115 D3
Bridle Way. Hod 115 D1
Bridlington Rd. Sth Ox 175 E4
Brierley Cl. Luton 46 B1
Briery Field. Chor 165 D3
Briery Way. Heml H 125 D2
Brigadier Ave. Enf 161 E1
Brigadier Hill. Enf 161 E1
Brighton Rd. Watf 154 A1
Brighton Way. Stev 50 A4
Brightview Cl. Bri Wd 140 C1
Brightwell Rd. Watf 167 D2
Brill Cl. Luton 46 B1
Brimfield Cl. Luton 46 C1
Brimsdown Ave. Enf 162 C1
Brinley Cl. Ches 162 B4
Brinsley Rd. Har 176 B1
Briscoe Cl. Hod 134 C4
Briscoe Rd. Hod 134 C4
Bristol Rd. Luton 45 D2
Britannia Ave. Luton 45 D2
Britannia Rd. Ches 162 C3
Britannia. Stand 55 F1
Brittain Way. Stev 51 D2
Britten Cl. Elst 169 E2
Britton Ave. St Alb 127 E2
Brixham Cl. Stev 50 A4
Brixton Rd. Watf 167 D4
Broad Acre. Bri Wd 140 C1
Broad Acres. Hat 129 F4
Broad Green Wood. Bay 132 C4
Broad Green. Bay 132 C4
Broad Mead. Luton 45 D2
Broad Oak Way. Stev 50 C1
Broad St. Heml H 124 B2
Broad Way The. Har 176 C1
Broad Wlk The. Norwd 174 B1
Broad Wlk. Harl 117 E1
Broadacres. Luton 45 F3
Broadcroft. Heml H 124 B3
Broadcroft. Letw 22 C1
Broadfield Cl. Had Cr 74 C1
Broadfield Ct. Har 176 C4
Broadfield Pl. Wel GC 110 A3
Broadfield Rd. Heml H 124 C2
Broadfield Rd. Wl Gr 69 D1
Broadfield Way. Had Cr 74 C1
Broadfield. Bis St 58 C1
Broadfield. Harl 117 F1
Broadfields. Gofs O 147 D1

adfields. H Wy 97 D1
oadfields. Har 176 A1
oadfields. Harp 85 F1
oadgate. Wa Aby 163 F3
oadhall Way. Stev 51 D1
oadlands Cl. Ches 162 B3
oadlawns Ct. Har 176 C1
oadleaf Ave. Bis St 76 B2
oadmead Cl. Pnr 175 F2
oadmead. Hit 35 D3
oadmeadow Ride. Hit 35 D2
oadmeads. Ware 93 E1
oadoak Ave. Enf 162 B2
oadstone Rd. Harp 107 E4
oadview. Stev 50 C3
oadwater Ave. Letw 22 C3
oadwater Cres. Stev 69 D4
oadwater Cres. Wel GC 110 B3
oadwater Dale. Letw 22 C3
oadwater La. Stev 51 E1
oadwater Rd. Wel GC 110 C3
oadwater. Berk 122 B3
oadwater. Pot B 145 D1
oadway Ave. Harl 118 A2
oadway The. Bla En 87 D3
oadway The. Hat 130 B3
oadway The. Pnr 175 F2
oadway The. Watf 167 E3
oadway. Letw 22 C3
rocket Rd. Hod 135 D3
rocket Rd. Stanb 110 A2
rocket View. Whea 108 B4
rockett Cl. Wel GC 110 A3
rockhurst Cl. Stan 176 C2
rocklesbury Cl. Watf 167 E4
rockley Hill. Stan 169 E1
rockswood La. Wel GC 110 A4
rockwell Shott. Wal 38 A1
rodewater Rd. Bor 170 A4
rodie Rd. Enf 161 E1
romborough Green. Sth Ox 175 E3
romet Cl. Watf 153 F1
romleigh Cl. Ches 148 C2
romley. Lon M 79 D2
rompton Cl. Luton 44 C4
ronte Cres. Heml H 105 D1
ronte Paths. Stev 51 E3
Brook Dri. Radl 155 F3
Brook Dri. Stev 69 D4
Brook End. Saw 97 E1
Brook Field. Ast 51 F1
Brook La. Berk 122 A3
Brook La. Saw 97 E1
Brook Rd. Bor 170 A4
Brook Rd. Ches 162 C3
Brook Rd. Saw 97 F1
Brook Rd. Sta Mo 59 F3
Brook St. Luton 63 E4
Brook St. Stot 11 F3
Brook St. Tri 100 A2
Brook View. Hit 35 E3
Brookbridge La. Dat 69 E1
Brookdene Ave. Watf 167 E1
Brookdene Dri. Norwd 174 C2
Brooke Cl. Bus 168 B1
Brooke Rd. Roystn 7 E4
Brooke Way. Bus 168 B1
Brooker Rd. Wa Aby 163 E3
Brookfield Cl. Tri 100 A2
Brookfield Gdns. Ches 148 B2
Brookfield La E. Ches 148 B2
Brookfield La W. Ches 148 B2
Brookfield La. Ast 51 F2
Brookfields. Saw 97 E1
Brookhill. Stev 68 C4
Brooklands Cl. Luton 44 B3
Brooklands Gdns. Pot B 158 C4
Brookmans Ave. Bro Pk 144 C3
Brooks Ct. Hert 112 C4
Brooksfield. Wel GC 111 D4
Brookshill Ave. Har 176 C3
Brookshill Dri. Har 176 B3
Brookshill. Har 176 B3
Brookside Cl. Barn 171 F2
Brookside Cres. Cuf 146 C2
Brookside Gdns. Enf 162 B1
Brookside. Hat 129 E3
Brookside. Hert 113 F3
Brookside. Hod 135 D3
Brookside. Letw 22 C3
Brookside. Pot B 158 A4
Brookside. Wa Aby 163 F4
Brookside. Watf 167 D1
Broom Cl. Ham St 148 A2
Broom Cl. Hat 129 F1
Broom Gr. Kneb 68 C3
Broom Gr. Watf 154 A1
Broom Hill. Heml H 123 F1
Broom Hill. Wl Gr 90 A4
Broom Wlk. Stev 50 C3
Broomer Pl. Ches 148 B1
Broomfield Ave. Ches 148 C3
Broomfield Cl. Welw 89 E2
Broomfield Rd. Welw 89 E2
Broomfield Rise. Abb L 153 E4
Broomfield. Chis 141 E2
Broomfield. Harl 118 A2
Broomhills. Wel GC 111 D4
Broomleys. St Alb 128 B3
Brooms Cl. Wel GC 89 E1
Brooms Rd. Luton 64 A4
Broomstick Hall Rd. Wa Aby 163 F3
Broomstick La. Bot 136 A1
Broughinge Rd. Bor 170 A4
Broughton Ave. Luton 45 E3
Broughton Hill. Letw 23 D3
Brow The. Watf 154 A3
Brown's Cl. Luton 44 B3
Brown's Rise. Buc Co 119 F2
Brownfield Way. Bla En 87 D3
Brownfields. Wel GC 110 C4
Browning Dri. Hit 35 D4
Browning Rd. Enf 161 E1
Browning Rd. Harp 86 B1
Browning Rd. Luton 44 A1
Brownlow La. Ched 80 A4
Brownlow Rd. Berk 122 B3
Brownlow Rd. Bor 170 A3
Browns Spr. Heml H 123 E4
Brox Dell. Stev 50 C3
Broxley Mead. Luton 44 B3
Bruce Grove. Watf 154 B1
Bruce Rd. Barn 171 F3
Bruce Rd. Har 176 C1
Bruce Way. Ches 162 B3
Brunel Rd. Stev 51 D4
Brunswick St. Luton 63 F4
Brushrise. Watf 154 A2
Brushwood Dri. Chor 164 B3
Brussels Way. Luton 44 B4
Bryan Rd. Bis St 76 C4
Bryanstone Rd. Ches 162 C3
Bryant Cl. Barn 171 F2
Bryant Ct. Harp 86 A2
Bryce Cl. Ware 93 E2
Buchanan Ct. Bor 170 B4
Buchanan Dri. Luton 64 A4
Buckettsland La. Ridge 157 F1
Buckettsland. Shen 157 E1
Buckingham Dri. Luton 46 B1
Buckingham Rd. Bor 170 B3
Buckingham Rd. Tri 99 F2
Buckingham Rd. Watf 154 B1
Buckland Rd. Dra B 99 D2
Buckland Rise. Pnr 175 E1
Bucklands The. Ric 165 D1
Buckle Cl. Luton 44 C4
Bucklers Cl. Hod 134 C1
Bucklersbury. Hit 34 C3
Bucknalls Cl. Watf 154 C4
Bucknalls Dri. Bri Wd 154 C4
Bucknalls La. Watf 154 C4
Bucks Alley. L Berk 132 B2
Bucks Ave. Watf 167 F1
Bucks Hill. Sar 152 B3
Buckthorn Ave. Stev 50 C2
Buckton Rd. Bor 156 C1
Buckwood La. Stu 82 B4
Buckwood Rd. Mark 83 E3
Buddcroft. Wel GC 111 D4
Bude Cres. Stev 50 A4
Bulbourne Cl. Berk 121 F3
Bulbourne Cl. Heml H 124 A1
Bulbourne Rd. Tri 100 B4
Bull La. Buck 27 E4
Bull La. Whea 108 A3
Bull Plain. Hert 113 E3
Bull Stag Green. Hat 130 B4
Bull's Cross. Enf 162 A2
Bullace Cl. Heml H 124 A2
Bullbeggars La. Pot En 123 D2
Bullen's Green La. Coln H 143 F4
Bullfields. Saw 97 F2
Bullhead Rd. Bor 170 B3
Bullock's Hill. St P W 49 D1
Bullock's La. Hert 113 E2
Bullrush Cl. Hat 130 A2
Bulls Cross Ride. Ches 162 C4
Bulls La. Wel Gr 144 C4
Bullsland Gdns. Chor 164 A2
Bullsland La. Chor 164 A2
Bullsmoor Cl. Enf 162 B2
Bullsmoor Gdns. Enf 162 A2
Bullsmoor La. Enf 162 B2
Bullsmoor Ride. Enf 162 B2
Bullsmoor Way. Enf 162 B2
Bullwell Cres. Ches 148 C1
Bulstrode La. Chipf 138 A3
Bulwer Link. Stev 50 C2
Buncefield La. Heml H 125 E3
Bungalows The. Harp 86 B2
Bunkers La. Heml H 139 D4
Bunnsfield. Wel GC 111 E4
Bunstrux. Tri 100 A2
Bunting Rd. Luton 44 A2
Buntingfold Rd. Puc 55 E2
Bunyan Cl. Pirt 20 B2
Bunyan Cl. Tri 100 A3
Bunyan Rd. Hit 34 C4
Bunyans Cl. Luton 45 D3
Burbage Cl. Ches 162 C4
Burchell Ct. Bus 168 B1
Burfield Cl. Hat 130 A4
Burfield Rd. Chor 164 B2
Burford Cl. Luton 31 D1
Burford St. Hod 135 D3
Burford Way. Hit 21 E1
Burfordstreet. Hod 135 D4
Burge End La. Pirt 20 B3
Burghley Ave. Bis St 76 B4
Burghley Ave. Bor 170 B2
Burghley Cl. Stev 69 D4
Burgoyne Hatch. Harl 118 A1
Burgundy Croft. Wel GC 110 C2
Burhill Gr. Pnr 175 F1
Burleigh Mead. Hat 130 B4
Burleigh Rd. Ches 162 C4
Burleigh Rd. Heml H 125 E1
Burleigh Rd. Hert 114 A4
Burleigh Rd. St Alb 128 A2
Burleigh Way. Cuf 146 C1
Burley Rd. Bis St 77 D2
Burley. Letw 11 F1
Burnell Rise. Letw 22 C3
Burnell Wlk. Letw 22 C3
Burnells Way. Sta Mo 59 F4
Burnet Cl. Heml H 124 C1
Burnett Ave. Henlw 10 A2
Burnett Sq. Hertng 112 C4
Burnham Cl. Enf 161 F1
Burnham Green Rd. Brn Gr 90 B3
Burnham Rd. Luton 46 A1
Burnham Rd. St Alb 128 A2
Burnley Cl. Sth Ox 175 E3
Burns Cl. Hit 35 D4
Burns Cl. Stev 51 E4
Burns Dri. Heml H 105 D1
Burns Rd. Roystn 7 E4
Burnsall Pl. Harp 107 E3
Burnside Cl. Hat 130 A4
Burnside Terr. Harl 118 C2
Burnside. Hertng 113 D3
Burnside. Hod 134 C3
Burnside. Saw 97 E1
Burnt Cl. Luton 44 C4
Burntfarm Ride. Ches 161 D4
Burntfarm Ride. Enf 161 D3
Burntmill Cl. Harl 117 E2
Burntmill La. H Wy 117 E2
Burr Cl. Lon C 142 C2
Burr St. Luton 63 F4
Burr's Pl. Luton 63 F4
Burrowfield. Wel GC 110 B2
Burrs La. Bark 17 E2
Bursland. Letw 22 B3
Burston Dri. Chis 141 E2
Burton Ave. Watf 167 D3
Burton Cl. Bla En 87 E3
Burton La. Gofs O 147 F2
Burtons Mill. Saw 97 F2
Burwell Rd. Stev 51 E2
Bury End. Pirt 20 B2
Bury Green Rd. Ches 148 A1
Bury Green. Heml H 124 B2
Bury Green. Whea 108 B4
Bury Hill Cl. Heml H 124 B2
Bury Hill. Heml H 124 B2
Bury Holme. Hod 148 C4
Bury La. Bram 91 D2
Bury La. Cod 67 F1
Bury La. Dat 69 E2
Bury La. Ric 165 E1
Bury La. Str 31 D3
Bury Mead Rd. Hit 21 F1
Bury Mead. Ch En 11 D4
Bury Meadows. Ric 165 E1
Bury Park Rd. Luton 63 E4
Bury Plntn. Roystn 7 F3
Bury Rd. Harl 118 B2
Bury Rd. Hat 130 B3
Bury Rd. Heml H 124 B2
Bury Rise. Fel 137 E3
Burycroft. Wel GC 89 F1
Burydale. Stev 69 D4
Burydell La. Pk St 141 E3
Burymead. Stev 36 B1
Burywick. Harp 107 D3
Bush Hall La. Hat 130 B4
Bush Spring. Bal 13 D1
Bushbarns. Ches 148 A1
Bushby Ave. Hod 134 C1
Bushel Wharf. Tri 100 A3
Bushell Green. Bus 176 B4
Bushey Cl. Wel GC 111 D3
Bushey Green. Wel GC 111 D3
Bushey Grove Rd. Bus 167 F3
Bushey Hall Dri. Bus 167 F3
Bushey Hall Rd. Bus 167 F3
Bushey Ley. Wel GC 111 D3
Bushey Mill Cres. Watf 154 B1
Bushey Mill La. Bus 167 F4
Bushey Mill La. Watf 154 B1
Bushfield Rd. Bov 137 E3
Bushmead Rd. Luton 45 F3
Bushwood Cl. Wel Gr 144 A4
Butcher's La. Hit 34 C3
Butcher's La. Pres 48 B3
Bute St. Luton 63 F4
Butely Rd. Luton 44 A3
Butlers Dri. Wa Aby 163 E1
Butlin Rd. Luton 63 D4
Butt Field View. St Alb 141 E4
Butterfield Green Rd. Luton 46 A3
Butterfield La. St Alb 141 F4
Butterfield Rd. Whea 108 B4
Butterfly La. Elst 169 D4
Buttersweet Rise. Saw 97 F1
Butterwick. Watf 154 C2
Buttlehide. Map Cr 172 B3
Buttondene Cres. Lo Naz 135 D1
Butts End. Heml H 124 A3
Butts The. Hod 148 C4
Buttsmead. Norwd 174 B2
Buxton Cl. St Alb 128 B3
Buxton La. Gu M 1 C2
Buxton Path. Sth Ox 175 E4
Buxton Rd. Luton 63 E4
Buzzard Rd. Luton 44 A2
By The Mount. Wel GC 110 B3
By-The-Wood. Watf 175 F4
Byde St. Hert 113 E4
Bye Way The. Har 176 C1
Byers Cl. Pot B 159 E3
Byeway The. Ric 173 F4
Byfield Cl. Luton 44 A1
Byfield. Wel GC 89 F1
Bygrave Rd. Bal 12 C1
Bylands Cl. Bis St 76 B3
Byng Dri. Pot B 159 D4
Byng Rd. Barn 171 E3
Byrd Wlk. Bal 24 A4
Byron Ave. Bor 170 A2
Byron Ave. Watf 167 E4
Byron Cl. Hit 35 D4
Byron Cl. Stev 51 E4
Byron Pl. Heml H 105 D1
Byron Rd. Har 176 C1
Byron Rd. Harp 86 A1
Byron Rd. Luton 44 A1
Byron Rd. Roystn 7 F4
Byslips Rd. Stu 82 C3
Byway The. Pot B 159 D3

Caddington Comm. Cad 83 F4
Caddis Cl. Stan 176 C2
Cade Cl. Letw 12 B1
Cades Cl. Luton 63 D3
Cades La. Luton 63 D3
Cadmore La. Ches 148 C1
Cadwell La. Hit 21 F1
Caernarvon Cl. Heml H 124 B2
Caernarvon Cl. Stev 69 D4
Caesars Rd. Whea 108 C4
Cage Pond Rd. Shen 156 C3
Cairn Way. Stan 176 C2
Caishowe Rd. Bor 170 A4
Caistor Cl. Stev 36 A1
Caldbeck. Wa Aby 163 E3
Caldecot Way. Hod 134 C1
Caldecote Gdns. Bus 168 C1
Caldecote La. Bus 168 C2
Caldecote Rd. Newn 12 C4
Calder Ave. Bro Pk 145 D3
Caldercote Rd. Cal 3 E1
Caldwell Rd. Sth Ox 175 E3
Caleb Cl. Luton 44 C1
Caledon Rd. Lon C 142 B3
California La. Bus 168 B1
California. Bal 12 C1
Callisto Ct. Heml H 124 C3
Calnwood Rd. Luton 44 A1
Calton Ave. Hertng 112 C4
Calton Ct. Hertng 112 C3
Calverley Cl. Bis St 76 C2
Calvert Rd. Barn 171 F4
Calverton Rd. Luton 45 D3
Camberley Pl. Harp 107 E3
Camborne Dri. Heml H 124 C4
Cambrian Way. Heml H 124 C3
Cambridge Cl. Ches 148 B1
Cambridge Cres. Knee 2 A4
Cambridge Dri. Pot B 158 C4
Cambridge Rd. Bar 17 F4
Cambridge Rd. Bark 17 F3
Cambridge Rd. Harl 118 B3
Cambridge Rd. Hit 22 B1
Cambridge Rd. Puc 55 E1
Cambridge Rd. Saw 97 F2
Cambridge Rd. St Alb 128 A1
Cambridge Rd. Sta Mo 59 F4
Cambridge Rd. Watf 167 E3
Cambridge St. Luton 63 F3
Cambridge Terr. Berk 122 B2
Cameron Dri. Ches 162 B3
Camfield. Wel GC 110 C1
Camford Way. Luton 44 A4
Camlet Way. Barn 159 E1
Camlet Way. St Alb 127 D2
Camp Rd. St Alb 128 A1
Camp View Rd. St Alb 128 A1
Campania Gr. Luton 45 D4
Campbell Cl. Hit 35 D4
Campers Ave. Letw 22 C3
Campers Rd. Letw 22 C3
Campers Wlk. Letw 22 C3
Campfield Rd. Hertng 113 D3
Campfield Rd. St Alb 128 A2
Campfield Way. Letw 22 B3
Campine Cl. Ches 148 B2
Campion Cl. Watf 154 A3
Campion Ct. Stev 50 B4
Campion Way. Roystn 7 F3
Campions Cl. Bor 157 D1
Campions The. Bor 157 D1
Campions The. Sta Mo 59 F4
Campkin Mead. Stev 51 E2
Campus Five. Letw 23 E4
Campus The. Wel GC 110 B4
Canada La. Ches 148 C2
Canadas The. Ches 148 C3
Canberra Cl. Knee 2 A3
Canberra Cl. St Alb 127 F4
Canberra Gdns. Luton 45 D3
Candlefield Cl. Heml H 139 D4
Candlefield Rd. Heml H 139 D4
Candlefield Wlk. Heml H 139 D4
Caneland Ct. Wa Aby 163 F3
Canfield. Bis St 76 C4
Cangels Cl. Heml H 124 A1
Canham Cl. Kim 66 B1
Cannix Cl. Stev 51 D1
Cannon La. Luton 46 A3
Cannon Rd. Watf 167 E2
Cannon St. St Alb 127 E2
Cannon's Cl. Gu M 1 C3
Cannons Cl. Bis St 59 D1
Cannons Mead. Sta Mo 59 E4
Cannons Meadow. Tewin 90 C1
Cannons Mill La. Bis St 59 D1
Canons Cl. Radl 156 A2
Canons Field. Whea 87 E1
Canons Field. Wl Gr 89 F4
Canons Gate. Harl 117 D1
Canons Rd. Ware 93 E1
Canonsfield Rd. Wl Gr 89 F4
Canopus Way. Norwd 175 D3
Canterbury Cl. Luton 44 C2
Canterbury Cl. Norwd 174 C2
Canterbury Ct. St Alb 127 F2
Canterbury Rd. Bor 170 A4
Canterbury Rd. Watf 167 D4
Canterbury Way. Cro Gr 166 B3
Canterbury Way. Stev 36 C1
Cape Rd. St Alb 128 A2
Capel Rd. Enf 162 A2
Capel Rd. Watf 167 F2
Capell Ave. Chor 164 B2
Capell Rd. Chor 164 B2
Capell Way. Chor 164 B2
Capella Rd. Norwd 174 C3
Capelvere Wlk. Watf 166 C4
Caponfield. Wel GC 111 D2
Cappell La. Sta Ab 115 E3
Capron Rd. Luton 44 C2
Captains Wlk. Berk 122 B2
Caractacus Cottage View. Watf 167 D2
Caractacus Green. Watf 166 C2
Caravan La. Ric 165 F1
Carbone Hill. Cuf 146 B3
Carde Cl. Hertng 112 C4
Cardiff Cl. Stev 69 D4
Cardiff Gr. Luton 63 E4
Cardiff Pl. Knee 2 A4
Cardiff Rd. Luton 63 E4
Cardiff Rd. Watf 167 D2
Cardigan St. Luton 63 E4
Cardinal Ave. Bor 170 A3
Cardinal Cl. Ham St 147 F3
Cardinal Gr. St Alb 127 D1
Cardy Rd. Heml H 124 A2
Carew Rd. Norwd 174 C2
Careys Croft. Nthch 121 F4
Carisbrook Rd. Luton 44 C1
Carisbrook. Chis 141 D3
Carisbrooke Ave. Watf 167 E4
Carisbrooke Rd. Harp 86 B1
Carleton Rd. Ches 148 C2
Carleton Rise. Welw 89 E3
Carlisle Ave. St Alb 127 E2
Carlton Cl. Bor 170 B3
Carlton Cl. Luton 45 E1
Carlton Cres. Luton 45 E2
Carlton Rd. Harp 86 A1
Carmelite Cl. Har 176 B1
Carmelite Rd. Har 176 B1
Carmelite Rd. Luton 44 A2
Carmelite Way. Har 176 B1
Carmelite Wlk. Har 176 B1
Carnaby Rd. Hod 134 C2
Carnarvon Rd. Barn 171 F3
Carnecie Rd. St Alb 127 E4
Carnegie Gdns. Luton 45 D4
Caro La. Heml H 125 D1
Carol Cl. Luton 45 D2
Caroline Pl. Watf 167 F2
Carpenders Ave. Watf 175 F4
Carpenders Cl. Harp 85 E2
Carpenter Way. Pot B 159 E3
Carpenters Rd. Enf 162 B2
Carpenters Wood Dri. Chor 164 A3
Carpenters Yd. Tri 100 A2
Carrigans. Bis St 76 C4
Carrington Ave. Bor 170 A2
Carrington Cl. Barn 171 D2
Carrington Cl. Bor 170 B2
Carrington Pl. Tri 100 A3
Carrington Sq. Har 176 B2
Carsdale Cl. Luton 45 D3
Cart Path. Watf 154 B3
Carteret Rd. Luton 46 B1
Carterhatch La. Enf 161 F1
Carters Cl. Ch En 11 D4
Carters Cl. Stev 51 E2
Carters Leys. Bis St 76 B4
Carters Way. Ch En 11 D4
Carters Wlk. Ch En 11 D4
Cartersfield Rd. Wa Aby 163 E3
Carthagena Est. Lo Naz 135 E2
Cartwright Rd. Roystn 7 E3
Cartwright Rd. Stev 37 E1

Carve Ley. Wel GC 111 D3
Cashio La. Letw 23 D4
Caslon Way. Letw 11 F1
Cassandra Gate. Ches 148 C2
Cassio Rd. Watf 167 D3
Cassiobridge Rd. Watf 166 C3
Cassiobury Dri. Watf 166 C4
Cassiobury Park Ave. Watf 166 C3
Castano Ct. Abb L 153 F4
Castellane Cl. Stan 176 C2
Castle Cl. Bus 168 A2
Castle Cl. Hod 115 E1
Castle Croft Rd. Luton 63 D3
Castle Gate Way. Berk 122 B3
Castle Hill Ave. Berk 122 B3
Castle Hill. Berk 122 B3
Castle Mead. Heml H 124 A1
Castle Mens. Berk 122 B2
Castle Rd. Enf 162 C1
Castle Rd. Hod 115 E1
Castle Rd. St Alb 128 A2
Castle Rise. Bla En 86 C1
Castle St. Berk 122 B2
Castle St. Bis St 76 C3
Castle St. Hert 113 E3
Castle St. Luton 63 F3
Castle St. Wing 60 A2
Castles' Cl. Stot 11 F4
Caterham Ct. Wa Aby 163 F3
Catesby Green. Luton 31 D1
Catham Cl. St Alb 128 A1
Cathedral Ct. St Alb 127 D1
Catherall Rd. Luton 45 D3
Catherine Cl. Heml H 125 D4
Catherine Rd. Enf 162 C2
Catherine St. St Alb 127 E2
Catisfield Rd. Enf 162 C1
Catkin Cl. Heml H 124 A2
Catlin St. Heml H 138 A4
Catsbrook Rd. Luton 45 D3
Catsdell Bottom. Heml H 139 E4
Catsey La. Bus 168 B1
Catsey Wood. Bus 168 B1
Catterick Way. Bor 169 F4
Cattlegate Hill. Nort 160 B4
Cattlegate Rd. Enf 160 B3
Cattsdell. Heml H 124 C3
Causeway Cl. Pot B 159 E4
Causeway The. Bis St 76 C4
Causeway The. Bre P 30 A1
Causeway The. Bun 40 C4
Causeway The. Fur P 43 D2
Causeway The. Knee 2 A3
Causeway The. P Bar 159 E4
Causeway The. Ther 15 F4
Cautherly La. Gt Am 115 D3
Cavan Dri. St Alb 127 E4
Cavan Rd. Red 106 A3
Cavell Rd. Ham St 148 A2
Cavell Wlk. Stev 51 E3
Cavendish Cres. Bor 170 A3
Cavendish Ct. Cro Gr 166 B2
Cavendish Rd. Barn 171 E3
Cavendish Rd. Luton 45 D1
Cavendish Rd. Mark 83 E3
Cavendish Rd. St Alb 127 F2
Cavendish Rd. Stev 50 A3
Cavendish Way. Hat 129 F3
Cawkell Cl. Sta Mo 59 E4
Caxton Hill. Hert 113 F3
Caxton Rd. Hod 115 D1
Caxton Way. Stev 50 A2
Caxton Way. Watf 166 B2
Cecil Cl. Bis St 77 E4
Cecil Cres. Hat 130 A4
Cecil Ct. Barn 171 E3
Cecil Rd. Ches 162 C4
Cecil Rd. Hert 113 E2
Cecil Rd. Hod 135 E4
Cecil Rd. Pot B 158 A4
Cecil Rd. St Alb 127 F2
Cecil St. Watf 154 A1
Cedar Ave. Ches 162 B3
Cedar Ave. Ick 21 F2
Cedar Cl. Gt Am 114 B4
Cedar Cl. Hert 113 D3
Cedar Cl. Pot B 145 D1
Cedar Cl. Saw 97 F1
Cedar Cres. Roystn 7 D3
Cedar Ct. St Alb 128 B2
Cedar Dri. Pnr 176 A2
Cedar Green. Hod 135 D3
Cedar Lawn Ave. Barn 171 F2
Cedar Park Rd. Enf 161 E1
Cedar Park. Bis St 76 B2
Cedar Pl. Norwd 174 B2
Cedar Rd. Berk 122 B2
Cedar Rd. Enf 161 E1
Cedar Rd. Hat 130 A2
Cedar Rd. Watf 167 E2
Cedar Way. Berk 122 B2
Cedar Wlk. Heml H 124 B1
Cedar Wlk. Wa Aby 163 E3
Cedar Wood Dri. Watf 154 A2
Cedars Ave. Ric 165 E1
Cedars Cl. Bor 170 A3
Cedars The. Harp 86 A1
Cedarwood Dri. St Alb 128 B2
Celandine Dri. Luton 45 D4
Celia Johnson Ct. Bor 170 B4
Cell Barnes Cl. St Alb 128 A1
Cell Barnes La. St Alb 128 A1
Cemetery Hill. Heml H 124 B1
Cemetery Rd. Bis St 76 C3
Cemmaes Court Rd. Heml H 124 B2
Cemmaes Meadow. Heml H 124 B2
Central App. Letw 22 C3
Central Ave. Ches 162 C3
Central Ave. Harl 117 E1
Central Ave. Henlw 10 A2
Central Dri. St Alb 128 B2
Central Rd. Harl 118 A2
Central Way. Norwd 174 C2
Centre Way. Wa Aby 163 E2
Century Rd. Hod 135 D4
Century Rd. Ware 93 E1
Cervantes Ct. Norwd 174 C2
Chace Ave. Pot B 159 E4
Chace The. Stev 50 C1
Chad La. Fla 84 B2
Chadwell Ave. Ches 148 B2
Chadwell Cl. Luton 45 F1
Chadwell Rd. Stev 50 A2
Chadwell Rise. Gt Am 114 A4
Chadwell. Gt Am 114 A4
Chaffinch La. Watf 166 C1
Chaffinches Green. Heml H 139 D4
Chagney Cl. Letw 22 C3
Chalet Cl. Berk 121 F2
Chalfont Cl. Heml H 125 D4
Chalfont La. Chor 164 A2
Chalfont La. Map Cr 172 B2
Chalfont Pl. St Alb 127 F2
Chalfont Rd. Map Cr 172 B4
Chalfont Way. Luton 46 B1
Chalfont Wlk. Pnr 175 E1
Chalgrove. Wel G C 111 D2
Chalk Dale. Wel GC 111 D4
Chalk Hill. Cok Gr 47 D3
Chalk Hill. Watf 167 F2
Chalk Hills. Bal 23 F3
Chalkdell Fields. St Alb 128 A4
Chalkdell Path. Hit 34 B4
Chalkdown. Stev 51 E4
Chalkfield. Letw 23 E2
Chalks Ave. Saw 97 E2
Challney Cl. Luton 44 B1
Chalton Rd. Luton 44 B3
Chamberlaines. Kin Gr 85 D2
Chambers La. Ick 21 F2
Chambers' St. Hert 113 E3
Chambersbury La. Heml H 139 D4
Champions Green. Hod 115 D1
Champions Way. Hod 115 D1
Chancellors Rd. Stev 36 B1
Chancery Cl. St Alb 128 B4
Chandlers La. Cha Cr 152 C1
Chandlers Rd. St Alb 128 B3
Chandlers Way. Hertng 113 D3
Chandos Cl. L Chal 150 B1
Chandos Rd. Bor 170 A4
Chandos Rd. Luton 44 C1
Chantry Cl. Bis St 76 C4
Chantry Cl. Enf 161 E1
Chantry Cl. Kin L 139 D1
Chantry La. Hat 129 F2
Chantry La. Hat 130 A2
Chantry La. Lon C 142 B3
Chantry Pl. Har 176 A1
Chantry Rd. Bis St 76 C4
Chantry Rd. Har 176 A1
Chantry The. Harl 118 A1
Chaomans. Letw 22 C2
Chapel Cl. L Gad 102 B3
Chapel Cl. Luton 45 E4
Chapel Cl. Watf 153 F3
Chapel Cotts. Heml H 124 B3
Chapel Croft. Chipf 152 A4
Chapel Croft. Nthch 121 F3
Chapel End La. Wils 99 E4
Chapel End. Bun 40 C4
Chapel End. Hod 135 D3
Chapel Hill. Sta Mo 59 F3
Chapel La. L Had 75 D4
Chapel La. Let Gr 112 A2
Chapel La. Lon M 79 D2
Chapel Pl. Stot 11 F3
Chapel Rd. Bre Gr 65 F4
Chapel Rd. Fla 84 A1
Chapel Row. Bis St 76 C3
Chapel Row. Hare 173 E1
Chapel St. Berk 122 B2
Chapel St. Heml H 124 B2
Chapel St. Hin 3 E3
Chapel St. Luton 63 F3
Chapel St. Tri 99 F2
Chapel Viaduct. Luton 63 F4
Chapelfields. Sta Ab 115 E2
Chapman Rd. Stev 36 A1
Chapmans End. Puc 55 E2
Chapmans Yd. Watf 167 E3
Chappell Ct. Tonw 92 C4
Chapter House Rd. Luton 44 A2
Chard Dri. Luton 31 D1
Chardins Cl. Heml H 123 F2
Charles St. Berk 122 A2
Charles St. Heml H 124 B1
Charles St. Luton 63 F4
Charles St. Tri 100 A2
Charlesworth Cl. Heml H 124 E1
Charlock Way. Watf 166 C2
Charlton Mead La. Hod 135 E3
Charlton Rd. Hit 34 B3
Charlton Way. Hod 135 D3
Charlwood Cl. Har 176 B2
Charlwood Rd. Luton 44 A1
Charmouth Ct. St Alb 128 A3
Charmouth Rd. St Alb 128 A3
Charndon Cl. Luton 31 D1
Charnwood Rd. Enf 162 A2
Chartley Ave. Stan 176 C2
Chartridge Cl. Barn 171 D2
Chartridge Way. Heml H 125 E2
Chartwell Cl. Wa Aby 163 F3
Chartwell Dri. Luton 45 F2
Chartwell Rd. Norwd 174 C2
Chasden Rd. Heml H 123 F3
Chase Cl. Ch En 11 D4
Chase Hill Rd. Ch En 11 D4
Chase St. Luton 63 F3
Chase The. Bis St 76 C3
Chase The. Gofs O 147 D2
Chase The. Heml H 124 C1
Chase The. Hert 113 F3
Chase The. Radl 155 F2
Chase The. Watf 166 C3
Chase The. Wl Gr 89 F4
Chaseside Cl. Ched 80 A4
Chaseways. Saw 118 B4
Chasten Hill. Hit 22 B4
Chatsworth Cl. Bor 170 A3
Chatsworth Ct. Stev 51 D1
Chatsworth Rd. Luton 45 D1
Chatteris Cl. Luton 44 B2
Chatterton. Letw 23 D3
Chatton Cl. Luton 46 C1
Chaucer Cl. Berk 121 F3
Chaucer Rd. Luton 45 E1
Chaucer Rd. Roystn 7 E4
Chaucer Way. Hit 35 E4
Chaucer Wlk. Heml H 105 D1
Chaul End La. Luton 44 C1
Chaul End Rd. Cad 44 A1
Chaul End Rd. Cad 62 B3
Chaulden House Gdns. Heml H 123 F1
Chaulden La. Heml H 123 F1
Chaulden Terr. Heml H 123 F1
Chauncy Ave. Pot B 159 E3
Chauncy Cl. Ware 93 E2
Chauncy Gdns. Clo 13 D1
Chauncy Rd. Stev 50 C3
Chaworth Green. Luton 44 B3
Cheapside. Luton 63 F4
Chedburgh. Wel GC 111 E4
Cheddington La. Lon M 79 E3
Cheddington Rd. Pit 80 B2
Cheffins Rd. Hod 114 C1
Chells La. Stev 51 E4
Chells Way. Stev 51 E3
Chelmsford Rd. Hertng 113 D3
Chelsing Rise. Heml H 125 E1
Chelsworth Cl. Luton 46 B1
Chelveston. Well GC 111 E4
Chelwood Ave. Hat 130 A4
Chelwood Cl. Norwd 174 B2
Chenduit Way. Stan 176 C3
Cheney Rd. Luton 44 B3
Chenies Ave. L Chal 150 B1
Chenies Ct. Heml H 125 D4
Chenies Green. Bis St 76 B3
Chenies Rd. Chor 164 B4
Chenies Way. Watf 166 C1
Chennells Cl. Hit 22 A1
Chennells. Hat 129 F2
Chequer La. Red 106 A2
Chequer St. Luton 63 F3
Chequer St. St Alb 127 E2
Chequers Bridge Rd. Stev 50 B3
Chequers Cl. Bun 40 B4
Chequers Cl. Pit 80 B2
Chequers Cl. Stot 12 A3
Chequers Field. Wel GC 110 B2
Chequers Hill. Fla 84 B1
Chequers La. Abb L 140 B1
Chequers La. Pit 80 B3
Chequers La. Pres 48 B4
Chequers Wlk. Wa Aby 163 F3
Chequers. Bis St 76 B4
Chequers. Hat 130 B4
Chequers. Wel GC 110 B2
Cheriton Cl. St Alb 128 B4
Cherry Bounce. Heml H 124 B3
Cherry Cl. Kneb 68 C2
Cherry Croft Gdns. Pnr 175 F2
Cherry Croft. Wel GC 89 E1
Cherry Dri. Roystn 7 F4
Cherry Gdns. Bis St 77 D4
Cherry Gdns. Saw 97 F2
Cherry Gdns. Tri 99 F2
Cherry Hill. Chis 141 D3
Cherry Hill. Chor 165 D3
Cherry Orch. Heml H 124 A3
Cherry Rd. Enf 162 B1
Cherry Tree Ave. Lon C 142 B3
Cherry Tree Cl. Arl 11 D2
Cherry Tree Cl. Luton 46 A1
Cherry Tree Green. Hertng 112 C4
Cherry Tree La. Buc Co 120 A2
Cherry Tree La. Harp 87 D1
Cherry Tree La. Heron 164 B1
Cherry Tree La. Pot B 159 D3
Cherry Tree Rd. Hod 135 D4
Cherry Tree Rd. Watf 154 A2
Cherry Tree Rise. Wal 38 A1
Cherry Trees. Henlw 10 A2
Cherry Way. Hat 130 A1
Cherry Wlk. Chor 165 E4
Cherrydale. Watf 166 C3
Cherrytree La. Heml H 125 E4
Chertsey Cl. Luton 64 B4
Chertsey Rise. Stev 51 E2
Cherwell Cl. Cro Gr 166 A2
Chesfield Cl. Bis St 76 C3
Chesford Rd. Luton 46 B2
Chesham Ct. Norwd 174 C2
Chesham Rd. Ash Gr 121 F1
Chesham Rd. Berk 122 A1
Chesham Rd. Bov 136 B2
Chesham Rd. Wigg 120 C4
Chesham Way. Watf 166 C2
Chess Cl. Chor 165 E3
Chess Cl. Lat 150 B2
Chess Hill. Chor 165 E3
Chess La. Chor 165 E3
Chess Vale Rise. Cro Gr 165 F2
Chess Way. Chor 165 D3
Chesswood Way. Pnr 175 E1
Chester Ave. Luton 44 C2
Chester Cl. Luton 44 C1
Chester Rd. Bor 170 B3
Chester Rd. Norwd 174 C2
Chester Rd. Stev 37 D1
Chester Rd. Watf 167 D3
Chesterfield Rd. Barn 171 E2
Chesterfield Rd. Enf 162 C1
Chesterton Ave. Harp 86 B1
Chestnut Ave. Chor 165 D2
Chestnut Ave. Henlw 10 B2
Chestnut Ave. Luton 44 B4
Chestnut Ave. Norwd 174 C1
Chestnut Ave. Ware 93 F2
Chestnut Cl. Bis St 76 C3
Chestnut Cl. Dagn 81 E3
Chestnut Cl. Pot En 123 D3
Chestnut Dri. Berk 122 B2
Chestnut Dri. Har 176 C1
Chestnut Dri. St Alb 128 B3
Chestnut La. Knee 2 A3
Chestnut La. N20 171 F1
Chestnut Rd. Enf 162 C2
Chestnut Rise. Bus 168 A1
Chestnut Wash. Ches 148 C2
Chestnut Wlk. Roystn 7 F3
Chestnut Wlk. Stev 36 B1
Chestnut Wlk. Watf 154 A1
Chestnut Wlk. Wl Gr 89 F4
Chestnuts The. Cod 67 F1
Chestnuts The. Fel 137 F4
Chestnuts The. Hert 113 E3
Cheverells Cl. Mark 83 E2
Cheverells Green. Mark 83 E2
Cheviot Cl. Bus 168 B2
Cheviot Cl. Luton 44 B4
Cheviot Rd. Luton 44 B4
Cheviots. Hat 130 A2
Cheviots. Heml H 124 C3
Cheyne Cl. Pit 80 B2
Cheyne Cl. Ware 93 E2
Chicheley Gdns. Har 176 B2
Chicheley Rd. Har 176 B2
Chichester Way. Watf 154 C3
Chigwell Hurst Ct. Pnr 175 E1
Chilcott Rd. Watf 153 F2
Chilcourt. Roystn 7 E3
Childwick Ct. Heml H 139 D4
Chiltern Ave. Bus 168 B2
Chiltern Cl. Berk 122 A3
Chiltern Cl. Bor 169 F4
Chiltern Cl. Bus 168 A2
Chiltern Cl. Gofs O 147 D2
Chiltern Cl. Ware 93 E2
Chiltern Ct. Harp 86 A1
Chiltern Dri. Ric 165 D1
Chiltern Gdns. Luton 44 C2
Chiltern Park Ave. Berk 122 A3
Chiltern Rd. Bal 23 F3
Chiltern Rd. Hit 35 D4
Chiltern Rd. St Alb 128 B4
Chiltern Rd. Wing 60 A2
Chiltern Rise. Luton 63 E3
Chiltern View. Letw 22 B3
Chiltern Way. Tri 100 B3
Chilterns The. Hit 35 D3
Chilterns The. Ken Co 82 C4
Chilterns. Hat 130 A1
Chilterns. Heml H 124 C3
Chilton Green. Wel GC 111 E3
Chilvers Bank. Bal 23 F4
Chilwell Gdns. Sth Ox 175 E3
Chinnery Hill. Bis St 76 C3
Chipperfield Rd. Bov 137 E2
Chipperfield Rd. Fel 138 B4
Chipperfield Rd. Kin L 138 B1
Chipping Cl. Barn 171 F3
Chippingfield. Harl 118 B2
Chishill Rd. Bar 9 D1
Chiswellgreen La. Chis 140 C3
Chobham St. Luton 63 F3
Chobham Wlk. Luton 63 F3
Cholesbury La. Buc Co 120
Cholwell Rd. Stev 51
Chorleywood Bottom. Chor 164
Chorleywood Cl. Ric 165
Chorleywood Rd. Chor 165
Chorleywood Rd. Ric 165
Chouler Gdns. Stev 36
Christ Church La. Barn 171
Christ Church Pas. Barn 171
Christchurch Cl. St Alb 127
Christchurch Cres. Radl 156
Christchurch Pl. Hert 113
Christchurch Rd. Heml H 124
Christchurch Rd. Tri 99
Christie Cl. Hod 134
Christie Rd. Stev 51
Christopher Ct. Heml H 138
Christopher Pl. St Alb 127
Church Cl. Cod 67
Church Cl. Cuf 146
Church Cl. L Berk 132
Church Cl. Norwd 174
Church Cl. Stu 82
Church Cres. Saw 97 F
Church Cres. St Alb 127 E
Church End. Bar 9 D
Church End. Ch En 11 D
Church End. Fla 84 E
Church End. Mark 83 E
Church End. Red 106 A
Church End. Sand 108 B
Church End. Wal 38 B
Church Field Path. Ches 148 B
Church Field. Ware 93 D
Church Green. Benn 52 B
Church Green. Harp 86 A
Church Hill. Bed 139 F
Church Hill. Ched 79 F
Church Hill. Hare 173 E
Church Hill. Hert H 114 A
Church La. Ashw 4 B
Church La. Bark 17 E
Church La. Berk 122 B
Church La. Bov 137 D
Church La. Ch En 11 D
Church La. Ched 80 A
Church La. Ches 148 B
Church La. Coln H 129 D
Church La. Dan En 71 F4
Church La. Gra 36 B
Church La. Gu M 1 C
Church La. Har 176 C
Church La. Hat 130 B3
Church La. Hod 148 B4
Church La. Kim 66 B
Church La. Kin L 139 D
Church La. Letw 12 B1
Church La. Mars 79 F1
Church La. Muc H 74 C2
Church La. Nort 146 A1
Church La. Reed 16 C3
Church La. Ric 165 D1
Church La. Roystn 7 E3
Church La. Sar 152 A2
Church La. Stap 92 A3
Church La. Stev 50 B4
Church La. Ther 15 F4
Church La. Thor 76 B2
Church Manor. Bis St 77 D4
Church Mead. Roy 116 A1
Church Mead. Stu 82 A2
Church Path. Gt Am 115 D3
Church Path. Hert 113 E3
Church Path. Ick 21 F2
Church Path. L Wym 35 F2
Church Rd. Cad 63 E1
Church Rd. Fla 84 A1
Church Rd. Gt Ha 77 F2
Church Rd. Heml H 125 E1
Church Rd. Hert 113 E4
Church Rd. Ivin 80 C3
Church Rd. Kin Wd 47 F2
Church Rd. L Berk 132 B2
Church Rd. L Gad 102 B4
Church Rd. L Hal 77 D1
Church Rd. Norwd 174 C2
Church Rd. Pit 80 C2
Church Rd. Pot B 145 D1
Church Rd. Pot En 123 D3
Church Rd. Sta Mo 59 F3
Church Rd. Stot 11 F3
Church Rd. Str 31 D3
Church Rd. Stu 82 A2
Church Rd. Watf 167 D4
Church Rd. Wel GC 110 B3
Church Row Mews. Ware 93 E1
Church St. Bal 12 C1
Church St. Bis St 76 C4
Church St. Bov 137 D2
Church St. Bun 40 C4
Church St. Gu M 1 C3
Church St. Hat 130 B3
Church St. Heml H 124 B3
Church St. Hert 113 E3
Church St. Luton 63 F4
Church St. Ric 165 F1
Church St. Saw 97 F1
Church St. St Alb 127 E2
Church St. Wa Aby 163 E3
Church St. Ware 93 E1

Church St. Watf 167 E3
Church St. Welw 89 E3
Church St. Whea 108 B4
Church St. Wing 60 A1
Church View. Hod 134 C2
Church View. Lon M 79 D2
Church Wlk. Bus 168 A2
Church Wlk. Saw 97 F1
Church Yd. Tri 100 A2
Churchfield Rd. Tewin 90 B1
Churchfield. Bar 9 D1
Churchfield. Harl 118 A1
Churchfield. Harp 107 E4
Churchfields. Hod 135 D2
Churchfields. Stand 55 F1
Churchgate Rd. Ches 148 A1
Churchgate St. Harl 118 C2
Churchgate. Ches 148 A1
Churchgate. Hit 34 C4
Churchill Rd. Luton 45 D1
Churchill Rd. St Alb 128 A2
Churchyard Wlk. Hit 34 C4
Churchyard. Hit 34 C4
Cicero Dri. Luton 45 D4
Cillocks Cl. Hod 135 D4
Claggy Rd. Kim 66 A1
Claire Ct. Ches 162 C4
Claire Ct. Pnr 175 F2
Clamp Hill. Stan 176 C3
Clapgate Rd. Bus 168 A2
Clare Cl. Elst 169 F2
Clare Cres. Bal 23 F3
Clare Ct. Norwd 174 C3
Clare Ct. St Alb 127 F1
Claremont Cres. Cro Gr 166 B2
Claremont Rd. Barn 159 E1
Claremont Rd. Har 176 C1
Claremont Rd. Luton 45 D1
Claremont. Bric 155 D4
Claremont. Ches 147 F1
Clarence Cl. Bus 168 C1
Clarence Rd. Berk 122 B2
Clarence Rd. Harp 86 A2
Clarence Rd. St Alb 128 A2
Clarence Rd. Sta Mo 59 F4
Clarendon Ct. Harp 86 A2
Clarendon Rd. Bor 170 A3
Clarendon Rd. Ches 148 B1
Clarendon Rd. Harp 86 A2
Clarendon Rd. Luton 45 F1
Clarendon Rd. Watf 167 D3
Clarion Cl. Gt Of 33 E1
Clark Rd. Roystn 7 E4
Clarke Way. Watf 154 A2
Clarke's Rd. Hat 130 A4
Clarke's Spring. Tri 100 C3
Clarkfield. Ric 173 D4
Clarks Cl. Ware 93 E2
Clarks Mead. Bus 168 B1
Claudian Pl. St Alb 127 D1
Claverhambury Rd. Wa Aby 149 F1
Claverley Green. Luton 46 C1
Claverton Cl. Bov 137 D2
Clay Hall Rd. Ken Co 82 C4
Clay Hill. Enf 161 E1
Clay La. Bus 168 C1
Clay La. Edg 170 A1
Claybury. Bus 168 A1
Claybush Rd. Ashw 4 B2
Claycroft. Wel GC 111 D4
Claydown Way. Cad 63 D1
Claygate Ave. Harp 85 F1
Claymore Dri. Ick 21 F3
Claymore. Heml H 124 C4
Claymores. Stev 50 C3
Clayponds. Bis St 77 D4
Cleall Ave. Wa Aby 163 E3
Cleave The. Harp 86 B1
Clement Pl. Tri 100 A2
Clement Rd. Ches 148 C2
Clements End Rd. Gt Ga 103 F4
Clements End Rd. Stu 82 C1
Clements Rd. Chor 164 B2
Clements St. Ware 93 F1
Clevedon Rd. Luton 46 A1
Cleveland Cres. Bor 170 B2
Cleveland Rd. Heml H 125 D3
Cleveland Rd. Mark 83 F3
Cleveland Way. Heml H 125 D3
Cleves Rd. Heml H 125 D4
Cleviscroft. Stev 50 C2
Clewer Cres. Har 176 B1
Clifford Cres. Luton 44 B3
Clifton Cl. Ches 148 C1
Clifton Rd. Luton 63 D4
Clifton Rd. Watf 167 D2
Clifton St. St Alb 127 F2
Clifton Way. Bor 170 A4
Clifton Way. Ware 93 E2
Climb The. Chor 165 D2
Clinton Ave. Luton 45 F2
Clinton End. Heml H 125 E2
Clitheroe Gdns. Sth Ox 175 E4
Clive Cl. Pot B 158 C4
Clive Par. Norwd 174 C2
Clive Way. Watf 167 E4
Cloister Garth. Berk 122 B2
Cloister Garth. St Alb 141 F4
Cloister Wlk. Heml H 124 B3
Cloisterlawns. Letw 22 C2
Cloisters Rd. Letw 23 D2
Cloisters Rd. Luton 44 A2
Cloisters The. Ric 165 F1
Cloisters The. Wel GC 110 B3
Clonard Way. Pnr 176 A2
Close The. Bal 23 F4
Close The. Bro Pk 144 C3
Close The. Bus 168 A2
Close The. Cod 67 F1
Close The. Harp 85 E2
Close The. Hin 3 E3
Close The. Luton 45 D3
Close The. Mark 83 F3
Close The. Pot B 159 D4
Close The. Radl 155 F3
Close The. Ric 165 E1
Close The. Roystn 7 F4
Close The. Wall 25 F3
Close The. Ware 93 F1
Closemead Cl. Norwd 174 B2
Clothall Rd. Bal 23 F4
Clothall Rd. Clo 24 B3
Clovelly Way. Stev 50 A4
Clover Cl. Luton 44 A2
Clover Way. Heml H 124 A2
Cloverfield. Wel GC 89 F1
Cloverland. Hat 129 F1
Clowns The. Harp 107 D3
Clump The. Chor 165 D2
Clusterbolts. Stap 92 A4
Clyde Rd. Roy 135 E2
Clyde Sq. Heml H 124 C4
Clyde St. Hert 114 A3
Clydesdale Cl. Bor 170 B2
Clydesdale Path. Bor 170 B2
Clydesdale Rd. Luton 44 A2
Clydesdale Rd. Roystn 7 F3
Clydesdale Wlk. Ches 148 C3
Clyfton Cl. Hod 148 C4
Clyston Rd. Watf 166 C2
Coach Dri. Hit 34 C3
Coachman's La. Bal 23 E4
Coates Dell. Watf 154 C3
Coates Rd. Elst 169 E1
Coates Way. Watf 154 C3
Cob Cl. Bor 170 B2
Cobb Green. Watf 154 A4
Cobb Rd. Berk 121 F2
Cobbett Cl. Ches 162 B2
Cobbetts Ride. Tri 99 F2
Cobbins The. Wa Aby 163 F3
Cobblers Wick. Wing 60 A2
Cobden St. Luton 45 F1
Cobham Rd. Ware 93 F1
Cobmead. Hat 130 A4
Cock La. Hod 134 B2
Cock La. Sta Gr 30 C2
Cockbush Ave. Hert 114 A4
Cocker Rd. Enf 162 B2
Cockfosters Rd. Barn 159 F1
Codicote Dri. Watf 154 B3
Codicote Heights. Cod 68 A1
Codicote Rd. A St L 88 B2
Codicote Rd. Welw 89 D3
Codicote Rd. Whea 87 F1
Codicote Rd. Whit 66 C3
Codicote Row. Heml H 105 D1
Codmore Wood Rd. Lat 150 B3
Coe's Alley. Barn 171 F3
Colburn Ave. Pnr 175 F2
Colchester Rd. Norwd 175 D1
Cold Christmas La. Thun 93 F3
Coldham Gr. Enf 162 C1
Coldharbour La. Bus 168 B2
Coldharbour La. Harp 86 B2
Cole Green La. Wel GC 111 D2
Cole Rd. Watf 167 D4
Colebrook Ave. Luton 44 B4
Coleman Green La. Sand 108 C2
Coleman Green La. Whea 109 D4
Coleman's La. Lo Naz 149 F3
Colemans Rd. Bre Wd 47 E1
Coleridge Cl. Ham St 147 F2
Coleridge Cl. Hit 35 D4
Coleridge Cres. Heml H 105 D1
Coles Green. Bus 168 B1
Coles Hill. Heml H 124 A3
Colesdale. Cuf 146 C1
Colestrete Cl. Stev 50 C3
Colestrete. Stev 50 C3
Coleswood Rd. Harp 107 E4
Colgrove. Wel GC 110 B3
Colin Rd. Luton 45 F1
Colindale Ave. St Alb 127 F1
College Ave. Har 176 C1
College Cl. Fla 84 A1
College Cl. Gt Am 114 B4
College Cl. Har 176 C2
College Ct. Ches 148 B1
College Hill Rd. Har 176 C1
College La. Hat 129 F2
College Pl. St Alb 127 E2
College Rd. Abb L 154 A4
College Rd. Ast C 78 B1
College Rd. Ches 148 B1
College Rd. Har 176 B1
College Rd. Hert H 114 B1
College Rd. Hod 134 C4
College Rd. St Alb 128 A1
College St. St Alb 127 E2
College Way. Norwd 174 B2
Collens Rd. Harp 107 D3
Collenswood Rd. Stev 51 D2
Collet Cl. Ches 148 B2
Collet Gdns. Ches 148 B2
Collett Rd. Heml H 124 B2
Collett Rd. Ware 93 E1
Colley Land. Chor 164 B3
Collingdon St. Luton 63 E4
Collings Wells Cl. Cad 62 C2
Collingtree. Luton 46 A2
Collingwood Dri. Lon C 142 B3
Collins Cross. Bis St 59 D1
Collison Cl. Hit 22 B1
Collyer Rd. Lon C 142 B2
Colmer Pl. Har 176 B2
Colne Ave. Ric 173 D4
Colne Ave. Watf 167 E2
Colne Gdns. Lon C 142 C2
Colne Mead. Ric 173 D4
Colne Way. Heml H 124 C4
Colne Way. Watf 154 C1
Colney Heath La. St Alb 128 C1
Colonade The. Ches 148 B2
Colonial Way. Watf 167 E4
Colonnade The. Ches 148 C2
Colonsay. Heml H 125 E1
Colston Cres. Gofs O 147 D2
Colts Cnr. Stev 51 D2
Colts Croft. Gt Ch 9 F1
Colts The. Bis St 76 C2
Coltsfield. Sta Mo 59 F4
Coltsfoot Dri. Roystn 7 F3
Coltsfoot Green. Luton 44 A3
Coltsfoot La. Dat 90 B4
Coltsfoot Rd. Ware 93 F2
Coltsfoot The. Heml H 123 F1
Coltsfoot. Wel G C 111 D2
Colvin Gdns. Enf 162 B2
Colwell Rise. Luton 46 C1
Colyer Cl. Har Gr 89 F2
Combe Rd. Watf 166 C2
Combe St. Heml H 124 B2
Comet Cl. Watf 153 F3
Comet Rd. Hat 129 F3
Comet Rd. Hat 129 F4
Comet Way. Hat 129 F3
Comet Way. Stanb 110 A1
Commerce Way. Letw 22 C3
Common Field. Wigg 100 B2
Common Gate Rd. Chor 164 C2
Common Green. Pot En 123 D3
Common La. Ashw 4 A3
Common La. Kim 66 A1
Common La. Kim 86 B3
Common La. Kin L 138 C2
Common La. Radl 155 F1
Common Rd. Chor 164 C4
Common Rd. Ken Co 82 C4
Common Rd. Stan 176 B4
Common Rd. Stot 11 F4
Common Rd. Stu 82 A2
Common Rise. Hit 22 A1
Common The. Chipf 151 F4
Common The. Hat 130 A3
Common The. Kin Gr 85 E2
Common The. Pot En 123 D3
Common The. Stan 176 C4
Common View Sq. Letw 23 D4
Common View. Letw 23 D4
Commonfields. Harl 117 F1
Commons La. Heml H 124 C2
Commons The. Wel GC 111 D2
Compton Ave. Luton 44 C2
Compton Gdns. Chis 141 D3
Compton Pl. Watf 175 F3
Comyne Rd. Watf 153 F2
Comyns The. Bus 168 B1
Concorde Dri. Heml H 124 B2
Concorde St. Luton 63 F4
Conduit La E. Hod 135 D3
Conduit La. Gt Ho 29 D1
Conduit La. Hod 135 D3
Coney Cl. Hat 130 A2
Coney Green. Saw 97 E2
Coneydale. Wel GC 110 B4
Congreve Rd. Wa Aby 163 F3
Conifer Cl. Ches 147 F1
Conifer Cl. Stev 51 E4
Conifer Wlk. Stev 51 E4
Coningesby Dri. Watf 166 C4
Coningsby Bank. St Alb 141 E4
Coningsby Cl. Wel G 144 B4
Coningsby Dri. Pot B 159 E3
Coniston Cl. Heml H 125 E1
Coniston Rd. Kin L 138 C2
Coniston Rd. Luton 44 C3
Connaught Cl. Heml H 125 D3
Connaught Gdns. Nthch 121 F4
Connaught Rd. Barn 171 E2
Connaught Rd. Har 176 C1
Connaught Rd. Harp 86 A1
Connaught Rd. Luton 44 C1
Connaught Rd. St Alb 127 E3
Connemara Cl. Bor 170 B2
Connop Rd. Enf 162 B1
Conquerors Hill. Whea 108 C4
Conquest Cl. Hit 34 C3
Constantine Cl. Stev 36 C1
Constantine Pl. Bal 13 D1
Convent Cl. Hit 34 C4
Conway Gdns. Enf 161 F1
Conway Rd. Luton 45 D1
Conyers. Harl 117 E1
Cook Rd. Stev 51 D4
Cook's Hole Rd. Enf 161 E1
Cooks Mead. Bus 168 A2
Cooks Spinney. Harl 118 A1
Cooks Vennel. Heml H 124 A3
Cooks Way. Hit 22 A1
Coombe Gdns. Berk 121 F3
Coombe Hill Rd. Ric 165 D1
Coombe Rd. Bus 168 B1
Coombe Rd. Kel 6 A1
Coombelands Rd. Roystn 2 C1
Coombes Rd. Lon C 142 B3
Cooper's Cl. Kim 66 A1
Cooper's Hill. Kim 87 D4
Cooper's La. Nort 145 F1
Coopers Alley. Hit 34 C4
Coopers Cl. Stev 51 E2
Coopers Cres. Bor 170 B4
Coopers Green La. St Alb 128 C3
Coopers Green La. Stanb 109 E1
Coopers Lane Rd. Nort 160 A3
Coopers Meadow. Red 106 A3
Coopers Rd. Pot B 145 E1
Coopers Wlk. Ches 148 B2
Cooters End La. Harp 85 F3
Copenhagen Cl. Luton 44 B4
Copmans Wick. Chor 164 B2
Coppens The. Stot 12 A3
Copper Beech Cl. Fel 137 F4
Copper Ct. Saw 97 F1
Copperfields. Roystn 7 E3
Copperfields. Wel GC 111 E3
Coppermill La. Map Cr 172 C2
Copperwood. Hert 113 F3
Coppice Cl. Hat 129 F1
Coppice Mead. Stot 11 F3
Coppice The. Watf 167 E2
Coppings The. Hod 115 D1
Coppins Cl. Berk 121 F2
Coppins The. Har 176 B2
Coppins The. Mark 83 E3
Copse Cl. Norwd 174 B1
Copse Hill. Wl Gr 90 A4
Copse The. Bis St 77 E4
Copse The. Heml H 123 F3
Copse Way. Luton 44 B4
Copse Wood Way. Norwd 174 B1
Copsewood Rd. Watf 167 D4
Copthorne Ave. Hod 134 C2
Copthorne Cl. Cro Gr 165 F2
Copthorne Rd. Cro Gr 165 F2
Copthorne. Luton 46 B2
Coral Gdns. Heml H 124 C2
Corbridge Dri. Luton 46 C1
Corby Cl. Chis 141 D3
Cordell Cl. Ches 148 C2
Corder Cl. St Alb 141 D4
Coreys Mill La. Stev 36 B1
Corinium Gate. St Alb 127 D1
Corinium Gdns. Luton 45 D4
Corn Mead. Wel GC 89 E1
Corncastle Rd. Luton 63 E3
Corncrake Cl. Luton 46 B3
Corncroft. Hat 130 A4
Cornel Cl. Luton 63 D4
Corner Hall Ave. Heml H 124 B1
Corner Hall. Heml H 124 B1
Corner Wood. Mark 83 E3
Cornerfield. Hat 130 A4
Corners. Wel GC 111 D4
Cornfield Rd. Bus 168 A3
Cornfields. Heml H 124 A1
Cornmill. Wa Aby 163 D3
Cornwall Cl. Ches 162 C3
Cornwall Ct. Pnr 175 F2
Cornwall Rd. Harp 86 A1
Cornwall Rd. Pnr 175 F2
Cornwall Rd. St Alb 127 F1
Coronation Ave. Roystn 7 E3
Coronation Rd. Bis St 76 C3
Coronation Rd. Ware 93 E1
Corringham Ct. St Alb 127 F2
Corton Cl. Stev 50 A4
Cory-Wright Way. Whea 87 F1
Cosgrove Way. Luton 62 C4
Cotefield. Luton 44 B2
Cotesmore Rd. Heml H 123 F1
Cotlandswick. Lon C 142 B3
Cotney Croft. Stev 51 E2
Cotswold Cl. St Alb 128 B4
Cotswold Gdns. Luton 44 B4
Cotswold. Heml H 124 C3
Cotswolds. Hat 130 A2
Cottage Cl. Cro Gr 165 F2
Cottered Rd. Thro 26 C1
Cotterells Hill. Heml H 124 B2
Cotterells. Heml H 124 B1
Cotton Dri. Hert 114 A4
Cotton Field. Hat 130 A4
Cotton Rd. Pot B 159 E4
Cottonmill Cres. St Alb 127 E1
Cottonmill La. St Alb 127 E1
Coulser Cl. Heml H 124 A3
Coulter Cl. Cuf 146 B2
Council Rd. Bis St 77 D4
Counters Cl. Heml H 124 A2
Countess Cl. Hare 173 E1
Coursers Rd. Coln H 143 E4
Coursers Rd. Lon C 143 D3
Courtaulds. Chipf 138 A1
Courtenay Ave. Har 176 B1
Courtenay Gdns. Har 176 B1
Courtfield Cl. Hod 135 D2
Courtfields. Harp 86 B1
Courtlands Cl. Watf 153 F1
Courtlands Dri. Watf 153 F2
Courtleigh Ave. Barn 159 E1
Courtway The. Watf 175 F4
Covent Garden Cl. Luton 44 C2
Coventry Cl. Stev 37 D1
Coverdale. Heml H 124 C3
Coverdale. Luton 44 A3
Covert Cl. Nthch 121 E3
Covert Rd. Nthch 121 E3
Covert The. Norwd 174 B1
Cow La. Bus 168 A2
Cow La. Tri 100 B2
Cow La. Watf 154 B2
Cowards La. Cod 88 C4
Cowbridge. Hert 113 E3
Cowdray Cl. Luton 46 B2
Cowles. Ham St 147 F2
Cowley Hill. Bor 157 D1
Cowper Cres. Hert 92 A1
Cowper Ct. Watf 154 A1
Cowper Rd. Berk 122 A2
Cowper Rd. Harp 86 B1
Cowper Rd. Heml H 124 A1
Cowper Rd. Mark 83 E3
Cowper Rd. Wel GC 110 C3
Cowper Rise. Mark 83 E3
Cowper St. Luton 63 F3
Cowpers Way. Tewin 90 B3
Cowridge Cres. Luton 46 A1
Cowslip Cl. Roystn 7 F3
Cowslip Hill. Letw 22 C4
Cowslips The. Wel GC 111 E3
Cox's Way. Arl 11 D3
Coxfield Cl. Heml H 124 C1
Coyney Green. Luton 45 E1
Cozens La E. Hod 134 C1
Cozens La W. Hod 134 C1
Cozens Rd. Ware 94 A1
Crab La. Aldhm 155 D3
Crab Tree La. Pirt 20 B2
Crab Tree Rd. Kneb 68 C2
Crabb's La. Sto P 43 F3
Crabtree Cl. Bus 168 A2
Crabtree Cl. Heml H 124 B1
Crabtree Ct. Heml H 124 C1
Crabtree Dell. Letw 23 E2
Crabtree La. Bal 23 F4
Crabtree La. Harp 107 E4
Crabtree La. Heml H 124 B1
Crackley Meadow. Heml H 125 D4
Cradock Rd. Luton 44 A1
Cragg Ave. Radl 155 F2
Cragside. Kneb 69 E4
Craig Mount. Radl 156 A2
Craigavon Rd. Heml H 124 C4
Craiglands. St Alb 128 B4
Craigs Wlk. Ches 148 B2
Craigweil Ave. Radl 156 A2
Cranborne Ave. Hit 34 B3
Cranborne Cl. Hert 113 E2
Cranborne Cl. Pot B 158 C4
Cranborne Cres. Pot B 158 C4
Cranborne Gdns. Wel GC 110 C3
Cranborne Rd. Ches 162 B4
Cranborne Rd. Hat 130 A3
Cranborne Rd. Hod 135 E4
Cranbourne Dri. Harp 107 E3
Cranbourne Dri. Hod 115 E1
Cranbourne Pl. Pot B 158 C4
Cranbourne Rd. Norwd 174 C1
Cranbrook Cl. Ware 93 E2
Cranbrook Dri. Luton 44 B4
Cranbrook Dri. St Alb 128 C2
Crane Mead. Ware 114 C4
Cranefield Dri. Watf 154 C3
Cranes Way. Bor 170 B2
Cranfield Cres. Cuf 146 C1
Cranleigh Cl. Ches 148 A2
Cranleigh Gdns. Luton 45 E2
Cranmer Cl. Pot B 145 E1
Cranmore Ct. St Alb 127 F2
Cranwell Gdns. Bis St 59 E1
Cravells Rd. Harp 107 E4
Crawford Rd. Hat 130 A4
Crawley Cl. Cad 63 E1
Crawley Dri. Heml H 124 C4
Crawley Green Rd. Luton 64 A4
Crawley Rd. Luton 63 E4
Crawley's La. Wigg 120 C4
Crecy Gdns. Red 106 A3
Creighton Ave. St Alb 141 E4
Crescent E. Barn 159 E1
Crescent Rd. Bis St 77 D3
Crescent Rd. Heml H 124 B2
Crescent Rd. Luton 63 F4
Crescent Rise. Luton 63 F4
Crescent The. Abb L 139 F1
Crescent The. Bri Wd 141 D1
Crescent The. Cad 62 C2
Crescent The. Cotrd 39 E4
Crescent The. Cro Gr 166 A2

Crescent The. Gos 35 D2
Crescent The. Harl 118 B3
Crescent The. Henlw 10 B2
Crescent The. Hit 21 E1
Crescent The. Letw 23 D3
Crescent The. Mars 80 A1
Crescent The. Pit 80 B2
Crescent The. Watf 167 E3
Crescent The. Welw 89 D2
Crescent W. Barn 159 E1
Cresset Cl. Sta Ab 115 E2
Cresswick. Whit 66 C4
Crest Dri. Enf 162 B1
Crest Park. Heml H 125 E2
Crest The. Gofs O 147 D2
Crest The. Luton 45 D4
Crest The. Saw 97 E1
Crest The. Ware 93 E2
Crest The. Wl Gr 89 E4
Cresta Cl. Dun 44 A1
Creswick Ct. Wel GC 110 B3
Crew Curve. Nthch 121 F4
Crews Hill. Nort 160 C3
Crib St. Ware 93 E1
Cricketer's Rd. Arl 11 D2
Cricketfield La. Bis St 76 C4
Crispin Field. Pit 80 B2
Croasdaile Rd. Sta Mo 59 F4
Croasdale Cl. Sta Mo 59 F4
Crocus Field. Barn 171 F2
Croft Cl. Chipf 138 A1
Croft End Rd. Chipf 138 A1
Croft Field. Chipf 138 A1
Croft Field. Hat 130 A3
Croft La. Chipf 138 A1
Croft La. Letw 12 A1
Croft Meadow. Chipf 138 A1
Croft Rd. Luton 46 A2
Croft Rd. Ware 93 E1
Croft The. Barn 171 F3
Croft The. Chis 141 D3
Croft The. Hod 148 C4
Croft The. Luton 44 B4
Croft The. Wars 94 C2
Croft The. Wel GC 110 C2
Croft Wlk. Hod 148 C4
Crofters End. Saw 97 F2
Crofters Rd. Norwd 174 C3
Crofters. Saw 97 F2
Crofts Path. Heml H 125 D1
Crofts The. Heml H 125 D1
Crofts The. Stot 11 F3
Croftwell. Harp 107 F4
Cromer Cl. L Gad 102 B2
Cromer Rd. Watf 154 B1
Cromer Way. Luton 45 E4
Crompton Rd. Stev 50 A3
Cromwell Ave. Ches 148 A1
Cromwell Cl. Bis St 77 B4
Cromwell Cl. St Alb 128 B4
Cromwell Green. Letw 23 D4
Cromwell Hill. Luton 45 E1
Cromwell Rd. Bor 169 F4
Cromwell Rd. Ches 148 A2
Cromwell Rd. Hert 114 A4
Cromwell Rd. Letw 23 D4
Cromwell Rd. Luton 45 E1
Cromwell Rd. Stev 51 E3
Cromwell Rd. Ware 93 F1
Cromwell Way. Pirt 20 B2
Crooked Mile. Wa Aby 163 E4
Crooked Way. Lo Naz 135 F1
Crookhams. Wel GC 90 A1
Crop Common. Hat 130 A4
Crosby Cl. Luton 45 D1
Cross La. Harp 107 E3
Cross La. Hert 113 D3
Cross Oak Rd. Berk 122 A2
Cross Rd. Ches 162 C3
Cross Rd. Hert 113 E4
Cross Rd. Watf 167 F2
Cross St. Letw 22 C4
Cross St. Luton 63 F4
Cross St. St Alb 127 E2
Cross St. Ware 93 F1
Cross St. Watf 167 E3
Cross Way The. Har 176 C1
Cross Way The. Luton 63 E3
Cross Way. Harp 86 B2
Crossbrook St. Ches 162 B4
Crossbrook. Hat 129 F2
Crossett Green. Heml H 125 E1
Crossfell Rd. Heml H 125 E1
Crossfield Cl. Berk 121 F2
Crossfield Rd. Hod 135 D4
Crossfields. St Alb 141 D4
Crossgates. Stev 50 C3
Crosslands. Cad 62 C2
Crossleys. Letw 11 F1
Crossmead. Watf 167 D2
Crossoaks La. Pot B 157 F3
Crossoaks La. Ridge 157 F3
Crosspath. Radl 156 A2
Crosspaths. Harp 85 E2
Crossway. Pnr 175 D1
Crossway. Wel GC 89 E1
Crossways. Berk 121 F2
Crossways. Heml H 125 E2
Crouch Hall Gdns. Red 106 A3
Crouch Hall La. Red 106 A3
Crouch La. Gofs O 147 E2
Crouchfield. Heml H 124 A1
Crouchfield. Hert 92 B1
Crow Furlong. Hit 34 B4
Crow La. Reed 16 C3
Crowborough Path. Sth Ox 175 E3
Crowland Rd. Luton 46 B3
Crown Cl. Saw 98 B1
Crown Pas. Watf 167 E3
Crown Rd. Bor 170 A4
Crown Rise. Watf 154 B3
Crown St. Red 106 A3
Crown Terr. Bis St 77 D4
Crownfield. Hod 135 D1
Croxdale Rd. Bor 170 A4
Croxley View. Watf 166 C2
Croxton Cl. Luton 45 D4
Crunell's Green. Pres 48 C3
Cubbington Cl. Luton 45 D4
Cubitts Cl. Har Gr 89 F2
Cuckmans Dri. Chis 141 D3
Cuckoo's Nest. Luton 64 A4
Cuffley Ave. Watf 154 B3
Cuffley Cl. Luton 44 C2
Cuffley Ct. Heml H 125 E4
Cuffley Hill. Gofs O 147 D1
Cullera Cl. Norwd 174 C2
Cullings Ct. Wa Aby 163 F3
Culver Rd. St Alb 127 F3
Culverden Rd. Sth Ox 175 D4
Culverhouse Rd. Luton 45 E2
Culworth Cl. Cad 62 C2
Cumberland Cl. Bed 139 F4
Cumberland Cl. Hert 113 E4
Cumberland Ct. St Alb 127 F2
Cumberland Dri. Red 106 A3
Cumberland St. Luton 63 F3
Cumberlow Pl. Heml H 125 E1
Cundalls Rd. Ware 93 F1
Cunningham Ave. Enf 162 C2
Cunningham Ave. St Alb 127 F1
Cunningham Hill Rd. St Alb 128 A1
Cunningham Rd. Ches 148 C2
Cupid Green La. Gt Ga 104 C2
Cupid Green La. Heml H 105 D1
Cupthall Cl. Gt Ha 77 F2
Curam Cl. Berk 122 B2
Curlew Cl. Berk 122 B2
Curlew Cl. Letw 11 F1
Curlew Rd. Luton 45 B3
Currie St. Hert 113 F3
Curtis Cl. Ric 165 D1
Curtis Rd. Heml H 125 E1
Curtis Way. Berk 122 B2
Curzon Rd. Luton 45 E1
Cussons Cl. Ches 148 A1
Cutenhoe Rd. Luton 63 F3
Cutforth Rd. Saw 97 F2
Cuttsfield Terr. Heml H 123 F1
Cuttys La. Stev 50 C3
Cwmbran Ct. Heml H 124 C4
Cygnet Cl. Bor 170 B4
Cygnet Cl. Norwd 174 B2
Cylers Thicket. Welw 89 E3
Cypress Ave. Enf 161 D2
Cypress Cl. Wa Aby 163 E3
Cypress Rd. Har 176 B1
Cypress Wlk. Watf 154 A2

Dacre Cres. Kim 66 B1
Dacre Gdns. Bor 170 B2
Dacre Green. Roystn 7 F3
Dacre Rd. Hit 35 D4
Dagger La. Elst 169 D2
Daggs Dell Rd. Heml H 123 F3
Dagnall Rd. Gt Ga 103 E3
Dagnalls. Letw 22 C1
Dalby Cl. Luton 44 A2
Dale Ave. Bla En 87 D3
Dale Cl. Hit 34 C2
Dale Cl. Pnr 175 D1
Dale Ct. Saw 97 E1
Dale Rd. Luton 63 E4
Dale The. Letw 22 C3
Dale The. Wa Aby 163 F3
Dales Path. Bor 170 B2
Dales Rd. Bor 170 B2
Daleside Dri. Pot B 158 C3
Dalewood. Harp 86 B1
Dalewood. Wel GC 111 E3
Dalkeith Rd. Harp 86 B1
Dallow Rd. Luton 63 D4
Dalroad Ind Est. Luton 63 D4
Dalton Gdns. Bis St 76 C2
Dalton St. St Alb 127 E2
Dalton Way. Whit 66 C4
Daltry Cl. Stev 36 B1
Daltry Rd. Stev 36 B1
Damask Cl. Wes 37 D4
Damask Green Rd. Wes 37 D4
Damask Green. Heml H 123 F1
Dammersey Cl. Mark 83 F2
Dancers End La. Dra B 99 E1
Dancers Hill Rd. Pot B 158 C2
Dancote. Kneb 68 C3
Dane Acres. Bis St 76 B4
Dane Bridge La. Gr Ty 75 D1
Dane Cl. Harp 86 B2
Dane Cl. Stot 11 F4
Dane End La. Hal Gr 37 F3
Dane End Rd. H Cr 72 C2
Dane O'Coys Rd. Bis St 58 C1
Dane Park. Bis St 76 B4
Dane Rd. Luton 45 E1
Dane St. Bis St 77 D4
Danebridge Rd. Gr Ty 75 D1
Danefield Rd. Pirt 20 B2
Danemead. Hod 115 D1
Danes The. Chis 141 E2
Danesbury La. Wl Gr 89 E4
Danesbury Park Rd. Wl Gr 89 E4
Danesbury Park. Hert 113 E4
Danescroft. Letw 12 A1
Danesgate. Stev 50 B3
Danestrete. Stev 50 B3
Daniells. Wel GC 111 D4
Danvers Croft. Tri 100 B3
Danziger Way. Bor 170 B4
Darby Dri. Wa Aby 163 E3
Darby Dri. Wl Gr 68 C2
Darcy Cl. Ches 162 C4
Dark La. Ches 148 A1
Dark La. Harp 107 E4
Dark La. San 15 D1
Dark La. Ware 93 F2
Dark La. Wing 60 B1
Darkes La. Pot B 159 D4
Darley Rd. Bre Gr 47 E1
Darnicle Hill. Ham St 147 D3
Darr's La. Nthch 121 E3
Darrington Rd. Bor 169 F4
Dart The. Heml H 125 D4
Darwin Cl. Heml H 105 D1
Darwin Cl. St Alb 127 F4
Darwin Gdns. Sth Ox 175 E3
Darwin Rd. Stev 51 D3
Dashes The. Harl 117 F1
Datchet Cl. Heml H 125 D4
Datchworth Turn. Heml H 125 E2
Davenham Ave. Norwd 174 C3
Daventer Dri. Stan 176 C2
Davies St. Hert 113 F3
Davis Cres. Pirt 20 B3
Davis' Row. Arl 11 D2
Davison Cl. Ches 148 B2
Davison Dri. Ches 148 B2
Davys Cl. Whea 108 C4
Dawes La. Sar 151 F2
Dawley Ct. Heml H 125 D4
Dawley. Wel GC 89 F1
Dawley. Wel GC 89 F1
Dawlish Cl. Stev 69 E4
Dawlish Rd. Luton 44 C2
Dawson Cl. Henlw 10 B3
Day's Cl. Roystn 7 E3
Dayemead. Wel GC 111 D2
Days Cl. Hat 129 F3
Days Mead. Hat 129 F3
De Havilland Cl. Hat 129 F3
De Havilland Way. Abb L 153 F4
De Vere Wlk. Watf 166 C4
Deacon Cl. St Alb 141 E4
Deacon's Hill Rd. Elst 170 A2
Deacon's Hts. Elst 170 A2
Deacons Cl. Bor 170 A3
Deacons Cl. Pnr 175 D1
Deacons Hill. Watf 167 E2
Deacons Way. Hit 21 E1
Deaconsfield Rd. Heml H 138 B4
Dead Woman's La. Pres 48 B3
Deadman's Ash La. Sar 152 A2
Deakin Cl. Watf 166 C1
Dean Field. Bov 137 D2
Dean The. Wing 60 A2
Dean's Gdns. St Alb 128 A4
Deane Ct. Norwd 174 C1
Deans Cl. Abb L 153 E4
Deans Cl. Tri 100 A2
Deans Furlong. Tri 100 A2
Deans Meadow. Dagn 81 E3
Deanscroft. Kneb 68 C3
Deansway. Heml H 138 C4
Deard's End La. Kneb 68 C3
Deards Wood. Kneb 68 C3
Debenham Rd. Ches 148 A2
Dee The. Heml H 124 C4
Deep Denes. Luton 46 A1
Deepdene. Pot B 158 B4
Deeping Cl. Kneb 68 C2
Deerfield Cl. Ware 93 E1
Deerings The. Harp 107 D2
Deerswood Ave. Hat 130 A2
Deeves Hall La. Shen 157 F3
Deimos Dri. Heml H 125 D3
Delahay Rise. Berk 122 A3
Delamare Rd. Ches 148 C1
Delamere Rd. Bor 170 A4
Delfcroft. Ware 93 E1
Delfield Cl. Cad 62 C2
Delius Cl. Elst 169 E2
Dell Cl. Harp 86 A2
Dell La. Bis St 77 D4
Dell La. L Hal 98 A4
Dell Meadow. Heml H 138 C4
Dell Rd. Enf 162 B1
Dell Rd. Nthch 121 E4
Dell Rd. Watf 154 A1
Dell Rise. Chis 141 D3
Dell Side. Watf 154 A1
Dell The. Bal 23 F3
Dell The. Cad 62 C2
Dell The. Hert 113 E2
Dell The. Luton 46 C1
Dell The. Norwd 174 C4
Dell The. Pnr 175 E1
Dell The. Radl 156 A2
Dell The. Roystn 7 E3
Dell The. St Alb 128 A2
Dell The. Stev 50 C3
Dellcot Cl. Luton 46 A2
Dellcott Cl. Wel GC 110 B4
Dellcroft Way. Harp 107 D3
Dellcut Rd. Heml H 125 D3
Dellfield Ave. Berk 122 A3
Dellfield Cl. Berk 122 A3
Dellfield Cl. Radl 155 F2
Dellfield Cl. Watf 167 D4
Dellfield Ct. Harl 118 B2
Dellfield Rd. Hat 130 A3
Dellfield. St Alb 128 A1
Dellfield. Wad 93 E4
Dellmeadow. Abb L 139 F1
Dellors Cl. Barn 171 E2
Dells The. Bis St 76 C4
Dells The. Heml H 125 D1
Dellsome La. Coln H 143 F4
Dellsome La. Wel Gr 144 A4
Dellsprings. Bun 40 C4
Dellwood Cl. Ric 165 D1
Delmar Ave. Heml H 125 E1
Delmerend La. Fla 84 B1
Delphine Cl. Luton 63 D3
Delta Gain. Watf 175 E4
Demontfort Rise. Ware 93 E2
Denbigh Rd. Luton 45 D1
Denby. Letw 23 D3
Dendridge Cl. Enf 162 A1
Dene La. Ast 51 F1
Dene Rd. Norwd 174 B2
Denes The. Heml H 138 C3
Denewood Cl. Watf 153 F1
Denham Cl. Heml H 125 D4
Denham Cl. Luton 44 C4
Denham La. C St P 172 A1
Denham Way. Bor 170 B4
Denham Way. Map Cr 172 C2
Denmark Cl. Luton 44 C4
Denmark St. Watf 167 D4
Denny Ave. Wa Aby 163 E3
Denny Ct. Bis St 59 D1
Denny's La. Ash Gr 121 F1
Densley Cl. Wel GC 110 B4
Denton Cl. Barn 171 E2
Denton Cl. Luton 44 A2
Denton Rd. Stev 50 C2
Dents Cl. Letw 23 E2
Derby Ave. Har 176 B1
Derby Rd. Luton 44 B1
Derby Rd. Roy 135 E2
Derby Rd. Watf 167 E3
Derby Way. Stev 51 D4
Derwent Ave. Luton 45 D4
Derwent Ave. Pnr 175 F2
Derwent Rd. Harp 85 E2
Derwent Rd. Heml H 125 E1
Derwent Rd. Henlw 10 A2
Derwent Rd. Luton 64 A4
Desborough Cl. Hert 92 B1
Desborough Dri. Tewin 90 B3
Desborough Rd. Hit 35 E4
Desmond Rd. Watf 153 F2
Deva Cl. St Alb 127 D1
Devereux Dri. Watf 153 F1
Devoils La. Bis St 76 C4
Devon Rd. Luton 64 A4
Devon Rd. Watf 167 E4
Devonshire Cl. Stev 69 D4
Devonshire Rd. Harp 86 A1
Devonshire Rd. Pnr 175 F1
Dewars Cl. Welw 89 E3
Dewes Green Rd. Sta Gr 30 C1
Dewgrass Gr. Enf 162 B2
Dewhurst Rd. Ches 148 B1
Dewpond Cl. Stev 50 B4
Dewsbury Rd. Luton 45 E3
Dexter Cl. Luton 31 D1
Dexter Rd. Barn 171 E2
Diamond Rd. Watf 154 A1
Dickens Cl. St Alb 127 E2
Dickens Ct. Heml H 105 D1
Dicket Mead. Welw 89 E3
Dickins Cl. Ham St 148 A3
Dickinson Ave. Cro Gr 166 A2
Dickinson Sq. Cro Gr 166 A2
Dickson. Ham St 147 F2
Dig Dag Hill. Ham St 147 F2
Digswell Hill. Welw 89 D1
Digswell La. Wel GC 89 F1
Digswell Park Rd. Wel GC 89 E2
Digswell Park Rd. Wel GC 89 F2
Digswell Rd. Wel GC 110 B4
Digswell Rise. Wel GC 110 C4
Dimmocks La. Sar 152 A2
Dimsdale Cres. Bis St 77 D3
Dimsdale St. Hert 113 E3
Dinant Link Rd. Hod 135 D4
Dinmore. Bov 137 D2
Dione Rd. Heml H 124 C3
Ditchfield Rd. Hod 115 D1
Ditchling Cl. Luton 46 B2
Ditchmore La. Stev 50 E
Divot Pl. Hert 114 A
Dixies Cl. Ashw 4 E
Dixon Pl. Bun 40 C
Dixons Hill Cl. Wel Gr 144 A
Dixons Hill Rd. Wel Gr 144 E
Dobb's Weir Rd. Roy 135 E
Docklands. Pirt 20 B
Doctors' Commons Rd. Berk 122 A
Dodds La. Heml H 104 C
Dodds La. Pic En 124 B
Dodwood. Wel GC 111 D
Dog Kennel La. Chor 164 C
Dog Kennel La. Hat 130 A
Dog Kennel La. Roy 7 E
Doggetts Way. St Alb 127 E
Dognell Green. Wel GC 110 A
Dolesbury Dri. Wl Gr 89 F
Dollis Brook Wlk. Barn 171 F
Dollis Valley Way. Barn 171 F
Dolphin Sq. Tri 100 A
Dolphin Way. Bis St 77 D
Dolphin Yd. Hert 113 E
Dolphin Yd. St Alb 127 E
Doncaster Cl. Stev 51 E
Doncaster Green. Sth Ox 175 E
Donkey La. Tri 99 F
Donne Cl. Roystn 7 E
Dorchester Ave. Hod 135 D
Dordans Rd. Luton 44 C
Dorel Cl. Luton 45 F
Dormans Cl. Norwd 174 B
Dormer Cl. Barn 171 E
Dormie Cl. St Alb 127 E
Dorrien's Croft. Berk 121 F4
Dorrington Cl. Luton 45 E1
Dorrofield Cl. Cro Gr 166 B2
Dorset Cl. Berk 121 F3
Douglas Ave. Watf 154 C1
Douglas Dri. Stev 51 D4
Douglas Gdns. Berk 122 A3
Douglas House. Ches 148 B2
Douglas Rd. Harp 85 F1
Douglas Rd. Luton 45 D1
Douglas Way. Wel GC 111 E3
Dove Cl. Bis St 76 C2
Dove Cl. Sta Mo 59 F4
Dove Ct. Hat 130 A2
Dove House La. Ken Co 82 B4
Dove La. Pot B 159 E3
Dove Park. Chor 164 B2
Dove Park. Pnr 176 A2
Dovedale Cl. Hare 173 E1
Dovedale. Stev 51 D2
Dovedale. Ware 93 E2
Dovehouse Croft. Harl 118 A1
Dovehouse Hill. Luton 46 A1
Dover Cl. Luton 45 D2
Dover Way. Cro Gr 166 B3
Doverfield. Gofs O 147 E1
Dowling Ct. Heml H 124 B1
Down Edge. Red 105 F3
Down Green La. Whea 108 A4
Downalong. Bus 168 B1
Downedge. St Alb 127 D2
Downes Rd. St Alb 128 A4
Downfield Cl. Hert H 114 B2
Downfield Rd. Ches 162 B4
Downfield Rd. Hert H 114 B3
Downfields. Wel GC 110 A2
Downhall Ley. Bun 40 C4
Downings Wood. Map Cr 172 B3
Downlands. Luton 44 B4
Downlands. Roystn 7 E3
Downlands. Stev 51 E4
Downlands. Wa Aby 163 F3
Downs Rd. Luton 63 E4
Downs The. Hat 130 A2
Downsfield. Hat 130 A1
Downside. Heml H 124 C2
Dragon Rd. Hat 129 F4
Drakes Cl. Ches 148 B2
Drakes Dri. Norwd 174 A1
Drakes Dri. St Alb 128 B1
Drakes Dri. Stev 51 D4
Drapers Way. Stev 50 B4
Drayson Cl. Wa Aby 163 F4
Drayton Ave. Pot B 158 C4
Drayton Rd. Bor 170 A3
Drayton Rd. Luton 44 A2
Driftway The. Heml H 124 C2
Driftwood Ave. Chis 141 D3
Drive The. Barn 171 F3
Drive The. Bla En 87 D4
Drive The. Chor 165 E2
Drive The. Gofs O 147 E2
Drive The. Harl 117 F1
Drive The. Harp 86 A1
Drive The. Hert 113 E4
Drive The. Hod 135 D4
Drive The. Lon C 142 A3
Drive The. Norwd 174 C1
Drive The. Pot B 158 C4
Drive The. Radl 156 A3
Drive The. Saw 97 F1
Drive The. Watf 153 E1
Drive The. Wl Gr 69 D1
Driver's End La. Cod 67 F2
Driveway The. Cuf 146 C2
Driveway The. Heml H 124 A1

mey Gdns. Har 176 C2
op La. Bric 155 E4
overs Way. Hat 130 A4
overs Way. St Alb 127 E2
ummond Dri. Stan 176 C2
ummond Ride. Tri 100 A3
ury La. Hun 95 E1
ycroft. Wel GC 110 C1
yden Cres. Stev 51 E4
yden Rd. Har 176 C1
ysdale Cl. Norwd 174 C2
bbs Knoll Rd. Gu M 1 C3
brae Cl. St Alb 127 D1
chess Cl. Bis St 77 B4
chy Rd. Barn 159 E1
ck La. Benn 52 C2
ck's Hill Rd. Norwd 174 A1
cketts La. Gr Ty 75 E1
cketts Mead. Roy 116 A1
cketts Wharf. Bis St 76 C3
cketts Wood. Thun 93 E4
ckling La. Saw 97 F2
ckmore La. Tri 99 F1
dley Ave. Ches 162 B4
dley Hill Cl. Wl Gr 89 F4
dley St. Luton 63 F4
dswell La. Nthch 121 E4
ugdale Ct. Hit 21 E1
ugdale Hill La. Pot B 158 C4
ugdales. Cro Gr 166 A3
uke St. Hod 135 D4
uke St. Luton 63 F4
uke St. Watf 167 E3
uke's La. Hit 34 C4
ukes Ride. Bis St 76 B4
ukes Way. Berk 122 A3
ulwich Way. Cro Gr 166 A2
umbarton Ave. Ches 162 B3
umfries Cl. Sth Ox 175 D4
umfries St. Luton 63 E3
uncan Cl. Wel GC 110 C3
uncan Way. Bus 167 F4
uncombe Cl. Hert 113 E4
uncombe Cl. Luton 45 E3
Duncombe Rd. Hert 113 E4
uncombe Rd. Nthch 121 F3
Dundale Rd. Tri 100 A2
Dunham's La. Letw 23 E3
Dunlin Rd. Heml H 124 C4
unlin. Letw 11 F1
Dunmow Ct. Luton 45 E1
Dunmow Rd. Birhr 77 F4
unmow Rd. Bis St 77 E4
Dunn Cl. Stev 50 C2
Dunnock Cl. Bor 170 A3
Dunny La. Chipf 151 F4
Dunny La. Sar 151 F3
Dunsby Rd. Luton 45 D3
Dunsley Pl. Tri 100 A2
Dunsmore Cl. Bus 168 B2
Dunsmore Rd. Luton 63 E3
Dunsmore Way. Bus 168 B2
Dunstable Cl. Luton 45 D1
Dunstable Pl. Luton 63 E4
Dunstable Rd. Cad 62 B2
Dunstable Rd. Dagn 81 E4
Dunstable Rd. Luton 44 B1
Dunstable Rd. Red 106 A4
Dunstable Rd. Stu 82 A3
Dunster Cl. Barn 171 E3
Dunster Cl. Hare 173 D1
Dunster Rd. Heml H 105 D1
Dunsters Mead. Wel G C 111 D2
Dunston Hill. Tri 100 A2
Durban Rd E. Watf 167 D3
Durban Rd W. Watf 167 D3
Durbar Rd. Luton 45 D1
Durham Cl. Saw 97 E1
Durham Cl. Sta Ab 115 D3
Durham Rd. Bor 170 B3
Durham Rd. Luton 64 A4
Durham Rd. Stev 37 D1
Durler Gdns. Luton 63 E3
Durrants Dri. Cro Gr 166 B3
Durrants Hill Rd. Heml H 138 B4
Durrants La. Nthch 121 F3
Durrants Rd. Berk 121 F3
Dury Rd. Barn 171 F4
Duxford Cl. Luton 45 D4
Duxons Turn. Heml H 125 D2
Dwight Rd. Watf 166 B1
Dyes La. Lan 49 F2
Dyes La. Stev 50 A2
Dyke La. Whea 108 C4
Dylan Cl. Elst 169 E1
Dymoke Green. St Alb 128 A4
Dymokes Way. Hod 115 D1
Dyrham La. Pot B 158 A2
Dysons Cl. Ches 162 B3

E Circular Rd. Luton 64 B4
Eagle Cl. Luton 44 A2
Eagle Ct. Hert 114 A4
Eagle Way. Hat 130 A2
Ealing Cl. Bor 170 B4
Earl St. Watf 167 E3
Earls Cl. Bis St 76 B3
Earls Hill Gdns. Roystn 7 E3
Earls La. Pot B 157 F3
Earls La. Ridge 157 F4
Earlsmead. Letw 22 C2
Easington Rd. Dan En 71 F4
Easingwood Gdns. Luton 62 C4
East Burrowfield. Wel GC 110 B2
East Cl. Chis 141 D3
East Cl. Hit 22 A1
East Cl. Stev 50 C3
East Comm. Harp 107 E4
East Dri. Lon C 142 A3
East Dri. Norwd 174 C4
East Dri. Saw 97 F1
East Dri. St Alb 128 C2
East Dri. Watf 154 A2
East End Way. Pnr 175 F1
East Flint. Heml H 123 F2
East Gate. Harl 117 E1
East Green. Heml H 139 D3
East Hill. Luton 45 D3
East La. Abb L 140 A1
East La. Bed 139 F2
East La. Whea 87 E1
East Lodge La. Enf 160 C2
East Mead. Wel GC 111 D2
East Mount. Whea 87 E1
East Park. Harl 118 B2
East Park. Saw 97 F1
East Rd. Bis St 77 D4
East Rd. Enf 162 B1
East Rd. Harl 118 A2
East Reach. Stev 51 D1
East Ridgeway. Cuf 146 C2
East Riding. Tewin 90 B3
East St. Heml H 124 B2
East St. Lily 32 B1
East St. Ware 93 E1
East View. Barn 171 F3
East View. Ess 131 F3
East View. St Ipp 35 E1
East Way. Wa Aby 163 E2
East Wlk. Harl 117 E1
Eastbourne Ave. Stev 50 A3
Eastbrook Rd. Wa Aby 163 F3
Eastbury Ave. Norwd 174 C3
Eastbury Cl. Norwd 174 C3
Eastbury Ct. St Alb 127 F2
Eastbury Pl. Norwd 174 C3
Eastbury Rd. Norwd 174 C2
Eastbury Rd. Watf 167 E2
Eastcheap. Letw 22 C3
Eastcote Dri. Harp 107 E3
Eastcott Cl. Luton 46 B1
Eastern Ave. Ches 162 C3
Eastern Ave. Henlw 10 B2
Eastern Way. Letw 12 A1
Eastfield Ave. Watf 167 E4
Eastfield Cl. Luton 46 B2
Eastfield Ct. St Alb 128 B3
Eastfield Par. Pot B 159 E4
Eastfield Rd. Ches 162 C4
Eastfield Rd. Enf 162 B1
Eastfield Rd. Roystn 7 F3
Eastgate. Stev 50 C3
Eastglade. Norwd 174 C3
Eastholm Green. Letw 23 D4
Eastholm. Letw 23 D4
Eastlea Ave. Watf 154 C1
Eastman Way. Heml H 125 D3
Eastmoor Park. Harp 107 E3
Eastnor. Bov 137 D2
Easton Gdns. Bor 170 C3
Eastor. Wel GC 90 A1
Eastwick Cres. Ric 172 C4
Eastwick Hall La. East 117 D3
Eastwick Rd. East 117 D2
Eastwick Rd. H Wy 117 F3
Eastwick Row. Heml H 125 D1
Eastwood Ct. Heml H 125 D2
Eaton Gate. Norwd 174 B2
Eaton Green Rd. Luton 46 C1
Eaton Rd. Heml H 125 D3
Eaton Rd. St Alb 128 A2
Eaton Valley Rd. Luton 46 A1
Ebberns Rd. Heml H 138 C4
Ebenezer St. Luton 63 E3
Ebury App. Ric 165 E1
Ebury Cl. Norwd 174 B3
Ebury Rd. Ric 165 E1
Ebury Rd. Watf 167 E3
Echo Hill. Roystn 7 E3
Eddy St. Berk 122 A3
Edenhall Cl. Heml H 125 E1
Edens Cl. Bis St 77 D4
Edens Mount. Saw 97 F2
Edgars Ct. Wel GC 110 C3
Edgbaston Rd. Sth Ox 175 D4
Edgcott Cl. Luton 31 D1
Edgecote Cl. Cad 62 C2
Edgehill Gdns. Luton 44 B4
Edgewood Dri. Luton 46 B3
Edgeworth Cl. Stev 51 E1
Edgware Way (Watford By-Ps). Elst 169 E1
Edgwarebury La. Elst 169 F1
Edinburgh Ave. Chor 165 D2
Edinburgh Cres. Ches 162 C3
Edinburgh Pl. Harl 118 A2
Edinburgh Sq. Knee 2 A3
Edinburgh Way. Harl 117 F2
Edison Rd. Stev 51 D3
Edkins Cl. Luton 45 F3
Edlyn Cl. Berk 121 F3
Edmonds Dri. Stev 51 E2
Edmund Beaufort Dri. St Alb 127 F3
Edmunds Rd. Hertng 112 C4
Edridge Cl. Bus 168 B2
Edulf Rd. Bor 170 A4
Edward Amey Cl. Watf 154 B2
Edward Cl. Abb L 153 F4
Edward Cl. St Alb 127 F1
Edward Ct. Wa Aby 163 F3
Edward St. Luton 45 F1
Edwyn Cl. Barn 171 E2
Egdon Dri. Luton 45 E3
Egerton Rd. Berk 122 A3
Eight Acres. Tri 100 A2
Eighth Ave. Luton 44 B4
Eisenberg Cl. Bal 13 D1
Elaine Gdns. Cad 63 D1
Elbow La. Hert H 114 A1
Elbow La. Stev 69 D4
Eldefield. Letw 22 B4
Elder Ct. Bus 176 C4
Elder Rd. Ware 93 F2
Elder Way. Stev 50 B2
Elderbeck Cl. Ches 148 A1
Elderberry Cl. Luton 46 A2
Elderberry Dri. Hit 35 D2
Elderberry Way. Watf 154 A2
Elderfield. Harl 118 B2
Eldon Ave. Bor 170 A4
Eldon Rd. Luton 44 B1
Eldon Rd. Roy 135 E2
Eleanor Ave. St Alb 127 E3
Eleanor Cross Rd. Ches 162 C3
Eleanor Gdns. Barn 171 E2
Eleanor Rd. Ches 162 C3
Eleanor Rd. Hert 113 E4
Eleanor Way. Ches 162 C3
Eleanor Way. Wa Aby 163 D3
Elfrida Rd. Watf 167 E2
Elgar Cl. Elst 169 E1
Elgin Dri. Norwd 174 C2
Elgin Rd. Ches 148 B1
Elgin Rd. Hod 148 C4
Elgood Ave. Norwd 175 D2
Eliot Rd. Roystn 7 E4
Eliot Rd. Stev 51 E3
Elizabeth Cl. Barn 171 E3
Elizabeth Cl. Lo Naz 149 E4
Elizabeth Cl. St Alb 128 B3
Elizabeth Ct. Watf 153 F1
Elizabeth Dri. Tri 100 A3
Elizabeth Rd. Bis St 76 C3
Elizabeth St. Luton 63 E3
Elizabeth Way. Harl 117 D1
Ellenborough Cl. Bis St 76 B3
Ellenbrook Cres. Hat 129 E3
Ellenbrook La. Hat 129 E2
Ellenhall Cl. Luton 45 E1
Ellerdine Cl. Luton 45 D2
Ellesborough Cl. Sth Ox 175 E3
Ellesfield. Welw 89 D3
Ellesmere Gr. Barn 171 F2
Ellesmere Rd. Berk 122 B2
Ellice. Letw 23 D2
Ellingham Cl. Heml H 125 D3
Ellingham Rd. Heml H 124 C2
Ellis Ave. Stev 50 C4
Elliswick Rd. Harp 86 A1
Ellwood Gdns. Watf 154 A3
Elm Ave. Cad 62 C2
Elm Ave. Watf 167 F1
Elm Cl. Wa Aby 163 E3
Elm Dri. Ches 148 C2
Elm Dri. Hat 130 A2
Elm Dri. St Alb 128 B2
Elm Gdns. Enf 161 E1
Elm Gdns. Wel GC 110 A3
Elm Gr. Berk 122 B2
Elm Green. Heml H 123 F3
Elm Grove. Bis St 77 D4
Elm Grove. Watf 154 A1
Elm Park Rd. Pnr 175 E1
Elm Park. Bal 23 F4
Elm Rd. Barn 171 F3
Elm Rd. Bis St 76 C4
Elm Rd. Hod 135 D3
Elm Rd. Ware 94 A1
Elm Terr. Har 176 B1
Elm Tree Wlk. Tri 100 A3
Elm Way. Ric 165 D1
Elm Wlk. Radl 155 F2
Elm Wlk. Roystn 7 F4
Elm Wlk. Stev 51 D2
Elmbank Ave. Barn 171 E3
Elmbridge. Harl 118 C2
Elmbrook Cl. Bis St 76 C2
Elmcote Way. Cro Gr 165 F2
Elmfield Cl. Pot B 158 C3
Elmfield Rd. Pot B 158 C3
Elmhurst Cl. Bis St 76 C4
Elmhurst Rd. Enf 162 B1
Elmoor Ave. Welw 89 D3
Elmoor Cl. Welw 89 D2
Elmore Rd. Luton 46 A1
Elmroyd Ave. Pot B 158 C3
Elmroyd Cl. Pot B 158 C3
Elms Rd. Har 176 C2
Elms The. Cod 67 F1
Elmscroft Gdns. Pot B 158 C4
Elmside Wlk. Hit 34 C4
Elmside. Ken Co 82 C4
Elmtree Ave. Cok Gr 46 C2
Elmwood Ave. Bal 23 F4
Elmwood Ave. Bor 170 A3
Elmwood Cres. Luton 45 F2
Elmwood. Saw 97 F1
Elmwood. Wel GC 110 A3
Elsinge Rd. Enf 162 B2
Elstree Hill N. Elst 169 E2
Elstree Hill S. Elst 169 E1
Elstree Rd. Bus 168 C1
Elstree Rd. Heml H 105 D1
Elstree Way. Bor 170 B4
Elton Ave. Barn 171 F2
Elton Park. Watf 167 D4
Elton Rd. Hert 113 E4
Elton Way. Bus 168 A4
Elveden Cl. Luton 45 F3
Ely Cl. Hat 129 F3
Ely Cl. Stev 37 D1
Ely Gdns. Bor 170 B2
Ely Pl. Wel GC 110 C3
Ely Rd. St Alb 128 A1
Ely Way. Luton 44 B2
Embleton Rd. Sth Ox 175 D4
Emerald Rd. Luton 44 A2
Emerton Cl. Nthch 121 F4
Emerton Garth. Nthch 121 F4
Emma's Cres. Sta Ab 115 D2
Emmanuel Lodge. Ches 148 B1
Emmanuel Rd. Norwd 174 C2
Emperor's Gate. Stev 51 E4
Empress Rd. Luton 44 C2
Endeavour Rd. Ches 148 C2
Enderby Rd. Luton 45 E3
Enderley Cl. Har 176 B1
Enderley Rd. Har 176 B1
Endersby Rd. Barn 171 E2
Endymion Rd. Hat 130 B3
Englefield. Luton 45 F2
Englehurst. Harp 86 B1
Enid Cl. Bri Wd 154 C4
Ennerdale Cl. St Alb 128 A1
Ennis Cl. Harp 107 E3
Ennismore Cl. Letw 23 E2
Enslow Cl. Cad 62 C2
Enterprise Centre The. Stev 50 A4
Enterprise Way. Luton 45 D4
Epping Green. Heml H 125 D4
Epping Way. Luton 44 B4
Ereswell Rd. Luton 45 D4
Erin Cl. Luton 45 D1
Ermine Cl. Ches 162 A4
Ermine Cl. Roystn 7 E4
Ermine Cl. St Alb 127 D1
Ermine Ct. Bun 40 C4
Ermine St. Thun 93 E4
Escot Way. Barn 171 E2
Esdaile La. Hod 135 D3
Eskdale Ct. Heml H 124 C3
Eskdale. Lon C 142 C2
Essendon Gdns. Wel GC 110 C3
Essex Cl. Luton 63 F3
Essex La. Abb L 153 E3
Essex Mead. Heml H 105 D1
Essex Rd. Bor 170 A3
Essex Rd. Hod 135 E3
Essex Rd. Stev 50 B4
Essex Rd. Watf 167 D4
Essex St. St Alb 127 F2
Estcourt Rd. Watf 167 E3
Ethelred Cl. Wel GC 110 C3
Etna Rd. St Alb 127 E2
Europa Rd. Heml H 124 C3
Euston Ave. Watf 166 C2
Evan's Cl. Cro Gr 166 A2
Evans Ave. Watf 153 F2
Evans Gr. St Alb 128 B4
Evedon Cl. Luton 44 C3
Evelyn Dri. Pnr 175 E2
Evelyn Rd. Dun 44 A1
Everard Cl. St Alb 127 E1
Everest Cl. Arl 11 D3
Everest Way. Heml H 125 D2
Evergreen Cl. Wl Gr 69 D1
Evergreen Rd. Ware 93 F2
Evergreen Way. Luton 45 D4
Everlasting La. St Alb 127 E3
Evron Pl. Hert 113 E3
Exchange Rd. Stev 50 C3
Exchange Rd. Watf 167 D3
Exchange Rd. Watf 167 D3
Exchange Yard. Hit 34 C4
Exeter Cl. Stev 37 D1
Exton Ave. Luton 46 A1
Eynsford Ct. Hit 34 C3
Eywood Rd. St Alb 127 E1

Faggots Cl. Radl 156 B2
Fair Cl. Bus 168 A1
Fair Oak Dri. Luton 45 F2
Fair View. Pot B 145 D1
Fairacre Ct. Norwd 174 C2
Fairacre. Heml H 138 C4
Fairacres Cl. Pot B 158 C3
Fairburn Cl. Bor 170 A4
Faircross Way. St Alb 128 A3
Fairfax Ave. Luton 44 B4
Fairfax Rd. Hert 113 F4
Fairfield Ave. Sth Ox 175 E4
Fairfield Cl. Harp 86 B1
Fairfield Cl. Radl 155 F1
Fairfield Dri. Hod 148 C4
Fairfield Rd. Hod 135 D4
Fairfield Way. Hit 35 E4
Fairfield Wlk. Ches 148 C2
Fairfield. Bun 40 C3
Fairfolds. Watf 154 C2
Fairford Ave. Luton 45 F2
Fairgreen Rd. Cad 62 C2
Fairhaven Cres. Sth Ox 175 D4
Fairhaven. Pk St 141 E2
Fairlands Way. Stev 50 B3
Fairlawns. Pnr 175 E1
Fairlawns. Watf 153 F1
Fairley Way. Ches 148 A2
Fairmead Ave. Harp 107 E4
Fairseat Cl. Har 176 C4
Fairthorn Cl. Tri 99 F2
Fairview Dri. Watf 153 F2
Fairview Rd. Stev 50 A3
Fairway Ave. Bor 170 A4
Fairway Cl. Chis 141 E2
Fairway Cl. Harp 107 D3
Fairway The. Abb L 153 E4
Fairway The. Norwd 174 C3
Fairway. Bis St 77 E3
Fairway. Gt Am 114 B4
Fairway. Heml H 138 C4
Fairway. Saw 97 F1
Fairways. Ches 148 B3
Fairways. Wa Aby 163 F3
Falcon Cl. Hat 130 A2
Falcon Cl. Norwd 174 C2
Falcon Cl. Saw 97 E1
Falcon Cl. Stev 51 E1
Falcon Ridge. Berk 122 B2
Falcon Way. Watf 154 C3
Falcon Way. Wel G C 110 C4
Falconer Rd. Bus 168 A2
Falconers Field. Harp 85 F2
Falconers Park. Saw 97 E1
Falconers Rd. Luton 46 A1
Falkirk Gdns. Sth Ox 175 E3
Falkland Rd. Barn 171 F4
Fallowfield Cl. Hare 173 E1
Fallowfield Wlk. Heml H 124 A3
Fallowfield. Luton 45 E2
Fallowfield. Stev 51 E2
Fallowfield. Wel GC 89 F1
Fallows Green. Harp 86 A2
Falstaff Gdns. St Alb 141 E4
Falstone Green. Luton 46 C1
Fanhams Hall Rd. Ware 93 F2
Fanhams Rd. Ware 93 F1
Fanshaw Ct. Hert 113 E4
Fanshawe Cres. Ware 93 E1
Fanshawe St. Hert 113 D4
Fanshaws La. Bric 133 E3
Fantail La. Tri 99 F2
Far End. Hat 130 A1
Faraday Cl. Watf 166 B2
Faraday Rd. Stev 51 D3
Faringdon Rd. Luton 44 B2
Faringford Cl. Pot B 159 E4
Farland Rd. Heml H 125 D2
Farley Farm Rd. Luton 63 D3
Farley Hill. Luton 63 E3
Farm Ave. Harp 85 E2
Farm Cl. Barn 171 E2
Farm Cl. Bor 156 B1
Farm Cl. Ches 148 B1
Farm Cl. Cuf 146 C2
Farm Cl. Hertng 113 D3
Farm Cl. Letw 12 A1
Farm Cl. Stev 50 C2
Farm Cl. Wel GC 110 B3
Farm Green. Luton 63 E3
Farm Hill Rd. Wa Aby 163 E3
Farm La. Chor 165 E3
Farm La. Stand 73 D4
Farm Pl. Berk 121 F3
Farm Rd. Chor 164 A2
Farm Rd. Norwd 174 B3
Farm Rd. Nwml E 85 D4
Farm Rd. St Alb 128 A2
Farm Way. Bus 168 A3
Farm Way. Hat 130 B4
Farm Way. Norwd 174 C3
Farmbrook. Luton 45 E4
Farmers Cl. Watf 154 A3
Farmhouse Cl. Ches 148 C3
Farmstead Rd. Har 176 B1
Farnham Cl. Bov 137 D2
Farnham Cl. Saw 97 E1
Farquhar St. Hert 113 E4
Farr's La. Nwml E 65 D1
Farraline Rd. Watf 167 D3
Farrant Way. Bor 169 F4
Farrer Top. Mark 83 F3
Farriday Cl. St Alb 127 F4
Farriers Cl. Bal 12 C1
Farriers Cl. Cod 67 F1
Farriers End. Ches 148 C3
Farriers Way. Bor 170 B2
Farriers. Gt Am 115 D3
Farringford Cl. Chis 141 D3
Farthing Dri. Letw 23 E2
Farthings The. Heml H 124 A2

Faverolle Green. Ches 148 B2
Faversham Cl. Tri 100 A2
Fawcett Rd. Stev 51 D4
Fawkon Wlk. Hod 135 D3
Fawn Ct. Hat 130 B4
Fay Green. Abb L 153 E3
Fayerfield. P Bar 159 E4
Feacey Down. Heml H 124 A3
Fearney Mead. Ric 165 D1
Fearnley Rd. Wel GC 110 B3
Fearnley St. Watf 167 D3
Fears Green. San 15 E2
Feather Dell. Hat 130 A3
Featherbed La. Fel 138 A4
Featherbed La. Heml H 138 B4
Featherston Rd. Stev 51 E2
Featherstone Gdns. Bor 170 B3
Federal Way. Watf 167 E4
Felden Cl. Watf 154 B3
Felden Dri. Fel 138 A4
Felden La. Fel 138 A4
Feldon Cl. Pnr 175 F2
Felix Ave. Luton 46 A1
Fell Path. Bor 170 B2
Fellowes La. Coln H 143 F4
Fellowes Way. Stev 51 D1
Fells Cl. Hit 34 C4
Felmersham Ct. Luton 63 D4
Felmersham Rd. Luton 63 D4
Felmongers. Harl 118 A1
Felstead Cl. Luton 45 F2
Felstead Rd. Ches 162 C4
Felstead Way. Luton 45 F2
Felton Cl. Bor 156 C1
Felton Cl. Ches 148 C3
Felton Cl. Luton 46 B1
Fen End. Stot 11 F4
Fennycroft Rd. Heml H 124 C4
Fensom's Alley. Heml H 124 B2
Fensom's Cl. Heml H 124 B2
Fenwick Cl. Luton 45 D3
Fermor Cres. Luton 46 B1
Fern Cl. Hod 148 C4
Fern Dells. Hat 129 F2
Fern Dri. Heml H 124 C1
Fern Gr. Wel GC 89 E1
Fern Way. Watf 154 A2
Ferndale Rd. Enf 162 C1
Ferndale Rd. Luton 63 D4
Ferndene. Bri Wd 154 C4
Ferndown Cl. Pnr 175 F2
Ferndown Rd. Sth Ox 175 E3
Ferndown. Norwd 175 D1
Fernecroft. St Alb 141 E4
Fernheath. Luton 31 D1
Fernhills. Abb L 153 E3
Fernleigh Ct. Har 176 A1
Fernleys. St Alb 128 B3
Ferns Cl. Enf 162 C2
Fernville La. Heml H 124 B2
Ferny Hill. Barn 159 F1
Ferrars Cl. Luton 44 A1
Ferrers La. Whea 108 A3
Ferrier Rd. Stev 51 E3
Ferryhills Cl. Sth Ox 175 E4
Feryngs Cl. Harl 118 B2
Fesants Croft. Harl 118 A2
Fetherstone Cl. Pot B 159 E4
Fiddle Bridge La. Hat 129 F3
Fidler Pl. Bus 168 A2
Field Cl. Harp 107 E4
Field Cres. Roystn 7 F4
Field End Cl. Luton 46 B2
Field End Cl. Watf 167 F1
Field Fare Green. Luton 44 A3
Field House Ct. Harp 86 A1
Field La. Letw 22 C2
Field Rd. Heml H 125 D2
Field Rd. Watf 167 F2
Field View Rd. Pot B 159 D3
Field View Rise. Bri Wd 140 C1
Field View. Barn 171 D3
Field Way. Bov 137 D2
Field Way. Hod 115 E1
Field Way. Ric 165 D1
Field's Ct. Pot B 159 E3
Fieldfare. Letw 11 F1
Fieldgate Rd. Luton 44 B1
Fieldings Rd. Ches 148 C1
Fields End La. Heml H 123 F3
Fields End. Tri 100 A3
Fieldway. Berk 122 B1
Fieldway. Sta Ab 115 D2
Fieldway. Wigg 100 B1
Fifth Ave. Harl 117 E1
Fifth Ave. Letw 23 E3
Fifth Ave. Watf 154 B2
Figtree Mill. Heml H 124 B2
Filey Cl. Stev 50 A4
Filmer Rd. Luton 44 C2
Finch Cl. Hat 130 A2
Finch Cl. Luton 44 A2
Finch La. Bus 168 A3
Finch Rd. Berk 122 A2
Finchdale. Heml H 124 A2
Finches The. Hit 35 D4
Finley Rd. Harp 86 B2
Finsbury Rd. Luton 44 B3
Finucane Rise. Bus 176 B4
Finway Rd. Heml H 125 D4

Finway. Luton 62 C4
Fir Cl. Stev 50 C1
Fir Station Alley. Barn 171 F4
Fir Tree Cl. Heml H 125 D1
Fir Tree Ct. Elst 169 F3
Fir Tree Hill. Cha Cr 153 D1
Firbank Dri. Watf 167 F1
Firbank Rd. St Alb 127 F4
Firecrest. Letw 11 F1
Firlands. Bis St 76 C3
Firs Cl. Hat 130 A2
Firs Cl. Hit 34 B4
Firs Dri. Bla En 87 E3
Firs La. Pot B 159 D3
Firs The. Ham St 147 F2
Firs The. St Alb 142 A4
Firs The. Wel GC 89 E1
Firs The. Wigg 100 B2
Firs Wlk. Norwd 174 B2
Firs Wlk. Tewin 90 C3
First Ave. Harl 117 F1
First Ave. Watf 154 B2
Firway Cl. Wl Gr 89 F4
Firway. Wl Gr 89 F4
Firwood Ave. St Alb 128 C2
Fish Hill. Roystn 7 E3
Fish St. Red 106 A3
Fish Street Farm. Red 106 A3
Fisher Cl. Kin L 139 D1
Fisher Rd. Har 176 C1
Fisher's Green Rd. Stev 50 A4
Fishers Cl. Ches 163 D3
Fishers Cl. Puc 55 E2
Fishers Green. Stev 36 A1
Fishers Mead. Puc 55 E2
Fishery Pas. Heml H 124 A1
Fishery Rd. Heml H 124 A1
Fishponds Rd. Hit 34 C4
Fishpool St. St Alb 127 E2
Fitzjohn Ave. Barn 171 F3
Fitzroy Ave. Luton 45 D2
Fitzwarin Cl. Luton 44 C4
Fitzwilliam Ct. Harl 118 C2
Five Acre Wlk. Wel GC 110 C3
Five Acres Ave. Bri Wd 140 C1
Five Acres. Lon C 142 B3
Five Acres. Sta M 59 F4
Five Oaks. Cad 62 C2
Five Springs. Luton 44 C3
Flags The. Heml H 125 D2
Flagstaff Rd. Wa Aby 163 D3
Flamstead End Rd. Ches 148 A2
Flamsteadbury La. Red 106 A2
Flash La. Enf 161 E2
Flatfield Rd. Heml H 125 D1
Flaunden Bottom. Lat 150 B2
Flaunden Hill. Flau 151 D3
Flaunden La. Bov 137 F2
Flaunden La. Fel 138 A3
Flaunden La. Flau 151 D4
Flavian Cl. St Alb 126 C1
Flax Mews. Mark 83 F3
Flecker Cl. Stan 176 C3
Fleet The. Roystn 7 E3
Fleetwood Way. Sth Ox 175 E3
Fleetwood. Letw 23 D2
Fleming Cl. Ham St 148 A3
Fleming Cres. Hertng 113 D3
Fletcher Way. Heml H 124 B3
Flexley Wood. Wel GC 90 A1
Flinders Cl. St Alb 128 A3
Flinders Cl. Stev 51 E3
Flint Cl. Luton 44 C4
Flint Rd. Letw 23 E4
Flint Way. St Alb 127 E4
Flora Gr. St Alb 127 F1
Floral Dri. Lon C 142 B3
Florence Ave. Luton 44 B3
Florence Cl. Watf 154 A2
Florence St. Hit 34 C4
Florida Cl. Bus 168 B1
Flowers Ind Est. Luton 63 F3
Fold Croft. Harl 117 D1
Foldingshott. Dat 69 E2
Follett Dri. Abb L 153 F4
Folly Ave. St Alb 127 E2
Folly Cl. Hit 35 D3
Folly Cl. Radl 155 F2
Folly Fields. Whea 87 D1
Folly La. Cad 62 C2
Folly La. St Alb 127 E2
Folly Pathway. Radl 155 F2
Folly The. Bun 40 B4
Folly The. Hert 113 E3
Folly View. Sta Ab 115 D2
Fontmell Cl. St Alb 127 F3
Fontwell Cl. Har 176 B2
Football Cl. Bal 12 C1
Forbes Ave. Pot B 159 E4
Ford Cl. Bus 168 B3
Ford Hill. L Had 75 D4
Ford St. Brag 55 F3
Fordham Cl. Ashw 4 B3
Fordham Rd. Roystn 7 F3
Fordwich Cl. Hertng 113 D3
Fordwich Mill. Hertng 113 D3
Fordwich Rd. Wel GC 110 B3
Fordwich Rise. Hertng 113 D3
Fore St. Harl 118 B2
Fore St. Hat 130 B3

Fore St. Hert 113 E3
Fore St. Wes 24 A1
Forebury Ave. Saw 97 F1
Forebury Cres. Saw 97 F1
Forebury The. Saw 97 F1
Forefield. Chis 141 D2
Forelands Pl. Saw 97 F2
Forest Ave. Heml H 124 B1
Forest Rd. Ches 148 B1
Forest Rd. Enf 162 C2
Forest Rd. Watf 154 A3
Forest Row. Stev 50 C1
Forest Wlk. Bus 167 F4
Foresters Cl. Ham St 147 F2
Foresthall Rd. Birhr 59 F2
Forge Cl. Chipf 152 A4
Forge Cl. Hit 34 C4
Forge End. Chis 141 D3
Forge La. Norwd 174 C2
Forge La. Welw 89 E3
Forres Cl. Hod 135 D4
Forrest Cres. Luton 46 A2
Forresters Dri. Wel GC 111 E3
Fortnums Acre. Stan 176 C2
Fortune La. Elst 169 E2
Forty Hill. Enf 161 F1
Forum The. Stev 50 B3
Fosman Cl. Hit 34 B4
Foster Cl. Stev 36 B1
Foster Dri. Hit 35 D3
Foster Rd. Heml H 124 A1
Foston Cl. Luton 44 C3
Fotherley Rd. Ric 172 C4
Founceley Ave. Dan En 71 F4
Fountain Pl. Wa Aby 163 E3
Fountain's Rd. Luton 45 E2
Four Acres The. Saw 98 A1
Four Acres. Stev 50 C4
Four Acres. Wel GC 110 C2
Four Limes. Whea 108 B4
Four Tubs The. Bus 168 B1
Fouracres Wlk. Heml H 138 C4
Fouracres. Letw 23 D2
Fourth Ave. Harl 117 E1
Fourth Ave. Letw 23 E4
Fourth Ave. Luton 44 B4
Fourth Ave. Watf 154 B2
Fovant Cl. Harp 107 E3
Fowley Cl. Ches 162 C3
Fowlmere Rd. Gt Ch 9 F4
Fox Alley. Watf 167 E2
Fox Cl. Bus 168 A3
Fox Cl. Elst 169 E2
Fox Cl. Wigg 100 B2
Fox Cnr. Gu M 1 C3
Fox Hill Rd. Gu M 1 C3
Fox Hill. Gu M 1 C3
Fox La. Ther 15 F4
Fox Rd. Stev 50 C2
Fox Rd. Wigg 100 B1
Foxbury Cl. Luton 45 E3
Foxcroft. St Alb 128 A1
Foxdell. Norwd 174 B2
Foxdells La. Bis St 58 C1
Foxdells. Bir Gr 112 B2
Foxes Cl. Hert 114 A3
Foxes Dr. Ches 148 A1
Foxfield Cl. Norwc 174 C2
Foxfield. Stev 51 E2
Foxglove Bank. Roystn 7 F3
Foxglove Cl. Hat 130 A2
Foxglove Way. Wl Gr 89 F4
Foxgloves The. Heml H 123 F1
Foxgrove Path. Sth Ox 175 E3
Foxhill. Luton 45 F3
Foxhill. Watf 154 A2
Foxholes Ave. Hert 113 F3
Foxhollows. Hat 130 A4
Foxley Dri. Bis St 77 D4
Foxley Gr. Har Gr 89 F2
Foxleys. Watf 175 F4
Foxton Rd. Hod 135 D3
Frampton Rd. Pot B 145 E1
Frampton St. Hert 113 E3
Francis Ave. St Alb 127 E3
Francis Cl. Hit 35 D3
Francis Rd. Hin 3 E3
Francis Rd. Ware 93 E1
Francis Rd. Watf 167 D3
Francis St. Luton 63 E4
Frank Martin Ct. Ches 148 A1
Frankland Cl. Watf 166 A1
Frankland Rd. Cro Gr 166 A2
Franklin Ave. Ches 148 A1
Franklin Cl. Coln H 129 F1
Franklin Cl. Pirt 20 B2
Franklin Gdns. Hit 22 A1
Franklin Rd. Watf 167 D4
Franklin's Rd. Stev 50 B4
Franks Cl. Henlw 10 A2
Fraser Rd. Ches 148 C2
Fred Millard Ct. Stev 50 C3
Frederick St. Luton 45 F1
Freeman Ave. Luton 45 D4
Freemans Cl. Hit 21 E1
Freewaters Cl. Ick 21 F2
Freman Dri. Bun 40 B4
French Horn La. Hat 130 A3
French Row. St Alb 127 E2
French's Cl. Sta Ab 115 D2

Frensham Dri. Hit 22 B1
Frensham. Ham St 148 A2
Freshwater Cl. Luton 44 C4
Freshwaters. Harl 117 F1
Fretherne Rd. Wel GC 110 B3
Friars Cl. Luton 63 D3
Friars Field. Nthch 121 F4
Friars Rd. Brag 56 A4
Friars Rd. Wes 24 A1
Friars Way. Bus 167 F4
Friars Way. Kin L 139 D1
Friars Way. Luton 63 D3
Friars Wlk. Tri 100 A2
Friars Wood. Bis St 77 E4
Friarscroft. Hod 135 D2
Friday Furlong. Hit 34 B4
Friedburg Ave. Bis St 76 B2
Friendless La. Fla 83 F2
Friesian Cl. Luton 44 A2
Frimley Rd. Heml H 123 F2
Fringewood Cl. Norwd 174 A1
Frinton Cl. Sth Ox 175 D4
Friston Green. Luton 46 B1
Frithsden Copse. Pop En 122 B4
Frithwood Ave. Norwd 174 C2
Frobisher Dri. Stev 51 D4
Frobisher Rd. St Alb 128 B1
Froghall La. Wal 38 A1
Frogmoor Ct. Ric 173 E4
Frogmoor La. Ric 173 E4
Frogmore Hill. Ast 70 A4
Frogmore Rd. Heml H 138 B4
Frogmore St. Tri 100 A2
Frogmore. Fro 141 F2
Frogs Hall La. Hault 53 F2
Frome Cl. Luton 44 C2
Frome Sq. Heml H 125 D4
Front St. Cad 63 E1
Front The. Pot En 123 D4
Frowick Cl. Wel Gr 144 A4
Frowyke Cres. Pot B 158 A4
Fry Rd. Stev 51 E3
Fulbeck Way. Har 176 B1
Fulford Gr. Sth Ox 175 D4
Fuller Ct. Bis St 77 D4
Fuller Gdns. Watf 154 A1
Fuller Rd. Watf 154 A1
Fuller Way. Cro Gr 166 A2
Fullers Cl. Wa Aby 163 F3
Fulling Mill La. Welw 89 D3
Fullmore Cl. Harp 86 B2
Fulmar Cres. Heml H 124 A2
Fulton Cl. Stev 50 B3
Fulton Cres. Bis St 77 E4
Furham Field. Pnr 176 A2
Furlay Cl. Hit 22 B4
Furlong Way. Gt Am 115 D3
Furlongs. Heml H 124 A2
Furrows The. Luton 45 D4
Furse Ave. St Alb 128 A4
Furtherfield. Abb L 153 F4
Furtherground. Heml H 124 C2
Furze Cl. Luton 45 E4
Furze Cl. Sth Ox 175 E3
Furze Gr. Roystn 7 F3
Furze Rd. Heml H 123 F1
Furze View. Chor 164 B2
Furzebushes La. Chis 140 C3
Furzedown Ct. Harp 86 A1
Furzedown. Stev 51 D2
Furzefield Rd. Wel GC 110 C2
Furzefield. Ches 148 A2
Furzehill Rd. Bor 170 A2
Furzen Cres. Hat 130 A1

Gable Cl. Abb L 153 F4
Gable Cl. Pnr 176 A2
Gables Ave. Bor 169 F3
Gables The. Heml H 124 B2
Gaddesden Cres. Watf 154 C3
Gaddesden Gr. Wel GC 111 E3
Gaddesden La. Red 105 E2
Gaddesden Row. Gt Ga 104 B3
Gade Ave. Watf 166 C3
Gade Bank. Cro Gr 166 B3
Gade Cl. Heml H 124 A3
Gade Side. Watf 153 F2
Gade Valley Cl. Bed 139 D2
Gade View Gdns. Abb L 153 E4
Gade View Rd. Fel 138 B4
Gadebridge La. Heml H 124 A3
Gadebridge La. Pic En 124 B3
Gadebridge Rd. Heml H 124 A2
Gadswell Cl. Watf 154 C2
Gage Cl. Roystn 7 E4
Gainsborough Ave. St Alb 127 F2
Gainsford Cres. Hit 22 B1
Gainswood. Wel GC 110 C3
Gall End La. Sta Mo 59 F4
Galley Green. Hod 115 D1
Galley Hill. Heml H 124 A3
Galley La. Barn 171 D3
Galleyhill Rd. Wa Aby 163 F4
Galloway Cl. Bis St 76 C4
Galloway Cl. Ches 148 C3
Galloway Rd. Bis St 58 C1
Gallows Hill La. Abb L 153 E4
Gallows Hill. Abb L 153 E4
Galston Rd. Luton 44 B4
Gammons La. Watf 154 A1

Gamnel Terr. Tri 100
Ganders Ash. Watf 154
Gangies Hill. H Wy 97
Gant Ct. Wa Aby 163
Ganton Wlk. Sth Ox 175
Ganymede Pl. Heml H 124
Gaping La. Hit 34
Garden Ave. Hat 130
Garden Cl. Barn 171
Garden Cl. Harp 107
Garden Cl. Roystn 7
Garden Cl. St Alb 128
Garden Cl. Watf 166
Garden Cl. Wl Gr 69
Garden Ct. Whea 87
Garden Field La. Berk 122
Garden Field. Ast 51
Garden La. Roystn 7
Garden Rd. Abb L 153
Garden Rd. Bun 40
Garden Rd. Wl Gr 69
Garden Row. Hit 34
Garden Terrace Rd. Harl 118
Garden Wlk. Roystn 7
Garden Wlk. Stev 50
Gardenia Ave. Luton 45
Gardens The. Bro Pk 144
Gardens The. Henlw 10
Gardens The. Stot 11
Gardens The. Watf 166
Gardiners La. Ashw .... 4 E
Garfield St. Watf .... 154 A
Garland Cl. Heml H .... 124 E
Garland Rd. Ware .... 93 F
Garnault Rd. Enf .... 161 F
Garner Dri. Ches .... 148 C
Garnett Cl. Watf .... 154 E
Garnett Dr. Bri Wd .... 140 C
Garrard Way. Whea .... 108 E
Garratts Rd. Bus .... 168 E
Garretts Mead. Luton .... 46 A
Garrowsfield. Barn .... 171 F
Garsmouth Way. Watf .... 154 E
Garston Cres. Watf .... 154 E
Garston Dri. Watf .... 154 B
Garston La. Watf .... 154 B
Garston Park Par. Watf .... 154 B
Garth Rd. Letw .... 22 C
Garth The. Abb L .... 153 E
Garthland Dri. Barn .... 171 E
Gartlet Rd. Watf .... 167 E
Gas La. Bark .... 17 E
Gascoyne Cl. Pot B .... 158 A
Gascoyne Way. Hert .... 113 E
Gate Cl. Bor .... 170 B
Gate End. Norwd .... 175 D
Gatecroft. Heml H .... 124 C
Gatehill Rd. Norwd .... 175 D
Gatehouse Mews. Bun .... 40 C
Gates Way. Stev .... 50 B
Gatesbury Way. Stand .... 55 E
Gatesdene Cl. L Gad .... 102 B
Gateshead Rd. Bor .... 170 A
Gateway Cl. Norwd .... 174 B
Gatwick Cl. Bis St .... 59 D
Gauldie Way. Stand .... 55 E
Gaunts Way. Letw 12 A1
Gaveston Dri. Berk .... 122 A
Gayland Ave. Luton .... 64 A
Gayton Cl. Luton .... 45 D
Gaywood Ave. Ches 148 B1
Gdns The. Bal 23 F4
Gean Wlk. Hat 130 A1
Geddes Rd. Bus 168 B3
Geddings Rd. Hod 135 D3
General Wlk The. Enf 162 C1
Gentlemens Field. Thun 93 D2
George La. Roystn 7 E3
George St W. Luton 63 F4
George St. Berk 122 B2
George St. Heml H 124 B2
George St. Hert 113 E3
George St. Luton 63 F4
George St. Mark 83 F3
George St. Watf 167 E3
George V Ave. Pnr 175 F1
George V Way. Sar 152 A2
George's Wood Rd. Bro Pk ... 145 D3
Georges Mead. Elst 169 E2
Georgewood Rd. Heml H 139 D4
Georgina Ct. Arl 11 D2
Gerard Ave. Bis St 76 C2
German Wlk. Letw 22 C3
Gernon Rd. Letw 22 C3
Gew's Car. Ches 148 B1
Giant Tree Hill. Bus 168 B1
Gibbons Cl. Bor 169 F4
Gibbons Cl. Sand 108 B1
Gibbons Way. Kneb 68 C3
Gibbs Cl. Ches 148 B1
Gibbs Couch. Watf 175 E4
Gibbs Field. Bis St 76 B3
Gibson Cl. Hit 35 D4
Gidian Ct. Chis 141 E2
Gifford's La. Hault 54 A1
Gilbert Rd. Hare 173 E1
Gilbert St. Enf 162 B1
Gilbert Way. Berk 122 A2
Gilbert's Hill. St Le 119 F2
Gilbey Ave. Bis St 77 D3

Gilbey Cres. Sta Mo 59 F4
Gilden Cl. Harl 118 C2
Gilden Way. Harl 118 C2
Gilder Cl. Luton 45 D4
Gilderdale. Luton 44 A3
Gilders. Saw 97 E1
Giles Cl. Sand 108 B1
Gillan Green. Bus 176 B4
Gilliam St. Luton 63 F4
Gillian Ave. St Alb 141 E4
Gills Hill La. Radl 155 F2
Gills Hollow. Radl 155 F2
Gills Mill. Radl 156 A2
Gilmour Cl. Enf 162 A2
Gilpin Green. Harp 86 B1
Gilpin Rd. Gt Am 114 C4
Gilpin's Gallop. Sta Ab 115 D2
Gilpin's Ride. Berk 122 B3
Gilsand. Wa Aby 163 F2
Gilsland. Wa Aby 163 F2
Ginns Rd. Sto P 43 E3
Gippeswyck Cl. Pnr 175 E1
Gipsy La. Hat 110 C1
Gipsy La. Kneb 68 C2
Gipsy La. Luton 64 A3
Gipsy La. Sta Mo 59 E2
Girdle Rd. Hit 22 A1
Girons Cl. Hit 35 D4
Girtin Rd. Bus 168 B3
Girton Ct. Ches 148 C1
Girton Way. Cro Gr 166 B2
Glade The. Bal 23 F4
Glade The. Letw 22 C2
Glade The. Wel GC 110 B4
Glades The. Heml H 123 F2
Gladeside. St Alb 128 B3
Gladeway The. Wa Aby 163 E3
Gladsmuir Rd. Barn 171 F4
Gladstone Ave. Luton 63 E4
Gladstone Rd. Dan En 71 F4
Gladstone Rd. Hod 135 D4
Gladstone Rd. Ware 93 E1
Gladstone Rd. Watf 167 E3
Glamis Cl. Ches 148 A1
Glamis Cl. Heml H 105 D1
Glanfield. Heml H 124 C3
Gleave Cl. St Alb 128 A2
Glebe Ave. Ch En 11 D4
Glebe Cl. Ess 131 F3
Glebe Cl. Heml H 138 C4
Glebe Cl. Pit 80 B3
Glebe Cl. Wat St 70 B2
Glebe Cotts. Ess 131 F3
Glebe Ct. Bis St 77 D4
Glebe La. Barn 171 D2
Glebe Rd. Hert 113 E4
Glebe Rd. Letw 23 D4
Glebe Rd. Welw 89 D3
Glebe The. Kin L 139 D1
Glebe The. Watf 154 B3
Glebelands. Harl 117 F2
Gleed Ave. Bus 176 B4
Glemsford Cl. Luton 44 A3
Glemsford Dri. Harp 86 B1
Glen Faba Rd. Roy 135 F3
Glen The. Heml H 124 C4
Glen The. Norwd 174 B2
Glen Way. Watf 153 F1
Glencoe Rd. Bus 168 A2
Glencourse Green. Sth Ox 175 E3
Glendale Wlk. Ches 148 C1
Glendale. Heml H 124 A2
Gleneagles Cl. Sth Ox 175 E3
Glenester Cl. Hod 115 D1
Glenferrie Rd. St Alb 128 A2
Glenfield Ct. Hert 112 C4
Glenfield Rd. Luton 45 E3
Glenhaven Ave. Bor 170 A3
Glenlyn Ave. St Alb 128 A1
Glenmire Terr. Sta Ab 115 E2
Glenview Rd. Heml H 124 A2
Glenville Ave. Enf 161 E1
Glenwood Cl. Stev 51 E1
Glenwood. Hod 134 C2
Glenwood. Wel GC 111 E3
Glevum Cl. St Alb 126 C1
Globe Cres. Far 58 B3
Globe Ct. Hert 113 E4
Globe Ct. Hod 148 C4
Gloucester Ave. Ches 162 C3
Gloucester Rd. Enf 161 E1
Gloucester Rd. Luton 63 F3
Glover Cl. Ham St 147 F2
Glovers Cl. Hert 113 E2
Glynde The. Stev 69 D4
Goat La. Enf 161 F1
Gobions Way. Pot B 145 D2
Goblins Green. Wel GC 110 B3
Goddard End. Ast 51 E1
Goddard End. Stev 69 E4
Goddards Cl. L Berk 132 B2
Goddfreys Cl. Luton 63 D3
Godfrey Cl. Stev 51 D2
Godfries Cl. Tewin 90 C2
Godsafe. Harl 118 C2
Goff's Oak Ave. Gofs O 147 E2
Goffs Cres. Gofs O 147 E1
Goffs La. Ches 147 F1
Goffs La. Gofs O 147 F1
Gold Crest Cl. Luton 44 A3
Golda Cl. Barn 171 E2
Goldcrest Way. Bus 168 B1
Goldcroft. Heml H 125 D1
Golden Dell. Wel GC 110 C1
Goldfield Rd. Tri 99 F2
Goldfinch Way. Bor 170 A3
Goldings Cres. Hat 130 A3
Goldings La. Wat 92 A1
Goldings. Bis St 77 D4
Goldington Cl. Hod 114 C1
Goldon. Letw 23 E2
Goldstone Cl. Ware 93 E1
Golf Cl. Bus 167 E3
Golf Club Rd. Bro Pk 145 D3
Golf Ride. Enf 161 D2
Gombard's Alley. St Alb 127 E2
Gombards. St Alb 127 E2
Gomer Cl. Cod 67 F1
Gonville Ave. Cro Gr 166 A2
Gonville Cres. Stev 51 E1
Goodey Meade. Heb En 52 C1
Goodrich Cl. Watf 154 A2
Goodwin Ct. Ches 148 C2
Goodwin Stile. Bis St 76 B3
Goodwins Mead. Ched 80 A4
Goodwood Ave. Enf 162 B1
Goodwood Ave. Watf 153 F2
Goodwood Cl. Hod 135 D4
Goodwood Path. Bor 170 A4
Goodwood Rd. Roystn 7 F3
Goodyers Ave. Radl 155 F3
Goose Acre. Bot 136 A1
Goose Acre. Ched 80 A4
Goose La. Gt Ha 98 C4
Gooseacre. Wel GC 110 C2
Gooseberry Hill S. Luton 45 D3
Gooseberry Hill. Luton 45 D4
Goosecroft. Heml H 123 F2
Goral Mead. Ric 165 E1
Gordon Ave. Stan 176 C2
Gordon Cl. St Alb 128 A1
Gordon Rd. Wa Aby 163 D3
Gordon St. Luton 63 E4
Gordon Way. Barn 171 F3
Gore La. Stand 73 E2
Gorham Dri. St Alb 141 F4
Gorle Cl. Watf 154 A2
Gorleston Cl. Stev 36 A1
Gorse Cl. Hat 129 F1
Gorselands. Harp 107 E4
Gorst Cl. Letw 22 C3
Gosforth La. Sth Ox 175 D4
Gosforth Path. Sth Ox 175 D4
Goshawk Cl. Luton 44 A2
Gosling Ave. Gt Of 33 E1
Gosmore Rd. Hit 34 C3
Gossamers The. Watf 154 C2
Gosselin Rd. Hert 113 E4
Gossom's End. Berk 122 A3
Gossoms Ride. Berk 122 A3
Gothic Way. Arl 11 D3
Gould Cl. Wel Gr 144 A4
Government Row. Enf 163 D1
Gowar Field. Pot B 158 A4
Gower Rd. Roystn 7 E4
Gowers The. Harl 118 A1
Grace Cl. Bor 170 B4
Grace Gdns. Bis St 76 C2
Grace Way. Stev 50 C4
Graces Maltings. Tri 100 A2
Graemes Dyke Rd. Berk 122 A2
Graham Ave. Hod 134 C1
Graham Cl. St Alb 127 E1
Graham Gdns. Luton 45 E2
Graham Rd. Har 176 C1
Grailands. Bis St 76 B4
Grammar School Wlk. Hit 34 C4
Grampian Way. Luton 44 B4
Granaries The. Wa Aby 163 E3
Granary Cl. Whea 108 B4
Granary La. Harp 86 B1
Granary The. Roy 116 A1
Granby Ave. Harp 86 B1
Granby Park Rd. Ham St 147 F2
Granby Rd. Luton 44 C1
Granby Rd. Stev 36 B1
Grandfield Ave. Watf 167 D4
Grange Ave. Luton 44 B3
Grange Ave. N20 171 F1
Grange Bottom. Roystn 7 F3
Grange Cl. Heml H 125 D1
Grange Cl. Hert 113 D3
Grange Cl. Hit 35 D2
Grange Cl. Mark 83 E3
Grange Court Rd. Harp 107 E3
Grange Ct. Hert 113 E4
Grange Ct. Wa Aby 163 E3
Grange Dri. Stot 11 F3
Grange Gdns. Gt Am 114 C4
Grange Hill. Welw 89 E3
Grange La. Aldhm 168 B4
Grange Park. Bis St 58 C1
Grange Rd. Bis St 77 D4
Grange Rd. Bus 167 F2
Grange Rd. Elst 169 F2
Grange Rd. Letw 22 C4
Grange Rd. Pit 80 B3
Grange Rd. Tri 100 B2
Grange Rd. Wils 79 E1
Grange Rise. Cod 67 F1
Grange St. St Alb 127 E2
Grange Wlk. Bis St 77 D4
Grangedale Cl. Norwd 174 C1
Grangeside. Bis St 59 D1
Grangewood. Pot B 145 D1
Gransden Cl. Luton 45 D4
Grant Gdns. Harp 86 A1
Grantham Cl. Roystn 7 D4
Grantham Gdns. Ware 93 F1
Grantham Green. Bor 170 B2
Grantham Rd. Luton 45 D1
Granville Dene. Bov 137 D2
Granville Gdns. Hod 115 D1
Granville Rd. Barn 171 E3
Granville Rd. Hit 22 B1
Granville Rd. Luton 63 D4
Granville Rd. Nthch 121 F3
Granville Rd. St Alb 127 F2
Granville Rd. Watf 167 E3
Grasmere Ave. Harp 86 B1
Grasmere Ave. Luton 45 D4
Grasmere Cl. Heml H 125 D1
Grasmere Cl. Watf 154 A4
Grasmere Rd. Luton 45 E4
Grasmere Rd. St Alb 128 A1
Grasmere Rd. Ware 93 F2
Grass Meadows. Stev 51 E4
Grass Warren. Tewin 90 C1
Grassington Cl. Bri Wd 141 D1
Grassy Cl. Heml H 124 A2
Gravel Hill. Heml H 124 A2
Gravel La. Heml H 124 A2
Gravel Path. Berk 122 A3
Gravel Path. Heml H 124 A2
Graveley Ave. Bor 170 B2
Graveley Dell. Wel GC 111 D3
Graveley La. Gt Wy 36 A3
Graveley Rd. Hit 35 F4
Gravelhill Terr. Heml H 124 A1
Gravely Ct. Heml H 125 E1
Gray's La. Hit 34 B4
Graylings The. Abb L 153 E3
Grays Cl. Roystn 7 E4
Grays Ct. Bis St 76 C4
Graysfield. Wel GC 111 D2
Grazings The. Heml H 124 C3
Great Braitch La. Hat 109 F1
Great Break. Wel GC 111 D3
Great Cambridge Rd. Ches 148 B2
Great Cambridge Rd. Enf 162 A2
Great Conduit. Wel GC 111 E4
Great Dell. Wel GC 89 E1
Great Elms Rd. Heml H 138 C4
Great Ganett. Wel GC 111 E2
Great Gr. Bus 168 A2
Great Hadham Rd. Bis St 76 B3
Great Heart. Heml H 124 C3
Great Heath. Hat 130 A4
Great Innings N. Wat St 70 B2
Great Innings S. Wat St 70 B2
Great Lawne. Dat 69 E1
Great Ley. Wel GC 110 C2
Great Meadow. Lo Naz 135 D1
Great Molewood. Hert 92 A1
Great North Rd. A St P 110 A4
Great North Rd. Barn 171 F3
Great North Rd. Bro Pk 145 D2
Great North Rd. Hat 130 A2
Great North Rd. Lem 110 A3
Great North Rd. Pot B 159 E3
Great North Rd. Rad 12 B2
Great North Rd. Stanb 110 A2
Great North Rd. Stot 12 B3
Great North Rd. Wel Gr 144 C4
Great North Rd. Wl Gr 89 F4
Great Palmers. Heml H 124 C4
Great Park. Kin L 139 D1
Great Plumtree. Harl 117 F1
Great Rd. Heml H 124 C2
Great Slades. Pot B 158 C3
Great Sturgess Rd. Heml H 123 F2
Great Whifes Rd. Heml H 124 C1
Greatfield Cl. Harp 85 E2
Greatham Rd. Watf 167 E3
Green Acres. Lily 32 B1
Green Acres. Stev 51 E1
Green Acres. Wel GC 110 C2
Green Cl. Bro Pk 144 C3
Green Cl. Ches 162 C4
Green Cl. Luton 44 B3
Green Cl. Stev 51 D1
Green Croft. Hat 130 A4
Green Dell Way. Heml H 125 E2
Green Drift. Roystn 7 D4
Green End La. Heml H 123 F2
Green End Rd. Heml H 124 A1
Green Hill Cl. Brag 55 F4
Green La. Ashw 4 C3
Green La. Bov 137 D2
Green La. Brag 55 F4
Green La. Cro Gr 165 F2
Green La. Harp 107 E4
Green La. Hat 109 F1
Green La. Heml H 125 E2
Green La. Hit 22 A1
Green La. Ivin 80 C3
Green La. Ken Co 82 C4
Green La. Lat 150 A3
Green La. Letw 23 E4
Green La. Lo Naz 149 D4
Green La. Luton 46 B2
Green La. Norwd 174 C2
Green La. St Alb 127 E4
Green La. St Alb 142 A4
Green La. Stanb 109 F2
Green La. Watf 167 E1
Green La. Wel GC 111 E3
Green Lane Cl. Harp 107 F4
Green Meadow. Pot B 145 D1
Green Oaks. Luton 45 F2
Green St. Bor 157 D1
Green St. Chen 164 B4
Green St. Chor 164 B3
Green St. Roystn 7 E4
Green St. Shen 157 D2
Green St. Stev 50 B4
Green The. Bis St 76 C2
Green The. Ched 80 A4
Green The. Ches 148 B2
Green The. Cod 67 F1
Green The. Cro Gr 165 F2
Green The. Ivin 80 B2
Green The. L Gad 102 B4
Green The. Luton 44 B3
Green The. Newn 12 C4
Green The. Old K 68 B3
Green The. Pet Gr 65 E2
Green The. Roystn 7 E3
Green The. Sar 152 A2
Green The. Stot 11 F4
Green The. Wa Aby 163 E3
Green The. Ware 93 E2
Green The. Wel GC 111 D2
Green The. Welw 89 D3
Green Vale. Wel G C 111 D3
Green View Cl. Bov 137 D1
Green Way Gdns. Har 176 C1
Green Way The. Har 176 C1
Green Wlk. Roystn 7 E3
Greenacre Cl. Pot B 158 C1
Greenacres. Bus 176 B4
Greenacres. Heml H 125 E1
Greenacres. Pit 80 B2
Greenall Cl. Ches 148 C1
Greenbank Rd. Watf 153 E2
Greenbank. Ches 148 A2
Greenbury Cl. Chor 164 B3
Greencoates. Hert 113 F3
Greene Field Rd. Berk 122 B2
Greene Wlk. Berk 122 B2
Greenfield Ave. Ick 21 E2
Greenfield Ave. Watf 175 F4
Greenfield La. Ick 21 F2
Greenfield Pas. Barn 171 F3
Greenfield Rd. Stev 50 C4
Greenfield St. Wa Aby 163 E3
Greenfield. Hat 130 B4
Greenfield. Roystn 7 D4
Greenfield. Wel GC 89 E1
Greenfields. Cuf 146 C1
Greenfields. Sta Mo 59 F4
Greengate. Luton 44 B4
Greenheys Cl. Norwd 174 C1
Greenhill Ave. Luton 45 F2
Greenhill Cres. Watf 166 C2
Greenhill Ct. Heml H 124 A1
Greenhill Park. Bis St 76 B3
Greenhills Cl. Chor 165 D2
Greenhills. Ware 93 E2
Greenland Rd. Barn 171 E2
Greenlane Ind Est. Letw 23 E4
Greenleas. Wa Aby 163 F3
Greenriggs. Luton 46 C1
Greenside Dri. Hit 34 B4
Greenside. Bor 157 D1
Greenstead. Saw 97 F1
Greensward. Bus 168 A2
Greenway The. Enf 162 B2
Greenway The. Pot B 159 D3
Greenway The. Ric 165 D1
Greenway The. Tri 99 F3
Greenway. Berk 122 A2
Greenway. Bis St 77 E3
Greenway. Harp 107 F4
Greenway. Heml H 125 D2
Greenway. Letw 23 D1
Greenway. Pnr 175 D1
Greenway. Wal 52 A4
Greenways. Abb L 153 F4
Greenways. Bun 40 B4
Greenways. Gofs O 147 D1
Greenways. Hertng 113 D3
Greenways. Luton 46 A3
Greenways. Stev 50 C3
Greenwood Ave. Ches 162 A4
Greenwood Cl. Ches 162 A4
Greenwood Dri. Watf 154 A3
Greenyard. Wa Aby 163 E3
Greer Rd. Har 176 B1
Gregories Cl. Luton 45 E1
Gregory Ave. Pot B 159 E3
Gregson Cl. Bor 170 B4
Grenadine Cl. Ham St 147 F2
Grenadine Way. Tri 100 A3
Grenville Ave. Hod 134 C1
Grenville Cl. Ches 162 B4
Grenville Ct. Chor 164 B3
Gresford Cl. St Alb 128 A2
Gresham Cl. Luton 64 B4
Gresham Ct. Berk 122 A2
Gresley Cl. Wel G C 110 C4
Gresley Ct. Enf 162 B2
Gresley Way. Stev 37 E1
Gresley Way. Stev 51 E2
Gresley Way. Stev 51 E4
Greville Cl. Wel Gr 144 B4
Greycaine Rd. Watf 154 B1
Greydells Rd. Stev 50 C4
Greyfriars. Ware 93 D2
Greyhound La. Pot B 158 A3
Greystoke Cl. Berk 122 A2
Grimsdyke Cres. Barn 171 E3
Grimsdyke Rd. Pnr 175 F2
Grimsdyke Rd. Wigg 100 B1
Grimston Rd. St Alb 127 F1
Grimstone Rd. L Wym 35 F2
Grimthorpe Cl. St Alb 127 E3
Grindcobbe Cl. St Alb 141 E4
Grinstead La. L Hal 98 B3
Groom Rd. Ches 148 C3
Grooms Cotts. Bot 136 A1
Groomsby Dri. Ivin 80 C3
Grosvenor Ave. Bed 139 E2
Grosvenor Ct. Cro Gr 166 B2
Grosvenor Rd W. Bal 12 C1
Grosvenor Rd. Bal 12 C1
Grosvenor Rd. Bor 170 A3
Grosvenor Rd. Hod 134 C2
Grosvenor Rd. Luton 45 D3
Grosvenor Rd. Norwd 174 C3
Grosvenor Rd. St Alb 127 F1
Grosvenor Rd. Watf 167 E3
Grosvenor Terr. Heml H 124 A1
Grotto The. Gt Am 114 A4
Ground La. Hat 130 A4
Grove Ave. Harp 107 E4
Grove Cres. Cro Gr 166 A3
Grove Ct. Wa Aby 163 D3
Grove Farm Park. Norwd 174 B3
Grove Gdns. Enf 162 B1
Grove Gdns. Tri 100 A3
Grove Hall Rd. Bus 167 F3
Grove Hill. Sta Mo 59 F4
Grove La. Ash Gr 136 B3
Grove Lea. Hat 130 A1
Grove Mead. Hat 129 F3
Grove Meadow. Wel GC 111 E3
Grove Mill La. Watf 153 E1
Grove Park Rd. Cad 63 D1
Grove Park. Tri 100 B3
Grove Path. Ches 162 A4
Grove Pl. Bis St 76 C4
Grove Rd West. Enf 162 B1
Grove Rd. Bor 170 A4
Grove Rd. Cad 63 D1
Grove Rd. Harp 107 E4
Grove Rd. Heml H 124 A1
Grove Rd. Hit 21 F1
Grove Rd. Luton 63 E4
Grove Rd. Norwd 174 B3
Grove Rd. Ric 173 D4
Grove Rd. Stev 50 B4
Grove Rd. Tri 100 A2
Grove Rd. Ware 93 F1
Grove The. Bro Pk 145 D2
Grove The. Bry Gr 75 F4
Grove The. Gt Ha 77 F2
Grove The. Lat 150 B2
Grove The. Luton 63 D3
Grove The. Pot B 159 E4
Grove The. Radl 156 A3
Grove Way. Chor 164 A2
Grove Wlk. Hert 113 E4
Grovedale Cl. Ches 147 F1
Groveland Way. Stot 12 A3
Grovelands Ave. Hit 22 B1
Grovelands. Chis 141 D2
Grovelands. Heml H 125 E3
Grover Cl. Heml H 124 B2
Grover Rd. Watf 167 E2
Grovesnor Cl. Bis St 76 B2
Grovewood Cl. Chor 164 A2
Grubb's Hill. Wa Aby 149 E1
Grubs La. Wild 145 E4
Guernsey Cl. Luton 44 A2
Guessens Ct. Wel GC 110 B3
Guessens Gr. Wel GC 110 B3
Guessens Rd. Wel GC 110 B3
Guessens Wlk. Wel GC 110 B4
Guildford Rd. St Alb 128 A1
Guildford St. Luton 63 F4
Guilfords. Harl 118 B3
Guinevere Gdns. Ches 162 C4
Gulland Cl. Bus 168 B2
Gullbrook. Heml H 124 A2
Gullet Wood Rd. Watf 154 A2
Gulphs The. Hert 113 E3
Gun La. Kneb 68 C2
Gun Meadow Ave. Kneb 69 D2
Gun Rd. Kneb 69 D2
Gun Road Gdns. Kneb 68 C2
Gunnels Wood Ind Est. Stev 50 B2
Gunnels Wood Rd. Stev 50 A3
Gurney Court Rd. St Alb 128 A3
Gurney's La. Hol 21 D4
Gwent Cl. Watf 154 B3
Gwynfa Cl. Wl Gr 89 E4
Gwynn's Wlk. Hert 113 F3
Gwynne Cl. Tri 100 A3
Gyford Walk. Ches 162 A4

Gypsy Cl. Gt Am 114 C2
Gypsy La. Abb L 153 E3
Gypsy La. Gt Am 114 C2

Hackforth Cl. Barn 171 D2
Hackney Cl. Bor 170 B2
Haddon Cl. Bor 170 A3
Haddon Cl. Heml H 125 D1
Haddon Cl. Stev 69 E4
Haddon Ct. Harp 86 A1
Haddon Rd. Chor 164 B2
Haddon Rd. Luton 63 F4
Hadham Rd. Bis St 76 B4
Hadham Rd. Stand 55 F1
Hadleigh Ct. Harp 107 F3
Hadleigh Ct. Hod 134 C1
Hadley Cl. Elst 169 F2
Hadley Gr. Barn 171 F4
Hadley Green Rd. Barn 171 F4
Hadley Green W. Barn 171 F4
Hadley Green. Barn 171 F4
Hadley Highstone. Barn 171 F4
Hadley Rd. Enf 160 A1
Hadley Ridge. Barn 171 F3
Hadlow Down Cl. Luton 45 D3
Hadrian Cl. St Alb 127 D1
Hadrian Way. Letw 23 E4
Hadrian's Wlk. Stev 51 E4
Hadrians Way. Bal 23 E4
Hadwell Cl. Stev 51 D2
Haelfoot. Letw 22 C3
Hagdell Rd. Luton 63 E3
Hagden La. Watf 166 C2
Haggerston Rd. Bor 156 C1
Hagsdell La. Hert 113 E3
Hagsdell Rd. Hert 113 E3
Haig Cl. St Alb 128 A1
Hailey Ave. Hod 115 D1
Hailey La. Hert H 114 C1
Hailey La. Hod 114 C1
Haines Way. Watf 154 A3
Haldens. Wel GC 89 F1
Hale Ct. Hert 113 E3
Hale Rd. Hert 113 E3
Hales Park Cl. Heml H 125 E2
Hales Park. Heml H 125 E2
Haleswood Rd. Heml H 125 D2
Half Acres. Bis St 76 C4
Half Moon La. Cad 63 E1
Half Moon La. Mark 84 A4
Half Moon Meadow. Heml H 125 D4
Halfacre La. Gt Ho 29 D1
Halfhide La. Ches 148 B3
Halfhides. Wa Aby 163 E3
Halfway Ave. Luton 44 B1
Halifax Rd. Heron 164 B1
Halifax Way. Wel Gc 111 F3
Hall Cl. Ric 165 D1
Hall Dri. Hare 173 E1
Hall Gdns. Coln H 143 E4
Hall Gr. Wel GC 111 D2
Hall Heath Cl. St Alb 128 A3
Hall La. Gt Ch 9 F1
Hall La. Gt Ho 29 D1
Hall La. Kim 66 B1
Hall Mead. Letw 22 B3
Hall Park Gate. Berk 122 B2
Hall Park Hill. Berk 122 B2
Hall Park. Berk 122 B2
Hall Place Gdns. St Alb 127 F2
Hallam Gdns. Pnr 175 F2
Halland Way. Norwd 174 B2
Halling Hill. Harl 117 F1
Hallingbury Cl. L Hal 77 D1
Hallingbury Rd. Bis St 77 D2
Hallingbury Rd. Saw 98 A2
Hallmores. Hod 135 D2
Hallowell Rd. Norwd 174 C2
Hallowes Cres. Sth Ox 175 D4
Hallside Rd. Enf 161 F1
Hallwicks Rd. Luton 46 A2
Hallworth Dri. Stot 11 F3
Halsey Dri. Hit 35 D4
Halsey Pl. Watf 154 A1
Halsey Rd. Watf 167 D3
Halstead Hill. Ches 147 F1
Halter Cl. Bor 170 B2
Haltside. Hat 129 F2
Halyard Cl. Luton 45 D3
Hamberlins La. Nthch 121 D4
Hambro Cl. Nwml E 85 F4
Hamburgh Ct. Ches 148 B2
Hamels Dri. Hert 114 A4
Hamilton Ave. Hod 135 D4
Hamilton Cl. Bric 155 D4
Hamilton Cl. Pot B 158 A3
Hamilton Mead. Bov 137 D2
Hamilton Rd. Abb L 153 E3
Hamilton Rd. Berk 122 A2
Hamilton Rd. St Alb 128 A2
Hamilton Rd. Sth Ox 175 D4
Hamilton St. Watf 167 E2
Hamlet Hill. Roy 135 F2
Hamlet The. Pot En 123 D4
Hammarskjold Rd. Harl 117 E1
Hammer La. Heml H 124 C2
Hammers Gate. Chis 141 D3
Hammond Cl. Ham St 147 F3
Hammond Cl. Stev 50 B3
Hammond La. Stanb 109 D2
Hammond Street Rd. Ham St 147 E3
Hammonds La. Sand 108 C2
Hammondswick. Harp 106 C2
Hamonte. Letw 23 E2
Hampden Cl. Letw 23 D4
Hampden Cres. Ches 162 A4
Hampden Hill Cl. Ware 93 F1
Hampden Hill. Ware 93 F1
Hampden Pl. Fro 141 F1
Hampden Rd. Har 176 B1
Hampden Rd. Hit 22 B1
Hampden Rd. Letw 23 D4
Hampden Rise. Roy 7 F2
Hampden Way. Watf 153 F2
Hampden. Kim 66 B1
Hampermill La. Watf 167 D1
Hampton Cl. Stev 69 E4
Hampton Gdns. Saw 118 B4
Hampton Rd. Luton 63 D4
Hamstel Rd. Harl 117 E1
Hamsworth Ct. Hert 112 C4
Hanbury Cl. Ches 148 C1
Hanbury Cl. Ware 93 F1
Hanbury Dri. Thun 93 E3
Hanbury Mews. Thun 93 E3
Hancock Ct. Bor 170 B4
Hancroft Rd. Heml H 124 C1
Hand La. Saw 97 E1
Handa Cl. Heml H 139 D4
Handcross Rd. Luton 46 B1
Handpost Hill. Cuf 146 A2
Handside Cl. Wel GC 110 B3
Handside Green. Wel GC 110 B4
Handside La. Wel GC 110 B3
Handsworth Cl. Sth Ox 175 D4
Hangar Ruding. Watf 175 F4
Hanger Cl. Heml 124 A1
Hangmans La. Wl Gr 89 F4
Hanover Cl. Stev 50 C1
Hanover Ct. Hod 135 D4
Hanover Green. Heml H 124 A1
Hanover Wlk. Hat 129 F1
Hanscombe End Rd. Aps En 19 E4
Hanselin Cl. Stan 176 C3
Hanswick Cl. Luton 46 A1
Hanworth Cl. Luton 45 E4
Hanyards End. Cuf 146 C2
Hanyards La. Cuf 146 B2
Happy Valley Ind Park. Bed 139 D2
Harbell Cl. Hert 114 A3
Harborne Cl. Sth Ox 175 E3
Harbury Dell. Luton 45 D4
Harcourt Rd. Bus 168 B2
Harcourt Rd. Tri 100 B2
Harcourt St. Luton 63 F3
Harding Cl. Luton 44 C4
Harding Cl. Red 106 A3
Harding Cl. Watf 154 B3
Hardings. Wel GC 111 E4
Hardwick Cl. Stev 69 E4
Hardwick Green. Luton 45 D4
Hardwick Pl. Lon C 142 B2
Hardy Cl. Hit 35 E4
Hardy Rd. Heml H 124 C2
Hare Cres. Watf 154 A4
Hare La. Hat 130 A2
Hare Street Rd. Bun 41 D4
Hare Street Rd. H St H 41 E4
Harebell. Wel GC 110 C2
Harebreaks The. Watf 154 A1
Harefield Pl. St Alb 128 B3
Harefield Rd. Luton 62 C4
Harefield Rd. Ric 173 F3
Harefield. Harl 118 A1
Harefield. Stev 51 E2
Harepark Cl. Heml H 123 F2
Harewood Rd. Sth Ox 175 D4
Harewood. Chor 165 E2
Hargrave Cl. Sta Mo 59 F4
Hargreaves Ave. Ches 162 A4
Hargreaves Cl. Ches 162 A4
Hargreaves Rd. Roystn 7 E3
Harkett Cl. Har 176 C1
Harkness Way. Hit 22 B1
Harkness. Ches 148 A1
Harlesden Rd. St Alb 128 A2
Harlestone Cl. Luton 31 D1
Harley Ct. St Alb 128 B4
Harlow Ct. Heml H 125 D4
Harlow Rd. Roy 116 B1
Harlow Rd. Saw 118 B4
Harlton Ct. Wa Aby 163 F3
Harmer Green La. Har Gr 90 A3
Harmsworth Way. N20 171 F1
Harness Way. St Alb 128 B3
Harold Cres. Wa Aby 163 E4
Harpenden Rd. St Alb 107 E1
Harpenden Rd. Whea 108 A4
Harpenden Rise. Harp 85 F2
Harpendon La. Red 106 A3
Harper La. Lon C 156 A4
Harps Hill. Mark 83 F3
Harpsfield Bwy. Hat 129 F3
Harptree Way. St Alb 128 A3
Harriet Way. Bus 168 B1
Harrington Ct. Hert H 114 B2
Harris La. Gt Of 33 E1
Harris La. Luton 46 A2
Harris La. Shen 157 D3
Harris Rd. Watf 154 A2
Harris's La. Ware 93 E1
Harrison Cl. Hit 34 C4
Harrison Cl. Norwd 174 B2
Harrison Wlk. Ches 148 B1
Harrisons. Birhr 59 E1
Harrogate Rd. Sth Ox 175 E4
Harrow Ct. Stev 50 C3
Harrow View. Har 176 B1
Harrow Way. Watf 175 F3
Harrow Weald Park. Har 176 B2
Harrow Yd. Tri 100 A2
Harrowden Rd. Luton 64 B4
Harrowdene. Stev 51 E2
Hart Hill Dri. Luton 63 F4
Hart Hill La. Luton 64 A4
Hart La. Luton 46 A1
Hart Rd. Harl 118 B3
Hart Rd. St Alb 127 E1
Hart Wlk. Luton 46 A1
Hartfield Ave. Elst 170 A2
Hartfield Cl. Elst 170 A2
Hartfield Ct. Ware 93 E1
Hartford Dri. Watf 166 C4
Hartforde Rd. Bor 170 A4
Harthall La. Bed 139 E2
Hartham La. Hert 113 E3
Hartland Ct. Hit 34 B4
Hartland Rd. Ches 148 B1
Hartley Rd. Luton 63 F4
Hartmoor Mews. Ches 162 B1
Harts Cl. Bus 168 A4
Hartsbourne Ave. Bus 176 B4
Hartsbourne Cl. Bus 176 B4
Hartsbourne Rd. Bus 176 B4
Hartsbourne Way. Heml H 125 E1
Hartsfield Rd. Luton 46 A1
Hartspring La. Bus 168 A4
Hartwell Gdns. Harp 85 F1
Harvest Cl. Luton 44 A2
Harvest Ct. Wl Gr 89 F4
Harvest End. Watf 154 B2
Harvest Mead. Hat 130 A4
Harvest Rd. Bus 168 A3
Harvey Rd. Cro Gr 166 A2
Harvey Rd. Lon C 142 B3
Harvey Rd. Stev 51 D3
Harveyfields. Wa Aby 163 E3
Harveys Hill. Luton 45 F3
Harwood Cl. Tewin 90 C1
Harwood Cl. Wel GC 89 F1
Harwood Hill. Wel GC 89 F1
Hasedines Rd. Heml H 124 A2
Haseldine Meadows. Hat 129 F2
Haseldine Rd. Lon C 142 B3
Hasketon Dri. Luton 44 A3
Haslewood Ave. Hod 135 D3
Haslingden Cl. Harp 85 E2
Hastings Cl. Stev 50 A4
Hastings St. Luton 63 E3
Hastings Way. Bus 167 F3
Hastings Way. Cro Gr 166 B3
Hastoe Hill. Has 119 F4
Hastoe La. Tri 100 A1
Hatch Green. L Hal 98 A4
Hatch La. Wes 24 A2
Hatching Green Cl. Harp 107 D3
Hatfield Cres. Heml H 124 C4
Hatfield Rd. Bir Gr 112 A2
Hatfield Rd. Hat 111 F2
Hatfield Rd. P Bar 159 E4
Hatfield Rd. St Alb 128 B2
Hatfield Rd. Watf 167 D4
Hathaway Cl. Luton 44 A1
Hathaway Ct. St Alb 128 C2
Hatherleigh Gdns. Pot B 159 E4
Hatters La. Watf 166 B2
Hatton Rd. Ches 148 B1
Havelock Rd. Kin L 138 C2
Havelock Rd. Luton 45 F1
Havelock Rise. Luton 45 F1
Haven Cl. Hat 129 F3
Havercroft Cl. St Alb 127 E1
Havers La. Bis St 76 C3
Havest Ct. St Alb 128 B4
Haward Rd. Hod 135 E4
Hawbush Rise. Welw 89 D3
Hawes Cl. Norwd 174 C2
Hawes La. Wa Aby 163 E1
Hawfield Gdns. Pk St 141 E3
Hawkbush Cl. Welw 89 D2
Hawkesworth Cl. Norwd 174 C2
Hawkfield. Letw 22 C4
Hawkfields. Luton 45 F3
Hawkins Cl. Bor 170 B4
Hawkins Hall La. Dat 69 F1
Hawks Dri. Fel 137 F4
Hawkshead La. Bro Pk 144 C2
Hawkshead Rd. Pot B 145 D1
Hawkshill. St Alb 128 A1
Hawksmead Cl. Enf 162 B2
Hawksmoor. Shen 157 D3
Hawkwell Dri. Tri 100 B2
Hawridge La. Chol 120 C1
Hawridge Vale. Chol 120 C1
Hawsley Rd. Harp 107 D2
Hawthorn Ave. Luton 46 A2
Hawthorn Cl. Harp 107 E4
Hawthorn Cl. Hertng 113 D4
Hawthorn Cl. Hit 34 C3
Hawthorn Cl. Roystn 7 F4
Hawthorn Cl. Watf 153 F1
Hawthorn Cres. Cad 62 C2
Hawthorn Gr. Enf 161 E1
Hawthorn Hill. Letw 22 C4
Hawthorn La. Heml H 123 F2
Hawthorn Rd. Hod 135 D4
Hawthorn Rise. Thor 76 C2
Hawthorn Way. Chis 141 D4
Hawthorn Way. Roystn 7 F4
Hawthorne Ave. Ches 162 A4
Hawthorne Cl. Ches 162 A4
Hawthorne Rd. Radl 156 A3
Hawthornes. Hat 129 F2
Hawthorns The. Berk 122 A3
Hawthorns The. Fel 137 F4
Hawthorns The. Map Cr 172 B3
Hawthorns The. Stev 51 D2
Hawthorns. Wel GC 110 B4
Hay Cl. Bor 170 B4
Hay La. Harp 86 A1
Haybourn Mead. Heml H 124 A1
Haycroft Rd. Stev 50 B4
Haycroft. Bis St 77 E4
Haydock Rd. Roystn 7 F3
Haydon Rd. Watf 167 F2
Hayes Cl. Luton 46 B3
Hayes Wlk. Ches 148 C3
Hayfield Cl. Bus 168 A3
Haygarth. Kneb 69 D2
Hayhurst Rd. Luton 44 A1
Hayley Bell Gdns. Bis St 76 C2
Hayley Comm. Stev 51 E2
Hayling Dri. Luton 46 B2
Hayling Rd. Sth Ox 175 D4
Haymeads La. Bis St 77 E3
Haymeads. Wel GC 89 F1
Haymoor. Letw 22 C4
Haynes Cl. Wel GC 111 D3
Haynes Mead. Berk 122 A3
Haysman Cl. Letw 23 D4
Haywood Cl. Pnr 175 E1
Haywood Ct. Wa Aby 163 F3
Haywood La. Ther 16 A3
Haywood Park. Chor 164 C2
Haywoods La. Roystn 7 F4
Hazel Cl. Ham St 147 F3
Hazel Cl. Har Gr 89 F2
Hazel Gdns. Saw 97 F2
Hazel Gr. Hat 129 F1
Hazel Gr. Stot 11 F3
Hazel Gr. Watf 154 A2
Hazel Gr. Wel GC 111 D4
Hazel Mead. Barn 171 D2
Hazel Rd. Berk 122 B2
Hazel Rd. Chis 141 D2
Hazel Tree Rd. Watf 154 A2
Hazelbury Ave. Abb L 153 E4
Hazelbury Cres. Luton 63 E4
Hazelcroft. Pnr 176 A2
Hazeldell Link. Heml H 123 F1
Hazeldell Rd. Heml H 123 F1
Hazeldell. Wat St 70 B2
Hazeldene. Ches 162 C3
Hazelend Rd. Sta Mo 59 D2
Hazelmere Rd. St Alb 128 B3
Hazelmere Rd. Stev 69 D4
Hazels The. Tewin 90 C1
Hazelwood Cl. Hit 34 C4
Hazelwood Cl. Luton 46 A2
Hazelwood Dri. Pnr 175 D1
Hazelwood Dri. St Alb 128 B2
Hazelwood La. Abb L 153 E4
Hazelwood Rd. Cro Gr 166 B2
Hazely. Tri 100 B2
Heacham Cl. Luton 44 A2
Headingley Cl. Ham St 147 F3
Headingley Cl. Stev 50 C4
Headstone La. Har 176 A1
Healey Rd. Watf 166 C2
Heath Ave. Roystn 7 E3
Heath Ave. St Alb 127 E3
Heath Brow. Heml H 124 B1
Heath Cl. Harp 107 E4
Heath Cl. Heml H 124 B1
Heath Cl. Luton 63 D3
Heath Cl. Pot B 145 D1
Heath Dri. Pot B 145 D1
Heath Dri. Ware 93 E2
Heath Farm La. St Alb 127 F3
Heath Hill. Cod 67 E1
Heath La. Cod 67 F1
Heath La. Heml H 124 B1
Heath La. Hert H 114 B1
Heath Rd. Bre Wd 47 E1
Heath Rd. Pot B 145 D1
Heath Rd. St Alb 127 F3
Heath Rd. Watf 167 F1
Heath Rd. Wl Gr 68 C1
Heath Row. Bis St 59 D1
Heath The. Bre Wd 47 E1
Heathbourne Rd. Bus 168 C1
Heathbrow Rd. Wl Gr 89 F4
Heathcote Ave. Hat 130 A4
Heather Rd. Wel GC 110 B2
Heather Rise. Bus 167 F4
Heather Way. Heml H 124 B2
Heather Way. Pot B 158 C4
Heather Way. Stan 176 C2
Heathermere. Letw 11 F1
Heathfield Cl. Cad 62 C2
Heathfield Cl. Pot B 145 D
Heathfield Ct. St Alb 127 F2
Heathfield Rd. Bus 167 F
Heathfield Rd. Hit 21 F1
Heathfield Rd. Luton 45 E
Heathfield. Roystn 7 D
Heathgate. Hert H 114 B1
Heathlands Dri. St Alb 127 F3
Heathlands. Wl Gr 68 C1
Heathside Cl. Norwd 174 B3
Heathside Rd. Norwd 174 B3
Heaton Dell. Luton 46 C1
Heay Fields. Wel GC 111 E4
Hebden Cl. Luton 44 A2
Hedge Row. Heml H 124 A3
Hedgebrooms. Wel GC 111 E4
Hedgerows The. Stev 51 E4
Hedgerows. Saw 97 F1
Hedges Cl. Hat 130 A3
Hedgeside Rd. Norwd 174 B3
Hedgeside. Pot En 123 D4
Hedley Rd. St Alb 128 A2
Hedley Rise. Luton 46 C1
Heights The. Heml H 124 C3
Helena Cl. Barn 159 E1
Hellards Rd. Stev 50 B4
Helmsley Cl. Luton 44 B3
Helston Cl. Pnr 175 F2
Helston Gr. Heml H 124 B4
Helston Pl. Abb L 153 F4
Hemel Hempstead Rd. Dagn 81 E1
Hemel Hempstead Rd. Heml H 125 F1
Hemel Hempstead Rd. L Gad 103 D4
Hemel Hempstead Rd. Red 105 F1
Hemel Hempstead Rd. St Alb 126 B1
Hemingford Dri. Luton 45 E3
Hemingford Rd. Watf 153 F2
Hemming Way. Watf 154 A2
Hemmings The. Berk 121 F2
Hemp La. Wigg 100 C1
Hempstall. Wel G C 111 D2
Hempstead La. Pot En 123 E3
Hempstead Rd. Bov 137 D3
Hempstead Rd. Kin L 139 D2
Hempstead Rd. Watf 153 F1
Henbury Way. Sth Ox 175 E4
Henderson Cl. St Alb 127 E4
Henderson Pl. Bed 139 F2
Hendon Wood La. NW7 171 D1
Henge Way. Luton 44 C4
Henry St. Heml H 138 B4
Henry St. Tri 100 A2
Hensley Cl. Hit 35 D3
Hensley Cl. Welw 89 E3
Hensteau Pl. Luton 46 B1
Henth The. Radl 156 A3
Herald Cl. Bis St 76 B3
Herbert St. Heml H 124 B2
Hereford Rd. Luton 44 A2
Hereward Cl. Wa Aby 163 E4
Herga Ct. Watf 167 D4
Heritage Cl. St Alb 127 E2
Herkomer Cl. Bus 168 A2
Herkomer Rd. Bus 168 A2
Hermitage Ct. Pot B 159 E3
Hermitage Rd. Hit 34 C4
Herne Rd. Bus 168 A2
Herne Rd. Stev 36 A1
Herneshaw. Hat 129 F2
Herns La. Wel GC 111 D4
Herns Way. Wel GC 111 D4
Heron Cl. Ric 173 E4
Heron Cl. Saw 97 E1
Heron Ct. Bis St 77 D4
Heron Dri. Luton 45 F3
Heron Dri. Sta Ab 115 E2
Heron Trading Est. Luton 44 B4
Heron Way. Hat 130 A2
Heron Wlk. Norwd 174 C3
Heronfield. Pot B 145 E1
Herongate Rd. Ches 148 C2
Herons Elm. Nthch 121 F4
Herons Way. St Alb 142 A4
Herons Wood. Harl 117 D1
Heronsgate Rd. Chor 164 A2
Heronslea. Watf 154 B2
Heronswood Pl. Wel GC 111 D3
Heronswood Rd. Wel GC 111 D3
Heronswood. Wa Aby 163 F3
Hertford End Ct. Norwd 174 C3
Hertford Rd. Enf 162 B2
Hertford Rd. Gt Am 114 C2
Hertford Rd. Hat 130 B4
Hertford Rd. Hod 134 C4
Hertford Rd. Stev 69 D4
Hertford Rd. Tewin 90 C1
Hertford Rd. Ware 93 E1
Hertford Rd. Wel GC 90 A1
Hertford Rd. Welw 89 E2
Hertingfordbury Rd. Hert 113 D3
Hertingfordbury Rd. Hertng 113 D3
Heswall Green. Sth Ox 175 D4
Hetchleys. Heml H 124 A3
Hewitt Cl. Whea 108 B4
Hewlett Rd. Luton 44 C3
Hexton Rd. Gt Of 33 F4
Hexton Rd. Lily 32 A2
Heydon Rd. Gt Ch 9 F2
Heydons Cl. St Alb 127 E3
Heyford Rd. Radl 155 F1

eysham Dri. Sth Ox 175 E3
eywood Dri. Luton 45 F1
ibbert Ave. Watf 154 B1
ibbert Rd. Har 176 C1
ibbert St. Luton 63 F3
ickling Cl. Luton 46 B1
ickling Way. Harp 86 B2
icks Rd. Mark 83 F3
idalgo Ct. Heml H 124 C3
ides The. Harl 117 E1
High Acres. Abb L 153 E4
High Ash Rd. Whea 108 B4
High Ave. Letw 22 C2
High Beech Rd. Luton 44 B4
High Canons. Shen 157 E1
High Cl. Chor 165 E2
High Cross. Aldhm 155 E1
High Dane. Hit 22 A1
High Dells. Hat 129 F2
High Elms Cl. Norwd 174 B2
High Elms La. Abb L 154 B4
High Elms La. Heb En 70 C4
High Elms. Harp 107 D3
High Firs Cres. Harp 107 E4
High Gr. Wel GC 110 B4
High House Est. Harl 118 C2
High La. Sta Mo 59 F4
High Mead. Luton 45 D2
High Meads. Whea 108 B4
High Oak Rd. Ware 93 E2
High Oaks Rd. Wel GC 110 A4
High Oaks. Enf 160 C1
High Oaks. St Alb 127 E4
High Plash. Stev 50 C3
High Rd Broxbourne. Hod 134 C1
High Rd Turnford. Ches 148 C3
High Rd Wormley. Hod 148 C4
High Rd. Aps En 19 F4
High Rd. Bus 168 B1
High Rd. Ess 131 F3
High Rd. Har 176 C1
High Rd. Hod 134 C2
High Rd. Stap 91 F3
High Rd. Wat 92 A2
High Rd. Watf 154 A3
High Ridge Rd. Fel 138 B4
High Ridge. Cuf 146 C2
High Ridge. Harp 85 F2
High Ridge. Luton 46 B1
High St. Abb L 139 F1
High St. Arl 11 D3
High St. Ashw 4 B2
High St. Bal 23 F4
High St. Bar 8 C1
High St. Bark 17 E2
High St. Barn 171 F3
High St. Bed 139 F2
High St. Berk 122 B2
High St. Bis St 76 C4
High St. Bov 137 D2
High St. Bun 40 C4
High St. Bus 168 A2
High St. Ch En 11 D4
High St. Ched 80 A4
High St. Ches 148 B2
High St. Cod 67 F1
High St. Coln H 129 D1
High St. Elst 169 E2
High St. Fla 84 A1
High St. Gos 34 C2
High St. Gra 36 B2
High St. Gt Of 33 E2
High St. Gu M 1 C2
High St. Har 176 C1
High St. Hare 173 E1
High St. Harl 118 B2
High St. Harp 86 A1
High St. Heml H 124 B2
High St. Hin 3 E3
High St. Hit 34 C4
High St. Hod 135 D3
High St. Hun 95 E1
High St. Kim 66 B1
High St. Kin L 139 D1
High St. Luton 44 B2
High St. Mark 83 F3
High St. Muc H 74 C2
High St. Norwd 174 C1
High St. Nthch 121 F3
High St. Pirt 20 B2
High St. Pot B 159 E4
High St. Puc 55 E2
High St. Red 106 A3
High St. Reed 16 C3
High St. Ric 165 F1
High St. Roy 116 A1
High St. Roystn 7 E3
High St. Sand 108 B1
High St. St Alb 127 E2
High St. Sta Ab 115 E2
High St. Stand 55 F1
High St. Stev 50 B4
High St. Stot 11 F3
High St. Tri 100 A2
High St. Wal 38 A1
High St. Ware 93 E1
High St. Wat St 70 B2
High St. Welw 89 E3
High St. Whea 87 E1
High St. Whit 66 C4
High St. Widf 95 F2
High Street Green. Heml H 125 D3
High Town Rd. Luton 45 F1
High View Ct. Har 176 C2
High View. Birhr 59 E2
High View. Chor 165 D3
High View. Hat 130 A1
High View. Hit 34 B4
High View. Mark 83 F2
High View. Watf 166 C2
High Wickfield. Wel GC 111 E3
High Wood Cl. Luton 62 C4
High Wood Rd. Hod 114 C1
High Wych La. Saw 97 D1
High Wych Rd. H Wy 117 F4
High Wych Rd. Saw 97 E1
High Wych Way. Heml H 105 D1
Higham Dri. Luton 46 B1
Highbanks Rd. Pnr 176 A2
Highbarns. Heml H 139 D3
Highbury Ave. Hod 135 D4
Highbury Rd. Hit 35 D4
Highbury Rd. Luton 45 E1
Highbush Rd. Stot 11 F3
Highclere Dri. Heml H 139 D4
Highcroft Rd. Fel 138 A3
Highfield Ave. Bis St 77 E3
Highfield Ave. Harp 107 E4
Highfield Cl. Norwd 174 C1
Highfield Cres. Norwd 174 C1
Highfield Dri. Hod 134 C1
Highfield La. Heml H 124 C3
Highfield La. St Alb 128 B1
Highfield La. Tyt 142 C4
Highfield Rd. Berk 122 B2
Highfield Rd. Bus 167 F2
Highfield Rd. Ham St 147 F3
Highfield Rd. Hert 113 E2
Highfield Rd. Luton 45 D1
Highfield Rd. Norwd 174 C1
Highfield Rd. Sand 108 A1
Highfield Rd. Tri 99 F2
Highfield Rd. Wigg 100 B2
Highfield Way. Pot B 159 D4
Highfield Way. Ric 165 D2
Highfield. Heml H 124 C3
Highfield. Letw 22 C2
Highfields. Cuf 146 C2
Highfields. Radl 155 F2
Highgate Gr. Saw 97 E1
Highgrove Ct. Ches 162 B3
Highland Dri. Bus 168 A1
Highland Dri. Heml H 125 D2
Highland Rd. Lo Naz 135 F1
Highland Rd. Norwd 174 C1
Highland Rd. Thor 76 C2
Highlands The. Pot B 145 E1
Highlands The. Ric 165 D1
Highlands. Hat 130 B4
Highlands. Roystn 7 F3
Highlands. Watf 167 E1
Highmead. Sta Mo 59 F4
Highmoor. Harp 86 A2
Highover Cl. Luton 46 A1
Highover Rd. Letw 22 B3
Highover Way. Hit 22 A1
Highview Cl. Pot B 159 E3
Highview Gdns. Pot B 159 E3
Highview Gdns. St Alb 128 B4
Highway The. Stan 176 C1
Highwood Ave. Bus 167 F4
Highwoodhall La. Heml H 139 E4
Hilbury. Hat 129 F2
Hilfield La S . Bus 168 C2
Hilfield La. Bus 168 B4
Hill Cl. Barn 171 E2
Hill Cl. Harp 86 B2
Hill Cl. Luton 45 E4
Hill Cl. Pic En 124 A4
Hill Common. Heml H 139 D4
Hill Crest. Pot B 159 E3
Hill Crest. Stev 50 C3
Hill Crest. Whit 66 C3
Hill Croft Cl. Luton 44 B3
Hill Dyke Rd. Whea 108 B4
Hill End La. St Alb 128 B1
Hill End Rd. Hare 173 E2
Hill Farm Ave. Watf 154 A3
Hill Farm Cl. Watf 154 A3
Hill Farm La. A St L 88 A3
Hill Farm La. Red 106 B1
Hill House Ave. Stan 176 C2
Hill Ley. Hat 129 F3
Hill Leys. Cuf 146 C2
Hill Rd. Cod 67 F1
Hill Rd. Norwd 174 B2
Hill Rise. Cuf 146 C2
Hill Rise. Luton 44 B4
Hill Rise. Pot B 159 E3
Hill Rise. Ric 165 D1
Hill Side. Ched 79 F4
Hill St. St Alb 127 E2
Hill The. Harl 118 B2
Hill The. Whea 108 B4
Hill Top. Bal 23 F4
Hill View. Buck 27 E4
Hill View. Nthch 122 A4
Hill View. Whit 66 C3
Hill's La. Norwd 174 C1
Hillary Cl. Luton 44 B4
Hillary Cres. Luton 63 E3
Hillary Rd. Heml H 125 D2
Hillary Rise. Arl 11 D3
Hillborough Rd. Luton 63 E3
Hillbrow. Letw 22 B2
Hillcrest Ave. Luton 45 E4
Hillcrest Rd. Shen 157 D3
Hillcrest. Bal 23 F4
Hillcrest. Hat 130 A3
Hillcroft Cres. Watf 175 D4
Hilldown Rd. Heml H 124 A3
Hillfield Ave. Hit 22 A1
Hillfield Rd. Heml H 124 B2
Hillfield. Hat 130 B4
Hillgate. Hit 22 A2
Hillhouse. Wa Aby 163 F3
Hilliard Rd. Norwd 174 C1
Hillingdon Rd. Watf 154 A3
Hillmead. Berk 122 A2
Hillmead. Stev 51 D3
Hillrise Ave. Watf 154 B1
Hillsborough Green. Sth Ox 175 D4
Hillshott. Letw 23 D3
Hillside Ave. Bis St 77 D4
Hillside Ave. Bor 170 A3
Hillside Ave. Ches 162 B4
Hillside Cl. Abb L 153 F4
Hillside Cres. Ches 162 B4
Hillside Cres. Enf 161 E1
Hillside Cres. Norwd 175 D1
Hillside Cres. Sta Ab 115 D2
Hillside Cres. Watf 167 F2
Hillside Gdns. Barn 171 F3
Hillside Gdns. Berk 122 B2
Hillside Gdns. Norwd 175 D2
Hillside La. Sta Ab 115 D2
Hillside Rd. Bus 167 F2
Hillside Rd. Chor 164 B2
Hillside Rd. Harp 85 F2
Hillside Rd. Luton 63 E4
Hillside Rd. Norwd 175 D2
Hillside Rd. Pnr 175 D2
Hillside Rd. Radl 156 A2
Hillside Rd. St Alb 127 F2
Hillside Rise. Norwd 175 D2
Hillside Terr. Hert 113 E2
Hillside Way. Wl Gr 90 A4
Hillside. Cod 67 F1
Hillside. Gt Am 114 A4
Hillside. Hat 130 A3
Hillside. Hod 134 C4
Hillside. Roystn 7 E3
Hillside. Stev 50 C3
Hillside. Wel GC 111 D2
Hilltop Cl. Ham St 147 F3
Hilltop Ct. Luton 63 E4
Hilltop Rd. Bed 139 E2
Hilltop Rd. Berk 122 B2
Hilltop. Red 105 F3
Hillview Cl. Pnr 175 F2
Hillview Cres. Luton 45 E4
Hillview Gdns. Ches 148 C2
Hillview Rd. Pnr 175 F2
Hilly Fields. Wel GC 111 E4
Hilmay Dri. Heml H 124 A1
Hilton Cl. Stev 50 A4
Hindhead Green. Sth Ox 175 E3
Hine Way. Hit 21 E1
Hinxworth Rd. Ashw 4 A2
Hinxworth Rd. Hin 3 E2
Hipkins. Bis St 76 C2
Hishbridge St. Wa Aby 163 F4
Hitchens Cl. Heml H 123 F2
Hitchin Hill Path. Hit 34 C3
Hitchin Hill. Hit 34 C3
Hitchin Rd. Arl 11 D1
Hitchin Rd. Gos 34 C2
Hitchin Rd. Gt Wy 35 F3
Hitchin Rd. Henlw 10 A3
Hitchin Rd. Hit 33 F4
Hitchin Rd. Kim 66 B1
Hitchin Rd. Letw 22 C2
Hitchin Rd. Luton 46 A2
Hitchin Rd. Pegs 19 E1
Hitchin Rd. Pirt 20 C1
Hitchin Rd. Stev 36 A1
Hitchin Rd. Stot 11 E2
Hitchin Rd. Wes 24 A1
Hitchin St. Bal 23 F4
Hither Field. Ware 93 F2
Hitherbaulk. Wel GC 110 C2
Hitherway. Wel GC 89 E1
Hitherwell Dri. Har 176 B1
Hive Cl. Bus 176 B4
Hive Rd. Bus 176 B4
Hive Rd. Har 176 C4
Hobart Walk. St Alb 127 F4
Hobbs Cl. Ches 148 B1
Hobbs Cl. St Alb 128 C1
Hobbs Cross Rd. Harl 118 C2
Hobbs Hill Rd. Heml H 138 C4
Hobbs Hill. Welw 89 E2
Hobbs Way. Wel GC 110 B3
Hobletts Rd. Heml H 124 C2
Hobsons Cl. Hod 114 C1
Hobsons Wlk. Tri 99 F3
Hobtoe Rd. Harl 117 D1
Hockerill St. Bis St 77 D4
Hockerill. Wat St 70 C2
Hocklands. Wel GC 111 E4
Hockwell Ring. Luton 44 B2
Hoddesdon Rd. Sta Ab 115 E2
Hodings Rd. Harl 117 E1
Hodwell. Ashw 4 B2
Hoe La. Enf 162 A1
Hoe La. Gt Am 114 B4
Hoe La. Lo Naz 135 F1
Hoe The. Watf 175 E4
Hoecroft. Lo Naz 135 F1
Hoestock Rd. Saw 97 E1
Hog Hall La. Dagn 81 D3
Hog La. Ash Gr 121 E1
Hogarth Ct. Bus 168 A1
Hogg End La. Heml H 125 F3
Hogg End La. Red 126 A3
Hogg La. Elst 169 D3
Hogges Cl. Hod 135 D3
Hogsdell La. Hert H 114 A2
Holbeck La. Ham St 147 F3
Holbein Gate. Norwd 174 C3
Holborn Cl. St Alb 128 B4
Holbrook Cl. Enf 162 A1
Holcroft Rd. Harp 86 B2
Holdbrook. Hit 35 D4
Holden Cl. Hert 113 F4
Holders La. Stev 51 F3
Holdings The. Hat 130 B4
Holecroft. Wa Aby 163 F3
Holford Way. Luton 31 D1
Holgate Dri. Luton 44 A2
Holkham Cl. Luton 44 A2
Holland Gdns. Watf 154 B2
Holland Rd. Luton 45 D1
Holland's Croft. Hun 95 E1
Holliday St. Berk 122 B2
Hollier Ct. Hat 130 A3
Holliers Way. Hat 130 A3
Hollies Cl. Roystn 7 F3
Hollies The. Heron 164 B1
Hollies The. Wigg 100 B2
Hollies Way. P Bar 159 E4
Hollow La. Hit 34 C4
Holloway La. Chen 151 E1
Holloway The. Dra B 99 E2
Holloways La. Wel Gr 144 B4
Holly Cl. Hat 129 F2
Holly Copse. Stev 50 C2
Holly Croft. Hertng 113 D4
Holly Dell. Hert 113 E2
Holly Dri. Berk 122 B2
Holly Dri. Pot B 159 D3
Holly Farm Cl. Cad 62 C2
Holly Gr. Pnr 175 F1
Holly Grove Rd. Bram 91 E2
Holly Hedges La. Bov 151 E4
Holly La. Kim 86 C3
Holly Leys. Stev 69 E4
Holly Rd. Enf 162 B2
Holly Rd. Wl Gr 69 D1
Holly Shaws. Stev 51 D1
Holly St. Luton 63 F3
Holly Tree Cl. Bot 150 A4
Holly Wlk. Harp 86 B1
Holly Wlk. Wel GC 89 E1
Hollybush Ave. Chis 141 D4
Hollybush Cl. Har 176 B1
Hollybush Cl. Heml H 123 E4
Hollybush Cl. Watf 167 E1
Hollybush Cl. Wl Gr 89 F4
Hollybush Hill. Lily 32 C1
Hollybush La. Dat 69 E2
Hollybush La. Fla 84 A2
Hollybush La. Harp 86 A2
Hollybush La. Heml H 123 F2
Hollybush La. Wel GC 110 C1
Hollybush La. Wel GC 110 C2
Hollybush La. Whit 66 A4
Hollybush Rd. Luton 46 B1
Hollybush Way. Ches 148 A2
Hollycross Rd. Ware 115 D4
Hollyfield Cl. Tri 100 B3
Hollyfield. Hat 130 A1
Hollyfield. Tri 100 B3
Hollyfields. Ches 148 C3
Hollygrove. Bus 168 B1
Holmbrook Ave. Luton 45 E3
Holmbury Cl. Har 176 C4
Holmdale Cl. Bor 169 F4
Holmdale. Letw 23 D3
Holme Cl. Ches 162 B4
Holme Cl. Hat 129 F4
Holme Lea. Watf 154 B3
Holme Park. Bor 169 F4
Holme Rd. Hat 129 F4
Holme Way. Stan 176 C2
Holmes Ct. St Alb 127 F2
Holmesdale. Enf 162 B2
Holmfield Cl. Luton 63 E3
Holmscroft Rd. Luton 44 C3
Holmshill La. Ridge 157 F1
Holmside Rise. Sth Ox 175 D4
Holmwood Rd. Enf 162 B2
Holroyd Cres. Bal 23 F4
Holt Cl. Elst 169 F3
Holt The. Heml H 124 C1
Holt The. Wel GC 111 E3
Holts Mdw. Red 106 A3
Holtsmere Cl. Luton 46 B1
Holtsmere Cl. Watf 154 B2
Holwell Hyde La. Wel GC 111 E2
Holwell Hyde. Wel GC 111 E2
Holwell Rd. Hol 21 D4
Holwell Rd. Pirt 20 C3
Holwell Rd. Wel GC 110 C3
Holy Cross Hill. Ham St 148 A4
Holyfield Rd. Wa Aby 149 E2
Holyrood Cres. St Alb 141 E4
Holywell Cl. Stu 82 B3
Holywell Ct. Luton 45 D2
Holywell Hill. St Alb 127 E1
Holywell Rd. Stu 82 A4
Holywell Rd. Watf 167 D2
Home Cl. Hod 148 C4
Home Cl. Luton 44 B2
Home Cl. Stot 11 F4
Home Farm Rd. Nthch 121 E4
Home Farm Rd. Ric 174 A3
Home Field. Barn 171 F2
Home Field. Pot En 123 D4
Home Ley. Wel GC 110 C3
Home Meadow. Wel GC 110 C3
Home Way. Ric 164 C1
Homedale Dri. Luton 44 B1
Homefield La. Lan 49 F1
Homefield Rd. Bus 168 A2
Homefield Rd. Chor 164 B3
Homefield Rd. Heml H 125 D1
Homefield Rd. Radl 155 F1
Homefield Rd. Ware 93 F1
Homefield. Bov 137 D2
Homeleigh Ct. Ches 148 A1
Homerfield. Wel GC 110 B4
Homerswood La. Welw 89 D1
Homerton Rd. Luton 45 D3
Homestead Ct. Wel GC 110 C2
Homestead La. Wel GC 110 C2
Homestead Moat. Stev 50 C3
Homestead Rd. Hat 130 A4
Homestead Rd. Ric 165 E1
Homestead Way. Luton 63 E3
Homewood Ave. Cuf 146 C2
Homewood La. Cuf 146 B2
Homewood Rd. St Alb 128 A3
Honey Bourne. Bis St 76 C3
Honey Brook. Wa Aby 163 F3
Honey La. Bun 40 C4
Honey La. Hert 113 E3
Honey La. Sta Gr 30 C2
Honey La. Wa Aby 163 F3
Honeycroft. Wel GC 110 B3
Honeycross Rd. Heml H 123 F1
Honeygate. Luton 45 F2
Honeymeade. Saw 118 B4
Honeysuckle Gdns. Hat 130 A2
Honeyway. Roystn 7 F3
Honeywood Cl. Pot B 159 E3
Hoo St. Luton 63 F3
Hoo The. Harl 118 B3
Hook Gate. Enf 162 A2
Hook La. Nort 159 F4
Hookers Way. Luton 44 B3
Hoops La. Ther 15 F3
Hope Green. Watf 154 A3
Hopewell Rd. Bal 23 E4
Hopground Cl. St Alb 128 A1
Hopkins Cres. Sand 108 A1
Hoppit Rd. Wa Aby 163 D3
Hopton Rd. Stev 50 A4
Horace Brightman Cl. Luton 45 D4
Horace Gay Gdns. Letw 22 C3
Hordle Gdns. St Alb 127 F1
Horn Hill. Whit 66 C3
Hornbeam Cl. Bor 170 A4
Hornbeam La. Wild 131 F1
Hornbeam Spring. Kneb 68 C2
Hornbeam Way. Ches 147 F1
Hornbeams Ave. Enf 162 B2
Hornbeams The. Harl 117 E1
Hornbeams The. Stev 51 D2
Hornbeams. Bri Wd 140 C1
Hornets The. Watf 167 D3
Hornhill Rd. Map Cr 172 B3
Horns Cl. Hert 113 E2
Horns Mill Rd. Hert 113 E2
Hornsby Cl. Luton 46 B1
Hornsfield. Wel GC 111 E4
Horrocks Cl. Ware 93 E2
Horse Hill. Bot 150 B4
Horsecroft Rd. Heml H 124 A1
Horselers. Heml H 139 D4
Horseshoe Cl. Ched 80 A4
Horseshoe Hill. Gt Ho 42 A4
Horseshoe La. Gt Ho 42 A4
Horseshoe La. N20 171 E1
Horseshoe La. Watf 154 B4
Horseshoe The. Heml H 125 E1
Horsham Cl. Luton 46 B1
Horsleys. Map Cr 172 B3
Horton Gdns. Heml H 105 D1
Hospital Rd. Arl 11 D2
Housden Cl. Whea 108 C4
House La. Ch En 11 D4
House La. Sand 108 A1
House La. St Alb 128 B4
Housewood End. Heml H 124 A3
Housman Ave. Roystn 7 E4
How Field. Harp 85 F2
How Wood. Chis 141 D2
Howard Agne Cl. Bov 137 D2
Howard Cl. Bus 168 C1

Howard Cl. Luton 45 D2
Howard Cl. St Alb 128 B1
Howard Cl. Wa Aby 163 E3
Howard Cl. Watf 154 A1
Howard Ct. Letw 23 D2
Howard Dri. Bor 170 B3
Howard Dri. Letw 23 D2
Howard Gate. Letw 23 D2
Howard Way. Harl 117 F1
Howards Cl. Pnr 175 D1
Howards Dri. Heml H 124 A3
Howards Wood. Letw 23 D2
Howardsgate. Wel GC 110 B3
Howe Dell. Hat 130 A3
Howe Rd. Heml H 125 D1
Howfield Green. Hod 115 D1
Howicks Green. Wel GC 111 D2
Howland Garth. St Alb 141 E4
Howlands. Wel GC 110 C2
Howton Pl. Bus 168 B1
Hoylake Gdns. Sth Ox 175 E3
Hubbards Rd. Chor 164 B2
Huckleberry Cl. Luton 45 D4
Hudnall La. L Gad 102 B4
Hudson Cl. St Alb 141 E4
Hudson Cl. Watf 153 F2
Hudson Rd. Stev 51 D4
Huggins La. Wel Gr 144 B4
Hughenden Rd. St Alb 128 B3
Hull La. Gr En 55 F4
Humberstone Cl. Luton 44 C1
Humberstone Rd. Luton 44 C1
Hunsdon Rd. Sta Ab 116 A3
Hunsdon Rd. Widf 95 F2
Hunsdon. Wel GC 111 E3
Hunston Cl. Luton 44 A3
Hunt Cl. St Alb 128 B3
Hunter Cl. Bor 170 B2
Hunter Cl. Pot B 159 D3
Hunter Wlk. Bor 170 B2
Hunter's La. Watf 153 F3
Huntercrombe Gdns. St Ox 175 E3
Hunters Cl. Bov 137 D1
Hunters Cl. Stev 51 E4
Hunters Cl. Stot 11 F3
Hunters Cl. Tri 100 A3
Hunters Oak. Heml H 125 D4
Hunters Park. Berk 122 A2
Hunters Reach. Ches 147 F1
Hunters Ride. Bric 155 D4
Hunters Way. Roystn 7 F3
Hunters Way. Wel GC 110 C2
Hunting Gate. Heml H 124 C4
Hunting Gate. Hit 22 A2
Huntingdon Cl. Hod 148 C4
Huntingdon Rd. Stev 50 A4
Hunton Bridge Hill. Abb L 153 E3
Hunts Cl. Luton 63 E3
Hunts Meadow. Wes 24 B1
Huntsmans Cl. Dagn 81 E3
Huntsmill Rd. Heml H 123 F1
Hurlock Way. Luton 44 B3
Hurst Cl. Bal 13 D1
Hurst Cl. Wel GC 111 E3
Hurst Dri. Ches 162 B3
Hurst Way. Luton 44 C3
Hurstlings. Wel G C 111 D2
Hutton Cl. Hertng 113 D3
Hutton Gdns. Har 176 B2
Hutton La. Har 176 B2
Hutton Wlk. Har 176 B2
Hyatt Ind Est. Stev 50 A3
Hyburn Cl. Bri Wd 140 C1
Hyburn Cl. Heml H 125 D1
Hyde Ave. Pot B 159 D3
Hyde Ave. Stot 11 F3
Hyde Cl. Barn 171 F3
Hyde Cl. Harp 86 A2
Hyde Green. Stev 51 D2
Hyde La. Bed 139 E3
Hyde La. Bov 137 D2
Hyde La. Chis 141 E2
Hyde La. Fro 141 E2
Hyde La. Pet Gr 65 E1
Hyde Mead. Lo Naz 149 F4
Hyde Meadows. Bov 137 D2
Hyde Rd. Cad 62 C2
Hyde Rd. Watf 167 D4
Hyde The. Stev 51 E2
Hyde The. Ware 93 D1
Hyde View Rd. Harp 86 A2
Hyde Vlly. Wel GC 110 C2
Hyde Way. Wel GC 110 C3
Hydean Way. Stev 51 D2
Hyperion Ct. Heml H 124 C3
Hyver Hill. NW7 170 B1

Ibberson Way. Hit 35 D4
Ickleford Rd. Hit 34 C4
Ickley Cl. Luton 44 A3
Icknield Cl. Ick 21 F2
Icknield Cl. St Alb 126 C1
Icknield Cres. Tri 100 A3
Icknield Green. Letw 22 C3
Icknield Rd. Luton 44 C2
Icknield Way E. Bal 12 C1
Icknield Way. Bal 12 C1
Icknield Way. Dra B 99 E2
Icknield Way. Letw 22 C3
Icknield Way. Luton 45 D4
Icknield Way. Tri 99 F2
Icknield Wlk. Roystn 7 F4
Ilford Cl. Luton 46 B2
Ilkley Rd. Sth Ox 175 E3
iller Cl. Pnr 175 E1
Imberfield. Luton 44 B2
Imperial Way. Watf 167 E4
Indells. Hat 129 F2
Industrial Park. Bor 170 B4
Ingelheim Ct. Stev 50 B4
Ingersoll Rd. Enf 162 B1
Inglefield. Pot B 145 D1
Ingles. Wel GC 89 F1
Ingleside Dri. Stev 36 A1
Inkerman Rd. St Alb 127 F1
Inkerman St. Luton 63 E4
Inn's Cl. Stev 50 B3
Innes Ct. Heml H 138 B4
Inskip Cres. Stev 50 C3
Ionian Way. Heml H 124 C3
Iredale View. Bal 13 D1
Iron Dri. Hert 114 A4
Irving Cl. Bis St 76 B2
Irving Cres. Ched 80 A4
Isabell Cl. Gofs O 147 E1
Isenburg Way. Heml H 124 B4
Isherwood Cl. Roystn 7 E4
Islington Way. Stev 36 C1
Itch La. Gravnd 57 E4
Iveagh Cl. Norwd 174 A1
Iveagh Ct. Heml H 124 B2
Ivel Ct. Letw 23 E2
Ivel Rd. Stev 50 B4
Ivel Way. Bal 24 A3
Ivel Way. Stot 11 F4
Ives Rd. Hert 113 D4
Ivinghoe Cl. St Alb 128 B4
Ivinghoe Cl. Watf 154 B2
Ivinghoe Rd. Bus 168 B1
Ivinghoe Rd. Ric 165 D1
Ivy House La. Berk 122 B2
Ivy House La. Pot En 122 B3
Ivy Rd. Luton 63 E4
Ivy Terr. Hod 135 E4
Ivy Wlk. Norwd 174 C1
Ivybridge. Hod 135 D2

Jackdaws. Wel GC 111 E3
Jackets La. Norwd 174 A2
Jacketts Field. Abb L 153 F4
Jackman's Pl. Letw 23 D3
Jackson Sq. Bis St 76 C4
Jackson St. Bal 12 C1
Jackson's La. Reed 16 C3
Jacksons Dri. Ches 148 A2
James Bedford Cl. Pnr 175 E1
James Cl. Bus 167 F2
James Way. Stev 50 B4
Jameson Ct. St Alb 127 F2
Jameson Rd. Harp 86 A2
Jarden. Letw 23 E2
Jarman Cl. Heml H 124 C1
Jarvis Cl. Barn 171 E2
Jarvis Cleys. Ham St 147 F3
Jasmine Gdns. Hat 130 A4
Jasons Hill. Bot 136 A1
Jasper Cl. Enf 162 B1
Jaywood. Luton 46 B3
Jeans Way. Dun 44 A1
Jeffrey Cl. Roystn 7 E4
Jeffries Rd. Ware 93 F1
Jellicoe Gdns. Stan 176 C2
Jenkins Ave. Bri Wd 140 C1
Jenkins La. Bis St 77 E3
Jenkins La. St Le 119 F2
Jenning Wood. Wl Gr 89 F4
Jennings Cl. Stev 50 C2
Jennings Rd. St Alb 128 A2
Jennings Way. Barn 171 E3
Jepps La. Roystn 7 E3
Jerome Dri. St Alb 127 D1
Jersey Cl. Hod 135 D4
Jersey La. St Alb 128 A3
Jersey Rd. Luton 44 A2
Jervis Ave. Enf 162 C2
Jervis Rd. Bis St 76 C3
Jessop Rd. Stev 37 D1
Jeves Cl. Bal 13 D1
Jillifer Rd. Luton 44 A1
Jinnings The. Wel GC 111 D2
Jocelyns. Harl 118 B2
Jocketts Hill. Heml H 123 F2
Jocketts Rd. Heml H 123 F1
Joel St. Norwd 175 D1
John Barker Pl. Hit 21 E1
John Ct. Hod 115 D1
John St. Luton 63 F4
John St. Roystn 7 E3
John Tate Rd. Hert 113 F3
Johnby Cl. Enf 162 C1
Johns La. Ash Gr 121 F1
Johns Rd. Bis St 59 D1
Johnson Ct. Heml H 124 C1
Joiner's Cl. Bot 136 A1
Joint The. Bark 17 D3
Joint The. Reed 16 C3
Jones Rd. Gofs O 147 D1
Jonquil Cl. Wel G C 111 D2
Jordan Cl. Watf 153 F2
Jordan's Way. Bri Wd 140 C1
Jordans. Wel GC 111 E4
Joyce Ct. Wa Aby 163 E3
Jubilee Ave. Lon C 142 B3
Jubilee Ave. Ware 93 F1
Jubilee Cl. Pnr 175 E1
Jubilee Cotts. Bun 40 B3
Jubilee Cres. Arl 11 D1
Jubilee Ct. Hat 130 A4
Jubilee Ct. Wa Aby 163 F3
Jubilee Memorial Ave. Stev 50 B4
Jubilee Rd. Letw 23 E4
Jubilee Rd. Stev 50 A4
Jubilee Rd. Watf 154 A1
Jubilee St. Luton 45 F1
Judge St. Watf 154 A1
Judge's Hill. Nort 145 F1
Julia Gate. Stev 51 E4
Julian's Ct. Stev 50 B4
Julian's Rd. Stev 50 A4
Julius Gdns. Luton 44 C4
Juniper Ave. Bric 155 D4
Juniper Cl. Hod 148 C3
Juniper Cl. Luton 44 C1
Juniper Gate. Ric 173 E4
Juniper Gdns. Wl Gr 89 F4
Juniper Gr. Watf 154 A1
Juniper Green. Heml H 123 F2
Juno Rd. Heml H 124 C3
Jupiter Dri. Heml H 124 C3
Juxon Cl. Har 176 A1

Kardwell Cl. Hit 35 D3
Katescroft. Wel GC 110 C1
Katherine Cl. Heml H 138 C4
Katrine Sq. Heml H 124 B4
Keats Cl. Heml H 105 D1
Keats Cl. Roystn 7 E4
Keats Cl. Stev 51 E4
Keats Way. Hit 35 E4
Keble Terr. Abb L 153 F4
Kecksy's. Saw 97 F2
Keepers Cl. Luton 46 B1
Keiths Rd. Heml H 125 D1
Keiths Wood. Kneb 68 C3
Kelbys. Wel GC 111 E4
Kelling Cl. Luton 45 E4
Kelly Cl. Bor 170 B4
Kelman Cl. Ches 162 C4
Kelmscott Cl. Watf 167 D2
Kelmscott Cres. Watf 167 D2
Kelshall St. Kel 15 F3
Kelshall. Watf 154 C2
Kelvin Cl. Luton 63 F3
Kelvin Cres. Har 176 C2
Kemble Cl. Pot B 159 E3
Kemp Pl. Bus 168 A2
Kempe Cl. St Alb 141 E4
Kempe Rd. Enf 162 B2
Kemprow. Aldhm 155 E2
Kemps Dri. Norwd 174 C2
Kempsey Cl. Luton 46 B1
Kendal Cl. Luton 44 B4
Kendale Rd. Hit 34 C3
Kendale Rd. Luton 44 A1
Kendale. Heml H 125 D1
Kendall Cl. Wel G C 110 C1
Kendals Cl. Radl 155 F2
Kenerne Dri. Barn 171 F2
Kenford Cl. Watf 154 A4
Kenilworth Cl. Bor 170 B3
Kenilworth Cl. Stev 69 E4
Kenilworth Cres. Enf 161 F1
Kenilworth Ct. Watf 167 D4
Kenilworth Dri. Bor 170 B3
Kenilworth Dri. Cro Gr 166 A3
Kenilworth Gdns. Sth Ox 175 E3
Kenilworth Rd. Luton 63 E4
Kennedy Ave. Hod 134 C3
Kennedy Cl. Ches 148 C2
Kennedy Cl. Pnr 175 F2
Kennedy Rd. Dan En 71 F4
Kennelwood La. Hat 130 A3
Kenneth Gdns. Stan 176 C2
Kenneth Rd. Luton 46 A1
Kenning Rd. Hod 135 D4
Kennington Rd. Luton 45 D2
Kensington Ave. Watf 166 C3
Kensworth Rd. Stu 82 B2
Kent Cl. Bor 157 E1
Kent Cres. Bis St 76 C2
Kent Rd. Luton 62 C4
Kent's La. Stand 55 F1
Kentish La. Bro Pk 145 E4
Kenton Gdns. St Alb 127 F1
Kenton La. Har 176 C2
Kents Ave. Heml H 138 B4
Kenwood Dri. Ric 172 C4
Kenworth Cl. Ches 162 B3
Kerdistone Cl. Pot B 145 D1
Kerr Cl. Kneb 68 C3
Kerri Cl. Barn 171 E3
Kershaw Cl. Luton 45 D4
Kershaw's Hill. Hit 34 C3
Kessingland Ave. Stev 36 A1
Kestrel Cl. Berk 122 B2
Kestrel Cl. Stev 51 E1
Kestrel Cl. Watf 154 C3
Kestrel Green. Hat 130 A2
Kestrel Way. Luton 44 A3
Kestrel Wlk. Letw 23 D2
Keswick Dri. Enf 162 B2
Keswick Rd. St Alb 128 A1
Kettering Rd. Enf 162 B1
Kettle Green Rd. Had Cr 74 C1
Ketton Cl. Luton 64 A4
Kewferry Dri. Norwd 174 B3
Kewferry Rd. Norwd 174 B3
Keyfield Terr. St Alb 127 E1
Keymer Cl. Luton 46 B2
Keynton Cl. Hertng 112 C4
Keysers Rd. Lo Naz 135 D1
Kibes La. Ware 93 F1
Kilbride Ct. Heml H 124 C4
Kilby Cl. Watf 154 B2
Kildonan Cl. Watf 166 C4
Kilfillan Gdns. Berk 122 A2
Kilmarnock Dri. Luton 45 F3
Kilmarnock Rd. Sth Ox 175 E3
Kiln Ave. L Chal 150 B1
Kiln Ground. Heml H 125 D1
Kiln House Cl. Ware 93 F1
Kiln La. Bot 150 A4
Kiln Way. Norwd 174 C2
Kilncroft. Heml H 125 D1
Kilnfield. Wel GC 89 F1
Kilsmore La. Ches 148 B1
Kilvinton Dri. Enf 161 E1
Kilworth Cl. Wel G C 111 D2
Kimberley Cl. Bis St 77 D3
Kimberley Rd. St Alb 127 E2
Kimberley. Letw 11 F1
Kimble Cl. Watf 166 C1
Kimble Cres. Bus 168 B1
Kimbolton Cres. Stev 69 D4
Kimbolton Green. Bor 170 B3
Kimps Way. Heml H 139 D4
Kimpton Bottom. Kim 86 C4
Kimpton Cl. Heml H 125 D4
Kimpton La. Luton 64 B4
Kimpton Pl. Watf 154 B3
Kimpton Rd. Bla En 87 D4
Kimpton Rd. Cod 88 C3
Kimpton Rd. Luton 64 A3
Kimpton Rd. Pet Gr 65 F1
Kimpton Rd. Welw 89 D3
Kimptons Cl. Pot B 158 B4
Kimptons Mead. Pot B 158 B4
Kinderscout. Heml H 125 D1
Kindersley Cl. Welw 89 E3
Kindersley Way. Abb L 153 E4
King Arthur Ct. Ches 162 C4
King Croft Rd. Harp 107 E4
King Ct. Berk 122 B3
King Edward Rd. Ches 162 C3
King Edward Rd. Shen 156 C3
King Edward Rd. Watf 167 F2
King Edward St. Fel 138 B4
King Edward's Rd. Ware 93 F1
King George Ave. Bus 168 A2
King George Cl. Stev 50 C3
King George Rd. Wa Aby 163 E3
King George Rd. Ware 93 F1
King George's Way. Whit 66 C3
King Georges Ave. Watf 166 C3
King Georges Cl. Hit 21 E1
King Harry La. St Alb 127 D1
King Harry St. Heml H 124 B1
King Henry's Mews. Ches 163 D1
King James Way. Roystn 7 E3
King James' Ave. Cuf 146 C1
King St. Bis St 76 C4
King St. Luton 63 F4
King St. Mark 83 F3
King St. Roystn 7 E3
King Street Mews. Bis St 76 C4
King's La. Chipf 152 A4
King's Rd. Ches 162 C3
King's Rd. Hert 114 A4
King's Rd. Hit 34 C4
King's Rd. Lon C 142 B3
King's Rd. St Alb 127 E2
King's Walden Rd. Gt Of 33 E1
Kingfisher Cl. Norwd 174 A1
Kingfisher Cl. Sta Ab 115 E2
Kingfisher Cl. Whea 87 E1
Kingfisher Lure. Bed 139 D1
Kingfisher Lure. Chor 165 D3
Kingfisher Rise. Stev 51 E1
Kingfisher Way. Bis St 77 D4
Kingham Rd. Wars 94 C3
Kinghamway. Luton 45 F1
Kings Ave. Heml H 138 C4
Kings Ave. Watf 167 D3
Kings Cl. Chipf 152 A4
Kings Cl. Norwd 174 C2
Kings Cl. Watf 167 E3
Kings Court. Berk 122 B3
Kings Ct. Bis St 77 D4
Kings Farm Rd. Chor 164 B2
Kings Hedges. Hit 34 B4
Kings Meadow. Bed 139 D2
Kings Rd. Barn 171 E3
Kings Rd. Berk 122 A2
Kings St. Watf 167 E3
Kings Walden Rise. Stev 51 E4
Kings Wlk. Roystn 7 E3
Kingsbridge Rd. Bis St 77 D4
Kingsbury Ave. St Alb 127 E2
Kingscroft. Wel GC 111 D4
Kingsdale Rd. Berk 122 A2
Kingsdown Ave. Luton 45 E
Kingsdown. Hit 35 D
Kingsfield Ct. Watf 167 E
Kingsfield Dri. Enf 162 B
Kingsfield Rd. Dan En 71 F
Kingsfield Rd. Watf 167 E
Kingsfield Way. Enf 162 B
Kingsfield. Hod 135 D
Kingshill Ave. St Alb 128 A
Kingshill Way. Berk 122 A
Kingsland Rd. Heml H 124 A
Kingsland Rd. Luton 63 F
Kingsland Way. Ashw 4 B
Kingsley Ave. Bor 169 F
Kingsley Ave. Ches 148 A
Kingsley Ct. Wel G C 110 C
Kingsley Rd. Luton 45 D
Kingsley Wlk. Tri 100 A
Kingsmead Rd. Bis St 77 D
Kingsmead. Ches 148 B
Kingsmead. Cuf 146 C
Kingsmead. Saw 97 F
Kingsmead. St Alb 128 B
Kingston Pl. Har 176 C
Kingston Rd. Luton 45 F
Kingston Vale. Roystn 7 F
Kingsway Ind Est. Luton 63 D
Kingsway Nrth Orbital Rd. Watf 154 A
Kingsway. Cuf 146 C
Kingsway. Luton 45 D
Kingsway. Roystn 7 E4
Kingsway. Stot 11 F4
Kingsway. Ware 93 E2
Kingswell Ride. Cuf 146 C
Kingswood Ave. Hit 35 E4
Kingswood Rd. Watf 154 A3
Kingwell Rd. Barn 159 E1
Kinross Cres. Luton 44 B4
Kinsbourne Cl. Harp 85 E2
Kinsbourne Cres. Harp 85 E2
Kinsbourne Green La. Kin Gr 85 D2
Kipling Cl. Hit 35 E4
Kipling Gr. Heml H 105 D1
Kipling Rd. Roystn 2 C1
Kipling Way. Harp 86 A1
Kirby Cl. Norwd 174 C2
Kirby Dri. Luton 45 D4
Kirkcaldy Green. Sth Ox 175 E4
Kirkdale Rd. Harp 86 A1
Kirklands. Wel GC 89 E1
Kirkwick Ave. Harp 86 A1
Kit's La. Wall 25 E4
Kitchener Cl. St Alb 128 A1
Kitching La. Stev 50 A3
Kite Field. Nthch 121 F4
Kite Way. Letw 22 C4
Kitsbury Rd. Berk 122 A2
Kitsbury Terr. Berk 122 A2
Kitson Way. Harl 117 E1
Kitswell Way. Radl 155 F3
Kitt's End Rd. Pot B 158 C1
Knap Cl. Letw 23 E4
Knebworth Ct. Bis St 76 B3
Knebworth Path. Bor 170 B3
Kneesworth Rd. Knee 2 C4
Kneesworth St. Roystn 7 E3
Knella Green. Wel GC 111 D3
Knella Rd. Wel GC 111 D3
Knight St. Saw 97 F1
Knights Cl. Bis St 76 B4
Knights Cl. Bun 40 B3
Knights Field. Luton 45 E1
Knights Templars Green. Stev 51 E4
Knightsbridge Way. Heml H 124 C2
Knightsfield. Wel GC 89 E1
Knoll Cres. Norwd 174 C1
Knoll Rise. Luton 45 F2
Knoll The. Hert 114 A4
Knolles Cres. Wel Gr 144 A4
Knolls Cl. Wing 60 A2
Knowl Piece. Hit 22 A2
Knowl Way. Elst 169 F2
Knowle Dri. Harp 107 E4
Knowle The. Hod 135 D3
Knutsford Ave. Watf 154 B1
Koh-I-Noor Ave. Bus 168 A2
Kristiansand Way. Letw 23 E4
Kymswell Rd. Stev 51 E2
Kynance Cl. Luton 46 A1
Kynaston Cl. Har 176 B2
Kynaston Wood. Har 176 B2
Kyrkeby. Letw 23 E2
Kytes Dri. Watf 154 B3

Laburnum Cl. Ches 162 B4
Laburnum Cl. Luton 45 E4
Laburnum Gr. Chis 141 D3
Laburnum Gr. Luton 45 D4
Laburnum Rd. Hod 135 D4
Lachbury Cl. Luton 63 D3
Lackmore Rd. Enf 162 B2
Lacre Way. Letw 23 E4
Ladbrooke Cl. Pot B 159 D4
Ladbrooke Dri. Pot B 159 D4
Ladies Gr. St Alb 127 E3
Lady Gr. Wel GC 110 C2
Lady's Cl. Watf 167 E3
Ladyhill. Luton 44 A3
Ladymeadow. Kin L 138 B2
Ladyshot. Harl 118 A1

ysmith Rd. Har 176 C1
ysmith Rd. Ivin 80 C3
ysmith Rd. St Alb 127 E2
ywalk. Map Cr 172 C3
ywell Prospect. Saw 98 A1
ywood Cl. Chor 165 E3
ywood Rd. Hertng 112 C3
don Sq. Heml H 124 B4
e Rd. Lo Naz 135 F1
e The. Bus 168 B1
e View. Pot B 159 E3
eland Cl. Har 176 B2
eside Pl. Lon C 142 B2
eside Rd. Ches 148 B2
eside. Elst 170 A2
eside. Tri 100 A3
eford Rd. Luton 46 B1
nb Cl. Hat 130 A2
nb La. Red 106 A3
nb Meadow. Arl 11 D2
nbert Ct. Bus 167 E3
nbourn Chase. Radl 155 F2
nbourn Gdns. Harp 85 F2
nbs Cl. Cuf 146 C1
nbs Cl. Dun 44 A1
nbton Ave. Ches 162 B3
ner La. Bla En 87 E2
ners Rd. Luton 46 A1
mmas Mead. Hit 21 F1
mmas Path. Stev 51 D2
mmas Rd. Ched 80 A4
mmas Rd. Wat St 70 B2
mmas Rd. Watf 167 E2
mmas Way. Letw 22 C4
mmasmead. Hod 148 C4
morna Cl. Luton 44 C3
morna Cl. Radl 156 A3
mpits. Hod 135 D3
msey Rd. Heml H 124 B1
ncaster Ave. Hit 34 C4
ncaster Ave. Luton 45 E4
ncaster Cl. Stev 36 C1
ncaster Dri. Bov 136 B2
ncaster Rd. Hit 34 C4
ncaster Rd. St Alb 127 F3
ncaster Way. Bis St 76 B4
ncaster Way. Welw 89 E2
ncastor Ave. Barn 159 E1
ncing Rd. Luton 46 B2
ncing Way. Cro Gr 166 A2
andau Way. Ches 148 C3
andford Cl. Ric 173 F4
andmead Rd. Ches 148 C1
ands End. Elst 169 E2
ane End. Hat 129 F1
ane Gdns. Bus 168 C1
anefield Wlk. Wel GC 110 B3
anercost Cl. Wl Gr 90 A4
angbridge Cl. Hit 35 D2
angdale Ave. Harp 86 B1
angdale Ct. Heml H 124 C3
angdale Gdns. Enf 162 B2
angdon St. Tri 100 A2
angfield Cl. Lo Naz 135 F1
angford Dri. Luton 46 A2
angham Cl. Luton 45 E4
angham Cl. St Alb 128 B4
angland Ct. Norwd 174 B2
angland Dri. Pnr 175 F2
angley Ave. Heml H 138 C4
angley Cres. Kin L 139 D1
angley Cres. St Alb 127 E3
angley Gr. Sand 108 B1
angley Hill Cl. Kin L 139 D1
angley Hill. Kin L 138 C1
angley La. Abb L 153 F4
angley Rd. Abb L 153 F4
angley Rd. Chipf 138 A1
angley Rd. Watf 167 D4
angley St. Luton 63 F3
angley Way. Watf 166 C4
angleybury La. Kin L 153 D2
angmead Dri. Bus 168 B1
Langthorne Ave. Stev 50 C3
Langton Gr. Norwd 174 B3
Langton Rd. Har 176 B2
Langton Rd. Hod 134 C3
Langwood Gdns. Watf 167 D4
Lankester Rd. Roystn 7 E3
Lannock Hill. Wes 23 F1
Lannock. Letw 23 E2
Lanrick Copse. Berk 122 B3
Lansdowne Cl. Watf 154 B2
Lansdowne Rd. Luton 45 E1
Lanthony Ct. Arl 11 D2
Lapwing Cl. Heml H 124 C4
Lapwing Dell. Letw 23 D2
Lapwing Rd. Luton 44 A2
Larch Ave. Bri Wd 140 C1
Larch Ave. Hit 35 D2
Larch Cl. Ham St 147 F2
Larch La. Wl Gr 89 F4
Larches Ave. Enf 162 B2
Larches The. Luton 45 E1
Larches The. Norwd 174 B2
Larches The. Nthch 121 E3
Larches The. Ware 93 E2
Larches The. Watf 167 F2
Larchwood Rd. Heml H 124 C3
Larchwood. Bis St 76 B3
Lark Rise. Hat 130 A2
Larke Way. Luton 44 B3
Larken Dri. Bus 168 B1
Larkens Cl. Puc 55 E2
Larkins Cl. Bal 12 C1
Larkinson. Stev 50 B4
Larks Ridge. Chis 141 D2
Larksfield. Ware 93 F2
Larkswood Rise. St Alb 128 B4
Larmans Rd. Enf 162 B2
Larsen Dri. Wa Aby 163 E3
Larwood Gr. Stev 51 D4
Latchmore Bank. L Hal 77 D1
Latchmore Cl. Hit 34 C3
Latimer Cl. Heml H 125 D4
Latimer Cl. Pnr 175 E1
Latimer Cl. Watf 166 C1
Latimer Ct. Ches 162 C3
Latimer Gdns. Pnr 175 E1
Latimer Rd. Lat 150 B1
Latimer Rd. Luton 63 F3
Lattimore Rd. St Alb 127 F2
Lattimore Rd. Whea 108 B4
Lauderdale Rd. Abb L 153 E3
Laughton Cl. Bor 170 B4
Laundry La. Lo Naz 149 F3
Laurel Ave. Pot B 158 C4
Laurel Cl. Heml H 124 C2
Laurel Fields. Pot B 158 C4
Laurel Park. Har 176 C2
Laurel Rd. St Alb 127 F2
Laurel Way. Ick 21 F2
Laureldene. Had Cr 74 C1
Laurels Cl. St Alb 141 D4
Laurels The. Ham St 147 F3
Laurels The. Pot En 123 E3
Lavender Cl. Ham St 147 F2
Lavender Ct. Bal 12 C1
Lavender Gdns. Enf 161 D1
Lavender Rd. Enf 161 E1
Lavender Way. Hit 34 B4
Lavender Wlk. Heml H 124 B3
Lavinia Ave. Watf 154 B3
Lavrock La. Ric 165 F1
Law Hall La. Whit 66 A4
Lawford Ave. Chor 164 B2
Lawford Cl. Chor 164 B2
Lawford Cl. Luton 63 E4
Lawn Ave. Kim 66 B1
Lawn Gdns. Luton 63 E3
Lawn La. Heml H 138 B4
Lawn The. Harl 118 A2
Lawn Vale. Pnr 175 F1
Lawns Cl. Gt Of 33 E1
Lawns Dri The. Hod 134 C1
Lawns The. Heml H 123 F2
Lawns The. Pnr 176 A2
Lawns The. St Alb 127 E2
Lawns The. Wel GC 89 E1
Lawrance Gdns. Ches 148 B2
Lawrance Rd. St Alb 127 E4
Lawrence Av. Sta Ab 115 E2
Lawrence Ave. Letw 23 D2
Lawrence Ave. Saw 97 F2
Lawrence Ave. Stev 50 C4
Lawrence Cl. Hertng 112 C4
Lawrence End Rd. Pet Gr 65 E2
Lawrence Moorings. Saw 97 F1
Laxton Cl. Luton 46 C1
Laxton Gdns. Bal 24 A4
Layard Rd. Enf 161 F1
Laybrook Cl. St Alb 128 A4
Layham Dri. Luton 46 C1
Layhill. Heml H 124 B3
Layston Meadow. Bun 40 C3
Layston Park. Roystn 7 E3
Lea Bushes. Watf 154 C2
Lea Cl. Bis St 59 D1
Lea Cl. Bus 168 A2
Lea Gr. Bis St 59 D1
Lea Mount. Gofs O 147 F2
Lea Rd. Harp 86 A2
Lea Rd. Hod 135 E4
Lea Rd. Luton 63 F4
Lea Rd. Wa Aby 163 D3
Lea Rd. Watf 154 A1
Lea Wlk. Harp 86 B2
Leaders Cl. Wing 60 A2
Leaf Cl. Norwd 174 B2
Leaford Cres. Watf 153 F1
Leaforis Rd. Ches 148 A2
Leagrave High St. Luton 44 A2
Leagrave Rd. Luton 45 D1
Leahoe Gdns. Hert 113 E3
Leamington Rd. Luton 45 D4
Leander Gdns. Watf 154 C1
Leas The. Bal 23 F4
Leas The. Bus 167 F4
Leas The. Heml H 139 D4
Leasey Bridge La. Harp 87 D1
Leat Cl. Saw 97 F2
Leathersellers Cl. Barn 171 F3
Leathwaite Cl. Luton 44 C3
Leaves Spring. Stev 51 D1
Leavesden Rd. Watf 154 A1
Leaview. Wa Aby 163 D3
Lebanon Cl. Watf 153 E2
Lectern La. St Alb 141 E4
Lecthmore Cl. Stev 50 B3
Leda Ave. Enf 162 B1
Ledgemore La. Gt Ga 103 F3
Ledwell Rd. Cad 62 C2
Lee Cl. Hert 113 E2
Lee Cl. Sta Ab 115 E2
Lee Farm Cl. Bot 136 A1
Leeches Way. Ched 80 A4
Leecroft Rd. Barn 171 F3
Leeming Rd. Bor 169 F4
Lees Ave. Norwd 174 C1
Leeside. Barn 171 F2
Leeswood Ct. Hert 112 C4
Leete Pl. Roystn 7 E4
Leggatts Cl. Watf 153 F2
Leggatts Rise. Watf 154 A2
Leggatts Way. Watf 154 A2
Leggatts Wood Ave. Watf 154 A2
Leggett Gr. Stev 50 C4
Leggfield Terr. Heml H 123 F2
Leghorn Cres. Luton 44 A2
Legions Way. Bis St 77 D4
Leicester Rd. Luton 44 C1
Leigh Comm. Wel GC 110 C2
Leigh Rodd. Watf 175 F4
Leighton Buzzard Rd. Gt Ga 103 F1
Leighton Buzzard Rd. Heml H 124 B2
Leighton Buzzard Rd. Pic En 124 B3
Leighton Rd. Har 176 B1
Leighton Rd. Wing 60 B2
Lemonfield Dri. Watf 154 C3
Lemsford Ct. Bor 170 B3
Lemsford La. Wel GC 110 A2
Lemsford Rd. Hat 130 A3
Lemsford Rd. St Alb 127 F2
Lemsford Village. Lem 109 F3
Lennox Green. Luton 46 C1
Lensbury Cl. Ches 148 C2
Leonard Ct. Har 176 B1
Leonard's Cl. Wl Gr 89 F4
Leslie Cl. Stev 51 E1
Letchfield. Bot 150 A4
Letchmore Rd. Radl 156 A2
Letchmore Rd. Stev 50 B4
Letchworth Cl. Sth Ox 175 E3
Letchworth Gate. Letw 23 D2
Letchworth La. Letw 22 C2
Letchworth Rd. Bal 23 F4
Letchworth Rd. Luton 45 D2
Leven Cl. Ches 162 B3
Leven Cl. Sth Ox 175 E3
Leven Dri. Ches 162 B3
Leven Way. Heml H 124 B4
Leveret Cl. Watf 154 A3
Leverstock Green Rd. Heml H 125 D2
Leverstock Green Rd. Heml H 125 E1
Leverstock Green Wy. Heml H 125 E1
Leverton Way. Wa Aby 163 E3
Lewes Way. Cro Gr 166 B3
Lewsey Rd. Luton 44 A2
Lexington Cl. Bor 170 A3
Lexington Ct. Pot B 158 B4
Lexington Way. Barn 171 E3
Ley Wlk. Wel GC 111 E3
Leyburne Cl. Men 61 E4
Leyburne Rd. Luton 45 D3
Leycroft Way. Harp 107 F4
Leyden Rd. Stev 50 B1
Leygreen Cl. Luton 64 A4
Leyhill Dri. Luton 63 D2
Leyland Ave. St Alb 127 E1
Leyland Cl. Ches 148 B1
Leys Ave. Letw 22 C3
Leys Cl. Hare 173 E1
Leys Rd. Heml H 124 C1
Leys The. St Alb 128 B3
Leys The. Tri 100 A2
Leysdown. Wel GC 111 E3
Leyton Green. Harp 86 A1
Leyton Rd. Harp 86 A1
Library Rd. Luton 63 F4
Lichfield Rd. Norwd 175 D1
Lichfield Way. Hod 134 C1
Liddel Cl. Luton 45 D2
Lidgate Cl. Luton 44 A3
Lighthorne Rise. Luton 45 D4
Lilac Cl. Ches 162 A4
Lilac Gr. Luton 44 B4
Lilac Rd. Hod 135 D4
Lilac Way. Harp 107 E3
Lilacs Ave. Enf 162 B2
Lilley Bottom Rd. Whit 66 B4
Lilley Bottom. Cok Gr 47 D3
Lilley Bottom. Kin Wd 47 E2
Lilley Bottom. Lily 46 C4
Lilleyhoo La. Lily 32 C1
Lilliard Cl. Hod 115 D1
Limberlost The. Wl Gr 89 D4
Limbrick Rd. Harp 107 D3
Limbury Rd. Luton 44 C2
Lime Ave. Bla En 87 D4
Lime Ave. Luton 44 B2
Lime Cl. Stev 51 E2
Lime Cl. Ware 93 F1
Lime Cl. Watf 167 E1
Lime Gr. N20 171 F1
Lime Gr. Roystn 7 F4
Lime Tree Pl. St Alb 127 F1
Lime Tree Wlk. Bus 176 C4
Lime Tree Wlk. Chor 165 D2
Lime Tree Wlk. Enf 161 E1
Lime Wlk. Heml H 124 C1
Limedene Cl. Pnr 175 E1
Limekiln La. Bal 23 F4
Limekiln La. Sta Mo 59 E3
Limes Cres. Bis St 77 D4
Limes Rd. Ches 162 C4
Limes The. Ch En 11 D4
Limes The. Hit 34 B3
Limes The. St Alb 127 F3
Limes The. Wel GC 111 D2
Limetree Ave. Nwml E 85 D4
Linacres. Luton 44 B2
Linbridge Way. Luton 46 C1
Linces Way. Wel G C 111 D2
Lincoln Cl. Bis St 76 B3
Lincoln Cl. St Alb 128 B4
Lincoln Cl. Wel GC 111 E4
Lincoln Ct. Berk 122 A2
Lincoln Ct. Bor 170 B2
Lincoln Dri. Cro Gr 166 A3
Lincoln Dri. Sth Ox 175 E4
Lincoln Rd. Luton 45 D1
Lincoln Rd. Stev 37 D1
Lincoln Way. Cro Gr 166 A3
Lindbergh. Wel GC 111 E3
Linden Cres. St Alb 128 B2
Linden Ct. Harp 107 D4
Linden Glade. Heml H 124 A1
Linden Lea. Watf 154 A3
Linden Rd. Luton 44 C2
Linden Rd. Red 106 A3
Lindencroft. Letw 12 A1
Lindens The. Bis St 76 C3
Lindens The. Fel 137 F4
Lindens The. Stev 50 C2
Lindley Cl. Harp 86 A2
Lindley Ct. Harp 86 A2
Lindlings. Heml H 123 F1
Lindsay Ave. Hit 35 D3
Lindsay Cl. Roystn 2 B1
Lindsey Cl. Bis St 58 C1
Lindsey Rd. Bis St 58 C1
Lindsey Rd. Luton 46 B1
Lindum Pl. St Alb 127 D1
Lingfield Cl. Norwd 174 C2
Lingfield Rd. Roystn 7 F3
Lingfield Rd. Stev 37 E1
Lingholm Way. Barn 171 E2
Linington Ave. Bot 136 A1
Link Dri. Hat 130 A3
Link Rd. Bus 167 E4
Link Rd. Wl Gr 89 F4
Link The. Letw 12 A1
Link Way. Bis St 76 C3
Link Wlk. Hat 130 A3
Linkfield. Wel GC 110 C1
Links Ave. Hert 114 A4
Links Dri. Elst 169 F3
Links Dri. Radl 155 F3
Links The. Ches 148 B3
Links View. St Alb 127 E3
Links Way. Cro Gr 166 B3
Links Way. uton 45 E4
Linkside Rd. Bis St 77 E3
Linksway. Norwd 174 B1
Linkway. Pnr 175 E1
Linkways E. Stev 50 C3
Linkways W. Stev 50 C3
Linley Dell. Luton 46 B1
Linnet Cl. Bus 168 B1
Linnet Cl. Letw 22 C4
Linnet Cl. Luton 44 A2
Linnet Wlk. Hat 130 A2
Linsey Cl. Heml H 139 D4
Linster Gr. Bor 170 B2
Linten Cl. Hit 35 E3
Linton Ave. Bor 169 F4
Lintott Cl. Stev 50 B3
Linwood Rd. Harp 107 E4
Linwood Rd. Ware 93 F2
Linwood. Saw 97 F1
Lion Ct. Bor 170 B4
Lion Yd. Kim 66 B1
Liphook Rd. Sth Ox 175 E3
Lippitts Hill. Luton 45 F3
Lismore. Heml H 125 E1
Lismore. Stev 51 E1
Lister Ave. Hit 34 C3
Liston Cl. Luton 44 A3
Little Acre. St Alb 127 E3
Little Acres. Gt Am 114 B4
Little Berries. Luton 44 C4
Little Bridge Rd. Berk 122 B2
Little Burrow. Wel GC 110 B2
Little Bushey La. Bus 168 B2
Little Chishill Rd. L Chis 18 B4
Little Church Rd. Luton 46 A2
Little Dell. Wel GC 110 B4
Little Ganett. Wel GC 111 E2
Little Gr. Bus 168 A3
Little Graylings. Abb L 153 F3
Little Green La. Cro Gr 166 A3
Little Green. Cro Gr 166 A3
Little Hardings. Wel GC 111 E4
Little Hayes. Kin L 139 D1
Little Heath La. Pot En 123 D2
Little Heath. L Hal 98 C2
Little Hill. Chor 164 B2
Little Hoo. Tri 99 F2
Little How Croft. Abb L 153 E4
Little Hyde. Stev 51 D2
Little La. Harp 107 E3
Little La. Pirt 20 B2
Little Lake. Wel GC 111 D2
Little Ley. Wel GC 110 C2
Little Martins. Bus 168 A2
Little Mead. Hat 130 A4
Little Mollards. Wing 60 A2
Little Moss La. Pnr 175 F1
Little Mundells. Wel GC 110 C4
Little Orchard Cl. Pnr 175 F1
Little Oxhey La. Sth Ox 175 E3
Little Oxhey La. Watf 175 F3
Little Park. Bov 137 D2
Little Piper's Cl. Gofs O 147 D1
Little Potters. Bus 168 C1
Little Rd. Heml H 124 C2
Little Ridge. Wel GC 111 D3
Little Rivers. Wel GC 111 D4
Little Thistle. Wel GC 111 E2
Little Tring Rd. Tri 99 F3
Little Twye Rd. Buc Co 119 F2
Little Wade. Wel GC 110 C2
Little Widbury La. Ware 93 F1
Little Widbury. Ware 93 F1
Little Windmill Hill. Sar 151 F4
Little Wlk. Harl 117 E1
Little Wood Croft. Luton 44 C4
Little Youngs. Wel GC 110 B3
Littlebrook Gdns. Ches 148 B1
Littlecote Pl. Pnr 175 F1
Littlefield Rd. Luton 46 A1
Littlegreen La. Cad 62 C2
Liverpool Rd. Luton 63 E4
Liverpool Rd. St Alb 127 F2
Liverpool Rd. Watf 167 D2
Livingstone Link. Stev 51 D4
Livingstone Wlk. Heml H 124 C4
Lloyd Way. Kim 66 B1
Loates La. Watf 167 E3
Loates Pasture. Sta Mo 59 E4
Local Board Rd. Watf 167 E2
Locarno Ave. Luton 44 B3
Lochnell Rd. Berk 121 F3
Lockers Park La. Heml H 124 A2
Locket Rd. Har 176 C1
Lockley Cres. Hat 130 A4
Lockleys Dri. Welw 89 E3
Lodge Ave. Elst 169 F2
Lodge Cl. Hert 113 E4
Lodge Cres. Ches 162 B3
Lodge Ct. Ick 21 F2
Lodge Dri. Chor 165 E3
Lodge Dri. Hat 130 B4
Lodge End. Cro Gr 166 B3
Lodge End. Radl 156 A3
Lodge Field. Wel GC 89 F1
Lodge La. Wa Aby 163 E2
Lodge Way. Stev 51 D1
Loftus Cl. Luton 44 A2
Lombardy Cl. Heml H 125 E1
Lombardy Dri. Berk 122 B2
Lombardy Way. Bor 169 F4
Lomond Rd. Heml H 124 B4
London Rd. Bal 23 F3
London Rd. Bar 8 C1
London Rd. Bark 17 E1
London Rd. Berk 122 B2
London Rd. Bis St 77 D3
London Rd. Bun 40 C3
London Rd. Bus 167 F2
London Rd. Dra B 99 D2
London Rd. Gos 35 D2
London Rd. Gt Am 114 C4
London Rd. Harl 118 B1
London Rd. Heml H 138 B4
London Rd. Hert 113 F3
London Rd. Hert H 114 A2
London Rd. Hit 34 C3
London Rd. Kneb 69 D3
London Rd. L Alm 49 D4
London Rd. Lan 49 E3
London Rd. Luton 63 F2
London Rd. Mark 83 F3
London Rd. Nwml E 85 D3
London Rd. Pot En 123 D1
London Rd. Ric 173 F4
London Rd. Roystn 7 E3
London Rd. Saw 97 F1
London Rd. Shen 156 C3
London Rd. St Alb 127 F1
London Rd. St Ipp 35 D1
London Rd. Stev 50 C1
London Rd. Tri 100 B2
London Rd. Wl Gr 69 D1
London Row. Arl 11 D2
Londrina Terr. Berk 122 B2
Long Acre. Harl 118 A2
Long Arrotts. Heml H 124 A3
Long Barn Cl. Watf 154 A4
Long Buftlers. Harp 107 F4
Long Chaulden. Heml H 123 F2
Long Cl. Luton 46 B2
Long Croft Dri. Ches 163 D3
Long Croft Rd. Luton 63 D4
Long Croft Rd. Map Cr 172 B3
Long Croft. Sta Mo 59 E4
Long Croft. Watf 167 D1
Long Cutt. Red 106 A3
Long Elmes. Har 176 B1
Long Elms Cl. Abb L 153 E3

Long Elms. Abb L 153 E3
Long Fallow. Chis 141 D2
Long Hyde. Stev 51 D2
Long John. Heml H 124 C1
Long La. Bov 150 B4
Long La. Heron 164 B1
Long La. Stev 51 F3
Long Leaves. Stev 51 D1
Long Ley. Ched 80 A4
Long Ley. Wel GC 111 E3
Long Marston Rd. Mars 79 F2
Long Meadow. Bis St 76 B3
Long Meadow. Mark 83 F3
Long Moor. Ches 148 C1
Long Ridge. Stev 51 E1
Long View. Berk 122 A3
Long Wlk. Wa Aby 163 D4
Longacres. St Alb 128 A2
Longbridge Cl. Tri 100 A3
Longcliffe Path. Sth Ox 175 D4
Longcroft Ave. Harp 85 F1
Longcroft Green. Wel GC 110 B3
Longcroft La. Bov 137 E3
Longcroft La. Wel GC 110 B3
Longcroft Rd. Stev 50 C4
Longcrofts. Wa Aby 163 F3
Longdean Park. Heml H 139 D4
Longfield Ave. Enf 162 B1
Longfield Dri. Luton 44 B1
Longfield Gdns. Tri 99 F2
Longfield La. Ches 148 A2
Longfield Rd. Harp 107 E4
Longfield Rd. Tri 99 F2
Longfield. Heml H 125 D1
Longfields. Stev 51 E1
Longlands Cl. Ches 162 B4
Longlands Rd. Wel GC 110 C3
Longlands. Heml H 125 D2
Longmans. Brag 55 F4
Longmead. Bun 40 B4
Longmead. Hat 130 A4
Longmead. Letw 22 C4
Longmead. Wl Gr 69 D1
Longmeadow Dri. Ick 21 F3
Longmore Cl. Map Cr 172 C3
Longmore Gdns. Wel GC 110 C3
Longspring. Watf 154 A1
Longwood Rd. Hertng 112 C4
Loning The. Enf 162 B1
Lonsdale Cl. Luton 45 D3
Lonsdale Cl. Pnr 175 F2
Lonsdale Ct. Stev 50 C4
Lonsdale Rd. Stev 50 C4
Lonsdale. Heml H 124 C3
Loom La. Radl 156 A2
Loom Pl. Radl 156 A2
Loop Rd. Wa Aby 163 D4
Lorane Ct. Watf 167 D4
Lord Mead La. A St L 88 B4
Lord St. Hod 134 B3
Lord St. Watf 167 E3
Lords Ave. Bis St 76 B4
Lords Meadow. Red 106 A3
Lords Wood. Wel GC 111 E3
Lordship Centre. Letw 23 D2
Lordship La. Letw 23 D2
Lordship Rd. Ches 148 A1
Lorne Rd. Har 168 C3
Lorraine Pk. Har 176 C2
Lorrimer Cl. Luton 45 F3
Lothair Rd. Luton 46 A2
Loudwater Dri. Chor 165 E3
Loudwater Hts. Chor 165 D3
Loudwater La. Chor 165 E3
Loudwater Ridge. Chor 165 E3
Louvain Way. Watf 154 A4
Lovatts. Cro Gr 166 A3
Love La. Abb L 139 F1
Love La. Ashw 4 A2
Love La. Kin L 138 C2
Love La. Pnr 175 E1
Lovel Cl. Heml H 124 A2
Lovell Cl. Hit 35 D3
Lovell Rd. Enf 162 A2
Low Hill Rd. Roy 135 F3
Lowbell La. Lon C 142 C2
Lower Barn. Heml H 138 C4
Lower Bourne Cl. Ware 93 E2
Lower Bourne Gdns. Ware 93 E2
Lower Clabdens. Ware 93 F1
Lower Dagnall St. St Alb 127 E2
Lower Emms. Heml H 125 E4
Lower End. Wing 60 A1
Lower Gower Rd. Roystn 7 E4
Lower Green. Tewin 90 C1
Lower Harpenden Rd. Nwml E 64 B2
Lower Hatfield Rd. Hertng 113 D2
Lower Hatfield Rd. L Berk 132 C4
Lower High St. Watf 167 E2
Lower Icknield Way. Drab 99 D3
Lower Icknield Way. Mars 80 A1
Lower Icknield Way. Wils 99 E4
Lower Innings. Hit 34 B4
Lower Island Way. Wa Aby 163 D2
Lower King St. Roystn 7 E3
Lower Kings Rd. Berk 122 B3
Lower Luton Rd. Bla En 86 C1
Lower Luton Rd. Harp 86 B2
Lower Luton Rd. Whea 87 D1
Lower Mardley Hill. Wl Gr 89 F4
Lower Paddock Rd. Watf 167 F2
Lower Park Cres. Bi St 76 C3
Lower Paxton Rd. St Alb 127 F1
Lower Plantation. Chor 165 E3
Lower Rd. Bed 139 D2
Lower Rd. Bre Wd 47 F1
Lower Rd. Chor 164 B2
Lower Rd. Gt Am 114 C4
Lower Rd. Heml H 139 D3
Lower Rd. L Hal 98 B4
Lower Sales. Heml H 123 F1
Lower Sean. Stev 51 D2
Lower Shott. Ham St 147 F3
Lower St. Sta Mo 59 F4
Lower Tail. Watf 175 F4
Lower Tub. Bus 168 B1
Lower Yott. Heml H 124 C1
Lowerfield. Wel GC 111 D3
Lowestoft Rd. Watf 167 D4
Lowfield La. Hod 135 D3
Lowfield. Saw 97 F1
Lowgate La. Sac Gr 72 A2
Lowlands. Hat 130 B4
Lowson Gr. Watf 167 F1
Lowswood Cl. Norwd 174 B1
Lowther Cl. Elst 169 F2
Loxley Rd. Berk 121 F3
Lucan Rd. Barn 171 F3
Lucas Ct. Wa Aby 163 F3
Lucas Gdns. Luton 45 D4
Lucas La. Ashw 4 C2
Lucas La. Hit 34 B4
Lucerne Way. Luton 45 E2
Lucks Hill. Heml H 123 F2
Ludgate. Tri 99 F2
Ludlow Ave. Luton 63 F2
Ludlow Mead. Sth Ox 175 D4
Ludlow Way. Cro Gr 166 B3
Ludwick Green. Wel GC 110 C3
Ludwick Way. Wel GC 110 C3
Lukes La. Lon M 79 E2
Lukes Lea. Mars 80 A1
Lullington Cl. Luton 46 B2
Lullington Garth. Bor 170 A2
Lulworth Ave. Gofs O 147 D1
Lumbards. Wel GC 90 A1
Lumen Rd. Roystn 7 E4
Lundin Wlk. Sth Ox 175 E3
Luring Rd. Berk 122 B2
Luton Dri The. Nwml E 64 A2
Luton La. Red 106 A4
Luton Rd. Cad 62 C2
Luton Rd. Cok Gr 46 C2
Luton Rd. Dun 44 A1
Luton Rd. Gt Of 33 D1
Luton Rd. Harp 85 F2
Luton Rd. Kim 66 A1
Luton Rd. Luton 44 A4
Luton Rd. Mark 83 F4
Luton Rd. Str 31 D3
Luton White Hill. Gt Of 33 D1
Luxembourg Cl. Luton 44 B4
Luynes Rise. Bun 40 B3
Lybury La. Red 105 F4
Lycaste Cl. St Alb 128 A1
Lych Gate. Watf 154 B3
Lydia Mews. Wel Gr 144 B4
Lydon Mead. Sand 108 B1
Lye Hill. Bre Gr 65 E4
Lye La. Bri Wd 141 D1
Lye La. Chis 141 D2
Lygetun Dri. Luton 44 C4
Lygrave. Stev 69 E4
Lyle's Row. Hit 34 C3
Lyles La. Wel GC 110 C4
Lymans Rd. Arl 11 D3
Lyme Ave. Nthch 121 E4
Lymington Rd. Stev 50 A4
Lymbury Ct. Watf 167 D3
Lynch Hill. Ken Co 83 D4
Lynch The. Hod 135 D3
Lyndale. Stev 50 C2
Lyndhurst Ave. Pnr 175 D1
Lyndhurst Cl. Harp 86 B1
Lyndhurst Dri. Harp 86 B1
Lyndhurst Gdns. Pnr 175 D1
Lyndhurst Rd. Luton 63 E4
Lyndon Ave. Pnr 175 F2
Lyne Way. Heml H 123 F3
Lyneham Rd. Luton 46 B1
Lynn Cl. Har 176 B1
Lynsey Cl. Red 106 A3
Lynton Ave. Arl 11 D3
Lynton Ave. St Alb 128 B1
Lynwood Ave. Luton 46 A2
Lynwood Dri. Norwd 174 C1
Lynwood Hts. Chor 165 E2
Lyon Way. St Alb 129 D2
Lys Hill Gdns. Hert 113 D4
Lysander Cl. Bov 137 D2
Lysander Way. Wel GC 111 E4
Lytham Ave. Sth Ox 175 E3
Lytton Ave. Enf 162 C1
Lytton Ave. Letw 22 C3
Lytton Fields. Kneb 68 C3
Lytton Gdns. Wel GC 110 B3
Lytton Rd. Pnr 175 F2
Lytton Way. Stev 50 A3
Lyttons Way. Hod 115 D1
Mabbutt Cl. Bri Wd 140 C1
Mabey's Wlk. H Wy 97 D1
Macaulay Rd. Luton 44 A1
Macdonnell Gdns. Watf 153 F2
Macer's La. Hod 148 C4
Macers Ct. Hod 148 C4
Mackenzie Sq. Stev 51 D2
Mackerel Hall. Roystn 7 D3
Maddles. Letw 23 E2
Maddox Rd. Harl 117 F1
Maddox Rd. Heml H 125 D2
Made Feld. Stev 50 C3
Madgeways Cl. Gt Am 114 C3
Madgeways La. Gt Am 114 C3
Magellan Cl. Stev 51 E3
Magna Cl. Harp 107 E3
Magnaville Rd. Bis St 76 C2
Magnaville Rd. Bus 168 C1
Magnolia Cl. Pk St 141 E3
Magpie Cres. Stev 51 E2
Magpie Hall Rd. Bus 176 C4
Magpie Wlk. Hat 130 A2
Magpies The. Luton 45 F3
Maiden St. Wes 24 B1
Maidenhall Rd. Luton 45 D1
Maidenhead St. Hert 113 E3
Maidenhead. Hert 113 E3
Main Ave. Norwd 174 B4
Main Par. Chor 164 B3
Main Rd. Bram 91 E2
Main Road N. Dagn 81 D3
Main Road S. Dagn 81 E2
Maitland Rd. Sta Mo 59 F3
Malden Rd. Bor 170 A3
Malden Rd. Watf 167 D4
Maldon Ct. Harp 86 A1
Malham Cl. Luton 44 C2
Malins Cl. Barn 171 E2
Mall The. Chis 141 E2
Mallard Gdns. Luton 45 D3
Mallard Rd. Roystn 7 E3
Mallard Rd. Stev 51 E1
Mallard Way. Norwd 174 B2
Mallard Way. Watf 154 C2
Mallion Ct. Wa Aby 163 F3
Mallories. Harl 117 F1
Mallow Wlk. Roystn 7 F3
Malm Cl. Ric 173 E4
Malmsdale. Wel GC 89 E1
Malt La. Radl 156 A3
Maltby Dri. Ches 162 A1
Maltby Dri. Enf 162 A1
Malthouse Ct. St Alb 127 E1
Malthouse La. Stot 12 A4
Malting La. Ald 101 E3
Malting La. Dagn 81 E3
Malting La. Gr En 55 F4
Malting La. Had Cr 74 C1
Maltings Cl. Clo 13 D1
Maltings Cl. Roystn 7 E4
Maltings Dri. Whea 108 B4
Maltings La. Gt Ch 9 F1
Maltings The. Abb L 153 E3
Maltings The. Heml H 124 B2
Maltings The. Wal 52 A4
Malus Cl. Heml H 125 D2
Malvern Cl. Hat 129 F3
Malvern Cl. St Alb 128 B4
Malvern Rd. Enf 162 C1
Malvern Rd. Luton 63 D4
Malvern Way. Cro Gr 166 A2
Malvern Way. Heml H 124 C3
Malzeard Rd. Luton 45 E1
Manan Cl. Heml H 125 E1
Manchester Cl. Stev 36 C2
Manchester St. Luton 63 F4
Mancroft Rd. Cad 62 C1
Mandela Ave. Harl 117 F1
Mandelyns. Nthch 121 E4
Mandeville Cl. Hert 113 E2
Mandeville Cl. Hod 134 C2
Mandeville Cl. Watf 153 F1
Mandeville Dri. St Alb 141 E4
Mandeville Rd. Enf 162 C2
Mandeville Rd. Hert 113 E2
Mandeville Rd. Pot B 159 E4
Mandeville Rise. Wel GC 110 B4
Mandeville. Stev 69 E4
Mangrove Dri. Hert 113 F2
Mangrove La. Bric 133 F4
Mangrove La. Hert 113 F2
Mangrove Rd. Hert 113 F2
Mangrove Rd. Luton 46 B1
Mangrove Rd. Man Gr 46 C2
Manland Ave. Harp 86 B1
Manland Way. Harp 86 B2
Manley Rd. Heml H 124 C2
Manly Dixon Dri. Enf 162 C1
Mannicotts. Wel GC 110 A3
Manor Ave. Heml H 138 B4
Manor Cl. Barn 171 F3
Manor Cl. Berk 122 B2
Manor Cl. Hat 129 F4
Manor Cl. Hert 113 E4
Manor Cl. Ick 21 F2
Manor Cl. Letw 22 C2
Manor Cotts. Norwd 174 C1
Manor Cres. Hit 35 D3
Manor Ct. Cad 62 C2
Manor Ct. Enf 162 A2
Manor Ct. Pot B 158 C4
Manor Dri. Chis 141 D2
Manor Farm La. Men 61 E4
Manor Farm Rd. Enf 162 A2
Manor House Dri. Stev 51 E4
Manor House Gdns. Abb L 153 E4
Manor Links. Bis St 77 E4
Manor Par. Hat 129 F4
Manor Pound Rd. Ched 80 A4
Manor Rd. Barn 171 F3
Manor Rd. Bis St 77 D4
Manor Rd. Bla En 86 C1
Manor Rd. Cad 62 C2
Manor Rd. Ched 79 F4
Manor Rd. Harl 118 B3
Manor Rd. Hat 129 F4
Manor Rd. Hod 135 D4
Manor Rd. Lon C 142 B3
Manor Rd. Luton 63 F3
Manor Rd. Pot B 159 D4
Manor Rd. St Alb 127 F2
Manor Rd. Sta Mo 59 F3
Manor Rd. Tri 100 A3
Manor Rd. Wa Aby 163 E3
Manor Rd. Watf 167 D4
Manor St. Berk 122 B2
Manor View. Stev 51 D1
Manor Way. Bor 170 B3
Manor Way. Ches 162 B4
Manor Way. Cro Gr 166 A3
Manor Way. Letw 22 C2
Manor Way. Pot B 145 D1
Manorside. Barn 171 F3
Manorville Rd. Fel 138 B4
Mansard Cl. Tri 100 A2
Manscroft Rd. Heml H 124 A3
Mansdale Rd. Red 105 F2
Manse Ct. Mark 83 F3
Mansfield Gdns. Hert 113 E4
Mansfield Rd. Bal 23 F4
Mansfield Rd. Luton 45 D1
Mansfield. H Wy 97 D1
Mansion Dri. Tri 100 A2
Manston Cl. Ches 148 B1
Manston Dri. Bis St 77 E4
Manton Dri. Luton 45 E2
Manton Rd. Hit 35 D3
Maple Ave. Bis St 76 B4
Maple Ave. St Alb 127 E4
Maple Cl. Bis St 76 B4
Maple Cl. Bus 167 F4
Maple Cl. Hat 130 A2
Maple Cl. Sta Ab 115 E2
Maple Gr. Bis St 76 B4
Maple Gr. Watf 167 D4
Maple Gr. Wel GC 110 C4
Maple Green. Heml H 123 F3
Maple Lodge Cl. Map Cr 172 C3
Maple Rd E. Luton 63 D4
Maple Rd W. Luton 63 D4
Maple Rd. Harp 85 F1
Maple Spring. Bis St 76 B4
Maple Way. Ken Co 82 C4
Maple Way. Roystn 7 F4
Maplecroft La. Lo Naz 135 F1
Maplefield. Chis 141 E1
Maples The. Hit 34 C3
Mapleton Cres. Enf 162 B1
Maplewood. Ware 93 E2
Maran Ave. Welw 89 E2
Mardley Ave. Wl Gr 90 A4
Mardley Dell. Wl Gr 69 D1
Mardley Hill. Wl Gr 89 F4
Mardley Hts. Wl Gr 90 A4
Mardley Wood. Wl Gr 89 F4
Mardleybury Ct. Wl Gr 69 D1
Mardleybury Rd. Wl Gr 69 D1
Mardyke Rd. Harl 118 A1
Marford Rd. Stanb 109 E3
Marford Rd. Whea 108 C4
Margaret Ave. St Alb 127 E3
Margaret Cl. Abb L 153 F4
Margaret Cl. Pot B 159 E3
Margaret Cl. Wa Aby 163 E3
Margeholes. Watf 175 F4
Margery Wood. Wel GC 90 A1
Maricas Ave. Har 176 B1
Marigold Pl. Harl 118 A2
Marina Gdns. Ches 148 B1
Mariner Way. Heml H 125 D1
Marion Cl. Bus 167 F4
Mark Hall Moors. Harl 118 A2
Mark Rd. Heml H 125 D3
Markab Rd. Norwd 175 D3
Markeston Green. Sth Ox 175 E3
Market Hill. Bun 40 C4
Market Hill. Roystn 7 E3
Market Oak La. Heml H 139 D4
Market Pl. Hat 130 A3
Market Pl. Hert 113 E3
Market Pl. Hit 34 C4
Market Pl. St Alb 127 E2
Market Pl. Watf 167 E3
Market Sq. Bis St 76 C4
Market Sq. Stev 50 B3
Market Sq. Wa Aby 163 E3
Market St. Bis St 76 C4
Market St. Harl 118 B2
Market St. Hert 113 E3
Market St. Watf 167 D3
Markfield Cl. Luton 45
Markgate Rd. Cad 84
Markham Rd. Luton 45
Marlands. Saw 97
Marlborough Cl. Bis St 76
Marlborough Cl. Wl Gr 89
Marlborough Gate. St Alb 127
Marlborough Rd. Luton 45
Marlborough Rd. Stev 51
Marlborough Rd. Watf 167
Marlborough Rise. Heml H 124
Marley Ct. Hod 148
Marley Rd. Wel GC 111
Marlin Cl. Berk 121
Marlin Copse. Berk 122
Marlin Hill. Has 120
Marlin Sq. Abb L 153
Marlins Cl. Chor 164
Marlins Meadow. Watf 166
Marlins The. Norwd 174
Marlins Turn. Heml H 124
Marlowe Cl. Stev 51
Marlowes. Heml H 124
Marnham Rise. Heml H 124
Marple Gdns. Wa Aby 163
Marquis Cl. Bis St 77
Marquis Cl. Harp 86
Marquis La. Harp 86
Marrilyne Ave. Enf 162
Marriott Rd. Barn 171
Marriott Rd. Luton 45
Marriotts Way. Heml H 124
Marryat Rd. Enf 162
Marschefield. Stot 11
Marsden Cl. Wel GC 110
Marsden Green. Wel GC 110
Marsden Rd. Wel GC 110
Marsh Cl. Ches 162
Marsh Hill. Wa Aby 149
Marsh La. Gt Am 114
Marsh La. Harl 118
Marsh La. Sta Ab 115
Marsh Rd. Luton 44
Marshal's Dri. St Alb 127
Marshall Ave. St Alb 127
Marshall Rd. Luton 46
Marshall's La. H Cr 72
Marshall's La. Sac Gr 72
Marshalls Heath La. Bla En 87
Marshalls Way. Bla En 86
Marshalswick La. St Alb 128
Marshcroft Dri. Ches 148
Marshcroft La. Tri 100
Marshe Cl. Pot B 159
Marshgate Dri. Hert 113
Marshgate. Stev 50
Marshmoor Cres. Hat 130
Marshmoor La. Wel Gr 144
Marsom Gr. Luton 45
Marston Cl. Heml H 125
Marston Ct. Lon M 79
Marston Gdns. Luton 45
Marston Rd. Hod 135
Marsworth Ave. Pnr 175
Marsworth Cl. Watf 166
Marsworth Rd. Pit 80
Marten Gate. St Alb 128
Martham Ct. Harp 86
Marthorne Cres. Har 176
Martian Ave. Heml H 124
Martin Cl. Hat 130
Martindale Rd. Heml H 123
Martinfield. Wel GC 110
Martingale Rd. Roystn 7
Martins Dri. Ches 148
Martins Way. Stev 36
Martins Way. Stev 37
Martins Wlk. Bor 170
Martlesham. Wel Gc 111
Martyr Cl. St Alb 141
Marwood Cl. Kin L 139
Marwoods Rd. Watf 167
Mary McArthur Pl. Sta Mo 59 F4
Mary Park Gdns. Bis St 76
Maryland. Hat 130 A3
Marymead Ct. Stev 69 D4
Marymead Dri. Stev 69 D4
Maryport Rd. Luton 45 D1
Masefield Ave. Bor 170 A2
Masefield Ave. Stan 176 C3
Masefield Ct. Harp 86 A2
Masefield Rd. Harp 86 A2
Masefield. Hit 35 E4
Mason Cl. Bor 170 B4
Mason Way. Wa Aby 163 F3
Masons Rd. Enf 162 B2
Masons Rd. Heml H 125 D2
Masters Cl. Luton 63 D3
Matching La. Bis st 76 B4
Mathams Dr. Bis St 76 B3
Matlock Cres. Luton 44 B1
Matlock Cres. Sth Ox 175 E4
Matthew Gate. Hit 35 D3
Mattocke Rd. Hit 21 E1
Maud Jane's Cl. Ivin 80 C3
Maude Cres. Watf 154 A1
Maulden Cl. Luton 46 B1
Maxted Cl. Heml H 125 E3
Maxted Rd. Heml H 125 E3
Maxwell Cl. Ric 173 D4

Maxwell Rd. Bor 170 A3
Maxwell Rd. Norwd 174 B2
Maxwell Rd. St Alb 128 A1
Maxwell Rd. Stev 50 A3
Maxwell Rise. Watf 167 F1
Maxwell's Path. Hit 34 B4
May Cl. St Alb 127 E3
May St. Gt Ch 9 F1
May St. Luton 63 F3
Maybury Ave. Ches 148 A2
Maycock Gr. Norwd 174 C2
Maycroft Rd. Ham St 147 F3
Maycroft. Letw 12 A1
Maycroft. Pnr 175 D1
Maydencroft La. Gos 34 C2
Maydwell Lodge. Bor 169 F4
Mayes Cl. Bis St 77 E4
Mayfair Cl. St Alb 128 B4
Mayfare. Cro Gr 166 B2
Mayfield Cl. Harl 118 C2
Mayfield Cl. Harp 85 F2
Mayfield Park. Bis St 76 B2
Mayfield Rd. Luton 46 A2
Mayfield. Wa Aby 163 E3
Mayfield. Wel GC 89 E1
Mayflower Ave. Heml H 124 B2
Mayflower Cl. Hertng 112 C2
Mayflower Cl. Lo Naz 135 F1
Mayflower Rd. Chis 141 D2
Mayhill Rd. Barn 171 F2
Maylands Ave. Heml H 125 D3
Maylands Rd. Sth Ox 175 E3
Maylin Cl. Hit 35 E4
Maylins Dri. Saw 97 E1
Maynard Ct. Wa Aby 163 F3
Maynard Dri. St Alb 141 E4
Maynard Pl. Cuf 146 C1
Maynard Rd. Heml H 124 B1
Mayne Ave. Luton 44 B2
Mayne Ave. St Alb 126 C1
Mayo Cl. Ches 148 B2
Mays La. Barn 171 E2
Mayshades Cl. Wl Gr 69 D1
Maythorne Cl. Watf 166 C3
Maytree Cres. Watf 153 F2
Maytree La. Stan 176 C2
Maytrees. Hit 35 D3
Maze Green Rd. Bis St 76 B4
Mazoe Cl. Bis St 76 C3
Mazoe Rd. Bis St 76 C3
Mc Adam Cl. Hod 135 D4
Mc Donald Ct. Heml H 130 A1
McGredy. Ches 148 A1
McKellar Cl. Bus 176 B4
Mckenzie Rd. Hod 135 D2
Mead Cl. Har 176 B1
Mead Cl. Stev 50 C3
Mead Ct. Sta Mo 59 E4
Mead Ct. Wa Aby 163 D3
Mead La. Hert 113 F4
Mead Pl. Ric 165 D1
Mead Rd. Shen 157 D3
Mead The. Ches 148 B1
Mead The. Hit 21 F1
Mead The. Watf 175 F4
Mead View. Sto P 43 F3
Mead Way. Bus 167 F4
Meadgate. Lo Naz 135 E2
Meadow Cl. Barn 171 F2
Meadow Cl. Berk 122 A1
Meadow Cl. Bri Wd 141 D1
Meadow Cl. Dat 69 E1
Meadow Cl. Enf 162 C1
Meadow Cl. Lon C 142 B2
Meadow Cl. St Alb 128 B3
Meadow Cl. Tri 100 A2
Meadow Cl. Wel Gr 144 B4
Meadow Croft. Hat 129 F3
Meadow Dell. Hat 129 F3
Meadow Green. Wel GC 110 B3
Meadow La. Pit 80 C2
Meadow Rd. Berk 122 A3
Meadow Rd. Bor 170 A4
Meadow Rd. Bus 168 A2
Meadow Rd. Heml H 139 D4
Meadow Rd. Luton 45 D2
Meadow Rd. Watf 154 A3
Meadow The. Wel GC 111 E4
Meadow Way The. Har 176 C1
Meadow Way. Bed 139 F2
Meadow Way. Cad 62 C2
Meadow Way. Chor 165 E1
Meadow Way. Cod 67 F1
Meadow Way. Gt Of 33 E2
Meadow Way. Heml H 138 A4
Meadow Way. Hit 34 B3
Meadow Way. Kin L 139 D1
Meadow Way. Letw 22 C3
Meadow Way. Pot B 159 D3
Meadow Way. Saw 98 A1
Meadow Way. Stev 50 C3
Meadow Way. Stot 11 F3
Meadow Way. Ther 16 A3
Meadow Wlk. Harp 107 E4
Meadow Wlk. Stand 55 F1
Meadowbank. Hit 35 D4
Meadowbank. Kin L 139 D1
Meadowbank. Watf 167 E1
Meadowbanks. Barn 171 D2
Meadowbrook. Tri 100 A3
Meadowcroft. St Alb 142 A4
Meadowcroft. Sta Mo 59 F4
Meadowcross. Wa Aby 163 F3
Meadowlands. Bis St 59 D1
Meadows The. Bre Wd 47 F1
Meadows The. Saw 98 B3
Meads La. Whea 87 E1
Meads The. Bri Wd 140 C1
Meads The. Letw 22 C3
Meads The. Luton 45 D2
Meads The. Nthch 121 F3
Meads The. Tri 100 A2
Meadview Rd. Gt Am 114 A4
Meadway Cl. Pnr 176 A2
Meadway The. Cuf 146 C1
Meadway. Barn 171 F3
Meadway. Berk 122 A2
Meadway. Coln H 143 E4
Meadway. Enf 162 B2
Meadway. Harp 107 F4
Meadway. Hod 135 D2
Meadway. Kneb 68 C2
Meadway. Stev 50 A3
Meadway. Wel GC 110 C2
Meautys. St Alb 127 D1
Medalls Link. Stev 51 D2
Medalls Path. Stev 51 D2
Medcalf Rd. Enf 162 C1
Medina Rd. Luton 45 D1
Medlows. Harp 85 F1
Medow Mead. Radl 155 F3
Medway Cl. Watf 154 B3
Medway Rd. Heml H 124 C4
Medwick Mews. Heml H 125 D4
Medworth Ave. Ches 162 B3
Mees Cl. Luton 31 D1
Meeting Alley. Watf 167 E3
Meeting House La. Bal 12 C1
Megg La. Chipf 138 A1
Melbourn Cl. Stot 11 F3
Melbourn Rd. Roystn 7 E4
Melbourn St. Roystn 7 E3
Melbourne Cl. St Alb 127 F4
Melbourne Ct. Wel GC 110 A3
Melbourne Rd. Bus 168 A2
Melford Cl. Luton 46 B1
Melings The. Heml H 125 D4
Melne Rd. Stev 69 D4
Melrose Ave. Bor 170 A2
Melrose Ave. Pot B 159 D4
Melrose Pl. Watf 153 F1
Melson St. Luton 63 F4
Melsted Rd. Heml H 124 A2
Melville Ct. Norwd 174 B2
Memorial Rd. Luton 44 C2
Mendip Cl. St Alb 128 B4
Mendip Rd. Bus 168 B2
Mendip Way. Heml H 124 C3
Mendip Way. Luton 44 B4
Mendlesham. Wel G C 111 F3
Mentley La E. Brag 55 E2
Mentley La W. Puc 55 E2
Mentley La. Gt Mu 54 C2
Mentmore Rd. Ched 79 F4
Mentmore Rd. St Alb 127 F1
Mentmore View. Tri 99 F3
Mepham Cres. Har 176 B2
Mepham Gdns. Har 176 B2
Mercer Pl. Pnr 175 E1
Mercers Row. St Alb 127 E1
Mercers. Heml H 124 C3
Merchant Dri. Hert 113 F4
Merchants Wlk. Bal 13 D1
Mercia Rd. Bal 24 A4
Mercury Wlk. Heml H 124 C3
Meredith Cl. Pnr 175 E2
Meredith Rd. Stev 51 D4
Meriden Way. Watf 154 C1
Meridian Way. Sta Ab 115 D3
Merle Ave. Hare 173 E1
Merling Croft. Nthch 121 F4
Merritt Wlk. Wel Gr 144 A4
Merrow Dri. Heml H 123 F2
Merrows Cl. Norwd 174 B2
Merry Hill Mount. Bus 168 A1
Merry Hill Rd. Bus 168 A1
Merryfield Cl. Bor 169 F4
Merryfields. St Alb 128 C2
Mersey Pl. Heml H 124 C4
Mersey Pl. Luton 63 E4
Merton Rd. Enf 161 E1
Merton Rd. Watf 167 D3
Metropolitan Station App. Watf166 C3
Meux Cl. Ches 162 A4
Meyer Green. Enf 162 A1
Meyrick Ave. Luton 63 E3
Mezen Cl. Norwd 174 B3
Michaels Rd. Bis St 59 D1
Micklefield Rd. Heml H 125 E2
Micklefield Way. Bor 156 C1
Micklem Dri. Heml H 123 F2
Midcot Way. Berk 121 F3
Middle Drift. Roystn 7 E3
Middle Furlong. Bus 168 A3
Middle La. Bov 137 D1
Middle Ope. Watf 154 A1
Middle Rd. Berk 122 A2
Middle Rd. Wa Aby 163 D4
Middle Row. Bis St 76 C3
Middle St. Lo Naz 149 F4
Middle Way The. Har 176 C1
Middle Way. Watf 154 A1
Middlefield Ave. Hod 135 D4
Middlefield Cl. St Alb 128 B3
Middlefield Rd. Hod 135 D4
Middlefield. Hat 130 A3
Middlefield. Wel GC 110 C2
Middlefields. Letw 11 F1
Middlehill. Heml H 123 F2
Middleknights Mill. Heml H 124 A3
Middleton Rd. Luton 46 B2
Middleton Rd. Ric 165 D1
Midhurst Gdns. Luton 45 E3
Midhurst. Letw 22 C4
Midland Cotts. Hit 22 A1
Midland Rd. Heml H 124 B2
Midland Rd. Luton 63 F4
Midway. St Alb 141 D4
Milburn Cl. Luton 31 D1
Mildmay Rd. Stev 37 D1
Mildred Ave. Bor 170 A3
Mildred Ave. Watf 167 D3
Mile Cl. Wa Aby 163 E3
Mile House Cl. St Alb 142 A4
Mile House La. St Alb 142 A4
Milestone Cl. Ast 51 E2
Milestone Rd. Hit 21 E1
Milestone Rd. Kneb 69 D3
Milford Cl. St Alb 128 B4
Milford Mill. Harp 86 B2
Milksey La. Gra 36 B3
Mill Bridge. Barn 171 F2
Mill Bridge. Hert 113 E3
Mill Cl. Heml H 139 D3
Mill Cl. Hit 35 E4
Mill Cl. Lem 110 A3
Mill Cl. Wing 60 A2
Mill Cnr. Barn 171 F4
Mill Farm Cl. Pnr 175 E1
Mill Field. Harl 118 B2
Mill Gdns. Tri 100 A2
Mill Green La. Wel GC 110 B1
Mill Green Rd. Wel GC 110 C3
Mill Hill. Roystn 7 F2
Mill La. Ches 148 C2
Mill La. Clap 57 E3
Mill La. Fla 84 A1
Mill La. Gos 34 C2
Mill La. Harl 118 C2
Mill La. Henlw 10 C2
Mill La. Hex 19 E2
Mill La. Hod 134 C1
Mill La. Hod 135 D1
Mill La. Kin L 139 D1
Mill La. L Hal 98 C2
Mill La. Mee 30 A3
Mill La. Saw 97 F2
Mill La. Stot 12 A3
Mill La. Ther 15 F4
Mill La. Wat St 70 C3
Mill La. Welw 89 E3
Mill La. Wes 24 B1
Mill La. Wing 60 B1
Mill Lane Cl. Hod 134 C1
Mill Race. Sta Ab 115 E2
Mill Rd. Gos 35 D2
Mill Rd. Hert 113 E3
Mill Rd. Roystn 7 E4
Mill Side. Sta Mo 59 F3
Mill St. Ashw 4 B2
Mill St. Berk 122 B2
Mill St. Bis St 77 D3
Mill St. Heml H 138 B4
Mill St. Luton 63 E4
Mill View Rd. Tri 99 F2
Mill Way. Bus 167 F4
Mill Way. Ric 164 C1
Millacres. Ware 93 E1
Millard Way. Hit 22 B1
Millbridge Mews. Hert 113 E3
Millbrook Rd. Bus 167 F4
Millcrest Rd. Gofs O 147 D2
Millcroft. Bis St 59 D1
Millers Ct. Hert 113 E3
Millers La. Sta Ab 115 E2
Millers Yard. Hert 113 E3
Millfield La. Cad 62 B1
Millfield La. Gos 34 C2
Millfield Rd. Luton 45 D2
Millfield Way. Cad 62 B2
Millfield Wlk. Heml H 125 D1
Millfield. Berk 122 B3
Millfield. Wad 93 F4
Millfield. Wel GC 111 E4
Millfields. Saw 97 F2
Millfields. Sta Mo 59 F3
Millhoo Ct. Wa Aby 163 F3
Millhouse La. Bed 140 A2
Millstream Cl. Hert 113 D3
Millstream Cl. Hit 22 A1
Millthorne Cl. Cro Gr 165 F2
Millwards. Hat 130 A1
Millway. Bre Wd 47 E1
Milne Cl. Letw 23 D2
Milne Field. Pnr 176 A2
Milner Cl. Watf 154 A3
Milner Ct. Bus 168 A2
Milneway. Hare 173 D1
Milton Ave. Barn 171 F2
Milton Cl. Roystn 2 B1
Milton Ct. Ham St 147 F3
Milton Ct. Wa Aby 163 E3
Milton Dri. Bor 170 A2
Milton Rd. Harp 86 A1
Milton Rd. Luton 63 E3
Milton Rd. Ware 93 E1
Milton St. Wa Aby 163 E3
Milton St. Watf 167 D4
Milton View. Hit 35 E4
Milverton Green. Luton 45 D4
Mimas Rd. Heml H 124 C3
Mimms Hall Rd. Pot B 158 B4
Mimms La. Ridge 157 E4
Mimms La. Shen 157 E3
Mimram Rd. Hert 113 D3
Mimram Rd. Welw 89 E3
Mimram Wlk. Welw 89 E3
Minchen Rd. Harl 118 A1
Minehead Way. Stev 50 A4
Minerva Dri. Watf 153 F2
Minorca Way. Luton 44 A2
Minsden Rd. Stev 51 E2
Minster Cl. Hat 130 A2
Minster Rd. Roystn 7 E4
Missden Dri. Heml H 125 E1
Mistletoe Hill. Luton 64 B4
Mistley Rd. Harl 118 A1
Miswell La. Tri 99 F2
Mitchell Cl. Bov 136 B2
Mitchell Cl. St Alb 141 E4
Mitchell Cl. Wel GC 111 E3
Mixes Hill Rd. Luton 45 F2
Mixies The. Stot 11 F3
Moakes The. Luton 44 C4
Moat Cl. Bus 168 A2
Moat La. Luton 45 D2
Moat La. Wing 60 A1
Moat The. Puc 55 E2
Moatfield Rd. Bus 168 A2
Moatside. Ans 29 D4
Moatwood Green. Wel GC 110 C3
Mobbsbury Way. Stev 51 D4
Mobley Green. Luton 46 A2
Moffats Cl. Bro Pk 145 D3
Moffats La. Bro Pk 144 C3
Moira Cl. Luton 44 B4
Moles La. Wyd 28 A2
Molescroft. Harp 85 E2
Molesworth. Hod 115 D1
Molewood Rd. Hert 113 D4
Mollison Ave. Enf 162 C1
Mollison Ave. Wa Aby 163 D2
Molteno Rd. Watf 167 D4
Momples Rd. Harl 118 A1
Monarch's Way. Ches 162 C3
Monastery Cl. St Alb 127 E2
Money Hill Rd. Ric 165 E1
Money Hole La. Wel GC 111 E3
Monica Cl. Watf 167 E4
Monklands. Letw 22 B3
Monks Cl. Hod 135 D2
Monks Cl. Letw 22 B3
Monks Cl. Red 106 A3
Monks Cl. St Alb 127 F1
Monks Horton Way. St Alb 128 A2
Monks Rise. Wel GC 89 E1
Monks View. Stev 50 C1
Monks Wlk. Bun 40 C4
Monks Wlk. Wel GC 89 E1
Monksmead. Bor 170 B3
Monkswick Rd. Harl 117 F1
Monkswood Ave. Wa Aby 163 E3
Monkswood Gdns. Bor 170 B3
Monkswood Way. Stev 50 C2
Monkswood. Wel GC 89 E1
Monmouth Rd. Watf 167 D3
Monro Gdns. Har 176 C2
Mons Ave. Bal 23 F3
Mons Cl. Harp 107 E3
Monson Rd. Hod 134 C2
Montacute Rd. Bus 168 C1
Montague Ave. Luton 44 B3
Montague Rd. Berk 122 A2
Montayne Rd. Ches 162 B4
Montesole Ct. Pnr 175 E1
Montfitchet Wlk. Stev 51 E4
Montgomerie Cl. Berk 122 A3
Montgomery Ave. Heml H 125 D2
Montgomery Dri. Ches 148 C2
Monton Cl. Luton 44 C3
Montrose Ave. Luton 45 E2
Montrose Rd. Har 176 C1
Moon La. Barn 171 F3
Moor End Rd. Heml H 124 B1
Moor Hall Rd. Harl 118 C2
Moor La. Ric 174 A4
Moor La. Sar 151 F2
Moor Lane Crossing. Watf 166 B1
Moor Mill La. Fro 141 F1
Moor Park Rd. Norwd 174 B2
Moor St. Luton 63 E4
Moor View. Watf 167 D2
Moore Rd. Berk 121 F3
Moorend. Wel GC 111 D2
Moorhurst Ave. Gofs O 147 D1
Moorland Gdns. Luton 63 E4
Moorland Rd. Harp 86 A2
Moorland Rd. Heml H 124 A1
Moorlands. Fro 141 F2
Moorlands. Wel GC 111 D2
Moormead Cl. Hit 34 B3
Moormead Hill. Hit 34 B3
Moors Ley. Wal 38 A1
Moors The. Wel GC 111 D4
Moors Wlk. Wel GC 111 E4
Moorside. Wel GC 111 D2
Moortown Rd. Sth Ox 175 E3
Morefields. Tri 100 A3
Moremead. Wa Aby 163 E3
Moreton Ave. Harp 85 F1
Moreton Cl. Ches 148 A2
Moreton End Cl. Harp 85 F1
Moreton End La. Harp 85 F1
Moreton Pl. Harp 85 F2
Moreton Rd. Luton 46 A1
Morgan Cl. Norwd 174 C2
Morgan Cl. Stev 36 B1
Morgan's Rd. Hert 113 E2
Morgan's Wlk. Hert 113 E2
Morgans Cl. Hert 113 E2
Morice Rd. Hod 134 C4
Morland Way. Ches 148 C2
Morley Gr. Harl 117 E1
Morley Hill. Enf 161 E1
Mornington Rd. Radl 156 A3
Mornington. Har Gr 90 A2
Morpeth Ave. Bor 156 C1
Morrell Cl. Luton 45 D4
Morris Cl. Henlw 10 B3
Morris Cl. Luton 44 C4
Morris Ct. Wa Aby 163 F3
Morris Way. Lon C 142 B3
Morriston Cl. Sth Ox 175 E3
Mortimer Cl. Bus 168 A2
Mortimer Cl. Luton 62 C4
Mortimer Hill. Tri 100 A2
Mortimer Rd. Roystn 7 F4
Mortimer Rise. Tri 100 A2
Morton Cl. Ivin 80 B2
Morton St. Roystn 7 E4
Morven Cl. P Bar 159 E4
Moss Cl. Pnr 175 F1
Moss Cl. Ric 173 E4
Moss Green. Wel GC 110 C2
Moss La. Pnr 175 F1
Moss Rd. Watf 154 A3
Moss Side. Bri Wd 140 C1
Moss Way. Hit 21 E1
Mossbank Ave. Luton 64 B4
Mossendew Cl. Hare 173 E1
Mostyn Rd. Bus 168 B2
Mostyn Rd. Luton 44 C2
Mott St. Wa Aby 163 E1
Motts Cl. Wat St 70 B2
Moulton Rise. Luton 63 F4
Mount Cl. Heml H 123 F2
Mount Dri. Pk St 141 E3
Mount Dri. Sta Mo 59 F3
Mount Garrison. Hit 34 C4
Mount Grace Rd. Luton 46 B3
Mount Grace Rd. Pot B 159 D4
Mount Pleasant Cl. Hat 130 B4
Mount Pleasant La. Bri Wd 140 C1
Mount Pleasant La. Hat 130 B4
Mount Pleasant Rd. Luton 44 C3
Mount Pleasant. Hare 173 D1
Mount Pleasant. Hert H 114 B2
Mount Pleasant. Hit 34 B3
Mount Pleasant. St Alb 127 E2
Mount Rd. Hertng 113 D3
Mount Rd. Whea 87 E1
Mount The. Bar 8 C1
Mount The. Chor 165 E2
Mount The. Ham St 147 E3
Mount The. Pot B 145 D1
Mount View. Enf 160 C1
Mount View. Lon C 142 C2
Mount View. Ric 165 D1
Mount Way. Wel GC 110 C2
Mountbatten Cl. St Alb 142 A4
Mounteagle. Roystn 7 E3
Mountfield Rd. Heml H 124 C2
Mountfield Rd. Luton 45 F1
Mountfitchet Rd. Sta Mo 59 F3
Mountjoy. Hit 22 B1
Mountside. Stan 176 C1
Mountview Rd. Ham St 147 F3
Mountview. Norwd 174 C2
Mountway Cl. Wel GC 110 C2
Mountway. Pot B 145 D1
Mowbray Cres. Stot 11 F4
Mowbray Gdns. Hit 35 D3
Mowbray Rd. Harl 118 A2
Moxes Wood. Luton 44 C4
Moxon St. Barn 171 F3
Mozart Ct. Stev 50 B3
Mud La. Harp 107 F3
Muddy La. Letw 22 C2
Muirfield Cl. Sth Ox 175 E3
Muirfield Green. Sth Ox 175 E3
Muirfield Rd. Sth Ox 175 E3
Muirhead Way. Kneb 68 C3
Mulberry Cl. Chis 141 D2
Mulberry Cl. Hod 148 C4
Mulberry Cl. Tri 100 A3
Mulberry Ct. Bis St 77 D3
Mulberry Ct. Heml H 124 B2
Mulberry Green. Harl 118 B2
Mulberry Terr. Harl 118 A2
Mullion Cl. Har 176 A1

Mullion Cl. Luton 46 A3
Mullion Wlk. Sth Ox 175 E3
Mullway. Letw 22 B3
Mundells Ct. Wel GC 110 C4
Mundells. Wel GC 111 D4
Munden Gr. Watf 154 B1
Munden Rd. Dan En 71 F4
Munden View. Watf 154 B2
Mundesley Cl. Stev 36 A1
Mundesly Cl. Sth Ox 175 E3
Mungo-Park Cl. Bus 176 B4
Munro Rd. Bus 168 A2
Muntings The. Stev 51 D2
Murchison Rd. Hod 115 D1
Muriel Ave. Watf 167 E2
Murray Cres. Pnr 175 E1
Murray Rd. Berk 122 A3
Murray Rd. Norwd 174 C2
Murrell La. Stot 12 A3
Murton Ct. St Alb 127 F2
Musgrave Cl. Ham St 147 F2
Musk Hill. Heml H 123 F1
Muskalls Cl. Ham St 148 A2
Muskham Rd. Harl 118 A2
Musleigh Manor. Ware 93 F1
Musley Hill. Ware 93 F1
Musley La. Ware 93 F1
Muswell Cl. Luton 45 D3
Mutchetts Cl. Watf 154 C3
Mutford Croft. Luton 46 B1
Mutton La. Pot B 158 C4
Myddelton Ave. Enf 161 F1
Myddleton Path. Ches 162 A4
Myddleton Rd. Ware 114 B4
Mymms Dri. Bro Pk 145 D2
Myrtle Gr. Enf 161 E1
Myrtle Green. Heml H 123 F2
Myrtleside Cl. Norwd 174 B2

N Luton Ind Est. Luton 44 A4
Nails La. Bis St 76 C4
Nairn Cl. Harp 107 E3
Nairn Green. Sth Ox 175 D4
Nan Aires. Wing 60 A2
Nancy Downs. Watf 167 E1
Nap The. Kin L 139 D1
Napier Cl. Lon C 142 B3
Napier Ct. Ches 148 A2
Napier Dri. Bus 167 F3
Napier Rd. Luton 63 E4
Nappsbury Rd. Luton 44 B3
Napsbury Ave. Lon C 142 B3
Napsbury La. St Alb 142 A4
Narrowbox La. Stev 51 E4
Nascot Pl. Watf 167 D4
Nascot Rd. Watf 167 D4
Nascot St. Watf 167 D4
Nascot Wood Rd. Watf 153 F1
Naseby Rd. Luton 63 D4
Nash Cl. Elst 169 F3
Nash Cl. Stev 51 D3
Nash Cl. Wel Gr 144 B4
Nash Green. Heml H 139 D3
Nash Mills La. Heml H 138 C3
Nash Rd. Roystn 7 E3
Nathaniel Wlk. Tri 100 A3
Nathans Cl. Welw 89 E3
Nayland Cl. Luton 46 C1
Nazeing New Rd. Hod 135 D1
Nazeing Rd. Lo Naz 135 E1
Neagle Cl. Bor 170 B4
Neal Cl. Norwd 175 D1
Neal Ct. Wa Aby 163 F3
Neal St. Watf 167 E2
Necton Rd. Whea 108 C4
Needham Rd. Luton 44 A3
Nelson Ave. St Alb 142 A4
Nelson Rd. Bis St 77 D3
Nelson Rd. Dagn 81 E3
Nelson St. Hert 113 D4
Nene Rd. Henlw 10 A2
Neptune Dri. Heml H 124 C3
Neston Rd. Watf 154 B1
Nether St. Widf 95 F2
Netherby Cl. Tri 100 B3
Nethercott Cl. Luton 46 B1
Netherfield La. Sta Ab 115 E2
Netherfield Rd. Harp 107 D2
Netherhall Rd. Roy 135 F3
Netherstones. Stot 11 F4
Netherway. St Alb 141 D4
Netley Dell. Letw 23 D2
Netteswell Cross. Harl 117 F1
Netteswell Rd. Harl 117 F2
Nettlecroft. Heml H 124 A1
Nettlecroft. Wel GC 111 D4
Nettleden Rd. Gt Ga 103 F1
Nettleden Rd. L Gad 102 B3
Nettleden Rd. Net 103 D1
Nettleden Rd. Pot En 123 D4
Nevell's Green. Letw 22 C4
Nevell's Rd. Letw 22 C3
Nevill Gr. Watf 167 D4
Neville Cl. Pot B 158 C4
Neville Rd. Luton 45 D3
New Barn La. Gt Ha 77 E1
New Barn La. L Hal 77 D1
New Barnes Ave. St Alb 142 A4
New Barns La. Muc H 74 C2
New Bedford Rd. Luton 45 E3
New Cl. Kneb 68 C3
New England Cl. Hit 34 C2
New England St. St Alb 127 E2
New Farm La. Norwd 174 C1
New Ford Rd. Ches 162 C3
New Forge Pl. Red 106 A3
New Greens Ave. St Alb 127 E4
New House Park. St Alb 142 A4
New Inn Rd. Hin 3 E3
New Kent Rd. St Alb 127 E2
New Par. Chor 154 B3
New Park Dri. Heml H 125 D2
New Park Rd. Hare 173 E1
New Park Rd. New St 146 B4
New Path. Bis St 76 C3
New Pl. Welw 89 D2
New Rd. Aldhm 168 C4
New Rd. Berk 122 B3
New Rd. Chipf 137 F1
New Rd. Cro Gr 166 A2
New Rd. Elst 169 E2
New Rd. Gt Ch 9 E3
New Rd. Har Gr 89 F2
New Rd. Harl 118 B2
New Rd. Henlw 10 A4
New Rd. Hert 113 E4
New Rd. Hert 114 A3
New Rd. Hod 135 D2
New Rd. L Had 75 D4
New Rd. Nthch 121 F4
New Rd. Radl 155 F1
New Rd. Sar 151 F1
New Rd. Shen 157 D3
New Rd. Stanb 110 A2
New Rd. Tri 100 A3
New Rd. Ware 93 E1
New Rd. Watf 167 E3
New Rd. Wils 99 E4
New Rd. Wl Gr 69 D1
New River Ave. Sta Ab 115 D2
New River Cl. Hod 135 D4
New St. Berk 122 B2
New St. Cad 63 E1
New St. Ched 79 F4
New St. Luton 63 E3
New St. Saw 97 F2
New St. Watf 167 E3
New Town Rd. Luton 63 F3
New Town St. Luton 63 F3
New Town. Cod 67 F1
New Wood. Wel GC 111 E4
Newark Cl. Roystn 7 E4
Newark Green. Bor 170 B3
Newark Rd. Luton 45 D1
Newberries Ave. Radl 156 A2
Newberries Par. Radl 156 A2
Newbiggin Path. Sth Ox 175 E3
Newbold Rd. Luton 45 D4
Newbolt Rd. Stan 176 C3
Newbury Ave. Enf 162 C1
Newbury Cl. Bis St 76 C4
Newbury Cl. Luton 44 C1
Newcombe Path. Shen 157 D3
Newcombe Rd. Luton 63 E4
Newcome Rd. Shen 157 D3
Newdigate Green. Hare 173 E1
Newdigate Rd E. Hare 173 E1
Newdigate Rd. Hare 173 E1
Newell La. Luf 38 B4
Newell Rd. Heml H 138 C4
Newell Rise. Heml H 138 C4
Newells Hedge. Ivin 80 B3
Newells. Letw 23 E2
Newfield La. Heml H 124 C2
Newfields. Wel GC 110 A3
Newford Cl. Heml H 125 D2
Newgate Cl. St Alb 128 B3
Newgate St. New St 146 B4
Newgate Street Vill. New St 146 C3
Newgate. Stev 51 D2
Newgatestreet Rd. Gofs O 147 E2
Newgatestreet Rd. Ham St 147 D3
Newground Rd. Ald 101 D2
Newhall Cl. Bov 137 D2
Newhall Ct. Wa Aby 163 F3
Newhouse Cres. Watf 154 A4
Newhouse Rd. Bov 137 D3
Newland Cl. Pnr 175 F2
Newland Cl. St Alb 142 A4
Newlands Ave. Radl 155 F3
Newlands Cl E. Hit 34 C2
Newlands Cl W. Hit 34 C2
Newlands La. Hit 34 C2
Newlands Pl. Barn 171 E2
Newlands Rd. Heml H 123 F2
Newlands Rd. Luton 63 E1
Newlands Rd. Nwml E 63 F1
Newlands Way. Pot B 145 D1
Newlands Wlk. Watf 154 B3
Newlands. Letw 23 D2
Newlyn Cl. Bri Wd 140 C1
Newlyn Cl. Stev 50 A3
Newlyn Rd. Barn 171 F3
Newman Ave. Roystn 7 F3
Newmans Dri. Harp 85 F1
Newmarket Rd. Roystn 7 F3
Newnham Cl. Luton 46 B1
Newnham Rd. Newn 12 C3
Newnham Way. Ashw 4 A1
Newport Cl. Enf 162 C1
Newport Mead. Sth Ox 175 E3
Newports. Saw 97 E1
Newquay Gdns. Sth Ox 175 D4
Newstead. Hat 129 F1
Newteswell Dri. Wa Aby 163 E4
Newton Cl. Harp 107 E3
Newton Cl. Hod 115 D1
Newton Dri. Saw 97 E1
Newton Rd. Har 176 C1
Newton Rd. Stev 51 D3
Newtons Way. Hit 34 C3
Newtown Cres. Bor 170 B3
Newtown Rd. Bis St 76 C3
Niagara Cl. Ches 148 B1
Nicholas Cl. St Alb 127 E4
Nicholas Cl. Watf 154 A1
Nicholas La. Hert 113 E3
Nicholas Pl. Stev 36 B1
Nicholas Rd. Elst 169 F2
Nicholas Way. Heml H 124 C3
Nicholas Way. Norwd 174 B1
Nicholls Cl. Red 105 F3
Nichols Cl. Luton 46 B1
Nicola Cl. Har 176 B1
Nicoll Way. Bor 170 B3
Nicolson Dri. Bus 176 B4
Nidderdale. Heml H 124 C3
Nightingale Ave. Knee 2 A3
Nightingale Cl. Luton 46 B3
Nightingale Cl. Radl 155 F2
Nightingale La. St Alb 142 B4
Nightingale Pl. Ric 165 E1
Nightingale Rd. Bus 168 A2
Nightingale Rd. Chor 165 E1
Nightingale Rd. Hit 34 C4
Nightingale Way. Bal 23 F3
Nightingale Wlk. Heml H 105 E1
Nightingale Wlk. Stev 51 E3
Nightingales. Wa Aby 163 F3
Nimmo Dri. Bus 168 B1
Ninefields. Wa Aby 163 F3
Ninesprings Way. Hit 35 D3
Ninian Rd. Heml H 124 C4
Ninning's La. Wl Gr 68 C1
Ninth Ave. Luton 44 B4
Niton Cl. Barn 171 E2
Niven Cl. Bor 170 B4
Nobles The. Bis St 76 B3
Nodes Dri. Stev 51 D1
Noke La. Chis 140 C2
Noke Shot. Harp 86 B2
Noke Side. Pk St 141 D2
Noke The. Stev 69 D4
Nokes The. Heml H 124 A3
Nokeside. Stev 69 D4
Norbury Ave. Watf 167 E4
Norfolk Ave. Watf 154 B1
Norfolk Gdns. Bor 170 B3
Norfolk Rd. Bun 40 C4
Norfolk Rd. Luton 64 A4
Norfolk Rd. Ric 165 F1
Norfolk Way. Bis St 76 C3
Norman Ave. Bis St 76 B3
Norman Cl. Wa Aby 163 E3
Norman Cres. Pnr 175 E1
Norman Ct. Pot B 145 E1
Norman Ct. Sta Mo 59 F4
Norman Rd. Luton 45 D1
Norman Rd. Welw 89 D2
Norman's La. Roystn 7 E3
Norman's Way. Sta Mo 59 F4
Normandy Ave. Barn 171 F3
Normandy Dri. Berk 122 A3
Normandy Rd. St Alb 127 E2
Normans Cl. Letw 11 F1
Normans La. Wl Gr 68 C1
Normansfield Cl. Bus 168 A1
Norris Cl. Bis St 77 E4
Norris Gr. Hod 134 C2
Norris Rd. Hod 135 D3
Norris Rise. Hod 134 C4
North App. Norwd 174 B4
North App. Watf 154 A3
North Ave. Letw 23 D4
North Ave. Shen 156 C4
North Barn. Lo Naz 135 D1
North Bridge Rd. Berk 122 A3
North Cl. Barn 171 E2
North Cl. Chis 141 D3
North Cl. Roystn 7 E4
North Common Rd. Red 106 A2
North Cotts. Lon C 142 A3
North Dri. H Cr 72 C1
North Dri. St Alb 128 C3
North Drift Way. Luton 63 D3
North Gate. Harl 117 E1
North Hill. Chor 164 C4
North Orbital Rd. Abb L 154 B4
North Orbital Rd. Bri Wd 140 C1
North Orbital Rd. Chis 141 D3
North Orbital Rd. St Alb 129 E1
North Orbital Rd. St Alb 141 F3
North Orbital Rd. Tyt 142 C4
North Pl. Hit 21 E1
North Pl. Wa Aby 163 D3
North Rd. Bal 12 C1
North Rd. Berk 122 A2
North Rd. Ches 162 C3
North Rd. Chor 164 B2
North Rd. Hertng 113 D4
North Rd. Hod 135 D4
North Rd. Stev 36 B1
North Ride. Welw 89 E3
North Riding. Bri Wd 141 D1
North Road Ave. Hertng 113 D4
North Road Gdns. Hert 113 D3
North St. Bis St 76 C4
North St. Lo Naz 135 F1
North St. Luton 45 F1
North Terr. Bis St 76 C4
North Way South. Letw 23 D3
North Western Ave. Bus 168 B3
North Western Ave. Elst 169 D1
North Western Ave. Watf 154 B2
Northam Rd E. Nort 146 C1
Northaw Cl. Heml H 125 D4
Northaw Rd W. Nort 160 A4
Northbrook Dri. Norwd 174 C2
Northbrook Rd. Barn 171 F2
Northcliffe Dri. N20 171 F1
Northcote. Pnr 175 D1
Northdown Rd. Hat 130 A1
Northend. Heml H 125 E1
Northern Ave. Henlw 10 B2
Northfield Gdns. Watf 154 B1
Northfield Rd. Ashw 1 B1
Northfield Rd. Bor 170 A4
Northfield Rd. Ches 162 C4
Northfield Rd. Harp 86 B2
Northfield Rd. Saw 97 F2
Northfield. Brag 55 F4
Northfield. Hat 130 A4
Northfields. Letw 11 F1
Northgate End. Bis St 76 C4
Northgate Path. Bor 156 C1
Northgate. Norwd 174 B2
Northlands. P Bar 159 E4
Northolt Ave. Bis St 59 D1
Northridge Way. Heml H 124 A2
Northview Rd. Luton 45 F1
Northway. Ric 165 F1
Northway. Wel GC 89 F1
Northwell Dri. Luton 44 C4
Northwick Rd. Sth Ox 175 E3
Northwood Cl. Ham St 147 F2
Northwood Hills Cir. Norwd 175 D1
Northwood Rd. Ric 173 F2
Northwood Way. Hare 173 E1
Northwood Way. Norwd 175 D1
Northwood. Wel GC 111 E3
Norton Bury La. Letw 12 B2
Norton Cres. Bal 23 F4
Norton Green Rd. Stev 50 B2
Norton Mill La. Letw 12 B2
Norton Rd. Bal 12 B1
Norton Rd. Letw 12 B1
Norton Rd. Luton 44 C2
Norton Rd. Stev 50 B2
Norton Rd. Stot 12 A2
Norton Way N. Letw 23 D4
Nortonstreet La. St P W 67 D4
Norvic Rd. Mars 80 A1
Norwich Cl. Stev 37 D1
Norwich Way. Cro Gr 166 A3
Norwood Cl. Hertng 112 C4
Nottingham Cl. Watf 154 A3
Nottingham Rd. Heron 164 B1
Nugent's Park. Pnr 175 F1
Nugents Ct. Pnr 175 F1
Nun's Cl. Hit 34 C4
Nunfield. Chipf 152 A4
Nunnery Cl. St Alb 127 F1
Nunnery La. Luton 45 D3
Nunnery Stables. St Alb 127 E1
Nuns La. St Alb 141 F4
Nunsbury Dri. Ches 148 C3
Nup End Cl. Wing 60 A2
Nup End La. Wing 60 A2
Nupton Dri. Barn 171 E2
Nurseries Rd. Whea 108 C4
Nursery Cl. Bis St 76 C3
Nursery Cl. Stev 69 D4
Nursery Fields. Saw 97 E1
Nursery Gdns. Tri 100 A2
Nursery Gdns. Ware 93 F1
Nursery Gdns. Wel GC 89 F1
Nursery Hill. Wel GC 89 F1
Nursery Rd. Bis St 76 C3
Nursery Rd. Ches 148 C3
Nursery Rd. Hod 115 D1
Nursery Rd. Lo Naz 135 E1
Nursery Rd. Luton 44 C3
Nursery Row. Barn 171 F3
Nut Gr. Wel GC 89 E1
Nut Slip. Bun 40 C3
Nutcroft. Dat 69 E1
Nutfield. Wel GC 90 A1
Nutleigh Gr. Hit 21 E1
Nye Way. Bov 137 D2
Nymans Cl. Luton 46 B2

Oak Ave. Bri Wd 141 D1
Oak Ave. Enf 160 C1
Oak Cl. Heml H 138 C4
Oak Cl. Wa Aby 163 E3
Oak Ct. Norwd 174 B2
Oak Dri. Berk 122 B2
Oak Dri. Saw 118 B4
Oak Farm. Bor 170 B2
Oak Glade. Norwd 174 A1
Oak Gr. Hat 129 F3
Oak Gr. Hert 113 F2
Oak Green Way. Abb L 153 F4
Oak Green. Abb L 153 F4
Oak La. Buc Co 120 A1
Oak La. Cuf 146 C2
Oak La. Gra 36 B2
Oak Path. Bus 168 A2
Oak Piece. Wl Gr 89 F4
Oak Rd. Luton 63 E4
Oak Rd. Wl Gr 69 D1
Oak St. Bis St 76 C3
Oak St. Heml H 138 C4
Oak Tree Cl. Hat 130 A3
Oak Tree Cl. Hert H 114 B2
Oak Tree Ct. Elst 169 E2
Oak Way. Harp 107 D3
Oak Wood. Berk 121 F2
Oakbank. Radl 156 A2
Oakcroft Cl. Pnr 175 D1
Oakdale Ave. Norwd 175 D1
Oakdale Cl. Sth Ox 175 E3
Oakdale Rd. Sth Ox 175 E3
Oakdale. Wel GC 89 E1
Oakdene Cl. Pnr 175 F2
Oakdene Rd. Heml H 138 C4
Oakdene Rd. Watf 154 A2
Oakdene Way. St Alb 128 B2
Oakdene. Ches 148 C1
Oaken Gr. Wel GC 110 C2
Oakfield Ave. Hit 35 D3
Oakfield Cl. Pot B 158 C4
Oakfield Rd. Harp 107 D3
Oakfield. Chor 165 D2
Oakfields Ave. Kneb 69 D3
Oakfields Cl. Stev 51 E1
Oakfields Rd. Kneb 69 D3
Oakfields. Stev 51 E1
Oakford Dri. Tri 99 F2
Oakhill Ave. Pnr 175 F1
Oakhill Dri. Welw 89 D3
Oakhill Rd. Map Cr 172 C3
Oakhill. Letw 23 E2
Oakhurst Ave. Harp 107 D3
Oakhurst Rd. Enf 162 B2
Oakington. Wel GC 111 E3
Oaklands Ave. Bro Pk 144 C2
Oaklands Ave. Watf 167 D1
Oaklands Cl. Bis St 59 D1
Oaklands Ct. Watf 167 D4
Oaklands Dri. Bis St 59 D1
Oaklands Gate. Norwd 174 C2
Oaklands La. Barn 171 D3
Oaklands La. St Alb 129 D2
Oaklands Park. Bis St 59 D1
Oaklands Rd. Ham St 147 F3
Oaklands Rd. N20 171 F1
Oaklands Rise. Wl Gr 89 F4
Oaklands. Berk 122 A2
Oaklea Cl. Wl Gr 89 F4
Oaklea Wood. Wl Gr 89 F4
Oaklea. Wl Gr 89 F4
Oakleigh Ct. Bis St 76 B4
Oakleigh Dri. Cro Gr 166 B2
Oakleigh Rd. Pnr 176 A2
Oakley Cl. Luton 44 B2
Oakley Rd. Harp 107 E4
Oakley Rd. Luton 44 C2
Oakmeade. Pnr 176 A2
Oakmere Ave. Pot B 159 E3
Oakmere Cl. Pot B 159 E4
Oakmere La. Pot B 159 E4
Oakridge Ave. Radl 155 F3
Oakridge La. Aldhm 155 E3
Oakridge. Bri Wd 140 C1
Oakroyd Ave. Pot B 158 C3
Oakroyd Cl. Pot B 158 C3
Oaks Cl. Hit 34 C3
Oaks Cl. Radl 155 F2
Oaks Cross. Stev 51 D1
Oaks The. Berk 122 A2
Oaktree Cl. Gofs O 147 E2
Oaktree Garth. Wel GC 110 C3
Oakview Cl. Ches 148 A2
Oakway. Stu 82 A4
Oakwell Cl. Stev 69 E4
Oakwood Ave. Bor 170 A3
Oakwood Cl. Stev 51 E1
Oakwood Dri. Luton 44 B4
Oakwood Dri. St Alb 128 B2
Oakwood Rd. Bri Wd 140 C1
Oakwood Rd. Pnr 175 D1
Oakwood. Wa Aby 163 F3
Occupation Rd. Watf 167 D2
Ochard House La. St Alb 127 E1
Oddfellows Ct. Hert 113 E3
Oddy Hill. Tri 100 B2
Odessey Rd. Bor 170 A4
Offa Rd. St Alb 127 E2
Offas Way. Whea 108 B4
Offley Hill. Gt Of 33 E2
Offley Rd. Hit 34 B3
Ogard Rd. Hod 135 E4
Okeley La. Tri 99 F2
Old Barn La. Cro Gr 165 F2
Old Bedford Rd. Luton 45 E3
Old Brewery Pl. Kim 66 B1
Old Charlton Rd. Hit 34 C3
Old Church La. Wad 93 F4
Old Cross. Hert 113 E3

Old Dean. Bov 137 D2
Old Drive The. Wel GC 110 A3
Old Farm. Ivin 80 B2
Old Fishery La. Heml H 123 F1
Old Fold Cl. Barn 171 F4
Old Fold La. Barn 171 F4
Old Fold View. Barn 171 E3
Old Forge Cl. Watf 154 A3
Old Forge Cl. Wel GC 89 F1
Old Forge Rd. Enf 161 F1
Old French Horn La. Hat 130 A3
Old Gammon Cl. Nort 174 B3
Old Garden Ct. St Alb 127 E2
Old Hale Way. Hit 21 F1
Old Hall Cl. Pnr 175 F1
Old Hall Dri. Pnr 175 F1
Old Harpenden Rd. St Alb 127 F3
Old Herns La. Wel GC 111 E4
Old Hertford Rd. Hat 130 B4
Old Highway. Hod 135 E4
Old House Ct. Heml H 124 C2
Old House La. Kin L 152 C2
Old House La. Lo Naz 149 F4
Old House Rd. Heml H 124 C2
Old Knebworth La. Old K 68 B4
Old La. Kneb 69 D3
Old Leys. Hat 130 A1
Old London Rd. Hert 113 F3
Old London Rd. St Alb 127 F1
Old Maple. Heml H 104 C1
Old Mill Gdns. Berk 122 B2
Old Mill La. L Hal 98 A3
Old Mill Rd. Abb L 153 E3
Old Nazeing Rd. Lo Naz 135 D1
Old North Rd. Knee 2 A2
Old North Rd. Roystn 7 E4
Old Oak Cl. Ch En 11 D4
Old Oaks. Wa Aby 163 F4
Old Orch. Pk St 141 E3
Old Orchard Mews. Berk 122 B2
Old Orchard. Luton 63 E3
Old Park Rd. Hit 34 C4
Old Parkbury La. Col St 141 F1
Old Rd. Harl 118 B3
Old Rectory Cl. Harp 86 A1
Old Rectory Dri. Hat 130 A3
Old Rectory Gdns. Whea 87 E1
Old Redding. Har 176 B3
Old School Cl. Cod 67 F1
Old School Green. Benn 52 C3
Old School Wlk. Arl 11 D2
Old School Wlk. Cad 63 E1
Old Shire La. Chor 164 A2
Old Sopwell Gdns. St Alb 127 F1
Old Uxbridge Rd. Map Cr 172 C2
Old Vicarage Gdns. Mark 83 E3
Old Watford Rd. Bri Wd 140 C1
Old's App. Watf 166 B1
Old's Cl. Watf 166 B1
Olden Mead. Letw 23 D2
Oldfield Cl. Ches 148 C2
Oldfield Dri. Ches 148 C2
Oldfield Farm Rd. Henlw 10 A2
Oldfield Rd. Heml H 123 F1
Oldfield Rd. Lon C 142 B3
Oldfield Rise. Whit 66 C4
Oldhall St. Hert 113 E3
Oldhouse Croft. Harl 117 F1
Oldings Cnr. Stanb 110 A1
Oldpark Ride. Ches 161 E4
Oldwood. Wl Gr 89 E4
Olive Taylor Ct. Heml H 124 C4
Oliver Cl. Heml H 138 C4
Oliver Cl. Pk St 141 E2
Oliver Rd. Heml H 138 C4
Oliver Rise. Heml H 138 C4
Oliver's Cl. Heml H 123 E4
Oliver's La. Stot 11 F4
Olleberrie La. Sar 151 E4
Olwen Mews. Pnr 175 E1
Olympus Rd. Henlw 10 A2
On-The-Hill. Watf 175 F4
Onslow Cl. Hat 130 A3
Onslow Cl. Hit 21 E1
Onslow Rd. Luton 44 B3
Opening The. Cod 88 C4
Openshaw Way. Letw 22 C3
Orbital Cres. Watf 153 F2
Orchard Ave. Berk 122 A2
Orchard Ave. Harp 85 F1
Orchard Ave. Watf 154 A4
Orchard Cl. Bor 169 F3
Orchard Cl. Bus 168 B1
Orchard Cl. Chor 164 B3
Orchard Cl. Cuf 146 C2
Orchard Cl. Gos 34 C2
Orchard Cl. Heml H 124 C3
Orchard Cl. L Berk 132 B2
Orchard Cl. Letw 22 C4
Orchard Cl. Radl 155 F2
Orchard Cl. St Alb 127 F1
Orchard Cl. Sta Ab 115 E2
Orchard Cl. Ware 93 E1
Orchard Cl. Watf 166 C4
Orchard Cl. Wing 60 A1
Orchard Cres. Stev 50 B4
Orchard Croft. Harl 118 A1
Orchard Dri. Chis 141 D3
Orchard Dri. Chor 164 B3
Orchard Dri. Watf 166 C4
Orchard Gdns. Wa Aby 163 E3
Orchard Mead. Hat 129 F3
Orchard Rd. Bal 12 C1
Orchard Rd. Barn 171 F3
Orchard Rd. Bis St 59 D1
Orchard Rd. Hit 22 A1
Orchard Rd. Roystn 7 D4
Orchard Rd. Stev 50 B4
Orchard Rd. Tewin 90 B2
Orchard Rd. Welw 89 E3
Orchard Sq. Hod 148 C4
Orchard St. Heml H 138 B4
Orchard St. St Alb 127 E1
Orchard The. Bal 23 F4
Orchard The. Hert 92 B1
Orchard The. Kin L 139 D1
Orchard The. Tonw 92 C4
Orchard The. Wel GC 110 B4
Orchard Way. Bov 137 D2
Orchard Way. Bre Wd 47 F1
Orchard Way. Gofs O 147 D2
Orchard Way. Henlw 10 A2
Orchard Way. Ivin 80 C3
Orchard Way. Kneb 68 C3
Orchard Way. Letw 22 C4
Orchard Way. Luton 44 B2
Orchard Way. Pot B 145 D2
Orchard Way. Ric 165 D1
Orchard Way. Roystn 7 E4
Orchards The. Saw 97 F2
Orchards The. Tri 99 F2
Ordelmere. Letw 11 F1
Ordnance Rd. Enf 162 C1
Oregon Way. Luton 45 D4
Organ Hall Rd. Bor 169 F4
Orion Way. Norwd 174 C3
Orlando Cl. Hit 35 D3
Ormesby Dri. Pot B 158 B4
Ormonde Rd. Norwd 174 B3
Ormsby Cl. Luton 63 F3
Ormskirk Rd. Sth Ox 175 E3
Oronsay. Heml H 125 D1
Orphanage Rd. Watf 167 E4
Orpington Cl. Luton 44 A2
Orton Cl. St Alb 128 A4
Orwell View. Bal 13 D1
Osborn Way. Wel G C 110 B3
Osborne Gdns. Pot B 145 D1
Osborne Rd. Ches 148 C2
Osborne Rd. Hod 135 D2
Osborne Rd. Luton 63 F3
Osborne Rd. Pot B 145 D1
Osborne Rd. Watf 154 B1
Osborne Way. Wigg 100 B1
Osbourne Ave. Kin L 138 C2
Osmington Cl. Tri 99 F2
Osprey Gdns. Stev 51 E1
Osprey Wlk. Luton 44 A3
Oster St. St Alb 127 E2
Osterley Cl. Stev 69 E4
Oswald Rd. St Alb 127 F1
Otley Way. Sth Ox 175 E4
otswold Ave. Bus 168 B2
Otter Gdns. Hat 130 A2
Otterspool La. Bus 154 C1
Otterspool Way. Bus 168 A4
Ottoman Terr. Watf 167 E3
Ottway Wlk. Welw 89 E2
Otways Cl. Pot B 159 D3
Oudle La. Muc H 74 C1
Oughton Cl. Hit 34 B4
Oughton Head Way. Hit 34 B4
Oughtonhead La. Hit 34 B4
Oulton Cres. Pot B 158 B4
Oulton Rise. Harp 86 B2
Oulton Way. Watf 175 F3
Oundle Ave. Bus 168 B2
Oundle Ct. Stev 69 E4
Oundle Path. Stev 69 E4
Oundle The. Stev 69 E4
Ousden Cl. Ches 148 C1
Ousden Dri. Ches 148 C1
Oval The. Henlw 10 B2
Oval The. Hod 148 C4
Oval The. Stev 37 D1
Overfield Rd. Luton 46 B1
Overstone Rd. Harp 86 B1
Overstone Rd. Luton 44 B1
Overstream. Chor 165 D3
Oving Cl. Luton 46 B1
Owen Jones Cl. Henlw 10 B3
Owens Way. Cro Gr 166 A3
owland Way. Letw 22 C3
Owles La. Bun 40 C3
Ox La. Harp 86 A2
Oxcroft. Bis St 76 C2
Oxen Rd. Luton 45 F1
Oxendon Dri. Hod 135 D3
Oxfield Cl. Berk 122 A2
Oxford Ave. St Alb 128 B1
Oxford Cl. Ches 148 B1
Oxford Cl. Knee 2 A4
Oxford Rd. Bre Wd 47 F1
Oxford Rd. Luton 63 F3
Oxford St. Watf 167 D2
Oxhey Ave. Watf 167 E1
Oxhey Dr. Sth Ox 175 D4
Oxhey La. Pnr 176 A2
Oxhey La. Watf 175 D4
Oxhey Rd. Watf 167 E1
Oxhey Ridge Cl. Norwd 175 D3
Oxlease Dri. Hat 130 A2
Oxleys Rd. Stev 51 E2
Oxleys The. Harl 118 C2

Pacatian Way. Stev 51 E4
Packhorse Cl. St Alb 128 B3
Packhorse La. Ridge 157 E4
Paddick Cl. Hod 134 C4
Paddock Cl. Hun 95 E1
Paddock Cl. Letw 23 D3
Paddock Rd. Bun 40 C4
Paddock The. Bis St 76 B2
Paddock The. Hat 130 A3
Paddock The. Hit 35 D3
Paddock The. Hod 135 D2
Paddock Way. Heml H 123 F2
Paddock Wood. Harp 107 F4
Paddocks Cl. Stev 51 D2
Paddocks The. Cod 67 F1
Paddocks The. Hert 114 A2
Paddocks The. Stev 51 D2
Paddocks The. Wel GC 111 D4
Padgets The. Wa Aby 163 F3
Page Cl. Bal 23 F3
Page Rd. Hert 114 A3
Pageant Rd. St Alb 127 E1
Pages Cl. Bis St 76 B3
Pages Croft. Berk 122 A3
Paine's La. Pnr 175 F1
Paines Orch. Ched 80 A4
Painters La. Enf 162 C2
Palace Cl. Kin L 139 D1
Palace Gdns. Roystn 7 E3
Palfrey Cl. St Alb 127 E3
Pallas Rd. Heml H 124 C3
Palmer Ave. Bus 168 A2
Palmer Cl. Hert 113 E4
Palmer Gdns. Barn 171 E2
Palmer Rd. Hert 113 E4
Palmers Gr. Lo Naz 135 F1
Palmers La. Bis St 76 C4
Palmers Rd. Bor 170 A4
Palmers Way. Ches 148 C1
Palmerston Cl. Wel GC 110 B3
Pamela Ave. Heml H 138 C4
Pamela Gdns. Bis St 76 C2
Pams La. Kim 66 B1
Pancake La. Heml H 125 E1
Pankhurst Cres. Stev 51 E3
Panshanger Dri. Wel GC 111 D3
Pantiles The. Bus 168 B1
Panxworth Rd. Heml H 124 B1
Paper Mill La. Stand 55 F1
Parade Ct. Tri 100 A2
Parade The. Radl 156 A2
Parade The. Sth Ox 175 E4
Parade The. Watf 167 D3
Paradise Cl. Ches 148 A2
Paradise Rd. Wa Aby 163 E3
Paradise. Heml H 124 B1
Parishes Mead. Stev 51 E2
Park Ave N. Harp 85 F1
Park Ave S. Harp 85 F1
Park Ave Trad Est. Luton 44 B4
Park Ave. Bis St 76 C2
Park Ave. Bus 167 F4
Park Ave. Chor 165 D3
Park Ave. Luton 44 B4
Park Ave. Pot B 159 E3
Park Ave. Radl 156 A3
Park Ave. St Alb 128 A2
Park Ave. Watf 167 D3
Park Cl. Bal 23 F4
Park Cl. Bro Pk 145 D3
Park Cl. Bus 167 E3
Park Cl. Har 176 B1
Park Cl. Hat 130 B3
Park Cl. Mark 83 E3
Park Cl. Ric 174 B3
Park Cl. Stev 51 D1
Park Cres. Bal 23 F4
Park Cres. Bor 169 F3
Park Cres. Har 176 B1
Park Ct. Harl 117 E1
Park Dri. Bal 23 F4
Park Dri. Har 176 B2
Park Dri. Pot B 159 D4
Park Dri. Puc 55 E2
Park Farm Cl. Henlw 10 B4
Park Farm La. Nut 18 B1
Park Gate. Hit 34 C3
Park Gdns. Bal 23 F4
Park Hill Rd. Heml H 124 A2
Park Hill. Harl 118 A2
Park Hill. Harp 85 F1
Park La. Bis St 76 C2
Park La. Ches 148 A2
Park La. Ches 162 B3
Park La. Coln H 129 E1
Park La. Hare 173 D1
Park La. Harl 117 E1
Park La. Heml H 124 B1
Park La. Hod 134 C2
Park La. Kim 66 B1
Park La. Kneb 68 C3
Park La. Old K 68 B3
Park La. Puc 55 E2
Park Lane Paradise. Ham St 148 A3
Park Mead. Harl 117 D1
Park Meadow. Hat 130 B3
Park Mews. Hat 130 B3
Park Mount. Harp 85 F2
Park Nook Gdns. Enf 161 E1
Park Pl. Hare 173 E1
Park Pl. Pk St 141 E2
Park Pl. Stev 50 B3
Park Rd. Barn 171 F3
Park Rd. Bus 168 A2
Park Rd. Ches 162 B3
Park Rd. Enf 162 C2
Park Rd. Heml H 124 B1
Park Rd. Hert 113 F3
Park Rd. Hod 135 D3
Park Rd. Nort 146 A1
Park Rd. Radl 156 A2
Park Rd. Ric 165 F1
Park Rd. Sta Mo 59 F3
Park Rd. Tri 100 A2
Park Rd. Ware 93 D1
Park Rd. Watf 167 D4
Park Rise Cl. Harp 85 F2
Park Rise. Har 176 C1
Park Rise. Harp 85 F2
Park Rise. Nthch 121 F3
Park Sq. Luton 63 F4
Park St W. Luton 63 F4
Park St. Bal 23 F4
Park St. Berk 122 A3
Park St. Hat 130 B3
Park St. Hit 34 C3
Park St. Luton 63 F3
Park St. Pk La 141 E2
Park St. Tri 100 A2
Park Street La. Bri Wd 141 D1
Park Street La. Chis 141 E2
Park Street La. Pk St 141 E2
Park The. Red 106 A3
Park The. St Alb 128 A3
Park Viaduct. Luton 63 F3
Park View Cl. Luton 44 B3
Park View Dr. Mark 83 E3
Park View Rd. Berk 122 A2
Park View Rd. Pnr 175 D2
Park View. Hat 130 B4
Park View. Hod 135 D3
Park View. Pnr 175 F1
Park View. Pot B 159 E3
Park View. Stev 51 D1
Park Way. Hit 34 C3
Park Way. Ric 165 E1
Parker Ave. Hert 113 E4
Parker Cl. Letw 22 C2
Parker St. Watf 167 D4
Parkers Field. Stev 51 E2
Parkfield Ave. Har 176 B1
Parkfield Cres. Har 176 B1
Parkfield Cres. Kim 66 B1
Parkfield Rd. Mark 83 E3
Parkfield. Chor 164 C3
Parkfield. Letw 23 E2
Parkfields. Wel GC 110 B3
Parkgate Rd. Watf 154 B1
Parkhurst Pl. Watf 167 E4
Parkhurst Rd. Hert 113 D4
Parkinson Cl. Whea 108 B4
Parkland Cl. Hod 115 D1
Parkland Dri. Luton 63 E3
Parklands. Roystn 7 F3
Parklands. Wa Aby 163 E4
Parkside Dri. Watf 166 C4
Parkside Rd. Norwd 174 C3
Parkside. Bun 27 E1
Parkside. Ches 162 C3
Parkside. Welw 89 E3
Parkway Cl. Wel GC 110 B3
Parkway Ct. St Alb 142 A4
Parkway Gdns. Wel G C 110 B3
Parkway. Saw 97 F1
Parkway. Stev 51 D1
Parkway. Wel GC 110 B3
Parkwood Cl. Hod 134 C2
Parkwood Dri. Heml H 123 F2
Parliament Sq. Hert 113 E3
Parndon Mill La. Harl 117 D2
Parnel Rd. Ware 93 F1
Parnell Cl. Abb L 139 F1
Parr Cres. Heml H 125 D4
Parrott's La. Buc Co 120 A2
Parrotts Cl. Cro Gr 166 A3
Parrotts Field. Hod 135 D4
Parson's Cl. Fla 84 A1
Parsonage Cl. Abb L 139 F1
Parsonage Cl. Tri 100 A2
Parsonage Ct. Tri 100 A2
Parsonage La. Alb 57 D3
Parsonage La. Birhr 59 F2
Parsonage La. Bis St 77 E4
Parsonage La. Wel Gr 144 A4
Parsonage Pl. Tri 100 A2
Parsonage Rd. Ric 165 E1
Parsonage Rd. Wel Gr 144 A4
Parsons Green Est. Stev 37 E1
Parthia Cl. Roystn 7 F3
Partridge Cl. Bus 168 B1
Partridge Hill. Ashw 4 B2
Partridge Rd. St Alb 127 E4
Parva Cl. Harp 107 E3
Parvills. Wa Aby 163 E4
Parys Rd. Luton 45 D3
Pascal Way. Letw 23 D4
Pasfield. Wa Aby 163 E3
Passingham Ave. Hit 35 D3
Paston Rd. Heml H 124 C3
Pasture Cl. Bus 168 B1
Pasture La. Bre Gr 65 F4
Pasture Rd. Letw 22 C2
Pastures The. Chis 141 D4
Pastures The. Hat 130 A2
Pastures The. N20 171 F1
Pastures The. Stev 51 E4
Pastures The. Ware 93 E2
Pastures The. Watf 167 E1
Pastures The. Wel GC 111 D2
Pastures Way. Luton 44 A2
Paternoster Cl. Wa Aby 163 F3
Paternoster Hill. Wa Aby 163 F4
Pathway The. Watf 167 E1
Patmore Cl. Bis St 76 B4
Patmore Link Rd. Heml H 125 E1
Patmore Rd. Wa Aby 163 F3
Patricia Gdns. Bis St 76 C3
Paul's Green. Ches 162 C3
Pauls La. Hod 135 D3
Paxton Rd. Berk 122 B2
Paxton Rd. St Alb 127 F1
Payne End. San 15 D1
Payne's Pk. Hit 34 C4
Paynes Cl. Letw 12 A1
Paynes La. Lo Naz 149 E4
Paynesfield Rd. Bus 168 C1
Pea La. Nthch 121 E4
Peace Gr. Wl Gr 90 A4
Peakes La. Ham St 147 F2
Peakes Way. Ham St 147 F2
Pear Tree Dell. Letw 23 D2
Pear Tree Wlk. Ham St 147 F3
Pearces Wlk. St Alb 127 E1
Pearman Dri. Dan En 71 F4
Pearsall Cl. Letw 23 D3
Pearson Ave. Hert 113 E2
Pearson Cl. Hert 113 E2
Peartree Cl. Heml H 124 A2
Peartree Cl. Wel GC 110 C3
Peartree Ct. Wel GC 110 C3
Peartree La. Wel GC 110 C3
Peartree Rd. Heml H 124 A2
Peartree Rd. Luton 46 B2
Peartree Way. Stev 51 D2
Peascroft Rd. Heml H 125 D1
Peasecroft. Cotrd 39 E4
Peasmead. Bun 40 B3
Pecham Ct. Wel GC 111 E3
Peck's Hill. Lo Naz 135 F1
Pedlars La. Ther 15 F4
Pedley Hill. Stu 103 D4
Peel Cres. Hert 113 E4
Peel Pl. Luton 63 E4
Peel St. Luton 63 E4
Peg's La. Hert 113 E3
Pegmire La. Bus 168 B4
Pegs La. Widf 95 E3
Pegsdon Cl. Luton 45 D4
Pegsdon Way. Pegs 19 F1
Peitley Hill. Fla 84 A1
Pelham Ct. Heml H 125 E2
Pelham Rd. Brag 55 F4
Pelhams The. Watf 154 B2
Pelican Way. Letw 11 F1
Pemberton Cl. St Alb 141 E4
Pembridge Chase. Bov 137 D2
Pembridge Cl. Bov 137 D2
Pembridge La. Bric 133 F1
Pembridge Rd. Bov 137 D2
Pembroke Ave. Enf 162 A1
Pembroke Ave. Luton 44 C2
Pembroke Cl. Hod 148 C4
Pembroke Dri. Gofs O 147 D1
Pembroke Rd. Bal 23 F4
Pembroke Rd. Norwd 174 B4
Pemsel Ct. Heml H 138 B4
Penda Cl. Luton 44 C4
Pendennis Ct. Harp 107 E4
Pengelly Cl. Ches 148 A1
Penhill. Luton 44 B3
Penman Cl. Chis 141 D2
Penn Cl. Chor 164 B2
Penn Rd. Chis 141 E2
Penn Rd. Ric 165 D1
Penn Rd. Stev 50 C2
Penn Way. Chor 164 B2
Penn Way. Letw 23 E2
Pennine Ave. Luton 44 B4
Pennine Way. Heml H 124 C3
Pennington La. Sta Mo 59 E4
Penningtons. Bis St 76 B3
Penny Croft. Harp 107 D2
Pennyfathers La. Har Gr 90 A2
Pennymead. Harl 118 A1
Penrose Ave. Watf 175 F4
Penrose Ct. Heml H 124 C4
Penscroft Gdns. Bor 170 B3
Penshurst Cl. Harp 85 E2
Penshurst Rd. Pot B 159 E4
Penshurst. Harl 118 B2
Pentland Rd. Bus 168 B2
Pentland. Heml H 124 C3
Pentley Cl. Wel GC 89 E1
Pentley Park. Wel GC 110 B4
Penton Dri. Ches 148 B1

Pentrich Ave. Enf 162 A1
Penzance Cl. Hare 173 E1
Peplins Cl. Bro Pk 144 C3
Peplins Way. Bro Pk 144 C3
Pepper Alley. Bal 23 F4
Pepper Hill. Gt Am 115 D2
Pepper Hill. Hert H 114 C3
Peppett's Green. Chol 120 A1
Pepsal End Rd. Fla 84 B4
Pepsal End. Stev 69 D4
Pepys Cres. Barn 171 E2
Pepys Way. Bal 23 F4
Percheron Dri. Luton 44 A2
Percheron Rd. Bor 170 B2
Percival Way. Luton 64 B4
Percy Rd. Watf 167 D3
Peregrine Cl. Watf 154 C3
Peregrine Rd. Luton 44 A2
Perham Way. Lon C 142 B3
Perimeter Rd. Hat 129 F4
Perivale Gdns. Watf 154 A3
Periwinkle Cl. Bark 17 E3
Periwinkle La. Hit 21 F1
Perowne Way. Stand 55 F2
Perram Cl. Ches 148 C3
Perriors Cl. Ham St 148 A2
Perry Dri. Roystn 7 F4
Perry Hill. Lo Naz 149 F4
Perry Mead. Bus 168 B2
Perrymead. Luton 46 C1
Perrysfield Rd. Ches 148 C2
Perrywood La. Bram 91 D3
Perrywood La. Wat St 91 D4
Petard Cl. Luton 44 A1
Peter's Pl. Nthch 121 F3
Peterlee Ct. Heml H 124 C4
Peters Ave. Lon C 142 B3
Peters Way. Kneb 68 C3
Peters Wood Hill. Gt Am 114 B4
Petworth Cl. Stev 69 E4
Pevensey Cl. Luton 46 B2
Pheasant Cl. Berk 122 B2
Pheasant Cl. Tri 100 A3
Pheasants Way. Ric 165 D1
Phillimore Pl. Radl 155 F2
Phillipers. Watf 154 C2
Phillips Ave. Roystn 7 E4
Phipps Hatch La. Enf 161 E1
Phoebe Rd. Heml H 124 C3
Phoenix Cl. Norwd 174 C3
Piccotts End La. Heml H 124 B4
Piccotts End La. Pic En 124 B3
Piccotts End Rd. Pic En 124 A4
Piccotts End. Pic En 124 B3
Pick Hill. Wa Aby 163 F4
Pickets Cl. Bus 168 C1
Picketts. Wel GC 89 F1
Pickford Hill. Harp 86 B2
Pickford Rd. Mark 83 E3
Picknage Rd. Bar 9 D1
Pie Cnr. Fla 84 A1
Pie Gdn. Fla 84 B1
Pig La. Bis St 77 D2
Pig's Nose. Bun 40 C4
Pigeonwick. Harp 86 A2
Piggotts La. Luton 44 B2
Piggotts Way. Bis St 76 C3
Piggottshill La. Harp 107 E4
Pightle Cl. Roystn 7 E4
Pilgrim Cl. Chis 141 E2
Pilgrim Cl. Watf 154 B3
Pilgrims Way. Stev 37 D1
Piltdown Rd. Sth Ox 175 E3
Pinchfield. Map Cr 172 C3
Pindar Rd. Hod 135 E4
Pine Cl. Ches 148 B2
Pine Cl. Norwd 174 C2
Pine Gr. Bis St 77 D3
Pine Gr. Bri Wd 140 C1
Pine Gr. Bro Pk 145 D3
Pine Gr. Bus 167 F4
Pine Gr. N20 171 F1
Pine Tree Cl. Heml H 124 B2
Pinecroft Cres. Barn 171 F3
Pinecroft. Heml H 138 C4
Pinelands. Bis St 58 C1
Pines Ave. Enf 162 A2
Pines Hill. Sta Mo 59 E3
Pines The. Bor 169 F4
Pinewood Ave. Pnr 176 A2
Pinewood Cl. Bor 170 B4
Pinewood Cl. Pnr 176 A2
Pinewood Cl. St Alb 128 B2
Pinewood Dri. Pot B 158 C4
Pinewood Gdns. Heml H 124 A2
Pinewood. Wel GC 110 C2
Pinfold Rd. Bus 167 F4
Pinford Dell. Luton 46 B1
Pinnacles. Wa Aby 163 F3
Pinnate Pl. Wel GC 110 C1
Pinner Green. Pnr 175 E1
Pinner Hill Rd. Pnr 175 E1
Pinner Hill. Pnr 175 D2
Pinner Park Ave. Har 176 B1
Pinner Park Gdns. Har 176 B1
Pinner Rd. Norwd 175 D1
Pinner Rd. Pnr 175 D1
Pinner Rd. Watf 167 F1
Pinnocks Cl. Bal 23 F4
Pinnocks La. Bal 23 F4
Pinto Cl. Bor 170 B2
Piper's Hill. Gt Ga 103 E2
Pipers Ave. Harp 107 E4
Pipers Cl. Red 106 A3
Pipers Hill. Net 103 E1
Pipers La. Cad 62 C1
Pipers La. Harp 107 F4
Pippens. Wel GC 89 F1
Pirton Cl. Hit 34 B3
Pirton Cl. St Alb 128 B4
Pirton Rd. Hit 34 B3
Pirton Rd. Hol 21 D4
Pirton Rd. Luton 44 B3
Pishiobury Dri. Saw 118 B4
Pishiobury Mews. Saw 118 B4
Pitsfield. Wel GC 89 E1
Pitstone Cl. St Alb 128 B4
Pittman's Field. Harl 117 F1
Pix Farm La. Heml H 123 E1
Pix Rd. Letw 23 D3
Pix Rd. Stot 11 F3
Pixies Hill Cres. Heml H 123 F1
Pixies Hill Rd. Heml H 123 F1
Pixmore Ave. Letw 23 D3
Pixmore Way. Letw 23 D3
Plaiston Way. Gt Ch 9 F1
Plaiters Cl. Tri 100 A2
Plaitford Cl. Ric 173 F4
Plantation Rd. Luton 44 B4
Plantation Wlk. Heml H 124 A3
Plash Dri. Stev 50 C3
Plashes Cl. Stand 55 E1
Plashets. Saw 98 B1
Plaw Hatch Cl. Bis St 77 D4
Pleasance The. Harp 85 E2
Pleasant Rd. Bis St 76 C4
Pleasant Rise. Hat 130 B4
Plewes Cl. Ken Co 82 C4
Plough Hill. Cuf 146 C1
Plough La. Chipf 152 A3
Plough La. Kin Wd 48 A3
Plough La. Pot En 123 D4
Ploughmans End. Wel GC 111 E3
Plover Cl. Berk 122 B2
Plum Tree Rd. Henlw 10 A1
Plummers La. Pet Gr 65 E1
Plumpton Cl. Luton 46 B2
Plumpton Rd. Hod 135 E4
Pluto Rise. Heml H 124 C3
Poets Green. Luton 44 A1
Polayn Garth. Wel GC 110 B4
Polegate. Luton 46 B1
Polehanger La. Heml H 123 F3
Poles Hill. Sar 151 F3
Poles La. Thun 93 E3
Poles Park. Thun 93 E3
Police Row. Ther 15 F4
Police Station La. Bus 163 A1
Pollard Gdns. Stev 50 C4
Pollards Cl. Gofs O 147 E1
Pollards Way. Pirt 20 B2
Pollards. Map Cr 172 B3
Pollicott Cl. St Alb 128 B4
Pollywick Rd. Wigg 100 B2
Polzeath Cl. Luton 64 B4
Pomeroy Cres. Watf 154 A2
Pomeroy Gr. Luton 45 F3
Pomfret Ave. Luton 63 F4
Pond Cl. Hare 173 E1
Pond Cl. Luton 44 A3
Pond Cl. Tri 100 A2
Pond Croft. Hat 129 F3
Pond La. Bal 23 F4
Pond Rd. Heml H 139 D3
Pondcroft Rd. Kneb 69 D2
Pondcroft. Wel GC 110 C3
Pondfield Cres. St Alb 128 A4
Pondside. Gra 36 B2
Pondsmeade. Red 106 A3
Pondwick Rd. Harp 85 F1
Pondwicks Cl. St Alb 127 E1
Pondwicks Rd. Luton 63 F4
Pooleys La. Wel Gr 144 B4
Pope's Rd. Abb L 153 F4
Popes La. Watf 154 A1
Popes Row. Ware 93 E2
Poplar Ave. Hat 129 E3
Poplar Ave. Luton 45 E4
Poplar Cl. H Cr 72 C1
Poplar Cl. Hit 35 D3
Poplar Cl. Pnr 175 E1
Poplar Cl. Roystn 7 F4
Poplar Dri. Roystn 7 F4
Poplar Rd. Ken Co 82 C4
Poplar Shaw. Wa Aby 163 F3
Poplars Cl. Hat 129 E3
Poplars Cl. Luton 46 A2
Poplars Cl. Watf 154 A4
Poplars The. Ch En 11 D4
Poplars The. Heml H 124 A1
Poplars The. Ick 21 F3
Poplars The. St Alb 142 A4
Poplars. Wel GC 111 D4
Popple Way. Stev 50 C3
Poppy Mead. Stev 50 C2
Poppyfields. Wel GC 111 E3
Porlock Dri. Luton 46 E1
Port Hill. Hert 113 E4
Port La. L Hal 77 D1
Port Vale. Hert 113 E3
Porters Cl. Bun 40 C4
Porters Hill. Harp 86 B2
Porters Wood. St Alb 127 F4
Portland Dri. Ches 162 A4
Portland Pl. Bis St 76 C4
Portland Pl. Hert H 114 B2
Portland Rd. Bis St 76 C4
Portland Rd. Luton 45 D1
Portland St. St Alb 127 E2
Portman Cl. Hit 21 E1
Portman Cl. St Alb 128 B4
Portmill La. Hit 34 C4
Post Office Rd. Harl 117 E1
Post Wood Rd. Gt Am 114 C4
Postfield. Wel GC 90 A1
Postwood Green. Hert H 114 B2
Potash La. Lon M 79 D3
Potten End Hill. Gt Ga 103 F1
Potter Heights Cl. Pnr 175 D2
Potter St. Bis St 76 C4
Potter St. Norwd 175 D1
Potter St. Pnr 175 D1
Potter Street Hill. Pnr 175 D2
Potters Field. St Alb 127 F4
Potters La. Bor 170 B4
Potters La. Stev 50 A2
Potterscrouch La. Chis 140 C4
Pottersheath Rd. Wl Gr 68 B1
Pottersmews. Elst 169 E2
Pottery Cl. Lutor 44 C4
Potton Rd. Gu M 1 C3
Pouchen End La. Heml H 123 E2
Poulteney Rd. Sta Mo 59 F4
Pound Ave. Stev 50 B3
Pound Cl. Lo Naz 149 F4
Pound Field. Watf 153 F2
Pound Green. Gu M 1 C3
Pound La. Shen 156 C3
Poundwell. Wel GC 111 D3
Powdermill La. Wa Aby 163 D3
Powdermill Way. Wa Aby 163 D3
Power Ct. Luton 63 F4
Powis Ct. Pot B 159 E3
Poynders Hill. Heml H 125 E2
Poynders Meadow. Cod 88 C4
Poynings Cl. Harp 107 F4
Poynters Rd. Dun 44 A1
Prae Cl. St Alb 127 D2
Praetorian Ct. St Alb 141 E4
Prescot Hill. Heml H 124 A3
Prescott Rd. Ches 148 C2
Presdales Dri. Gt Am 114 C4
President Way. Luton 64 B4
Preston Gdns. Enf 162 C1
Preston Gdns. Luton 45 F1
Preston Path. Luton 45 F1
Preston Rd. Gos 34 C1
Preston Rd. Pres 48 C4
Prestwick Cl. Luton 45 F3
Prestwick Dri. Bis St 59 D1
Prestwick Rd. Sth Ox 175 E3
Pretoria Rd. Watf 167 D3
Pretty Cnr. Norwd 175 D3
Priestleys. Luton 63 D4
Primary La. Saw 98 B1
Primary Way. Arl 11 D2
Primett Rd. Stev 50 B4
Primrose Cl. Arl 11 D2
Primrose Cl. Hat 130 A2
Primrose Ct. Stev 50 B4
Primrose Gdns. Bus 168 A1
Primrose Hill Rd. Stev 50 B4
Primrose Hill. Bed 139 D2
Primrose La. Arl 11 D2
Primrose Path. Ches 162 A4
Primrose View. Roystn 7 F3
Prince Andrew's Cl. Roystn 7 E3
Prince Edward St. Berk 122 B2
Prince Park. Heml H 124 A1
Prince St. Watf 167 E3
Prince Way. Luton 64 B4
Prince's St. Stot 11 F4
Princes Ave. Enf 162 C2
Princes Ave. Watf 167 D3
Princes Cl. Berk 122 A3
Princes Ct. Bis St 76 B4
Princes Gate. Bis St 76 B4
Princes Mews. Roystn 7 E3
Princes St. Ware 93 E1
Princess St. Luton 63 E4
Printers Way. Harl 118 A3
Priors Cl. Hert 114 A2
Priors Hill. Pirt 20 B2
Priors Wood Rd. Hert 114 B2
Priory Ave. Harl 118 B3
Priory Cl. Hod 135 D3
Priory Cl. Hod 148 C4
Priory Cl. N20 171 F1
Priory Cl. Roystn 7 F3
Priory Cl. Stan 176 C4
Priory Ct. Berk 122 B2
Priory Dell. Stev 50 C3
Priory Dri. Sta Mo 59 F3
Priory Dri. Stan 176 C4
Priory End. Hit 34 C3
Priory Gdns. Berk 122 B2
Priory Gdns. Luton 45 E2
Priory La. L Wym 35 F2
Priory La. Roystn 7 E3
Priory Orch. Fla 84 A1
Priory St. Hert 113 E3
Priory St. Ware 93 E1
Priory View. Bus 168 C1
Priory View. L Wym 35 F2
Priory Way. Hit 34 C2
Priory Wlk. St Alb 141 F4
Proctor Way. Luton 64 B4
Proctors Way. Bis St 77 D2
Progress Way. Luton 44 A4
Prospect La. Harp 107 D2
Prospect Pl. Welw 89 E3
Prospect Rd. Ches 148 B1
Prospect Rd. St Alb 127 E1
Protea Way. Letw 23 D3
Providence Gr. Stev 50 C4
Providence Way. Bal 23 F4
Prowse Ave. Bus 176 B4
Pryor Gdns. Stot 11 F4
Pryor Cl. Abb L 153 F4
Pryor Rd. Bal 23 F4
Pryor Way. Letw 23 E3
Pryors Cl. Bis St 77 D3
Puddephat's La. Fla 104 C4
Pudding La. Bar 9 D1
Pudding La. Heml H 124 A3
Pudgell The. Gt Ch 9 F1
Puller Rd. Barn 171 F3
Puller Rd. Heml H 124 A1
Pulleys Cl. Heml H 123 F2
Pulleys La. Heml H 123 F2
Pulter's Way. Hit 35 D3
Pumphill. Bre P 30 A1
Punch Bowl La. Heml H 125 E3
Punch Bowl La. Red 126 A4
Purbrock Ave. Watf 154 B2
Purcell Cl. Bor 169 E4
Purcell Cl. Brn Gr 90 C3
Purkiss Rd. Hert 113 E2
Purlings Rd. Bus 168 A2
Pursley Gdns. Bor 157 D1
Purway Cl. Luton 44 C4
Purwell La. Hit 35 E4
Putney Rd. Enf 162 B2
Puttenham Cl. Sth Ox 175 E4
Putteridge Rd. Luton 46 B2
Putterills The. Harp 86 A1
Putters Croft. Heml H 124 C4
Puttocks Cl. Wel Gr 144 B4
Puttocks Dri. Wel Gr 144 B4
Pyghtle The. Bun 40 B4
Pyghtle The. Luton 63 D4
Pyms Cl. Letw 23 D4
Pynchbek. Bis St 76 C2
Pynchon Paddocks. L Hal 98 B4
Pytchley Cl. Luton 45 F3

Quadrangle The. Wel GC 110 B4
Quadrant The. Letw 22 C3
Quadrant The. St Alb 128 A3
Quadrant The. Stev 50 B2
Quaker La. Wa Aby 163 E3
Quaker Rd. Ware 93 F2
Quakers La. P Bar 159 E4
Quantock Cl. Luton 45 D4
Quantock Cl. St Alb 128 B4
Quantock Rise. Luton 45 D4
Quantocks. Heml H 124 C3
Quartermass Cl. Heml H 124 A2
Quartermass Rd. Heml H 124 A2
Queen Anne's Cl. Stot 12 A3
Queen Hoo La. Dat 90 C3
Queen Mary's Ave. Watf 166 C3
Queen St. Chipf 152 A4
Queen St. Hit 34 C4
Queen St. Pit 80 B2
Queen St. St Alb 127 E2
Queen St. Stot 12 A3
Queen St. Tri 100 A2
Queen's Cl. Saw 97 F2
Queen's Ct. St Alb 128 A2
Queen's Dri The. Ric 164 C1
Queen's Dri. Ches 163 D3
Queen's Pl. Watf 167 E3
Queen's Rd. Ches 162 C3
Queen's Rd. Harp 107 D4
Queen's Rd. Hert 113 E3
Queen's Rd. Watf 167 E3
Queen's Sq The. Heml H 124 C2
Queens Ave. Watf 166 C2
Queens Ave. Watf 167 D3
Queens Cl. Sta Mo 59 F4
Queens Cres. Bis St 76 C3
Queens Cres. St Alb 128 A3
Queens Ct. Hert 113 E3
Queens Dri. Abb L 153 F4
Queens Head Wlk. Hod 148 C4
Queens Rd. Barn 171 E3
Queens Rd. Berk 122 A3
Queens Rd. Roystn 7 E4
Queens Rd. Ware 93 F1
Queens Way. Ches 162 C3
Queens Way. Shen 156 C4
Queensway Cres. Watf 154 A3
Queensway. Hat 130 A3
Queensway. Heml H 124 C2
Queensway. Roystn 7 E4
Queensway. Stev 50 B3
Queenswood Dri. Hit 22 B1
Quendon Dri. Wa Aby 163 E3
Quickbeams. Wel GC 90 A1
Quickley Brow. Chor 164 A
Quickley La. Chor 164 E
Quickley Rise. Chor 164 E
Quickmoor La. Sar 152 E
Quickswood. Luton 45 D
Quickwood Cl. Chor 165 D
Quills. Letw 23 E
Quinces Croft. Heml H 124 A
Quincey Rd. Ware 93 E
Quinn Ct. Brag 55 F
Quinta Dri. Barn 171 E
Quinton Way. Wa Aby 163 E

Raans Rd. L Chal 150 A
Raban Cl. Stev 51 E
Rabley Heath Rd. Cod 68 A
Radburn Way. Letw 23 E
Radcliffe Rd. Hit 35 D
Radlett La. Shen 156 C
Radlett Park Rd. Radl 156 A
Radlett Rd. Aldhm 155 E
Radlett Rd. Col St 141 F
Radlett Rd. Fro 141 F
Radlett Rd. Watf 167 E
Radstone Pl. Luton 46 C
Radwell La. Radw 12 B
Raebarn Gdns. Barn 171 D
Raffin Cl. Dat 69 E
Raffin Green La. Dat 69 F
Raffin Park. Dat 69 F
Ragged Hall La. Chis 140 C
Raglan Ave. Ches 162 B3
Raglan Gdns. Watf 167 D1
Rags La. Ham St 147 F2
Railway Pl. Hert 113 F3
Railway Rd. Ches 162 C3
Railway St. Hert 113 E3
Railway Terr. Bed 139 D2
Rainbow Ct. Watf 167 E2
Rainier Cl. Ches 148 B1
Rainsford Rd. Sta Mo 59 F4
Raleigh Cres. Stev 51 D4
Raleigh Gr. Luton 44 B1
Rally The. Ch En 11 D4
Ralston Way. Sth Ox 175 E4
Ram Gorse. Harl 117 D1
Ramblers Way. Wel GC 111 E3
Rambling Way. Pot En 123 E3
Ramerick Gdns. Arl 11 D1
Ramney Dri. Enf 162 C1
Ramparts The. St Alb 127 D1
Ramridge Rd. Luton 46 A1
Ramsay Cl. Hod 134 C1
Ramsbury Rd. St Alb 127 F1
Ramsdell. Stev 50 C3
Ramsey Cl. Bro Pk 145 E2
Ramsey Cl. St Alb 128 A1
Ramson Rise. Heml H 123 F1
Rand's Cl. Hol 21 D4
Rand's Meadow. Hol 21 D4
Randalls Ride. Heml H 124 C3
Randals Hill. Stev 51 E2
Randon Cl. Har 176 A1
Ranelagh Rd. Heml H 125 D2
Ranleigh Wlk. Harp 107 E3
Rannoch Wlk. Heml H 124 B4
Ranock Cl. Luton 44 B4
Ranskill Rd. Bor 170 A4
Ransom Cl. Hit 34 C2
Rant Meadow. Heml H 125 D1
Ranworth Ave. Hod 115 D1
Ranworth Ave. Stev 69 E4
Ranworth Cl. Heml H 124 B1
Raphael Dri. Watf 167 E4
Rasehill Cl. Chor 165 E2
Rathlyn. Heml H 139 D4
Ratty's La. Hod 135 E3
Raven Cl. Ric 165 E1
Raven Ct. Hat 130 A2
Ravenbank Rd. Luton 46 B3
Ravenhill Way. Luton 44 A2
Ravens La. Berk 122 B2
Ravens Wharf. Berk 122 B2
Ravenscroft Park. Barn 171 E3
Ravenscroft. Harp 107 E3
Ravenscroft. Watf 154 C3
Ravensdell. Heml H 123 F2
Ravensthorpe. Luton 46 A2
Ravenswood Park. Norwd 175 D2
Rawdon Dri. Hod 135 D3
Ray's Hill. Chol 120 B1
Rayburn Rd. Heml H 124 A3
Raydon Rd. Ches 162 B4
Rayfield. Wel GC 89 E1
Raymer Cl. St Alb 127 F2
Raymond Cl. Abb L 153 E4
Raymonds Cl. Wel GC 110 C2
Raymonds Plain. Wel GC 110 C2
Raynam Cl. Bis St 77 E4
Raynham Rd. Bis St 77 E4
Raynham St. Hert 113 F3
Raynham Way. Luton 46 B1
Raynsford Rd. Ware 93 F1
Raynton Rd. Enf 162 B1
Recreation Ground. Sta Mo 59 F3
Rectory Cl. Ess 131 F3
Rectory Cl. Hun 116 B4
Rectory Cl. Thor 76 B2
Rectory Gdns. Hat 130 A3
Rectory La. Berk 122 B2

Rectory La. Dat 69 E1
Rectory La. Far 58 B3
Rectory La. Kin L 139 D2
Rectory La. Ric 165 E1
Rectory La. Shen 157 D4
Rectory La. Stev 36 B1
Rectory La. Wat St 70 B2
Rectory Rd. Ric 165 E1
Rectory Rd. Wel GC 89 D1
Rectory Wood. Harl 117 E1
Red House Cl. Gt Am 114 C4
Red Lion Ct. Bis St 77 D4
Red Lion La. Heml H 139 D3
Red Lodge Gdns. Berk 122 A2
Red Rails. Luton 63 E3
Red Rd. Bor 169 F4
Red White and Blue Rd. Bis St 59 D1
Redan Rd. Ware 93 F2
Redbourn La. Harp 106 C3
Redbourn Rd. Heml H 125 D4
Redbourn Rd. Red 106 B1
Redbourn Rd. St Alb 126 C3
Redbournbury La. Red 106 B1
Redcar Dri. Stev 50 A3
Redding La. Red 105 F4
Reddings Ave. Bus 168 A2
Reddings The. Bor 169 F3
Reddings. Heml H 125 D1
Reddings. Wel GC 110 B4
Redferns Cl. Luton 63 D3
Redgrave Gdns. Luton 44 C4
Redhall Cl. Hat 129 F1
Redhall Dri. Hat 129 F1
Redhall La. Cha Cr 165 F4
Redhall La. Hat 129 F1
Redheath Cl. Watf 153 F2
Redhill Rd. Hit 34 B4
Redhoods Way E. Letw 22 C4
Redhoods Way W. Letw 22 C3
Redlands Rd. Enf 162 C1
Redmire Cl. Luton 44 A3
Redrick La. H Wy 117 F3
Redricks La. Saw 118 A4
Redvers Cl. Bis St 59 D1
Redwood Cl. Sth Ox 175 E3
Redwood Dri. Heml H 124 C1
Redwood Dri. Luton 44 B4
Redwood Rise. Bor 157 D1
Redwood Way. Barn 171 E2
Redwoods. Hert 113 E4
Redwoods. Wel GC 89 E2
Redwoods. Wl Gr 89 F4
Reedham Cl. Bri Wd 141 D1
Reedings Way. Saw 97 F2
Reeds Cres. Watf 167 E4
Reedsdale. Luton 46 C1
Reeves Ave. Luton 45 D2
Regal Ct. Tri 100 A2
Regency Cl. Bis St 76 C4
Regency Ct. Hod 148 C4
Regent Cl. St Alb 128 B4
Regent Ct. Stot 11 F4
Regent Ct. Wel G C 110 C3
Regent St. Luton 63 F4
Regent St. Stot 11 F4
Regent St. Watf 154 A1
Regents Cl. Radl 156 A3
Regina Cl. Barn 171 E3
Reginald Rd. Norwd 174 C2
Reginald St. Luton 45 F1
Rendlesham Ave. Radl 155 F1
Rendlesham Cl. Ware 93 D1
Rendlesham Rd. Enf 161 E1
Rendlesham Way. Chor 164 B2
Rennison Cl. Ham St 147 F2
Renshaw Cl. Luton 46 C1
Repton Cl. Luton 44 C3
Repton Green. St Alb 127 E3
Repton Way. Cro Gr 166 A2
Reson Way. Heml H 124 A1
Reston Cl. Bor 157 D1
Reston Path. Bor 157 D1
Retford Cl. Bor 157 D1
Retreat The. Abb L 153 E4
Revels Cl. Hert 113 E4
Revels Rd. Hert 113 E4
Reynard Way. Hert 114 A3
Reynard's Way. Bri Wd 140 C1
Reynards Rd. Wl Gr 89 D4
Reynolds Cl. Heml H 124 A2
Reynolds Cres. Sand 128 A4
Rhee Spring. Bal 13 D1
Rhodes Ave. Bis St 76 C3
Rhodes Way. Watf 167 E4
Rib Vale. Hert 92 B1
Ribbledale. Lon C 142 C2
Ribblesdale. Heml H 124 C3
Ribocon Way. Luton 44 A4
Rice Cl. Heml H 124 C2
Richard Stagg Cl. St Alb 128 B1
Richards Cl. Bus 168 B1
Richards Cl. Luton 63 D3
Richardson Cl. Lon C 142 C2
Richfield Rd. Bus 168 B1
Richmond Cl. Bis St 77 B4
Richmond Cl. Ches 148 B1
Richmond Cl. Ware 93 D2
Richmond Ct. Hod 134 C2
Richmond Ct. Luton 45 F1
Richmond Ct. P Bar 159 E4
Richmond Dri. Watf 166 C4
Richmond Gdns. Har 176 C2
Richmond Hill. Luton 45 F1
Richmond Rd. P Bar 159 E4
Richmond Way. Cro Gr 166 B3
Richmond Wlk. St Alb 128 B4
Rickfield Cl. Hat 130 A2
Rickmansworth La. C St P 172 A3
Rickmansworth Rd. Chor 164 C3
Rickmansworth Rd. Hare 173 E2
Rickmansworth Rd. Norwd 174 B2
Rickmansworth Rd. Pnr 175 D1
Rickmansworth Rd. Watf 166 C3
Rickyard Cl. Luton 46 A2
Rickyard Meadow. Red 106 A3
Rickyard The. Ashwell 4 B2
Riddy Hill Cl. Hit 35 D3
Riddy La. Hit 35 D3
Riddy La. Luton 45 E3
Riddy The. Cod 88 C4
Ridge Ave. Harp 85 F2
Ridge Ave. Letw 23 D3
Ridge La. Watf 153 F1
Ridge Lea. Heml H 123 F2
Ridge Rd. Letw 23 D3
Ridge St. Watf 154 A1
Ridge The. Barn 171 F2
Ridge The. Norwd 174 C2
Ridgedown. Red 106 A3
Ridgehurst ve. Watf 153 F3
Ridgeview Cl. Barn 171 E2
Ridgeway Cl. Heml H 138 C3
Ridgeway Ct. Pnr 176 A2
Ridgeway The. Cod 67 F1
Ridgeway The. Cuf 146 B2
Ridgeway The. Enf 160 B2
Ridgeway The. Hertng 112 C4
Ridgeway The. Hit 34 B3
Ridgeway The. Radl 155 F1
Ridgeway The. St Alb 128 B4
Ridgeway The. Ware 93 E2
Ridgeway The. Watf 153 F1
Ridgeway. Berk 121 F2
Ridgeway. Harp 85 F2
Ridgeway. Ken Co 82 C4
Ridgeway. L Had 57 D1
Ridgeway. Ric 165 D1
Ridgeway. Stev 50 C3
Ridgeway. Wel GC 111 D3
Ridgewood Dri. Harp 85 F2
Ridgewood Gdns. Harp 85 F2
Ridgmont Rd. St Alb 127 F1
Ridgway Rd. Luton 45 F1
Ridings The. Bis St 76 B2
Ridings The. Hertng 113 D3
Ridings The. Lat 150 B2
Ridings The. Mark 83 F3
Ridings The. Stev 51 D2
Ridler Rd. Enf 161 F1
Ridlins End. Stev 51 E1
Riley Rd. Enf 162 B1
Ringshall Dri. Rin 102 A4
Ringshall Rd. Dagn 81 D2
Ringshall Rd. Rin 81 D1
Ringtail Pl. Clo 13 D1
Ringway Rd. Chis 141 D2
Ringwood Rd. Luton 45 E3
Ripley Rd. Enf 161 E1
Ripley Rd. Luton 44 B1
Ripley Way. Ches 148 A1
Ripley Way. Heml H 123 F2
Ripon Rd. Stev 37 D1
Ripon Way. St Alb 128 B4
Rise The. Bal 23 F4
Rise The. Elst 169 F2
Rise The. Pk St 141 E3
Risedale Cl. Heml H 138 C4
Risedale Hill. Heml H 138 C4
Risedale Rd. Heml H 138 C4
Rising Hill Cl. Norwd 174 B2
Risingholme Cl. Bus 168 A1
Risingholme Cl. Har 176 C1
Risingholme Rd. Har 176 C1
Ritcroft Cl. Heml H 125 D1
Ritcroft Dri. Heml H 125 D1
Ritcroft St. Heml H 125 D1
Ritz Ct. Pot B 159 D4
Rivenhall End. Wel GC 111 E3
River Ave. Hod 135 D4
River Cl. Ches 163 D3
River Ct. Ick 21 F2
River Hill. Fla 84 A1
River Mead. Hit 21 E1
River Meads. Sta Ab 115 E2
River Park Ind Est. Berk 122 A3
River Park. Heml H 124 A1
River St. Ware 93 F1
River View. Wel GC 89 F1
River Way. Harl 118 A3
River Way. Luton 44 C3
Riverfield La. Saw 97 F2
Riverford Cl. Harp 86 A2
Rivermill. Harl 117 E1
Riversend Rd. Heml H 138 B4
Rivershill. Wat St 70 C2
Riverside Ave. Lo Naz 135 D1
Riverside Cl. Kin L 139 D1
Riverside Cl. St Alb 127 F1
Riverside Cotts. Sta Ab 115 E2
Riverside Dri. Ric 165 E1
Riverside Gdns. Berk 122 A3
Riverside Path. Ches 148 B1
Riverside Rd. Luton 45 D3
Riverside Rd. St Alb 127 F1
Riverside Rd. Watf 167 D2
Riverside Wlk. Bis St 76 C4
Riverside. Bis St 76 C4
Riverside. Bun 40 C4
Riversmead. Hod 135 D3
Riversmeet. Hert 113 D3
Rivett Cl. Bal 13 D1
Roan Wlk. Roystn 7 F3
Robbery Bottom La. Wl Gr 90 A4
Robbs Cl. Heml H 124 A3
Robe End. Heml H 123 F3
Robert Ave. St Alb 141 E4
Robert Cl. Pot B 158 C3
Robert Wallace Cl. Bis St 58 C1
Roberts Rd. Watf 167 E2
Roberts Way. Hat 129 F2
Roberts Wood Dri. C St P 172 A3
Robertson Cl. Ches 148 C3
Robin Cl. Sta Ab 115 E2
Robin Hill. Berk 122 B2
Robin Hood Dri. Bus 167 F4
Robin Hood Dri. Har 176 C2
Robin Hood La. Hat 130 A3
Robin Hood Meadow. Heml H 124 C4
Robin Mead. Wel GC 90 A1
Robin Way. Cuf 146 C2
Robins Nest Hill. L Berk 132 B3
Robins Rd. Heml H 125 D1
Robins Way. Hat 129 F1
Robinsfield. Heml H 124 A2
Robinson Ave. Gofs O 147 D2
Robinson Cl. Bis St 76 C3
Robinson Cres. Bus 168 B1
Robinsway. Wa Aby 163 F3
Robinswood. Luton 45 F3
Robsons Cl. Ches 148 B1
Rochester Ave. Luton 46 B2
Rochester Way. Cro Gr 166 A3
Rochford Ave. Wa Aby 163 E3
Rochford Cl. Ches 148 C3
Rochford Dri. Luton 46 C1
Rochford Rd. Bis St 59 E1
Rock Rd. Roystn 7 E4
Rockfield Ave. Ware 93 E2
Rockingham Way. Stev 50 C2
Rockley Rd. Luton 63 D4
Rockliffe Ave. Kin L 139 D1
Rockways. Barn 170 C2
Rode Heath. Luton 44 B2
Roden Cl. Harl 118 C2
Rodgers Cl. Elst 169 E2
Rodney Avenue. St Alb 128 A1
Rodney Cres. Hod 135 D4
Roe Cl. Stot 11 F3
Roe End La. Mark 83 D2
Roe Green Cl. Hat 129 F2
Roe Green La. Hat 129 F3
Roe Hill Cl. Hat 129 F2
Roebuck Cl. Luton 63 D3
Roebuck Gate. Stev 50 C1
Roebuck Retail Park. Stev 50 C1
Roedean Ave. Enf 162 B1
Roedean Cl. Luton 46 B2
Roefields Cl. Fel 138 A4
Roehyde Way. Hat 129 F1
Roestock Gdns. Coln H 129 F1
Rofant Rd. Norwd 174 C2
Rogate Rd. Luton 46 B3
Roger's La. Ans 29 D3
Rogers Ruff. Norwd 174 B1
Roland St. St Alb 128 A1
Rolleston Cl. Ware 93 E2
Rollswood Rd. Wl Gr 89 D4
Rollswood. Wel GC 110 C2
Rollys La. Ashw 4 B2
Roman Cl. Hare 173 D1
Roman Gdns. Abb L 139 D1
Roman La. Clo 24 A4
Roman Rd. Luton 44 C2
Roman Rd. Welw 89 E3
Roman St. Hod 135 D4
Roman Vale. Harl 118 B3
Roman Way. Mark 83 F3
Roman Way. Puc 55 E2
Roman Way. Welw 89 E3
Romany Cl. Letw 22 B3
Romeland Hill. St Alb 127 E2
Romeland. St Alb 127 E2
Romeland. Wa Aby 163 E3
Romilly Dri. Watf 175 F3
Rondini Ave. Luton 45 D2
Rook Tree Cl. Stot 12 A3
Rook Tree La. Stot 12 A3
Rooke's Alley. Hert 113 F3
Rookery Dri. Luton 45 F3
Rookery The. Sta M 59 F4
Rookes Cl. Letw 23 D2
Rooks Hill. Chor 165 E3
Rooks Hill. Wel GC 110 B3
Rooks Nest La. Ther 16 A3
Rookwood Dri. Stev 51 D1
Rosary Ct. Pot B 145 D1
Rose Gdns. Watf 167 D2
Rose La. Whea 87 E1
Rose Lawn. Bus 168 B1
Rose Mead. Pot B 145 E1
Rose Meadow. Hay St 41 F2
Rose Vale. Hod 135 D3
Rose Wlk. Radl 156 A2
Rose Wlk. St Alb 128 B3
Rose Wood Cl. Luton 45 F1
Roseacre Gdns. Wel GC 111 E3
Roseacres. Saw 97 E2
Rosebank. Wa Aby 163 F3
Roseberry Ct. Watf 167 D4
Roseberry Way. Tri 100 A3
Rosebery Ave. Harp 85 F1
Rosebery Rd. Bus 168 A1
Rosebery. Bis St 77 E3
Rosebriar Wlk. Watf 153 F2
Rosecroft Dri. Watf 153 F2
Rosecroft La. Wl Gr 90 A4
Rosedale Ave. Ches 147 F1
Rosedale Cl. Bri Wd 140 C1
Rosedale Cl. Luton 44 B4
Rosedale Way. Ches 148 A2
Rosedale. Wel GC 89 F1
Roseheath. Heml H 123 F2
Rosehill Cl. Hod 134 C3
Rosehill Gdns. Abb L 153 E4
Roselands Ave. Hod 114 C1
Rosemary Cl. Harl 118 B2
Rosemont Cl. Letw 22 C3
Rosewood Ct. Heml H 123 F2
Rosewood Dri. Enf 161 D2
Roslyn Cl. Hod 134 C1
Ross Cl. Har 176 B2
Ross Cl. Hat 130 A4
Ross Cl. Luton 63 D3
Ross Cres. Watf 154 A2
Ross Way. Norwd 174 C3
Rossfold Rd. Luton 44 B4
Rossgate. Heml H 124 A3
Rossington Ave. Bor 156 C1
Rossiter Fields. Barn 171 F2
Rosslyn Cres. Luton 45 E3
Rosslyn Rd. Watf 167 D3
Rossway Dri. Bus 168 B2
Rossway La. Wigg 121 D4
Rossway. Cad 63 D1
Roswell Cl. Ches 148 C1
Rothampstead Ave. Harp 86 A1
Rother Cl. Watf 154 B3
Rother Field. Luton 46 B2
Rotheram Ave. Luton 63 D3
Rotherfield. Enf 162 B1
Rothesay Rd. Luton 63 E4
Rotten End Hill. Pot En 123 F4
Roughdown Ave. Heml H 138 A4
Roughdown Rd. Heml H 138 A4
Roughdown Villas Rd. Heml H 138 A4
Roughs The. Norwd 174 C4
Roughwood Cl. Watf 153 F1
Round Mead. Stev 51 E2
Round Wood. Kin L 138 C2
Roundabout La. Wl Gr 89 F4
Roundcroft. Ham St 147 F3
Roundfield Ave. Harp 86 B2
Roundhaye. Puc 55 E2
Roundhedge Way. Enf 160 C1
Roundhills. Wa Aby 163 F3
Roundings The. Hert H 114 B1
Roundmoor Dri. Ches 148 C1
Roundway The. Watf 166 C2
Roundwood Cl. Hit 22 B1
Roundwood Cl. Wl Gr 89 E4
Roundwood Dri. Wel GC 110 B4
Roundwood Gdns. Harp 85 F1
Roundwood La. Harp 85 E2
Roundwood Park. Harp 85 F2
Rounton Dri. Watf 153 F1
Rounton Rd. Wa Aby 163 F3
Rousebarn La. Cro Gr 166 B3
Rowan Cl. Bric 155 D4
Rowan Cl. Luton 63 D4
Rowan Cl. St Alb 128 C2
Rowan Cl. Wes 37 D4
Rowan Cres. Letw 22 C4
Rowan Cres. Stev 50 C4
Rowan Dri. Hod 148 C4
Rowan Way. Harp 107 E4
Rowan Wlk. Hat 130 A1
Rowans The. Bal 23 F4
Rowans The. Heml H 124 A2
Rowans. Wel GC 90 A1
Rowcroft. Heml H 123 F1
Rowel Field. Luton 46 B1
Rowington Cl. Luton 46 C1
Rowland Pl. Norwd 174 C2
Rowland Rd. Stev 50 C2
Rowlands Ave. Pnr 176 A2
Rowlands Cl. Ches 148 B1
Rowlatt Dri. St Alb 127 D1
Rowley Cl. Watf 167 F2
Rowley Green Rd. Barn 171 D2
Rowley La. Bor 170 C3
Rowley's Rd. Hert 113 F4
Rowney Gdns. Saw 118 B4
Rowney La. Sac Gr 72 A3
Rowney Wood. Saw 97 E1
Roy Rd. Norwd 174 C2
Royal Ave. Ches 162 C3
Royal Ct. Heml H 138 C4
Royal Ct. Tri 101 D3
Royal Oak Cl. Chipp 27 E3
Royal Oak La. Pirt 20 B2
Royal Rd. St Alb 128 A2
Royce Cl. Hod 134 C1
Roydon Ct. Heml H 105 D1
Roydon Lodge Chalet Est. Roy 116 B1
Roydon Rd. Harl 116 C1
Roydon Rd. Sta Ab 115 F2
Royse Gr. Roystn 7 E2
Royston Cl. Hert 113 D3
Royston Gr. Pnr 176 A2
Royston Park Rd. Pnr 176 A3
Royston Rd. Ashw 14 A3
Royston Rd. Bal 12 C1
Royston Rd. Bar 8 C2
Royston Rd. Bark 17 E3
Royston Rd. Byg 13 E1
Royston Rd. St Alb 128 A1
Rucklers La. Chipf 138 A2
Rucklers La. Kin L 138 B2
Ruckles Cl. Stev 50 C3
Rudd Cl. Stev 51 D2
Rudham Gr. Letw 23 E2
Rudolph Rd. Bus 168 A2
Rudyard Cl. Luton 44 B2
Rue De St Lawrence. Wa Aby 163 E3
Rueley Dell Rd. Lily 32 B1
Rugby Way. Cro Gr 166 A2
Ruins The. Red 106 A3
Rumballs Cl. Heml H 139 D4
Rumballs Rd. Heml H 139 D4
Rumbold Rd. Hod 135 E4
Runcie Cl. St Alb 128 A4
Runcorn Cres. Heml H 124 C4
Rundells. Letw 23 E2
Runfold Ave. Luton 45 D3
Runham Cl. Luton 44 A2
Runham Rd. Heml H 124 C1
Runley Rd. Luton 62 C4
Runnalow. Letw 22 C4
Runsley. Wel GC 90 A1
Ruscombe Dri. Chis 141 E3
Rush Cl. Sta Ab 115 E2
Rushall Green. Luton 46 B1
Rushby Mead. Letw 23 D3
Rushby Pl. Letw 23 D3
Rushby Wlk. Letw 23 D3
Rushden Rd. Ro Gr 26 A4
Rushen Dri. Hert H 114 B2
Rushendon Furlong. Ivin 80 C3
Rushes Ct. Bis St 77 D3
Rushfield Rd. Ware 93 F2
Rushfield. Pot B 158 B3
Rushfield. Saw 97 F1
Rushleigh Ave. Ches 148 B1
Rushleigh Green. Bis St 76 B2
Rushmere La. Ash Gr 136 A2
Rushmoor Cl. Ric 173 E4
Rushton Ave. Watf 154 A2
Ruskin Ave. Wa Aby 163 F3
Ruskin Cl. Ham St 147 F3
Ruskin La. Hit 35 E4
Rusper Green. Luton 46 B2
Russell Ave. St Alb 127 E2
Russell Cl. Ken Co 82 C4
Russell Cl. Stev 51 D1
Russell Cres. Watf 153 F2
Russell Ct. Bri Wd 141 D1
Russell La. Watf 153 E2
Russell Pl. Heml H 138 A4
Russell Rd. Enf 161 F1
Russell Rd. Norwd 174 B3
Russell Rise. Luton 63 E3
Russell St. Hert 113 E3
Russell St. Luton 63 E3
Russell's Ride. Ches 162 C4
Russell's Slip. Hit 34 C3
Russellcroft Rd. Wel GC 110 B4
Russettwood. Wel GC 111 E3
Rutherford Cl. Stev 50 A3
Rutherford Way. Bus 168 C1
Ruthin Cl. Luton 63 E3
Ruthven Ave. Ches 162 B3
Rutland Cres. Luton 64 A4
Rutland Gdns. Heml H 124 C2
Rutts The. Bus 168 B1
Rydal Way. Luton 44 C3
Ryde The. Hat 130 B4
Ryder Ave. Ick 21 E2
Ryder Cl. Bov 137 D2
Ryder Cl. Bus 168 A2
Ryder Way. Ick 21 E2
Ryders Ave. Coln H 129 F2
Rye Cl. Harp 86 A2
Rye Gdns. Bal 13 D1
Rye Hill. Harp 86 A2
Rye Rd. Hod 135 E4
Rye Rd. Sta Ab 115 E1
Rye St. Bis St 58 C1
Ryecroft Cl. Heml H 125 E1
Ryecroft Cres. Barn 171 D2
Ryecroft Ct. St Alb 128 C2
Ryecroft Way. Luton 46 A2
Ryecroft. Hat 129 F2
Ryecroft. Stev 50 C4
Ryefeld Cl. Hod 105 D1
Ryefield Cres. Norwd 175 D1
Ryefield. Luton 31 D1
Ryelands Heath. Luton 46 C1
Ryelands. Wel GC 110 C2
Ryley Cl. Henlw 10 A2
Ryman Ct. Chor 164 B2

Rymill Cl. Bov 137 D2
Ryton Cl. Luton 63 D4

Saberton Cl. Red 105 F2
Sacombe Green Rd. Sac 71 F2
Sacombe Pound. Sac 71 F2
Sacombe Rd. Cha En 92 A2
Sacombe Rd. Heml H 123 F3
Sacombe Rd. Hert 92 B1
Sacombs Ash La. H Wy 96 C4
Saddlers Cl. Bal 23 F4
Saddlers Cl. Bor 170 B2
Saddlers Cl. Pnr 176 A2
Saddlers Path. Bor 170 B2
Sadleir Rd. St Alb 127 F1
Sadlers Way. Hertng 113 D3
Sadlier Rd. Stand 55 F1
Saffron Cl. Ch En 11 D4
Saffron Cl. Hod 134 C4
Saffron Hill. Letw 22 C3
Saffron La. Heml H 124 A2
Saffron St. Roystn 7 F3
Sainfoin End. Heml H 125 D3
St Agnells Ct. Heml H 125 D4
St Agnells La. Heml H 125 D4
St Albans Dri. Stev 36 C1
St Albans Hill. Heml H 124 C1
St Albans La. Bed 140 A3
St Albans Link. Stev 36 C1
St Albans Rd East. Hat 130 A3
St Albans Rd W. Hat 129 E3
St Albans Rd. Abb L 154 B4
St Albans Rd. Barn 171 F4
St Albans Rd. Cod 88 C4
St Albans Rd. Harp 107 D4
St Albans Rd. Heml H 124 C1
St Albans Rd. Pot B 158 B2
St Albans Rd. Red 106 B2
St Albans Rd. Sand 128 A4
St Albans Rd. Watf 154 B2
St Andrew St. Hert 113 E3
St Andrew's Ave. Harp 85 F1
St Andrew's Cl. Cad 63 D1
St Andrew's Pl. Hit 34 C4
St Andrew's Rd. Fel 138 B4
St Andrews Dri. Stev 36 C1
St Andrews Rd. Sth Ox 175 E4
St Andrews Wlk. Cad 63 E1
St Ann's Rd. Luton 63 F4
St Anne's Cl. Ham St 147 F2
St Anne's Rd. Hit 34 C4
St Anne's Rd. Lon C 142 B2
St Annes Cl. Sth Ox 175 E3
St Anthonys Ave. Heml H 125 D1
St Audreys Cl. Hat 130 A1
St Audreys Green. Wel GC 110 C3
St Augustine Ave. Luton 45 E2
St Augustine Cl. Hit 34 C4
St Augustines Cl. Hod 134 C2
St Augustines Dri. Hod 134 C2
St Bernard's Rd. St Alb 127 F2
St Bernards Cl. Luton 45 E2
St Brelades Pl. St Alb 128 B4
St Catharine's Rd. Hod 135 D2
St Catherine's Ct. Hod 135 D2
St Catherines Ave. Luton 45 D2
St Clare Ct. Wal 52 A4
St Cross Ct. Hod 135 D2
St Cuthbert's Rd. Hod 115 E1
St Cuthberts Gdns. Pnr 175 F2
St David's Cl. Heml H 125 E1
St David's Dri. Hod 134 C2
St Davids Cl. Stev 36 C1
St Dunstan's Rd. Hun 116 B4
St Edmund's Way. Harl 118 B2
St Edmunds. Berk 122 B2
St Ethelbert Ave. Luton 45 E2
St Etheldreda's Dri.Hat 130 B3
St Faiths Cl. Hit 22 A1
St Francis Cl. Pot B 159 E3
St Francis Cl. Watf 167 D1
St George's Drive. Watf 175 F3
St George's Rd. Enf 161 F1
St George's Rd. Fel 138 B4
St George's Rd. Watf 154 A1
St George's Way. Stev 50 B3
St Giles Rd. Cod 67 F1
St Giles' Ave. Pot B 158 A3
St Helen's Cl. Whea 108 B4
St Heliers Rd. Sand 128 A4
St Ives Cl. Har Gr 89 F2
St Ives Cl. Luton 45 D2
St James Rd. Harp 86 A2
St James Rd. Watf 167 D2
St James' Ave. Luton 45 D2
St James's Rd. Gofs O 147 E2
St John Cl. Luton 63 D3
St John's Ave. Harl 118 B2
St John's Cl. Pot B 159 E3
St John's Cres. Sta Mo 59 F4
St John's Ct. Harp 107 E4
St John's Ct. Hert 113 E3
St John's La. Sta Mo 59 F4
St John's Path. Hit 34 C3
St John's Rd. Arl 11 D2
St John's Rd. Harp 107 E4
St John's Rd. Heml H 124 A1
St John's Rd. Hit 34 C3
St John's Rd. Sta Mo 59 F4
St John's Rd. Watf 167 D4
St John's St. Hert 113 E3
St John's Terr. Enf 161 E1
St John's Well Ct. Berk 122 A3
St John's Well La. Berk 122 A3
St Johns Cl. Welw 89 E3
St Johns Ct. St Alb 128 A3
St Johns Wlk. Harl 118 B2
St Johns. Stand 55 F2
St Josephs Cl. Luton 45 D2
St Julian's Rd. St Alb 127 E1
St Katherines Cl. Ick 21 E2
St Katherines Way. Berk 122 A3
St Laurence Dri. Hod 148 C4
St Lawrence Cl. Abb L 139 F1
St Lawrence Cl. Bov 137 D2
St Lawrence Way. Bri Wd 140 C1
St Lawrences Ave. Luton 45 E2
St Leonard's Rd. Hert 113 E4
St Leonards Cl. Bus 167 F3
St Leonards Cl. Hert 113 F4
St Leonards Cres. Sand 108 B1
St Leonards Ct. Sand 108 B1
St Leonards Rd. Lo Naz 149 F4
St Luke's Ave. Enf 161 E1
St Luke's Cl. Luton 44 C1
St Margaret's Cl. Berk 122 B2
St Margaret's Rd. Hod 115 D1
St Margarets Ave. Luton 45 D2
St Margarets Cl. Str 31 D3
St Margarets Way. Heml H 125 E2
St Margarets. Stev 50 C1
St Mark's Cl. Coln H 129 D1
St Mark's Cl. Hit 21 E1
St Martin's Ave. Luton 45 F1
St Martin's Rd. Kneb 69 D3
St Martins Cl. Harp 86 B2
St Martins Cl. Sth Ox 175 E3
St Mary's Ave. Norwd 174 C3
St Mary's Ave. Nthch 121 E3
St Mary's Ave. Stot 11 F3
St Mary's Cl. Letw 22 C1
St Mary's Cl. Pirt 20 B2
St Mary's Cl. Stev 51 F1
St Mary's Ct. Heml H 124 B2
St Mary's Ct. Welw 89 E2
St Mary's Dri. Sta Mo 59 F3
St Mary's La. Hertng 112 C2
St Mary's La. Red 106 A2
St Mary's Rd. Ches 148 B1
St Mary's Rd. Heml H 124 B2
St Mary's Rd. Luton 63 F4
St Mary's Rd. Stand 55 E1
St Mary's Rd. Watf 167 D3
St Mary's Rise. Bre Wd 47 E1
St Mary's Sq. Hit 34 C4
St Mary's Way. Bal 23 F3
St Marys Cl. Heml H 124 B2
St Marys Cl. Welw 89 E3
St Marys Wlk. St Alb 128 A4
St Matthews Cl. Luton 63 F4
St Matthews Cl. Watf 167 E2
St Michael's Cres. Luton 45 E2
St Michael's Ct. St Alb 127 D2
St Michael's Mount. Hit 35 D4
St Michael's Rd. Hod 135 D2
St Michael's St. St Alb 127 D2
St Michaels Ave. Heml H 125 D1
St Michaels Cl. Harp 107 E4
St Michaels Rd. Hit 35 D4
St Michaels Way. Pot B 145 D1
St Mildred's Ave. Luton 45 D2
St Monicas Ave. Luton 45 D2
St Neots Cl. Bor 157 D1
St Nicholas Cl. Elst 169 E2
St Nicholas Mount. Heml H 123 F2
St Olam's Cl. Luton 45 D3
St Olives. Stot 11 F3
St Paul's Rd. Heml H 124 C2
St Paul's Rd. Luton 63 F3
St Pauls Pl. St Alb 128 A2
St Pauls Way. Wa Aby 163 E3
St Pauls Way. Watf 167 E4
St Peter's Ave. Ch En 11 D4
St Peter's Cl. Barn 171 D2
St Peter's Cl. Bus 168 B1
St Peter's Cl. Ric 165 D1
St Peter's Cl. St Alb 127 E2
St Peter's Rd. St Alb 127 F2
St Peter's St. St Alb 127 E2
St Peters Cl. Hat 130 A3
St Peters Hill. Tri 100 A2
St Peters Rd. Luton 63 D4
St Peters Way. Chor 164 A3
St Rowans Cl. Barn 159 E1
St Saviour's Cres. Luton 63 E3
St Stephen's Ave. St Alb 141 D4
St Stephen's Cl. St Alb 141 D4
St Stephen's Hill. St Alb 127 E1
St Stephen's Rd. Enf 162 B1
St Stephens Rd. Barn 171 E2
St Thomas Dri. Pnr 175 F1
St Thomas Pl. Whea 108 B4
St Thomas's Rd. Luton 46 A2
St Vincent Dri. St Alb 128 A1
St Vincent's Way. Pot B 159 E3
St Winifreds Ave. Luton 45 E2
St Yon Cl. St Alb 128 C2
Sale Dri. Bal 13 D1
Salisbury Ave. Harp 85 F1
Salisbury Ave. St Alb 128 A2
Salisbury Cl. Bis St 76 C3
Salisbury Cl. Pot B 159 E4
Salisbury Cres. Ches 162 B4
Salisbury Gdns. Wel GC 110 C3
Salisbury Rd. Bal 12 C1
Salisbury Rd. Barn 171 F3
Salisbury Rd. Enf 162 C1
Salisbury Rd. Harp 86 B2
Salisbury Rd. Hod 135 E4
Salisbury Rd. Luton 63 E3
Salisbury Rd. Stev 37 D1
Salisbury Rd. Watf 154 A1
Salisbury Rd. Wel GC 111 D3
Salisbury Sq. Hat 130 B3
Salisbury Sq. Hert 113 E3
Sally Deards La. Cod 68 A2
Salmon Meadow Footpath. Heml H 138 C4
Salmons Cl. Ware 93 E2
Saltars Way. Luton 44 B2
Saltdean Cl. Luton 46 B2
Salter's Cl. Berk 121 F3
Salters Gdns. Watf 167 D4
Saltfield Cres. Luton 44 B2
Salusbury La. Gt Of 33 E1
Salwey Cres. Hod 134 C2
Samian Gate. St Alb 126 C1
Sampson Ave. Barn 171 E2
Sancroft Rd. Har 176 C1
Sanctuary Cl. Hare 173 E2
Sandalwood Cl. Luton 45 D4
Sanday Cl. Hem H 125 D1
Sandbrook La. Wils 79 E1
Sanderling Cl. Letw 22 C4
Sanders Cl. Heml H 138 C4
Sanders Cl. Lon C 142 B2
Sanders Rd. Heml H 139 D4
Sandfield Rd. St Alb 128 A2
Sandgate Rd. Luton 44 B1
Sandhurst Ct. Harp 107 E3
Sandifield. Hat 130 A1
Sandle Rd. Bis St 77 D4
Sandmere Cl. Heml H 125 D1
Sandon Cl. Tri 99 F2
Sandon Rd. Ches 148 B1
Sandover Cl. Hit 35 D3
Sandown Rd. Stev 37 E1
Sandown Rd. Watf 154 B1
Sandpit La. St Alb 128 B3
Sandpit Rd. Wel GC 110 C2
Sandridge Cl. Heml H 105 D1
Sandridge Rd. St Alb 127 F3
Sandridgebury La. Sand 108 A1
Sandringham Cres. St Alb 128 B4
Sandringham Rd. Pot B 145 D1
Sandringham Rd. Watf 154 B1
Sandringham Way. Ches 162 B3
Sandy Cl. Herts 113 D3
Sandy Gr. Hit 34 C3
Sandy La. Bus 168 B3
Sandy La. Norwd 175 D3
Sandy Lodge Ct. Norwd 174 C3
Sandy Lodge La. Norwd 174 C4
Sandy Lodge Rd. Ric 174 B4
Sandy Lodge Way. Norwd 174 C3
Sandycroft Rd. L Chal 150 B1
Sanfoin Rd. Luton 44 A2
Sanfoine Cl. Hit 35 E4
Santers La. Pot B 158 C3
Santingfield N. Luton 63 D3
Santingfield S. Luton 63 D3
Saottfield Cl. Sand 108 B1
Sappers Cl. Saw 97 F1
Saracens Head. Heml H 125 D2
Sargents. Stand 55 F1
Sarratt La. Chor 165 E3
Sarratt Rd. Sar 165 F4
Sarum Pl. Heml H 124 C4
Sarum Rd. Luton 44 C2
Saturn Way. Heml H 124 C3
Sauncey Ave. Harp 86 A1
Sauncey Wood La. Kim 86 C3
Sauncey Wood. Kim 86 B2
Saunders Cl. Letw 23 E4
Savoy Cl. Hare 173 E1
Sawbridgeworth Rd Saw 98 A1
Sawbridgeworth Rd Saw 98 C2
Sawells. Hod 134 C1
Sawtry Cl. Luton 45 D3
Sawtry Way. Bor 157 D1
Sawyers La. Pot B 158 B3
Sawyers Way. Heml H 124 C2
Saxon Ave. Stot 11 F4
Saxon Cl. Harp 86 B2
Saxon Cl. Letw 11 F1
Saxon Ct. Bor 169 F4
Saxon Rd. Luton 45 E1
Saxon Rd. Welw 89 D2
Saxon Rd. Whea 108 B4
Saxon Way. Bal 13 D1
Saxon Way. Wa Aby 163 E3
Saxtead Cl. Luton 46 B1
Sayer Way. Kneb 68 C2
Sayes Gdns. Saw 97 F1
Sayesbury Ave. Saw 97 F2
Sayesbury Rd. Saw 97 F1
Saywell Rd. Luton 46 A1
Scarborough Ave. Stev 50 A4
Scatterdells La. Chipf 138 A1
Scholar's Ct. Coln H 143 E4
Scholar's Hill. Wars 95 D2
Scholars Wlk. Hat 130 A1
School Cl. Stev 51 D2
School Gdns. Pot En 123 D3
School La. Ast 51 F1
School La. Bar 9 D1
School La. Bric 155 D4
School La. Bus 168 A1
School La. Ess 131 F3
School La. Gt Of 33 E2
School La. Harl 117 F1
School La. Hat 130 B3
School La. Luton 44 B2
School La. Pres 48 C3
School La. Tewin 90 C1
School La. Wat St 70 C2
School La. Welw 89 D2
School Mead. Abb L 153 E4
School Rd. Pot B 145 E1
School Row. Heml H 123 F1
School Wlk. Letw 23 D3
Schubert Rd. Elst 169 E2
Scot Gr. Pnr 175 F2
Scots Hill Cl. Cro Gr 165 F2
Scots Hill. Cro Gr 165 F2
Scots Mill La. Cro Gr 165 F2
Scott Ave. Sta Ab 115 D2
Scott Cl. Roystn 2 B1
Scott Rd. Bis St 76 C3
Scott Rd. Stev 51 D3
Scott's Rd. Gt Am 114 B4
Scotts Cl. Gt Am 114 B4
Scotts View. Wel G C 110 B3
Scottswood Cl. Bus 167 F4
Scottswood Rd. Bus 167 F4
Scrubbitts Park Rd. Radl 156 A2
Scrubbitts Sq. Radl 156 A2
Seabrook Rd. Bed 139 E2
Seabrook. Luton 44 B2
Seacroft Gdns. Sth Ox 175 E4
Seaford Cl. Luton 46 B2
Seaforth Dri. Ches 162 B3
Seaman Cl. Pk St 141 E3
Searches La. Bed 140 B2
Seaton Rd. Heml H 124 C1
Seaton Rd. Lon C 142 B3
Seaton Rd. Luton 44 C2
Sebright Rd. Barn 171 E3
Sebright Rd. Heml H 124 A1
Sebright Rd. Mark 83 F3
Secker Cres. Har 176 B1
Second Ave. Letw 23 E3
Second Ave. Watf 154 B2
Sedbury Cl. Luton 45 D3
Sedge Green. Lo Naz 135 F2
Sedge Green. Roy 135 F2
Sedgwick Rd. Luton 44 A3
Seebohm Cl. Hit 21 E1
Seeleys. Harl 118 B2
Sefton Ave. Har 176 B1
Sefton Cl. St Alb 127 F2
Sefton Rd. Stev 37 D1
Selbourne Rd. Luton 45 D1
Selby Ave. St Alb 127 E2
Selden Hill. Heml H 124 B1
Sele Rd. Hert 113 D3
Selina Cl. Luton 44 B4
Sellers Cl. Bor 170 B4
Sells Rd. Ware 93 F1
Sellwood Dri. Barn 171 E2
Selsey Dri. Luton 46 B2
Selwyn Ave. Hat 129 F2
Selwyn Cres. Hat 129 F3
Selwyn Dri. Hat 129 F3
Sempill Rd. Heml H 138 C4
Senate Pl. Stev 37 D1
Sequoia Cl. Bus 168 B1
Sequoia Park. Pnr 176 A2
Serby Ave. Roystn 7 E4
Sergehill La. Bed 140 A3
Service Rd The. Pot B 159 D4
Seven Acres. Norwd 175 D2
Sevenoaks Ct. Norwd 174 B2
Severalls The. Luton 46 A2
Severn Dri. Enf 162 A1
Severn Way. Watf 154 B3
Severnmead. Heml H 124 C3
Severnvale. Lon C 142 C2
Sewardstone Rd. Wa Aby 163 E2
Sewardstone St. Wa Aby 163 E3
Sewardstone Way. Wa Aby 163 E2
Sewell Cl. St Alb 128 C2
Sewell Harris Cl. Harl 118 A1
Sewells. Wel GC 89 F1
Seymour Ave. Luton 63 F3
Seymour Cl. Pnr 175 F1
Seymour Cres. Heml H 124 C2
Seymour Mews. Saw 118 C4
Seymour Rd. Luton 63 F3
Seymour Rd. Nthch 121 F3
Seymour Rd. St Alb 127 F3
Shackledell. Stev 50 C1
Shacklegate La. Whit 66 C3
Shackleton Spring. Stev 51 D2
Shackleton Way. Wel GC 111 E3
Shady Bush Cl. Bus 168 B1
Shady La. Watf 167 D4
Shaftenhoe End Rd. Bar 9 D1
Shaftesbury Ct. Stev 50 C2
Shaftesbury Rd. Luton 45 D
Shaftesbury Rd. Watf 167 E
Shaftesbury Way. Bed 139 E
Shaftesbury Way. Roystn 7 F
Shakespeare Rd. Harp 86 A
Shakespeare Rd. Luton 44 A
Shakespeare St. Watf 154 A
Shakespeare. Roystn 7 E
Shalcross Dri. Ches 148 C
Shallcross Cres. Hat 130 A
Shangani Rd. Bis St 76 C
Shanklin Cl. Ches 147 F
Shanklin Cl. Luton 45 D
Shanklin Gdns. Sth Ox 175 E
Shantock Hall La. Bov 136 B
Shantock La. Bov 136 B
Sharmans Cl. Har Gr 89 F
Sharpcroft. Heml H 124 B
Sharpenhoe Rd. Str 31 D
Sharpes La. Heml H 123 D
Sharples Green. Luton 45 D
Shaw Cl. Bus 176 C
Shaw Cl. Ches 148 B
Shaws The. Wel GC 111 E
Shearwater Cl. Stev 51 E
Sheepcot Dri. Watf 154 B
Sheepcot La. Watf 154 A
Sheepcote La. Whea 87 F
Sheepcote Rd. Heml H 124 C
Sheepcote. Wel GC 111 D
Sheepcroft Hill. Stev 51 E
Sheephouse Rd. Heml H 124 C
Sheering Dri. Harl 118 C
Sheering Lower Rd. Harl 118 C
Sheering Lower Rd. Saw 98 A1
Sheering Mill La. Saw 97 F1
Sheering Rd. Harl 118 C3
Sheethanger La. Fel 138 A4
Shefton Rise. Norwd 175 D2
Sheldon Cl. Ham St 147 F3
Shelford Rd. Barn 171 E2
Shelley Cl. Norwd 174 C3
Shelley Cl. Roystn 2 B1
Shelley Ct. Harp 86 A1
Shelley Rd. Luton 44 A1
Shelly Cl. Hit 35 E4
Shelton Way. Luton 46 A2
Shenley Ct. Heml H 125 D4
Shenley Hill. Radl 156 A2
Shenley La. Lon C 142 B2
Shenley Rd. Bor 170 A3
Shenley Rd. Heml H 125 E4
Shenleybury Cotts. Shen 156 C4
Shenleybury. Shen 142 C1
Shenstone Hill. Berk 122 B3
Shephall Green La. Stev 51 D1
Shephall Green. Stev 51 D1
Shephall La. Stev 51 D1
Shephall View. Stev 51 D3
Shephall Way. Stev 51 E2
Shepherd Cl. Roystn 7 F3
Shepherd's La. Chor 164 B2
Shepherd's La. Ric 164 C1
Shepherds Ct. Hert 92 B1
Shepherds Green. Heml H 123 F1
Shepherds La. Stev 50 A3
Shepherds Mead. Hit 21 F1
Shepherds Rd. Watf 166 C3
Shepherds Way. Bro Pk 145 E2
Shepherds Way. Harp 85 E2
Shepherds Way. Ric 165 D1
Shepherds Wlk. Bus 176 B4
Shepley Mews. Ches 163 D1
Sheppard Cl. Enf 162 A1
Sheppards Cl. St Alb 127 F3
Shepperton Cl. Bor 170 B4
Sheppey's La. Abb L 139 E1
Sheraton Cl. Elst 169 F2
Sherborne Ave. Luton 45 E3
Sherborne Way. Cro Gr 166 A3
Sherd Cl. Luton 44 C4
Sheredes Dri. Hod 134 C2
Sherfield Ave. Ric 173 F4
Sheridan Rd. Luton 45 E1
Sheridan Rd. Watf 167 E1
Sheriff Way. Watf 154 A3
Sheringham Ave. Stev 50 A4
Sheringham Cl. Luton 45 E4
Sherington Ave. Pnr 176 A2
Shernbroke Rd. Wa Aby 163 F3
Sherrardspark Rd. Wel GC 110 B4
Sherwood Ave. Pot B 158 C4
Sherwood Ave. St Alb 128 A3
Sherwood Rd. Luton 45 D1
Sherwood. Letw 22 C4
Sherwoods Rd. Watf 167 F1
Sherwoods Rise. Harp 107 E4
Shetland Cl. Bor 170 B2
Shillington Rd. Aps En 19 F3
Shillington Rd. Pirt 20 A3
Shillitoe Ave. Pot B 158 C4
Shingle Cl. Luton 45 D4
Shire Cl. Ches 148 C3
Shire La. Buc Co 120 A3
Shire La. C St P 172 A3
Shire La. Chor 164 B2
Shire La. Has 119 F4
Shiremeade. Elst 169 F2
Shires The. Luton 45 E1
Shires The. Roystn 7 F3

Shirley Cl. Ches 148 B1
Shirley Cl. Hod 148 C4
Shirley Cl. Stev 51 E4
Shirley Rd. Abb L 153 F4
Shirley Rd. Luton 63 E4
Shirley Rd. St Alb 127 F1
Shooters Dri. Lo Naz 135 F1
Shootersway La. Berk 121 F2
Shootersway Park. Berk 121 F2
Shootersway. Berk 121 F2
Shoplands. Wel GC 89 E1
Shoreham Cl. Stev 50 A4
Short La. Ast 51 F2
Short La. Bri Wd 140 C1
Shortcroft. Bis St 77 E4
Shortlands Green. Wel GC 110 C3
Shortmead Dri. Ches 162 C4
Shothanger Way. Fel 137 E3
Shott La. Letw 23 D3
Shrub Hill Rd. Heml H 123 F1
Shrubbery Gr. Roystn 7 E2
Shrubbery The. Heml H 123 F2
Shrublands Ave. Berk 122 A2
Shrublands Rd. Berk 122 A3
Shrublands The. Pot B 158 C3
Shrublands. Bro Pk 145 D3
Shrubs Rd. Ric 173 F2
Shugars Green. Tri 100 A3
Sibley Ave. Harp 107 F4
Sibley Cl. Luton 46 A2
Sibthorpe Rd. Wel Gr 144 B4
Siccut Rd. L Wym 35 F2
Sicklefield Cl. Ham St 147 F3
Siddons Rd. Stev 51 E3
Sidford Cl. Heml H 123 F2
Sidings The. Hat 129 F2
Sidmouth Cl. Sth Ox 175 D4
Sidney Terr. Bis St 76 C3
Silam Rd. Stev 50 C3
Silecroft Rd. Luton 64 A4
Silk Mill Ct. Watf 167 D1
Silk Mill Rd. Watf 167 D1
Silk Mill Way. Tri 100 A3
Silver Cl. Har 176 B2
Silver Dell. Watf 153 F2
Silver Hill. Shen 157 E2
Silver St. Ans 29 D3
Silver St. Ashw 4 B2
Silver St. Ches 147 E1
Silver St. Gu M 1 C2
Silver St. Luton 63 F4
Silver St. Sta Mo 59 E3
Silver St. Wa Aby 163 E3
Silver Trees. Bri Wd 140 C1
Silverbirch Ave. Stot 11 F4
Silverdale Rd. Bus 167 F2
Silverfield. Hod 134 C1
Silverthorn Dri. Heml H 139 D4
Silverwood Cl. Norwd 174 B1
Simmonds Rise. Heml H 124 B1
Simon Dean. Bov 137 D2
Simpson Dri. Bal 23 F4
Simpsons Ct. Bal 23 F4
Sinderby Cl. Bor 169 F4
Sinfield Cl. Stev 51 D3
Singlets La. Fla 84 B1
Sir Herbert James Village The. Luton 44 B2
Sir Peter's Way. Stu 81 E3
Sirita Cl. Har 176 B1
Sirus Rd. Norwd 175 D3
Sish Cl. Stev 50 B3
Sish La. Stev 50 B3
Siskin Cl. Bor 170 A3
Sisson Cl. Stev 51 E1
Sitwell Gr. Stan 176 C3
Six Acres. Heml H 139 D4
Six Hills Way. Stev 50 B2
Sixth Ave. Letw 23 E3
Sixth Ave. Watf 154 B2
Skegness Rd. Stev 50 A4
Skegsbury La. Pet Gr 65 F1
Skelton Cl. Luton 31 D1
Skidmore Way. Ric 165 F1
Skimpans Cl. Wel Gr 144 B4
Skimpton Rd. Luton 44 A1
Skipton Cl. Stev 68 C4
Skua Cl. Luton 44 A3
Skys Wood Rd. St Alb 128 A4
Slade Ct. Radl 156 A2
Sleaford Green. Sth Ox 175 E4
Sleapcross Gdns. St Alb 129 E1
Sleaps Hyde. Stev 51 E1
Sleapshyde La. St Alb 129 E1
Sleddale. Heml H 124 C3
Sleets End. Heml H 124 A3
Slimmons Dri. St Alb 128 A4
Slip La. St P W 68 A3
Slipe La. Hod 148 C4
Slipe The. Ched 80 A4
Sloansway. Wel GC 90 A1
Slype The. Bla En 87 D3
Small Acre. Heml H 123 F2
Smallcroft. Wel GC 111 D4
Smallford La. St Alb 129 D1
Smallwood Cl. Whea 108 C4
Smarts Green. Ham St 147 F3
Smeaton Cl. Wa Aby 163 F4
Smith St. Watf 167 E3
Smith's End La. Bar 8 C1
Smithfield. Heml H 124 B3
Smiths La Mall. Luton 63 F4
Smiths La. Ham St 147 E3
Smithy The. L Had 57 D1
Smug Oak La. Bri Wd 141 E1
Smug Oak La. Fro 141 F1
Snailswell La. Ick 21 F3
Snatchup. Red 106 A3
Snells Mead. Bun 40 C4
Snipe The. Wes 24 A1
Snowford Cl. Luton 45 D4
Snowley Par. Bis St 59 D1
Soham Rd. Enf 162 C1
Solesbridge Cl. Chor 164 C3
Solesbridge La. Chor 165 D4
Sollershott E. Letw 22 C2
Sollershott W. Letw 22 C2
Solomon's Hill. Ric 165 E1
Solway Rd S. Luton 45 D2
Solway Rd. Luton 45 D2
Solway. Heml H 124 C3
Somerby Cl. Hod 135 D1
Someries Rd. Harp 86 B2
Someries Rd. Heml H 123 F3
Somers Rd. Wel Gr 144 B4
Somers Sq. Wel Gr 144 B4
Somers Way. Bus 168 B1
Somersby Cl. Luton 63 F3
Somerset Ave. Luton 46 A1
Somerset Rd. Enf 163 D1
Somersham. Wel GC 111 E3
Soothouse Spring. St Alb 127 F4
Sopers Rd. Cuf 146 C1
Sopwell La. St Alb 127 E1
Sorrel Cl. Luton 45 D4
Sorrel Cl. Roystn 7 F3
Sorrel Garth. Hit 35 D3
Sotheron Rd. Watf 167 E3
Souberie Ave. Letw 22 C3
Souldern St. Watf 167 D2
South App. Norwd 174 B4
South ark Ave. Chor 164 C2
South Bank Rd. Nthch 121 F3
South Cl. Bal 23 F4
South Cl. Barn 171 F3
South Cl. Chis 141 D3
South Cl. Pnr 175 E1
South Cl. Roystn 7 D4
South Cottage Dri. Chor 164 C2
South Cottage Gdns. Chor 164 C2
South Dri. Cuf 146 C1
South Dri. St Alb 128 C2
South Drift Way. Luton 63 D3
South Hill Cl. Hit 35 D3
South Hill Rd. Heml H 124 B2
South Ley. Wel GC 110 C2
South Mimms By-Ps. Pot B 157 F4
South Par. Wa Aby 163 E3
South Park Gdns. Berk 122 A3
South Pl. Harl 118 A2
South Pl. Hit 34 B4
South Rd. Bal 23 F4
South Rd. Bis St 77 D3
South Rd. Chor 164 B2
South Rd. Harl 118 A2
South Rd. Hat 130 A1
South Rd. Luton 63 E3
South Rd. Stand 55 F1
South Riding. Bri Wd 141 D1
South St. Bis St 76 C3
South St. Hert 113 E3
South St. Sta Ab 115 E2
South View Rd. Pnr 175 D2
South View. Letw 22 C3
South Way. Abb L 153 F3
South Way. Hat 129 F1
South Way. Wa Aby 163 E2
South Weald Dri. Wa Aby 163 E3
Southacre Way. Pnr 175 E1
Southall Cl. Ware 93 E1
Southbrook Dri. Ches 148 B2
Southbrook. Saw 97 F1
Southdown Ct. Hat 130 A1
Southdown Ind Est. Harp 107 E4
Southdown Rd. Harp 107 D4
Southdown Rd. Hat 130 A1
Southend Cl. Stev 50 B4
Southern Ave. Henlw 10 B2
Southern Rise. Nwml E 85 F4
Southern Way. Letw 22 C4
SouthernWood Cl. Heml H 125 D2
Southfield Ave. Watf 154 B1
Southfield Rd. Ches 162 C4
Southfield Rd. Hod 135 D4
Southfield Way. St Alb 128 B3
Southfield. Barn 171 E2
Southfield. Brag 55 F4
Southfield. Wel GC 110 B2
Southfields. Letw 11 F1
Southfields. Stand 55 F1
Southgate Rd. Pot B 159 E3
Southgate. Stev 50 B2
Southmead Cres. Ches 148 C1
Southmill Rd. Bis St 77 D3
Southsea Ave. Watf 167 D3
Southsea Rd. Stev 50 A4
Southview Cl. Ham St 147 F3
Southview Rd. Harp 86 B2
Southwark Cl. Stev 37 D1
Southwold Rd. Watf 154 B1
Soval Ct. Norwd 174 B2
Sowerby Ave. Luton 46 B2
Sparhawke. Letw 12 A1
Sparrow Cl. Luton 44 A2
Sparrows Herne. Bus 168 B1
Sparrowswick Ride. St Alb 127 E4
Spayne Cl. Luton 45 D4
Spear Cl. Luton 44 C3
Speedwell Cl. Luton 45 D4
Speke Cl. Stev 51 E3
Spellbrook La E. Spel 97 F4
Spellbrook La W. Spel 97 F4
Spellbrooke. Hit 34 B4
Spencer Ave. Ham St 147 F3
Spencer Cl. Sta Mo 59 F3
Spencer Gate. St Alb 127 F3
Spencer Pl. Sand 108 B1
Spencer Rd. Har 176 C1
Spencer Rd. Luton 45 E1
Spencer St. Hert 113 F4
Spencer St. St Alb 127 E2
Spencer Way. Heml H 124 A3
Spencer Wlk. Chor 165 E2
Spenser Cl. Roystn 2 B1
Spenser Rd. Harp 86 B1
Sperberry Hill. St Ipp 35 D1
Sphere Ind Est The. St 128 A1
Spicer St. St Alb 127 E2
Spicers La. Harl 118 B2
Spicersfield. Ham St 148 A2
Spinney Cl. Hit 35 D3
Spinney La. Wl Gr 68 B1
Spinney Rd. Luton 44 B4
Spinney St. Hert 114 A3
Spinney The. Bal 23 F4
Spinney The. Harp 85 F2
Spinney The. Hert 113 F3
Spinney The. Hod 134 C2
Spinney The. Pot B 159 E4
Spinney The. Stev 51 E4
Spinney The. Watf 167 D4
Spinney The. Wel GC 110 C3
Spittlesea Rd. Luton 64 B3
Spooners Dri. Chis 141 E2
Spratts La. Ken Co 82 C4
Spreckley Cl. Henlw 10 A3
Spring Cl. Bor 170 A4
Spring Cl. Hare 173 E1
Spring Cl. Lat 150 B2
Spring Court Rd. Enf 161 D1
Spring Crofts. Bus 168 B3
Spring Dri. Stev 69 D4
Spring Field Rd. Berk 122 A3
Spring Gdns. Watf 154 B2
Spring Hills. Harl 117 D1
Spring La. Cotrd 39 E3
Spring La. Heml H 124 A2
Spring Pl. Luton 63 E3
Spring Rd. Kin Gr 85 D2
Spring Rd. Letw 22 C3
Spring View Rd. Gt Am 114 A4
Spring Way. Heml H 125 D3
Spring Wlk. Hod 134 B1
Springfield Cl. Cro Gr 166 A2
Springfield Cl. Pot B 159 E4
Springfield Cres. Harp 86 A2
Springfield Rd. Ches 162 C4
Springfield Rd. Heml H 124 C2
Springfield Rd. Luton 45 E3
Springfield Rd. St Alb 128 A1
Springfield Rd. Watf 154 A3
Springfield. Bus 168 B1
Springfield. St Alb 129 D2
Springfields House. Wel GC 110 B2
Springfields. Hod 134 C2
Springfields. Wa Aby 163 F3
Springfields. Wel GC 110 A2
Springhall La. Saw 97 F1
Springhall Rd. Saw 97 F1
Springhead. Ashw 4 B2
Springle La. Hod 114 C1
Springs The. Hert 113 F4
Springs The. Hod 148 C3
Springshott. Letw 22 C3
Springwell Ave. Ric 173 D4
Springwell La. Hare 173 D3
Springwood Cl. Hare 173 E1
Springwood Wlk. St Alb 128 B3
Springwood. Ham St 148 A3
Spruce Way. Chis 141 D2
Spur Cl. Abb L 153 E3
Spur The. Ches 148 B2
Spur The. Stev 50 C2
Spurrs Cl. Hit 35 D4
Square The. Brag 55 F4
Square The. Chipp 27 E3
Square The. Heml H 124 B2
Square The. Hoc 148 C4
Square The. Red 105 F3
Square The. Saw 97 F1
Square The. Watf 154 A1
Squires Cl. Bis St 76 B4
Squires Ride. Heml H 104 C1
Squirrels Cl. Bis St 76 C4
Squirrels The. Bus 168 B2
Stackfield. Harl 118 A2
Stacklands. Wel GC 110 A2
Staddles. L Hal 98 A4
Stafford Cl. Ches 148 A1
Stafford Dri. Hod 135 D2
Stafford Rd. Har 176 B2
Staffords. Harl 118 C2
Stag Green Ave. Hat 130 B4
Stag La. Berk 122 A3
Stag La. Chor 164 B2
Stagg Hill. Barn 159 F2
Stainer Rd. Bor 169 E4
Stains Cl. Ches 148 C2
Stake Piece Rd. Roystn 7 E3
Stakers Ct. Harp 86 A1
Stamford Ave. Roystn 7 E4
Stamford Cl. Har 176 C2
Stamford Cl. Pot B 159 E4
Stamford Rd. Watf 167 D4
Stanborough Ave. Bor 157 D1
Stanborough Cl. Wel GC 110 B3
Stanborough Green. Wel GC 110 B2
Stanborough La. Wel GC 110 B2
Stanborough Rd. Wel GC 110 B2
Stanbury Ave. Watf 153 F1
Standard Rd. Enf 162 C1
Standfield. Abb L 139 F1
Standhill Cl. Hit 34 C3
Standhill Rd. Hit 34 C3
Standon Hill. Stand 55 E1
Standon Mews. Stand 55 F1
Standon Rd. L Had 56 C2
Standring Rise. Heml H 138 A4
Stane Cl. Bis St 58 C1
Stane Field. Letw 23 D2
Stane St. Bal 13 D1
Stanelow Cres. Stand 55 E1
Stanford Rd. Luton 46 A1
Stangate Cres. Bor 170 C2
Stanhope Ave. Har 176 B1
Stanhope Rd. Barn 171 E2
Stanhope Rd. Ches 162 C3
Stanhope Rd. St Alb 127 F2
Stanier Rise. Nthch 121 F4
Stanley Ave. Chis 141 D3
Stanley Gdns. Bor 169 F4
Stanley Gdns. Tri 99 F2
Stanley Rd. Hert 113 F3
Stanley Rd. Norwd 175 D1
Stanley Rd. Stev 51 D4
Stanley Rd. Str 31 D3
Stanley Rd. Watf 167 E3
Stanley St. Luton 63 E3
Stanmore Cres. Luton 44 C2
Stanmore Rd. Stev 50 B4
Stanmore Rd. Watf 167 D4
Stanmount Rd. Chis 141 D3
Stannington Path. Bor 170 A4
Stanstead Dri. Hod 135 D4
Stanstead Rd. Hert 114 A3
Stanstead Rd. Hert H 114 C3
Stanstead Rd. Hod 115 D1
Stansted Hill. Gr Ty 75 D1
Stansted Rd. Birhr 59 E2
Stansted Rd. Bis St 59 D1
Stanton Cl. St Alb 128 B4
Stanton Rd. Luton 44 B1
Staplefield Cl. Pnr 175 F2
Stapleford Rd. Luton 46 B2
Stapleford. Wel GC 111 E3
Stapleton Cl. Pot B 159 E4
Stapleton Rd. Bor 157 D1
Stapley Rd. St Alb 127 E2
Stapylton Rd. Barn 171 F3
Star St. Ware 93 F1
Starling La. Cuf 146 C2
Statam Cl. Luton 31 D1
Station App. Ches 162 C3
Station App. Chor 164 B3
Station App. Harp 86 A1
Station App. Hit 35 D4
Station App. Kneb 68 C3
Station App. Norwd 174 C2
Station App. Radl 156 A2
Station App. Sth Ox 175 E4
Station Cl. Bro Pk 144 C3
Station Cl. Pot B 158 C4
Station Mews. Pot B 159 D4
Station Pl. Letw 22 C3
Station Rd. Abb L 139 D1
Station Rd. Ald 101 D3
Station Rd. Arl 11 D2
Station Rd. Bal 12 C1
Station Rd. Berk 122 A3
Station Rd. Bis St 77 D4
Station Rd. Bor 170 A3
Station Rd. Bric 155 D4
Station Rd. Bun 40 C4
Station Rd. Ched 79 F4
Station Rd. Cuf 146 C1
Station Rd. Had Cr 74 C1
Station Rd. Har Gr 89 F2
Station Rd. Harl 117 E2
Station Rd. Harl 118 B2
Station Rd. Harp 86 B1
Station Rd. Heml H 124 B1
Station Rd. Henlw 10 A2
Station Rd. Hod 135 D2
Station Rd. Ivin 80 C3
Station Rd. Kneb 69 D3
Station Rd. Let Gr 112 A1
Station Rd. Letw 22 C3
Station Rd. Lon M 79 D2
Station Rd. Luton 44 C3
Station Rd. Luton 63 F4
Station Rd. Odsey 5 E1
Station Rd. Puc 55 E2
Station Rd. Radl 156 A2
Station Rd. Ric 165 E1
Station Rd. Saw 97 F2
Station Rd. St Alb 129 D2
Station Rd. Sta Ab 115 E2
Station Rd. Sta Mo 59 F3
Station Rd. Stand 55 F1
Station Rd. Ste Mo 5 D4
Station Rd. Tri 100 B2
Station Rd. Ware 93 F1
Station Rd. Wat St 70 B2
Station Rd. Watf 167 D4
Station Rd. Wel Gr 144 B3
Station Rd. Whea 87 E1
Station Way. Letw 22 C3
Staveley Rd. Luton 44 B1
Steeplands. Bus 168 A1
Steeple View. Bis St 76 C4
Stephens Cl. Luton 46 A2
Stephens Way. Red 105 F3
Stepnells. Mars 80 A1
Sterling Ave. Ches 162 B3
Sterling Rd. Enf 161 E1
Stevenage Cres. Bor 169 F4
Stevenage Rd. Hit 35 D3
Stevenage Rd. Kneb 68 C4
Stevenage Rd. L Wym 35 E2
Stevenage Rd. St Ipp 35 D2
Stevenage Rd. Wal 51 F4
Stevenage Rise. Heml H 124 C4
Stevens Green. Bus 168 B1
Steward Cl. Ches 148 C1
Stewardstone St. Wa Aby 163 E3
Stewart Cl. Abb L 153 F4
Stewart Rd. Harp 86 A1
Stewarts The. Bis St 76 C3
Stile Plntn. Roystn 7 F3
Stilton Path. Bor 157 D1
Stirling Cl. Stev 69 E4
Stirling Cnr. Barn 170 B2
Stirling Way. Bor 170 B2
Stirling Way. Wel GC 111 F3
Stobart Cl. Kneb 68 C3
Stock La. News 8 B1
Stockbreach Cl. Hat 130 A3
Stockbreach Rd. Hat 130 A3
Stockens Dell. Kneb 68 C2
Stockens Green. Kneb 68 C2
Stockers Farm Rd. Ric 173 E4
Stockfield Ave. Hod 135 D4
Stockholm Way. Luton 44 C4
Stocking La. Nut 18 B1
Stockings La. L Berk 132 B3
Stockingstone Rd. Luton 45 F2
Stockport Rd. Heron 164 B1
Stocks Rd. Ald 101 E4
Stockwell Cl. Ches 148 A2
Stockwell La. Ches 148 A2
Stockwood Cres. Luton 63 E3
Stone Cross. Harl 117 E1
Stonecroft. Kneb 68 C3
Stonecross Cl. St Alb 127 F2
Stonecross Rd. Hat 130 A4
Stonecross. St Alb 127 F2
Stonehills. Wel GC 110 B4
Stonelea Rd. Heml H 138 C4
Stoneleigh Ave. Enf 162 A1
Stoneleigh Cl. Ches 162 B3
Stoneleigh Cl. Luton 45 D4
Stoneleigh. Saw 97 E2
Stoneley. Letw 11 F1
Stonemead. Wel GC 89 E2
Stones Alley. Watf 167 D3
Stoneways Cl. Luton 44 B3
Stoney Common Rd. Sta Mo 59 E3
Stoney Common. Sta Mo 59 F3
Stoney Croft. Ald 101 E3
Stoney La. Bov 137 E3
Stoney La. Chipf 137 F1
Stoney Pl. Sta M 59 F3
Stoneycroft. Heml H 124 A2
Stoneycroft. Wel GC 111 D4
Stoneyfield Dri. Sta Mo 59 F3
Stoneygate Rd. Luton 44 B2
Stonleigh Dri. Hod 115 D1
Stonnells Cl. Letw 22 C4
Stony Croft. Stev 50 C3
Stony Hills. Cha En 92 B4
Stony La. Chen 150 B1
Stony La. T Gr 47 E2
Stonyshotts. Wa Aby 163 F3
Stookslade. Wing 60 A2
Stopsley Way. Luton 46 A2
Storehouse La. Hit 34 C3
Storey St. Heml H 138 B4
Stormont Rd. Hit 21 F1
Stornoway. Heml H 125 D1
Stort Lodge. Bis St 76 B4
Stort Mill. Harl 118 A3
Stort Rd. Bis St 76 C3
Stortford Hall Park. Bis St 77 D4
Stortford La. Stand 55 F1
Stortford Rd. Hod 135 E4
Stortford Rd. L Had 57 E1
Stortford Rd. L Hal 98 C2
Stotfold Rd. Cal 3 E1
Stotfold Rd. Ch En 11 D4
Stotfold Rd. Letw 22 B2

Stotford Rd. Radw 12 B4
Stow The. Harl 117 F1
Stox Mead. Har 176 B1
Strafford Cl. Pot B 159 D4
Strafford Ct. Kneb 69 D3
Strafford Gate. Pot B 159 D4
Strafford Rd. Barn 171 F3
Straits The. Wa Aby 163 D4
Strangers Way. Luton 44 B2
Strangeways. Watf 153 F2
Stratfield Dri. Hod 134 C2
Stratfield Rd. Bor 170 A4
Stratford Rd. Luton 45 D1
Stratford Rd. Watf 167 D4
Stratford Way. Heml H 138 A4
Stratford Way. Watf 167 D4
Strathmore Ave. Hit 21 F1
Strathmore Ave. Luton 63 F3
Strathmore Rd. Whit 66 C3
Strathmore Wlk. Luton 63 F3
Stratton Ave. Enf 161 E1
Stratton Gdns. Luton 45 E2
Strawberry Field. Hat 130 A1
Strawberry Field. Luton 44 C4
Strawfields. Wel GC 111 D4
Strawmead. Hat 130 A4
Strawplait Way. Arl 11 D2
Strayfield Rd. Enf 161 D1
Street The. Brag 55 F4
Street The. Chipf 152 A4
Street The. Fur P 43 D2
Street The. Hault 53 F2
Street The. Saw 98 C1
Street The. Wall 25 E4
Stretton Way. Bor 156 C1
Stringers La. Ast 51 F1
Stroma Cl. Heml H 125 E1
Stronsay. Heml H 125 E1
Stuart Ct. Elst 169 E2
Stuart Dri. Hit 35 D4
Stuart Dri. Roystn 7 E4
Stuart Pl. Luton 63 E4
Stuart Rd. Welw 89 D2
Stuart St. Luton 63 E4
Stuart Way. Ches 162 A4
Stuarts Cl. Heml H 124 B1
Stud Green. Watf 154 A4
Studham La. Dagn 81 E2
Studham La. Stu 82 A4
Studio Way. Bor 170 B4
Studios The. Bus 168 A2
Studlands Rise. Roystn 7 F3
Studley Rd. Luton 45 E1
Sturgeon's Way. Hit 22 A1
Sturlas Way. Ches 162 B3
Styles Cl. Luton 46 B1
Such Cl. Letw 23 D4
Sudbury Rd. Luton 44 A3
Suffolk Cl. Bor 170 B2
Suffolk Cl. Lon C 142 B3
Suffolk Cl. Luton 44 A2
Suffolk Rd. Pot B 158 C4
Suffolk Rd. Roystn 7 F3
Sugar La. Heml H 123 D1
Sulgrave Cres. Tri 100 B3
Sullivan Cres. Hare 173 E1
Sullivan Way. Elst 169 E2
Summer Ct. Heml H 124 B3
Summer Dale. Wel GC 89 E1
Summer Gr. Elst 169 E2
Summer Hill. Elst 170 A2
Summer St. Cad 63 E1
Summer Wlk. Mark 83 F3
Summerfield Cl. Lon C 142 B3
Summerfield Rd. Luton 62 C4
Summerfield Rd. Watf 154 A2
Summerfield. Hat 130 A1
Summerhouse La. Bus 168 B4
Summerhouse La. Hare 173 D2
Summerhouse Way. Abb L 139 F1
Summerlands Rd. St Alb 128 B4
Summers Rd. Luton 46 B1
Summerswood La. Ridge 157 F2
Summit Rd. Pot B 144 C1
Sumpter Yd. St Alb 127 E1
Sun Hill. Roystn 7 E3
Sun La. Harp 86 A1
Sun St. Bal 23 F4
Sun St. Hit 34 C3
Sun St. Saw 98 A1
Sun St. Wa Aby 163 E3
Sunderland Ave. St Alb 128 A2
Sundon Park Rd. Luton 44 B4
Sunmead Rd. Heml H 124 B3
Sunningdale. Bis St 76 C3
Sunningdale. Luton 45 F2
Sunny Bank. Ched 79 F4
Sunny Hill. Bun 40 C4
Sunnybank Rd. Pot B 159 D3
Sunnydell. Chis 141 D3
Sunnyfield. Hat 130 B4
Sunnyhill Rd. Heml H 124 A2
Sunnyhill Rd. Map Cr 172 B2
Sunnyside Rd. Hit 35 D3
Sunnyside. Sta Mo 59 F3
Sunridge Ave. Luton 45 F1
Sunrise Cres. Heml H 138 C4
Sunset Dri. Luton 45 F2
Sunset View. Barn 171 F4
Surrey Pl. Tri 100 A2
Sursham Ct. Mark 83 F3
Sussex Cl. Hod 135 D4
Sussex Pl. Luton 46 B1
Sussex Rd. Watf 154 A1
Sutcliffe Cl. Bus 168 B3
Sutcliffe Cl. Stev 51 D4
Sutherland Ave. Cuf 146 B2
Sutherland Cl. Barn 171 F3
Sutherland Ct. Wel GC 110 C4
Sutherland Pl. Luton 63 E3
Sutherland Way. Cuf 146 C2
Sutton Acres. L Hal 98 B4
Sutton Cl. Hod 134 C2
Sutton Cl. Tri 100 A3
Sutton Cres. Barn 171 E2
Sutton Gdns. Luton 44 B3
Sutton Path. Bor 170 A4
Sutton Rd. St Alb 128 A2
Sutton Rd. Watf 167 E3
Swallow Cl. Bus 168 B1
Swallow Cl. Chor 165 E1
Swallow Cl. Luton 44 A2
Swallow End. Wel GC 110 C3
Swallow Gdns. Hat 130 A2
Swallow La. St Alb 142 A4
Swallowdale La. Heml H 125 D3
Swallowfields. Wel GC 110 C3
Swallows The. Wel GC 89 F1
Swallows. Harl 118 B2
Swan La. Gu M 1 C2
Swan Pike Rd. Enf 163 D1
Swan St. Ashw 4 B2
Swanfield Rd. Ches 162 C3
Swangley's La. Kneb 69 D2
Swanhill. Wel GC 90 A1
Swanland Rd. Pot B 158 A4
Swanland Rd. Wa En 144 A2
Swanley Bar La. Pot B 145 D2
Swanley Cres. Pot B 145 D1
Swanmead. Luton 44 A3
Swannells Wood. Stu 82 B2
Swans Cl. St Alb 128 C1
Swanstand. Letw 23 E2
Swanston Path. Sth Ox 175 E4
Swasedale Rd. Luton 45 D3
Sweet Briar. Wel GC 111 D3
Sweetbriar Cl. Heml H 124 A3
Sweyns Mead. Stev 51 E4
Swift Cl. Letw 22 C4
Swift Cl. Roystn 2 B1
Swifts Green Cl. Luton 46 A3
Swifts Green Rd. Luton 46 A3
Swinburne Ave. Hit 21 E1
Swinburne Cl. Roystn 2 B1
Swing Gate La. Berk 122 B1
Swingate. Stev 50 B3
Swinnell Cl. Knee 2 A3
Swiss Ave. Watf 166 C3
Swiss Cl. Watf 166 C3
Sycamore Ave. Hat 130 A2
Sycamore Cl. Bus 167 F4
Sycamore Cl. Ham St 147 F2
Sycamore Dri. Pk St 141 E2
Sycamore Dri. Tri 100 A2
Sycamore Rd. Cro Gr 166 B2
Sycamore Rise. Berk 122 B2
Sycamores The. Bal 23 F4
Sycamores The. Bis St 77 D3
Sycamores The. Fel 137 F4
Sydney Rd. Watf 166 C2
Sylam Cl. Luton 44 C4
Sylvan Cl. Heml H 125 D1
Sylvan Way. Wel GC 111 E3
Sylvandale. Wel GC 111 E3
Sylvia Ave. Pnr 175 F2
Symonds Green La. Stev 50 A3
Symonds Green La. Stev 50 A3
Symonds Green Rd. Stev 50 A4

Tabbs Cl. Letw 23 D4
Takeley Cl. Wa Aby 163 E3
Talbot Ave. Watf 167 F1
Talbot Ct. Heml H 124 B1
Talbot Rd. Har 176 C1
Talbot Rd. Hat 130 A4
Talbot Rd. Luton 45 F1
Talbot Rd. Ric 165 F1
Talbot St. Hert 113 F3
Talbot Way. Letw 12 B1
Tall Trees. Roystn 7 F3
Tallack Cl. Har 176 C2
Tallents Cres. Harp 86 B2
Tallis Way. Bor 169 F4
Tamar Green. Heml H 124 C4
Tamarisk Cl. St Alb 127 F4
Tamworth Rd. Hert 113 F4
Tancred Rd. Luton 46 A2
Tanfield Cl. Ham St 148 A2
Tanfield Green. Luton 46 C1
Tanglewood Cl. Stan 176 C4
Tanglewood. Wl Gr 90 A4
Tanners Cres. Hert 113 E2
Tanners Hill. Abb L 154 A4
Tanners Way. Hun 116 B4
Tanners Wood La. Abb L 153 F4
Tannery Cl. Roystn 7 E3
Tannery Drift. Roystn 7 E3
Tannery The. Bun 40 C4
Tannsfield Dri. Heml H 124 C3
Tannsmore Cl. Heml H 124 C3
Tansycroft. Wel GC 111 D4
Tanworth Cl. Norwd 174 B2
Tanworth Gdns. Pnr 175 E1
Tany's Dell. Harl 118 A2
Tanyard La. A St L 88 A4
Tapster St. Barn 171 F3
Taransey. Heml H 125 D1
Tarpan Way. Ches 148 C3
Tarrant Dri. Harp 107 E4
Tassell Hall. Red 105 F3
Tatlers La. Ast 51 F2
Tatsfield Ave. Lo Naz 149 E4
Tattershall Dri. Heml H 105 D1
Tattle Hill. Bram 91 F1
Tattlers Hill. Wing 60 A2
Taunton Ave. Luton 46 A1
Taverners. Heml H 124 C3
Tavistock Ave. St Alb 141 E4
Tavistock Cl. Pot B 159 E4
Tavistock Cl. St Alb 141 E4
Tavistock Cres. Luton 63 F3
Tavistock Rd. Watf 167 E4
Tavistock St. Luton 63 F3
Taylor Cl. St Alb 128 A4
Taylor St. Luton 63 F4
Taylor's Hill. Hit 34 C3
Taylor's Rd. Stot 3 D1
Taylor's Rd. Stot 11 F4
Taylors Ave. Hod 135 D3
Taylors La. Barn 171 F4
Taywood Cl. Stev 51 D1
Teasdale Cl. Roystn 2 B1
Teasel Cl. Roystn 7 F3
Tedder Ave. Henlw 10 A3
Tedder Rd. Heml H 125 D2
Tee Side. Hert 114 A4
Teesdale. Heml H 124 C3
Telford Ave. Stev 51 D3
Telford Cl. Watf 154 B2
Telford Ct. St Alb 127 F1
Telford Rd. Lon C 142 B2
Telford Way. Luton 63 E4
Telmere Ind Est. Luton 63 F3
Telscombe Way. Luton 46 B2
Temperance St. St Alb 127 E2
Tempest Ave. Pot B 159 E4
Templar Ave. Bal 23 F3
Templars Dri. Har 176 B2
Templars La. Pres 48 B3
Temple Cl. Ches 162 A4
Temple Cl. Hit 34 B2
Temple Cl. Watf 166 C4
Temple Ct. Hert 92 B1
Temple Fields. Hert 92 B1
Temple Gdns. Ric 174 A3
Temple La. Tonw 92 C4
Temple Mead. Heml H 124 B3
Temple Mead. Roy 116 A1
Templepan La. Cha Cr 152 C1
Templewood. Wel GC 89 E1
Tempsford Ave. Bor 170 B3
Tempsford. Wel GC 111 E3
Temsford Cl. Har 176 B1
Tenby Dri. Luton 44 C2
Tene The. Bal 23 F4
Tennand Cl. Ham St 147 F3
Tennison Ave. Bor 170 A2
Tennyson Ave. Hit 35 E4
Tennyson Ave. Wa Aby 163 F3
Tennyson Cl. Roystn 2 B1
Tennyson Rd. Chis 141 D3
Tennyson Rd. Harp 86 A2
Tennyson Rd. Luton 63 F3
Tenth Ave. Luton 44 B4
Tenzing Gr. Luton 63 E3
Tenzing Rd. Heml H 125 D2
Teresa Gdns. Ches 162 B3
Terminus St. Harl 117 E1
Terrace Gdns. Watf 167 D4
Terrace The. Tri 100 A2
Tethys Rd. Heml H 124 C3
Tewin Cl. St Alb 128 B4
Tewin Cl. Tewin 90 B3
Tewin Ct. Wel GC 110 C4
Tewin Hill. Tewin 90 C2
Tewin Rd. Heml H 125 E2
Tewin Rd. Wel GC 110 C4
Thackeray Cl. Roystn 2 B1
Thames Ave. Heml H 124 C4
Thames Ct. Luton 45 D2
Thamesdale. Lon C 142 C2
Thatchers Croft. Heml H 124 C4
Thatchers End. Hit 35 E4
Thaxted Way. Wa Aby 163 E3
Thaynesfield. P Bar 159 E4
Thelby Cl. Luton 44 C3
Thele Ave. Sta Ab 115 E2
Thele Est. Sta Ab 115 F2
Theobald Cres. Har 176 B1
Theobald St. Bor 169 F4
Theobald's Cl. Cuf 146 C1
Theobald's La. Ches 162 B4
Theobald's Rd. Cuf 146 C1
Theobalds Park Rd. Enf 161 D2
Therfield Rd. St Alb 127 E3
Thetford Gdns. Luton 45 F3
Thieves' La. Hertng 112 C3
Thieves' La. Hertng 112 C4
Third Ave. Letw 23 E4
Third Ave. Luton 44 B4
Third Ave. Watf 154 B2
Thirlestone Rd. Luton 44 B1
Thirlestone. St Alb 127 F2
Thirlmere Dri. St Alb 128 A1
Thirlmere Gdns. Norwd 174 B2
Thirsk Rd. Bor 157 D1
Thirston Path. Bor 170 A4
Thistle Cl. Heml H 123 F1
Thistle Gr. Wel GC 111 E2
Thistle Rd. Luton 63 F4
Thistlecroft. Heml H 124 A1
Thistles The. Heml H 124 A2
Thistley La. Gos 34 C1
Thomas Rochford Way. Ches 148 C3
Thompsons Cl. Harp 86 A1
Thorley High. Thor 76 C1
Thorley Hill. Bis St 76 C3
Thorley La. Bis St 76 C2
Thorley La. Thor 76 B2
Thorley Park Rd. Bis St 76 C2
Thorn Ave. Bus 168 B1
Thorn Gr. Bis St 77 D3
Thornage Cl. Luton 45 E4
Thornbera Cl. Bis St 76 C2
Thornbera Gdns. Bis St 76 C2
Thornbera Rd. Bis St 76 C2
Thornbury Cl. Hod 115 D1
Thornbury Cl. Stev 69 D4
Thornbury Gdns. Bor 170 B3
Thornbury. Harp 86 B1
Thorncroft. Heml H 125 D1
Thorndyke Ct. Pnr 175 F2
Thornfield Rd. Bis St 76 C4
Thornhill Rd. Luton 44 C1
Thornhill Rd. Norwd 174 B3
Thornton Gr. Pnr 176 A2
Thornton Rd. Barn 171 F3
Thornton Rd. Pot B 145 E1
Thornton St. Hert 113 E3
Thornton St. St Alb 127 E2
Thorpe Cres. Watf 167 E1
Thorpe Rd. St Alb 127 E1
Thorpefield Cl. St Alb 128 B3
Thrales Cl. Luton 44 C4
Three Cherry Tree La. Heml H 125 E4
Three Close La. Berk 122 B2
Three Corners. Heml H 125 D1
Three Houses La. Lan 67 F3
Three Stiles. Benn 52 C2
Thremhall Ave. Bis St 77 F4
Thricknells Cl. Luton 44 C4
Thrift Farm La. Bor 170 B4
Thrimley La. Far 58 A3
Thristers Cl. Letw 23 D2
Thrums. Watf 154 A1
Thrush Ave. Hat 130 A2
Thrush Gr. Chor 165 E1
Thrush La. Cuf 146 C2
Thumbswood. Wel GC 111 D2
Thumpers. Heml H 124 C3
Thundercourt. Ware 93 E1
Thundridge Cl. Wel GC 111 E3
Thurgood Rd. Hod 135 D4
Thurlow Cl. Stev 36 B1
Thurnall Ave. Roystn 7 E3
Thurnall Cl. Bal 23 F4
Tibbles Cl. Watf 154 C2
Tibbs Hill Rd. Abb L 139 F1
Tiberius Rd. Luton 44 C3
Tichborne. Map Cr 172 B3
Tile Kiln Cl. Heml H 125 D1
Tile Kiln Cres. Heml H 125 D1
Tile Kiln La. Heml H 125 D1
Tilecroft. Wel GC 89 E1
Tilehouse Cl. Bor 169 F3
Tilehouse La. Map Cr 172 C1
Tilehouse St. Hit 34 C3
Tilgate. Luton 46 B2
Tillers Link. Stev 51 D1
Tillotson Rd. Har 176 A2
Tilsworth Wlk. St Alb 128 B4
Timber Orch. Wat 92 A1
Timber Ridge. Chor 165 E3
Timbercroft. Wel GC 89 F1
Timbers Ct. Harp 85 F1
Times Cl. Hit 21 E1
Timplings Row. Heml H 124 A3
Timworth Cl. Luton 46 B1
Tingeys Cl. Red 106 A3
Tinkers La. Wigg 121 D3
Tintagel Cl. Heml H 124 B4
Tintagle Cl. Luton 45 D2
Tintern Cl. Harp 85 E2
Tintern Cl. Stev 69 D4
Tippendell La. Chis 141 E3
Tippet Ct. Stev 50 B2
Tiree Cl. Heml H 125 D1
Titan Rd. Heml H 124 C3
Titchfield Rd. Enf 162 C1
Tithe Barn Cl. St Alb 141 E4
Tithe Cl. Cod 67 F1
Titian Ave. Bus 168 C1
Titmus Cl. Stev 50 C3
Tiverton Ct. Harp 107 F3
Tiverton Rd. Enf 159 F4
Toddington Rd. Luton 44 B3
Toland Cl. Luton 44 B1
Tolcarne Dri. Pnr 175 D1
Tollgate Cl. Chor 164 C3
Tollgate Rd. Coln H 143 F4
Tollgate Rd. Enf 162 B2
Tollpit End. Heml H 124 A3
Tolmers Ave. Cuf 146 C2
Tolmers Gdns. Cuf 146 C1
Tolmers Mews. Cuf 146 C3
Tolmers Rd. Cuf 146 C2
Tolpits Cl. Watf 166 C2
Tolpits La. Watf 166 C1
Tom's Hill. Cha Cr 152 C1
Tom's La. Bed 139 E2
Tomkins Cl. Bor 169 E4
Toms Croft. Heml H 124 C1
Toms Field. Hat 129 F2
Toms Hill Rd. Ald 101 E3
Tooke Cl. Pnr 175 F1
Toorack Rd. Har 176 B1
Tooveys Mill Cl. Kin L 139 D2
Topstreet Way. Harp 107 E4
Torquay Cres. Stev 50 A4
Torquay Dri. Luton 44 B2
Torridge Wlk. Heml H 124 C4
Torrington Dri. Pot B 159 E4
Torrington Rd. Berk 122 A2
Torvey Cl. Lon C 142 B3
Torwood Cl. Berk 121 F2
Torworth Rd. Bor 157 D1
Tot La. Birhr 59 E2
Totteridge Comm. N20 ..... 171 E1
Totteridge La. N20 ..... 171 E1
Totteridge Rd. Enf 162 B1
Totteridge Village. N20 ..... 171 F1
Totts La. Wal 38 B1
Toulmin Dri. St Alb 127 E4
Tounshend St. Hert 113 F3
Tovey Ave. Hod 135 D4
Tovey Cl. Lo Naz 149 F4
Tower Cl. Berk 122 A2
Tower Cl. L Wym 35 F2
Tower Hill La. Sand 108 C2
Tower Hill. Chipf 137 F1
Tower Hill. Muc H 74 C1
Tower Rd. Cod 67 F1
Tower Rd. Luton 64 A4
Tower Rd. Ware 93 F1
Tower St. Hert 113 E4
Tower Way. Luton 64 A4
Towers Rd. Heml H 124 C2
Towers Rd. Pnr 175 F1
Towers Rd. Stev 50 B2
Town Centre. Hat 130 A3
Town Farm Cres. Stand 55 F1
Town Fields. Hat 130 A3
Town La. Benn 52 C2
Town Mead Rd. Wa Aby 163 E3
Towne Rd. Roystn 7 E3
Townfield. Chor 165 E1
Townley. Letw 23 E2
Townsend Ave. St Alb 127 F2
Townsend Cl. Bark 17 E2
Townsend Cl. Harp 85 F1
Townsend Dri. St Alb 127 E3
Townsend La. Harp 85 F1
Townsend Rd. Harp 86 A1
Townsend Way. Norwd 174 C2
Townsend. Heml H 124 B3
Townsley Cl. Luton 63 F3
Trafalgar Ave. Hod 134 C1
Trafford Cl. Stev 36 C1
Trafford Ct. Stev 50 A4
Traherne Cl. Hit 34 C3
Trapstyle Rd. Ware 93 D1
Travellers Cl. Wel Gr 144 B4
Travellers La. Hat 130 A2
Treacle La. Rus 25 F2
Treacy Cl. Bus 176 B4
Trebellan Dri. Heml H 124 C2
Tree Cl. Ham St 147 F2
Treehanger Cl. Tri 100 A2
Treetops Cl. Norwd 174 B3
Trefoil Cl. Luton 44 A2
Trefusis Wlk. Watf 166 C4
Tregelles Rd. Hod 135 D4
Tremaine Gr. Heml H 124 C4
Trent Cl. Stev 50 C4
Trent Rd. Luton 45 D2
Tresco Rd. Berk 121 F3
Tresilian Sq. Heml H 124 C4
Trevalga Way. Heml H 124 C4
Trevellance Way. Watf 154 B3
Trevelyan Way. Berk 122 A3
Trevor Cl. Stan 176 C2
Trevor Rd. Hit 35 D4
Trevose Way. Sth Ox 175 E4
Trewenna Dri. Pot B 159 E4
Triangle The. Hit 34 C3
Trident Rd. Watf 153 F3
Triggs Way. Cok Gr 46 C2
Trimley Cl. Luton 44 A3
Trinder Rd. Barn 171 E2
Tring Ford Rd. Tri 100 A4
Tring Hill. Dra B 99 E2
Tring Rd. Lon M 79 E2
Tring Rd. Nthch 121 E4
Tring Rd. Wils 79 E1
Tring Rd. Wing 60 B1
Trinity Cl. Bis St 76 C3
Trinity Cl. Hert H 114 B2
Trinity Cl. Norwd 174 C2
Trinity Gr. Hert 113 E4
Trinity Hall Cl. Watf 167 E4

Trinity La. Ches 162 C4
Trinity Mens. Heml H 125 E1
Trinity Pl. Stev 50 B3
Trinity Rd. Hert H 114 B2
Trinity Rd. Luton 45 D2
Trinity Rd. Stev 50 B3
Trinity Rd. Stot 11 F4
Trinity Rd. Ware 93 F1
Trinity St. Bis St 76 C3
Trinity Way. Bis St 76 C3
Tristram Rd. Hit 22 A1
Triton Way. Heml H 124 C3
Trooper Rd. Ald 101 E3
Trotter's Gap. Sta Ab 115 F2
Trotters Bottom. Pot B 158 A1
Trout Rise. Chor 165 D3
Troutstream Way. Chor 165 D3
Trowbridge Gdns. Luton 45 F2
Trowley Bottom. Fla 105 D4
Trowley Hill Rd. Fla 84 A1
Trowley Rise. Abb L 153 F4
Truemans Rd. Hit 21 E1
Trumper Rd. Stev 36 C1
Trumpington Dri. St Alb 141 E4
Trundlers Way. Bus 168 C1
Truro Gdns. Luton 45 D3
Trust Rd. Ches 162 C3
Tucker St. Watf 167 E2
Tucker's Row. Bis St 76 C3
Tudor Ave. Ches 162 A4
Tudor Ave. Watf 154 B1
Tudor Cl. Ches 162 A4
Tudor Cl. Hat 129 F1
Tudor Cl. Hun 116 B4
Tudor Cl. Stev 36 B1
Tudor Cres. Enf 161 E1
Tudor Ct. Bor 169 F4
Tudor Ct. Hit 34 B3
Tudor Dri. Watf 154 B1
Tudor Hill. Heml H 124 B1
Tudor Manor Gdns. Watf 154 B4
Tudor Parade. Ric 165 D1
Tudor Rd. Har 176 B1
Tudor Rd. Luton 45 D1
Tudor Rd. Pnr 175 E1
Tudor Rd. St Alb 127 F4
Tudor Rd. Welw 89 D2
Tudor Rd. Whea 108 C4
Tudor Rise. Hod 134 C1
Tudor Way. Hertng 113 D4
Tudor Way. Ric 165 D1
Tudor Way. Wa Aby 163 E3
Tudor Wlk. Watf 154 B1
Tuffnells Way. Harp 85 E2
Tunnel Wood Cl. Watf 153 F1
Tunnel Wood Rd. Watf 153 F1
Tunnmeade. Harl 118 A1
Turf La. Gra 36 A2
Turkey St. Enf 162 B1
Turmore Dale. Wel GC 110 B3
Turnberry Ct. Sth Ox 175 E4
Turnberry Dr. Bri Wd 140 C1
Turner Cl. Stev 36 B1
Turner Rd. Bus 168 B3
Turner's Hill. Ches 148 B1
Turners Cl. Bram 91 E2
Turners Cl. Harp 86 B2
Turners Hill. Heml H 124 C1
Turners Orch. Chor 165 B2
Turners Rd N. Luton 46 A1
Turners Rd S. Luton 46 A1
Turnpike Dri. Luton 31 E1
Turnpike La. Ick 21 F2
Turnstones The. Watf 154 C2
Turpin's Ride. Roystn 7 E3
Turpin's Rise. Stev 50 C1
Turpin's Way. Bal 23 F4
Turpins Chase. Wl Gr 89 F4
Turpins Cl. Hertng 112 C3
Turpins Ride. Wl Gr 89 F4
Tuxford Cl. Bor 156 C1
Tweed Cl. Berk 122 A3
Twelve Acres. Wel GC 110 C2
Twelve Leys. Wing 60 A2
Twickenham Gdns. Har 176 C2
Twigden Ct. Luton 44 C3
Twinwoods. Stev 50 C2
Twist The. Wigg 100 B1
Twitchell The. Bal 23 F4
Two Acres. Wel GC 110 C2
Two Beeches. Heml H 124 C4
Two Dells La. Ash Gr 136 A3
Two Oaks Dri. Brn Gr 90 B3
Two Waters Rd. Heml H 124 B1
Twyford Bury La. Bis St 77 D2
Twyford Busns Cntr The. Bis St77 D2
Twyford Cl. Bis St 77 D3
Twyford Dri. Luton 46 B1
Twyford Gdns. Bis St 76 C2
Twyford Rd. Bis St 77 D3
Twyford Rd. St Alb 128 B4
Tye End. Stev 69 D4
Tyfield Cl. Ches 148 B1
Tylers Cl. Kin L 138 C2
Tylers Cswy. New St 132 B1
Tylers Hill Rd. Bot 150 A4
Tylers Mead. Luton 45 F3
Tylers Way. Bus 168 C2
Tylers Wood. Brn Gr 90 B3
Tylers. Harp 86 B1
Tylersfield. Abb L 154 A4
Tynedale. Lon C 142 C2
Tynemouth Dri. Enf 162 A1
Tynfield Rd. Hod 115 D1
Typledean Cl. Heml H 124 B3
Tysoe Ave. Enf 162 C1
Tythe Rd. Luton 44 B3
Tyttenhanger Green. Tyt 142 C4

Uckfield Rd. Enf 162 B1
Ufford Cl. Har 176 A2
Ufford Rd. Har 176 A2
Ullswater Rd. Heml H 125 E1
Underacres Cl. Heml H 125 D2
Underwood Rd. Stev 36 B1
Union Green. Heml H 124 B3
Union St. Barn 171 F3
Union St. Luton 63 F3
Union Terr. Bun 40 C4
Unity Rd. Enf 162 B1
University Cl. Bus 168 A3
Unwin Cl. Letw 22 C2
Unwin Pl. Stev 51 E2
Unwin Rd. Stev 51 E2
Updale Cl. Pot B 158 C3
Uplands Ave. Hit 35 D3
Uplands Dri. Bro Pk 145 D3
Uplands The. Bri Wd 140 C1
Uplands The. Harp 107 D2
Uplands. Brag 55 F3
Uplands. Cro Gr 165 F2
Uplands. Luton 44 B4
Uplands. Stev 51 E4
Uplands. Ware 93 F1
Uplands. Wel GC 89 E1
Upper Ashlyns Rd. Berk 122 A2
Upper Barn. Heml H 138 C4
Upper Clabdens. Ware 93 F1
Upper Culver Rd. St Alb 127 F3
Upper Dagnall St. St Alb 127 E2
Upper Ditch. Watf 167 F1
Upper George St. Luton 63 E4
Upper Green Rd. Tewin 90 C1
Upper Green. Tewin 90 B2
Upper Hall Park. Berk 122 B1
Upper Heath Rd. St Alb 127 F3
Upper Highway. Abb L 153 E3
Upper Hill Rise. Ric 165 D2
Upper Icknield Way. Dra B 99 D2
Upper Icknield Way. Pit 80 C1
Upper Icknield Way. Tri 100 B4
Upper Lattimore Rd. St Alb 127 F2
Upper Marlborough Rd. St Alb127 F2
Upper Maylins. Letw 23 E2
Upper Paddock Rd. Watf 167 F2
Upper Park. Harl 117 D1
Upper Sales. Heml H 123 F1
Upper Sean. Stev 51 D2
Upper Shot. Wel GC 111 D4
Upper Shott. Ham St 147 F3
Upper Station Rd. Radl 156 A2
Upper Tail. Watf 175 F4
Upper Tilehouse St. Hit 34 B4
Upperfield Rd. Wel GC 110 C3
Upperstone Cl. Stot 11 F3
Upshire Rd. Wa Aby 163 F4
Upton Ave. St Alb 127 E2
Upton Cl. Luton 45 E3
Upton Cl. Pk St 141 E3
Upton Lodge Cl. Bus 168 B1
Upton Rd. Watf 167 D3
Upwell Rd. Luton 46 A1
Uranus Rd. Heml H 124 C3
Urban Rd. Bis St 77 D4
Uxbridge Rd (Hatch End). Pnr175 F2
Uxbridge Rd (Pinner). Pnr 175 E1
Uxbridge Rd. Har 176 B2
Uxbridge Rd. Pnr 176 A2
Uxbridge Rd. Ric 173 D4

Vadis Cl. Luton 44 C4
Vale Ave. Bor 170 A2
Vale Cl. Harp 85 E2
Vale Ct. Whea 108 B4
Vale Dri. Barn 171 F3
Vale Rd. Bus 167 F2
Valence Dri. Ches 148 A2
Valency Cl. Norwd 174 C3
Valerian Way. Stev 37 E1
Valerian Way. Stev 51 E4
Valerie Cl. St Alb 128 A2
Valeside. Hertng 113 D3
Vallans Cl. Ware 93 E2
Vallansgate. Stev 51 D1
Valley Cl. Hert 113 E3
Valley Cl. Stu 82 A2
Valley Cl. Wa Aby 163 E4
Valley Cl. Ware 93 D1
Valley Green The. Wel GC 110 B4
Valley Green. Heml H 105 D1
Valley l. Pnr 175 D1
Valley La. Fla 83 F1
Valley Rd. Berk 121 F3
Valley Rd. Chor 165 D2
Valley Rd. Cod 67 F1
Valley Rd. Letw 22 B4
Valley Rd. St Alb 127 F4
Valley Rd. Stu 82 A2
Valley Rd. Wel GC 110 A3
Valley Rise. Bla En 86 C1
Valley Rise. Roystn 7 F3
Valley Rise. Watf 154 A3
Valley The. Whit 66 C4
Valley View. Barn 171 F2
Valley View. Gofs O 147 E1
Valley Way. Stev 51 D2
Valley Wlk. Cro Gr 166 B2
Valleyside. Heml H 123 F2
Vanda Cres. St Alb 127 F1
Vantorts Cl. Saw 97 F1
Vantorts Rd. Saw 97 F1
Vardon Rd. Stev 50 C4
Varna Cl. Luton 45 D2
Varney Cl. Ches 148 A2
Varney Cl. Heml H 123 F2
Varney Rd. Heml H 123 F2
Vaugham Rd. Harp 86 A1
Vaughan Mead. Red 106 A2
Vaughan Rd. Stot 11 F4
Vauxhall Rd. Heml H 125 D2
Vauxhall Rd. Luton 64 A3
Vauxhall Way. Luton 46 A1
Vega Cres. Norwd 174 C3
Vega Rd. Bus 168 B1
Velizy Ave. Harl 117 E1
Venetia Rd. Luton 46 A2
Ventnor Gdns. Luton 45 D4
Venus Hill. Bov 151 D4
Ver Rd. Red 106 B3
Ver Rd. St Alb 127 E2
Vera Ct. Watf 167 E1
Verdure Cl. Watf 154 C4
Verity Way. Stev 51 D4
Veritys. Hat 130 A3
Verney Cl. Berk 121 F3
Verney Cl. Tri 100 B3
Vernon Ave. Enf 162 C2
Vernon Dri. Hare 173 E1
Vernon Rd. Bus 167 F2
Vernon Rd. Luton 63 E4
Vernon's Cl. St Alb 127 F1
Verulam Cl. Wel GC 110 C3
Verulam Gdns. Luton 44 C3
Verulam Pas. Watf 167 D4
Verulam Rd. Hit 34 C4
Verulam Rd. St Alb 127 E2
Verwood Rd. Har 176 B1
Vespers Cl. Luton 44 A1
Vesta Ave. St Alb 141 E4
Vesta Rd. Heml H 124 C3
Viaduct Rd. Gt Am 114 C4
Viaduct Way. Wel GC 89 F1
Vian Ave. Enf 162 C2
Vicarage Cl. Ch En 11 D4
Vicarage Cl. Heml H 124 B1
Vicarage Cl. Nort 145 F1
Vicarage Cl. St Alb 141 E4
Vicarage Cl. Stand 55 F1
Vicarage Cswy. Hert H 114 A2
Vicarage Gdns. Fla 84 A1
Vicarage Gdns. Mars 80 A1
Vicarage Gdns. Pot En 123 D4
Vicarage La. Bov 137 D2
Vicarage La. Ivin 80 C3
Vicarage La. Kin L 138 C1
Vicarage La. Wat 92 A2
Vicarage Rd Prec. Watf 167 D3
Vicarage Rd. Bun 40 C4
Vicarage Rd. Mars 80 A1
Vicarage Rd. Pit 80 C2
Vicarage Rd. Pot En 123 D4
Vicarage Rd. Ware 93 F1
Vicarage Rd. Watf 167 D2
Vicarage Rd. Wigg 100 B1
Vicarage St. Luton 63 F4
Vicarage Wood. Harl 118 A1
Victoria Cl. Ric 165 E1
Victoria Cl. Stev 50 B4
Victoria Cres. Roystn 7 E4
Victoria La. Barn 171 F3
Victoria Pas. Watf 167 D3
Victoria Rd. Berk 122 B2
Victoria Rd. Bus 168 A1
Victoria Rd. Harp 86 A1
Victoria Rd. Hit 34 B4
Victoria Rd. Wa Aby 163 E3
Victoria Rd. Watf 154 A1
Victoria St. Luton 63 F3
Victoria St. St Alb 127 F2
Victors Way. Barn 171 F3
Victory Rd. Berk 122 A3
View Rd. Pot B 159 E4
Vigors Croft. Hat 129 F2
Villa Rd. Luton 63 E4
Village St. Lan 49 F1
Villiers Cres. St Alb 128 B3
Villiers Rd. Watf 167 F2
Villiers St. Hert 113 F3
Villiers-Sur-Marne Ave. Bis St 76 B3
Vincent Cl. Ches 148 C2
Vincent Ct. Norwd 174 C1
Vincent Rd. Luton 44 B3
Vincent. Letw 23 E2
Vincenzo Cl. Wel Gr 144 B4
Vine Cl. Wel GC 110 C4
Vine Gr. H Wy 117 F3
Vineyard Hill. Nort 146 A1
Vineyard The. Ware 94 A1
Vineyard The. Wel GC 89 F1
Vineyards Rd. Nort 146 A1
Vineyards The. Ware 94 A1
Vinters Ave. Stev 50 C3
Violet Ave. Enf 161 E1
Violet Way. Chor 165 E3
Violets La. Fur P 43 D3
Virgil Dri. Hod 148 C4
Viscount Cl. Luton 45 D3
Vivian Cl. Watf 167 D1
Vivian Gdns. Watf 167 D1
Vixen Dri. Hert 114 A3
Vyse Cl. Barn 171 E3

Wacketts. Ham St 148 A2
Waddesdon Cl. Luton 46 B1
Waddington Rd. St Alb 127 E2
Wade The. Wel GC 111 D2
Wades The. Hat 130 A1
Wadesmill Rd. Cha En 92 B2
Wadesmill Rd. Hert 92 B1
Wadesmill Rd. Ware 93 E1
Wadham Rd. Abb 153 F4
Wadhurst Ave. Luton 45 E2
Wadley Cl. Heml H 124 C1
Wadnall Way. Kneb 68 C2
Waggon Rd. Barn 159 E1
Wagon Rd. Pot B 159 D2
Wagon Way. Chor 165 E3
Wain Cl. Pot B 145 D1
Wakefields Wlk. Ches 162 B4
Walcot Ave. Luton 46 A1
Waldeck Rd. Luton 63 E4
Waldegrave Park. Harp 86 B1
Walden End. Stev 50 C2
Walden Pl. Wel GC 110 B4
Walden Rd. Wel GC 110 B4
Waleran Cl. Stan 176 C3
Waleys Cl. Luton 44 C4
Walfords Cl. Harl 118 B2
Walk The. Hertng 113 D3
Walk The. Pot B 159 D4
Walkern Rd. Benn 70 A4
Walkern Rd. Stev 50 B4
Walkern Rd. Stev 51 E4
Walkern Rd. Wal 52 B3
Walkern Rd. Wat St 70 B3
Walkers Cl. Harp 107 E4
Walkers Rd. Harp 107 D4
Wallace Way. Letw 22 A1
Waller Ave. Luton 44 C2
Waller Dr. Norwd 175 D1
Waller St Mall. Luton 63 F4
Waller's Cl. Gt Ch 9 F1
Wallers Way. Hod 115 D1
Wallingford Wlk. St Alb 141 E4
Wallington Rd. Clo 13 E1
Wallington Rd. Wall 14 A1
Walmar Cl. Barn 159 E1
Walnut Ave. Bal 24 A4
Walnut Cl. Chis 141 D2
Walnut Cl. Hit 35 D3
Walnut Cl. Luton 46 A2
Walnut Cl. Stot 11 F3
Walnut Ct. Wel GC 110 C2
Walnut Dri. Bis St 76 B2
Walnut Gr. Heml H 124 B2
Walnut Gr. Wel GC 110 C2
Walnut Green. Bus 167 F4
Walnut Tree Ave. Saw 97 F2
Walnut Tree Cl. Ches 162 B4
Walnut Tree Cl. Hod 135 D3
Walnut Tree Cl. Stev 51 E2
Walnut Tree Cres. Saw 97 F2
Walnut Tree Rd. Pirt 20 B2
Walnut Tree Wlk. Gt Am 114 C3
Walnut Way. Ick 21 F2
Walpole Cl. Pnr 176 A2
Walsh Cl. Hit 34 B4
Walsham Cl. Stev 69 E4
Walshford Way. Bor 157 D1
Walsingham Cl. Hat 129 F4
Walsingham Cl. Luton 45 E4
Walsingham Way. Lon C 142 B2
Waltham Gdns. Enf 162 B1
Waltham Rd. Hit 34 C3
Waltham Rd. Lo Naz 149 F3
Walton Gdns. Wa Aby 163 D3
Walton Rd. Bus 167 E3
Walton Rd. Gt Am 114 B4
Walton Rd. Hod 135 E4
Walton St. St Alb 127 F3
Walverns Cl. Watf 167 E2
Wandon Cl. Luton 46 B2
Wannions Cl. Bot 136 A1
Wansford Park. Bor 170 C3
Warburton Cl. Har 176 B2
Ward Cl. Ham St 148 A2
Ward Cl. Ware 93 E1
Ward Cres. Bis St 76 C3
Warden Hill Cl. Luton 45 E4
Warden Hill Gdns. Luton 45 E4
Warden Hill Rd. Luton 45 E4
Wardown Cres. Luton 45 F1
Ware Park Rd. Hert 113 F4
Ware Rd. Gt Am 115 D1
Ware Rd. Hert 113 F3
Ware Rd. Hod 135 D4
Ware Rd. Sac 71 E1
Ware Rd. Tonw 92 C4
Ware Rd. Wat St 71 D2
Ware Rd. Widf 95 E2
Wareham's La. Hert 113 E3
Warenford Way. Bor 170 A4
Wareside Cl. Wel GC 111 D3
Wareside. Heml H 105 D1
Warham Rd. Har 176 C1
Warmark Rd. Heml H 123 F3
Warneford Pl. Watf 167 F2
Warner Rd. Gt Am 114 B4
Warners Ave. Hod 134 C2
Warners Cl. Stev 51 E2
Warners End Rd. Heml H 124 A2
Warren Cl. Hat 130 A4
Warren Cl. Letw 22 B4
Warren Dale. Wel GC 89 E1
Warren Dri The. Nwml E 64 B1
Warren Gr. Bor 170 B3
Warren Green. Hat 130 A4
Warren La. Clo 24 B4
Warren La. Stan 176 C4
Warren Park Rd. Hert 113 E4
Warren Rd. Bus 168 B1
Warren Rd. Luton 62 C4
Warren Rd. St Alb 141 E4
Warren Terr. Hert 113 E4
Warren The. Harp 107 D3
Warren The. Radl 156 A3
Warren The. Roystn 7 E3
Warren Way. Har Gr 89 F2
Warrenfield Cl. Ches 162 A4
Warrengate La. Pot B 144 B1
Warrengate Rd. Wa En 144 B2
Warrensgreen La. Wa Gr 37 E3
Warton Green. Luton 46 C1
Warwick Ave. Cuf 146 B2
Warwick Cl. Bus 168 C1
Warwick Cl. Cuf 146 B2
Warwick Cl. Hert 113 E2
Warwick Dri. Ches 148 B2
Warwick Gdns. Pot B 158 C1
Warwick Rd E. Luton 63 D4
Warwick Rd W. Luton 63 D4
Warwick Rd. Bis St 77 D3
Warwick Rd. Bor 170 B3
Warwick Rd. Enf 162 C1
Warwick Rd. St Alb 127 F3
Warwick Rd. Stev 51 E3
Warwick Way. Cro Gr 166 B3
Wash La. Pot B 158 B3
Wash The. Hert 113 E3
Wash The. Sto P 43 D3
Washington Ave. Heml H 124 C4
Watchlytes. Wel GC 111 E3
Watchmead. Wel GC 111 D3
Water End Rd. Heml H 123 E4
Water La. Bed 139 D1
Water La. Berk 122 B2
Water La. Bis St 76 C4
Water La. Bov 137 D1
Water La. Hert 113 E3
Water La. Hit 21 F1
Water La. Sta Mo 59 F3
Water La. Watf 167 E3
Water Row. Ware 93 E1
Waterbeach. Wel GC 111 E3
Watercress Cl. Stev 51 E3
Waterdale. Hert 113 E2
Waterdell La. Gos 35 D1
Waterend La. A St P 88 B1
Waterend La. Red 106 A3
Waterend La. Whea 109 E4
Waterfield. Wel GC 111 D4
Waterford Comm. Wat 92 A1
Waterford Green. Wel GC 111 D3
Watergate The. Watf 175 E4
Waterhouse St. Heml H 124 B1
Waterloo La. Hol 21 D3
Waterman Cl. Watf 167 D2
Waterman's Yd. Watf 167 E3
Watermead Rd. Luton 44 C3
Watermill Est. Bun 40 C3
Watermill La. Hert 113 E4
Waters Dri. Ric 165 F1
Waterside. Berk 122 B2
Waterside. Kin L 139 D1
Waterside. Lon C 142 C2
Waterside. Sta Mo 59 F3
Waterside. Wel GC 90 A1
Waterslade Green. Luton 45 D3
Watery La. Fla 84 C2
Watery La. Hat 129 F2
Watery La. Lon C 142 B2
Watery La. Mars 79 F1
Watford By-Ps. Elst 169 D1
Watford Field Rd. Watf 167 E2
Watford Heath. Watf 167 E1
Watford Rd. Abb L 153 E3
Watford Rd. Chis 141 D3
Watford Rd. Cro Gr 166 A2
Watford Rd. Elst 169 E2
Watford Rd. Kin L 153 D4
Watford Rd. Radl 155 F2
Watford Rd. St Alb 141 D4
Watling Cl. Heml H 124 C3
Watling Knoll. Radl 155 F3
Watling St. Pk St 141 E3
Watling St. St Alb 141 E4
Watling View. St Alb 141 E4
Watlington Rd. Harl 118 B2
Watson Ave. St Alb 127 F3

Watson's Walk. St Alb 127 F1
Watton Rd. Dat 69 F1
Watton Rd. Kneb 69 D3
Watton Rd. Ware 93 E1
Watton Rd. Wat St 70 A1
Watts Cl. L Had 57 E1
Waulds Bank Dri. Luton 44 C4
Wavell Cl. Ches 148 C2
Waveney Rd. Harp 86 B2
Waveney. Heml H 124 C4
Waverley Cl. Stev 69 D4
Waverley Gdns. Norwd 175 D1
Waverley Rd. St Alb 127 E3
Waxhouse Gate. St Alb 127 E2
Waxwell Cl. Pnr 175 E1
Waxwell La. Pnr 175 E1
Wayre St. Harl 118 B2
Wayre The. Harl 118 B2
Waysbrook. Letw 23 D2
Wayside Ave. Bus 168 B2
Wayside The. Heml H 125 E1
Wayside. Chipf 138 A1
Wayside. Pot B 159 E3
Waysmeet. Letw 23 D2
Waytemore Rd. Bis St 76 C3
Weald La. Har 176 B1
Weald Rise. Har 176 C1
Wealdwood Gdns. Pnr 176 A2
Weall Green. Watf 154 A4
Weatherby Rd. Luton 44 B1
Weavers Rd. Tri 99 F2
Webb Rise. Stev 51 D4
Webber Cl. Elst 169 E2
Wedgewood Cl. Norwd 174 B2
Wedgewood Way. Stev 37 D1
Wedgwood Ct. Stev 37 E2
Wedgwood Park. Stev 37 E1
Wedmore Rd. Hit 35 D3
Wedon Way. Byg 4 B2
Weedon Cl. Henlw 10 B3
Weighton Rd. Har 176 B1
Welbeck Cl. Bor 170 A3
Welbeck Rd. Luton 63 F4
Welbeck Rise. Harp 107 E3
Welbury Ave. Luton 45 E4
Welch Pl. Pnr 175 E1
Welclose St. St Alb 127 E2
Welham Cl. Wel Gr 144 B4
Welham Manor. Wel Gr 144 B4
Well App. Barn 171 E2
Well Croft. Heml H 124 A2
Well End Rd. Shen 157 E1
Well Garth. Wel GC 110 C3
Well Green. Bram 91 E2
Well La. Cra 61 D4
Well La. Harl 117 D1
Well Rd. Barn 171 E2
Well Rd. Nort 145 F1
Well-Row. Bay 132 C3
Wellands. Hat 130 A4
Wellbury Terr. Heml H 125 E2
Wellcroft Cl. Wel GC 111 D2
Wellcroft Rd. Wel GC 111 D2
Wellcroft. Ivin 80 C3
Wellen Rise. Heml H 138 C4
Wellers Gr. Ches 148 A2
Wellesley Ave. Norwd 174 C3
Wellesley Cres. Pot B 158 C3
Wellfield Ave. Luton 44 B4
Wellfield Cl. Hat 130 A3
Wellfield Rd. Hat 130 A3
Wellgate Rd. Luton 44 B1
Wellhouse Cl. Luton 63 D4
Wellhouse La. Barn 171 E3
Wellingham Ave. Hit 21 E1
Wellington Ave. Pnr 175 F1
Wellington Dri. Wel GC 111 E3
Wellington Pl. Knee 2 A3
Wellington Rd. Lon C 142 B3
Wellington Rd. Pnr 175 F1
Wellington Rd. St Alb 128 A1
Wellington Rd. Stev 51 E3
Wellington Rd. Watf 167 D4
Wellington St. Hert 113 D4
Wellington St. Luton 63 E3
Wells Cl. Harp 85 F2
Wells Yard. Watf 167 D3
Wellside Cl. Barn 171 E3
Wellstones. Watf 167 D3
Wellswood Cl. Heml H 125 D2
Welsummer Way. Ches 148 B2
Weltmore Rd. Luton 44 C3
Welwyn By Pass Rd. Welw 89 E2
Welwyn Ct. Heml H 124 C4
Welwyn Rd. Herts 112 C4
Wendover Cl. Harp 86 B1
Wendover Cl. St Alb 128 B4
Wendover Dri. Welw 89 E3
Wendover Way. Bus 168 B2
Wendover Way. Luton 45 F2
Wengeo La. Ware 93 D1
Wenlock St. Luton 63 F4
Wensley Cl. Harp 107 E3
Wensley Dale. Luton 45 F1
Wensleydale. Heml H 124 C3
Wensum Way. Ric 165 E1
Wentbridge Path. Bor 157 D1
Wentworth Ave. Elst 169 F2
Wentworth Ave. Luton 44 B3
Wentworth Cl. Pot B 159 D4
Wentworth Cl. Watf 153 F1
Wentworth Cotts. Hod 134 C1
Wentworth Dri. Bis St 76 B3
Wentworth Rd. Barn 171 E3
Wentworth Rd. Hert 113 E2
Wenwell Cl. Dra B 99 D2
Wesley Ave. Hert 113 E3
Wesley Cl. Arl 11 D2
Wesley Cl. Gofs O 147 E2
Wesley Rd. Mark 83 F3
Wessex Dri. Pnr 175 F2
West Alley. Hit 34 C4
West Ave. Bal 23 F4
West Ave. Chis 141 D3
West Burrowfield. Wel GC 110 B2
West Chantry. Har 176 A1
West Cl. Barn 171 D2
West Cl. Hit 22 A1
West Cl. Hod 135 D4
West Cl. Stev 50 C3
West Comm. Harp 107 D3
West Common Cl. Harp 107 D3
West Common Gr. Harp 107 D3
West Common Way. Harp 107 D3
West Dene. Gt Ga 104 A4
West Dri. Arl 11 D2
West Dri. Har 176 B2
West Dri. Watf 154 A2
West Drive Gdns. Har 176 B2
West End La. Barn 171 E3
West End Rd. Bric 147 F4
West End Rd. Ched 79 F4
West End. Ashw 4 B2
West Gate. Harl 117 E1
West Hill Rd. Hod 135 D4
West Hill Rd. Luton 63 F3
West Hill. Hit 34 B4
West Hyde La. C St P 172 A2
West La. Gt Of 33 E1
West La. Pirt 20 B3
West Leith. Tri 99 F1
West Mead. Wel GC 111 D2
West Rd. Berk 122 A3
West Rd. Bis St 76 C3
West Rd. Harl 118 A2
West Rd. Saw 97 E2
West Rd. Sta Mo 59 F3
West Reach. Stev 50 C1
West Riding. Bri Wd 140 C1
West Riding. Tewin 90 B3
West Side Centre. Luton 63 E4
West Side. Hod 148 C3
West Sq. Harl 117 E1
West St. Hert 113 E3
West St. Lily 32 B1
West St. Ware 93 E1
West Valley Rd. Fel 138 B4
West View Gdns. Elst 169 E2
West View Rd. St Alb 127 E2
West View. Hat 130 A4
West View. Letw 22 C3
West Way. Harp 86 B1
West Way. Ric 165 D1
West Way. Wa Aby 163 D1
Westall Cl. Hert 113 E3
Westall Mews. Hert 113 E3
Westbourne Rd. Luton 45 D1
Westbrook Cl. Ste Mo 5 D4
Westbury Cl. Hit 34 B4
Westbury Gdns. Luton 45 F2
Westbury Pl. Letw 22 C3
Westbury Rd. Norwd 174 C4
Westbury Rd. Watf 167 D2
Westbush Cl. Hod 114 C1
Westcott. Wel GC 111 E4
Westcroft Cl. Enf 162 B1
Westcroft Ct. Hod 135 D2
Westell Cl. Bal 24 A4
Westerdale. Heml H 124 C3
Westerdale. Luton 44 A3
Western Ave. Henlw 10 A2
Western Cl. Letw 11 F1
Western Rd. Lo Naz 135 F1
Western Rd. Luton 63 E3
Western Rd. Tri 99 F2
Western Way. Letw 11 F1
Westfield Ave. Harp 86 A2
Westfield Ave. Watf 154 B1
Westfield Cl. Bis St 76 C4
Westfield Cl. Ches 162 C4
Westfield Cl. Hit 34 B4
Westfield Ct. St Alb 128 B3
Westfield Dri. Harp 86 A2
Westfield La. Hit 34 B4
Westfield Park. Pnr 175 F2
Westfield Pl. Harp 86 A2
Westfield Rd. Berk 121 F3
Westfield Rd. Bis St 76 C4
Westfield Rd. Harp 86 A2
Westfield Rd. Hert 113 E4
Westfield Rd. Hod 134 C4
Westfield Wlk. Ches 162 C4
Westfield. Wel GC 111 D4
Westfields. St Alb 141 D4
Westgate. Stev 50 B3
Westholm. Letw 22 C4
Westland Dri. Bro Pk 144 C2
Westland Rd. Kneb 69 D3
Westland Rd. Watf 167 D4
Westlea Ave. Watf 154 C1
Westlea Cl. Hod 148 C4
Westlea Rd. Hod 148 C4
Westlecote Gdns. Luton 45 E2
Westly Wood. Wel GC 111 D4
Westmeade Cl. Ches 148 A1
Westmill La. Ick 21 E1
Westmill Rd. Hit 21 E1
Westmill Rd. Thun 93 D2
Westminster Ct. St Alb 127 E1
Westmorland Ave. Luton 44 C3
Weston Ave. Roystn 7 E4
Weston Rd. Stev 36 C1
Weston Way. Bal 23 F4
Westray. Heml H 125 E1
Westridge Cl. Heml H 123 F2
Westview Ct. Elst 169 E2
Westview Rise. Heml H 124 B2
Westway. Luton 46 B2
Westwick Cl. Heml H 125 E1
Westwick Row. Heml H 125 F1
Westwood Ave. Hit 35 D3
Westwood Cl. Pot B 145 D1
Wetherby Cl. Stev 51 E4
Wetherby Rd. Bor 169 F4
Wetherby Rd. Enf 161 E1
Wetherfield. Sta Mo 59 E4
Wetherne Link. Luton 44 B3
Wexham Cl. Luton 44 C4
Weybourne Cl. Harp 86 B1
Weybourne Dri. Luton 45 E4
Weymouth St. Heml H 138 B4
Whaley Rd. Pot B 159 E3
Wharf La. Nthch 121 E4
Wharf La. Ric 165 F1
Wharf Rd. Bis St 76 C3
Wharf Rd. Heml H 124 A1
Wharf Rd. Hod 148 C4
Wharfedale. Heml H 124 C3
Wheat Cl. St Alb 128 A4
Wheat Croft. Bis St 76 C2
Wheat Hill. Letw 22 C4
Wheatbarn. Wel GC 111 D4
Wheatcotes. Dat 69 E1
Wheatcroft. Ches 148 A2
Wheatfield Ave. Harp 107 D3
Wheatfield Cres. Roystn 7 F3
Wheatfield Rd. Harp 107 D2
Wheatfield. Hat 130 A3
Wheatfield. Heml H 124 B3
Wheatfields. Saw 118 B3
Wheathampstead Pl. Whea 87 E1
Wheathampstead Rd. Harp 107 F4
Wheatlands. Stev 51 E4
Wheatley Cl. Saw 97 E1
Wheatley Cl. Wel GC 111 D2
Wheatley Rd. Wel GC 111 D2
Wheatleys. St Alb 128 B3
Wheatlock Mead. Red 106 A3
Wheatsheaf Dri. Ware 93 D2
Wheatsheaf Rd. Hun 95 E1
Wheelers Cl. Lo Naz 135 F1
Wheelers La. Heml H 124 C1
Wheelright Cl. Bus 168 A2
Whempstead La. Wat St 71 D3
Whempstead Rd. Heb En 52 C1
Whetstone Cl. Wl Gr 89 F4
Whinbush Gr. Hit 34 C4
Whinbush Rd. Hit 34 C4
Whippendell Hill. Chipf 138 B1
Whippendell Rd. Watf 166 C2
Whipperley Ring. Luton 63 D3
Whipperley Way. Luton 63 E3
Whisper Wood. Chor 165 D3
Whitby Rd. Luton 45 E1
White Bear. Sta Mo 59 F4
White Crofts. Stot 11 F3
White Gate Gdns. Har 176 C2
White Hart Cl. Bun 40 C4
White Hart Dri. Heml H 124 C1
White Hart Rd. Heml H 125 D1
White Hedge Dri. St Alb 127 E3
White Hill. Ash Gr 136 B4
White Hill. Fla 105 D4
White Hill. Heml H 123 F1
White Hill. Ric 174 A2
White Hill. Wal 38 B1
White Hill. Welw 89 D2
White Horse La. Brn Gr 90 B4
White Horse La. Lon C 142 C3
White Horse La. Wl Gr 69 D1
White La. L Alm 49 E4
White Lion St. Heml H 138 B4
White Orchs. N20 171 F1
White Post Field. Saw 97 E1
White Shack La. Cha Cr 152 C1
White Stubbs La. Bay 133 D1
White Stubbs La. Bric 133 E1
White Stubbs La. Hod 134 B1
White Way The. Stev 51 E4
Whitebarns La. Fur P 43 D3
Whitebarns. Fur P 43 D3
Whitebeam Cl. Ham St 147 F3
Whitebeams. Chis 141 E2
Whitebeams. Hat 130 A1
Whitebroom Rd. Heml H 123 F3
Whitechurch Cl. Luton 46 B1
Whitechurch Gdns. Letw 23 E2
Whitecroft Rd. Luton 64 A4
Whitecroft. St Alb 142 A4
Whitefield Ave. Luton 44 B4
Whitefields Rd. Ches 148 B2
Whitefriars Ave. Har 176 C1
Whitefriars Dri. Har 176 C1
Whitefriars Trad Est. Har 176 B1
Whitegale Cl. Hit 35 D3
Whitegates Cl. Cro Gr 166 A3
Whitehall Cl. Lo Naz 135 F1
Whitehall La. Bis St 58 C1
Whitehall Rd. Bis St 58 C1
Whitehands Cl. Hod 134 C3
Whitehart Cross. Bov 136 B2
Whitehicks. Letw 12 A1
Whitehill Ave. Luton 63 E3
Whitehill Ct. Berk 122 B3
Whitehill Rd. Hit 35 D3
Whitehill. Berk 122 B3
Whitehorn Way. Luton 63 D3
Whitehorse St. Bal 12 C1
Whitehorse Vale. Luton 45 D4
Whitehouse Ave. Bor 170 A3
Whitehouse La. Bed 140 B2
Whitehurst Ave. Hit 21 F1
Whitelands Ave. Chor 164 B3
Whiteleaf Rd. Heml H 138 B4
Whiteley Cl. Dan En 71 F4
Whiteley La. Buck 27 E4
Whitesmead Rd. Stev 50 C4
Whitestone Wlk. Heml H 124 A3
Whitethorn La. Letw 23 D2
Whitethorn. Wel GC 111 D3
Whitewaites. Harl 117 F1
Whiteway. Letw 23 E2
Whitewaybottom La. Pet Gr 66 A2
Whitewebbs La. Enf 161 F2
Whitewebbs Rd. Enf 161 E2
Whitewood Rd. Berk 122 A2
Whitfield Way. Ric 164 C1
Whitings Cl. Harp 86 B2
Whitings Rd. Barn 171 E2
Whitlars Dri. Kin L 138 C2
Whitley Rd. Hod 135 D4
Whitney Dri. Stev 36 B1
Whittingham Cl. Luton 46 C1
Whittingstall Rd. Hod 135 D4
Whittington La. Stev 50 C2
Whittington Way. Bis St 76 C2
Whittle Cl. Henlw 10 A2
Whittlesea Cl. Har 176 B2
Whittlesea Path. Har 176 B1
Whittlesea Rd. Har 176 B1
Whitwell Cl. Luton 45 D4
Whitwell Rd. Watf 154 B2
Whitworth Jones Ave. Henlw 10 B3
Whitworth Rd. Stev 37 D2
Whomerley Rd. Stev 50 C2
Whydale Rd. Roystn 7 F3
Whytingham Rd. Tri 100 B2
Wick Ave. Whea 108 B4
Wick Hill. Ken Co 82 C4
Wick Rd. Wigg 120 B4
Wick The. Hert 92 B1
Wicken Fields. Ware 93 E2
Wickets The. Luton 45 E1
Wickfield Cl. Wl Gr 69 D1
Wickham Cl. Hare 173 E1
Wickham Rd. Har 176 B1
Wickham Way. Stand 55 E2
Wicklands Rd. Hun 116 B4
Wickmere Cl. Luton 45 E4
Wickstead Ave. Luton 44 C2
Wickwood Ct. St Alb 128 A2
Widbury Gdns. Ware 93 F1
Widbury Hill. Ware 94 A1
Widford Rd. Had Cr 95 F4
Widford Rd. Hun 95 E1
Widford Rd. Wel GC 111 D3
Widford Terr. Heml H 105 D1
Widgeon Way. Watf 154 C2
Widmore Dri. Heml H 125 D3
Wieland Rd. Norwd 175 D2
Wiggenhall Rd. Watf 167 E2
Wigginton Bottom. Wigg 120 C4
Wigmore La. Luton 46 B1
Wigmores N. Wel GC 110 B4
Wigmores S. Wel GC 110 B3
Wigram Way. Stev 51 D2
Wilbury Cl. Letw 22 B4
Wilbury Hills Rd. Letw 22 B3
Wilbury Rd. Letw 22 C4
Wilbury Way. Hit 22 A1
Wilcot Ave. Watf 167 F1
Wilcox Cl. Bor 170 B4
Wild Cherry Dri. Luton 63 E3
Wild Oaks Cl. Norwd 174 C2
Wilderness. Berk 122 B2
Wildwood Ave. Bri Wd 140 C1
Wildwood La. Stev 50 C2
Wildwood. Norwd 174 B2
Wilford Cl. Norwd 174 B2
Wilga Rd. Welw 89 D3
Wilkin's Green La. St Alb 129 E2
Willenhall Cl. Luton 45 D4
William Covell Cl. Enf 160 C1
William Pl. Stev 51 D2
William St. Berk 122 B2
William St. Bus 167 E3
William St. Luton 45 F1
William St. Mark 83 F3
Williams Way. Radl 156 B2
Williamson St. Luton 63 F4
Willian Church Rd. Will 23 D
Willian Rd. Hit 22 C
Willian Rd. Will 23 D
Willian Way. Bal 23 F
Willian Way. Letw 23 D
Willinghall Cl. Wa Aby 163 E
Williton Rd. Luton 46 B
Willoughby Cl. Hod 134 C
Willoughby Rd. Harp 86 A
Willoughby Way. Hit 35 D
Willow Cl. Bis St 76 C
Willow Cl. Gt Ho 42 A
Willow Cl. Ham St 147 F
Willow Cl. Reed 16 B
Willow Cres. St Alb 128 B
Willow Dene. Bus 168 C
Willow Dene. Pnr 175 E
Willow Dri. Barn 171 F
Willow Edge. Kin L 139 D
Willow End. Norwd 175 D
Willow Gr. Wel GC 89 E
Willow Green. Bor 170 B
Willow La. Hit 34 B3
Willow La. Watf 167 D
Willow Mead. Saw 97 F1
Willow Path. Wa Aby 163 F3
Willow Way. Chis 141 D
Willow Way. Harp 86 B2
Willow Way. Hat 129 F1
Willow Way. Heml H 124 A3
Willow Way. Luton 44 C3
Willow Way. Pot B 159 D3
Willow Way. Radl 155 F2
Willow Wlk. Wl Gr 89 E4
Willowby Ct. Lon C 142 B3
Willowdene. Ches 148 C2
Willowgate Trading Est. Luton 44 A4
Willowmead. Hertng 113 D3
Willows Cl. Pnr 175 E1
Willows Link. Stev 51 D1
Willows The. Hit 35 D3
Willows The. Ric 173 D4
Willows The. St Alb 142 A4
Willows The. Stev 51 D1
Willows The. Watf 167 D1
Willowside Way. Roystn 7 E4
Willowside. Lon C 142 C2
Wilsden Ave. Luton 63 E3
Wilshere Ave. St Alb 127 E1
Wilshere Cres. Hit 35 E4
Wilshere Rd. Welw 89 D2
Wilsmere Dri. Har 176 C2
Wilsons La. Ashw 4 B2
Wilstone Dri. St Alb 128 B4
Wilton Cl. Bis St 77 D4
Wilton Cres. Hert 113 E2
Wilton Rd. Hit 21 F1
Wilton Way. Hert 113 E2
Wiltshire Rd. Stev 51 D2
Wimborne Cl. Saw 97 E1
Wimborne Gr. Watf 153 F1
Wimborne Rd. Luton 63 E4
Wimple Rd. Luton 44 A1
Winch Cl. Cod 88 C4
Winch St. Luton 45 F1
Winchdells. Heml H 139 D4
Winches Farm Dri. St Alb 128 B2
Winchester Cl. Bis St 76 B2
Winchester Cl. Stev 37 D1
Winchester Rd. Norwd 174 C1
Winchester Way. Cro Gr 166 A2
Winchfield Way. Chor 165 E1
Windermere Ave. St Alb 128 A1
Windermere Cl. Chor 164 B2
Windermere Cl. Heml H 125 E1
Windermere Cres. Luton 44 C3
Windhill Fields. Bis St 76 C4
Windhill Old Rd. Bis St 76 C4
Windhill. Bis St 76 C4
Windhill. Wel GC 111 D4
Winding Hill. Muc H 75 D2
Winding Shot. Heml H 124 A2
Winding Shott. Bram 91 E2
Windmill Ave. St Alb 128 B4
Windmill Cl. Bark 17 E3
Windmill Cl. Ivin 80 C3
Windmill Cl. Wa Aby 163 F3
Windmill Dri. Cro Gr 165 F2
Windmill Field. Gt Am 114 B4
Windmill Fields. Harl 118 C2
Windmill Hill. Chipf 151 F4
Windmill Hill. Sar 151 F4
Windmill La. Barn 170 C2
Windmill La. Bus 168 C1
Windmill La. Ches 148 C1
Windmill Rd. Bre Wd 47 E1
Windmill Rd. Heml H 124 C1
Windmill Rd. Luton 63 F4
Windmill Rd. Mark 84 A3
Windmill St. Bus 168 C1
Windmill Way. Had Cr 74 C1
Windmill Way. Tri 99 F2
Windmore Ave. Pot B 158 B4
Windridge Cl. St Alb 127 D1
Winds End Cl. Heml H 125 D3
Windsor Cl. Bor 170 A4
Windsor Cl. Bov 137 D2
Windsor Cl. Ches 148 A1
Windsor Cl. Norwd 175 D1
Windsor Cl. Stev 69 D4

Windsor Cl. Welw 89 D2
Windsor Dri. Hertng 112 C4
Windsor Gdns. Bis St 77 B4
Windsor Rd. Barn 171 E2
Windsor Rd. Enf 162 B2
Windsor Rd. Har 176 B1
Windsor Rd. Roystn 7 F3
Windsor Rd. Watf 154 B1
Windsor Rd. Welw 89 D2
Windsor St. Luton 63 E3
Windsor Way. Ric 165 D1
Windward Cl. Enf 162 B2
Windy Rise. Dan En 71 F4
Winford Dri. Hod 134 C1
Wingate Gdns. Welw 89 D3
Wingate Rd. Luton 44 C1
Wingate Way. St Alb 128 A1
Wingrave Rd. Lon M 79 E1
Wingrave Rd. Tri 100 A3
Winifred Rd. Heml H 138 B4
Winkfield Cl. Luton 44 A1
Winkwell. Heml H 123 E1
Winnington Rd. Enf 162 B1
Winsdon Hill. Luton 63 E3
Winsdon Rd. Luton 63 E3
Winslow Cl. Luton 45 E2
Winslow Rd. Wing 60 A2
Winston Cl. Hit 34 B4
Winston Cl. Stan 176 C2
Winston Ct. Har 176 A2
Winston Gdns. Berk 121 F2
Winston Way. Pot B 159 D3
Winstre Rd. Bor 170 A4
Winters La. Wal 38 B1
Winterscroft Rd. Hod 134 C4
Winton App. Cro Gr 166 B2
Winton Cl. Letw 23 E4
Winton Cl. Luton 45 E3
Winton Cres. Cro Gr 166 A2
Winton Dri. Ches 148 C1
Winton Dri. Cro Gr 166 B2
Winton Rd. Ware 93 F1
Wisden Rd. Stev 36 C1
Wisemans Gdns. Saw 97 E1
Wistlea Cres. Coln H 129 D1
Wistow Rd. Luton 45 D3
Witchford. Wel GC 111 E3
Withy Cl. Luton 44 A2
Witney Cl. Pnr 175 F2
Witter Ave. Ick 21 F2
Wiveton Cl. Luton 45 E4
Woburn Ave. Bis St 77 B4
Woburn Cl. Bus 168 B2
Woburn Cl. Stev 69 E4
Wodecroft Rd. Luton 45 D3
Wolsey Ave. Ches 147 F1
Wolsey Rd. Heml H 124 B1
Wolsey Rd. Norwd 174 B4
Wolston Cl. Luton 63 E4
Wolves Mere. Wl Gr 69 D1
Wood Cl. Hat 130 A3
Wood Common. Hat 130 A4
Wood Cres. Heml H 124 C1
Wood Dri. Stev 51 D1
Wood End Hill. Harp 85 E2
Wood End La. Fla 104 C4
Wood End Rd. Harp 85 E2
Wood End. Chis 141 E2
Wood Farm Rd. Heml H 124 C1
Wood Green Cl. Luton 46 A3
Wood Green Rd. Luton 46 B3
Wood La. Heml H 124 B1
Wood Lane End. Heml H 125 D2
Wood St. Barn 171 E3
Wood St. Luton 63 F3
Wood Vale. Hat 130 A3
Wood View. Cuf 146 C2
Wood View. Heml H 124 A3
Woodacre Dri. Wl Gr 90 A4
Woodbine Gr. Enf 161 E1
Woodbridge Cl. Luton 44 C2
Woodbrook Gdns. Wa Aby 163 F3
Woodbury Hill Path. Luton 45 F1
Woodbury Hill. Luton 45 F1
Woodcock Hill. Ric 173 F3
Woodcock Hill. Sand 108 C1
Woodcock Rd. Luton 63 D4
Woodcock Rd. Stev 51 E1
Woodcote Cl. Ches 148 B1
Woodcroft Ave. Sta Ab 115 E2
Woodfall Ave. Barn 171 F2
Woodfield Ave. Norwd 174 C3
Woodfield Cl. Sta Mo 59 F3
Woodfield Dri. Heml H 125 E1
Woodfield Gdns. Heml H 125 E1
Woodfield La. New St 145 F4
Woodfield Rd. Radl 156 A2
Woodfield Rd. Stev 36 B1
Woodfield Rd. Wel GC 110 C3
Woodfield Rise. Bus 168 B1
Woodfield Terr. Sta Mo 59 F3
Woodfield Way. St Alb 128 B3
Woodfields. Sta Mo 59 F3
Woodford Cres. Pnr 175 D1
Woodford Rd. Watf 167 E4
Woodforde Cl. Ashw 4 C2
Woodgate Cres. Norwd 175 D2
Woodgate. Watf 154 A3
Woodgreen Way. Ches 162 C4
Woodhall Ave. Pnr 175 F1
Woodhall Cl. Hert 113 E4
Woodhall Ct. Wel GC 110 C3
Woodhall Dri. Pnr 175 F1
Woodhall Gate. Pnr 175 E2
Woodhall Gr. Bis St 76 B3
Woodhall La. Heml H 124 C3
Woodhall La. Shen 156 C2
Woodhall La. Sth Ox 175 E3
Woodhall La. Wel GC 110 C2
Woodham Way. Sta Ab 115 E2
Woodhouse Eaves. Norwd 175 D3
Woodhurst Ave. Watf 154 B2
Woodhurst. Letw 22 C4
Woodland Ave. Heml H 124 A1
Woodland Ave. Luton 45 D2
Woodland Cl. Heml H 124 A1
Woodland Cl. Tri 99 F1
Woodland Dri. St Alb 128 B2
Woodland Dri. Watf 166 C4
Woodland La. Chor 164 B3
Woodland Mount. Hert 113 F3
Woodland Pl. Heml H 124 A1
Woodland Rd. Hert H 114 B2
Woodland Rd. Map Cr 172 B3
Woodland Rise. Stu 82 A4
Woodland Rise. Wel GC 110 B4
Woodland Way. Bal 23 F3
Woodland Way. Gofs O 147 D2
Woodland Way. Stev 51 D1
Woodland Way. Wl Gr 89 F4
Woodlands Ave. Berk 122 B2
Woodlands Cl. Bor 170 A3
Woodlands Cl. Hod 135 D3
Woodlands Dri. Bed 139 E2
Woodlands Dri. Hod 135 D2
Woodlands Dri. Stan 176 C2
Woodlands Meade. Wes 37 D4
Woodlands Rd. Bed 139 D2
Woodlands Rd. Bus 167 F2
Woodlands Rd. Enf 161 E1
Woodlands Rd. Hert 113 F3
Woodlands Rd. Thun 93 E3
Woodlands. Bis St 77 E4
Woodlands. Bro Pk 145 D3
Woodlands. Harp 85 F2
Woodlands. Radl 156 A3
Woodlands. Roystn 7 F3
Woodlea Gr. Norwd 174 B2
Woodley Rd. Ware 93 F1
Woodman Rd. Heml H 124 C1
Woodmans Yd. Watf 167 E3
Woodmere Ave. Watf 154 C1
Woodmere. Luton 31 D1
Woodmill Mews. Hod 135 D4
Woodpecker Cl. Bus 168 B1
Woodpecker Cl. Hat 129 F1
Woodridge Way. Norwd 174 C2
Woodridings Ave. Pnr 175 F1
Woodridings Cl. Pnr 175 F2
Woods Ave. Hat 130 A3
Woods The. Norwd 175 D3
Woodshots Meadow. Watf 166 B2
Woodside Rd. Abb L 154 A4
Woodside Rd. Bri Wd 140 C1
Woodside Rd. Cad 63 D2
Woodside Rd. Har Gr 89 F2
Woodside Rd. Norwd 174 C2
Woodside. Bis St 77 E4
Woodside. Elst 169 F3
Woodside. Hert H 114 B1
Woodside. Watf 154 A2
Woodstock Cl. Hert H 114 A2
Woodstock Rd N. St Alb 128 A2
Woodstock Rd S. St Alb 128 A2
Woodstock Rd. Bus 168 C1
Woodstock Rd. Hod 134 C2
Woodville Ct. Watf 167 D4
Woodward Gdns. Stan 176 C2
Woodwaye. Watf 167 E1
Woodwicks. Map Cr 172 B3
Woolands. Chis 141 E2
Woolgrove Rd. Letw 22 A1
Woollam Cres. St Alb 127 E4
Woollard St. Wa Aby 163 E3
Woolmans Cl. Hod 134 C1
Woolmer Dri. Heml H 125 E2
Woolmers La. Let Gr 112 A1
Woolners Way. Stev 50 B3
Woolston Ave. Letw 23 D2
Wootton Cl. Luton 45 D4
Wootton Dri. Heml H 124 C4
Worcester Rd. Hat 129 F3
Worcesters Ave. Enf 162 A1
Wordsworth Cl. Roystn 2 B1
Wordsworth Rd. Harp 86 A2
Wordsworth Rd. Luton 44 A1
Works Rd. Letw 23 E4
Worley Rd. St Alb 127 E2
Wormley Lodge Cl. Hod 148 C4
Worsted La. H St H 41 F4
Wortham Rd. Roystn 7 F2
Wortham Way. Stev 51 D2
Wragles The. Bis St 77 D3
Wratten Cl. Hit 34 C3
Wratten Rd E. Hit 34 C3
Wratten Rd W. Hit 34 C3
Wrayfields. Stot 12 A4
Wren Cl. Kim 66 A1
Wren Cl. Luton 46 B3
Wren Cl. Stev 51 D3
Wren Cres. Bus 168 B1
Wren Wood. Wel GC 111 D4
Wrenbrook Rd. Bis St 76 C3
Wrensfield. Heml H 124 A2
Wrestlers Cl. Hat 130 B4
Wrexham Terr. Roystn 7 E4
Wright Cl. Whea 108 C4
Wright's Buildings. Watf 167 D4
Wright's Green La. L Hal 98 B4
Wrights Meadow. Wal 52 A4
Wrights Orch. Ast 51 F1
Wrotham Rd. Barn 171 F4
Wroxham Ave. Heml H 124 B1
Wroxham Gdns. Enf 161 D2
Wroxham Gdns. Pot B 158 B4
Wroxham Way. Harp 86 B2
Wulfrath Way. Ware 93 E2
Wulwards Cl. Luton 63 D3
Wyatt Cl. Ick 21 E2
Wyatt's Cl. Chor 165 D3
Wyatts Rd. Chor 165 D3
Wyburn Ave. Barn 171 F3
Wych Elm La. Wl Gr 68 C1
Wych Elm. Harl 117 E1
Wych Elms. Chis 141 D2
Wychdell. Stev 69 E4
Wychford Dri. Saw 97 E1
Wychwood Ave. Luton 45 F2
Wychwood Way. Norwd 174 C2
Wycliffe Cl. Luton 45 E3
Wycombe Way. Luton 45 E4
Wycombe Way. St Alb 128 A3
Wyddial Green. Wel GC 111 D3
Wyddial Rd. Bun 40 C4
Wye The. Heml H 125 D4
Wyedale. Lon C 142 C2
Wykeham Rise. N20 171 F1
Wyken Cl. Luton 45 D4
Wyldwood Cl. Harl 118 B3
Wyllyotts Cl. Pot B 158 C4
Wyllyotts La. Pot B 158 C4
Wyllyotts Pl. Pot B 158 C4
Wylo Dri. Barn 171 D2
Wymondley Cl. Hit 35 D4
Wymondley Rd. Gt Wy 35 F4
Wymondley Rd. Hit 35 D3
Wymondley Rd. Will 23 D1
Wynchgate. Har 176 C2
Wynchlands Cres. St Alb 128 B2
Wynd The. Letw 22 C3
Wyndham Rd. Luton 44 B1
Wyndhams End. Wel G C 110 C1
Wynlie Gdns. Pnr 175 D1
Wynn Cl. Bal 13 D1
Wyrley Dell. Letw 23 D2
Wyton. Wel GC 111 E3
Wyvern Cl. Luton 44 C2

Yardley Ave. Pit 80 B2
Yardley. Letw 23 E2
Yarmouth Rd. Stev 50 A4
Yarmouth Rd. Watf 154 B1
Yeats Cl. Roystn 2 B1
Yeomanry Dri. Clo 13 D1
Yeomans Ave. Harp 85 E2
Yeomans Dri. Ast 51 F1
Yeomans Ride. Heml H 105 D1
Yeovil Rd. Luton 46 A1
Yew Cl. Ham St 147 F2
Yew Gr. Wel GC 111 E3
Yew Tree Cl. Bot 136 A1
Yew Tree Cl. Ivin 80 C3
Yew Tree Ct. Bov 137 D2
Yew Tree Ct. Heml H 124 A1
Yew Wlk. Hod 135 D3
Yewlands. Hod 135 D3
Yewlands. Saw 97 F1
Yews Ave. Enf 162 A2
Yewtree End. Chis 141 D2
York Cl. Kin L 139 D1
York Cres. Bor 170 B4
York Rd. Ches 162 C3
York Rd. Hit 34 C4
York Rd. Norwd 175 D1
York Rd. St Alb 127 F2
York Rd. Stev 36 C1
York Rd. Watf 167 E2
York St. Luton 63 F4
York Terr. Enf 161 E1
York Way. Roystn 7 D4
York Way. Watf 154 C2
York Way. Welw 89 E2
Yorke Rd. Cro Gr 166 A2
Youngfield Rd. Heml H 123 F2
Youngs Rise. Wel GC 110 B3
Youngsbury La. Wad 93 F4
Yule Cl. Bri Wd 140 C1

Zambesi Rd. Bis St 76 C3

OS STREET ATLASES

CSA94

	Hardback (Quantity / Total)	Softback	Pocket (Quantity / Total)	
	£12.99	£8.99	£4.99	
Berkshire	£ ISBN 0-540-05992-7	£ ISBN 0-540-05993-5	£ ISBN 0-540-05994-3	£
Buckinghamshire	£ ISBN 0-540-05989-7	£ ISBN 0-540-05990-0	£ ISBN 0-540-05991-9	£
East Essex	£ ISBN 0-540-05848-3	£ ISBN 0-540-05866-1	£ ISBN 0-540-05850-5	£
West Essex	£ ISBN 0-540-05849-1	£ ISBN 0-540-05867-X	£ ISBN 0-540-05851-3	£
North Hampshire	£ ISBN 0-540-05852-1	£ ISBN 0-540-05853-X	£ ISBN 0-540-05854-8	£
South Hampshire	£ ISBN 0-540-05855-6	£ ISBN 0-540-05856-4	£ ISBN 0-540-05857-2	£
Hertfordshire	£ ISBN 0-540-05995-1	£ ISBN 0-540-05996-X	£ ISBN 0-540-05997-8	£
East Kent	£ ISBN 0-540-06026-7	£ ISBN 0-540-06027-5	£ ISBN 0-540-06028-3	£
West Kent	£ ISBN 0-540-06029-1	£ ISBN 0-540-06031-3	£ ISBN 0-540-06030-5	£
Nottinghamshire	£ ISBN 0-540-05858-0	£ ISBN 0-540-05859-9	£ ISBN 0-540-05860-2	£
Oxfordshire	£ ISBN 0-540-05986-2	£ ISBN 0-540-05987-0	£ ISBN 0-540-05988-9	£
Surrey	£ ISBN 0-540-05983-8	£ ISBN 0-540-05984-6	£ ISBN 0-540-05985-4	£
East Sussex	£ ISBN 0-540-05875-0	£ ISBN 0-540-05874-2	£ ISBN 0-540-05873-4	£
West Sussex	£ ISBN 0-540-05876-9	£ ISBN 0-540-05877-7	£ ISBN 0-540-05878-5	£
	£10.99			
Warwickshire	£ ISBN 0-540-05642-1			£

I enclose a cheque/postal order for £
made payable to ***Reed Book Services*** *or please debit my* Access / American Express / Visa *account by* £

Name

Address

Postcode

Account number

Expiry date

Signature

Please tick this box if you do not wish your name to be used by other carefully selected organisations that may wish to send you information about other products and services

◆ ***Free postage and packing*** ◆ *All available titles will normally be dispatched within 5 working days of receipt of order, but please allow up to 28 days for delivery.*

Registered office: Michelin House, 81 Fulham Road, London SW3 6RB. Registered in England No 1974080